MEMOIR

OF THE

OPERATIONS OF THE BRITISH ARMY

IN

INDIA

DURING THE

MAHRATTA WAR OF 1817, 1818, & 1819.

MEMOIR

OF THE

OPERATIONS OF THE BRITISH ARMY

IN

INDIA,

DURING THE

MAHRATTA WAR OF 1817, 1818, & 1819.

ILLUSTRATED BY MAPS AND TOPOGRAPHICAL PLANS.

BY

LIEUT.-COLONEL VALENTINE BLACKER,

COMPANION OF THE MOST HONOURABLE ORDER OF THE BATH, AND

QUARTERMASTER-GENERAL OF THE ARMY OF FORT ST. GEORGE.

LONDON:

PRINTED FOR BLACK, KINGSBURY, PARBURY, AND ALLEN,

LEADENHALL-STREET.

1821.

PRINTED BY S. AND R. BENTLEY,
DORSET STREET, SALISBURY SQUARE, LONDON.

THE OFFICERS

OF THE

BRITISH ARMY IN INDIA.

FELLOW SOLDIERS,

The original object of Dedications, to gain currency for a Work under the patronage of some powerful name, forms no part of the motive with which I address you. Your decision on subjects of Literature will not be admitted by the Public, as infallible; though you are the best judges of the truth of the facts, and justness of the opinions, which are introduced in the following pages.

A lively interest in your Fame, a grateful attachment to our common Service, and a sincere Friendship for many of you, conspire in prompting me to offer you this Memoir. I am anxious that your merits and services may ever be exhibited to the public view; and though I do not pretend to the credit of being actuated solely by this desire, it forms an important part of my motives. I assert this with a confidence, the sincerity of which, I trust, the freedom of my language throughout this work will testify. Candour of speech is, or ought to be, a characteristic of our profession; I have therefore, without hesitation, treated of your merits and deficiencies, as they have appeared to me, with an impartiality which will, I hope, be received as the highest compliment.

You have done your duty in war, by bringing it to a successful termination. It behoves you now to acquit yourselves equally well in peace. The proper motives of a Soldier are Patriotism and Love of Fame. Of these excitements, neither can have any valuable operation, without constant and attentive study of the Military Profession. The objects abounding in this pursuit cannot here be enlarged on with propriety; yet, I may be permitted to remark, that an interval of peace is the fittest time for reflecting upon them, as, during active service, there is little leisure for more than observation. Such ardour of improvement will correct those imperfections, of which you have your share; and will render you still more worthy of a better history of your exploits than you have now before you.

That you will never have a more zealous historian, I may venture to affirm; and with assurances of the just pride I feel, in belonging to the same Army with yourselves,

I remain

Your most devoted and faithful Comrade,

VALENTINE BLACKER.

PREFACE.

An Author who offers himself for the first time to the Public is usually occupied in anxiously considering the most effectual method of avoiding their severity, and securing the protection of their indulgence. In pursuance of this design, some place all their confidence in the novelty of their subject; or, if it has already been discussed, in their additional information, and the new lights in which facts are exposed. Should no one, however, have described the same events, they consider themselves imperiously called on to rescue from total oblivion a subject which all others have abandoned. They wish, indeed, that an abler pen had undertaken the task, and plead an evident necessity, to secure a lenient judgment. Should an author pursue the profession of arms, he may even consent to term himself an "unlettered soldier," with the probable expectation of being allowed to possess, instead of the knowledge of books, a familiarity with scenes of life, the most important to States from their results, and most interesting to individuals from their vicissitudes and dangers.

If, thus, only a few are either instructed or amused; if even in a solitary instance, the Reader shall be guarded against the dangerous consequences of ignorance, the candidate for indulgence declares himself entirely content. In the modesty of his own pretensions, he founds his claim to the forbearance of others. Some, however, candidly confess as their object, a desire to amuse their leisure hours. Others boldly declare their intention of edifying the world by their opinions. There are those also, who consider their professional or official situation as having constituted them the proper historians of certain events in which they have participated. Old *Montluc** freely avows, as the intention of his *Commentaries*, the excitement of his countrymen to glorious actions, through the emulation of his exploits. However natural this style may be to a *Gascon*, to the better taste of the present day it will be more agreeable to propose self-instruction and excitement, from contemplating the behaviour of others. Whether a Military Author make this his own object, or induce it in his Readers, he will necessarily benefit the public service.

While, in the present instance, the Author disclaims all intention of writing for the edification of others, he is conscious of having had opportunities, which fall to the lot of few, of forming opinions respecting the Military Service of India. It does not follow, that he has fully profited by the occasion; yet reflections grounded on the observations of twenty-two years unremitting service in that part of the British empire, and referring to numerous facts, are entitled to the consideration, if not to the approval, of the less experienced. The events which form the subject of the following Memoir are worthy of attention, at least on account of their important consequences; and, under this view, they may, possibly, engage even the general reader, however indifferent to military affairs. But to interest the public at large, as it never formed the object of the Author, so is it by no means his present expectation. To be rendered popular, the Memoir must be divested of the professional details, which form the principal value of a Military work. It must be interspersed abundantly with affecting incidents, and private anecdotes; with the adventures of individuals, and florid descriptions. These topics, unfortunately, so far from holding a conspicuous situation in a work of information, should be carefully withheld from any interference with essential points, the contemplation of which is alone capable of confer-

* Blaise de Montluc, who died in 1577, aged 77 years, sixty of which he had passed in military service during the reigns of Francis I., Henry II., and Henry III. By the latter prince, he was created a Marshal of France. Montluc's "Mémoires ou Commentaires de sa Vie et des Affaires Mémorables de son tems" were reprinted at Paris in 1746. Henry IV. used to describe them as "La Bible des Guerriers." Vid. "Nouv. Dict. Hist." *Paris*, 1772. Tom. iv. p. 598.

ring instruction. However amusing, in an idle hour, may be a history of individuals, unless its details exhibit characteristic features, which illustrate human nature under views belonging to the subject of such a history, it is evidently extraneous. It is, indeed, as prejudicial to the integrity of a work, as, in the present instance, would be the substitution of a romantic description of the beauties of a prospect, for a topographical delineation of a field of battle.

The leading object of a Military Commentary should be the information of professional men. Thus they may, by reflection, derive instruction, and consequently promote the service of their country. It is not, therefore, with a view to recreation, but to careful study, that such a work should be perused; nor should attention to the amusement of the Reader's mind be suffered to distract it from essential objects. These embrace a variety of circumstances, relating to the strength and composition of armies—their efficiency; and the peculiarities in their method of warfare: military character, and proficiency in the modern art of war: arms, and even clothing. Descriptions of important encampments, marches in the vicinity of an enemy, and orders of battle, must be minute to be beneficial; and as these are to be understood only by topographical description, its value becomes doubly enhanced. Ascending to more general topics, the geographical positions of the several belligerent powers bear to the project of a campaign the same relation, as the details of ground to armies within each other's sight; and a study of their frontiers involves considerations connected with both views. Their interests, power, and resources, as well as the applicable parts of their previous history, are considerations no less important.

Though these topics refer principally to facts and circumstances, yet, on many accounts, the introduction of individual names will be indispensable. Without dwelling on the occasional clearness it gives to the narrative, it must be allowed, without hurting its main objects, to encrease its interest. Other arguments, founded on a supposed regard to equity, have been used in support of the same principle; but the propriety of these is questionable. If their tendency be at all to advance individual fame, at the expense of the due importance of principles and facts, they should surely be avoided, even under the most plausible pretences. That a man who serves his Country well in a high and responsible situation, is entitled to the good-will and applause of his fellow-subjects, as well as of his Prince, is undeniable. He runs great risks, both of person and reputation; and submits to privations, and diminution of freedom, unexperienced in other walks of life. If to these sacrifices be added, devotion to his Country's service, uncontaminated by a view to personal emolument through the exercise of his functions, such an individual is entitled to be ranked with those whose existence has conferred most honour on the human race: but these numerous qualities, added to successful exertion, are of rare occurrence, and limit the field of impartial panegyric within narrow bounds. Even such praise is incompatible with the pure objects of a Military work. It would be the assumption of an unnecessary freedom with the Reader: for, unless the Author be esteemed a final dictator, his encomiums can only be received as the results of his own admiration. With all due deference to the generous character of that sentiment, it has much tendency to mislead; and, in a judicious Reader, will be more likely to excite distrust than confident acquiescence.

An Officer, fitted for a situation of high responsibility, will necessarily possess a certain education, and be accustomed to reflection. Such a man is not be excited through his vanity; and on those who have no worthier motive of action, than the desire of exciting the admiration of others, example is thrown away. There must be, derived from nature and improved by habit, an internal principle, whose operation alone will be permanent; whether the main object proceed from patriotism, or a love of fame. Facts clearly defined, and circumstances satisfactorily explained, will form to such Readers the grounds of impartial judgment, respecting the characters and conduct of the principal actors. The mere introduction of their names, therefore, for the reasons already mentioned, leaves open to them the only sure road to permanent fame. Nor is it improper here to advert to the frequent custom of recording, in the body of a Military Memoir, the names of Officers killed and wounded. If they hold important commands, such distinction appears necessary, because the removal of their talents or inabilities from a post of consequence, may materially affect the conduct and success of the war. Otherwise the indication of the numbers appears to be sufficient in the Narrative; leaving the insertion of individual names to the Appendix, where that course may be practicable. If so much moderation be proper in the notice of Officers, it is equally advisable respecting troops; and a continual aim at exalting their exploits can be calculated only to dazzle the imagination. The same principle applies to the circumstances attending battles and sieges. If the perils and labours belonging to them are related in superlative terms and hyperbolical expressions, it is evident that there is in the description a deviation from the reality. Such a method is calculated not only to produce an exaggerated impression, but likewise to divert the attention from the main object, which is that of overcoming similar difficulties. Thus the more sober the narrative, the more will it offer of facts for instruction. On the other hand, the risk of appearing dull to the generality of readers is not less manifest. Thus numerous are the obstacles in the way of reconciling instruction with general amusement.

If it be permitted to an author to advert to the style of his own work, or to mention the difficulties of expression by which he has been embarrassed, they may be explained in a summary manner, by a reference to the principal objects of description. The history of warfare since the beginning of the world cannot exhibit an example of more unremitting movements than is furnished by this Memoir. Marches and countermarches, when so frequently repeated, cannot be described in varied language. Not only the same words, but the same order must occur. Yet to treat them generally or loosely, would be to sacrifice all the advantage which may be derived from particular information respecting them. The author can vouch, from his own experience, for the great importance of knowing what movements have been made on former occasions, by what description of force, and in what times;

and that, under certain circumstances, such information affords the safest ground of calculation, from the principle, that what has been once done, may be done again. A similar difficulty attends the description of sieges, of which there were very many during the late war. To describe them familiarly would afford no precise instruction, and to adopt the style of a journal would not accord with the rest of the work. Yet a diurnal form is certainly the most distinct method of conveying the required information on such a subject. The author has endeavoured to combine both methods; but confesses himself doubtful of his success.

To these considerations may be added, the necessity of frequently inserting dates, and the designations of corps. Both these, however unfriendly to eloquence, appeared indispensable to a Military commentary. They have therefore been scrupulously preserved, as well as the strength of detachments on all occasions of service. Such minutiæ cannot be invented; and therefore become valuable even as pledges for the fidelity of a narrative. While two approved historians, *Guicciardini* and *Davila*, are cited as abounding in details, it will not be denied that some popular military histories have been written under a total disregard of dates. Of this fact "The retreat of the ten thousand," "Cæsar's Commentaries," and Polybius's History, are sufficient examples. Still, however justly admired are these productions, they afford no conclusion against the principle contended for. Though it was of less importance to the objects of those works, yet even in them the deficiency in this respect produces an effect more favourable to the desire of pleasing, than to the means of instruction. In fact, the pleasure of the reader was the chief object of most of the ancient writers, to which was rendered subservient every other consideration. But the example has not been followed by the generality of historians, as will appear on a comparison of the best ancient and modern histories. It is still less worthy of imitation in the instance of a professional work. The great importance of facts and circumstantial information in this case, gives the narrative, in some measure, the character of a voyage on discovery, or of a process in experimental philosophy; the popular description of which may be fitted to teach a smattering of science, but not to confer or improve scientific knowledge. A considerable difficulty attaches to attempts at literary composition by all men in offices of much writing, arising from the unavoidable habit of confining their compositions to one description of subject. Words are used with a particular import, for want of others expressly belonging to the case, particularly in a far distant country. Writers in India, therefore, are never likely to succeed in works of taste *.

In a Memoir of this kind, the reader will reasonably expect to be informed from what sources the facts related are derived. On this head the author has so little reason to complain of any deficiency, that he exposes himself, by a display of the abundance of his materials, to the charge of having failed in making the most advantageous use of them. Occupying an important staff situation in the Army of the Deckan, he was in the confidence of his Commander-in-Chief, Sir Thomas Hislop, under whose orders he conducted all the correspondence respecting the movements of the several Divisions under the Lieutenant-general's command. Where this public source failed, he was supplied through the medium of private letters from his friends, both during the war and after its conclusion. As the object for which he called for information was fully known, he considers himself authorized to refer to those papers, should the intelligence so obtained be ever questioned.

But in fact there is scarcely a single assertion advanced, for which there are not several authorities, and many can be proved from the author's personal observation. As, however, this source of information, and the others which have been mentioned, refer principally to the Army of the Deckan, he found himself uninformed on many points respecting the operations of the Grand Army. Hewas therefore induced to visit the Bengal Presidency, where alone his wants could be

* Sir William Jones's Works come not within the scope of this observation.

supplied. The public records were thrown open to him, by the liberality of the Governor-general. The facilities afforded to his enquiries by the suavity and accommodating disposition of the highest official characters at Calcutta, also demand the expression of his gratitude for a reception which forms a striking contrast with the vulgar insolence of office. He can boast of similar liberality from Sir John Malcolm, and the Residents at Hydrabad, Poonah, and Nagpoor. To the friendship of F. Warden, Esq. the Chief Secretary of the Bombay Government, he is also indebted for most valuable materials. Gratifying as it would be to the Author's private feelings to continue this enumeration, he is forced to curtail it, from a regard to the Reader; but not without adding the name of Captain James Hanson, who conducted for him some important enquiries, with as much ability as good-nature and industry. These sources of information respect the geographical descriptions, as well as the substance of the Memoir. In their collection, and in the acquisition of topographical plans, he is greatly indebted to the extra-labours of all the Officers of the Quartermaster-general's department. The maps which accompany this work are therefore offered with confidence, as superior to any that have ever been published respecting Central India, though minute detail has generally been avoided, as injurious to the perspicuity of Military geography. For their construction from a mass of detached materials, he is indebted to the intelligent and diligent aid derived from Captain T. P. Ball, Assistant-Quartermaster-general.

For the official returns of killed and wounded in the Appendix, access was open to the Adjutant-general's office, the proper repository of those documents, as well as of the reports of actions and of commendatory orders and reports. None of any other description respecting the conduct of the troops are to be found on record. How far this circumstance could stand as evidence of their correctness, would be an important point for examination, were any opinions on this subject derived from them. But they have been entirely disregarded under this view; for a vicious style has manifestly crept into this species of composition, emanating from the highest to the lowest authority.

In almost all armies there will be detected some partiality of the General or other Commanding-officer in distributing praise; but that is not the fault in the present instance. It is an indiscriminate application of superlative expressions*, which banishes all gradation, and leaves no distinction between the most exalted and most moderate merit. To such excess has this practice extended, that at length the pen is dropt, with an avowal of inability to find words for the description of remaining excellencies. With this confession, they are dismissed as indescribable; in imitation of the painter, who, having exhausted every expression of grief, finished by drawing a veil over the principal figure. Reports of actions are in so many cases equally inconclusive, that, excepting as an outline, they afford little information. Long and general descriptions are given of trifling affairs, in terms important enough for the conflict of armies and the loss of thousands; but they are easily reduced to their proper level, by the investigation of facts and circumstances, the real loss of the British troops in the return, and the probable loss of the enemy inferred from many accounts. No common standard being easily established for the preparation of reports, they are left at the mercy of individual characters; of which, in one respect, they do not form a bad criterion. It therefore follows that some officers display, in diffuse detail, petty services, which by others † would be altogether omitted.

Though few wars possess greater variety of incident than abounds in that which has been recently terminated, it is probable the account of

* The Duke of Wellington's reports always maintain a sobriety of style which renders them intelligible.

† The reduction of Paar Gheer, once an important place under the first Mahratta Ruler, with that of more than thirty other forts of different degrees of consequence, was effected under Brigadier General Munro's orders without their ever being reported: so little did he consider them worthy of notice.

it which is now given will be considered as abundantly long. A more summary narrative, however, would have been unnecessary; and would not have suited its declared intention. How far the importance of the subject entitles it to be treated at such length, may possibly be considered with more impartiality out of India. Yet if *here* be a tendency to confer too much importance on events in this quarter of the British Empire, there is not less danger of their being neglected by the public at home. Compared with the events of vital consequence at their own doors, the transactions of India lose much of their interest, except among a few who have relatives or friends in this country. The high rank* of the actors, and the strength of the armies engaged in Europe, give them a splendour denied to Indian warfare, where a Lieutenant will occasionally exercise the functions of a Lieutenant-colonel, and a Colonel command a division. At the same time the real dignity of events ought to depend on facts and their results to mankind, and are a worthier object of the contemplation of a philosopher. Yet even here the field is narrowed, for, as the reviewers remark: "It is very difficult to be philosophical about the details of warfare---about marches and sieges, howitzers and lieutenant-colonels, stratagems, alarms, manœuvrings, fightings, and runnings away"---of all which there is abundance in the following pages.

Not only is the rank of the officers, employed in great commands, lower in India than in Europe, but the military operations, it must be allowed, are more simple, and consequently neither afford so much interest, nor require the same calculation or caution. The want of skill in the Commandant of a fort relieves his adversary from the practice of many precautions and expedients. Owing, indeed, to a deficiency of perseverance or means of defence on the part of a garrison, the greater number of sieges have been reduced to little more than *demonstrations*.

---

* Although it may be said, we had "a kingdom for a stage, Princes to act, and Monarchs to behold the swelling scene," yet they were very unimportant characters compared with the Potentates of Europe.

Equal simplicity prevails throughout the general conduct of the campaign. The practicability or difficulty of roads is even more considered, and with good reason, than the opportunities which may be furnished by any movement, to the enterprises of the enemy. On the field of battle, there occur but few instances of parts of a position being taken and retaken, or long contested. There are few batteries carried and recaptured*, and few difficult predicaments or uncertain situations arising out of an enemy's manœuvre. This will be manifest from an inspection of the topographical plans, none of which require repetition, for the exhibition of new positions on the same ground.

But if the service of India is thus reduced within narrow scientific bounds, its dangers † are not inferior to those in European service; nor is there less exercise for the virtues of bravery and constancy, as may be deduced from the following details; and these displayed in a climate, whose influence tends to debilitate the mind as well as the body. An efficient military system, under vigilant superintendence, has always prevailed in some part of the Eastern empire, and has kept alive the military spirit, like the sacred fires which are never extinguished. In India the mind of the officer has scarcely any opportunity of being weaned from his profession; his home is distant, and he can fly to no other society or scenes where he may cease to reflect that he is a soldier. His service is against declared enemies; for he is not even employed against an unarmed mob. ‡ The very circumstance also of wearing his

---

* The instance of the Nepaul War forms scarcely an exception.

† The following recapitulation of casualties in action during the war, will illustrate this point, if it be recollected how few European Officers are ever present with Native corps.

Number of European Commissioned Officers Killed and Wounded.	Of the Bengal Presidency	18
	—— Madras ditto	104
	—— Bombay ditto	12
	Total	134

To which might be added, in justice to this subject, the extraordinary number who have died during the latter campaign, and immediately afterwards, from the severity of service.

‡ The singular instance to the contrary occurred at Seringapatam, in 1800.

military uniform on all occasions (excepting at a few stations) is, however trivial it may appear, calculated to maintain the *esprit de corps* undiminished. The common marches of corps in India for mere change of quarters, bear the semblance of war, and are accompanied by forms and circumstances of actual service, which are impracticable either in the United Kingdom, or any of the Colonies. On these grounds is ventured the general assertion, that during peace a British corps in India is at any time fitter for field service, than one in Europe.

Under such circumstances, the generality of officers cannot avoid attaining a considerable share of proficiency in their art. Even for excellence in the highest walk, the India service boasts of having unfolded the talents of a genius who has outshone and conquered his rivals. The Madras Army pride themselves on this distinction; and the individuals of it who served under Sir Arthur Wellesley add to the common feeling, the cherished recollection of acquaintance* with a General who has risen even to the pinnacle of fame, and the highest rank of a subject. Indisputable merit alone can attain such elevation under the British Government. This places the pre-eminence of the *Sepoy General* on a different footing from the fame of many heroes who have risen by Court favour.†

---

* It is said that the Duke of Wellington recollects the acquaintances of Major-general Wellesley; and his Grace has given most substantial proof of the constancy of his Eastern friendships.

† Although the great Condé is deservedly esteemed a genius in war, and had latterly to struggle against Court intrigues, he was forced into command of the French army by Court favour, when only twenty-one years of age, before he could possibly have formed his character, when he was quite inexperienced, and was therefore placed under the tutelage of old Mareschal de l'Hôpital, to be thus prevented from doing wrong. His genius, however, forced the Marshal's trammels on the occasion of the first battle, and, at that early age, exhibited not only talents, but a judgment scarcely credible. The accounts of this warrior having come down to posterity, through the medium of panegyrics, (those master falsifiers of facts,) and the vain expositions of French writers, there is almost room to distrust so miraculous a phenomenon. What man will find in his own breast, or in his observations, the evidence of such self-confidence at that age, or of that of the page of Gustavus Adolphus, who, at the age of eighteen, ventured to change the orders of his Prince on the field of battle? These instances of precocity certainly appear incredible; but they are in reality little more singular than the circumstance of Mareschal Turenne growing more venturous as he grew old.

It might have been gratifying to the reader to find here a portraiture of the various Native characters whose names have been introduced; and it is confessed that such an addition would have served to elucidate some circumstances of the war. But the information on this subject, which is in the Author's possession, being very defective, would appear quite insulated, from the want of further materials for completing a general view. Great difficulty attends the acquisition of knowledge respecting the characters of individuals among the Natives of India; and when obtained, it is not particularly interesting.

The only remaining topic which appears to require notice here, respects the geographical and topographical plans, which exceed in number those commonly attached to military works. Without them no commentary is completely intelligible; and it is only to be regretted, that, in general, it is impracticable to supply them so abundantly as on the present occasion. To the professional student they are invaluable; and even the general reader will be gratified by the geographical plans. The collection of materials, both for them and for the Memoir, has delayed the completion of this work beyond the period originally proposed. This, perhaps, should not be considered a subject of regret, as it afforded more opportunity for a satisfactory conclusion. On some points information may be still wanting; but it must necessarily be trifling, for otherwise it would have been found in the records to which the Author has had access. As the further suspense, to command minute precision, would however lead to an indefinite delay, it has appeared inexpedient to lose a favourable opportunity, which cannot recur during this season, for dispatching the work in its present shape from India. The Author would fain excuse its deficiencies, by a reference to the multiplicity of his official business; but he is aware of the weakness of such apologies, and that when a man assumes the character of an Author, he is liable to every responsibility belonging to a voluntary act. While the public are grateful for information submitted to them, they will bear ready evidence against perverse or mistaken views and errors of judgment; but above all faults, they will resent the freedom of a writer, who appears carelessly before their tribunal; for the general position may be safely maintained, that however common is the spectacle of labour fruitlessly bestowed, a work of permanent value is only accomplished by toilsome perseverance.

Madras, March 13, 1820.

CONTENTS.

BOOK I.

CHAPTER I.

CAUSES OF THE WAR.

CHAPTER II.

VIEW OF MILITARY FORCES.

CHAPTER III.

OPENING OF THE CAMPAIGN.

CHAPTER IV.

RUPTURE ON THE PART OF THE PEISHWAH.

CHAPTER V.

EXPULSION OF THE PINDARRIES FROM SOUTHERN MALWAH.

CHAPTER VI.

DISPERSION AND FLIGHT OF THE PINDARRIES BEYOND THE CHUMBUL.

CHAPTER VII.

RUPTURE ON THE PART OF THE BHOOSLAH.

CHAPTER VIII.

SUBMISSION AND RE-ESTABLISHMENT OF THE BHOOSLAH.

CHAPTER IX.

HOSTILITIES WITH HOLKUR.

CHAPTER X.

PEACE WITH HOLKUR.

BOOK II.

CHAPTER I.

PURSUIT OF THE PEISHWAH TO THE REDUCTION OF SATARA.

Flight of Bajee Rao to the Southward; pursued by the Fourth Division, 176. Flight and Pursuit to the Northward, 176. Return of the Peishwah towards Poonah, and consequent Alarm there, 178. Gallant Defence of Koreigaum, 179. Successful Retreat to Serroor, 181. Reflections on this Exploit, 182. European Troops in India, how to be considered, 184. Return of the Fourth Division to Serroor, 185. March of the Deckan Reserve from Chinnoor to Punderpoor, 186. Countermarch to secure a Convoy, 186. Pursuit of the Peishwah to the Southward, 187. Reflections on the Service of Cavalry, 188: on Horse-Artillery, 189. The Peishwah turned to the Northward, 190. The Pursuit resumed by the Fourth Division, 190. Junction of both Divisions, and Reduction of Satara, 192.

CHAPTER II.

EXPULSION OF THE PINDARRIES FROM THE LEFT OF THE CHUMBUL.

Separation of Ameer Khan's Army, 194. Detachment of a Light Force from the Centre and Third Divisions of the Grand Army, under Major-general Brown, and recall of Lieut.-colonel Philpot's Detachment, 195. Major-general Brown's Attack of the insubordinate Remains of Holkur's Army at Rampoora, 195. Advance of the Head-quarters of the Second Division to Sanganeir, 196. Advance of the Goozerat Division to Burra-Sadree, 197. Captain Grant's Detachment at Jawud, 198. Re-assembly of the Second Division at Shapoorra, 198. Lieutenant-colonel Russell's Detachment from the Deckan Army at Purtabghur, and Reinforcement of Captain Grant's Detachment on the Advance of the Guickwar Contingent, 199. Operations of the Goozerat Division in Meywar, 199. Return of Captain Grant's Detachment to Mundissoor, 201. Parties of Kurreem and Wassil Mahomud's Durrahs flying to the Eastward, are attacked and dispersed, with much Loss, by a Detachment from the Fifth Deckan Division, 202. Preparations for the Countermarch of the Head-quarters of the Army of the Deckan, 203. Return to Mehidpoor; and Detachments under Major Lushington and Captain Grant to the Goozerat Frontier, 204. The Army at Oojein, 205. Movements of Captain Grant's Detachment, 206. The Army at Indoor, 206. Movements of Major Lushington's Detachment, 207. Sir John Malcolm at Neemuj, 208. Major-general Brown's successful Attack of Jeswunt Rao Bhao, 208. Return to the Chumbul, 210. Sir John Malcolm at Jawud, 210. Operations of the Second Division of the Grand Army in Meywar, 211. Submission of Beema Baee's Force to Sir William Grant Keir, 211. Reflections on the Pursuit of the Pindarries, 213.

CHAPTER III.

DISLOCATION OF THE GRAND ARMY.

Retirement of the Head-quarters of the Marquis of Hastings, and Centre Division of the Grand Army, from the Sind, 215. Return of the Second Division to Quarters, 216. March of the Fifth Deckan Division to the Bhetwah in pursuit of Kurreem's and Wassil Mahomud's Pindarries, 218. Cheettoo's Durrah dispersed near the Nerbuddah, 219. Operations of Lieutenant-colonel Mac Morine from Hoossingabad, 220. Return of Brigadier-general Hardyman's Force to Quarters, 221. Return of Brigadier-general Toone's Force to Quarters, 222. Operations of Major Macpherson from Hoossingabad, 222. Expulsion of Gunput Rao's Party from the Nagpoor Territory, 223. March of the Second Division of the Deckan Army from Nagpoor, for the Reduction of the Ceded Districts West of the Wurdah, 224. March of Colonel Pollock's Detachment, and Progress of the Second Division to Ootran, 224. Establishment of Holkur's Authority about Indoor, entrusted to the Goozerat Force, 225. Head-quarters of the Deckan Army recross the Nerbuddah, 226. Progress of the First Division to the Taptee, 227. Unexpected Hostility of the Garrison of Talneir, 228. Reconnaissance and Description of Talneir, 229. Attack of the Place, 230. Assault by the Gates, 231. Reflections on this Service, 232. Considerations on *Coups de Main* in general, 233. Comparison of the usual Means employed, 234. Reflections on the Engineer Establishment in India, 236.

CHAPTER IV.

ESTABLISHMENT OF THE RAJAH OF SATARA, AND EXPULSION OF THE PEISHWAH FROM THE POONAH TERRITORY.

Re-organization of the Fourth Division and Reserve, 238. Siege of Singhur, 239. Capitulation, 240. Reduction of Poorunder, 241. Occupation of the remaining Forts between Satara and Poonah, 242. Colonel Deacon's Marches North of the Godavery, and Departure of Sulabut Khan, 242. March in pursuit of Gunput Rao to Ahmednuggur, and Return of Sulabut Khan, 244. Reduction of Places between Ahmednuggur and Poonah, 244. Operations of Lieutenant-colonel Prother's Detachment in the Southern Kokun, 245. Operations above the Ghats, 247. March of the Fourth Division from Satara, in Pursuit of the Peishwah, 248. Cavalry Combat at Ashtee, 249. Parallel between the Defeat of Gokla and Dhoondeah Waugh, 251. Reflections on this Affair, and its Results, 252. Considerations respecting the British and Mahratta Governments, 254. Re-establishment of the Rajah of Satara, 255. Movements of Lieutenant-colonel Pollock's Detachment, 256. March of the Head-quarters of the Deckan Army through the Valley of Khandesh, 257. March of the First and Second Divisions to the Godavery, 257. Movements of the Enemy, and of the Fourth Division, 258. Re-organization of the Hydrabad and Poonah Divisions, 259. Termination of Sir Thomas Hislop's Command of the Army of the Deckan, 261.

CHAPTER V.

ESTABLISHMENT OF HOLKUR'S AUTHORITY IN WESTERN MALWAH, AND EXPULSION OF THE PEISHWAH FROM THE DECKAN.

Sir John Malcolm's Movement from Jawud to Oojein, 264. Detachments from the Goozerat Force at Indoor, in Search of Pindarries, 264. Junction of Colonel Huskisson's Detachment, and Return to Baroda, 265. Dispatch of the captured Ordnance and Field Hospital from Mehidpoor, 266. Lawless Tribes in Western Malwah, 267. Reduction of the Soandees, 267. Expulsion of Cheettoo from the right Bank of the Nerbuddah, 268. Return of the Russell Brigade to the Deckan, 269. Hostile Design of the Nagpoor Rajah defeated by the Seizure of his Person, 270. March of Colonel Adams's Force to Hingunghat, and of Colonel Scot's to Chanda, 271. Combined Arrangements of the Hydrabad and Poonah Divisions for the Attack of Bajee Rao's Army, 271. Brigadier-general Doveton's March from Jaulnah to Panderkaorah, 272. Brigadier-general Smith's Progress down the Godavery, 273. Dispersion of Bajee Rao's Army by Colonel Adams's Attack at Seonee, 274. Results of this Action, 275. Pursuit of Bajee Rao's Army by Brigadier-General Doveton's Force, 275. Pursuit taken up by Brigadier-general Smith, 276. Return of the Hydrabad Division to Jaulnah, 277. Return of the Poonah Division to Serroor, 277. Reflections on the Peishwah's Conduct, 278. His Military Stratagems, 279. Reflections on the Marches of Armies, 281. Comparison of those in Europe with those in India, 282. Bad Roads, and consequent heavy Gun-Carriages, the Impediments to the Movements of Indian Armies, 283.

CHAPTER VI.

REDUCTION OF THE SOUTHERN MAHRATTA COUNTRY.

Brigadier-general Munro's Situation at Dharwar in December 1817, 285. Commencement of Operations by the Reduction of Places South of the Mulpurba, 286. Incursion of a Body of Pindarries into the British Territory, 288. March of Brigadier-general Munro's Force beyond the Mulpurba, 289. Capture of Badaumee, 290. Occupation of the Country between the Mulpurba and Gutpurba, 291. Operations before Belgaum, to the Construction of breaching-Batteries, 292. Reduction of the Place on Capitulation, 293. Reflections on this Success and consequent Arrangements, 294. March of Brigadier-general Pritzler's Force from Satara for the Investment of Wassota, 295. Fall of that Place, and Liberation of the Prisoners, 296. Return to Satara, and Separation of the Madras and Bombay Troops, 297. Junction with Brigadier-general Munro's Force, 297. Collected Amount of the Reserve, 298. March to Sholapoor, and Description of the Enemy's Strength and Position, 299. Escalade of the Pettah, 300. Defeat of Gunput Rao's Attack, 300. Flight and Dispersion of Bajee Rao's Infantry, 301. Reflections on the Arms of Cavalry, 302. Surrender of Sholapoor, 304. Considerations on the Number of Mahratta Forts, 305. Importance of Fortresses in general, 305. Application of these Reflections to the Case of India, 306.

CHAPTER VII.

SUBJUGATION OF THE KOKUN, AND THE NORTHERN PARTS OF THE POONAH TERRITORY.

Operations of Lieut.-colonels Kennedy and Imlach from Severndroog and Malwan, 309. March of Lieut.-colonel Prother's Detachment to Ryghur, 310. Capitulation of the Fortress, 312. Its former Importance, 312. Dislocation of the Kokun Field Force, 313. Return of the Reserve to Dharwar and Hooblee, 314. Detachments in the Jooneer and Ahmednuggur Districts, 315. Sir Thomas Hislop's Return to the Madras Presidency, 317. March of Lieutenant-colonel Mac Dowell's Detachment to the Khandesh Ghats, 317. Siege and Capture of Rajdeir, 318. Countermarch to the Godavery, 320. Siege and Surrender of Trimbuck, 321. Inadequacy of the Means of further Operations, 322. Defence of Soanghcer, 323. Description of Malleygaum, 323. Investment and Construction of the Batteries, 324. Unsuccessful Assault, on the 29th of May, 326. Abandonment of the Attack of the West Face, 327. Successful Operations after the Arrival of the Bombay Train, 328. Comparison of the Force of both Parties, and Loss of the Besiegers, 330. Qualities of an Engineer, 331. Lieutenant-colonel Mac Dowell's Detachment assumes its Monsoon Position, 332.

CHAPTER VIII.

REDUCTION OF THE PLACES IN THE INTEREST OF APPAH SAIB BHOOSLAH.

Re-organization of Major-general Marshall's Division, 333. Subjugation of the Saughur District, 334. Treacherous Conduct of the Killedar of Mundalah towards Major O'Brien, 336. Investment of the Fort of Mundalah by General Marshall's Division, 337. Establishment of the Batteries, 338. Storm of the Town and Surrender of the Fort of Mundalah, 339. Trial of the Killedar for Rebellion and Treachery, 341. March of the Saughur Force towards Chouraghur, which is consequently evacuated, 342. Escape of Appah Saib, Ex-Rajah of Nagpoor, 343. Lieutenant Johnson's successful Attack of the Pindarrics at Goruckpoor, 344. Arrival of the Force at Saughur, and Major Lamb's unsuccessful Attack of Satunwarree, 344. Evacuation of Satunwarree, and Return of Major Lamb's Detachment, 346. Creditable Behaviour of Scindiah's Contingent, 347. Uselessness of Native Auxiliary Horse in general, 348. Considerations respecting the Maintenance of Irregular Horse in the British Service, 349. March of Colonel Adams's Force against Chanda, 350. Establishment of the Batteries against the Town, 352. Capture by Storm, 353. Comparison of the Attack of Indian and European Forts, 355. Causes which produced the imperfect Defence of Places during the Campaign, 356. Return of the Nerbuddah Division to Hoossingabad, 357.

CHAPTER IX.

SUBMISSION OF THE PEISHWAH, AND DISSOLUTION OF THE MAHRATTA CONFEDERACY.

March of the Hydrabad Division from Jaulnah to Boorhaunpoor, 358. Bajee Rao's Application to Sir John Malcolm for friendly Intercession, 360. Considerations which dictated the Conduct observed by Sir John Malcolm, 361. Disposition of Sir John Malcolm's Division during the Negotiations, 362. Interview between Bajee Rao and Sir John Malcolm, 363. Ultimatum dispatched to the Ex-Peishwah, 365. His reluctant Surrender on Conditions, 366. Reflections respecting the Necessity of the Terms granted, 367. Return of the Hydrabad Division to Quarters, 369. March of Sir John Malcolm with the Ex-Peishwah towards the Nerbuddah, 370. Mutiny of the Arabs, 371. Suppression of the Mutiny, 372. Reflections on this Service, 373. Arrival at Mhow, and Confirmation of the Convention, 374. Comparison of the British with Native Governments, 375. Difficulty attending a fair Judgment respecting Indian Affairs, 376. Mutability of Indian Empires, 378.

CHAPTER X.

EXPULSION OF APPAH SAIB FROM THE NAGPOOR TERRITORY.

Reasons for continuing this Memoir after the Dissolution of the Mahratta Confederacy, 380. Distribution of the British Forces, 381. Elevation of the young Rajah of Nagpoor, 382. Destruction of Captain Sparkes's Detachment, 383. March of British Detachments into the unsettled Districts, 384. March of Brigadier-general Doveton's Light Force from Jalnah to Ellichapoor, 385. Detention of this Reinforcement by inclement Weather, 387. Destruction of the Enemy's Garrison of Mooltye, 387. Captain Gordon's successful Attack of Compta, 388. Major Wilson's successful Attack of Ambaghur, 390. Major Wilson's successful Attack of Pourree, 391. Evacuation of Amlah before Captain Jones's Detachment, 392. Major Bowen's successful Attack of Boordye, 392. Lieutenant Cruickshanks's successful Excursion into the Hills, 393. Arrival of Cheettoo Pindarry at Patchmurree, 394. Unsuccessful Efforts of the Ghoands North of the Hills, 395. Last Efforts of Appah Saib at the Close of 1818, 396. Combined Dispositions for his Attack and Interception, 397. Siege of Jilpy-Aumneir by Lieutenant-colonel Pollock's Detachment, 397. Renewal of Operations in Khandesh, 399. Reduction of Ummulneir, and Separation of the Field Force, 400. Combined Movement into the Mahadeo Hills, 401. Appah Saib's Escape from Patchmurree, 402. Brigadier-general Doveton's March to Boorhaunpoor, 404. Reflections on the Events described in this Chapter, 404.

CHAPTER XI.

TERMINATION OF THE WAR.

APPENDIX.

MEMOIR

OF THE

OPERATIONS OF THE BRITISH ARMY

IN

INDIA

DURING THE

MAHRATTA WAR OF 1817, 1818, & 1819.

BOOK I.

CHAPTER I.

CAUSES OF THE WAR.

Retrospect of Political Relations with the Native Powers subsequent to the War of 1803. *Peishwah. Bhooslah. Holkur and Scindiah. Pindarries. Lord Minto's Administration. Peishwah. Bhooslah. Holkur. Lord Hastings's Administration. Peishwah. Nizam. Bhooslah. Augmented Force in the Deckan. Irruption of the Pindarries. Necessity of destroying their Power. Prospects connected with the Attack of the Pindarries. Extensive means of the British Government. Exercise of a special Authority necessary in the Deckan. Sir Thomas Hislop. Sir John Malcolm. Primary Object of the Military Operations subsequently changed.*

Retrospect of political relations with Native Powers subsequent to the War of 1803.

THE political events which immediately followed the general Mahratta War of 1803, and those which preceded that of 1817, have already been laid before the public in a manner so satisfactory, as may obviate the necessity of entering at length into considerations with which probably the reader is familiar. This remark would be more incontrovertible, did such publications supply a connected account of the occurrences which occupied all the time between those periods. As there are, however, considerable blanks, it is trusted that a short retrospect of the series of events which intervened, will prove acceptable, as furnishing the desired connection, so far as relates to the objects of the present Memoir.

Peishwah.

The conclusion of the Mahratta War of 1803 left the British Government in India at peace with all the Native Powers, without, however, destroying the seeds of future hostility. The Peishwah's alliance was by many deemed insecure; and the Duke of Wellington, whose situation at that time gave him opportunities of observing the progress of affairs, and of officially declaring his opinions, formed the lowest estimate of Bajee Rao's* character and government.

Bhooslah.

The Rajah of Nagpoor, through the agency of others whose conduct he might, when convenient, disavow, committed, under the mask of friendship, actions which sufficiently demonstrated that he was not cordially attached to the new order of things. He engaged, likewise, in intrigues with Scindiah and Holkur to such an extent, as led to the supposition, if not to the absolute belief, that by a confederacy of those three powers, the war would be renewed.

Holkur and Scindiah.

Holkur, however, was the first to commence hostilities, unaided by any public support from other quarters, though, not improbably, encouraged by hopes of future assistance. The course of that war, which was terminated in 1805, is sufficiently known. Scindiah, the year before, through fear of Holkur's encroachments on him, while labouring under the disastrous effects of his late campaign, had concluded a treaty of defensive alliance with the British Government. Yet, when he perceived how much their arms were occupied by the contest with Holkur, he could not resist the temptation of again trying his strength. He, [illegible], marched from Saughur, and arrived on the Chumbul when Holkur was at Bhurtpoor, the Rajah of which he had engaged in his cause. These events occupied a considerable time; during which the operations at Bhurtpoor terminated, and Holkur shewed a disposition so pacific, that Lord Lake hastened by speedy marches to attack Scindiah. The latter fled with the greatest precipitation from Subbulghur, when, finding Holkur subdued, and a peace subsequently concluded with him by the British Government, he, also, was willing to make a new treaty, which took place in November 1805.

Pindarries

Thus was the general peace restored, as it respected the British dominion; but the States of Scindiah and Holkur, which had been accustomed to live by plunder, continued to desolate most of the country now denominated Central India. Under this state of things, was gradually and imperceptibly formed a power which, though still under the sanction of an avowed subjection to the rulers of Malwah, gained sufficient strength, with time, to extort territory from them under various pretences, and to wrest

* The Peishwah's.

some lands from the petty Chiefs adjoining. These losses produced occasional efforts to reduce to obedience those freebooters denominated Pindarries, in the first instance by persuasion, and when that failed, by treachery. But the seizure of the Chiefs by Scindiah diminished neither the spirit nor the numbers of their followers, and they were at length liberated by him, on the promise of paying a large ransom, at a fixed period. Thus let loose in 1807, they again headed their followers, and spread devastations on all sides, sparing, however, the territories of Scindiah, in order to retain the support of his name and authority.

Lord Minto's administration.

The foregoing occurrences refer to the Governments of Lord Wellesley, Lord Cornwallis, and Sir George Barlow. Lord Minto arrived in India during the year last mentioned, when peace, the excursions of Pindarries excepted, prevailed throughout the country. From his Lordship's pacific * policy this peace would have continued, but for the unjustifiable conduct of neighbouring Powers. In 1808, Runjeet Sing, the Chief of Lahore, threatened to subdue, and annex to his dominion, the petty Seik States lying to the south of the Sutlej, which, for a long series of years, had been dependant on the empire of Delhi. Under these circumstances, they claimed the protection of the British Government. This was granted by assembling a respectable force, under General St. Leger, who marched towards the Sutlej, while Mr. C. T. Metcalfe † proceeded on a mission to Runjeet Sing. As the result, the latter abandoned his designs on the southern Seiks; and uninterrupted amity has, ever since, subsisted between both governments.

Peishwah.

To return to the Mahrattas. The Peishwah's affairs had proceeded in a peaceful tenor till 1812, when his attempts to subvert the southern

---

* This expression must be taken entirely with reference to the Native Powers, without examining where that Nobleman placed the line which should separate the propriety of forbearance from that of chastisement. Charged as he was with the reduction of all the French and Dutch possessions east of the Cape, he had abundant cause for avoiding war in India, during a period occupied in distant operations, which were conducted with energy, and terminated with the most brilliant success.

† This gentleman, whose name, from frequent employment in affairs of delicacy and trust, is well known as a diplomatic agent, was, till lately, Political Resident at Delhi; and is now (1820) Secretary, to the Governor General, in the secret and political department.

Jaghiredars * led to an interference for their protection. These it had always been the British policy to support, consistently with their performance of the service due to the Poonah Government. The Peishwah was induced to wave some of his extravagant pretensions, while the Jaghiredars were obliged to renew their obedience, and their services, which, till then, had been either refused or tardily granted. But the British Government was, afterwards, constantly called upon, to prevent, on the one side, unjust exaction, and to enforce, on the other, subordination and respect.

Bhooslah.

During the life of Raghojee Bhooslah, nothing occurred to disturb the peace, or the seeming harmony, which subsisted with the Nagpoor Government. Indeed, according to the natural course of things, it should have been greatly improved by the conduct of the British Government, during Lord Minto's administration, in 1809, when the Nagpoor Power was considerably endangered in consequence of the invasion of Ameer Khan.† Then the movements of a respectable division of the Madras army, under the late Major-general Sir Barry Close, from the Deckan, and of a similar corps, under Sir Gabriel Martindell, from Bundelcund, relieved the Nagpoor army from the distressing situation of being invested in a position where, for some weeks, it was forced to engage in a daily skirmish for water.

Holkur.

Since the peace with Holkur, in January 1806, the most amicable terms had subsisted between that Power and the British Government. Almost the only intercourse, however, which occurred, was on the occasion of the reception, at Holkur's court, of Mohiput Ram ‡; the invasion of the Nizam's and Peishwah's territories by Wahid Allee Khan Bungush §, and

---

* These were Chiefs considered, latterly, though not originally, as feudatories of the Peishwah. They principally occupied the Mahratta country south of the Kistnah, from whence their general appellation.

† The name of this Chief occurs in the campaign, of 1805, with Holkur. He commanded a large body of horse, who crossed the Ganges, and were pursued by the British cavalry under Major-general Smith, till their final retreat beyond the Jumnah.

‡ He was one of the Nizam's ministers. Having shewn himself inimical to the existing relations between that *Durbar* and the British Government, he was expelled from his office in 1807, and placed himself at the head of an insurrection. The Hydrabad Subsidiary Force marched to suppress his party, which was pursued to the extremity of the Deckan.

§ This was a Chief, who having collected a formidable body of soldiers of fortune, was surprised at Aumulnair, in Khandesh, by the Hydrabad Subsidiary Force, under Brigadier-general Doveton, in 1808, and his force destroyed or dispersed.

Ameer Khan's attack on the Rajah of Nagpoor. Jeswunt Rao Holkur became deranged in 1808; and from that period till his death, in 1811, he took no active part in the government of his dominions. He was succeeded by his son, the present Mulhar Rao Holkur, then about six years of age.

Lord Hastings, on his arrival in India, as Governor-general and Commander-in-Chief, in 1813, found the relations with the Native Powers such as have been cursorily described. In a short time, however, his Lordship's attention was drawn to the conduct of the Nepaul State; and the experience, early obtained, of the effects of forbearance on the part of the British Government, induced him to adopt those spirited measures, with the success of which the public are well acquainted. Lord Hastings's administration

For some time previous to 1815, the Poonah Court had been disturbed by intrigues to displace the minister Sedasheo Bhao Munkaisur. In the course of that year they gained much ground; the Peishwah having been persuaded to bring into public notice his personal favourite Trimbuckjee Deinglia. It was during the period of *his* power that Gungadhur Shastree, the accredited agent from the Guickwar State, was assassinated in the streets of Punderpoor, to which place he had attended the Peishwah's Court for purposes of devotion. As Trimbuckjee was universally considered as the promoter of this murder, though it was subsequently undoubted that he was but an instrument employed for that purpose by the Peishwah, the interference of the British Government was found necessary, for his disgrace and punishment. The details of his apprehension, confinement, and escape from Taunah, in September 1816, are sufficiently known. The latter event was followed, in the early part of the ensuing year, by an insurrection, of which he was the head, about the Mahadeo hills, south of Poonah. The Peishwah not only evading the adoption of measures to reduce Trimbuckjee's power, but also scarcely acknowledging its existence, the Subsidiary Force was marched to the vicinity of Poonah, and terms of a new alliance, more efficient than that now subsisting had proved, were offered for his Highness's acceptance. The security required for the performance of these terms, and which he was unable to reject, was the surrender into British possession of the forts of Ryeghur, Singhur, and Poorunder. Accordingly, after the treaty of June 1817, they were immediately occupied by British garrisons. Peishwah.

While these commotions prevailed in the Court of Poonah, occurrences at the Nizam's *Durbar* produced, on the Resident's part, the application Nizam.

of military force, to assert the British predominancy. This measure was, in its result, successful, and the Nizam's son, who was at the head of the insubordinate party, was sent to reside in the fort of Golconda.

Bhooslah

Rajah Raghojee Bhooslah died in the early part of 1816, and was succeeded by his imbecile son Moodajee, who, by incapacity and total blindness, was rendered unfit to govern. A Regent was therefore appointed, by the principal members of the State, who desired and obtained the concurrence of the British Government. This Regent was Appah Sahib, who succeeded his cousin Moodajee, on the *Musnud* becoming vacant soon afterwards by his death. During the short regency of Appah Sahib, the object of a subsidiary alliance, which had long been a desideratum, was accomplished at his express solicitation. These events, under Lord Hastings's administration, with reference to the States of Nepaul, Poonah, Hydrabad and Nagpoor, it was necessary to relate, as they produced the gradual augmentation of the British forces* in the Deckan previous to the war.

Augmented force in the Deckan.

Irruptions of the Pindarries.

How far the removal of a large force, to a distance from the British frontier, might have induced the Pindarries to expect that they should find it ill protected, is, perhaps, a consideration of little importance. It is, however, probable, that seeing they had already exhausted the districts of the Deckan, where their incursions had, likewise, become more difficult, they were induced to fix on a less impoverished, though more distant, field of plunder. Accordingly, in the early part of 1816 and 1817, they entered the British territory, under the Madras Presidency, in large bodies. Notwithstanding the previous dispositions for the prevention of their incursions, and the activity of the troops in the vicinity of their routes, they succeeded in materially injuring the country, and left no reason to suppose their chastisement such, as to preclude the probability of their return.

Necessity of destroying their power.

These aggressions called for the most spirited conduct on the part of the British Government; and the communications on this subject to the several Mahratta powers, through whose tolerance, if not encouragement, the Pin-

* From 1814, successive reinforcements, according to the exigency of affairs, had made them amount, at the date of the treaty of Poonah, to one squadron of horse artillery, eight regiments of Native light cavalry, two companies and a half of European foot-artillery with an equal number of gun Lascars, three regiments of European foot; four companies of rifles, three battalions of light infantry, thirty-two battalions of the line, and five companies of pioneers, Native.

darries existed on so formidable a footing, should have convinced them that the proposed measures would be most effectually executed. The result of defensive measures had been already ascertained by the experience of several years. Not only had the expense of that system been proved to be ruinous, but the unremedied evil was, as undoubtedly, found to be rapidly increasing. In fact, it will appear, that in the natural course of things, affairs could not have had another result. The Pindarries were situated on the Nerbuddah, in the centre of a circle, of which the British Government had to defend the circumference, with the exception of a small portion, extending from Goozerat to the nearest point of the Jumnah. This part, forming the south-eastern boundary of Rajahpootana, was, however, that alone which the Pindarries abstained from molesting; but it was occupied by plunderers of as formidable a character under another name. Ameer Khan had succeeded in establishing himself permanently in Jeypoor and Joupoor. As these countries were nearly exhausted by his army, it appeared that he had scarcely any option, but that of relying on the plunder of the neighbouring British possessions, for its future subsistence. To dwell longer on this point is evidently superfluous; for, in proportion as it was ruinous and inefficacious to attempt the defence of a circumference, the opposite points of which might be threatened at the same moment, so was the concentric attack of this source of annoyance advantageous and indispensable.

(Map 1.)

Prospects connected with the attack of the Pindarries.

All the Native Powers concurred in deploring the evil of the predatory system which prevailed in the midst of them, and testified every possible alacrity to contribute to its suppression. These professions, which were probably intended to diminish the ardour of the British Government, were not sufficient to lull it into a confidence in their sincerity. Less suspicion might have been entertained of the Nagpoor State, with which the greatest cordiality prevailed; and the conclusion of the treaty of the 13th of June, with the Peishwah, seemed to promise at least that no counteraction would arise from that quarter. On Scindiah, Holkur, and Ameer Khan, there was less reason to depend. The former was long known to participate in the plunder of the Pindarries, in return for the protection of his authority. Of Holkur's Government, no better opinion could be formed, although any intercourse with it had for a considerable time ceased, and its dispositions remained, in some degree, to be surmised. Ameer Khan, whose dominion existed only with the presence of his army, was notoriously acknowledged to be the supporter of plunder and rapine against regular government. In contemplating, therefore, the plan of a campaign for the extermination of the Pindarries, it behoved the Governor-general to provide at the same time against a combination of the substantive Powers. He thus would frustrate a measure which tended to establish an active foreign controul in the heart of India. He would also relieve the British territories from an annoyance, which, there was reason to suspect, was viewed by the Native Powers with a secret satisfaction.

Extensive means of the British Government.

The provision of means for this purpose was projected on the most ample scale; for it has always been the policy of Lord Hastings's administration, to bring forward, in military operations, such an overwhelming force, as either to deter, or rapidly to crush, opposition. From what has been premised, it will appear that the first and immediate theatre of war would be the Valley of the Nerbuddah, but that, after the expulsion of the Pindarries from that line, the operations were liable to extend to any part of Malwah or the Deckan, according to the direction of their flight, and to the part which, under those circumstances, the substantive Powers might appear to adopt. Those countries forming generally what is denominated Central India, are nearly surrounded by the British possessions. They are therefore open to the separate entrance of armies drawn from the three Presidencies. With regard to the Deckan, it was already occupied, as has been mentioned, by a large British force. On that side, therefore, it was only required, that what reinforcements could be spared should be added from the territories of Madras and Bombay. The *demonstrations* on the northern and eastern parts of Malwah were the peculiar province of the Bengal army. On the western frontier, the means of bringing forward a strong corps of Bombay troops, existed in Goozerat.

Exercise of a special authority necessary in the Deckan

A combination so extensive, under the direction of one authority, has nothing exactly similar, or parallel to it, in European warfare. The armies which attacked the power of Buonaparte, after the failure of the Russian expedition, were indeed drawn from points scarcely more distant than were the corps lately co-operating in India; yet, the combination against him was formed by the coalition of many crowned heads. This remark is offered to exhibit the peculiar character of a general war in India, arising from the vast extent of the theatre; the numerous lines of operations; the successive changes of their objects, owing to the uncertain councils of the Native Powers; the length of the communications, and the necessity of previously collecting extraordinary supplies of money and provisions, where the system of levying contributions in an enemy's country, is not practised by the British armies. Even the means of transport are maintained entirely independent of the resources of the country, through which the movements of an army are conducted. These are the principal considerations of a government, in preparing for war. Yet, however well they might be digested in the present instance, the contemplation of the delays and uncertainties attending all distant communications through the theatre of operations, and the necessity, under particular circumstances, of an immediate conclusion of political arrangements, without a previous reference, pointed out the expediency of a special controul and responsibility being exercised in the Deckan, subject to general instructions, and such occasional direction, as the Governor-general, who resolved on taking the field in person, should consider necessary to be applied.

In selecting for such distinguished authority an officer deserving of proportionate confidence, Lord Hastings acknowledged that his rank should be sufficiently elevated, to justify the supercession of the Residents at Hydrabad, Nagpoor, and Poonah. Also, that he should be aided in the exercise of his powers, by a Political Agent from the Governor-general, to be the channel of correspondence with those functionaries, and of negotiations with the Native States and Chiefs. Pursuant to these views, his Excellency, Lieutenant-general Sir Thomas Hislop, Bart. Commander in Chief of the army of Fort St. George, was directed to assume "the personal command of all the troops in the Deckan, and the general controul, subject to the authority of the Governor-general in Council only, of the military operations, and political negotiations and arrangements, connected with the proposed service in that quarter of India;"* and farther, to consider himself "subject eventually, in the conduct of operations in the field, to the authority of the Commander in Chief in India."† Sir John Malcolm, K. C. B. and K. L. S. was, at the same time, appointed for the purposes already mentioned, to be the Governor-general's Political Agent at Sir Thomas Hislop's head-quarters, on the grounds of "his acknowledged abilities, judgment, experience, and his extensive and accurate acquaintance with every branch of our British political interests."‡ In making these

Sir Thomas Hislop

* Supreme Government to the Government of Fort St. George, 10th May, 1817.

† Supreme Government to Sir Thomas Hislop, 10th May, 1817.

‡ Governor-general's Minute, 10th May, 1817.

arrangements, however, it was not intended that the duties of the Residents should be unnecessarily interrupted; and it was therefore expressly declared, that "the authority vested in Sir Thomas Hislop does not extend to the regular and established functions of the Residents; nor is it to give him any interference in the details of their official duties, or in the affairs of the courts at which they reside." For so delicate a situation, few persons were so well qualified as Sir Thomas Hislop. His unassuming character gave entire security to the Supreme Government, that no strained interpretation of the extensive political controul vested in him, would derange the dispositions they contemplated. In the spirit of these arrangements it was resolved, that the officers at that time in command of corps in the field, should not be unnecessarily superseded. The rank of Brigadier-general being also considered suitable to the extent of command proposed for those following, the same was conferred, by the Supreme Government, on Colonels Toone, D'Auvergne, Arnold, Hardyman, Watson, and Frith, serving under the Bengal Presidency; on Colonels Munro*, Doveton, Malcolm, Floyer, and Pritzler, serving under the Madras Presidency; and on Colonel Smith, serving under the Presidency of Bombay. Thus a provision was made for the eventual employment of the Political Agent, Sir John Malcolm, in a military capacity, pursuant to Lord Hastings's view of enabling Sir Thomas Hislop "to avail himself of that officer's services on any distinct military command, on which he may find it expedient to employ an officer in his particular confidence."†

Sir John Malcolm

Primary object of the Military operations subsequently changed.

It may be proper to mention, that these orders of the Supreme Government were dated on the 10th of May, 1817; at which period the affairs at Poonah, previous to the treaty, were in that unsettled state which has been described. Accordingly, Sir Thomas Hislop's instructions embraced, in the first instance, the object of reducing the Peishwah's power. The presence of the Poonah Subsidiary Force having, however, been found sufficient for this purpose, as already noticed, the campaign was proposed to be opened by the attack of the Pindarries; leaving the assumption of the Cessions, in the southern Mahratta country, to be effected by means of a corps assembled on the Toombudra. This was placed under the command of Colonel Thomas Munro, a name too well known to require, through any eulogium here, an introduction to the reader's acquaintance.

* Colonel J. Munro was later in receiving his Brigadier-general's commission than the other officers on whom it was conferred.

† Governor-general's Minute, 10th May, 1817.

CHAPTER II.

VIEW OF MILITARY FORCES.

Transactions at the Native Courts immediately previous to the War. At Gwalior. At Poonah. At Nagpoor. Estimate of the Amount of the Enemy's Force, including the Nizam, and excluding the Guickwar. Army of Scindiah. Of Holkur. Of the Peishwah. Of the Bhooslah. Of the Nizam. Of Ameer Khan. Of the Pindarries. Reflections on the Composition of a Native Army. Origin of Regular Corps in the Native Service. Description of their Cavalry and Infantry. Of their Artillery and Engineering. Detail and Amount of British Forces: and of Auxiliaries. Comparison of the Amount of the Field Armies, with the Extent and Population of the Country producing them. Its Revenues. Review of the former Armies of India.

THE political negotiations at the several Native Courts, subsequent to the Governor-general's resolution of introducing a British army into the heart of India, are intimately connected with a view of the plans adopted for the opening and prosecution of the campaign. Thus, however it has been the Author's object to confine himself to subjects of a nature purely military, some reference to such negotiations he finds to be indispensable. Transactions at the Native Courts immediately previous to the war.

The situation of Scindiah's dominions, both politically and geographically, gave it a primary importance in the contemplation of a war for the extirpation of the Pindarries; accordingly, early measures were adopted to engage the power of that government in support of the British designs; or, failing in that object, to preclude, at least, its opposition. The uncertainty of Scindiah's councils, while it rendered this task extremely difficult, served, at the same time, to prevent that Chief from assuming a position declaredly hostile. The insubordination of his army, added to some other circumstances, also contributed to produce occurrences of a vexatious nature. By the last Treaty of Poonah, the Peishwah ceded, in perpetuity, to the British Government, all right and sovereignty over his possessions north of the Nerbuddah. These were bordering on the territories of Dowlut Rao Scindiah, with which they were in some instances intermixed; a circumstance which presented an obvious cause of difference At Gwalior.

with a Mahratta State. A force in Scindiah's service, consisting of some battalions of infantry with guns, under the command of Major Hartoon, entered the district of Deorree, seized on Ghoorjama, one of its dependencies, and subsequently attempted to levy contributions on the town of Deorree itself. In reply to remonstrances, on the part of the British Resident, against this aggression, Scindiah disclaimed the acts of his officer, and affected to dispatch orders for his immediate recal. These, however, being disregarded, Scindiah would neither punish him for the alleged disobedience, nor permit his ally to assist in chastising the perpetrators of these acts of hostility, though he admitted his own inability to controul them. Such conduct is frequent with the Native Powers of India; as suited to their loose system of government, by enabling them occasionally to disavow a participation in acts for which they may be called to account. In the same spirit of unsatisfactory alliance, applications for the protection of their families and support of themselves, were received from the Pindarry Chiefs, by Scindiah, while professing his anxious desire to suppress them. Their Vakeels actually resided in his camp, as well as the British Resident, till the course of military operations rendered useless their longer continuance. Such conduct, on the part of Scindiah, not only encouraged the efforts of the Pindarries, but declared to India that he was really adverse to their expulsion.

(Map II.)

At Poonah.

By the fourth Article of the Treaty of Poonah, concluded in June 1817, the Peishwah had engaged to hold no communication with any Power whatsoever, except through the British Resident with his Highness. Yet, before the end of the following month, that officer had reason to suspect, that negotiations for a general confederacy against the British interests were in progress, at the particular instigation of the Peishwah. Intelligence arrived from several quarters, detailing the intrigues of his emissaries at the camps of Scindiah, Holkur, and Ameer Khan. At the same time he was affecting to concert, with the British Resident, the most effectual means of crushing the Pindarries. For this ostensible purpose, a large body of horse and foot was assembled, under his own immediate direction; while the organization of a separate corps was placed, by the sixth Article of the late Treaty, in the hands of the Resident. This was proposed to consist of three thousand foot and five thousand horse. They were to be commanded by British officers, and regulated by them on the principles which already obtained in an auxiliary corps maintained by his Highness the Nizam.

At Nagpoor.

The Rajah of Nagpoor had in like manner agreed, to place at the disposal of the British authority at his Court, a contingent of three thousand horse and two thousand foot, to be commanded and organized by British officers. The delays however which occurred, in bringing forward this contingent, became a source of constant expostulation on the part of the Resident, and indicated how little the Rajah was disposed to observe the terms of the existing alliance. Nor did this circumstance afford the only cause to suspect the sincerity of his professed wish to continue on terms of friendship. During the suspicious proceedings at Poonah, shortly after the Treaty with the Peishwah, he had carried on direct negotiations with that Prince, in positive violation of the alliance under which he derived his right to the British protection of his dominions. Subsequently, indeed, he expressed his contrition for this conduct; and his professions, though not calculated on, might be thought sincere, till the opening of the campaign. Then it appeared, that, during the interval, he had surrendered the fort of Hoossingabad as a post and depôt for the Nagpoor Subsidiary Force.

Estimate of the amount of Enemy's Force.

In proceeding to form an estimate of the forces of the several Native Powers, against whose opposition it was necessary to provide, difficulties present themselves sufficient to discourage the undertaking, were it not indispensable to the plan of this Memoir. In pursuing this object, it will be necessary not only to employ documents dated before the opening of the war, but likewise to anticipate occasionally the use of such information, collected during the subsequent operations, as will give a more definite idea on this head, than can be derived from vague conjectures, regarding the secret preparations for meditated hostility. The real force of the Pindarries is thus undetermined. They have always endeavoured to make their power appear as formidable as possible. For this purpose, they spread abroad reports, the falsehood of which few were disposed to detect. Their system was altogether that of terror. Practising the expedients of a civilized nation in modern times, they maintained emissaries, throughout the sphere of their influence, to publish exaggerated accounts of their successes, and to contradict or suppress occasional rumours of their reverses. In the presumptuous language of their pretensions, Cheettoo did not hesitate to propose himself to Scindiah, as an instrument for the expulsion of the British from India. He probably participated in the general opinion, that the British Government had not the power of expelling the Pindarries, considering how ineffectual had hitherto proved the attempts at controuling them.

including the Nizam;

In this enumeration, the irregular force of the Nizam is likewise included, notwithstanding the difficulty of deciding whether he should be considered able, as well as inclined, to be hostile. His personal character was inactive and imbecile; while the discontented spirit of some of his sons, added to the restlessness of a numerous armed population, rendered dubious, at the least, the turn which affairs might take, at Hydrabad, under the supposition of British reverses. It is however certain, that, in the instructions to Sir Thomas Hislop, he was directed to provide for the support of the British predominancy at that capital. Secret overtures were also made to the Nizam on the part of the Peishwah, through agents dispatched for that purpose, but who were secured by the activity of the Resident.

excluding the Guickwar.

It may be a question whether the Guickwar Government should not be included in the enumeration of eventual enemies, considering that it was a Mahratta State. The Bombay Government evinced considerable apprehensions respecting its attachment, after the ruptures at Poonah and Nagpoor, and the march of the British force from Baroda. Yet, as the Governor-general denied the necessity of this apprehension, and as a body of Guickwar irregular horse absolutely joined, though tardily, the British force in Malwah, the remaining military resources of that Government have been considered as entirely neutral.

Army of Scindiah.

An estimate of Scindiah's force, dated at Gwalior the 11th of October, 1817, and derived through the most authentic means procurable, describes it as follows:

(Map II.)

	Horse.	Foot.	Golandauze	Field-guns
Scindiah's Head Quarters, at Gwalior	5,000	3,000		
Baptiste . . . . [illegible]	1,000	5,500		
Bapoojee Scindiah . . . . Ajemeer	3,000	2,000		
Jeswunt Rhao Bhao . . . Jawud	1,500	2,000		
Ambajee Punt . . . . . . Budnawur	1,500	2,000		
Anna Bukhshee . . . . . Shajehanpoor	1 000	1,000		
Belonging to the district of Gwalior	1,250	250		
Five hundred men is the general strength of a battalion, and to each is commonly attached four or five field-pieces, making	—	—	—	140
Allowing ten to twelve Golandauze to each gun	—	—	1,500	
Total	14,250	15,750	1,500	140

Or 31,500 fighting Men, and 140 Light Guns.*

* This estimate will probably be found not to exaggerate Scindiah's force. Some years previously, it was computed by Sir John Malcolm, when at that Chief's *Durbar*, to amount to eighteen thousand horse, nine thousand five hundred foot, and seven hundred Golandauze; total, 28,200

The following statement of Holkur's force was derived, by Sir John Malcolm, from official documents at Poonah, in September 1817. Of Holkur.

INFANTRY AND ARTILLERY.

	Men.	Guns.
Commanded by Purseram Dada.		
Park of Artillery	—	35
Golandauze, 350; Gun Lascars and Pioneers, 200	550	
2 Battalions, containing each 507 men 1 Battalion, containing . . 407 men 1 Battalion, containing . . 357 men } Including Golandauze, Gun Lascars, and Pioneers	1,271	
4 Guns to each Battalion	—	16
Ballakao Inglia.		
2 Battalions, including Golandauze, &c.	814	8
Juggunnaut Rao.		
1 Battalion, including Golandauze, &c.	507	4
2 Battalions, including Golandauze, 607 men, and 4 guns each	1,214	8
Ram Deen.		
2 Battalions, including Golandauze, 507 men, and 4 guns each	1,014	8
Ghuffoor Khan and Roshun Beg.		
1 Battalion, including Golandauze, 707 men, and 4 guns . . .	707	4
1 Battalion, including Golandauze, 351 men, and 4 guns . . .	351	4
Attached to Holkur's Head-Quarters.		
1 Battalion, including Golandauze, 500 men, and 4 guns . .	500	4
Battery of 8 guns, with 156 Golandauze, Gun Lascars, &c. . .	156	8
Horse Artillery, 156, including Pioneers, Gun Lascars, &c. . .	156	8
Personal Guards { Bundelas . . 300; Meiwattees . 400 }	700	
ABSTRACT.		
Golandauze . . . . 890 14 Battalions . . . . 5,450 Personal Guards . . . . 700 Gun Lascars and Pioneers 900	7,940	107
Cavalry.		
Contingent of the Jaghiredars . . . . 3,000 Silledar Horse . . . . 12,000 Pagah Horse 5,000	20,000	
Total . . .	27,940	107*

men: and subsequently, by Mr. Strachey, to sixteen thousand horse, and seventeen thousand six hundred foot, with one hundred and thirty seven guns. It appears therefore, that more difference has gradually obtained in the composition of Scindiah's army, than in its numbers, during the period of peace between the two Governments.

* It was the opinion however of Sir John Malcolm, who, with the Resident at Poonah, took much trouble to ascertain the strength of Holkur's army, that since the date of the above state-

Of the Peishwah.

The British Resident at Poonah estimated the force of the Peishwah, at the opening of the campaign, at twenty-five thousand horse and twenty-five thousand foot. Of the latter, one half were considered as distributed in the various forts of his dominions, and the other half disposable for field operations. The following estimate, subsequently made with much research, is not widely different:

	Horse.	Foot.	Guns.
Bapoo Gokla	11,200	6,000	
Vinchoorkur	3,000	1,000	
Narropunt Aptey	2,000	2,000	
Abba Poorundhurree	1,150	500	
Trimbuckjee Deinglia	1,000	500	
Nepunkur	1,000	500	
Waman Rao Aptey	1,000		
Mor Dixit	700		
Rastey	500	200	
Hurree Munishwar	500	200	
Various Chiefs of less note, whose quotas did not exceed 500 men	5,950	2,900	
Guns attached to different Chiefs, including the Peishwah's own	—	—	37
Total in the Field* .	28,000	13,800	37

(Map II.)

Of the Bhooslah

There appears to be no better method of computing the strength of the Rajah of Nagpoor's army, than by adding to the estimated amount of the force engaged with Brigadier-general Doveton's division in December, the troops stationed at the same time in the Valley of the Upper Nerbuddah. Nor does it appear that any other military means, worthy of being mentioned, were

ment, the infantry had been encreased, and the cavalry diminished. He accordingly concluded, from the report of spies, compared with other sources of information, that the foot amounted to about twelve thousand men, and the horse to the same number, making a total of twenty-four thousand men. The justness of this estimate appears to be, in a great measure, supported by an official report of the Resident at Nagpoor, dated the 5th September, 1815. In this it is mentioned, that the Holkur Government were desirous of relying on their infantry, and that their cavalry could not be taken at less than ten thousand.

* Exclusive of the above number, there were 17,300 foot, and an unknown number of guns in the garrisons of Poorunder, Singhur, Wassota, Maha and Ryeghur, Koaree, Lhoghur, Sholapoor, Pandaughur, Satara, Purtabghur, with several others of less note; besides an unestimated number of hereditary soldiers, who served for lands, and garrisoned many places, especially in the Kokun.

distributed in other parts of the Nagpoor dominions. The enemy's force, on the above-mentioned occasion, was represented to be :—

	Horse.	Infantry.	Guns.
In the field at Nagpoor	12,600	8,500	85
In the City	—	4,600	
In the Valley of the Nerbuddah, with other small detachments	3,166	4,726	
Total . . .	15,766	17,826	85

The amount of regular force* which might be brought forward by the Nizam's Government is calculated on the following principles :—In 1815, it was stated from the public returns to be equal to 29,004 horse, and 42,737 foot. It was concluded, however, from the best sources of information, not really to exceed two-thirds of those numbers, or about fifty thousand men of every arm. Of this number, twenty thousand foot would have been of the best description. The horse would probably have amounted to twenty-five thousand, while, of inferior foot, which would be of no use in the field, the numbers would have been unlimited. If, therefore, the Nizam's efficient force, for service in the field in case of a rupture, be taken at forty-five thousand men, it will not be overcharged. At the same time, this may be considered as not likely to be much below the mark; the active levies of men and horse by all the surrounding States having reduced his means of recruiting to much narrower bounds, than would have controuled him under other circumstances. of the Nizam,

In 1809-10, Ameer Khan's Power was at its zenith. He commanded between thirty and forty thousand horse, many of them, however, composed of Pindarries. His connection with Mahomud Shah Khan, who maintained an army on the resources of the Joupoor State, also gave him the disposal of twelve thousand disciplined infantry, six thousand cavalry, five hundred and fifty golandauze, and one hundred and twelve pieces of ordnance. It appears that, subsequently, Ameer Khan's Power became considerably reduced ; for when, in May 1817, Sir John Malcolm's inquiries were directed at Calcutta, through the best channels of information regarding that chief's military force, it was estimated at only twelve thousand horse, several indifferent battalions, and between two and three hundred guns. of Ameer Khan

* It is here assumed that the regular infantry and reformed horse, commanded by European officers, would adhere to the British interests.

of the Pindarries.

In 1814, the Pindarries were estimated by Captain Sydenham, Political Agent in Berar, to consist of the following numbers.

		Horse.	Foot.	Guns.
Scindiah Shahee, or adherents of Scindiah	Cheettoo	8,000	500	10
	Dost Mahomud	6,000	800	5
	Kooshal Koowar and Namdar Khan	4,000		
	Total	18,000	13,000	15
Holkur Shahee, or adherents of Holkur.	Kadir Bukhsh	1,200	200	3
	Tookao	1,000		
	Shah Khan and Buhadoor Khan	800		
	Total	3,000	200	3
	Grand Total	21,000	1,500	18

The author of this computation, who had superior opportunities for forming it, and spared no pains in his researches, concludes, that the number of horse may, without exaggeration, be taken at twenty thousand. Of these, one half may be considered fit for military service, and the remainder calculated only for the work of devastation and plunder, under the protection of the former. In July 1817, Colonel Adams, commanding the Nagpoor Subsidiary Force, the head-quarters of which were at Hoossingabad, in the almost immediate vicinity of the Pindarries, estimated them at twenty thousand horse and foot, and twenty-two guns. Nor does it appear that better means have existed than he possessed, of determining their numbers. Yet the fact, that these bodies, when an opportunity has offered of ascertaining their amount, have always been found less numerous than they were reported, will make it proper to take them at a reduced estimate. It may not be far from the truth, to assume the total at fifteen thousand horse, fifteen hundred foot, and twenty guns. These will be considered as the numbers permanently attached to the Pindarry leaders; for, doubtless, they have occasionally far exceeded that amount. Captain Tod, when attached to the Residency with Scindiah, a short time previous to the war, assumed their numbers to be, at one time, forty-one thousand. This probably arose from their being joined at that particular period by volunteers, for a plundering excursion, from several Native armies. These, if considered as Pindarries on the present occasion, would probably be twice included in the general total. The disposition of the mind, especially when under alarm, to magnify objects indefinitely, contributes not a little to swell the numbers* of an irregular body in idea and report. Squadrons and battalions, from their distinct and compact formation, are to be contemplated separately, like individuals; while the same number of troops, particularly horse, scattered over a plain, may appear almost innumerable. On this account, hyperbolical expressions* are continually applied to considerable bodies of irregular horse, and never to regular corps.

The following recapitulation of hostile forces offers an estimate of their aggregate amount.

	Horse.	Foot.	Guns.
Scindiah	14,250	16,250	140
Holkur	20,000	7,940	107
Peishwah	28,000	13,800	37
Bhooslah	15,766	17,826	85
Ameer Khan	12,000	10,000	200
Nizam	25,000	20,000	
Pindarries	15,000	1,500	20
Total	130,016	87,316	589

Reflections on the composition of a Native army.

In contemplating the Native force which has been enumerated, one of the first circumstances which will strike a military reader, unacquainted with Indian armies, is the great disproportion of cavalry to infantry. The cause must be sought in circumstances common to nearly all the countries of the East; for under almost every Asiatic Government, cavalry is the prevailing force. The formation of regular infantry has arisen generally from a connection with Europeans. Nor is this system confined to Asia: it prevailed in Europe within the period of modern history, till expelled by the progress of civilization; and it now maintains its ground only in Turkey. In ancient history, the states of Greece and Rome appear as the only seats of civilization, compared with surrounding nations; and, by their infantry, they augmented their power or maintained their existence. In the Roman legions, the cavalry formed but an inconsiderable proportion; while the armies they defeated, in the subjugation of the African and Asiatic part of their empire, consisted almost entirely of horse. An immature civilization appears therefore to be one cause of this prevalence of cavalry, aided, in

* In both French and English relations of the late Russian campaign, the Cossacks are called clouds and swarms, and represented as flights of locusts, as well from their countless number as from their devastations; yet their aggregate amount did not exceed forty thousand with all the divisions of the Russian army.

some countries, by the facility of multiplying horses. The indispensable necessity of maintaining some order among infantry, for their own preservation, has been acknowledged in all times. To effect this object, some degree of coercive regulation is requisite; but this can only exist steadily with a regular Government. Under a contrary state of things, a love of uncontrouled license is the ruling passion of all the individuals of a country. On horseback alone, and in the plain, can this be effectually enjoyed. The irregularity of Governments therefore appears to be another cause. Accordingly it will be found that, in many instances, an Asiatic State must be satisfied with being served on horseback, or not at all. Again, the exterior of cavalry-service bears an imposing appearance of grandeur and power, which, in the vain, flatters self-love, while it inspires terror among the ignorant. These are particularly moved by whatever affects the eye, as are savages, by brilliant colours; and, in like manner, it is found that the young, even in civilized countries, always prefer the service of the cavalry

Origin of regular corps in the Native service.

Calculated as that arm is for offensive, rather than for defensive operations, it receives from this circumstance additional splendour. During the conquests of the Mahrattas, their forces consisted entirely of horse, and they had chiefly horse to contend with. They may be said to have first come in contact with regular infantry, in their wars with the Nizam, when a small disciplined corps, with a few guns, under French officers, baffled all their attempts to break them. This corps had forced the Nizam to receive it as his principal support, after one of the most brilliant acts * ever performed by a small body surrounded by enemies. The Mahrattas, after their experience of the efficacy of this arm, immediately gave their attention to the formation of infantry and artillery; but neither the nature of their government, nor their character or physical constitution, were calculated to give full effect to this change. Infantry best succeeds among a people with robust bodies and obstinate minds; whereas the Mahrattas are the most subtle of nations, and the most delicately framed. They were obliged to call in the aid of Europeans to form their corps, which were almost entirely recruited from other casts of Hindoos, and from Mahomedans. These were certainly the most powerful infantry that ever existed under a Native Government in India; but they were nearly destroyed in the war of 1803; and the Treaties that followed provided against the return of Europeans for

---

* See Orme's History of India. London 1775. 4to edition. Vol. I. page 155.

their reformation. All the towns in the Mahratta country being walled, and capable of some defence, it was found that they could be retained, under even a partial degree of subjection, only by means of infantry and guns. This circumstance obliged the Governments to maintain those arms, even after they had experienced their inability to stand against a British army, in consequence of a general action with whom their guns were taken and their infantry destroyed.

Description of their Cavalry and Infantry

Previously to the war, several of the Mahratta Chiefs were represented as declaring, that their hope could rest only on a return to their original method of warfare, by which their numerous cavalry acted on the offensive, and carried devastation and dismay into their enemies' territories. But their cavalry has since become widely different from what it was in those times. The breed of horses has been neglected, and they are neither numerous nor generally fit for military service. The principal division of the cavalry is into *russalahs**, which may be considered on the footing of a regiment. Their strength is indeterminate, depending entirely on the influence and the rank of the nobleman who commands them. Any inferior division, such as a *braderree*, or association, under a Jemidar, is equally indefinite. The men who serve on horseback are Mahomedans, Rajpoots, and Brahmins. The pay of a private, finding his own horse, varies from twenty to fifty rupees † a month. It is frequently regulated by the appearance of the man and the goodness of his steed. As the continuance of the pay depends on the service of the one as well as of the other, it is not extraordinary that the safety of the horse should never be unnecessarily endangered. This circumstance appears to be one of the principal vices in the cavalry-service of the Native Powers. They are equipped with a fire-arm and a weapon of cut or thrust; the former of which is a blunderbuss, pistol, or matchlock, and the latter a lance or sabre; but the lance and blunderbuss never go together. The infantry is composed of various degrees of efficiency. The most hardy of all are the Arabs, and their immediate descendants, who receive higher pay than other casts. Every substantive Native Power had a portion of these troops; and they are in general fully to be depended on, but particularly in the defence of walls.

* This opportunity is embraced of mentioning, that a Russalah of British irregular horse consists of 1,000 men in the Deckan, and of 100 in Hindoostan.

† In some instances it will even amount to much more.

The Sindees, or the inhabitants of the lower Indus, are held next in consideration; so much so, as to be occasionally confounded with the Arabs in the enumeration of these troops. The Gossyes have been always considered as good troops. They are a Hindoo cast of peculiar habits, scattered over different parts of India. Among other professions, they pursue that of arms, and may be ranked in the same degree with Rohillahs, Jats, and Seiks. The remaining descriptions of all casts who serve on foot, such as Telingas, Beders, &c., may be considered as of an equal standard: they form the bulk of the disciplined corps and inferior irregulars. The division of the infantry is into regular and irregular: but the latter is, on account of the less discipline, considered as the higher service. In some instances they are called *Nujeeb* (literally, Noble), and would not deign to stand sentry, or perform any fatiguing duty, considering it their only business to fight, and to protect the person of their Prince. In like manner, they consider a uniform dress and the carriage of a musket as derogatory to their dignity; their arms being a matchlock or blunderbuss, and a sword. The Allygools answer nearly the same description, being bodies of tried fidelity, and reserved for services of great danger. The pay of an Arab is generally twelve rupees a month, and from that it descends, as to other casts, by various gradations, to five. Notwithstanding this description of irregular foot, they are in many instances divided into *pultuns*, like the regulars. These bodies consist of five hundred men at the highest average. To each is commonly attached from two to four guns, with a proportion of golandauze (men who load the gun), of khalassees or those who serve at the drag-ropes, drivers, and bildars or pioneers.

Of their Artillery and Engineering.

From this proportion of ordnance attached to a battalion, it might be expected that its number, in a Native army, would swell to a considerable amount. This apparent consequence will, however, vanish, when it is considered how few are the battalions, and that the numbers of guns are not affected by the number of cavalry. Besides the artillery attached to the troops in line, there is, with every Native army, a park, where are placed their heavier batteries, their howitzers, and mortars. These mortars are of little use in their hands, and therefore only maintained in trifling numbers; while less science being required for the practice of guns, they are served in a manner which always surprises those who examine the inferiority of their equipment and construction. The service of the artillery is held in the same estimation as that of the cavalry, and the same casts are found in both. They are armed with a sword, receive higher pay than the infantry, excepting the Arabs, and are deservedly esteemed the best troops in the Native service. In the art of fortification, the Natives of India are still less advanced. In this country, it is in the same state as it was in Europe before the introduction of the regular systems. Even though some judicious works have been constructed by European engineers for Indian powers, they appear to have neither imitated the example nor appreciated its superiority. They place their reliance more in a strong profile than in a judicious plan; of the advantages of the former, the rudest people are a judge, whereas some degree of science is required to comprehend the merits of the latter. Nothing can speak more forcibly their ignorance of the attack and defence of fortified places, than that their superiority is decidedly manifest when acting on the defensive. In fact, a Native army scarcely ever succeeds in taking a place which attempts resistance: it is generally reduced to terms of composition, through the distress caused by a large force lying around it. On the contrary, some very vigorous defences have been made, and sieges prolonged, both by a determined defence of the breach, and by bold sallies to the trenches. Mining has found its way into some parts of India, but not generally; and there are but few instances of its being practised with much effect.

Detail and amount of the British Forces.

Many of the principal stations of the Bengal Army nearly approached the frontiers of the Mahratta territory. Thus only a few distant movements were necessary, in order to hold in readiness on that side a sufficient amount of force to take the field, whenever the state of politics should render that measure expedient. Accordingly, in the month of September 1817, the troops under orders for field-service amounted to two squadrons of European and Native horse-artillery, two regiments of dragoons, six regiments of Native cavalry, thirteen companies of European and Native foot-artillery, five battalions of European foot, and twenty-four battalions of Native infantry, besides five corps of irregular horse, and twenty-three companies of pioneers, gun-lascars, and miners. On the side of Goozerat were held in readiness, one regiment of dragoons, two companies of European artillery, one battalion of European foot, four battalions of Native infantry, and four companies of pioneers and gun-lascars. In the southern Mahratta country was Brigadier-general Munro's force, consisting of half a squadron of horse-artillery, three squadrons of dragoons, four squadrons of Native cavalry, two companies of European foot artillery, one battalion of right flank companies of European foot, four companies of Native rifles, one battalion of Native light infantry, two battalions of Native infantry of the line, and five companies of pioneers and gun-lascars To these corps, the force noticed in the First Chapter (p. 6.) as already in the Deckan, being added, with a few variations, gives a total of British regular troops amounting to four squadrons of horse artillery, sixteen squadrons of dragoons, forty-four squadrons of Native cavalry, twenty-five companies of foot artillery ([illegible] golandauze), ten battalions of European foot, sixty-three of Native infantry, forty-eight companies of pioneers and gun-lascars, and of irregular troops four corps of horse.

and of Auxiliaries

It will here be proper to take into the account of regular troops available for the war, those corps in the pay of the Nizam and of the Peishwah, whose services were at the orders of the British government.

These were the Russell brigade, consisting of two battalions of Native infantry, one company of golandauze, and one company of gun-lascars; the Berar infantry of four battalions of Native infantry, one company of golandauze, and one company of gun-lascars; the Poonah brigade of two battalions of Native infantry, two companies of golandauze, one company of pioneers; and Salabut Khan's brigade of two battalions of Native infantry, and three companies of golandauze. The irregular horse in the Nizam's service, commanded by European officers, were equal to four thousand men. Those to be raised for the Peishwah amounted only to one thousand three hundred and fifty, though proposed to be five thousand. The contingent of Dowlut Rao Scindiah, though called for at the commencement of the war, was not ready to be brought into the field till the month of February 1818, when it consisted of four thousand horse. The Mysore silladars amounted likewise to four thousand. The last and lowest arm, which was as much considered in a political as in a military view, was the aid invited from petty Native states in alliance, or with whom there was hitherto no immediate intercourse. The Jaghirdars on the west of the Jumnah, were called on to furnish small quotas of irregular horse, according to their means. The same requisition was addressed to the chiefs bordering on Bundelcund. Subsequent proposals of a similar nature were made to the several Rajpoot States, who might be considered as having no common interest with the Mahrattas. These negotiations, however, may be viewed as having little effect beyond that of neutralizing the efforts of the parties to whom they were addressed. The aids supplied by those under the immediate protection of the British Government were inconsiderable, and by the remainder co-operation was tardily afforded, or only agreed to at the end of the campaign.

	Horse.	Infantry.	Guns.
The Guickwar State brought forward	2,000		
Begum Sunnoo, two Pultuns (Nujeebs)	—	1,000	8
Fyze Mahummud Khan, one Pultun (Nujeebs)	400	800	3
Uhmud Bukhsh Khan	2,000	250	
Rajah of Macheree	500	500	2
Rajah of Bhurtpoor	1,200		
Nabob of Bhopal	800		
Rajah of Rewah	300		
Total..	7,200	2,550	13 *

The total of forces described amounted to the following numbers:

	Europeans.	Natives.	Total.	Grand Total.
Horse Artillery	836	178	1,014	3,716
Foot Artillery	1,652	1,050	2,702	
European Cavalry	2,247	—	10,053	10,053
Native Cavalry	—	7,806		
European Infantry	8,474	—	68,887	68,887
Native Infantry	—	60,413		
Pioneers, Gun-Lascars, and Native Miners, &c.	—	4,935	—	4,935
Total of Regulars....	13,209	74,382	—	87,591

	Horse.	Foot.	
British Irregular Horse	5,773		
Hydrabad Irregular Horse	4,000		
Poonah Irregular Horse	1,350		
Scindiah's Irregular Horse	4,000		
Mysore Irregular Horse	4,000		
Total of Irregular Horse, commanded by European Officers	19,123		
Irregular Contingents, commanded by Natives ..	7,200	2,550	
Grand Total of Irregulars	26,323	2,550	28,873
Grand Total of British and Allied Forces	—	—	116,464

* The above enumeration does not specify the Dholpoor contingent of horse, whose numbers were never well ascertained, nor were they withdrawn from the Chumbul; but they may be fairly considered as included in the total, for that is composed of the nominal numbers, which invariably, on similar occasions, exceeds the real amount by a considerable proportion.

	Guns.
Guns with the Grand Army	124
Guns with the Deckan Army	158
Guns with the Irregular Contingents, commanded by Natives	13
Total number of Guns of all calibers	295

Comparison of the amount of the field armies, with the extent and population of the country producing them.

(Map I.)

The whole Military force belonging to Powers allied for and against the British interests, and available for field service, appears, from the preceding investigation, to amount to 333,800 men. The country whose resources were drawn forth on the present occasion, extends from the Sutlej to Cape Comoree *(Comorin)*, and from the mouth of the Nerbuddah to that of the Burmpootur, containing nearly one million British square miles. Of these, the British possessions, and those of protected Powers, whose fidelity was unsuspected, amounted to 552,000* square miles; while the remainder was equal to 428,000† British square miles. These might be fairly considered as hostile to the British interests. The governments of some petty States avoided, indeed, to declare themselves by any overt measures; yet their relaxed rule permitted the enemy to draw resources, particularly in men and horses, from their country, without any limitation. Again, the regular infantry and reformed horse in the Nizam's service were principally raised in the Deckan, and at the same time were taken into the calculation of British means. If, therefore, the assistance derived from the country of the enemy, be set off against that which they derived from neutral governments, the superficial contents of the latter, equal to 6,000 square miles, must be deducted from the extent of country assumed as hostile to

* Bengal Presidency, including Oude and protected frontier States	326,000
Madras Presidency, including Mysore, Travancore, Kurnool	210,000
Bombay Presidency and Goozerat, &c.	16,000
Total	552,000
† Scindiah and Dependencies; Holkur and Dependencies	81,000
Peishwah and Dependencies	60,000
Bhooslah and Dependencies	124,000
Nizam and Dependencies	97,000
Part of Rajahpootana	60,000
Remaining petty States	6,000
Total	428,000
Grand Total	980,000

the British interests, which will thus be reduced to 422,000 British square miles. It might be satisfactory, if a comparison were also made of the population of the several Belligerent Powers ; but the difficulty, not to say, impossibility, of gaining any information on this subject, worthy of confidence, renders the attempt fruitless. Within the Company's territories, where the best means of calculation should exist, the population, previous to the Nepaul war, has been variously estimated, at forty, at fifty, and even at sixty millions. It is therefore evident that any conclusion on this subject must be entirely vague.

Its revenues

An accurate knowledge of their revenues would not be much more conducive to the object of appreciating the efforts of the different States, indicated by the number of fighting men which they brought into the field. The Peishwah, whose clear revenue was two crores and ten lacs of rupees annually, and who was certainly the richest of the active hostile Powers, did not produce a much larger army than Holkur, who may be considered as the poorest.* To this chief the Peishwah paid a subsidy, to encourage his exertions. The Nizam, with an annual revenue of nearly three crores of rupees, is supposed able to bring forward an army as large, in proportion to his revenue, as the Peishwah; while the Bhooslah, on a nett revenue of sixty-five lacs, and Scindiah, with only fifty-five thousand rupees more, came into the field in respectable force, which appeared to bear no calculable proportion to the funds at their disposal. The soldiers in the army of a Native Power, who are entirely devoid of patriotic sentiment, consist of all casts and of all nations of India, and even of some nations beyond India. Thus the population of the country actually at war, is a criterion no better than the revenue, the deficiencies of which are frequently compensated by the contributions and plunder derived from the theatre of operations. How far this system is efficient, may be inferred by a reference to the subsistence of the French armies in the wars of the Revolution. An army maintained in time of profound peace may be in proportion to the revenue, if regularly paid; but under a Native Government that would be an extraordinary circumstance, and would demand a more regular system of rule than they are found to possess. As long as an Indian army is able to carry on offensive operations, recruits will flow in from all quarters. Perhaps, therefore,

* Holkur's annual revenue has been estimated at thirty-six lacs and a half of rupees; but he was supposed to have much treasure in jewels.

the character of the war in which a Native Power is engaged may be of as much importance* as its revenue, its population, or the superficial contents of its territory. Ameer Khan's Power in 1809-10 is a forcible instance to establish this point. He had neither territory nor population under his acknowledged dominion, and the revenue which he derived through his influence in Holkur's government, was very incommensurate to his military force. But whatever may be the compound ratio which shall express the military force of a country, it is evident that the Indian armies brought into the field in 1817 were very weak, in comparison with the resources which would be derived from a country of similar extent in cultivated Europe.

If, in former periods, the numbers of fighting men it produced were much more numerous, it will follow that the country has since become impoverished. Such, indeed, appears, from the evidence of many other circumstances, to be the case in Central India; while the British possessions have become richer, as well as more extensive. At the famous battle of Pamput in 1761, when the Mahrattas had reached their summit of power, and pretended to the universal empire of Hindoostan, they produced two hundred thousand men in one army against the Mahomedans, computed at one hundred and fifty thousand. India has never again beheld three hundred and fifty thousand combatants engaged in one field. The rival

---

* Even under the more regular governments of Europe, the military force of a nation will not be found more proportionate to the above elements of calculation. The population of European Russia is estimated at thirty-five millions, and in 1807, could produce an army in the field of two hundred thousand men. In 1812 she brought forward three hundred and twenty-seven thousand; while France, from a population of fifty-one millions, including the kingdom of Italy, the Illyrian Provinces, and the departments of Holland, Italy, and Germany, opposed her with four hundred and fifteen thousand five hundred men, independent of her army in Spain. In 1808 France made great efforts, but they produced no more than two hundred and fifty thousand men; while England at the same time, with a population of only fifteen or sixteen millions, maintained two hundred and thirty thousand, exclusive of two hundred thousand militia, seamen, and marines. There is, consequently, no direct proportion between the population and the military force of a nation, which as little depends on the territorial extent. Great Britain and Ireland contain about one hundred and eight thousand square miles, European Russia one million two hundred thousand, and the territory lately under French influence about three hundred and seventy-five thousand square miles. The revenue would therefore appear a better criterion; but this again is modified by the expense to the Government of each soldier, which differs in different States, and is greatest of all in England.

The above estimates are chiefly derived from "Paisley's Military Policy," and a late Memoir of the Campaign of 1812, in Russia.

Powers of that day have ever since been declining, though Scindiah established a temporary ascendancy by his acquisition of the seat of the Mogul empire, and the custody of the Prince, which seemed again to inspire the Mahrattas with hopes of exclusive dominion. At the battle of Kurdla or Pareinda, in 1795, between the Nizam and the confederate Mahrattas,—

	Horse.	Foot.	Guns.
The former brought into action	44,650	43,540	108
And the latter	73,600	38,000	192
Making in all	118,250	81,540	300

But, though this number contained the full extent of the Nizam's resources, the entire Mahratta force was by no means brought forward; twenty-six regular battalions only were present, and ten thousand horse and foot of Purseram Bhao's were on their way to join. In 1803,—

	Battalions.	Guns.	Horse
Scindiah brought forward an army of	68	422	41,500
The Bhooslah	15	60	30,000
Holkur had at the same time, though not then opposed to the British, an army of	24	200	30,900
Shumshur Buhadoor	4	20	10,000
Making a Total of	111	702	112,400
Estimating the Battalion at 550 men each, including golandauze, they will be			61,050

which makes a total of 173,450 fighting men, and 702 field-guns. At the same time the British Government were enabled to produce in the field an army of fifty-five thousand regular troops, besides the irregular horse supplied by its Allies. The difference of the positions in which the Belligerent parties stood at the commencement of the late war, consisted in the Peishwah having joined the confederacy, while Scindiah was deterred from declaring himself; and in the British Power having become richer by the acquisitions of Cuttack, Bundelcund, cessions in Goozerat, and conquests from Scindiah on the Jumnah and the Ganges.

CHAPTER III.

OPENING OF THE CAMPAIGN.

Reflections on the Importance of small Bodies of British Troops in India. Arrival of the Marquis of Hastings at Cawnpoor, and Formation of the Grand Army into Divisions and Brigades. Arrival of Sir Thomas Hislop's Head-quarters at Hydrabad, and Formation of the Army of the Deckan. Proposed Plan and Period for opening the Campaign. Inclemency of the Weather in the Deckan during September 1817, *and actual Distribution of the Troops. Previous Reliefs. March of Corps and Detachments from Sekunderabad. March of Corps and Detachments from Serroor and Punderpoor. Continued Inclemency, and consequent change of the proposed Routes. March of the Corps of the First and Third Divisions from Jaulnah. Departure of the Head-quarters of the Deckan Army from Hydrabad. March of the Second Division. March of the Fourth Division. Partial assembling of the First and Third Divisions on the Nerbuddah, and Dispositions on that River. Arrival of the Head-quarters at Hurdah, and Orders to the Second and Fourth Divisions. Proposed Dispositions at Nagpoor. Assembly of the Fifth Division at Hoossingabad. Advance of the Marquis of Hastings with the Centre Division to the Sind, and of the Second Division to the Chumbul. Predicament to which Scindiah was reduced by these Movements. Conditions proposed to him, and Treaty of the 5th November. Advance of the Third Division. Advance of the Force under Brigadier-general Hardyman. Dispositions of Brigadier-general Toone's Force. Preparation for the Movement of the Reserve. Goozerat Force. Reduction of Soondoor by the Deckan Reserve. Dispositions of the Madras Government for the Protection of their Provinces.*

Reflections on the importance of small bodies of British Troops in India

PREVIOUSLY to describing the events with which the campaign opened, it may be proper to apprize the reader unacquainted with Indian Military details, that it will be necessary to notice the movements of much smaller bodies than would claim the same attention in the history of European warfare. This necessity arises from the important part acted by numbers of British troops apparently insignificant when compared with the extensive theatre throughout which they were distributed.

The history of India, since the middle of the last century, is an abundant illustration of this point. If a parallel were attempted between the battles which imposed the Treaties of Presburg and Tilsit, with those which produced the Treaties of Surgee-Anjengaum and Deogaum, it will be found that the former victories were gained by a number of regular troops at least twelve* or fifteen times larger than those which acquired the latter. Previously to 1803, the British Power, so far from opposing itself to a confederacy, found it expedient to form one in its favour for the attack of a powerful enemy. Accordingly, in both the wars with Tippoo Sultaun, the Nizam and Peishwah were engaged to bring forward large contingents. The three Presidencies then contributed to the formation of a force capable of reducing the fortress of Seringapatam. This force amounted, in 1792, to thirty-one thousand; and, in 1799, to thirty-seven thousand three hundred and seventy-nine regular troops. As the British Power extended, it came in contact with more enemies; and it became necessary to meet them at many points. The army, which had been augmented with the increase of territory, was therefore divided into several corps, each of which was capable of meeting any body of the enemy liable to be opposed to it. These corps may be compared, in many respects, to the legions of the Romans; two of which formed a Consular army, and amounted to nine thousand men. The legions composed the army of the State, and its main strength, like the regular troops of the British service. But, in both cases, the numbers, with time and extension of dominion, were found to be inadequate. The Romans, in their wars with Hannibal, perceived the want of irregular cavalry. This deficiency they supplied, by taking into pay, Gauls, Germans, and Numidians; as in the Mysore wars the British called in the aid of Moguls and Mahrattas. What was employed, in the first instance, as a temporary expedient, was subsequently organized into a permanent system. By Roman officers, a selection from the troops of the allies was marshalled, under the appellation of "extraordinaria," according to their own discipline. These form a striking coincidence with the corps supplied by Native Powers in alliance, under the names of regular infantry, reformed horse, &c.

Arrival of Marquis of Hastings at Cawnpoor, and formation of the Grand Army into Divisions and Brigades. (Map I.)

The Marquis of Hastings embarked at Calcutta on the 9th of July. On the 13th of September he arrived at Cawnpoor, in order to regulate the preparations for the campaign, and the negotiations with the Native Powers, from the nearest convenient position. His Lordship was attended by such Civil-

---

* The French Army that entered Austria, before the battle of Austerlitz, contained 200,000 men; at the battle of Jena, the French had 80,000 men, and, at Eylau, 90,000. The British Troops, in the battle of Assye, were 4,500 men, at Laswarree 7,500, and at Argaum 9,500.

officers as he required for the transaction of extraordinary business in the Political and Military departments of the Government, and by all the Head-quarters' departments of the army. From Cawnpoor was published the following order for the formation of the troops, which had been held in readiness for field service, into divisions and brigades.

GRAND ARMY.

(Plan 1.) HIS EXCELLENCY THE MOST NOBLE THE COMMANDER-IN-CHIEF.

FIRST or CENTRE DIVISION,

Major-general Brown commanding.

First Brigade of Cavalry.

Lieutenant-colonel Philpot, 24th Light Dragoons, to command.

3d Regiment Native Cavalry.
His Majesty's 24th Light Dragoons.
7th Regiment Native Cavalry.

First Brigade Infantry.

Brigadier-general d'Auvergne, to command.

2d Battalion 25th Native Infantry.
His Majesty's 87th Regiment of Foot.
1st Battalion 29th Native Infantry.

Third Brigade of Infantry.

Colonel Burrell, 13th Native Infantry, to command.

2d Battalion 11th Native Infantry.
1st ditto 24th ditto.
2d ditto 13th ditto.

Second Brigade of Infantry.

Colonel Dick, 9th Native Infantry, to command.

2d Battalion 1st Native Infantry.
Flank Battalion.
1st Battalion 8th Native Infantry.

THE SECOND, OR RIGHT DIVISION.

Major-general R. S. DONKIN commanding.

Second Brigade of Cavalry.

Lieutenant-colonel Westenra, 8th Light Dragoons commanding
1st Regiment Native Cavalry,
His Majesty's 8th Light Dragoons,
Colonel Gardiner's Irregulars.

Fourth Brigade of Infantry.

Lieutenant-colonel Vamennon, 12th Native Infantry, commanding
2d Battalion 12th Native Infantry,
His Majesty's 14th Foot,
1st Battalion 27th Native Infantry,
1st ditto 25th ditto.

THE THIRD, OR LEFT DIVISION.

Major-general D. MARSHALL commanding.

Third Brigade of Cavalry.

Colonel Newberry, 24th Light Dragoons, commanding,
4th Regiment Native Cavalry,
2d Rohillah Horse,
Four Russalahs 3d Rohillah Horse.

Fifth Brigade of Infantry.

Brigadier-general Watson to command.
1st Battalion 1st Native Infantry,
1st ditto 26th ditto,
1st ditto 7th ditto.

Sixth Brigade of Infantry.

Lieutenant-colonel Price, 28th Native Infantry, commanding.
1st Battalion 14th Native Infantry,
2d ditto 28th ditto.

THE RESERVE DIVISION.

Major-general Sir D. OCHTERLONY, Bart. G. C. B. commanding.

Fourth Brigade of Cavalry.

Lieutenant-colonel A. Knox, 2d Native Cavalry, commanding.
2d Regiment Native Cavalry,
Two Corps of Colonel Skinner's Horse.

Seventh Brigade of Infantry.
Colonel Huskisson, His Majesty 67th, to command.
2d Battalion 5th Native Infantry,
His Majesty's 67th Regiment of Foot,
1st Battalion 6th Native Infantry.

Eighth Brigade of Infantry.
Brigadier-general Arnold commanding.
2d Battalion 7th Native Infantry,
1st ditto 28th ditto,
Detachment Simroor Battalion,
2d Battalion 19th Native Infantry.

Arrival of Sir Thomas Hislop's Head-quarters at Hydrabad, and formation of the Army of the Deckan.

(Map II.)

During the time that the Marquis of Hastings was on the river, Sir Thomas Hislop, and the head-quarters of the Madras army, arrived on the 12th of August, at Hydrabad. They were joined there a few days afterwards by Sir John Malcolm, who had been deputed from the Presidency to Hydrabad and Poonah, for the purpose of holding certain communications at those courts, connected with the proposed arrangements for the opening of the campaign. The troops which were destined to join the Army of the Deckan, were ordered, on the 27th of August*, to be formed into divisions and brigades, in the following order, with a view to their assuming the positions which should be assigned to them when the season for commencing operations should arrive.

(Plan 2.)

THE FIRST, OR ADVANCED DIVISION,
under the personal command of
His Excellency Lieutenant-general Sir THOMAS HISLOP, Bart. Commander-in-Chief.

Light Artillery Brigade.
Captain-Lieutenant H. Rudyerd commanding.
The Troop of Horse-Artillery, and the Cavalry Gallopers incorporated with it,
The Rocket Troop,

Cavalry Brigade.
Major Lushington commanding.
4th Regiment Light Cavalry,
Detachment of His Majesty's 22d Light Dragoons,
8th Regiment Light Cavalry.

* Part of this order took place at a subsequent date; but is now anticipated to give a collected view of the formation of the army.

Light Brigade.

Lieutenant-colonel Deacon commanding.

The Rifle Corps,

1st Battalion 3d or Palamcottah Light Infantry,

1st ditto 16th or Trichinopoly ditto,

2d ditto 17th or Chicacole ditto.

First Infantry Brigade.

Lieutenant-colonel Thompson commanding.

Flank Companies His Majesty's Royal Scots,

1st Battalion 7th Regiment Native Infantry,

Madras European Regiment.

Second Infantry Brigade.

Lieutenant-colonel Robert Scott commanding.

1st Battalion 14th Regiment Native Infantry,

2d ditto 6th ditto.

THE SECOND, OR HYDRABAD DIVISION.

Brigadier-general J. Doveton commanding.

Cavalry Brigade.

Major H. Munt commanding.

Three Brigades Horse-Artillery,

6th Regiment Light Cavalry.

First Brigade of Infantry.

Lieutenant-colonel N. Macleod commanding.

His Majesty's Royal Scots,

2d Battalion 13th Regiment Native Infantry,

2d ditto 24th ditto.

Second Brigade of Infantry.

Lieutenant-colonel Mackellar commanding.

1st Battalion 11th Regiment Native Infantry,

2d ditto 14th ditto,

1st ditto 12th, or Wallajahbad Light Infantry,

1st ditto 2d Regiment Native Infantry.

Berar Brigade.

Major Pitman commanding.

Four Battalions Native Infantry,

Detail of Artillery, Eight Guns,

Reformed Horse.

Hydrabad Brigade.

Colonel Sir Augustus Floyer, K. C. B. commanding.
1st Battalion 22d Regiment Native Infantry,
1st ditto 21st ditto,
Five Companies Madras European Regiment,
Detail of Artillery,
1st Battalion 8th Regiment Native Infantry.

THE THIRD DIVISION.

Brigadier-general Sir J. MALCOLM, K. C. B. and K. L. S.

Colonel Patrick Walker, Brigadier.

One Brigade Horse Artillery,
3d Regiment Light Cavalry,
Five Companies 1st Battalion 3d or Palamcottah Light Infantry,
Russell Brigade { 1st Regiment, 2d Regiment,
Ellichapoor Contingent, Two Battalions and Four Guns,
4000 Mysore Horse.

THE FOURTH, OR POONAH DIVISION.

Brigadier-general SMITH, C. B. commanding.

Cavalry Brigade.

Lieutenant-colonel Colebrooke commanding.
Three Brigades Horse-Artillery,
2d Regiment Madras Light Cavalry,
Light Battalion.

First Infantry Brigade.

Lieutenant-colonel Milnes commanding.
1st Battalion 2d Regiment Bombay Native Infantry,
His Majesty's 65th Regiment Foot.

Second Infantry Brigade.

Lieutenant-colonel Fitzsimons commanding.
1st Battalion 3d Regiment Bombay Native Infantry,
2d ditto 15th ditto Madras ditto.

Third Infantry Brigade.

2d Battalion 9th Regiment Bombay Native Infantry,
2d ditto 1st ditto.

THE FIFTH, OR NAGPOOR DIVISION.

Lieutenant-colonel J. W. ADAMS, C. B. commanding.

First Infantry Brigade.

Lieutenant-colonel M'Morin commanding.

1st Battalion 10th Regiment Native Infantry,
2d ditto 23d ditto,
1st ditto 19th ditto.

Second Infantry Brigade.

Major Popham commanding.

2d Battalion 10th Regiment Native Infantry,
1st ditto 23d ditto,
1st ditto 19th ditto.

Reserve Brigade.

Lieutenant-colonel Gahan commanding.

Three Troops Native Horse-Artillery,
5th Regiment Native Cavalry,
6th ditto,
1st Rohillah Cavalry,
Light Infantry Battalion.

THE RESERVE DIVISION.

Brigadier-general MUNRO commanding.
Brigadier-general PRITZLER, second in command.

Artillery.

Lieutenant-colonel Dalrymple commanding.
Detachment Madras Artillery.

Cavalry Brigade.

Major Doveton, 7th Light Cavalry, commanding.
His Majesty's 22d Light Dragoons,
7th Regiment Madras Cavalry.

Infantry Brigade.

Colonel Hewitt, C. B. commanding.
European Flank Battalion,
Four Companies Madras Rifle Corps,
2d Battalion 4th Regiment Native Infantry,
2d ditto 12th ditto.

THE GOOZERAT DIVISION.

Major-general Sir WILLIAM GRANT KEIR, K. M. T.

Cavalry Brigade.

Lieutenant-colonel the Honourable L. Stanhope commanding.
His Majesty's 17th Dragoons,
Flank Battalion.

First Infantry Brigade.

Lieutenant-colonel Elrington commanding.
His Majesty's 47th Regiment,
2d Battalion 7th Regiment.

Second Infantry Brigade.

Lieutenant-Colonel Corsellis commanding.
Grenadier Battalion,
1st Battalion 8th Regiment.

Proposed plan and period for opening the Campaign.

At this time, Sir Thomas Hislop was suddenly attacked by a severe and dangerous illness, which rendered him, for a few weeks, incapable of business. It was justly considered a fortunate circumstance, that he had already issued the necessary orders for the formation of his army, and the preliminary disposition of the several divisions. In pursuance of these, the correspondence connected with the movement and assembly of the troops was conducted without detriment to the service, during his unavoidable detention at Hydrabad. (Map II.) Sir John Malcolm was deputed to Nagpoor, on the 3d of September, for the arrangement of certain concerns with the Bhooslah Government. He was directed, after effecting that service, to repair to Oomrouttee, in order to join his own or the Third Division. He was also to assume there the personal command of the First Division, should the indisposition of Sir Thomas Hislop prevent his head-quarters from previously arriving at that point of assembly. It was proposed that, by the 20th of October, these two divisions should descend into the Valley of the Nerbuddah; making, from a position near Hurdah, such a disposition of posts along the river below Hoossingabad, as should guard the passage of it against the Pindarries; while, above that place, a similar arrangement should be effected by the Fifth Division. At the same period, it was intended that the Second Division should occupy the lines of the Payne-Gunga and the Poornah, above and below the Berar Ghats. The Fourth Division was destined to continue the lines of defence to the left, by corps on the Upper

Godavery and the Gheernah, above and below the Ghats of Khandesh. This plan had been submitted to Lord Hastings shortly after Sir Thomas Hislop's arrival at Hydrabad. It received his Lordship's approbation, though the periods of assembly of the different divisions were deemed too late, considering the advancement of the season, and the fall of the rivers on the side of Bengal. It had been Lord Hastings's intention, in the hopes that the movements on the side of the Deckan would have been more forward, to occupy advanced positions near Scindiah's frontier on the 10th of October; and that the Third Division of the Grand Army should at the same time be in position at Callinger, for immediate co-operation with the troops from the Deckan against the Pindarries. This part of the arrangement it was found inconvenient to alter; but the assembly of the Centre and Right Divisions, and of the Reserve, at Secundra, Agra, and Delhi, was postponed till the 20th of October.

Inclemency of the weather in the Deckan during September 1817, and actual distribution of the troops.

It happened that this year there had been an uncommon drought in Hindoostan: while in the Deckan, the monsoon, which should have gradually subsided in the month of September, augmented its violence in a manner unexampled during the last twenty-five years. Combined with this untoward circumstance, which delayed the commencement of operations on the side of the Deckan, was the necessity of relieving some of the Native corps at Jaulnah, whose long employment in advance had considerably impaired their efficiency. A large portion of the troops had but recently taken up their monsoon-quarters, having been employed on field-service till an unusually late period of the year. This was especially the case with those composing the Reserve. These assembled at Darwar so late as the middle of August, with a detachment which had been actively employed under Colonel Robert Scot in Khandesh, and did not arrive at Jaulnah till the 19th of August.

(Map II)

At this time the troops, of which the divisions were to be formed, were distributed in the following manner:—

Darwar	Two Horse-Artillery Guns.	
	Two Squadrons of Dragoons.	
	One Regiment of Native Cavalry.	
	Two Companies of Foot-Artillery.	
	One Battalion (Eight Flank Companies) European Infantry.	
	Four Companies of Rifle Corps,	Native.
	Two Battalions of the Line,	Native.
Punderpoor	Half a Company of Foot-Artillery.	
	One Battalion of Light Infantry,	Native.
	One Battalion of the Line,	Native.

Sekunderabad	Six Horse-Artillery Guns.	
	One Rocket Troop.	
	One Squadron of Dragoons.	
	One Regiment of Native Cavalry.	
	One Battalion of European Infantry.	
	One Battalion of Light Infantry,	Native.
	Five Battalions, including the Russell Brigade of the Line,	
	Three Companies of Pioneers.	
Jaulnah	Half Squadron of Horse-Artillery.	
	One Regiment of Native Cavalry.	
	Two Companies of Foot-Artillery.	
	One Battalion of European Infantry.	
	Four Companies of the Rifle Corps,	Native.
	Two Battalions of Light Infantry,	
	Six Battalions of the Line,	
	Five Companies of Pioneers.	
Nagpoor	Three Troops of Native Cavalry.	
	One Company of Artillery.	
	Two Battalions of the Line—Native.	
Hoossingabad	One Regiment of Native Cavalry.	
	One Company of Foot-Artillery.	
	One Battalion of Light Infantry.	
	Three Battalions of the Line.	
	One Company of Pioneers.	
Sohagpoor	Five Russalahs of Rohillah Cavalry.	
	One Battalion and four Companies of the Line—Native.	
Gurhwarra	Three Troops of Native Cavalry.	
	One Battalion of the Line—Native.	
Jubbulpoor	Five Russalahs of Rohillah Cavalry.	
	Five Companies of a Battalion of the Line—Native.	
Near Poonah	Six Horse-Artillery Guns.	
	Two Regiments of Native Cavalry with Gallopers.	
	Four Companies of European Infantry.	
	Six Companies of Light Infantry---Native.	
At Poonah	Detail of Foot-Artillery.	
	Four Battalions of the Line---Native.	
Near Ahmednuggur	Detail of Foot-Artillery.	
	One Company of European Infantry.	
	Two Battalions of the Line---Native.	
Coreegaum on the Beemah	Company of Foot-Artillery.	
	One Battalion of European Infantry.	
	Three Battalions of the Line---Native.	
Garrisons of Ahmednuggur, Serroor, and Posts communicating with the Godavery	Detail of Foot-Artillery.	
	One Battalion of the Line---Native.	
	Details of Sick and Convalescents from all the Corps, and Detachment of the Force	

In pursuance of the project for opening the campaign on the side of the Deckan, the necessary orders were issued for the movements of the troops. These, for the sake of perspicuity, it will be proper to follow, without interruption, till the arrival of the Advance on the banks of the Nerbuddah, in the position contemplated by Lord Hastings for the fulfilment of his views on that side of Malwah. In the description of their progress, should there appear an unnecessary detail, let it be recollected that their sufferings and privations in their preparatory movements, were among the greatest hardships of the campaign. Nor can a more effectual way be adopted, of conveying to the reader a suitable idea respecting the march of troops in the Deckan at that season, or the important consideration of the delays which must be anticipated, when the exigencies of the service may require an exertion, which under less imperious circumstances it would be injudicious to demand. Previous Reliefs

Three battalions of Native infantry, viz. the 2d battalion of the 8th regiment, the 1st battalion of the 21st regiment, and the 1st battalion of the 22d regiment, were put in motion from Jaulnah to Sekunderabad*; in order to relieve there the 1st battalion of the 2d regiment, the 1st battalion of the 11th regiment, and the 2d battalion of the 24th regiment of Native infantry, destined to join the Second Division of the army. The two first of those corps commenced their march on the 29th of August, and proceeding by the route of Seiloo, arrived on the 13th of September opposite to Keir on the Godavery; in crossing which river, they were occupied till the end of the month. This detention enabled the 1st battalion of the 22d regiment of Native infantry, which marched from Jaulnah on the 20th of September, to overtake the 2d battalion of the 8th regiment and the 1st battalion of the 21st regiment of Native infantry; and the three battalions continued their route on the 4th of October to Sekunderabad, where they arrived on the 24th of the same month. The 1st battalion of the 2d regiment of Native infantry marched from Sekunderabad on the 27th of August, and proceeding by the route of Oudgheer and Purtoor, arrived at Jaulnah on the 8th of October. The 1st battalion of the 11th regiment of Native infantry commenced its movement towards Jaulnah on the 6th of September; but was so much delayed in its progress, that its route was subsequently changed at Keir, where it arrived on the 14th of October. The 6th regiment of (Map II)

* The name of the British cantonment near Hydrabad.

Native cavalry marched from Sekunderabad under orders for Jaulnah, on the 1st of September; but its route was changed likewise at the Godavery, where it arrived, at the point of Keir, on the 11th of October, by the route of Amudabad and Oudgheer.

March of corps and detachments from Sekunderabad.

A detachment, consisting of the following troops, marched in the latter days of August from Sekunderabad, with the Head-quarters departments, for the point of assembly of the First Division of the army.

(Map II.)

A half Squadron of Horse-Artillery,
A Squadron of His Majesty's 22d Dragoons,
Head-quarters, and one Wing of the Madras European Regiment,
The 1st Battalion 3d Regiment, or Palamcottah Light Infantry,
and half of the 1st Battalion of Pioneers.

This detachment proceeded under the command of Lieutenant-colonel Macgregor Murray, Deputy Adjutant general of His Majesty's forces in India, by the route of Nuwaubpet, Jogheepet, and Nizampet, to Nandeir on the Godavery, where it arrived on the 16th of October; having detached from the Manjerra, for the Third Division, four companies of the 1st battalion of the 3d regiment, or Palamcottah light infantry, to Oomrouttee. At the latter river, the detachment was joined by the rocket troop, which marched from Hydrabad on the 10th of September, having arrived there from St. Thomas's Mount on the 6th of that month. The Russell brigade, consisting of two corps of infantry, with four six-pounder field-pieces, marched from Bellarum, near Sekunderabad, on the 13th of September, under orders to proceed with all practicable expedition to Oomrouttee, where it arrived on the 27th of October, by the route of Begaurpet, Nuwaubpet, Nandeir, and Bassim.

March of corps and detachments from Serroor and Punderpoor

(Map II.)

On the 5th of September, the 4th and 8th regiments of Native cavalry, and the 1st battalion of the 14th regiment of Native infantry, commenced their march from the neighbourhood of Serroor, and continued their progress to Jaulnah, where they arrived on the 10th of October, by the route of Wamboory, Toka, and Ganderpoor. The field detachment commanded by Lieutenant-colonel Thompson, which had passed the beginning of the monsoon at Punderpoor, commenced the passage of the Beemah on the 13th of September; and arrived at Jaulnah, under the command of Lieutenant-colonel Pollock, by the route of Singwarree and Rakisbaun, on the 13th of October. Colonel Thompson had, for a considerable period, suffered from a disease, which threatened the most fatal consequences from a further continuance in the field. The prospect of an approaching opportunity of serving his country had, however, rendered him deaf to medical advice, till the period of recovery was past. An attempt was at length made to convey him to the coast; but he expired at the village of Mulliat, in his way to Poonah, on the 28th of September. A division of Mysore irregulars, amounting to fifteen hundred horsemen, which had been likewise stationed at Punderpoor, preceded, on the 2d of September the march of this force; which was joined on the 12th by two horse-artillery guns, that left Darwar on the 17th of August, and arrived by the route of Beejapoor. For the purpose of relieving the 1st and 5th regiments of Native cavalry, which had been continued on field service beyond the British frontier during an extraordinarily long period, those corps had been put in motion from Jaulnah on the 5th of August for Ellore and Bellary. A few days after the arrival of the former at Sekunderabad, on the 27th of August, the 2d regiment of Native cavalry commenced its march from Ellore, and reached Hydrabad on the 29th of September, from whence it proceeded on the 3d of October, for the head-quarters of the Fourth Division, by the route of Oudgheer and Jaulnah. The only remaining corps destined for field service, which, in the beginning of September continued stationary, were the 2d battalion of the 15th regiment, and the 2d battalion of the 24th regiment of Native infantry. The time of their departure from Sekunderabad, was dependent on their relief; after which, the former was directed to join the Fourth, and the latter the Second Division.

Continued inclemency, and consequent changes of the proposed routes.

The late period at which the western monsoon attained its extreme violence, has been already noticed. The impediments this unexpected occurrence opposed to the progress of the troops marching to their destined points, may be inferred from the delay attending their arrival. In some instances they found it impossible to move for several days; in others, they could only accomplish the advance of a few miles. The passage of the Manjerra and Beemah was arduous and tedious beyond all former example: independently of which, every little rivulet had become unfordable; while the Godavery, menacing by its extensive inundation the destruction of some corps, swept off a portion of their followers and cattle. The spirit and zeal which pervaded the whole army on the present occasion, excited these troops to make extraordinary exertions under great privations; but their cattle of every description were materially reduced in vigour and numbers, and the efficiency of their camp equipage and appointments was impaired in a similar degree. The loss of time, however, threatened to prove the most extensive evil. It was therefore deemed necessary to advance the point of assembly of the First and Third Divisions, in order that a respectable corps might be in position on the Nerbuddah at the period originally proposed. Thus they might obviate any disappointment to the public service, arising from a failure of combination with the dispositions on the side of Bengal. Hurdah was fixed on as a central point from whence to make the desired dispositions, with whatever troops should first arrive there. It was also resolved, that the corps belonging to the First Division should attempt the passage of the Taptee, in the direction of Boorhaunpoor; while those of the Third Division should march round the source of that river by Mooltye. This was the most certain, but the most circuitous route; while the other, though little more than half the distance, might prove eventually the most tedious, from the probable inconvenience of crossing the Taptee with cavalry and extensive departments, under circumstances of unforeseen difficulty. In order to guard most effectually against delay, an officer of the Quartermaster-general's department was detached with an escort from Jaulnah. He was directed to fix on the most advisable point for gaining the right bank of the Taptee; with reference not only to the passage of the river, but also to the nature of the road communicating with both banks, and to other local circumstances affecting the movements and supply of an army. The point of Changdeo, at the confluence of the Poornah and Taptee, was judiciously selected by Lieutenant Strahan, who likewise succeeded in collecting from both rivers a considerable number of flat-bottomed boats, with a view to the passage of them at their junction.

(Map II)

March of corps of the First and Second Divisions from Jaulnah. (Map II)

The 1st battalion of the 7th regiment of Native infantry, with two six-pounder field-pieces and detail of artillery, was ordered to escort such materials from Jaulnah as should be necessary for further facilitating this important operation. It was accompanied by half of the 1st battalion of pioneers, and the engineers' department under Lieutenant Davis, the senior officer of that corps, to whom was entrusted the immediate preparation of such expedients as should be found most applicable to the pressing exigency of the service. This corps commenced its march on the 20th of September, and proceeded by the route of Adjunta, Jambool, and Wuzzurkeira, to Changdeo. There, on account of the impediments still opposed by the continuance of the monsoon, it did not arrive till the 4th of October. A flying-bridge was established without delay, in the expectation of the early approach of the advanced corps, consisting of four six-pounder field-pieces with a proportion of artillery-men, four companies of rifles, the 2d battalion of the 6th regiment of Native infantry, the 1st battalion of the 16th regiment, and the 2d battalion of the 17th regiment, both light-infantry corps: the whole commanded by Lieutenant-colonel Robert Scot. Its progress was, however, delayed by the sudden rise of the Poornah above the Ghats; so that, though it marched from Jaulnah on the 26th of September, it had not crossed the Taptee before the 12th of October, having marched by Jaokera and Sumroad. It was joined on the right bank of the river by two companies of pioneers belonging to the detachment at Changdeo. Lieutenant-colonel Scot's corps was followed by the 4th and 8th regiments of Native cavalry, with four galloper-guns, and flank companies of his Majesty's Royal Scots. These had marched from Jaulnah on the 11th of October, under the command of Major Lushington, and crossed the Taptee on the 18th of the same month, that river having then become fordable. The remainder of the First Division at Jaulnah consisted of the whole of the commissariat, ordnance, and pay departments, the 1st battalion of the 14th regiment of Native infantry, and two howitzers, with detail of artillery-men, and one company of the 1st battalion of pioneers. This convoy and escort, which was subsequently joined by the two horse-artillery guns from Darwar, commenced its march on the 13th of October, and proceeded under the command of Lieutenant-colonel Mackintosh, Deputy Commissary-general, by the route of Salood to the Taptee, which it crossed at Changdeo on the 27th. It was joined on the right bank by the 1st battalion of the 7th regiment of Native infantry, and two six-pounder field-pieces, whose longer continuance on the river had now become unnecessary.

In order to describe the movements of the several parts of the Third Division, it is necessary to return to the month of September. On the 20th, Colonel Walker marched from Jaulnah with two horse-artillery guns and the 3d regiment of Native cavalry, by the route of Hewerkeir, Meiker, and Bassim. This corps arrived on the 19th of October at Oomrouttee, under the command of Lieutenant-colonel Russell, and was there joined by the four companies of the 1st battalion of the 3d regiment, or Palamcottah light infantry, which had halted since the 15th. Its progress had been considerably delayed by the swollen state of the Poornah above the Ghats, and the other obstacles produced by the inclemency of the season. Every endeavour was used by officers and men to surmount these difficulties, lest the general plans for the opening of the campaign should be affected by their slow progress. Their veteran commandant, Colonel Walker, sunk under the struggle; and thus closed, in arduous exertion for the promotion of the public service, a life which, during thirty-five years of honourable and eventful employment, had been dedicated to his profession from an early age. This melancholy event occurred at Sirpoor, on the 12th of October; and the lamented remains of this gallant Officer were interred at Bassim, on the following day, with military honours and unfeigned regret. In the mean time, the Mysore horse, commanded by Captain James Grant, advanced from Jaulnah, by Jafferrabad, Lackunwarree, Ellichapoor, and the Debanuggur Ghat, to Beitool, for the purpose of joining, or following, Brigadier-general Malcolm. Having concluded his mission to Nagpoor, he had left that place for the Nerbuddah, to assume the command of the troops assembling at Hurdah, previously to the arrival there of Sir Thomas Hislop.

Departure of Head-quarters of the Deckan army from Hydrabad (Map II.)

His Excellency was sufficiently recovered from his severe illness to move with his Staff from Sekunderabad on the 1st of October. Though still suffering from the natural consequence of so dangerous an attack, he overtook Lieutenant-colonel Murray's detachment at Nandeir, on the 16th of that month. Here the escort was divided into two parts, of which the lightest, consisting of the rocket-troop, a squadron of his Majesty's 22d dragoons, and three companies of the 1st battalion of the 3d regiment of [illegible], was selected for the immediate escort of the Head-quarters, and was joined by five hundred Silladar horse from Mysore. The remainder, consisting of the half squadron of horse-artillery, the Madras European regiment, and three companies of the 1st battalion of the 3d regiment, with four companies of pioneers, was left to follow as quickly as possible, and to bring on all the heavy equipment of the Head-quarters. The light detachment marched from Nandeir on the 19th of October, halted at Bassim on the 23d, and on the 27th arrived at Ambee-Taaklee. There Brigadier-general Doveton repaired to the Head-quarters, to receive his orders for opening the campaign with the Second Division of the army.

March of the Second Division (Map II.)

That Officer left Jaulnah on the 15th of October, and arrived on the 23d at Meiker, by the route of Sindkeir, with a half squadron of horse-artillery, one company of foot-artillery with ten six-pounders and two howitzers;

his Majesty's Royal Scots, excepting the flank companies; the 1st battalion of the 12th regiment, or Wallajahbad light-infantry; the 2d battalion of the 13th regiment, and the 2d battalion of the 14th regiment, of Native infantry. At Meiker, he was joined by the 6th regiment of Native cavalry, and the 1st battalion of the 11th regiment of Native infantry, on the 28th and 30th; both corps having marched from Keir on the Godavery, by Kotarry and Bassim.

While these movements took place in Berar on the right, the Fourth Division, commanded by Brigadier-general Smith, C. B., was advancing on the left towards Khandesh. Lieutenant-colonel Milnes, with the light-artillery, consisting of two five-and-a-half-inch howitzers, and fourteen six-pounders, of which six were horse-artillery; his Majesty's 65th foot, the 1st battalion of the 2d regiment, the 1st battalion of the 3d regiment, the 2d battalion of the 9th regiment, of Bombay Native infantry, and the light company of the 2d battalion of the 15th regiment of Madras Native infantry, commenced the passage of the Gore River, near Serroor, on the 3d of October, and arrived by the route of Ahmednuggur and Toka, at Unkota, in rear of the Unkye-Junkye pass, on the 20th of that month. On the same day, Brigadier-general Smith, C. B., arrived in position between Byzapoor and Kassurbanee Ghat, about eighteen miles to the right of Unkota; having crossed the Gore River on the 8th and 9th, and followed the route of the left corps as far as Toka. These positions were taken up with a view to cover the country in their rear, and to enable the troops to descend into the Valley of Khandesh, when that measure should become necessary. All the heavy ordnance and commissariat supplies were left in depôt at Ahmednuggur; and the 1st battalion of the 4th regiment of Bombay Native infantry was held disposable, to bring them forward if required. Other dispositions were likewise in view for the completion of the proposed strength of the Fourth Division, and for the maintenance of a well-connected line of communication between its head quarters and Poonah. These could not immediately take place, as they depended on the arrival of the Bombay European regiment from that Presidency, the 2d regiment of Madras Native cavalry, and the 2d battalion of the 15th regiment of Madras Native infantry from Sekunderabad.

March of the Fourth Division. (Map II.)

On the 7th of October, Brigadier-general Sir John Malcolm was joined at Amneir by the contingent of Sulabut Khan, Nawaub of Ellichapoor, from which he made a selection of one thousand two hundred horse, and one battalion of regular infantry, with four guns drawn by horses; the remainder, con-

Partial assembly of the First and Third Divisions on the Nerbuddah, and dispositions on that river. (Map II.)

sisting of about five hundred horse and four hundred regular infantry, returned to the Ellichapoor territory, to contribute to its defence; and were employed in guarding the passes leading into it from the Valley of the Upper Taptee.

The Ellichapoor contingent arrived by the Shawpoor Ghat, at Sindkeir, near Hoossingabad, on the 18th of October. In consequence of the reports received, by Sir John Malcolm, of the rapid fall of the Nerbuddah, a detachment from that corps was sent immediately to the Bugglatur Ghat, being the point which would first become fordable below Hoossingabad. Lieutenant-colonel Scot's detachment arrived at Hurdah on the 22d of October, from the Taptee, by Sewul, Peepload, and Charwah. Major Lushington's detachment followed by the same route, and arrived at Hurdah on the 29th of October. Lieutenant-colonel Mackintosh's detachment joined, in the beginning of November, at the same point, and by the same route. Immediate measures were adopted by Lieutenant-colonel Scot, under the orders of Brigadier-general Sir John Malcolm, for the occupation of all the Ghats on the Nerbuddah likely to become early fordable. The principal of these were, the Chipaneer, Cheechode, Bugglatur, Patkaira, and Burkeisur Ghats. At each of these a post of Native infantry, under an European officer, was established before the end of October. Brigadier-general Sir John Malcolm had then personally taken the command of the troops assembled at Hurdah, having concluded such business as previously detained him for some time at Hoossingabad. He was accompanied by the Ellichapoor contingent, and the Mysore horse; the latter amounted to about three thousand six hundred men, exclusive of the party attending his Excellency the Commander-in-Chief.

Arrival of the Head-quarters at Hurdah, and Orders to the Second and Fourth Divisions. (Map II.)

The Head-quarters of the army crossed the Poornah at Eedulabad on the 30th of October, and the Taptee, above Boorhaunpoor, on the 1st of November On the 10th, Sir Thomas Hislop entered the camp at Hurdah; and was received by a line under arms, composed of troops ardent to engage in a campaign of distant operations, and hopeful of finding a more tangible foe than the Pindarries had proved themselves, when laying waste the southern countries. On the 13th of November, Major Andrews' detachment, which pursued the route of the Head-quarters, joined the army at Hurdah, accompanied by the 2d battalion of the 14th regiment of Native infantry. This corps left Meiker on the 27th of October, and followed up the march of Major Andrews' detachment from Mulkapoor, at which place it arrived on the 1st of November, by the route of Koatlee.

Of the four companies of pioneers marching with this detachment, three had been ordered to join the Second Division; which, with one company ordered back from Changdeo to Jaulnah, completed the number destined for Brigadier-general Doveton's force. The pioneers attached to the First Division were consequently composed of two companies which joined Lieutenant-colonel Scot's detachment at the Taptee, one company which marched with Lieutenant-colonel Mackintosh's detachment from Jaulnah, and the company which arrived with Major Andrews. The company of pioneers ordered to Jaulnah, was intended to join a small battering-train which marched from that place for Mulkapoor on the 7th of November, with the 1st battalion of the 2d regiment of Native infantry, by the Adjunta Ghat and Lohaee. This train of ordnance * was designed for the eventual siege of Asseerghur, which there was early reason to contemplate. The Second Division was held in view for the performance of that service; and in order that it might be conveniently situated for the same, without abandoning the defensive objects which have been described, Brigadier-general Doveton was directed to move his head-quarters to a position immediately in the rear of Mulkapoor, either above or below the Berar Ghats. Orders were at the same time sent to Brigadier-general Smith, directing his descent into the valley in his front, where it was proposed that he should leave one brigade of infantry, and with the remainder advance his head-quarters through the Seindwah Ghat to the Nerbuddah, to complete the occupation of that river.

Pursuant to this disposition, Brigadier-general Doveton was directed to extend his views to the left of the line, which had been originally assigned to his division, and to issue such occasional instructions to the brigade designed to be left on the Gheernah by the Fourth Division, as should be necessary for its defensive co-operation. Connected with General Doveton's line of operations, which extended beyond the Wurdah, were the proposed dispositions in front of Nagpoor.

Proposed dispositions at Nagpoor.

(Map II.)

In the beginning of November, the Nagpoor auxiliary corps amounted to three hundred horse and two thousand foot; and was proposed to be employed in conjunction with a respectable body of regular troops from Nagpoor. A troop of Bengal cavalry, and four hundred Madras Native infantry, were destined for the position of Nuggurdoon, near Ramteak,

* Consisting of two eighteen-pounders, two iron twelves, and two mortars, with one thousand rounds for each gun, and five hundred shells for each of the mortars.

H

having on each flank a detachment of two hundred Madras infantry, and one troop of Bengal cavalry. One of these was to be posted in the direction of the Wyne-Gunga, and the other towards Pandoorna. The Rajah of Nagpoor was expected to contribute a considerable body of his best horse, to be employed in protecting the villages, and intercepting any Pindarries who might attempt to pass the right of the line near Sanghee. The main body of the auxiliary contingent was destined for Chuparra; from thence to occupy the country on that parallel, between the eastern avenue by Heerapoor on the right, and that on the left by Hurrye and Amburwana. One thousand Nagpoor horse were likewise to be posted on the Upper Taptee, near Meisdee, from whence their movements were to extend to Mooltye on the right, and to Meil on the left. The detachment which arrived under the command of Lieutenant-colonel Russell at Oomrouttee (p. 45), prosecuted its march by Amneir, Mooltye, the Shawpoor Ghat, and Seeonee, towards the Nerbuddah, at the Ford of Bugglatur, where it arrived on the 15th of November. This route was the same commonly pursued by troops marching between the Wurdah and the Nerbuddah: but for the ascertainment of a more direct road to the lower parts of the latter river, a company of the 1st battalion of the 3d regiment was detached from the vicinity of Beitool, by the way of Saolleeghur, under Lieutenant Meredith, from whom a most satisfactory report was received. The Russell brigade was detained at Oomrouttee for some days, in order that it might escort a convoy of treasure and provisions collected at that place. During its march, which followed the route of Lieutenant-colonel Russell's detachment, it dropped two companies at Beitool, under orders received to establish there a post of communication.

Assembly of the Fifth Division at Hoossingabad.

(Map II.)

The Fifth Division of the army, composed of troops which had been occupied in the defence of the Valley of the Nerbuddah till the commencement of the monsoon, was found conveniently situated, at its close, for the operations of the present campaign. Only a few movements were necessary for enabling it to cross the river. A detail of Native artillery, and four six-pounder field-pieces, marched from Hoossingabad on the 18th of October for Gurhwarra. Three troops of the 6th regiment of Bengal Native cavalry arrived at Hoossingabad from Gurhwarra on the 3d of November. The 1st battalion of the 23d regiment of Bengal Native infantry arrived at the same point, from Sohagpoor, on the 6th; and on the same day, the first Rohillah horse, with the exception of two hundred men, left at Gurhwarra and Sohagpoor, arrived from the latter place and Jubbulpoor. But while troops were assembling at Hoossingabad for the prosecution of active operations in advance of the Nerbuddah, a storm was gathering about the capital, in the rear, which demanded immediate attention. Colonel Adams accordingly received orders to detach to Nagpoor a suitable reinforcement; and on the 12th of November, Lieutenant-colonel Gahan marched with three troops of the 6th regiment of Bengal Native cavalry with a detail of gallopers attached, and the 1st battalion of the 22d regiment of Bengal Native infantry with two six-pounder field-pieces, under instructions to proceed with all practicable expedition to the above-mentioned point. This detachment was, however, subsequently halted at Sindkeir, till a requisition for its advance should be received from Mr. Jenkins, the Resident at Nagpoor; to whom the arrangement which had taken place was accordingly notified.

Advance of the Marquis of Hastings with the Centre Division to the Sind, and of the Second Division to the Chumbul.

(Map II.)

Having conducted to their first base of operations the Advance, which, having far to march for this purpose, were necessarily first in motion, it is proper to return to the dispositions which, during the same period, were adopted on the side of Hindoostan. The Head-quarters of the Marquis of Hastings having continued at Cawnpoor from the 14th of September to the 12th of October, proceeded by the route of Akburpoor to Secundra, where his Lordship arrived on the 20th in the personal command of the Grand Army in the field. His march was accompanied from Cawnpoor by the following troops, under the orders of Major-general Brown, forming part of the Centre Division.

The Rocket Troop.
The Corps of Miners and Engineer's Park.
The Experimental Dromedary Corps.
His Majesty's 24th Light Dragoons.
His Majesty's 87th Foot.
1st Battalion 24th Regiment Native Infantry.
2d ditto 25th ditto.

The European and Native Artillery,
with the Battering and Light Field-Trains, consisting of—

Two	24	Pounders,	Iron.	
Four	12	ditto	Brass.	
Four	6	ditto	ditto.	
Four	5½	inch Howitzers		To be joined by Four more from Keitah.

On the 25th of October, Lord Hastings' Head-quarters, and the Centre Division, marched by Sherghur to Sunkerpoor, where they halted till the 28th, having crossed the Jumnah between those places by a temporary bridge, which, with the approach to it, had been constructed with much labour and ingenuity. On the 29th the march was continued; and proceeding by Soharee, Jaloan, Danoura, Sekunderpoor, and Jedowsa, his Lordship's Head-quarters arrived at Mahewa, near the Seoora or Seeoonda Ghat, on the river Sind, on the 7th of November. Combined with the movements of the Centre Division of the Grand Army to the Sind, was that of the Right Division, commanded by Major-general Donkin, to the Chumbul. This corps assembled in the latter end of October in camp, near Agra, where it was joined, early in November, by the irregular quota of the Rajah of Bhurtpoor, and on the 5th commenced its march for Dholpoor, by the left bank of the Chumbul, which forms the northern boundary of Scindiah's dominions. It arrived in position, agreeably to previous arrangement, on the 8th. This movement having completed Lord Hastings's combination, as it was immediately directed against Scindiah, here will be the proper place to examine these positions, and the objects proposed by them.

Predicament to which Scindiah was reduced by these movements.

His Lordship, prior to this period, had received the most undoubted proof that Scindiah was pledged to the Pindarries, to support them; and was aware that his taking the field would be followed by the resistance of Ameer Khan, as well as by that of other Powers, whose hostility he was instigating. Scindiah's negotiations were conducted with all the secrecy in his power, and he flattered himself with complete success in that respect; but the admirable dexterity with which all his schemes were detected, and even copies of his correspondence obtained, forms by no means the least happy part of his Lordship's arrangements. The possession of the most correct information, while it enabled Lord Hastings to adopt the plan most suitable to the actual state of affairs, relieved him from all ties founded on anterior treaties. Under these circumstances it appeared possible, without an actual struggle, to reduce Scindiah to submission; and all the preparations for this purpose were conducted with so much order and secrecy, as to promise every success. Accordingly, on the advance of the army (Map II.) across the Jumnah, Scindiah suddenly found himself pressed from opposite directions, by the approach, to points on his frontier within two marches of himself and his capital, of two strong divisions, which were interposed between him and all his corps, whose situation has been noticed (p. 14). The position of the Centre Division likewise covered the Company's territories from any diversion that might be attempted by Scindiah in that direction. It was also equally well calculated for the interception of any Pindarries who might attempt to gain Gwalior by a route east of the Sind. At the same time, the Second or Right Division, at Dholpoor, opposed itself to the junction with Ameer Khan's principal force, then besieging Maharajpoor, of that portion of them which was about Seronge, as well as the corps serving in Holkur's country.

The importance of these positions will be better understood by considering the peculiar features of this part of Malwah. About twenty miles south of Gwalior, a ridge of steep broken woody hills extends uninterruptedly from the Sind to the Chumbul. This ridge is passable for carriages or bodies of cavalry in two places only; while, perhaps, in all other points, it may not be found practicable even to single horsemen. One of the passes is within about four miles of the Chumbul; and the other on the banks of the Sind, where the chain slopes down to the river, near Narwur. From this peculiarity of ground, the alternatives between which Scindiah had to choose, in the event of his not submitting to the dictates of the Governor-general, were, either to shut himself up in Gwalior, or to repair to his distant dominions and the Pindarries. In the former case, a single brigade entrenched, would block up the only outlet from the fortress, while the rest of the British force in that quarter might reduce the provinces of Gwalior and Gohud. In the latter supposition, he would begin his contest by sacrificing his fine train of brass artillery, amounting to nearly one hundred and fifty pieces; for, if left in Gwalior, it must speedily fall with the place, which would be starved into surrender. If he attempted to take it with him, he would be overtaken before he could get it up the Ghats; and in either case, by occupying the gorges of the hills, his richest provinces were secured against him for ever.

Conditions proposed to him, and Treaty of the 5th of November.

Scindiah, while in this predicament, was pressed to accede to the following propositions: To supply a contingent of five thousand select horse, to be placed under the command of a British officer, with an assignment for their maintenance for two years, on the tribute payable by the States of Jondpoor, Boondee, and Kotah; and to relinquish, for three years, the payment made by the British Government to himself and certain members of his family, in consequence of former treaties: To continue in his actual position, and on no account to quit it without the acquiescence of the Governor-general: To resign to the occupation of a British garrison the forts of Asseerghur and Hindia, during the war, as places of security and depôts for the British army: To receive a British force near his person, in order to check his refractory and disobedient officers, and to preserve the tranquillity of his country: To agree that the several corps of his army should occupy, during the war, certain positions to be fixed on by the Governor-general; and that a British officer should reside with each to secure the fulfilment of this condition: That the British Government should be relieved from the restrictions established by the treaty of 1805, which precluded their forming engagements with the States of Oodeipoor, Joadpoor, and Kotah, and with the State of Boondee, and other substantive States on the left bank of the Chumbul. It is no part of the design of this Memoir to describe the negotiations through which these important points were carried. The Resident's arguments were backed by the advance of an overwhelming force, and his instructions were proportionably peremptory.* Considerable management was, however, still necessary to accomplish them without any struggle on the part of Scindiah, as especially desired by the Governor-general. After much and frequent discussion of the several points, they were finally acceded to on the 5th of November, with the exception of that which provided for the reception of a British force near the Maharajah's person. Lord Hastings ratified the treaty on the following day, probably not without doubts of the sincerity with which Scindiah might be now acting. This may be inferred from the positions his Lordship's Head-quarters continued to maintain after the conclusion of these engagements.

* Captain Close, though labouring under severe indisposition at this important period, continued to conduct the functions of a Political Minister at Scindiah's Court with entire success, till towards the close of the war, when he was obliged to seek change of air, by a sickness, aggravated most probably by the extreme solicitude naturally produced by the momentous and critical state of affairs in which he was engaged. He had early used the freedom of suggesting in considerable detail, the arrangements, even of a military nature, on the side of Malwah, which he conceived necessary to the success of a war that should commence with the attack of the Pindarries; and had the satisfaction of finding their wisdom confirmed by the general adoption of the Marquis of Hastings.

Advance of the Third Division.

(Map II.)

It has been mentioned (p. 39) that the Third or Left Division of the Grand Army, commanded by Major-general Marshall, was to assemble at Callinger on the 10th of October. Accordingly its head-quarters and the majority of the troops were actually there on that day. The objects to which the attention of this corps was directed, were the co-operation with the advanced divisions of the Army of the Deckan, for the expulsion of the Pindarries; the protection of the frontier of Bundelcund against their incursions; and the frustration of their eventual attempts at escaping by the south-east towards the Nagpoor frontier, on being expelled, by the proposed combination of movements, from their permanent positions. The first of these objects was certainly the most practicable; and required in the commencement the advance of the force to such a position as should be properly situated for a fresh point of departure, when the Deckan divisions should be prepared to cross the Nerbuddah. A route by Huttah promised to answer this purpose, and the march of the division was accordingly commenced in that direction on the 13th; though some of the troops, and a considerable portion of the commissariat supplies, had not yet joined. On the 19th, Major-general Marshall's head-quarters were at Punnah, having arrived there by the Bisram-Gunje Ghat, where he halted in order to be joined by supplies, which he much needed. At this time two troops of the 2d Rohillah cavalry were stationed at Azeemghur. Four troops of Baddeley's horse and a company of pioneers, on their march from Cawnpoor and Kalpee, had not yet joined. At Lohargaum were stationed two troops of the 2d Rohillah cavalry, and three companies of the 1st battalion of the 14th regiment of Native infantry. After these arrangements, the division advanced by Semeerah and Huttah, where it arrived on the 27th, and halted till the 4th of November; during which period it was overtaken by such detachments as were on the road to join. As these movements deprived Bundelcund of the protection of an active force, the deficiency was now supplied by a detachment which marched on the 1st of November from the Centre Division at Seeoonda, and consisted of two squadrons of Native cavalry, the dromedary corps, and three companies of light infantry, under Major Cumming. This detachment moved by Koonch, and the Kunchun Ghat to Raat, near Keitah, and was left at liberty to take up such further positions as should best defeat any eventual attempt of the Pindarries. From Huttah a route was taken to Reillee, where the division arrived on the 12th of November, by the way of Gurracota. It was here necessary to halt, as well to bring up treasure and stores expected by the route of Lohargaum, as to await the advance of the Deckan divisions. During the latter part of the march, a party of Pindarries from Wassil Mahomud's camp, passed near to Saughur and Benaikaputtun, and from thence down the Dhamaunee Ghat into the Chanderi district. They were represented to amount to four hundred horse, and returned to Gungee-Basowda on the 5th of November, after having plundered Mow Raneepoor and many of Baptiste's* village. While in the Saghur country, the division was plentifully supplied; but the chief Bennaik Row, whose feudal allegiance had been transferred by the treaty of Poonah to the British Government, positively refused to supply any part of his contingent of six hundred and sixty-six horse.

Advance of the force under Brigadier-gen Hardyman. (Map I.)

On the left of the Third Division a force was directed to assemble under the orders of Brigadier-general Hardyman, to continue the line towards the south-east. That officer accordingly marched with the 8th regiment of Native cavalry, and the 2d battalion of the 8th regiment of Native infantry, from Mirzapoor, early in October, and arrived at Mhow on the 11th, at which place he was joined eight days afterwards by his Majesty's 17th foot, which marched from the former point on the 10th. On the 23d Brigadier-general Hardyman was at Oomree, about twelve miles from the river Toonse, with the 8th cavalry, having left the Native battalion at Mhow, and stationed the European regiment at Mungamma (or Mungowah), between the latter place and Rewah. At the same time he opened communications with the Third Division and the post of Lohargong on his right; and with Brigadier-general Toone's force on his left. He was joined in the beginning of November by about two hundred and fifty irregular horse, furnished, unwillingly, by the Rajah of Rewah. As at this time the before-mentioned Pindarries, from Wassil Mahomud's camp, appeared likely to be driven by the troops in Bundelcund, in the direction of his part of the line of general defence, he proceeded with the cavalry (Map II.) to Sohal, forty miles west of Rewah, on the 7th of November, and ordered the 17th foot to assume a position near the latter place. A squadron of cavalry was subsequently detached to the Buddenpoor Ghat to look to-

* An officer in Scindiah's service, who held Jaghires for the payment of troops.

towards the direction of Changdeo and the road between Bellary and Jubbulpoor, where Major Richards commanded, with whom a communication was also established; but the cavalry post was soon afterwards withdrawn, and joined its head-quarters on the right bank of the Toonse.

Dispositions of Brigadier-general Toone's force.

Brigadier-general Toone's detachment was destined to terminate the line of general defence to the left, by dispositions on the Upper Soan for the protection of the southern frontier of Bahar. Its head-quarters, his Majesty's 24th foot, the 2d battalion of the 4th regiment of Native infantry, four six-pounders, and two hundred and twenty-five irregular horse, were, on the 16th of October, encamped at Baroon; and on the 6th of November at Oontarree. From thence was made a distribution of posts, to occupy the principal passes, and to maintain communications between them and Brigadier-general Hardyman's extreme post of Burdee. The Ramghur battalion, commanded by Major Roughsedge, though not forming a part of Brigadier-general Toone's detachment, was in co-operation with it for the defence of the frontier, by detachments from its head-quarters at Hazareebaugh; and by the supply of the irregular horse, serving with Brigadier-general Toone, which were collected in that district, and furnished by the Rajah of Singrowla. A post was likewise established at Kidmir, about eighteen miles south of Oontarree, to command the passes of the Kunnur river. Across these it was apprehended the Pindarries might advance from the Ghats of Dhumna and Lackenpoor, in the Sirgooja country. This district is a dependency of the province of Chaoteesghur, belonging to Nagpoor, and immediately adjoining the British districts of Palamao and Chotah Nagpoor. On this account Brigadier-general Toone was directed to combine with his protection of the British possessions under the Bengal Presidency, a co-operation with the military dispositions in Chaoteesghur, as well for the protection of the Rajah's territory (p. 50) as for the interception of any bodies of Pindarries who might attempt to pass through them to the northern Sirkars under the Madras Presidency. (Map I)

Preparation for the movement of the Reserve. (Map II)

The Reserve Division of the Grand Army, as already mentioned, was directed to assemble on the 20th of October, under Major-general Sir David Ochterlony at Delhi; and from thence to march, as soon as fully equipped, to Rewarree. The objects immediately assigned to this division, were the controul of Ameer Khan, the interception of Pindarries who might retreat by the north-west, and the support of the Rajahpoot States, should they evince a desire to come under British protection. As the movements consequent on these views were later than those of the other divisions, their description will be postponed; but it was thought advisable to refer here to the field position of the Reserve, in order to give a better idea of the general military combination.

Goozerat force. For the same purpose it is necessary to take into consideration the proposed employment of the Goozerat force, which was ultimately brigaded for field service, in the order already anticipated. (p. 38.) To it was attached the Guickwar contingent of two thousand horse, with which James Williams, Esq. was appointed to reside, as a channel of communication for its conduct. The purposes for which this division was destined, were the protection of the Goozerat frontier against eventual (Map II.) inroads of the Pindarries, their interception, should they attempt to cross the Lower Nerbuddah, and a general co-operation with the Army of the Deckan in the event of a war with the Mahratta Powers. To render this project more effectual, Sir Thomas Hislop was vested with authority to "assume the direction and controul of that force in the same manner as if it constituted a part of" his "own army, so long as it should be acting in prosecution of the same objects." In consequence of some disturbances at Pahlanpoor, in the northern quarter of Goozerat, a part of the field force was detached at the end of October, under Colonel Elrington, for the reduction of that district to its customary state. This object being entirely unconnected with the general operations in view, it appears unnecessary here to enter into a particular description of the projects which it embraced; while some reference to it was requisite in order to account for the delay of the re-assembly of the division till the latter end of November.

Reduction of Soondoor by the Deckan Reserve. It might be considered equally unnecessary to describe, in this place, the operations of Colonel Munro's force at Soondoor in October, which delayed its being in position for offensive operations in the Deckan till the end of November, did it not appear that the instigations of the Peishwah for its employment on the former service, proceeded from his secret schemes for a rupture; when it would be for his advantage to direct to distant objects as many of the British troops as possible. (Map II.) This corps was destined ultimately to form a reserve on the parallel of Kulburga, to be applicable as circumstances might require, either to incline towards the capitals Hydrabad and Poonah, or to fall back for the protection of the British frontier in the direction of Ellore or Bellary. One thousand of the Nizam's horse were to be posted at Sooriapet on the right; and it was expected that the troops of the southern Mahratta Jaghirdars on the left, would act under the orders of the officer commanding the Reserve, in the general co-operation on that line. The adoption of this disposition, at the same time that the other divisions were on march to their advanced positions, was prevented by the plan proposed for the reduction of the Valley of Soondoor, at the solicitation of the Peishwah. This Prince had long pressed the British Government for their assistance in the acquisition of this small tract of territory, which was maintained in a state of insubordination by a feudatory, and which contained a temple of great sanctity, that his highness occasionally visited. The most convenient force for this purpose was that at Darwar; and preparations were accordingly made for its movement early in October, with the exception of the 2d battalion of the 4th regiment of Native infantry, and two six-pounder field-pieces, which were proposed to be left under the command of Major Newall, for the occupation of that place, Kooshgul, and Ranee-Bidnoor. On the 11th of October all the ordnance department and artillery marched from Darwar for Humpsagur on the Toombudra, under the command of Lieutenant-colonel Dalrymple; and were followed on the 13th by Colonel Munro with the remainder of the force.*

On the 20th of October Colonel Munro divided his force into two parts, of which one, consisting of the cavalry, with the exception of a half squadron of dragoons and a half squadron of Native cavalry, was placed on the left bank of the river, in charge of the sick, and of the heavy baggage; and the other crossed over by basket-boats to Humpsagur. This operation was completed on the 23d, and the force was there joined by the head-quarters and three companies of the 2d battalion of pioneers from Bellary. On the 27th of October Colonel Munro entered the Valley of Soondoor by the Kanaweehullee Ghat, when the fort was surrendered, and, on the same

---

* Consisting of two squadrons of his Majesty's 22d dragoons, the 7th regiment of Native cavalry, the European battalion, consisting of flank companies of his Majesty's 34th, 53d, 69th, and 84th regiments, four companies of rifles, and the 2d battalion of the 12th regiment of Native infantry.

day, occupied by a British garrison, consisting of a part of the rifle corps, which were subsequently relieved by two companies of the 2d battalion of the 12th regiment of Native infantry. There being no further occasion for the services of this force south of the Toombudra, it returned immediately to Humpsagur, at which point it completed its passage to the left bank on the 5th of November; having previously sent into Bellary all heavy equipments which might render it unfit for active field operations. On the 7th of November Colonel Munro delivered over the command of the force to Colonel Hewett, C. B., with instructions to put it in motion for the position assigned to the Reserve, in three divisions. Of these, the cavalry, forming the first, were to march on the 9th. The European flank battalion, artillery, rifles, and pioneers, forming the second, were to march on the 10th; and the 2d battalion of the 12th regiment of Native infantry, and the commissariat supplies, forming the third and last, were to march on the 11th. Colonel Munro then returned to Darwar; Brigadier-general Pritzler, appointed to the Reserve, being at this time far advanced on his return from Hydrabad, to assume the command. These several corps proceeded by the route of Kanagherry to Chinnoor, and were finally formed, on the 16th of November, into the Reserve Division of the Army of the Deckan.

Dispositions of the Madras Government for the protection of their Provinces.

Previously to closing this chapter, which has been designed to comprise the detail of all previous military dispositions, as well defensive as offensive, it will be proper to notice the exertions made by the Madras Government to cover its provinces, under the prospect of the Reserve being diverted from that service. These exertions, considering the paucity of means available, may be deemed as surprising as they were praiseworthy; and were rewarded by their salutary effects, when the country was subsequently entered by a body of Pindarries, who passed with impunity all the corps in advance. (Map I.) From the most western point of the British frontier on the Toombudra, a chain of posts distantly connected was established along that river, till its junction with the Kistnah at Moorkondah. From thence it followed the course of the latter river to Chintapilly, and afterwards took the course of the eastern Ghats to the Chilka Lake, terminating in that direction the Presidency of Fort St. George. These posts were established at various distances in rear of the line of frontier, and threw forward smaller parties to the passes of the rivers and hills in their front. The number of troops employed on this service amounted to six squadrons of dragoons, six squadrons of Native cavalry, nine battalions of Native infantry, besides five thousand horse and foot belonging to the Rajah of Mysore, who continued the chain to the left. This force, distributed along a line of eight hundred and fifty miles in length, necessarily reduced the strength of each post to a small number. Experience, however, had already shewn that the Pindarries were to be deterred by the smallest party of infantry posted ; and that they were to be beaten from their ground by the unexpected attack of a single company. Their object being plunder, it was natural for them to avoid all contest, which could only impair their numbers without adding to their booty.

CHAPTER IV.

RUPTURE ON THE PART OF THE PEISHWAH.

Suspicious Conduct of the Peishwah. How evinced. Apprehensions of the Resident. Countermarch of the Fourth Division. Consequent Dispositions of the Second Division. States of Force at the three Deckan Capitals. Change of Position of the Poonah Detachment and its Reinforcement. Situation of the Resident. Abrupt Declaration of War. Abandonment and Destruction of the Residency. Position of the Enemy. Colonel Burr's Dispositions. Attack of the Peishwah. Defeat of the Peishwah. Reflections. Importance of European Troops. Barbarous Treatment of British Officers. March of the Fourth Division. Arrival near Poonah. Position of the Enemy. Preparations for Attack. Contest at the Yelloura Ford. Flight of the Peishwah. Subsequent Arrangements. Reflections. Routes pursued by the Enemy, and Capture of their Guns.

Suspicious conduct of the Peishwah;

THE Division commanded by Brigadier-general Smith, C. B., had scarcely taken up its positions for the protection of the territories of the Peishwah, when that Prince exhibited unequivocal demonstrations of hostility against the Power engaged in his defence.

how evinced.

During the preparations for the opening of the campaign, he had shewn great apparent zeal for co-operation against the common enemy, the Pindarries. The British Government, to testify their confidence in his faith, restored to him the fortresses of Ryeghur, Singhur, and Poorunder, which had been ceded in occupancy, as pledges for his fulfilment of the treaty of the preceding June.

For this ostensible purpose, he was extraordinarily active in raising troops, both horse and foot; and gave higher pay for military service than had been usual either in the Poonah or neighbouring States. At the same time he discovered a decided unwillingness to let any part of his army leave the vicinity of the capital, for the purpose of contributing to the defence of the frontier; and every obstruction was secretly opposed to the levy of irregular auxiliary horse, which at this time the British Government was raising through the means of its own officers.

However convinced the Resident at Poonah must have been, by these and other practices, of the sinister designs of the Peishwah, a circumstance betrayed itself in its consequences, which could not fail to give considerable alarm. Apprehensions of the Resident.

A large portion of the Bombay Army were constantly recruited from the Peishwah's territory, and particularly from the Kokun, where their families generally resided. A spirit of desertion suddenly appeared in some corps above the Ghats, which might seem unaccountable, till it was discovered that their families had been dispossessed of their habitations, and exposed to great distress by the Peishwah's servants.

At length affairs had so far approached the impending crisis, that the Honourable Mr. Elphinstone found himself called on to apply, however unwillingly, to Brigadier-general Smith for the immediate return of the troops north of the Godavery ; as the Peishwah had assembled, in a menacing position, an army of no less than twenty-five thousand horse, and ten thousand foot, with several guns. The Fourth Division broke up from its field-positions in the first days of November, and was re-assembled at Fooltamba on the 4th. It here awaited a further requisition for its speedy advance on the capital till the 6th, when it continued its route in that direction. At the same time the light battalion, which had been posted with two six-pounder field-pieces in the Valley of Serroor, was ordered, on the first alarm, to repair to Poonah. All small details were called in; while the 2d regiment of Madras cavalry was ordered to march on Toka, as a more direct route for its junction. Countermarch of the Fourth Division. (Map VII)

As soon as Brigadier-general Doveton received reports of Brigadier-general Smith's retrograde movements, he judiciously countermanded the march of the battering-train on Mulkapoor; and directed the engineers' park and department, which had moved from that place to Changdeo on the 1st of November, to join him above the Ghats. The head-quarters of the Second Division marched from Meiker on the 12th of November, and arrived by the route of Ootradpett, Soonah, and Wurrood, at Jafferrabad, on the 15th. They were here joined by the battering-train, which countermarched from Sunnoad on the 16th, and arrived by the route of Adjunta. Consequent dispositions of the Second Division. (Map VII)

The engineers' park and department arrived on the 16th by the route of Jeypoor, Koatlee, Chickly, and Wurrood, having marched from Mulkapoor on the 12th of November.

In order to fill, in some measure, the void occasioned by the march of the Fourth Division southward, two thousand of the Nizam's reformed horse, commanded by Captain Davies, and one battalion of the Nizam's regular infantry, were ordered by Brigadier-general Doveton to assume the vacant position above the Khandesh Ghats.

States of Force at the three Deckan capitals. (Map II.)

At this period, the amount of force left at the three capitals of the Deckan was distributed as follows:—

At Sekunderabad ..	Detail of Artillery.
	Left Wing of the Madras European Regiment.
	The 2d Battalion of the 8th Regiment of Native Infantry.
	1st .. Ditto .... 21st .. Ditto .... Ditto.
	1st .. Ditto .... 22d .. Ditto .... Ditto.
	Two Companies of Bengal Native Infantry (Resident's Escort.)
At Poonah	Detail of Artillery.
	2d Battalion of the 1st Regt. of Bombay Native Infantry.
	2d .... Ditto .. 6th .. Ditto .... Ditto.
	1st.... Ditto .. 7th .. Ditto .... Ditto.
	1st.... Ditto .. Poonah Brigade...... Ditto.
	Two Companies of Bengal Native Infantry (Resident's Escort.)
At Nagpoor	Three Troops of the 6th Regiment of Bengal Cavalry.
	Details of Madras Cavalry and Foot Artillery.
	1st Battalion of the 20th Regt. of Madras Native Infantry.
	1st..Ditto ...... 24th .... Ditto .... Ditto.
	Two Companies of Bengal Native Infantry (Resident's Escort.)

While these movements took place at a distance from Poonah, at that capital it had become unsafe for any persons belonging to the British camp to quit their lines. Lieutenant Shaw, of the auxiliaries, was, on the 1st of November, dismounted, within two miles of the Residency, by three of the Peishwah's horsemen, and speared in the thigh. On the same day, the British brigade at Poonah changed its ground from the immediate vicinity of the city to a more tenable position, at the distance of about three miles, leaving a small guard in charge of their cantonments. This measure had become absolutely necessary, not only on account of the weakness of a position, towards which the enemy were closing in from all directions, thus

Change of position of the Poonah detachment, and its reinforcement. (Plan 4.) (C C)

depriving the brigade of the advantages of its discipline; but likewise owing to the unremitting endeavours of the Peishwah to corrupt the fidelity of the Native troops, to which they were the more exposed in proportion to their vicinity to the city. The left of the new position was *appuied* on the Kirkee bridge, over the Moolla river, and its right on the village of Kirkee. This position was rather too extensive for the troops which occupied it; but it had the advantage of [illegible] the water, and communicating directly with the Residency, and the great roads of Serroor and Bombay.

It happened, fortunately, that the Bombay European regiment, with detachments of his Majesty's 65th foot and of Bombay artillery, which were on their march from the coast to the Poonah Division, had not yet passed that capital towards their northern destination. This reinforcement entered the camp at Kirkee on the 30th of October, after a forced march of thirty miles from the bottom of the Ghats.

Situation of the Resident.

On the morning of the 5th of November, the British Resident still occupied the Residency at the Sungum*, having augmented his guard to several hundred men. The head-quarters of the Peishwah's brigade, commanded by Captain Ford, were at Dapooree, but one battalion only was present, and with it were three field-pieces. This brigade was raised and disciplined by European officers, under the Peishwah's immediate orders, as has been already mentioned; but on the present occasion more reliance was placed on their attachment to them, than to their Prince. The small guard which had been left in the cantonment was withdrawn, and joined the troops at the Residency; while in the city so unusual a tumult prevailed, that the Resident thought the cause of it should be ascertained on sufficient authority. (Plan 4.)

Abrupt declaration of war.

He wished to employ, on this occasion, the services of Captain Ford, who had been long used to confidential conferences with the Peishwah, and was intimately acquainted with the Minister, Mor Dixit; but the latter discouraged him from persevering in his attempt, stating that Bajee Rao was going to the Parbuttee †, and that the bustle in question arose solely from the [illegible] of the troops who were to accompany his Highness.

---

* This word signifies, in the Sanscrit, the confluence of two streams; which, in this instance, were the Moota and Moolla.

† A hill on the south side of the City of Poonah, on the top of which is a Pagoda of considerable celebrity.

Could the assignment of this reason have satisfied the Resident, the deception would have had but a short continuance; for at about two o'clock P. M. a confidential officer on the part of the Peishwah arrived at the Residency, and delivered in an insolent manner a message from his master, desiring, among other things, that the European regiment should be sent away, the Native brigade reduced to its usual strength, and that the cantonments should be removed to a place to be pointed out by the Peishwah. Mr. Elphinstone declared his incompetency to depart from the arrangements ordered by the Governor-general, and that he was prepared for any emergency necessary to their maintenance, while he lamented the infatuation which prompted the Peishwah to make such extraordinary demands. The officer then departed with a threatening gesture, desiring the Resident to abide the consequences.

Abandonment and destruction of the Residency (Plan 4) (*B,B,B,B.*)

It was no longer safe to occupy the Residency; and as the guard was held in readiness to move at the shortest notice, Mr. Elphinstone, with his suite, commenced their retreat up the left bank of the Moota river, which they crossed near the Sungum, and recrossed by the Kirkee bridge into the camp. The Peishwah's troops now entering the gardens of the Residency, set fire to every thing combustible, and in a short time destroyed the buildings, furniture, and records.

Position of the enemy

At the distance of about three miles to the north-westward of the city of Poonah, lie some hills, between which passes the road to Bombay. In that direction the Peishwah's army was assembled since morning, in expectation of orders for attacking the British force, to which it was opposite.

A high ridge of ground extended between the two positions, which were distant more than two miles. On each side flowed, in the lower ground, the Moota river, which doubled round the rear of the British camp. Many ravines and water-courses joined the bed of the river from the high ground round which it flowed, and were calculated to impede any distant flank movement along the bank of the river.

(*a, a, a, a*)

The enemy's position was on strong commanding ground. In front were a rivulet and some walled gardens; his left was at the Gunneiskund *

* This action is called by the Natives the Combat of Gunneiskund, and the British Reports style it that of Kirkee. The Battle of Argaum in 1803, is likewise called by the name of Narnulla. Nor are the instances of two names to the same action confined to India. Two of the most

hills, his right on the Residency, and in his rear a chain of mountains. The Vinchoor horse were on the left, the guns and infantry in the centre, and large bodies of cavalry on the right and along the rear. The Mahratta army was immediately commanded by Gokla: the Peishwah having retired to the top of the Parbuttee, to have a distant and elevated view of the action. Mor Dixit, the Minister, held a respectable command, though more considered as a politician than a soldier.

Colonel Burr's dispositions.

Colonel Burr commanded the British force, and had been engaged since his removal to Kirkee in the establishment of a post for the security of his stores, treasure, provisions, and sick, before the expected crisis. He now found himself enabled to leave them under the protection of the 2d battalion of the 6th Bombay Native infantry, greatly weakened by small detachments, but reinforced by such details as he considered unfit to bring into action. This position, in which were placed two iron twelve-pounders, was committed to the charge of Major Roome.

During the retreat of the Resident from the Sungum, Colonel Burr was required to move forward to meet the enemy, already in motion to commence the action. The Colonel was informed that the Poonah battalion was marching to join him from its cantonment at Dapooree, situate about two miles distant in a westerly direction. The force accordingly selected a position about a mile further in advance. It was joined by the Resident (D,D) with the guard from the Sungum, and formed, in expectation of receiving here the reinforcement under Captain Ford. In the centre were the Bombay European regiment, the Resident's escort, and a detachment of the 2d battalion of the 6th regiment; on the right and left were the 2d battalion of the 1st, and the 1st battalion of the 7th regiments, and on each of their outer flanks two guns.

Attack of the Peishwah.

It was now about four P. M.; and as the Dapooree battalion approached, the force again advanced, while the enemy threw forward his cavalry in masses on the right and left, for the purpose of passing to the rear of the British force, between it and the river. Immediately afterwards, a brisk cannonade opened from their centre. The Dapooree battalion was still

---

important battles in which the British arms have been engaged on the Continent, are in the same predicament: that of Blenheim is called by the French and Bavarians Hochstedt, and that of Waterloo, St. Jean.

about one thousand yards distant from the right of the line, and offered a (r, e.) tempting inducement to a corps of the enemy, who hoped to cut it off while yet detached. Mor Dixit commanded this body of cavalry, and is said to have been excited to undertake so brilliant an enterprize, in consequence of some sarcastic remarks made by Gokla, with reference to his former pursuits, and his supposed disposition in favour of the English. (F.) As he approached the right flank of the battalion, that wing was promptly thrown back, and when the distance was considered short enough for ample execution, an animated fire was commenced from the battalion and its three field-pieces, which obliged the enemy to desist, and continue his (ff.) movement towards Kirkee. He was here received by the two twelve-pounders which had been placed in position; and having lost the leader, Mor Dixit, who was shot in the mouth during the attack of the battalion, this body of the enemy, discouraged from any further attempt in that quarter, turned towards the rear of the British line.

On the left flank a more decided attack was sustained from the enemy's (c) centre, from whence was sent forward a select body of infantry, consisting of about three thousand Arabs and Gossyes, who advanced in solid column against the 1st battalion of the 7th regiment. Their attack was checked by a warm and decided reception, which induced them to retire. Their confusion presented a temptation to their opponents to follow up the impression, without orders. The eagerness of this movement was the cause of a partial disorder, which was not neglected by the enemy's horse. Of these, a body of three hundred, consisting of the most resolute, sur- (d.) rounding the Zereeput flag*, advanced to cover the retreat of the infantry. They forced their way through the British line; but a reinforcement of two companies of Europeans, timely supplied by Colonel Burr's orders, having enabled the 1st battalion of the 7th regiment to rally expeditiously, the attack was soon repulsed, and its repetition abandoned.

On the junction of Captain Ford's battalion, which formed on the flank at which it arrived, little alteration was made in the previous dispositions. The additional guns from Dapooree being placed on the right flank, those which had formerly occupied that position were moved to the centre. At the same time, the light companies of the 7th regiment, which had hitherto

---

* The flag of the State.

preceded the line, were sent to the rear to oppose the *demonstrations* of the enemy's horse, who had turned the right flank. Colonel Burr again advanced; and finding his line much galled by numerous skirmishers, who occupied some garden inclosures, and a *nullah* in his front, he detached all the remaining light infantry to dislodge them: a service which was effected as it became dark.

Defeat of the Peishwah. (*G, G*)

The enemy had now resumed his original position, and was engaged in drawing off his guns towards the city. The British force was in possession of the field of battle; and probably from prudence, as well as want of day-light, considered it unadvisable to persist in a further attack. The troops accordingly marched back to their camp at Kirkee, with the exception of the Dapooree corps, which returned to its insulated cantonments; so well satisfied were the victors that no molestation would be attempted during the night. Lieutenant-colonel Burr found, on his return, that Lieutenant-colonel Osborne had arrived to relieve him. Having, with that officer's permission, issued his orders of acknowledgments to the troops, he resigned his command. The loss of the enemy was estimated at about five hundred killed and wounded, while that of the British force amounted to eighty-six of all ranks*.

Reflections.

It will probably appear surprising, that the Peishwah's army should not have made more impression on so small a regular force†, which continued to advance after its flanks were turned, and while a large body of cavalry was hanging on its rear. The farther forward also that the British force moved, the more opportunity was afforded to the enemy's numbers to act; as the field became more extensive, and they came more within the command of the enemy's position, which had several strong features. These disadvantages attending the advance of the force, if considered, were preferred to the probable consequences of maintaining merely the original position. Colonel Burr reports officially, that he received a requisition from the British Resident to move out and attack the Mahratta force. Mr. Elphinstone, it is probable, admitted into the calculation which prompted this measure, a large share of the political effect he anticipated from an act so spirited. Had it not been adopted, the British force would have been possibly obliged to sustain the reiterated attacks of several days.

---

* Vide Appendix. A.

† About two thousand eight hundred men in action.

Heavy batteries would have been brought against them to do execution from beyond the reach of the British field-pieces. These batteries it would have been necessary to take by a rapid advance, without cavalry to cover so hazardous a measure, surrounded also by hordes of horse, and opposed by a heavy body of infantry confident in the protection of their guns. A just appreciation of the character of the Peishwah's army, furnished an additional argument in favour of the bold measure of becoming the assailant; and the prompt and well-served fire of the artillery, had a full share with the infantry in justifying the confidence unlimitedly placed in the British force.

Importance of European troops.

Notwithstanding the good behaviour of the Native troops, the seasonable arrival of the Europeans from Bombay must be considered as, independent of the numerical reinforcement, of incalculable importance. This arm gives a solidity to all formations in Indian warfare, which has no substitute. Its presence excites the emulation of the Native troops, who, while they exult in shewing themselves as daring in attack as their European fellow-soldiers, will tacitly concede* to them the honour of forming the rallying point under a reverse. This feeling arises, in a certain degree, from their being considered in this country as an indissoluble band, which may be diminished but not dispersed, and in which may be found a practical instance of the effect of that systematic combination which characterizes the arrangements of the British Government with respect to its most subordinate branches. The Native Powers, with much reason, omit not to compare such conduct with their own improvident proceedings; nor need a more striking instance to this point be desired, than the conduct of the enemy both before and after the battle of Kirkee. On the former occasion, the junction of the Bombay European regiment was not prevented, though the crisis must have been resolved on; and on the latter, the flank battalion, with one thousand irregular horse, were permitted to march from Serroor to camp at Kirkee, though foes so numerous were lying unemployed about (Map VI.) Poonah. With this reinforcement, which arrived on the 6th, there could be no grounds for apprehension of a further attack from the Peishwah; and the force continued in its position, awaiting the arrival of the division under Brigadier-general Smith.

---

* A striking instance of this occurred in the defeat of Colonel Baillie's detachment, at the fatal battle of Poololoor.—See *Wilks's History of India*, vol. II. p. 217, 4to Edition.

It will not, perhaps, be considered as irrelevant to the subject of this narrative, to notice the barbarous behaviour of the Peishwah's troops to some individual officers of the British army, who were unfortunately intercepted on their way to join. Captain Vaughan, of the 15th regiment of Madras Native infantry, had recently returned from England, and was accompanied by a brother just entering the service. Having landed at Bombay, he resolved on proceeding to join his corps by the way of Poonah; and was in company, it should seem, with Colonel Osborne during part of the journey. The latter is said to have recommended the most rapid progress to join the force at Kirkee, on account of the suspicious state of affairs at Poonah; but, finding his advice neglected, he went on alone. Arrived on the 5th of November within a few miles of Poonah, he received, with the noise of the cannon from Gunneiskund, a corroboration of the intelligence given to him by some villagers. These humanely advised him to abandon the high road of the capital, and to cross the country to the British position. The two Vaughans were, a few days afterwards, intercepted by a body of horse, at the village of Wurgaum, twenty-two miles from Poonah. They were driven forward in the most insulting manner a few miles to Tullygaum, where they were unrelentingly put to death, by being hanged on a tree on the Poonah side of the town. Barbarous treatment of British officers.

Cornets Hunter and Morrison, of the 1st and 2d regiments of Madras Native cavalry, were on their way to Poonah when the rupture took place there. On the 6th of November, they were surrounded by a party of the Peishwah's troops at the village of Urille, sixteen miles east of the capital, where they were obliged to fortify themselves, by means of their baggage, in a *choultry*. The guard which accompanied them consisted of a Havildar and twelve Sepoys. Till their ammunition was expended, they resolutely continued their defence. That being at length exhausted, their assailants were enabled to occupy the roof of the building, through which they made holes and fired down. Further exertion being now unavailing, these officers, after a gallant resistance of several hours, reluctantly surrendered. They were removed, under circumstances of great hardship and privation, to the Fort of Kangoorree, in the Kokun. After about nine weeks confinement there, they were obliged to exchange their prison, with little amelioration, for Wassota.

The march of the Fourth Division from the Godavery, on the 6th of November, has already been noticed. That corps reached Ahmednuggur March of the Fourth Division

(Map VI.) without molestation, in three marches; and on the 8th took possession of the Pettah. It was here joined by the battering-train, with extensive military and provision stores, which had been formerly left at this point; and continued its route by the high road to Poonah. After passing Serroor, the openness of the country, and the vicinity of the Peishwah's army, exposed the division to considerable annoyance, encumbered as it was by large departments, and destitute of all regular cavalry. This circumstance necessarily impeded its progress to the capital, being obliged to march with great precaution, and subject to frequent interruptions. The irregular horse attached to the Fourth Division were continually employed. On the 11th about four hundred, under Captain Spiller, successfully attacked a more numerous body of the enemy's cavalry, who lost an officer of rank, and about fifty killed and wounded. They succeeded, however, in carrying off two thousand bullocks near Condapoor. On the 12th they made another shew of opposition; but on this, as well as the former occasion, suffered severely.

Arrival near Poonah.

The light troops and irregular cavalry at Kirkee moved out on the evening of the 12th, to meet the march of the Fourth Division. This arrived in the vicinity of Poonah on the 13th of November, and took up ground between the Kirkee bridge and a small hill on the left bank of the (Plan 5.) (A.) Moota-Moolla river: the former being in the rear, and the latter extending along the right towards the front. As this hill commanded a ford, situate a little lower down the river, it was occupied in the morning of the 14th, and a six-pounder was mounted on it in the course of the day.

Position of the Enemy.

At this time the enemy were encamped on the opposite side of the river (a, a, a.) at Garpeer, the old cantonment of the British brigade, which they outflanked in both directions. Their principal battery was on their left; but they had some guns scattered along their centre, and on their right, where was a mangoe *tope* and *nullah*. Parts of their position were within range of an eighteen-pounder in the British battery on the small hill, near the Yelloura ford, already mentioned. The remaining ford was close to the Sungum, and about half as distant from the enemy's camp as the other, which was separated upwards of a mile. The Sungum ford was, however, a mile and a half from the British camp, while the Yelloura ford was within a third of that distance.

Preparations for attack.

On the evening of the 14th, the Bombay European regiment, and two corps of Native infantry, joined the head-quarters of the Fourth Division from Kirkee; and preparatory movements were made during the night for attacking the enemy's position at day-light on the following morning. The Yelloura ford, by which the troops should have crossed the river, being, however, found impassable for guns, the troops returned to their camp. On the 15th, pioneers were set to work on the ford, and the day was passed in trifling skirmishes of the irregular horse, and in annoying the enemy from the battery on the hill.

Contest at the Yelloura Ford.

On the 16th, the enemy appeared disposed to prevent the repair of the ford, of which, probably, they were not previously aware, and sent down parties of Arabs to interrupt the work. These were followed, in the afternoon, by large bodies prepared to dispute the passage, for which at this time dispositions were making on the part of the British. The left wing* was, in fact, placed for this purpose under the command of Lieutenant-colonel Milnes. After a contest of some hours, during which the enemy even crossed the river, that officer succeeded in establishing himself, with his guns, on the right bank. The enemy seemed to attach great importance to the result of this operation, from the struggle they made to frustrate it, and the repeated reinforcements they sent forward; but they were ultimately driven back with considerable loss, and at eleven o'clock P. M. all firing ceased. The loss on this occasion, on the British side, amounted to fifteen killed and sixty-eight wounded, including, in the latter, one European commissioned officer.† (E)

Flight of the Peishwah.

On the morning of the 17th, at three o'clock, the remaining troops in Brigadier-general Smith's camp, with the exception of such as were necessary for its protection, moved out under the Brigadier-general's command, and crossed the river at the Sungum ford. This wing consisted of his Majesty's 65th foot, the 1st battalion of the 2d regiment, the 1st battalion of the 3d regiment, the 2d battalion of the 9th regiment, the flank battalion, and horse artillery. At day-break both wings, followed by the irregular horse, were in motion against the enemy; but the latter had already abandoned all intention of maintaining their ground. They had, no doubt, anticipated an

G. G. G G. and F. F. F. F.

* Consisting of the Bombay European regiment, the Resident's escort, the 2d battalion of the 1st, the 2d battalion of the 6th, and the 1st battalion of the 7th regiments of Native infantry; one company of the light battalion, with two twelve-pounders, six six-pounders, and two five-and-a-half inch howitzers.

† Vide Appendix. B.

attack that morning, in consequence of the events of the preceding evening. The dawn of light, therefore, served only to shew the fruitlessness of the attempt against a flying enemy, out of reach. They had left their camp standing, and a few hundred Arabs remained in the city. These, through the Resident's influence with the inhabitants, were prevailed on to withdraw. In the course of the day the British standard was elevated on the Peishwah's palace, and guards established in peaceable possession of the city, wherein were found from forty to fifty guns, with a considerable quantity of military stores.

Subsequent arrangements.

It will be unnecessary to descant on the importance of this result, by which the resources of a populous city were brought into action for the furtherance of the campaign. Grain of every kind had risen to an exorbitant price at Kirkee after the 5th; but considerable relief was afforded by the arrival of the head-quarters of the Fourth Division. One brigade was placed in the old cantonments at Garpeer. The remainder of the division encamped near the Sungum, across the great road leading from Poonah to Bombay. The conduct of the troops merits the praise of alacrity and fortitude during these operations, having been severely harassed on the march from Serroor; and the division of Lieutenant-colonel Milne's, which carried the passage of the river at the Yelloura ford on the evening of the 16th, is entitled to additional encomium. The Peishwah had used many endeavours to corrupt the fidelity of the Native troops; but it is officially recorded, that at this period not a Sepoy had deserted to the enemy since the beginning of the war.

Reflections.

From a comparison of many accounts, it appears that the enemy did not expect to be attacked on the morning of the 15th, and were probably unprepared, either for effectual resistance or sudden retreat. If this supposition be well founded, there will be the greater reason for regretting the disappointment in the first attempt of the Yelloura ford, or that its impracticability had not been ascertained previously to the troops quitting their lines for attack. It appears to have been afterwards too late to decide on the adoption of the ford near the Sungum.

Such uniform success in general attends the British arms in India, that the first object of solicitude, on most occasions, is to bring the enemy to action. It will not, therefore, appear surprising that the troops composing the Fourth Division should have lamented the occurrence which deprived them of an opportunity of attacking an enemy, against whom they had much reason to be exasperated. It is the fate even of many successful military operations, that some circumstance comes to light, of which the previous ignorance is a matter of temporary regret. There is seldom, indeed, a victory which cannot be imagined to have been capable of a nearer approach to complete success. The uneasiness of this reflection is, however, soon lost in the exultation on the general issue; a consolation which was not wanting on the occasion in question.

Routes pursued by the Enemy, and capture of their guns. (Map VI.)

The enemy retreated on the morning of the 17th in the direction of the Ghats south of Poonah; the Peishwah and Gokla taking the route of Poonadur or Poorundur, and other parts of their army that of Singhur. To overtake the guns which accompanied the fugitives, a detachment commanded by Captain Turner, consisting of four horse-artillery guns, the light battalion and light companies of his Majesty's 65th and Bombay European regiment, with a party of irregular horse, was sent in pursuit. They arrived at the foot of the hill fort on the evening of the 19th, in time to capture fourteen pieces of ordnance, with tumbrils, and some booty. The detachment returned to camp on the morning of the 21st, having destroyed the captured ammunition, and disabled the guns which could not be brought off. However desirable it might be that the Peishwah's army should be immediately followed in force, many preparations were necessary, as well for an unremitting pursuit, as for the establishment of military security in the city of Poonah. Thus Brigadier-general Smith found himself constrained to relinquish that object for some days. The future operations of the Fourth Division will therefore be resumed hereafter; only observing here, that the 2d regiment of Madras Native cavalry joined with a supply of grain on the 18th, by the route of Jaulnah, Aurungabad, Ahmednuggur, (Map II.) and Serroor, without having experienced any opposition.

CHAPTER V.

EXPULSION OF THE PINDARRIES FROM SOUTHERN MALWAH.

Pindarries affected by the Treaty with Bhopal. Their Plans. Their supposed Strength and Position. Plan for their Attack. Passage of the Nerbuddah by the Fifth Division. By the Third Division. Fresh Arrangements consequent on the Rupture at Poonah. Prospect of Asseerghur refusing to surrender. Sir Thomas Hislop's Reasons for returning towards the Deckan. Preparations for the Siege of Asseerghur; and Reinforcement of Nagpoor. Colonel Deacon's Detachment. Occupation of Hindia. Countermarch and Return of the Head-quarters of the Army of the Deckan, and Passage of the Nerbuddah. Combined Advance of the Third and Fifth Divisions of the Army of the Deckan, and of the Left Division of the Grand Army. Flight of the Pindarries, and Co-operation of the Third Division of the Grand Army. Cheettoo's adopted Son taken. Fresh Departure of the Deckan Divisions. Third Division of the Grand Army at Seronge. Sir John Malcolm's Communications with Scindiah's Officers. Ambajee Punt's Corps. Demonstrations of Holkur's Army: Favour Cheettoo's Escape from the Third Division, which countermarches. Advance of the Head-quarters and First Division from the Nerbuddah. Detachment to Oonchode. Goozerat Division called forward. Head-quarters ascend the Ghats at Oonchode. Third Division called in. Head-quarters arrive at Oojein. Position of the Army described. Reflections on Indian Encampments; and on the number of Followers with an Army, particularly with a Madras Army. So much Ground occupied by an Indian Encampment unprejudicial.

Pindarries affected by the Treaty with Bhopal.

AS the period when the Nerbuddah would become fordable approached, the Pindarries became proportionably sensible of the danger of their situation, and were solicitous to acquire a secure asylum for their families and their property. They had hitherto been much at variance among themselves; but the approach of a common danger reconciled their differences, and taught them the necessity of unanimity. There were no forts in their vicinity capable of offering resistance, except such as were in the Bhopal territory. Of Islamnuggur, one of these, according to report, they had designed to possess themselves; but they probably were soon aware that no place could be deemed secure so near the British forces. They had likewise reason to apprehend the active hostility of the Nabob of Bhopal, who at this time entered into engagements with Sir John Malcolm. By these he agreed, in order to obtain the British protection, and to recover some lost territory, to deliver up the fort of Goolgaon, to co-operate against the Pindarries, to hold no intercourse with other Powers, and to submit to British arbitration in all matters of dispute, with several minor conditions.

Their Plans

But the Pindarry chiefs continued to receive every encouragement from Scindiah, who conferred on them dresses of honour, and gave them promises of support. They were in immediate communication with the commandants of his principal corps, and particularly with Baptiste and Jeswunt Rao Bhao. From the latter they received invitations to join, when they should be obliged to fly; and as his position at Jawud was distant from all the British corps, this direction promised more security than any other part of Malwah. They sent agents to Kotah also; but Zalim Sing, the chief of that place and its dependencies, was too prudent to prefer their friendship to the proferred alliance of the British Government. He accordingly received Captain Tod from the Residency, at Gwalior, as an accredited agent to settle the terms of a treaty, and to direct his conduct during the present critical times. Should all the views of the Pindarry chiefs in Malwah fail, they looked to a refuge in the southern parts of Rajahpootana.* The access to these was least likely to be closed against them, and they already were making their arrangements for conveying their valuables to Koomulneir in Meywar.

During these speculations, Kurreem Khan's cantonment was burnt, by which he suffered considerable loss, and was superstitiously inclined to interpret the occurrence as a bad omen. It was occasionally proposed among them, that they should cross the Nerbuddah, and proceed to the rear of the British forces. It appears, however, that ultimately they arrived at no determined plan, so that their subsequent conduct was left to depend entirely on future accidents, and on such temporary expedients as should suggest themselves.

position.

In the beginning of November the Pindarries were understood to be in position on a line extending from Bhilsah to Shujawulpoor. Their left, or

* In like manner when Holkur was pursued by Lord Lake into the Punjab, in 1805, he sent his family and treasure into Meywar.

(Map III.) Wassel Mahomud's *durrah*, consisted of eight thousand horse of all descriptions, with five guns. The *durrahs* of Kurreem Khan and the Holkur Shahee, consisting of about eight thousand horse and foot, with five or six guns, occupied a central position; and Cheettoo's *durrah* of seven thousand horse and foot, and ten guns, had formed the right. But this disposition had been partially changed as the river became fordable, and Sir Thomas Hislop decided on the following plan for their attack and expulsion.

Plan for their attack.

It was proposed, that the Third Division, reinforced from the First, should cross the river at the Bugglatur Ghat, and advance by the route of Ashta.

The Fifth Division was at the same time to cross at the Goondree Ghat, near Hooshingabad, and to march by Rasseen.

Major-general Marshall, commanding the Left Division of the Bengal Army, was expected to advance on Bhilsah from Reillee on the right, in order to co-operate in the attack, or intercept any bodies of fugitive Pindarries who might endeavour to escape by the direction of Bundelcund, or the upper part of the Nerbuddah.

A detachment of the First Division, under the immediate command of Lieutenant-colonel Deacon, and subject to the orders of Sir John Malcolm, was to cross at Hindia, and to ascend the Malwah Ghats at Oonchode. From thence it was to act either as a Reserve to the Third Division, or to intercept the enemy flying to the westward.

It was anticipated that the several columns would gain their respective points of attack or co-operation, on or about the 22d of November; and that at the same time, the Right and Centre Divisions of the Grand Army would be at their positions to continue the pursuit, should the Pindarries approach the Dooab, or attempt to escape across the Chumbul below Kotah. In pursuance of this plan of operations, the following movements succeeded:

On the 13th of November the 1st battalion of the 7th regiment marched from Hurdah and relieved all the detachments of the 2d battalion of the 6th regiment of Native infantry, which had been broken up for the defence of the Ghats; and its head-quarters were established near Hindia.

Passage of the Nerbuddah by the Fifth Division;

On the 14th of November, the Fifth Division began to cross the Nerbuddah at the appointed Ghat. On the 15th, its head-quarters, with the

5th regiment of Bengal cavalry, eight hundred Rohillah horse, the 1st battalions of the 19th and 23d regiments of Bengal infantry, wanting their light companies, and the light battalion of the six companies, with four brass twelve-pounders, two six-pounders, four brass howitzers, two galloper-guns, and a proportion of European and Native artillerymen, were on the right bank of the river.

by the Third Division.

(Map III.)

On the 15th of November the head-quarters of the Third Division, with two horse-artillery guns, one regiment of cavalry, and galloper-guns, the 1st battalion of the 3d regiment, six companies of the 2d battalion of the 6th regiment, with two six-pounders, one company of pioneers, and three thousand five hundred Mysore horse, crossed at the Bugglatur Ghat and Hindia; leaving their sick and heavy baggage there until the arrival of the Russell brigade.

On the 16th of November the Reserve, consisting of two squadrons of Native cavalry, with gallopers, the 1st battalion of the 16th regiment, or Trichinopoly light infantry, four companies of the 2d battalion of the 6th regiment of Native infantry, with two field-pieces, half a company of pioneers, and five hundred Mysore horse, crossed at Hindia.

Fresh arrangements consequent on the rupture at Poonah.

Accounts of the attack on the British position at Poonah were received by his Excellency Sir Thomas Hislop, at Hurdah, on the night of the 15th. A dispatch was instantly sent to recal Sir John Malcolm, in order that such further measures should be concerted as might arise out of the new posture of affairs. This measure obliged the Third Division to halt on the 16th, till rejoined by its commanding officer.

On the same day it was determined that the Reserve should be broken up, and the Third Division reinforced. The four companies of rifles were accordingly ordered from Hurdah to cross the river at Hindia, and to proceed with the four companies of the 2d battalion of the 6th regiment to join Brigadier-general Sir John Malcolm on the 17th. The remainder of the Reserve rejoined the First Division on the following day at Hurdah, with the exception of the two six-pounders, and detail of artillery ordered to reinforce the corps at Hindia, to which had likewise been added a company of the Madras European regiment.

Prospect of Asseerghur refusing to surrender.

The treaty concluded with Dowlut Rao Scindiah has already been noticed. Among other articles, it provided that the forts of Asseerghur and Hindia should be placed in possession of the British army during the war, as depôts and posts of communication. The former of those places was allowed to retain its Killedar, with a small guard of honour about his person.

It was apprehended, however, that the orders from Scindiah's *durbar* for their surrender, and particularly that relating to Asseerghur, might not, when received, meet immediate obedience. This suspicion appears likewise to have prevailed at the discussion of the treaty; in which it was made a condition, that should the Killedar refuse submission, the fort might be besieged by the British army at the expense of the Maharaj.

The Killedar, Jeswunt Rao Laar, maternal uncle of his sovereign, held the government of Scindiah's principal possessions south of the Nerbuddah. There was at this time the greater reason to suppose he would refuse obedience to the order of surrender, as he was actually employed in laying in the necessary provisions against a siege, and in augmenting his garrison. Nor would this state of open insubordination have been surprising under a Native Government, which might at the same time have sent secret counter-orders: so natural was this occurrence considered by Scindiah's *durbar*, that on their being warned of the consequent expense to their Government for the reduction of the place, they are said to have simply demanded, however absurdly, to be informed what that expense would amount to.

Sir Thomas Hislop's reasons for returning towards the Deckan.

The expectation of the eventual siege of Asseerghur, connected with the actual state of affairs at Poonah and Nagpoor, and with the possible contingencies at Hydrabad, induced Sir Thomas Hislop to resolve on carrying towards a quarter where appearances were so threatening, his own head-quarters, besides dispatching such light reinforcements as might proceed with expedition in advance. In pursuance of this determination, Brigadier-general Sir John Malcolm was vested with the general command of that part of the Deckan Army in Southern Malwah. Advice was also sent to the officer commanding the Goozerat force, describing the new dispositions which had been made for the service in front of the Nerbuddah.

Preparations for the Siege of Asseerghur, (Map V.)

Brigadier-general Doveton was ordered to send his engineers' park, his battering train, and his Majesty's Royal Scots, down the Berar Ghats to Jypoor-Koatly, in order that they might be conveniently situated for joining the First Division, in the event of undertaking the siege of Asseerghur. Two days afterwards this reinforcement was directed to advance to Mulkapoor.

and reinforcement of Nagpoor.

Lieutenant-colonel Gahan was ordered, on the 17th, to continue his march from Sindkeir to Nagpoor; whilst Brigadier-general Doveton, on the 19th, was directed to reinforce, with two six-pounders, the 2d battalion of the 24th regiment of Native infantry, which left Sekunderabad on the 28th of October for Bassim. He was also to instruct that corps to take the route of Nagpoor.

Colonel Deacon's detachment.

Brigadier-general Smith had made urgent applications for aid in cavalry, from the Second Division, during his march towards Poonah; but on account of the extensive objects imposed on Brigadier-general Doveton, that officer found himself incapable of complying with the requisition. The corps, however, which had been detached, under Captain Davies, from the Second Division, to assume the position originally occupied by the Fourth, was directed, from Head-quarters, to march immediately after Brigadier-general Smith. At the same time a detachment was formed at Hurdah, to occupy Khandesh, in its room, as soon as possible. This force consisted of two squadrons from the 4th and 8th regiments of Native cavalry, with two galloper-guns, the 2d battalion of the 17th regiment, and the Ellichapoor contingent. These, as already noticed, consisted of eight hundred regular infantry, twelve hundred horse, and four guns.

Lieutenant-colonel Deacon, commanding this detachment, marched on the 20th of November, and was furnished with a route by Charwah, Kundwah, Kurgoun, and the Seindwah Ghat. This was the shortest that could be adopted, though in some degree uncertain, from having never yet been followed by any body of British troops. (Map VII.)

Occupation of Hindia

After these dispositions, the Head-quarters and the First Division changed ground to Koolurdah on the 21st, the day on which the orders for Hindia and Asseerghur were received. Scindiah's principal officer at Hurdah, to whom Hindia was subordinate, was summoned to receive the order and give the necessary instructions for the surrender of that place. This was promised, after considerable hesitation, and many remarks on the informality of the document presented; but when the time arrived for executing the engagement, Mahratta-like, nothing was offered but an attempt at evasion.

An officer was accordingly dispatched, on the 22d, with a party of horse, to demand the fort on the strength of the order. He arrived, in the vicinity of the place, at night-fall. The hour of shutting the gates had not yet come, and as they were remissly guarded, the darkness enabled the party suddenly to enter. Having thus gained possession of the gates, they kept it till a detachment of the 1st battalion of the 7th regiment of Native infantry arrived from the neighbouring camp, when the garrison reluctantly surrendered.

Countermarch and return of the Head-quarters of the Army of the Deckan; (Map VII.)

On the 24th of November, the Head-quarters of the army, and First Division, marched upon their return southward to Mundalah, on the Machuck *nullah*, and, on the 25th, encamped at Charwah. Sir Thomas Hislop, on his arrival at this place, was overtaken by dispatches from the Marquis of Hastings, earnestly pressing his return towards Malwah, where his co-operation was of importance for the success of plans which were approaching their maturity. At the same time, the Fourth Division and the Reserve were placed at the disposal of the Honourable Mr. Elphinstone; who, by the same order, was empowered to decide immediately on whatever questions should arise out of the Peishwah's conduct and the course of events at Poonah.

Fresh orders became necessary for the Second Division. Brigadier-general Doveton was directed to summon Asseerghur, and to lay siege to it, in the event of a refusal to surrender. Information of these instructions were sent to Lieutenant-colonel Deacon, with orders for his detachment to take up the position near Jafferabad, which would be vacated by the Second Division, and to maintain an open communication between the [illegible]'s head-quarters and Jaulnah, the principal depôt of the Second Division.

On the 29th, Sir Thomas Hislop arrived with the First Division at Hindia, by the route of Roalgaum and Runnye.

[illegible] (Map III.)

On the following day, the passage of the Nerbuddah was commenced by means of large and commodious flat-bottomed boats, collected from different points of the river; and on the 2d of December, the whole of the troops and departments were encamped, with the Head-quarters, near Nemawur, on the right bank.

Combined advance of the Third and Fifth Divisions of the Army of the Deckan, and of the Left Division of the Grand Army.

In the mean time the Third Division, reinforced under the command of Brigadier-general Sir John Malcolm, marched on the 18th of November to Sundulpoor, to Hurringaum on the 19th, and from thence, in two marches, to Ashta, by the Kirvunnee Ghat, being one of the best passes into Malwah from a southern direction. During this operation, which was principally in the country subject to Cheettoo Pindarry, Sir John Malcolm re-established in authority the servants of Dowlut Rao Scindiah and the Nabob of Bhopal, to whose governments it previously belonged. On arriving at Ashta on the 21st, intelligence was received concerning the Pindarries, that their only camps, which had been within thirty miles of that point, had moved in a northerly direction, on the British troops crossing the river. Sir John Malcolm [illegible] resolved to proceed with celerity towards the same quarter, on a combined plan with the division under Lieutenant-colonel Adams, with whom he was in continual communication.

Flight of the Pindarries;

As soon as this corps crossed the Nerbuddah, the *durrah* of Wassil Mahomud, which was in its front, moved to Imlanee, on the road to Seronge. Lieutenant-colonel Adams, following the same route, arrived at Chickload on the 20th. Having learnt that the abovementioned chief and Kurreem Khan had passed with their *durrahs* to the southward, he sent a detachment in pursuit of them under Major Clarke, and proposed, should the intelligence of their route prove correct, to follow in the same direction. It appears, however, that the Pindarries were not prepared to enter the Deckan, which, on many accounts, there was reason to suppose considerable bodies of them might attempt, in order to distract the plans for attacking them. Colonel Adams accordingly marched, on the 22d, to Rasseen, where he received intimation of the advance and proposed progress of the Left Division of the Grand Army under Major-general Marshall.

and co-operation of the Third Division of the Grand Army.

This corps, on the 18th of November, was near Reillee, at the Jaum Ghat, and was from thence to march by Saghur and Ratghur to Gungee Basowda, where it was expected to arrive on the 27th. The Fifth Division was to march on the 24th from Rasseen, in the direction of Beirseeah, and to arrive there on the 26th, previously establishing a post and depôt at Goolgaon, on the frontier of the Bhopal country. At the same time information was received that the *durrah* of Kurreem Khan had moved on the night of the 20th from Beirseeah towards Agra Burkeira, and that Wassil Mahomud had moved to Gootwa Doonga, with the intention of proceeding to Sherghur.

Cheettoo's adopted Son taken.

Sir John Malcolm, after establishing a post at Ashta, marched from that place, as proposed, in pursuit of Cheettoo, and on the 24th of November reached the village of Mynapoor. Intelligence being here received, that some of the enemy occupied the Fort of Talyne, within the distance of a forced march for cavalry, twelve hundred Mysore horse were in the early part of the night sent forward, in the expectation that they would surround the place, at day-break, on the following morning. Captain James Grant, to whom this service was entrusted, completely succeeded in the execution of it, after a rapid movement of thirty-two miles, which deprived the garrison of any means of escape, and induced them to surrender at discretion. They consisted of some horsemen and about fifty infantry, under the command of Wahad Kour, one of Cheettoo's chiefs, and his adopted Son. The Third Division arrived on the 25th at Shujawulpoor; and at Talyne on the 26th.

Fresh departure of the Deckan Divisions

The three divisions acting from the southward and eastward, having now arrived at points of a line equally advanced, and the enemy taking a northerly and westerly direction, the future projects for their destruction or expulsion were to be adopted from this new base, in rear of which, as far as the Nerbuddah, whatever enemies might be concealed, there were none who avowed themselves. In pursuance of this design, the next points fixed for the movements of the divisions under General Marshall, Colonel Adams, and Sir John Malcolm, were Ragooghur, Rajghur, and Soosneir, it being understood that they would be adhered to according to circumstances, and the motions of the enemy. Colonel Adams dropped half his ordnance at Beirseeah on the 1st of December, under the protection of five companies of Native infantry; and was at Rajghur on the 4th. The inimical dispositions of the Killedar of that place, who refused to let him purchase any supplies, induced him to continue his march on the 7th towards Munnohur Thannah, nineteen miles north-north-east of Rajghur, where he arrived with his division on the following day. This position, being within the Kotah territory, was well calculated for its protection, and for the supply of the troops while expecting the combinations of other divisions, or waiting for further information respecting the movements of the enemy, who were said to have gone far in advance, in the direction of Kolarus and Narwur.

Third Division of the Grand Army at Seronge.

For the co-operation of the Third Division of the Grand Army, Major-general Marshall proposed to divide it into two parts, of which one, containing every impediment to active movement, should be left at Seronge, and the remainder, equipped for expedition, should be carried forward on the proposed line. This measure however was delayed; and the Major-general explained his motives for halting, from the 30th of November to the 7th of December, to have been, the distance of the Pindarries from his division, compared with their vicinity to the Centre Division; the apprehension of driving them across the fords of the Jumnah; and his doubts respecting the security of his guns and baggage, in the event of a general rupture, if left at Seronge, a place under the authority of Ameer Khan,

All the information received by Sir John Malcolm concerning the movements of the Pindarries, had induced him to consider the *durrah* of Cheettoo as his peculiar object. This chief, from the period at which the British troops crossed the Nerbuddah, had taken a more westerly course than either Kurreem or Wassil Mahomud, who, consequently, remained as the objects of the other divisions. At this time Scindiah had three corps in the field, near the western parts of Malwah. One was under Jeswunt Rao Bhao, in Meywar. The others were between the Calee Sind and Seeprah rivers, under Ambajee Punt and Annah Bhao. To the first of these it was thought probable that Cheettoo would fly for protection. A correspondence, for the purpose of defeating that expectation, was accordingly opened with Jeswunt Rao Bhao, by Sir John Malcolm; who likewise made the other two commanders acquainted with his objects, and his hopes of their assistance against a common enemy. But all those commanders of Scindiah's troops were suspected, with too much reason, to be so averse to the destruction of the Pindarries, as to forbid any well-founded reliance on their co-operation. As the British troops were however approaching these corps, this communication was considered as necessary, even with a view of holding a check on their possible counteraction.

Sir J. Malcolm's communications with Scindiah's officers.

The Russell brigade, belonging to the Third Division, had been left in the rear, as already noticed, when that force crossed the river; but had been instructed to follow up the route of its head-quarters to Ashta, and from thence to strike off to Saurungpoor. To effect there the junction of this corps, the Third Division marched from Talyne on the 1st of December. On crossing the Calee Sind, to take up the proposed ground of encampment, intelligence was received of the advance of Ambajee Punt's corps, marching to the same place. It appeared that they were in a state of mutiny, having confined their commander, with whom they had refused to permit a Native officer, previously sent forward by Sir John Malcolm, to hold any conference. They declared their intention of marching direct to Gwalior, to recover arrears of pay long due. As their proposed route, however, would pass close to the position of the Third Division, and probably interfere with the expected junction of the Russell brigade on the following day, Sir John Malcolm deemed it necessary to insist on their halting without further advance. This proposition was received with that vociferous indignation which might be expected from an armed multitude without a leader; but on seeing preparations made to flank their road, should they advance

Ambajee Punt's corps.

further, they prudently halted. This corps, consisting of six weak battalions with thirty guns, remained perfectly calm while in the vicinity of the British force, and on the 5th continued its march.

Demonstrations of Holkur's army

On the 2d of December the Russell brigade having joined the head-quarters of the Third Division, arrangements were made for the rapid movement of the principal part of the force, lightly equipped, leaving every thing cumbrous to follow under a reserve. This consisted of the eight battalion companies of the 1st battalion of the 6th regiment, and twelve companies of the Russell brigade, with six six-pounder field-pieces, and four hundred irregular horse. The detachment with which Sir John Malcolm proposed making a forced march to the westward of Nalkeira, having received intelligence of the presence of the Pindarry enemy there, consisted of four horse-artillery guns, one regiment of cavalry with gallopers, twenty companies of light infantry including the rifles, the 1st battalion of the 3d, and flank companies of the 1st battalion of the 6th regiments, and the Russell brigade, with three thousand Mysore horse. This portion of the division arrived on the 3d at Burghur; and there learned that Cheettoo, having met with opposition at Burroad, on the Kotah frontier, had turned southerly towards Mehidpoor, and encamped within a few miles of the army of Mulhar Rao Holkur. This information did not however prevent Sir John Malcolm from continuing his march; and on the following day he reached Augur. There he had more opportunity of ascertaining the real state of affairs, both from his greater proximity to the position of Holkur's army, and his easier communication with Captain Tod, the Political Agent at Kotah.

Favor Cheettoo's escape from the Third Division, which countermarches.

To say that the designs of Holkur's Government were neutral, would be to draw a conclusion too favourable from their *demonstrations*. It was evident that Cheettoo had escaped to the north-westward, under the protection of their military proceedings; and they publicly gave out, that they were in march to join the Peishwah by the route of Indoor and Myheyswur. (Map II.) The strength of their army was, however, too considerable to be attacked by a corps fitted only for the pursuit of Pindarries; and Sir John Malcolm seeing the propriety of approaching the head-quarters of Sir Thomas Hislop, (Map III & IV.) countermarched on the 6th towards Shajehanpoor, where he was rejoined by his reserve and baggage. On the 8th the Third Division arrived at Turrana, and halted there during the 9th and 10th, having detached six hundred Mysore horse to the First Division, in pursuance of instructions to that effect. (Map IV.) On the 11th it moved to Ursoda, three miles south-west of

Tajpoor, in expectation of further orders from Head-quarters, as promised to Sir John Malcolm.

Advance of the Head quarters and First Division from the Nerbuddah. (Map III)

The movements of the First Division of the Army of the Deckan have been brought down (p. 82) to the 2d of December, when it was at Nemawur, on the right bank of the Nerbuddah, opposite to Hindia. The solicitude with which the Marquis of Hastings directed the return of Sir Thomas Hislop's head-quarters northwards, evinced that the eventual extent of his measures were not confined to the mere expulsion or reduction of the Pindarries. The equivocal conduct of Holkur's army, which shortly afterwards became known, gave further evidence of the steady foresight with which his Lordship contemplated the means of executing his plans.

Detachment to Oonchode.

Sir Thomas Hislop was now situated favourably for resuming the immediate direction of the operations of the divisions which had been previously sent across the Nerbuddah. Having formed the resolution of advancing on the high road to Oojein, which, after crossing the Calee Sind near its source, keeps on the left of that river, he sent forward instructions to the Third Division to continue on the right of the same stream, unless there should be an opportunity, by crossing to the left bank, to strike at the Pindarries. The greater part of the detachment of Mysore horse, which had remained with the head-quarters, had been sent towards Pandoorna on the 1st, with a company of Native infantry, to reinforce a detachment under Captain Lucas, employed in collecting Brinjarries. Sir John Malcolm was, therefore, called upon to send one thousand of that contingent to Oonchode, to meet the First Division; as, without this arm, there were not sufficient means, either for pursuing effectually any Pindarries who might turn back by that route, or for preventing small parties of them from annoying the line of march or distant foragings. The reasonable apprehension, that some of the Pindarries, who were pressed from many quarters, might endeavour to penetrate into the Deckan by the way of Myheyswur, which had been left open by the sudden countermarch of the Fourth Division to Poonah, induced Sir Thomas Hislop to send forward, on the 1st, a detachment to Oonchode, as a suitable position from whence to obtain intelligence, and to act accordingly. Major Lushington, who commanded this detachment, consisting of four squadrons of the 4th and 8th Native cavalry, two flank companies of Native infantry, and a detachment of the 16th light infantry, arrived at Sutwass on the 4th, and at Oonchode on the 6th, without being able to overtake any party of Pindarries; though a night march had been

(Map II) (Map III)

made for that purpose from Bejawar, where intelligence was received of their route.

On the 3d of December the Head-quarters and First Division moved to Sundulpoor, a short distance, to allow of the easy junction of some part of the commissariat, which had not yet crossed the river. On the 4th, the whole marched to Soankeir.

The Goozerat Division called forward.

The Goozerat division had received intimation of the return of the Head-quarters of the Army of the Deckan to the Nerbuddah, for operations in Malwah, and were directed (p. 58) by the Marquis of Hastings to place themselves under the orders of Sir Thomas Hislop, as soon as their progress should bring them in co-operation with the divisions of the Army of the Deckan. His Excellency accordingly dispatched instructions from Soankeir to Sir William Grant Keir, requiring his advance from Baroda to Oojein by the great road of the Dawud Ghat, unless the former communications should have already carried his division too far in the direction of the Lower Nerbuddah.

The Head-quarters ascend the Ghats at Oonchode.

It was found necessary to halt at Soankeir, on the 5th, in order to complete some arrangements consequent on the recent passage of the river. This opportunity was used for examining the Toorreea Ghat ascending into Malwah, which promised a shorter line to Oojein by Soankutch. Yet, though a practicable way was traced to the foot of the pass, the ascent, which was only a pathway, was found to be too steep, intricate, and narrow, for the advance of the army. There were, in fact, no vestiges nor tradition of its having been ever traversed by carriages. The route of Oonchode was accordingly pursued, and the Head-quarters arrived on the 6th of December at Bejawar, and on the 7th at Oonchode, where Major Lushington's detachment rejoined.

The Third Division called in.

Sir Thomas Hislop having now contemplated the attainment of the objects for which the Third Division had been reinforced, deemed it necessary to recall Sir John Malcolm, in order to reorganize the plans of operation with reference to the *demonstrations* offered by Holkur's Government, and to the circumstance of all the Pindarries having been expelled from Southern Malwah. The orders for this purpose directed the Third Division to shape its countermarch in the direction of Tajpoor, near Oojein, and to expect further instructions respecting a specific point of junction. On the 8th of December, the Head-quarters of the Army of the Deckan arrived at Peepleea, on the 9th at Nappa Keira, on the 10th at Singwarra, and on the 11th of De-

(Map IV.)

cember at Duttana-Muttana. Sir John Malcolm came into his Excellency's camp in the afternoon from the Third Division, encamped at Ursoda, distant about eight miles; and returned the same night with orders to carry his division on the following morning to Oojein, where ground would be allotted to it in the vicinity of the Head-quarters' camp.

Head-quarters arrive at Oojein

The enemy's horse had not hitherto offered any molestation to the advance of the First Division. The only armed body which appeared was the corps of Annah Bhao, encamped at the distance of two miles from Duttana-Muttana, in an easterly direction. There was, however, reason to expect that the foragers would shortly experience annoyance, as some private camels had already been carried off from the Third Division by straggling parties of horse. On the 12th of December the Head-quarters, and First and Third Divisions of the Army of the Deckan, marched past Oojein, and crossing the Seeprah at a ford opposite the north-west angle of the city, encamped on the left bank of that river; the rifles and 2d battalion of the 6th regiment of Native infantry, which had been detached with Sir John Malcolm from Hindia, rejoining the First Division.

Position of the Army described

The suspicion with which the city contemplated the presence of the British army, forbade any particular investigation of its interior state, nor had any person in the army much leisure to inquire regarding its interesting antiquities. A satisfactory sketch of its environs on the river side, was made by the officers of the Quartermaster-general's department. This will be found in *Plan* 6, representing the position of the army while halting on that ground. All the gates of the city were carefully guarded, to prevent the entrance of any armed body; but individuals were allowed to enter and to make purchases in the bazar. A corps of a dubious character, consisting of some hundred horse and foot, were encamped on the banks of the river, opposite to the western gate of the city; but these moved off at night-fall, and their subsequent route was not ascertained. The city was also supposed to contain a number of concealed enemies, expecting events which might encourage them to declare themselves. With a view therefore to this circumstance, and to the position of Holkur's camp, the British army assumed a position fronting the ford by which they had crossed the river, and which led to one gate of the city, while, on the remaining avenue to the right, a strong picket was placed to watch the ford in that direction. To the right and left of the camp were deep ravines, which extended from the river far to the rear, and were only passable where

(Plan 6.)

high roads crossed them. The country to the rear was alone open, and there strong pickets were placed on all the avenues leading into the camp, notwithstanding that the Goozerat Division was advancing from that direction. As the road to Mehidpoor led out from the left flank, the Third Division was encamped across it, *en potence* to the First, and at some distance, on an eminence which faced the position of Holkur's army. These, and further particulars respecting the situation of the army near Oojein, will be more evident on a reference to the *Plan*. It has been considered proper to describe them so minutely, as, previously to the arrival of the army in the vicinity of Oojein, there had been but little occasion to take an enemy into consideration, in selecting a position with reference to its immediate localities.

Reflexions on Indian Encampments;

In latter times, the British armies in India have marched many hundred miles, after leaving their own frontier, before they arrived within reach of a tangible enemy. The convenience of the troops, and the facility of their movements, are consequently, under such circumstances, the primary considerations. It will always gratify a military eye to contemplate a position facing the enemy's direction, and commanding the ground in its front with its flanks well covered, and its rear unembarrassed. If, however, no enemy exist within a calculable distance, an exclusive attention to such circumstances, must be considered only as the blind gratification of feelings founded on habit and precept, and unfit to enter into competition with considerations connected with the transportation of an army to a distant theatre of war. These considerations are, principally, the facility with which the troops and the various departments of an Indian army may enter their camp from the roads, and leave it again to resume their march. The more avenues by which this operation can be performed, the better, considering the multitude of followers who are necessarily excluded from the highway allotted to the troops and wheel-carriages. With regard to the ground of encampment itself, an abundant supply of water in its immediate vicinity must be considered as the first and most indispensable requisite. This, though an article necessary in all countries, is not required in such quantity elsewhere as in India, where an army is accompanied by innumerable attendants and cattle.

and on the number of Followers with an Army.

The maintenance of this number of followers, and the propriety of permitting them to accompany an army, are questions on which the narrators of military operations in India have occasionally touched, without drawing any very decided conclusion. That the reduction of the number of followers is possible, cannot be doubted. It must at the same time be confessed, that, so much attention being necessary to enforce a regulation for that purpose, a question arises whether the benefit to be derived is worth the care of its accomplishment. When the late General Agnew commanded a force employed to reduce the rebellious Polygars of the southern division, he found it prudent to reduce the number of his followers, on entering a district, in which he should be insulated while he remained there, and obliged to depend almost entirely on the supplies he carried with his force. The expedient adopted was an order restricting the proportion of private followers which would be allowed to individuals of every rank, and directing that such followers, as well as the public servants of departments, should each receive a ticket from their several superiors or masters. Also, that within a certain time after the publication of this regulation, all followers not provided with certificates, should withdraw from the camp to an assigned place, and there await orders for their future return. In the event of disregarding such orders, the offenders would be punished and drummed out of the camp. This arrangement had the desired effect; and the separation once made, none of the discarded followers could return, on account of the intervention of the enemy.

In almost every campaign in India a line will be found, beyond which no individuals can follow the army after a considerable advance has been made; consequently, a separation once effected, will have a result as complete as in the foregoing instance. But arrangements of this description should be made previously to the troops leaving their quarters; for if suddenly promulgated at an advanced point, so much desertion would probably take place, as to produce greater inconvenience than would accrue from a superfluity of followers. This will arise from a state of things commonly known in India. Almost every Native arrived at a mature age, has a family, or several relations, depending on him for their support. Therefore, unless they can be left at a secure place, in the receipt of a certain subsistence, they must be allowed to accompany him on whom they depend, or he will desert, sooner than abandon them. The supposed pre-arrangement, for obvious reasons, will appear difficult to be effected, from its extent and other causes, even with respect to private servants. When, therefore, the numbers of public attendants attached to the cavalry and the great supply departments are taken into the calculation, it will not seem extraordinary that this part of the question has been considered as a matter of opinion; and that measures have seldom been adopted to reduce the number of an army's followers, which consist, beyond comparison, more of people out of employ, than of public and private servants. It has been asserted by some officers of great experience, that this multitude is of positive advantage; as, having no prescribed duty to perform, they have leisure to bring into the camp, from the neighbouring country and towns, supplies that otherwise would be probably abandoned. Thus they not only feed themselves, but relieve the commissariat, which is obliged to supply the soldier, when rice cannot be had in the bazar below a certain rate. This argument necessarily supposes the army to be moving in an enemy's country, from which the inhabitants having fled, it remains for the followers to discover their hidden grain and to bring it in. That instances of a favourable result from such a state of things have occurred, there can be little doubt, or, probably, that opinion would never have been formed or declared; yet, in extensive [illegible] the inhabitants do not generally abandon their villages at the approach of a British force, but, on the contrary, frequently prefer their protection to that of the army of their own sovereign. Even during the Mysore war, which may be cited as an exception, it has been fully ascertained that the inhabitants were forcibly driven from their villages by the Sultaun's numerous horse. If, in petty operations against former Polygars, the villages were abandoned, this arose from local and particular causes, which have ceased to exist. If it be allowable for followers to seize the property of the villagers when the owners are absent, they can scarcely be expected to discern the justice of forbearance when the inhabitants may occasionally be present. Thus is engendered a habit of plunder which cannot be kept within bounds, even by capital punishments—that deplorable and too frequent expedient suggested by the impatience of uncontrouled power. It appears, then, that the more numerous the followers, the more prevalent will be this species of evil, which can scarcely be counterbalanced by even the supposed advantage to be derived from them.

particularly with a Madras Army.

The enormous estimates of the multitudes which follow a British army, are probably taken more from instances under the Madras Presidency than on the Bengal and Bombay establishments. This difference may be traced in the history of British India. So unremitting has been the field service of the Madras army through more than half a century, that a large population has continued during many years, who were born in a camp, and are so habituated to field service, that it has become their most natural state. Multitudes, consequently, are on all occasions ready to move, with an alacrity which will not be found under the sister Presidencies, where the intervals of peace have been longer, or where the operations have had a more confined theatre. Unless, therefore, coercive measures be adopted for restricting the number of followers with a Madras army, they will probably continue as numerous as at present, till a long interval of peace shall have exterminated a generation habituated from youth to a roving life. To this explanation it may be added, that it has been long the habit of the Madras, more than of the Bengal Sepoys, to carry their women to camp; and indeed there are certain regulations in favour of the latter, which renders the movement of their families unnecessary. In the mean while this questionable evil continues; for notwithstanding many officers of rank who have served in Europe, are, on taking the field in India, struck with what appears a monstrous and insupportable impediment, yet none have ventured on the labour of controuling a custom, which the natural course of events has produced and supported with all its disadvantages.

So much ground occupied by an Indian Camp unprejudicial.

This being the case, it becomes necessary to give more ground for an encampment than is required in Europe. There are, it is true, other causes, such as the quantity and size of the camp equipage; and with regard to the cavalry in particular, the distance from each other at which horses must be picketed. But these considerations are immaterial causes, compared with that of the multitude of followers, for giving so large a front in proportion to the number of fighting men. For were that fundamental principle of preserving an equality between the front of the camp and the space required for the formation of the troops invariably observed, the lines of a corps would require an extent of depth inconveniently disproportionate to its front. This explanation appears necessary on the first description of a position of the army, in order to account for circumstances which otherwise may be misunderstood. It is but rarely that an Indian enemy attacks a British force in position; and this will afford a further reason for consulting convenience so much in the distribution of encampments. Detachments have, no doubt, been attacked, but by considerable armies; and as the motions of large bodies must always be discovered in sufficient time to admit of making the proper dispositions of a small force, no injury has been hitherto sustained in consequence of the existing system of encampment. An instance to this effect has occurred in the attack at Poonah, and will be found hereafter in that at Nagpoor. Many similar examples also occur in the wars of Hyder Allee; and one very apposite, in 1799, in Tippoo's attack of the advance of the Bombay army at Seedaseer.

CHAPTER VI.

DISPERSION AND FLIGHT OF THE PINDARRIES BEYOND THE CHUMBUL.

Movement of the Head-quarters of the Grand Army from the Sind to the Bheitwah. Treacherous Conduct of Scindiah. Treaty with Ameer Khan. Return of Lord Hastings to the Sind. March of the Second Division of the Grand Army towards the Upper Chumbul. Its Separation for the Attack of the Pindarries. Resumption of the Pursuit of the Pindarries by the Third Division. By Colonel Philpot's Detachment. The Pindarries force the Kotah Frontier, and are overtaken by the Third Division. Opposed in Front, they abandon their Baggage, &c. to the Second Division. Flying to the Southward, they are pursued by the Fifth Division of the Deckan Army, till they cross the Upper Chumbul. Cheettoo protected by Jeswunt Rao Bhao. Return of the Third Division to the Eastward. Investigation of the Causes of the Escape of the Pindarries. Their Escape accounted for.

HOWEVER well chosen might be the position of the Marquis of Hastings' Head-quarters on the banks of the Sind, for the preservation of the advantages already gained by the treaty with Scindiah, it was found necessary to relinquish it, on account of a dreadful pestilence which ravaged the camp of the Centre Division.

This destructive disease, since denominated *cholera spasmodica*, advanced from the countries about the head of the bay where it first made its appearance, and, almost as soon as the troops began to move, was felt on the Jumnah.

Movement of the Head-quarters of the Grand Army from the Sind to the Bheitwah. (Map III.)

Under the impression that a situation might be found more favourable to the health of the army than the banks of the Sind, Lord Hastings, on the 10th of November, directed his march by Terrait, Talgaon, and Seleia, to Erich, on the right bank of the Bheitwah, in the neighbourhood of which was a comparatively elevated country; but the disorder, so far from abating, increased to a degree which rendered all movement most embarrassing. The march of the troops was strewed with the victims of this malady, which latterly attacked the Europeans, though the Natives, from their habit of low diet, appeared most exposed to it. Of the latter, two hundred and upwards are said to have died in one day. This produced so great an alarm among the followers, that desertions succeeded, to the amount of several thousands.

Treacherous conduct of Scindiah.

The Head-quarters and Centre Division of the Grand Army occupied the ground near Erich from the 20th of November to the end of that month. During this time, Lord Hastings received information respecting the secret machinations of Scindiah, who thought the British troops were crippled beyond what was really the case. This he considered as a favourable opportunity for breaking the treaty recently concluded. The Pindarries being at this time attacked in the south of Malwah, he invited them to retire to Gwalior by a particular route, engaging to join them as soon as they arrived within a certain distance. However the Governor-general might formerly have been only suspicious of Scindiah's sincerity, he could have little doubt on this head, on receiving copies of his letters to the Pindarry chiefs—a transaction which was corroborated by the Maharajah's unsatisfactory conduct in other respects. He shewed so little desire to produce the contingent of five thousand horse, agreeably to the fourth article, that Captain Blacker, the officer appointed to superintend that corps, was necessitated, under the instructions of the Resident, to commence a levy for Scindiah in the neighbourhood of his own capital. The positions allotted to the detached corps of Scindiah's army, in pursuance of the sixth article, were (Map II) Ajemeer, Koomulneir, Bahadoorghur, and Oojein; yet it has been seen, that the corps of Ambajee Punt, from the latter place, was met at Saurungpoor by Sir John Malcolm's division; and it also occurred, that a party of troops marched from Gwalior about the same time for Bhilsah, though it was particularly stipulated that there should be no movement of any part of the Maharajah's army. To these facts was added the corroborated information of the negotiations carried on by Scindiah with the Nepaul and Seik Governments. Though little apprehensions were entertained of the first breaking with the British Government, the activity of the other, in military preparations, was reasonably calculated to excite a wide and alarming distrust.

Treaty with Ameer Khan.

The negotiations with Ameer Khan had at the same time arrived at a favourable issue, by the treaty concluded between that chief, through a confidential agent, and Mr. Metcalfe, the resident at Delhi; and which was ratified by the Governor-general on the 15th of November. It consisted of six articles; and provided for the guarantee of the Ameer's Jaghires to himself and heirs, on the condition that he should disband his army, surrender his guns, assist in the destruction of the predatory system, hold the small force he was allowed to retain, at the requisition of the British Government, and relinquish all connection with other Powers. Yet nothing could be effected, supposing even his best intentions, till the near approach of Sir David Ochterlony's division should afford him, by its support, the power of executing these engagements. It was, however, well known to the Governor-general, that he was pledged to assist Scindiah, should that chief take the field. This event was also to be followed by the co-operation of Nana Govind Rao, ruler of certain territories in Malwah, which had been ceded to the British Government by the treaty of June with the Peishwah. The proceedings of Holkur's Government have been noticed (p. 86); and it was now quite impossible to foretell what measures it would ultimately adopt. While one party was resolute for marching to the support of the Peishwah, the Regent Mother made overtures, through the Resident at Delhi, for the protection of the British Government; in consequence of which, the Political Agent at Kotah, on account of his convenient situation, was authorized to treat with her. This view of the state of affairs will account for the Governor-general's anxiety, on learning that the Head-quarters and First Division of Sir Thomas Hislop's army were retiring from the Nerbuddah, instead of advancing into Malwah, where the demands of the service appeared to his Lordship incomparably more important than in the Deckan.

Return of Lord Hastings to the Sind.

(Map III.)

Such was the state of things when the expulsion of the Pindarries from Southern Malwah was effected by the divisions from the Nerbuddah and Bundelcund. The flight of the two *durrahs* was exactly in the direction prescribed to them by Scindiah; and as this route was left open by the movement of the First Division to Erich, Lord Hastings hastened his return to the Sind, notwithstanding the distressing prevalence of the epidemic. A detachment, consisting of the cavalry-brigade under Colonel Philpot, and one battalion of Native infantry, had been formed, and separated from the Head-quarters, for expeditious movement wherever required, since the 18th of November. It then marched by Samptur and Ihansee to Burwa-Saghur, and there halted from the 24th to the 3d of December. It then received orders to march immediately to the Sind, and, should intelligence be received there of the flight of the Pindarries towards Gwalior, to cross that river and attack them. The detachment accordingly marched on the 4th; and on the 7th arrived at Sonari, by the route of Ihansee and Delteah. On the 8th it passed the ford, and encamped at Cheemuck, a position commanding the only road between Narwur and Gwalior. Contemporary with the order for this movement, were instructions directing Major Cumming to march his detachment (p. 55) with all expedition to Teearree; and to Brigadier-general Frith to detach half the 2d battalion of the 2d regiment, with two field-pieces, to the fords on the Chumbul, at Dholpoor. On the 2d of December the Centre Division was at Labeira, on the 6th at Imroke, on the 8th at Bundoor, and on the 10th at the Sonari ford, where it was within twenty-eight miles of Gwalior, and considerably nearer than Scindiah's position to the pass of Narwur. The western Ghat, near the Chumbul, as well as the ford at Dholpoor, were at the same time, by his Lordship's pre-arrangement, occupied by the Right Division; and the fords of the Jumnah by detachments from the frontier stations. By throwing the advanced guard of the Centre Division across the Sonari ford, as has been described, and making it move to the left to occupy a position behind a small river which runs into the Sind, all communication, by the Narwur line, was cut off between the Pindarries and Scindiah, who was unable to attack this post without placing himself between two fires. What has been premised will be sufficient to shew, that the future operations of the campaign entirely depended on the movement or quiescence of Scindiah, on whom, consequently, all eyes were turned. This importance attaching to his conduct demanded a particular description of the Marquis's position, by which Scindiah was so completely controuled.

March of the Second Division of the Grand Army towards the Upper Chumbul.

After the conclusion of the treaty with Scindiah, the necessity for the presence of the Right Division at Dholpoor appeared no longer pressing. Major-general Donkin was accordingly ordered to ascend the left bank of the Chumbul, leaving at the ford abovementioned a battalion of Native infantry, some ordnance and irregular cavalry. The 2d battalion of the 12th regiment of Native infantry, two six-pounders, a *russalah* consisting of one hundred and forty of Gardner's horse, and a considerable party of the Dholpoor contingent, were allotted to this service. The head-quarters and remainder of the division marched from their position on the 13th of November. The route lay by Roopass, Beana, and Hindoon, at which place the division arrived on the 20th; and on the 23d at Oodye, within two miles of Kooshalghur, where it halted for instructions from the Head-quarters.

(Map III)

An agent from Ameer Khan here presented himself with a friendly message from his master, who engaged to afford every protection to the communication in the rear of the Second Division, which necessarily passed through territory occupied by his posts. This assurance was the more satisfactory, as the treaty with the Khan was still unexecuted, and as this division had other objects to pursue which obliged it to offer its rear to his position. Its presence was earnestly called for on the right bank of the Chumbul, as well for the interception of the Pindarries on the Kotah frontier, as to offer to Holkur an opportunity of abandoning the warlike faction of his Government, should he find it most expedient to retire in that direction.

Its separation for the attack of the Pindarries.

Accordingly, Major-general Donkin, having satisfactorily established his commissariat depôt at Koosh-hulghur, continued his march on the 2d of December, followed by the 2d battalion of the 12th regiment, which had been previously recalled from Dholpoor, and was subsequently replaced by a wing of the 2d battalion of the 2d regiment from Agra. On the 5th he crossed the Bunnass, near Bhugwunt-ghur, with a part of his division lightly (Map III.) equipped, consisting of the cavalry-brigade, horse-artillery, and four companies of Native infantry, leaving under the command of Colonel Vanrenen the infantry-brigade and foot-artillery. On the 8th, the head-quarters of the Second Division reached Dubblanna by forced marches; and halted on the 9th, in consequence of intelligence from Kotah. At the same time the 2d battalion of the 12th regiment of Native infantry were ordered to march to the Lakeiree pass; while General Donkin, on the 10th, renewing his march on information of the movements of the Pindarries, encamped at Boondee that day, and on the 11th at Thekerea. Here the division's head-quarters again halted for supplies from the rear, the cattle with Colonel Vanrenen's detachment being unable to move with rapidity. On the 13th, however, the whole division crossed the Chumbul at the Gummuck Ghat, eight miles below Kotah. On the 14th, the division again separated, and the head-quarters and lightly equipped part made a forced march of twenty-one miles to Sooltaunpoor, where it was ascertained that the Pindarries, having attempted to enter Harrowtie by the Oomree pass, close to Digdowlie, were repulsed by the Kotah troops.

Resumption of the pursuit of the Pindarries by the Third Division.

It will be recollected that the *durrahs* of Kurreem Khan and Wassil Mahomud, when retreating before Colonel Adams's division, took the direction of Kolarus and Narwur (p. 84.) As the pursuit of them brought the troops acting from the southward into immediate co-operation with the

Second Division, it becomes necessary to recur to the movements from that quarter, in order to render the further detail perspicuous. Major-general Marshall, on the 8th of December, marched from Seronge, and arrived by the route of Mogulserye, and Shadowra, at Nyaserye, where, on the 12th, he separated his division into two parts. The first lightly equipped, under his immediate orders, consisted of the whole of the cavalry, three battalions of infantry, and six guns, besides the galloper-brigade; leaving under Colonel Price, the 2d battalion of the 28th regiment of Native infantry, the remainder of the artillery, the moveable hospital, stores and heavy baggage. The Major-general continued his route in the direction of Kolarus, the previous information of the movements of the Pindarries giving reason to suppose them on the northern road; but after crossing the Sind, it turned towards Bijrawun, satisfactory intelligence having been received that they had passed to the westward.

(Map III.)

By Colonel Philpot's detachment.

This will be understood by a reference to the march of Colonel Philpot's detachment to Cheemuck, where it anticipated the arrival of the Pindarries moving towards Gwalior. They had already reached Narwur with that intent. Here, finding their further progress obstructed, they turned, on the 6th of December, south-west, into the district of Thurye; and on this information Colonel Philpot marched on the 9th through the hills to Magrone. Finding here that he was far in the rear of the enemy, more closely pursued by other detachments, he returned by Mustoora to Cheemuck, where he arrived on the 14th. The Pindarries finding themselves thus pressed from three quarters by British troops, preferred encountering those of Kotah.

The Pindarries force the Kotah frontier, and are overtaken by the Third Division.

On the 8th, the united *durrahs* of Kurreem and Wassil Mahomud marched from Pooree. On the 9th they were at B[illegible], where they were desirous of depositing their families, on account of the difficulties attending their flight. Failing in this object, and not effecting their passage of the hills west of Pooree and north of Shahabad, which were guarded by the Kotah troops, they fell back to the Neem Ghat on the Koorah river; and following the skirts of the hills, attacked the Ghat at Laddanah, near Seersee, on the 12th. They succeeded in forcing it that evening, after long opposition from four hundred of the Kotah troops, and encamped the next day at Bechola, or Beechee Tal, to let their baggage and rear rejoin them from the bottom of the Ghat. In this situation they were heard of, by General Marshall, at Bijrawun, about twenty-two miles distant. He marched at twelve o'clock on the night of the 13th; but owing to the bad road, did not arrive at the foot of the Ghat till two o'clock the afternoon following. The Pindarries were at this time still at Beechee Tal; but soon after, receiving information of the approach of the British troops, they moved off with their families and baggage, leaving a body of a thousand horse to cover their rear. General Marshall's cavalry immediately mounted the Ghat, preceded by an advance-guard of infantry, and followed by the 1st battalion of the 14th regiment dragging up the galloper-guns, the remaining infantry and guns being left in the rear. As soon as the cavalry got sight of the Pindarry rear-guard, Colonel Newberry, commanding them, pushed on in advance of the infantry to the attack, and succeeded in destroying about forty or fifty of them. The remainder escaped, by dispersing in all directions. The cavalry returned to Beechee Tal, after a pursuit of ten miles, and rejoined the division, having lost ten men killed and wounded, and twenty-six horses. On the 16th, General Marshall continued the pursuit to Keelwarra, a distance of nineteen miles, which he found strewed with baggage that had been abandoned, with a brass gun. On the following day he arrived at the Parbuttee, on the road to Barra, to which place the cavalry had been sent in advance to capture some thousand head of Brinjarrie cattle. The division reassembled here on the 18th, with the exception of the detachment left at Nyaserye.

Opposed in front, they abandon their baggage, &c. to the Second Division

It will be recollected, that the Head-quarters of the Right Division, commanded by Major-general Donkin, were at Sooltaunpoor on the 14th. On the following morning, the light brigade moved on to Kullana, on the Sind. Intelligence was there received of General Marshall's attack of the Pindarries, on the previous day, at Beechee Tal; and on the night of the 16th, it was satisfactorily ascertained that the pursuit had driven Kurreem Khan's *durrah* into their vicinity. Accordingly, on the 17th, early in the morning, the light-brigade was in motion, and came up with their baggage and bazars before day-light. The few Pindarries guarding them fled, and the family of Kurreem Khan remained prisoners. Refuge had been demanded for them in a neighbouring fort; which being refused, they were on their return to the *durrah*, accompanied by an elephant and some articles of regalia. Thirty-two camels, laden, were also brought in by Colonel Gardner, from another party of three or four hundred, whom he had been sent, on the same morning, to attack with the frontier horse. At this time the division was distributed in the following manner:—the head-quarters, cavalry brigade, horse-artillery, and four companies of Native infantry, at

Mungrol; one battalion, with four pieces of artillery, at Pattun, on the Chumbul; another battalion, with two guns, at the Lakeiree pass; and the remainder of the infantry and artillery, with the camp equipage, commissariat depôt, and heavy baggage, at Kullana.

Flying to the southward, they are pursued by the Fifth Division of the Deckan Army.

The Pindarries, having found all access to the Chumbul opposed by these and previous dispositions, had turned short to the southward from Bamoleah, on the night of the 16th, when pressed by General Marshall. They directed their course between the Sind and Parbuttee rivers, upon Sherghur and Gogul Chuppra, abandoning to their pursuers, as has been seen, every thing likely to hamper their flight. But in this direction they were destined again to fall in with enemies; for Colonel Adams arrived on the 15th at Gogul Chuppra, by the route of Meergwass, from Munnohur Thannah, where it will be recollected he was encamped on the 8th (p. 84), and which he left on the 13th. On the 17th, in the forenoon, he detached his cavalry from Jeelwarra on the Parnuddee. Major Clarke, commanding this body, made a march of thirty miles, the same day, up the right bank of that river, in pursuit of the Pindarries. At Oothara he found that a party of his irregulars, who here rejoined him, had been hanging on the rear of the two *durrahs*, without being able to make any impression, and that they had fled by the way of P'hool Burroad. But want of provisions, and the fatigue of the detachment, induced the Major to halt a few hours; after which the pursuit was continued. The favour evidently shewn, by the subjects of Kotah, to the enemy, prevented afterwards his getting satisfactory information concerning them. His subsequent pursuit, therefore, consisted of a continual change of direction, under great distress for provisions, till he was rejoined, on the 19th, by his supplies and equipage, near Burroad. From thence he marched again on the following morning, in search of a body of the enemy said to be at Peeplcea, about twelve miles in a westerly direction, and succeeded in dispersing them and destroying a few, fifteen being found dead. The principal effect of this movement was to hurry still more the flight of the *durrahs* to Rajghur-Pattun, where they arrived, greatly dispirited and disunited, on the 21st. On the same day, Major Clarke's detachment likewise rejoined its head-quarters. In the mean while, Colonel Adams prosecuted his march according to the information he received. This had carried him, in the first instance, north, by Luckerakeirry to Katrow, on the Parbuttee; but subsequently learning the direction of the Pindarries, in their flight from Barra, he arrived on the 22d at Eklara, by the route of Moraseed and the Barouda Ghat; having been greatly impeded in his progress by the heavy rains which had lately fallen. This inclemency of the weather obliged him to halt on the 23d. Learning that evening, that a body of the enemy had just descended the Tara Ghat, near to which they had for some days been concealed by the subjects of Kotah, and from which asylum they were forced by the movement of a party of the Bhopal horse on their flank, he immediately detached the 1st Rohillah cavalry, commanded by Captain Roberts, to overtake them. This service he performed in a very creditable manner. After a march of nearly fifty miles, coming up with about four hundred of the enemy near Chubar, he pursued them, during two hours, through rocks and jungles. The loss of the Rohillahs amounted to five men and nine horses, while only sixty or seventy of the enemy were supposed to have escaped. These were probably the same party which had been attacked, on the morning of the 17th, by Gardner's horse from General Donkin's division. The two *durrahs* continued their flight towards Augur. Learning near that place, that Holkur's army had been defeated, and was retreating towards Hinglaisghur, as will be related hereafter, they turned back towards Chupperguttah, on the Oornuddy, seven miles west of Soosneir. Here they halted for some time, in consequence of interruptions, but subsequently resumed their march by a *detour*, which brought them, on the 27th, to Gungraur. From thence they crossed the Chumbul, to join the remains of Holkur's army. At the same time, Colonel Adams was marching by Seirhoo Googurnee and Kotra on Soosneir, where he arrived on the 1st of January, having experienced continued obstructions from the inclemency of the weather. He halted here on the 2d and 3d, and continued his march by Oodeipoor to Gungraur. There he was obliged to halt, from the 6th, in expectation of commissariat supplies, which were on the route from his rear division, escorted by a detachment under Major Logie. Here it will be proper to leave this force, which consisted of one thousand two hundred and fifty regular and irregular cavalry, one thousand four hundred and ninety regular Native infantry, and six pieces of ordnance, of which two were twelve-pounders, two six-pounders, and two five-and-a-half-inch howitzers.

(Map IV.)

Cheettoo protected by Jeswunt Rao Bhao.

It is time to notice the movements of Cheettoo Pindarry, who exhibited great sagacity in conducting the retreat of his *durrah*, said to amount to eight thousand men, without suffering diminution from the forces in pursuit of him. Having thrown himself in the rear of Holkur's army (p. 86), which a portion of his Pindarries joined, he subsisted for some time, in security, in the country about the Chumbul, till the advance of his enemies obliged him to cross that river. For some days previous to the 20th he was encamped at Singollee, about twenty-five miles south-west of Kotah; when, by invitation from Jeswunt Rao Bhao, he proceeded to Jawud, having previously sent his baggage and families to the jungles about Koomulneir. General Donkin, on hearing that Cheettoo had crossed the Chumbul, ordered Lieutenant-colonel Kelly, with five companies of Native infantry from Pattun, to occupy the Boondee pass, and then proceeded with the cavalry of the Second Division and Colonel Vanrenen's detachment to the Gynta Ghat. There he halted till the 28th, when having learned Cheettoo's movement to Jawud, he recalled the detachment from the Boondee pass.

Return of the Third Division to the eastward. (Map III)

General Marshall, after his attack of the Pindarries, had been recalled to his former position in Southern Malwah, by orders from Lord Hastings, and countermarched from Barra as he was preparing for a further pursuit of the enemy. This had now become unnecessary, as they had fled towards Colonel Adams's line of operations, and he had got into General Donkin's line. On the 21st he was at Keelwarra, where he received orders to detach his horse-artillery, the 4th regiment of Native cavalry, four *russalahs* of Rohillah cavalry, one battalion of Native infantry, and a company of pioneers, to join Major-general Brown, at a point to be assigned by that officer, whose operations will be described hereafter. He was also directed to place the 1st battalion of the 7th regiment, the 1st battalion of the 26th regiment, two twelve-pounders, two five-and-a-half-inch howitzers, and six six-pounders, under Brigadier-general Watson, with instructions to repair to the Centre Division of the Grand Army. With the remainder of the division, General Marshall retraced his march to Beirseah; and Brigadier-general Watson proceeded to the Centre Division by the route of Budderwass and Kolarus.

Investigation of the causes of the Escape of Pindarries.

After seeing the manner in which the Pindarries escaped from so many corps, employed in driving them to the confines of Malwah and Rajahpootana, it is important to investigate the causes of their having suffered so little loss from their pursuers. Their retreat from the Nerbuddah was commenced too soon, maintained with too much diligence, and conducted too decidedly, to leave any probability of their being overtaken at the commencement of the campaign against them. But the case was altered with respect to the joint *durrahs* of Kurreem Khan and Wassil Mahomud, when they took the road to Narwur on the strength of Scindiah's invitation; while Cheettoo, who always exhibited more marks of sagacity than any of the other Pindarry Chiefs, adopted decidedly, from the first, a north-westerly course, which obviated all possibility of his being intercepted. His character appears likewise, in other respects, to have been comparatively superior; for when Sir John Malcolm came to take possession of some of the places which had been under his rule, he found all the indications of a regular government, as far as such a state of things could exist in Malwah. The halt of the Third Bengal Division at Seronge, the subsequent slowness of its movement, and of that of the Fifth Deckan Division, with guns drawn by bullocks along bad roads, enabled Wassil Mahomud's and Kurreem Khan's *durrahs* to escape from Narwur with impunity, across the heads of both columns. The difficulties of movement with ordnance were still further increased by the rains, which prevailed with great violence from the middle of December. Here the question suggests itself, how came these divisions to hamper themselves with a description of arm so little adapted to the pursuit of Pindarries? To this it must be answered, in candour to the commanding officers concerned, that they had sufficient cause at the opening of the campaign to anticipate the possibility, if not probability, of finding themselves suddenly opposed by a formidable Mahratta corps, or by united corps of Mahrattas and Pindarries. In such a case, which was not overlooked by the highest authorities, and was referred to in their instructions, the absence of artillery might have exposed them to a serious check, which very few officers, after long service, will voluntarily hazard. Sir John Malcolm marched the lightest of all the divisions from the southward, having never with his head-quarters, when engaged in the pursuit, any troops besides cavalry, light infantry, and galloper-guns. In the course of his consequent rapid movement, which certainly gave Cheettoo no time to rest till he crossed the Seeprah, Sir John found himself, on one occasion, unexpectedly in presence of a corps of infantry and thirty guns, which, however, he was enabled to overawe; though he was latterly checked in his pursuit of Cheettoo by Holkur's army. It is not meant to be concluded from this statement, that even with the whole of his division the same consequence must not have ensued; but that, such events having occurred, there was ample possibility for the other divisions on his right to find themselves in situations more inextricable. This reasoning will not apply with equal force to the march of the divisions from Nyaserye and Munnohur

Thannah. There was little or no reason to suppose that any Power would oppose itself between the Pindarries and their pursuers, after their flight from Narwur. Thus, with the advanced party, any ordnance besides galloper-guns must be considered as superfluous. Even these it would have been proper to leave behind, on approaching the enemy; for, since Pindarries have been first attacked, never has a gun been brought to bear upon them. A couple of pieces, with a few men, whether horse or foot, who may be too much jaded, after a long march, for the exertion of attack, will afford excellent protection for such provisions and followers as may be in the rear, and be required to halt during the pursuit. This was precisely the case in the instance of Major Lushington's attack of the Pindarries at Cowah, on the 26th of December 1816, with the 4th regiment of Madras cavalry. After a forced march of fifty-three miles in fourteen hours, he dropped his guns with the jaded horses; or he could never have crowned so admirable an exertion with the success of that day. When Colonel Adams sent forward his cavalry alone on the occasions which have been related, as much success attended that measure, as the distance of the head-quarters of the division permitted. This remoteness was indeed a great disadvantage. The impossibility, on that account, of keeping the parties supplied, always checked their progress, and enabled the enemy, even when most pressed, to countermarch in the front of their pursuers.

Their Escape accounted for.

While examining the conduct of the divisions which followed the Pindarries through Malwah, the wretched state of the cattle which carried their supplies must not be overlooked. These were a continual clog on rapid movements, particularly after the setting-in of the rains; and obliged the head-quarters of every division to halt occasionally for their arrival from the rear. If any question arise out of this hindrance, it must be referred to the system of their commissariat, and to whatever difficulties might be experienced in deriving supplies from the country and establishing a free bazar, which high rates, with good management, seldom fail to invite. An army is, in most situations, more or less controuled in its movements by a necessary attention to its provisions; but it may be considered as undoubted, that wherever the system of issuing from the public store to the private followers of an Indian field force shall prevail, that force will be inevitably shackled by its department of supply. The Second Bengal Division appears to have been equally held back by its bullocks. Whenever it attempted to move rapidly, it was obliged to make a subsequent halt for the approach of the supplies, and thus to forego whatever advantage was proposed to be secured by a forced march. Yet, by judicious positions on both banks of the Chumbul, in a country of passes, it prevented a single Pindarry from crossing that river below Kotah. The part of it with Major-general Donkin was also well composed for an impression on the enemy in a direct pursuit. But no part of them, except Kurreem Khan's baggage-guard, ever appeared; and their main body was then too near the other divisions to justify a pursuit, to the abandonment of other objects of importance.

It was represented from both General Marshall's and Colonel Adams's divisions, that the escape of the Pindarries was favoured by the subjects of Kotah. These were possibly actuated by their fears of future visitation, should they aid the British troops with information. In some cases they even shut their gates, and refused to sell to them any provisions. If under all the circumstances which have been described, the Pindarries escaped with the loss of their baggage only, it may not be a matter of much surprise. It will indeed ever be impossible for a regular force, whose movements are guided by rules, to overtake a mounted enemy, who voluntarily abandon their followers, and every impediment to flight. They are even regardless of that principle of association which, on ordinary occasions, obtains among them. Much, however, was gained by forcing them to throw away their valuables, and disperse. Thus the inhabitants of the country, now convinced of the ruin of their cause, relinquished their fears, and shewed a disposition to retaliate, by plundering in their turn.

The hardy horses on which the Pindarries were mounted, were admirably calculated for the two most important manœuvres which they had occasion to perform. One was a rapid passage through a country, to the point to be plundered, so as to anticipate any intelligence of their approach; and the other by as expeditious a return, to escape the chastisement of their atrocious aggressions. Their most valuable articles they carried with them on the horses they rode. But even of these articles they were prepared to disencumber themselves, when their further preservation was likely to endanger their safety. Last of all they would abandon even their horses, when local circumstances rendered their escape on foot necessary or most practicable. But such an exigency seldom occurred, as their cattle were habituated to travel by the most rugged paths, and consequently, in the worst ground, would have the greatest advantage over their pursuers. It may be deemed surprising that the Pindarries, or a large portion of them, did not turn to the southward, from the first. Let it, however, be recollected, that though they had distressed the inhabitants of the British districts which they entered, they had themselves suffered severely during the last excursion, before they regained their own stations. Many of them were killed, many lost their horses, and but few returned with any booty. They had therefore reason to suppose, that in consequence of the experience gained, still more efficient precautions would be adopted for their interception. This reasoning, added to their expectation of a Mahratta combination in their favour, will be sufficient to account for the line of conduct they pursued. One party of Pindarries did, however, separate themselves from the principal hordes, and passed between all the corps in the field, to the Toombudra, as will be more particularly described hereafter.

CHAPTER VII.

RUPTURE ON THE PART OF THE BHOOSLAH.

Suspicious Conduct of the Rajah. Precautionary Measures of the Resident. Occupation of the Seetabuldee Hills by the British Brigade. Commencement of Hostilities by the Rajah's Troops. They gain Possession of the lesser Hill. Their Cavalry defeated and their Infantry repulsed at all Points. Reflections on this Defence. Comparison of the Actions at Poonah and Nagpoor. Considerations respecting Civil Residents. Arrival of Lieutenant-colonel Gahan's Detachment. Hostile Indications in various Parts of the Nagpoor Country. Force on the Nerbuddah concentrated at Hoossingabad. Brigadier-general Hardyman's March to Jubbulpoor. Defeat of the Enemy there.

IT is proper, from a regard to the order of time, here to suspend the relation of affairs in Malwah, and to return to events in the Deckan, the most considerable of which occurred at Nagpoor. These have been slightly noticed, in accounting for certain movements which were necessarily mentioned in the course of the preceding narrative. They will now be described with the minuteness which their importance deserves.

Suspicious conduct of the Rajah.

Throughout the early part of November, the intercourse with the Rajah of Nagpoor still continued on terms the most friendly, though frequent reports were conveyed to the Resident* of the sinister designs which he entertained, and of his secret correspondence with Scindiah and the Peishwah. He was stated, on the most respectable authority, to have the intention of sending off his treasures to the fortress of Chanda, and of repairing thither himself, under the pretence of a visit of religious ceremony. At the same time, none of his troops were sent forward to their advanced positions, as had been stipulated; and Captain Bayley, who was placed in immediate superintendance of the auxiliary contingent, was scarcely permitted to look at the corps assembled under that name. A force of about

* Richard Jenkins, Esq.

eight thousand horse, and as many foot, was already near the capital; and an active additional levy of troops, for the Rajah's service, was carried on, even in Malwah. Those already raised were held in readiness for immediate action; and it was reported that the principal officers had been recommended to send away their families to distant places of more security. During this state of things, an extraordinary coincidence in the information received at Nagpoor, by the Resident, and at Hurdah, by Sir John Malcolm, could not fail to attract attention. Even so early as September, Mr. Jenkins received intelligence that agents on the part of Cheettoo Pindarry had been admitted to the Rajah's presence, and sent back, with an honorary dress, as a present to their master, inviting also his junction with the Nagpoor troops, for the destruction of the British force. At Hurdah it was ascertained, in the beginning of November, that these agents had passed through that place, on their return to Cheettoo, in the middle of October, and had confidentially declared, to an individual there, their own errand and the objects of the Rajah.

Precautionary measures of the Resident

So little satisfaction was gained by any expostulation on the part of the Resident, that it became necessary for him to adopt his own measures immediately, for the security of the British interests at Nagpoor. The first of these was to recall Lieutenant-colonel Scot's detachment from the vicinity of Ramteak (p. 50.) This force was altogether very inconsiderable; but no other was immediately available, and its situation was contemplated with great anxiety. On the 14th of November, intelligence arrived of the Peishwah's attack of the brigade at Poonah on the 5th. As this event corroborated all the unfavourable appearances in the Rajah's conduct, a requisition was sent to Captain Hare, at Beitool, (p. 50,) for the immediate countermarch of the Russell brigade, to Nagpoor. Lieutenant-colonel Gahan's detachment was also called on to advance from the vicinity of H[illegible] (p. 80.) The requisition to Captain Hare was countermanded on the following day, in consideration of the expected advance of Lieutenant-colonel Gahan; and would indeed have been fruitless, as the Russell brigade was already near the Nerbuddah. But the order for the Lieutenant-colonel's advance was repeated, on the 20th, in more pressing terms, on account of the encreasing danger at the capital. By an uncommon coincidence, the treaty at Gwalior had been concluded on the same day that the rupture took place at Poonah, and the information of both events was received on the same day, the 14th, at Nagpoor. The Resident was thus enabled, at the *durbar*, to discuss both occurrences, with reference to each other; and to draw from them, arguments suited to the discouragement of the hostile intentions supposed to be entertained. The Rajah's expressions were still friendly and conciliatory; but insufficient to lull the Resident's suspicions, which were further strengthened by his subsequent conduct in opposition to the most pressing remonstrances. A *khillaat** arrived from the Peishwah, which had been dispatched shortly after the Treaty of Poonah, with the cognizance of the Resident there. But as the relations between the contracting parties had changed, while it was on the road, from peaceful to hostile, Mr. Jenkins protested against its reception by the Rajah, as inconsistent with his alliance with the British Government. The other disregarded these representations. Having first received the *khillaat* in public *durbar* with the usual forms, he proceeded, on the 24th, to his principal camp on the west side of the town. There he was received with uncommon demonstrations of pomp, and with every ceremony indicative of his having received the dignity of *Serraputtee*, or General in Chief of the Armies of the Mahratta Empire.

Occupation of the Seetabuldee Hills by the British brigade.

If any shadow of doubt remained on the Resident's mind, respecting the Rajah's intention to imitate the Peishwah's example, it arose from a consideration of his pusillanimous character. The greatest degree of vigilance was, however, maintained at the Residency, owing to the universal opinion among all classes in Nagpoor, that the British lines would be immediately attacked. Accordingly, on the following day, the brigade under Lieutenant-colonel Hopeton Scot's command, moved from its lines to the Residency, and took possession of the double hill of Seetabuldee, which formed a strong and convenient post. This measure had been delayed as long as possible, and luckily was delayed no longer, supposing it more judicious than to remain in the cantonment; for a party of Arabs evinced an intention of seizing the same position at the very moment they were anticipated by the British troops. Yet, such was the duplicity of the Rajah, that even amidst these occurrences he pretended a desire of maintaining terms of amity with the British, and, to concert the best means for that purpose, desired the attendance of the Resident's Moonshee. The latest communication from Mr. Jenkins to the Rajah, conveyed an account of the Peishwah's expulsion from Poonah on the 17th, and was made on

* Dress of honour.

the morning of the 25th, to which was returned a friendly and congratulatory reply. As a last measure of precaution, and which could be no longer delayed, expresses were sent off to General Doveton's division, urging the most expeditious movement towards Nagpoor for the succour
(Plan 7.) of the brigade. The hill of Seetabuldee, standing close to the Residency,
(A. B) which it divides from the city of Nagpoor, consists of two eminences, distant from each other three hundred yards, and connected by a low and narrow ridge. The soil of which the hill is composed is much mixed with rocks, so as to render extremely difficult, if not fruitless, any hasty attempt to entrench its summits. Fronting the city, which is distant about a mile, and separated from Seetabuldee by an intervening tank called the
(B.) Jumma Taulao, the eminence has least elevation on the left. Being, however, within musquet range, its occupation was evidently necessary to the maintenance of the new position, particularly as on that side the suburbs of the city approached close to the base of the smaller hill. The 1st battalion of the 24th regiment of Native Infantry was therefore placed in possession of it, and the remainder of the infantry and guns occupied
(C.) the principal eminence of Seetabuldee. The cavalry were in the rear of the Residency, which, on that side, was open to the plain.

Commencement of hostilities by the Rajah's troops.

In front, and on both flanks of the British position, extended a village of mud huts, which adjoined the foot of the hill, and gave cover to the enemy, who were noticed, throughout the 26th, to be gradually collecting.
(C. c.) This movement, connected with the arrival of five guns, left no room to doubt that immediate hostilities were intended. As night approached, Lieutenant-colonel Scot adopted suitable measures of precaution. He was engaged in distributing sentries opposite the quarter occupied in force by the Arabs, when they opened a fire of musquetry on his small party, who forbore returning it, while attempts were made to convince the enemy that no molestation was intended. These endeavours having been disregarded, the party gave their fire, and retreated to the top of the hill, under a discharge of musquetry from the village. This was the signal for the attack to commence against the other side of the hill, and a severe fire was maintained on both sides through the whole of the night. The enemy, who had been, during the day, engaged in bringing forward some guns with their infantry, completed their arrangements in the course of the night; and the day-light of the morning of the 27th exhibited to the British troops occupying an insulated position, enemies and batteries opposed to them in every

direction, to the estimated amount of eighteen thousand men and thirty-six guns.

Who gain possession of the lesser hill.

The 1st battalion of the 24th regiment of Native infantry having suffered greatly during the night, were reinforced by a party from the 1st battalion of the 20th regiment. Yet, at five o'clock in the morning, they were found to be so much reduced by casualties and fatigue, that Colonel Scot deemed his force insufficient to maintain the whole of the lesser eminence. He therefore withdrew the remains of the 1st battalion of the 24th regiment of Native infantry, relieving them by the Resident's escort, commanded by Captain Lloyd. These were ordered to confine their position to the immediate summit, which had been strengthened by a breastwork of bags of grain. This posture of affairs continued till nine o'clock, when the enemy made a desperate charge, in powerful force, up the face of the lesser height, and carried it. All that had been anticipated from their occupation of this part of the position immediately ensued. The brigade had now but little superiority of ground to compensate for their disparity of numbers. Consequently, their loss of men and officers rapidly increased. The enemy, encouraged by success, gave fresh ardour to their attacks, closed in from all directions, and threatened to enter the Residency, in rear of the British position, which contained the wives and families of both officers and men of the brigade.

Their cavalry defeated, and their infantry repulsed at all points.

At this crisis, Captain Fitzgerald, commanding the three troops of Bengal cavalry, reinforced by the detail of the Madras cavalry, forming part of the Resident's escort, discerned, with admirable sagacity, the importance of a daring effort in the plain, which might repel the presumption with which the enemy contemplated the posture of affairs. With his small but compact body, in opposition to the most express injunctions, (devoted and generous disobedience!) he made a decided charge against their principal mass of horse, who, unable to resist so much impetuosity, broke in all directions, and abandoned a small battery by which they had been supported. This, likewise, was attacked with equal success; the infantry attached to it being cut to pieces, and the guns immediately turned against the flying enemy; after which they were brought into the Residency in triumph.* This exploit was witnessed by the troops on Seetabuldee, with

* This resembles a feat performed by a similar body of Austrian cavalry; but supported by a particular disposition of infantry, to prove the advantages of which, it is adduced. "I saw,"

those sentiments which may be easily imagined as resulting from a consideration of its brilliancy, connected with a conviction of their own dangerous situation. It induced the immediate resolution of recovering the lost height by a combined attack of the cavalry and infantry. The execution was, at first, delayed in expectation of the return of the cavalry, till a tumbril in possession of the enemy at the point to be possessed, blew up; when a simultaneous sentiment in favour of an instant attack so forcibly operated, that the commanding officer could with difficulty prevent the principal position from being abandoned. Where such ardour existed, the result which followed might be easily anticipated. The enemy were driven from the lesser eminence, and their battery taken: nor here did the movement cease. The victors followed their success into the Arab village, and captured in the plain two guns, which were immediately spiked. The enemy, however, soon became sensible of their recent misconduct, and evinced an intention of retrieving their loss, by reassembling in force at the foot of the hill. A well-timed charge, of a troop of cavalry, led by Cornet Smith round the base of the hill, took them unexpectedly in flank, and terminated their hopes of success. The fire henceforth slackened, and at twelve o'clock at noon had entirely ceased. No confident statement has been made of the enemy's loss, though it has been generally estimated at three hundred. That on the British side amounted to three hundred and sixy-seven*, including fifteen European commissioned officers; and exceeded one-fourth of the number of fighting men under arms.

Reflections on this defence.

The good conduct of the troops on this occasion requires no comment, and the dispositions made for the defence of the British interests at Nagpoor, appear to have been judicious. There were probably good reasons for withdrawing the 1st battalion of the 24th regiment of Native infantry, on the morning of the 27th, from the smaller height, and for expecting that the escort, with a trifling reinforcement, would be sufficient to maintain possession of its summit. Of the justness of this supposition there could be no doubt, had the breastwork been respectable enough not to be easily surmounted; or had it possessed a small ditch in its front, which

---

says General Lloyd, "at Silistria in Turkey, two squadrons attack a column or mass of above six thousand Turks in this manner, whom they defeated and dispersed in less than three minutes." Vol. i. p. 58.

* See Appendix. C.

might have exposed the enemy to the fire of the musquetry from behind the grain-bags. In the attack of such a position, what the assailants suffer will be during the approach; which, if the charge be rapid, will be inconsiderable, and this being scarcely seen by them, they will not be deterred. Arrived at this breastwork, they are as much covered by it as those within, unless indeed it have flanking parts; and if it be easily surmountable, there appears no reason to expect that it will not be attempted, and with success. Even a despicable ditch will oblige the assailants to remain for some time sufficiently distant from the breastwork, to be exposed to a severe fire. During this delay they will contemplate their loss and danger, and be most probably induced to relinquish the attempt, however practicable.

If such a position be attacked on all sides, and there be no more troops for its defence than are sufficient to man the breastwork, it is evident that no part can be held in reserve. But were the case otherwise, perhaps the best employment of that reserve would be to sally out and take the enemy in flank by a circuit of the position, if the nature of the ground permit this movement. The result can scarcely be doubted; and the issue of a similar operation is happily illustrated in the success of Cornet Smith's charge round the base of the hill. This part of the action has demanded a fuller consideration, as it was evidently the crisis of the defence.

Comparison of the actions at Poonah and Nagpoor

Though some circumstances respecting the situation of the British brigades at Poonah and Nagpoor make them proper subjects for a parallel, yet there were several, and these striking dissimilarities. Colonel Burr's force was double the strength of Colonel Scot's, and possessed a corps of Europeans; while to Colonel Scot's a small body of cavalry was attached. Colonel Burr advanced into the plain, while Colonel Scot's paucity of numbers confined him to a strong position. The action at Kirkee was from its nature necessarily terminated in a short time; while that at Seetabuldee continued during eighteen hours, till both nature and hope exhausted, obliged the assailants to relinquish further attack. The enemy's force appears, on both occasions, to have been nearly equal; but at Poonah their horse were brought more into action. On the British side, the Civil functions of the Resident were, on both occasions, temporarily suspended; and they were obliged to join the troops under arms for personal safety. The situation of a Resident at Indian Courts is dissimilar to that of a resident Ambassador in Europe, and cannot be described by any comparison with the diplomatic department at home. Such is the controul which the power of the British Government enables them to exercise, that they would more resemble a Roman Proconsul, were the military character annexed to their situation. Yet though they cannot take the command of troops, without a military commission, they exercise judgment on military measures. A reader unacquainted with Indian affairs, will have seen, probably not without considerable surprise, in the relation of the rupture at Poonah, that the Resident called on the commanding officer to quit his position, and to attack the enemy, prepared for action, in theirs. If there be such a thing as a question purely military, it must be such an one as this. However, therefore, the commanding officer's obedience or disobedience to such a requisition might affect his subsequent employment by the Government, he would probably feel confident in the opinion of a court-martial, on his asserting the exercise of his own judgment on a field of battle, with due deference to his own commission, after the Resident had been obliged to fly from the violence of the Power to whom he was accredited.

Considerations with regard to Civil Residents.

It may be presumed that difficulties have been experienced in describing an exact line of demarcation for the authority of a Resident; and that it has been regulated by circumstances and occasional decisions on particular points of reference. The present state of things has gradually arisen from the employment of Civil officers in the capacity of Residents; and the assertion may be safely ventured, that no Military Resident has ever interfered so much as Civilians* with the exercise of the military command. Whence, it may be demanded, should this arise? From the silent operation of a habit of deference, among soldiers, to a higher military commission —from a respect for their profession, which considers as indecent the degradation of an officer of rank—or from a conviction of the necessity of

* If an attempt were made to discover a similar occurrence in Europe to the ordinary power exercised by political Residents in India, it would be in the instance of Sir John Moore's campaign in Spain. The commanding officer's opinion was at variance with that of the diplomatic agent with the Central Junta, and public injury naturally followed; but from any subsequent conduct of the Government generally known, it does not appear that any advantage was expected from trammelling the judgment of the commanding officer, or that the latter has been blamed for asserting and acting on his own opinion. This instance will not however form an exact parallel with that noticed in the text, were even the interference with the military commission equally strong; for as Great Britain was at war not *with* Spain, but *for* her, Mr. Frere's powers were in their full vigour at the time in question.

military experience in judging of military matters. It may be argued on this subject, that as the practice remains unaltered, under a Governor-general possessing the high military commission of a General and Commander-in-Chief, and who has all his life evinced an ardent love of his profession, this circumstance must be received as favourable to its existence, and demonstrative of its expediency. Under perfect ignorance of his Lordship's opinion on this subject, it can only be said, that, probably, a reference has never been distinctly made by the commanding officer of a subsidiary force, or that the subject has never been obtruded for decision by an opposition on one side, equal to the encroachment on the other. Lord Hastings, on his arrival in India, found the three Residencies in the Deckan filled by Civil gentlemen of acknowledged talents. This circumstance considerably recommended, however indirectly, whatever might favourably affect their situations; and the late transactions of the campaign have shewn them to possess all the personal qualities necessary in the situations of danger to which they have been exposed. But these transactions afford no contradictions to the general experience, that however all men of education may be considered as equally brave, self-possession depends principally on habit. Political courage has a special character of its own; and so has that quality of the mind which will enable the possessor to contemplate with firmness the nearest approach to certain dissolution, unaccompanied by violence, noise, and conflict; but where circumstances so opposite to those of Civil life are brought before the already-occupied and unaccustomed mind, there will be no cause for surprise, if, confused and overpowered, it shrink from the trial. In the two present instances, a previous intimacy with scenes of assault was familiar to the individuals in question, and during the last Mahratta war they had acquired much knowledge and experience of military affairs. These and similar remarks, however, tend only to prove, that while Residencies shall be exposed to barbarous attacks, and it shall be considered sound policy, but for which it will be difficult to find conclusive arguments derived from principle, to employ in charge of them gentlemen of the Civil service, the public interests will be best advanced by procuring, if practicable, men of endowments such as have been described.

Arrival of Lieutenant-colonel Gahan's detachment.

It will be recollected, that on the 17th of November, Lieutenant-colonel Gahan was ordered to march his detachment, with all practicable expedition, from Sindkeir, near Hoossingabad, to Nagpoor. He accordingly, on

(Map VII.) the 20th of that month, commenced his progress, and on the 24th reached Beitool, a distance of seventy-five miles, in five marches. On the 26th he had advanced thirty-one miles further; and on receiving in the evening of that day an express from Lieutenant-colonel Scot, requiring his accelerated advance, he marched twenty miles further on the following morning, to Pandoorna. Here he separated his detachment into two parts. One of these, composed of three troops of cavalry, six companies of Native infantry, and the gallopers, proceeded under his own command. The other part, consisting of four companies of Native infantry, and two field-pieces, remained under Lieutenant Anquetil to bring up the baggage. That officer was joined by a company of Madras Native infantry, commanded by Captain Lucas, who had been employed on a commissariat duty, [illegible] Bringarries. Lieutenant-colonel Gahan, at eight P. M. of the 27th, marched again, and arrived, at nine A. M. of the 28th, at Omree, a distance of twenty-six miles. Here he halted a few hours, after which, continuing his route, he reached Nagpoor at four A. M. of the 29th, a distance of twenty-four miles.* Every account received from Nagpoor, immediately after the action at that place, concurred in representing the Rajah as much humbled by the failure of his attack, of which he evidently declined a repetition. This appeared by the removal of all his guns and troops from the vicinity of the British position. The brigade, therefore, though for many successive nights they slept on their arms, yet felt secure against any future aggression, particularly on the arrival of Lieutenant-colonel Gahan's detachment, with the expectation of early reinforcements from other quarters.

Hostile indications in various parts of the Nagpoor country

While affairs at Nagpoor had been gradually ripening to a rupture, other parts of the dependant country were disposed not less hostilely to the British troops posted in their vicinity. In the Valley of the Nerbuddah this feeling was evident, from the middle of November, particularly around Gurhwarra, where Lieutenant-colonel Mac Morine commanded a detach-

---

* It has been considered necessary to describe this march minutely, not only on account of its importance as connected with the state of affairs at Nagpoor, but also because both the period it occupied and the distance marched, are misrepresented in a Calcutta paper, the *Times* of the 3d of February, 1818. The inflated accounts, under the head of letters from the camp in all the papers of that Presidency, of the smallest military feat by any of the troops of the Bengal Establishment, are in the true style of eastern amplification, and very imprudently do an injury to the character of an army which is independent of such attempts to increase its celebrity. These appeared again in the *Asiatic Journal*, published in London.

ment from the Fifth Division, and at Jubbulpoor, where Major Richards was stationed with three companies of Native infantry and a detachment of Rohillah horse. Further to the eastward, similar demonstrations were exhibited to Brigadier-general Toone, by the people of the Bhooslah's frontier province of Sirgooja, who, by parties of armed men, shut up all the Ghats of that line in his front, and prevented any communication through them. The most active levies of troops were set on foot by the Rajah's officers, silently at first; and in the principal towns all strangers were rigidly examined, on the suspicion of their being in the British employ. Such of the Native Authorities as were least devoted to the Mahratta cause were removed, and others established in power, of a more zealous and warlike disposition.

Force on the Nerbuddah concentrated at Hoossingabad.

The first effect of these demonstrations appeared at Jubbulpoor. In the beginning of December the enemy assembled there in so much force, that Major Richards was obliged to abandon his cantonment with a part only of his baggage, and to fall back to the Nerbuddah, by the road towards Gurhwarra. He was preceded by a valuable convoy which had arrived in his vicinity, by the way of the Myheer Valley. Following this convoy, he continued his retreat to form a junction with Colonel Mac Morine. That officer was likewise joined by all his outposts on the river. These he had called in, considering them exposed to the danger of being separately cut off; as the remoteness of their situation precluded them from succouring each other. The same measure was also adopted by Major Macpherson, who commanded at Hoossingabad. He was, moreover, required to concentrate his troops, in consequence of demands for escorts with grain and ordnance, at this time called for from the depôt under his charge. The detachments united under Colonel Mac Morine, commenced their movement westerly on the 10th of December, for the safe conveyance of the convoy and stores belonging to his force, to the central depôt at Hoossingabad, where he arrived on the 20th, after a march without intermission. The enemy were now in full occupation of the Valley of the Nerbuddah, and the Colonel was engaged in organizing his means for operating actively against such bodies of them as by their number might be tangible.

Brigadier-general Hardyman's march to Jubbulpoor, and defeat of the Enemy there.

The force of Brigadier-general Hardyman, in the beginning of December, was still in the Rewah territory, occupying the positions (p. 56, 57) which he had assumed, in the previous month, for the interception of the Pindarries. As soon, however, as intelligence of the menacing posture of affairs at Nagpoor was received by Lord Hastings, orders were dispatched to him to move down to the Nerbuddah, and to attend to the requisitions of the Resident at the capital for his further advance. Should he, however, there receive undoubted information of the positive commencement of hostilities, he was directed to push on with his reinforcement with all expedition. The Brigadier-general, accordingly, commenced his march on the 7th of December from Myhee, with the 8th regiment of cavalry, and was followed by his Majesty's 17th foot, and the 2d battalion of the 8th regiment of Native infantry, from Rewah and Mhow. (Map II.) The former of these joined him on the 10th at Buddenpoor. On the 11th (Map VIII.) his head-quarters were at Doura, from the 13th to the 16th at Bellharree, and on the 17th at Talwah, having received repeated accounts during his progress, of Major Richards's detachment having been obliged to fall back to Nutwarra, near the river. The force with which Brigadier-general Hardyman continued his march, consisted of a regiment of cavalry, a regiment of European foot, and four guns; the Native battalion being so far in the rear, that it was directed to halt at Bellharree till a favourable opportunity should offer for its junction. On his approach to Jubbulpoor on the 19th, Brigadier-general Hardyman found the enemy drawn up and (Plan 8.) strongly posted to oppose his possession of that place. They were in numbers about three thousand, of whom about one thousand were horse, and stationed on the left. Their right was on a rocky eminence, where they had (A. A.) likewise four brass guns. The Brigadier-general placed his guns in the centre with three companies of the 17th foot on each side of them, and two (B. B.) companies in their rear. He sent two squadrons, under Major O'Brien, round the left of the enemy to cut them off from the river, masked his guns by another squadron, and held a squadron in rear of his left as a reserve. On arriving near enough to the enemy's centre, the guns being unmasked, opened with Shrapnel shells, and were immediately answered. A fire was kept up for about a quarter of an hour, when the enemy's infantry wavered; on which the reserve squadron was ordered to charge the battery. This service was gallantly performed, and the artillerymen sabred and pistoled at their guns. The advance squadron then attempted to charge the infantry, who had descended into the plain; but they reascended the emi- (E. E.) nence, and obliged it to return under a heavy fire. On this, one wing of the 17th foot was brought up by the Brigadier-general to storm the height; and effected the same by a strenuous exertion, which ended in a severe loss to the enemy. Those who fled into the plain, down the opposite side, were mostly intercepted by the advance squadron, which made a *detour* round their right, as the 17th ascended. This affair, which appears to have been creditably conducted and executed, occupied about two hours. Should any doubt arise respecting the propriety of attacking the enemy's battery on strong ground, with cavalry, the question will probably be decided by a reference to the small loss of British troops, amounting only to twelve men and twenty horses; among the former were three European* and one Native officer. In the course of that night and the following morning, the enemy abandoned the town and *gurree* of Jubbulpoor, leaving behind them nine pieces of ordnance and various military stores. Brigadier-general Hardyman immediately continued his march towards the Nerbuddah; from whence he pursued his route by Chupprah. There he arrived on the 26th, and was met by a dispatch from the Resident at Nagpoor, dated the 20th, dispensing with his further advance, and [illegible] him to direct his entire attention to such enemies as might shew themselves about the upper part of the river, in consequence of Colonel Mac Morine's movement to Hoossingabad. The Brigadier-general returned to Jubbulpoor on the 1st of January, when he was joined by the 2d battalion of the 8th regiment of Native infantry: this after the affair of the 19th had been ordered on from Belharree, and halted in order to favour the junction of commissariat supplies and treasure expected from the rear, without which his force was unprepared for further operations.

* Vide Appendix. D.

CHAPTER VIII.

SUBMISSION AND RE-ESTABLISHMENT OF THE BHOOSLAH.

Situation of the Second Division of the Deckan Army. March to the Relief of the Nagpoor Brigade. Disposition for the Attack of the Rajah. Description of the British and Enemy's Position. Submission of the Rajah, and Attack of his insubordinate Army. Its defeat with the Loss of Camp Equipage and Guns. Reflections on the Action of the 16th of December. The Garrison of Nagpoor hold out, after the Dispersion of the Field Army. Description of the City, as a Place of Strength. Operations against the City. Unsuccessful Assault of the Jumma Durwazza. Camp of the Enemy's Horse beaten up by Major Munt's Detachment. Capitulation of the Arabs. Reflections on the Attack of the City and its Failure. Reflections on the Capitulation. March of the Arabs to Khandesh. March of Colonel Deacon's Detachment from Hurdah to Jafferabad.

Situation of the Second Division of the Deckan Army

IN pursuance of the orders addressed to Brigadier-general Doveton, with a view to the eventual siege of Asseerghur (p. 82), that officer ordered his small battering-train and engineer's park, with his Majesty's Royal Scots, and eight companies of the 1st battalion of the 2d regiment of Native infantry, down a Ghat to the eastward of Badoolah, by the route of Chickly, Pulladug, and Tarrapoor, to Koatlee. This detachment accordingly marched on the 24th of November, under the command of Lieutenant-colonel Macleod of his Majesty's Royal Scots: the Head-quarters of the Second Division still remaining at Jafferabad. It will be recollected that Captain Davies's detachment, which took up the position of the Fourth Division on its retrograde movement, was ordered to follow Brigadier-general Smith to Poonah, on account of his great want of cavalry, and considering that the vacancy so occasioned would be shortly filled up by the arrival of Lieutenant-colonel Deacon's detachment. At the time, however, when this order was received, affairs in that quarter had considerably changed, in consequence of the appearance of Kadir Baldoo and Moorroo Pundit, partisans of the Peishwah, who occupied strong positions, and influenced a considerable party in the country. It accordingly appeared impracticable, viewing the spirit of Sir Thomas Hislop's orders, to deprive that line, of Captain Davies's detachment, previously to the arrival of Lieutenant-colonel Deacon's force; and Brigadier-general Doveton found himself justified in maintaining the existing dispositions.

March to the relief of the Nagpoor brigade. (Map V.)

On the 29th of November, Brigadier-general Doveton received a dispatch from the Resident at Nagpoor, dated on the 25th, requesting, in consequence of the designs evinced by the Rajah, that he would march immediately on Ellichapoor; and if he did not receive further advice, that he would continue his advance on the capital. The Second Division accordingly moved, at ten o'clock of the same day, from Jafferabad, proposing to proceed by forced marches. At this time Major Pitman commanded a detachment of the Nizam's troops, consisting of two battalions with guns, and a thousand reformed horse, at Mortizapoor, near Oomrouttee. He likewise received a requisition, from the Resident at Nagpoor, for his speedy advance. It was the more important that this corps should reach a convenient situation, as the 2d battalion of the 24th regiment of Native infantry, not having received the order directing them to march on Oomrouttee, had joined Brigadier-general Doveton's head-quarters, at Jafferabad, on the 22d of November. On the arrival of the division at Lackenwarree, on the 1st of December, further dispatches were received from Mr. Jenkins, which determined the Brigadier-general to take the direct road to Nagpoor. He learned at the same time, that Major Pitman, on a similar requisition, was pushing forward with all practicable expedition. These appearances induced the Brigadier-general to order Lieutenant-colonel Macleod's detachment, with the battering-train, to follow as quickly as possible, conceiving the immediate siege of Asseerghur to be an object comparatively of no importance. On the 4th of December he was at Koorunkeir, and there receiving authentic accounts of the failure of the Bhooslah's attack, he directed the battering-train to halt at Akolah under the protection of the 1st battalion of the 2d regiment, and his Majesty's Royal Scots to continue their march to Nagpoor. On the 5th, information was received at Bapoory that the two chiefs at the head of the Peishwah's party above the Khandesh Ghats, having found it impracticable, on account of the vigilance of Captain Davies's detachment, to unite their forces and keep the field, had severally dispersed. General Doveton accordingly directed that corps to proceed, as previously ordered, to join Brigadier-general Smith, leaving eight hundred reformed horse, under Lieutenant Hamilton, in the vicinity of Byzapoor. But this was subsequently countermanded, in obedience to orders from Sir Thomas Hislop, and Lieutenant Hamilton's party was ordered to Akolah. On the 7th, the Head-quarters of the Second Division were joined at Oomrouttee by the Royal Scots, and on the following day they were at Sevungaum. It was the Brigadier-general's intention to reach Nagpoor on the 13th; but having in the meanwhile received an urgent request to use greater expedition, he arrived there by forced marches, on the 12th, with—

The Horse Artillery,
6th Regiment of Native Cavalry,
The Royal Scots,
Wallajahbad Light Infantry, and
Flank Companies of the { 1st Battalion of the 2d Regiment,
1st Battalion of the 11th Regiment,
2d Battalion of the 13th Regiment,
2d Battalion of the 24th Regiment, } Native Infantry,

and occupied a position in rear of the Residency and the Nagah river. Major Pitman's detachment, with the exception of a few hundred horse left at the Wurdah, had previously arrived on the 5th; and on the 13th, the rear of the Second Division, under Lieutenant-colonel Mackellar, rejoined its Head-quarters.

Disposition for the attack of the Rajah.

Ever since the 26th of November the Rajah had evinced his desire to come to terms with the Resident; but Mr. Jenkins, conscious of the weakness of his ground till the brigade should be reinforced, waved all negotiation in the absence of Brigadier-general Doveton's division. The excessive fatigue which the troops had endured, on their recent march, rendered necessary some days' rest, previous to any other arduous undertaking. This consequently postponed a communication to the Rajah, of the conditions which would be offered him. On the afternoon of the 15th, all the stores and baggage were sent to the foot of the Seetabuldee hills, as to a secure position, under the protection of the 1st battalion of the 20th regiment, the 1st battalion of the 24th regiment, and a battalion of the Nizam's infantry; (Plan 9.) and the troops under the immediate command of the Brigadier-general, slept (*A. A.*) on their arms, that night, in order of battle. After these preparations, the Rajah was allowed till the morning to accept of the terms which had been previously proposed to him. They were as follows:—To repair in person to the Residency;—to surrender his guns, and order his troops to disperse immediately;—to cede the Valley of the Nerbuddah, including the fortresses of Chouraghur and Mundalah, with certain districts above the Ghats, and east of the Wyne Gunga;—to place the contingent of horse under the command of British officers, and the collection of his revenue under the superintendence of the Resident. His acquiescence was received at the appointed hour; but as he delayed to come into the Residency as required, the troops got into motion early in the day, and assumed a position on the right of the Residency and opposite to the enemy, whose most advanced post was distant about a mile and a half. The cavalry-brigade, commanded by Lieutenant-colonel Gahan, was on the right, and was composed of the 6th Bengal and 6th Madras Native cavalry, with a horse-artillery battery of six six-pounder field-pieces. To the cavalry succeeded, on their left, the infantry-brigade of Lieutenant-colonel Macleod, consisting of a wing of his Majesty's Royal Scots, the Wallajahbad light-infantry, the 2d battalion of the 13th regiment of Native infantry, the 1st battalion of the 22d regiment of Bengal Native infantry, and the flank-companies of the 1st battalion of the 2d regiment of Native infantry. Next, that of Lieutenant-colonel Mackellar, composed of a division of his Majesty's Royal Scots, the 2d battalion of the 24th regiment of Native infantry, and a detachment of horse-artillery. On the left of the whole line were a division of his Majesty's Royal Scots, the 1st battalion of the 11th regiment of Native infantry, a detachment of foot-artillery and sappers and miners, forming the brigade of Lieutenant-colonel Scot. The line was supported by a reserve of infantry *, under the command of Lieutenant-colonel Stewart; and the principal battery, under Lieutenant-colonel Crosdill commanding the artillery, was immediately in rear of Lieutenant-colonel Macleod's brigade, ready to be brought into action when required. Of the remaining foot-artillery guns, four were attached to Lieutenant-colonel Scot's brigade, and two to that of Lieutenant-colonel Mackellar. The Berar infantry, under Major Pitman, were in the rear of Lieutenant-colonel Scot's brigade, but were not brought into action, being sent back, as soon as the line advanced, to escort the baggage of the division to its new ground. (B. B.)

Description of the British and the Enemy's position.

On the left of the British position was an enclosed garden, and beyond it the Nagah Nuddee, a small river which ran from hence past the enemy's right, and would consequently cover the flank of a movement from either side. Three parallel ravines, terminating in the bed of the river, crossed the space which intervened between the British infantry and the enemy;

* The 2d battalion of the 13th regiment of Native infantry, from the 1st brigade.

but in front, and to the right of the cavalry, the country was open and unintersected. The enemy's order and position, being less regular, is more difficult to be described. It was masked by the inequalities of the ground, and by several *pettahs*, between and around which was a thick plantation of trees. His advanced post occupied this cover, in front of which, towards
(1.) the right, was a heavy battery of fourteen guns, in rear of a ravine. In rear of the *pettahs* was a tank towards the left, from the extremity of which a
(3, 4, 5.) ravine extended to the river. In rear of this ravine were other batteries, of various numbers of guns; while to the left of the tank was a third battery of six guns. Along the rear of these points was drawn up the enemy's army of twenty-one thousand men, of whom fourteen thousand were horse. Between the batteries and the *pettahs* was an open space, to give a favourable effect to their guns. On their left was a deep ravine, and their rear was quite open. It only remains to be explained, that beyond the river lay the city of Nagpoor, from the walls of which all the movements, on both sides, could be perceived.

Submission of the Rajah, and Attack of his insubordinate army.

Matters were in this state when, at nine A. M., after many efforts to procrastinate decisive measures, the Rajah arrived at the Residency, and promised that all his guns should be surrendered to the British troops at twelve o'clock at noon, by an agent whom he sent to attend on Brigadier-general
(b, b, b.) Doveton. The whole force accordingly got into motion, in battalion-columns of divisions, from the right, followed by the reserve in line, and marched on parallel lines towards the enemy, all the intervening ravines being passable. The enemy were unprepared to defend the first battery of fourteen guns, which were taken possession of, and placed under the charge of Lieutenant-colonel Scot's brigade. On entering the plantation and passing between the *pettahs*, a sharp fire of musquetry opened from that of Sookandurree, on the right of the British infantry. This did not interrupt their advance into the plain beyond it, within cannon-range of the enemy's main position. Here the line of infantry formed, previous to their attack of the batteries in
(g, h, i.) their front, from which an incessant fire was maintained. In the mean while
(a, a, a.) the cavalry brigade and horse-artillery moved round the *pettahs* in the same order as the infantry, having a reserve of one hundred men from each regiment, and their gallopers in rear of the columns of regiments. As soon as they had passed Sookandurree on their left, they found themselves in front of the enemy's left battery, which was supported by a strong corps of
(f, f.) horse and foot. They immediately formed the line, to be prepared for

whatever design might be entertained; and were not long in suspense, for the enemy's guns immediately opened. The brigade instantly charged, carried the battery, and drove before them the corps supporting it, which fled towards their right. The pursuit was continued in that direction by the rear of the tank, till a second battery of the enemy opened. This was (3) carried in the same style, when the brigade was obliged to halt for the recovery of order, and to let the horse-artillery form battery. They had already advanced considerably beyond the infantry, and their insulated situation encouraged a body of the enemy's horse in their front to evince an intention of charging in turn. But the timely fire of the horse-artillery, which opened with happy effect on so deep a mass, checked their advance; and the cavalry being re-formed, followed up the impression, and continued their pursuit while they could keep up with the fugitives.

Which is defeated, with the loss of their Camp Equipage and Guns.

The second battery which the cavalry charged, remained but a short time in their possession, as their attention was immediately directed to the force supporting it. The enemy accordingly resumed their guns, and were prepared to re-open them against the British line of infantry advancing between the tank and the river. The brigades under Lieutenant-colonels Macleod and Mackellar were now ordered to charge the enemy's right battery, (h, h) and executed these orders with gallantry and success; advancing afterwards against the enemy's right, which retired before them. The centre battery was attacked by the reserve under Lieutenant-colonel Stewart, with (g, g) similar effect. On both occasions, the artillery under Lieutenant-colonel Crosdill, materially contributed to the successful result. It was now half-past one; the enemy had been driven from all their positions, they left their camp standing, and forty elephants, with forty-one guns in battery, besides twenty-three in a neighbouring depôt. The light infantry were sent forward to support the pursuit by the cavalry, which continued about five miles; and the force encamped on the Nagah river, fronting it and the city. The loss of the enemy on this occasion was principally in the pursuit, and therefore difficult to be estimated; but it may be concluded, from their early abandonment of their position, that it was inconsiderable. On the side of the British force, there were one hundred and forty-one* killed and wounded. The wounds being chiefly by cannon-shot, many subsequent deaths were the consequence.

---

* Vide Appendix. E.

Reflections on the Action of the 16th of December.

From the occurrences of this day, it appears, that either the enemy were unprepared for the attack, or there was some division in their councils. The Rajah either gave, or withheld, the order for his troops to surrender his guns. In the latter case, it is not surprising that they considered it necessary to make some attempt at repelling an unexpected advance on them, and that the first battery was abandoned from want of time to bring up troops to its support. All the guns in it were found, however, primed and loaded, and were evidently intended for resistance. Had the Rajah given orders for their surrender, it is as little surprising that those orders should be disregarded on his abandoning his troops. As they consisted of several separate corps, there was also the less chance of an union of opinion in regard to their own defence. Had their plans been concerted, it was evidently their policy to throw all their infantry among the *pettahs*, and to oblige the British to form in its front for the attack; and when beaten out, they had always a retreat open on the city, or to their cavalry. Their guns likewise should have occupied the same position as proposed for their infantry, who would have defended them, and been defended in return. They were of no use, and likely to be of none, to their cavalry; nor were their cavalry likely to be of more use to the guns; for between them, if the expression may be allowed, there was no natural sympathy. The guns of an Indian army, in a field of action, are generally immovable, and their cavalry are all motion. The object of the batteries is to fire as long as possible previously to being taken; and of the horse, to secure their retreat, if discomfited, unfettered by any incumbrance. But it would be an idle speculation to investigate further what might have been the best dispositions for an army not resolved on profiting by the best. Their design evidently was, to maintain their ground till the batteries were stormed, in the hopes that during that operation some occasion might offer, favourable to their action, without risk; and as soon as the batteries should be taken, to retreat as quickly as possible from a hopeless posture. Let not this digression be supposed to detract at all from the merit of the British troops, or of their commander, on this occasion. The whole disposition was admirably calculated for the service to be performed, particularly as it regarded the cavalry; though their impetuosity in abandoning all connection with the infantry, while the enemy yet maintained their ground, incurred a risk, for which success forms the best apology. The movements of the infantry are described as resembling the manœuvres of a peaceable field-day. Under the experienced officer who commanded, they insured a result subject to no contingency but that of a greater or less amount of loss in its accomplishment.

The Garrison of Nagpoor hold out, after the dispersion of the Field Army.

The field army of Nagpoor was, in consequence of the events of the 16th of December, in a manner broken up. The chiefs who remained with the divided troops, were unsupported by the authority of the Rajah, and they were naturally expected to act in detached parties, unless some officer of influence should arise among them and assemble their forces. The horse were scattered over the country, but a considerable body was collected about Ramteak. In the city, however, there was a sturdy band of five thousand Arabs and Hindoostanees, who insisted on extraordinary terms before they would surrender, even at the order of the Prince they served. Their arrears were paid by the Rajah, and every security was offered for their march out of his territories, but without effect. It became necessary therefore to besiege them, and the battering-train from Akolah, where it had been left, (p. 123.) was ordered on for this purpose.

Description of the City as a place of strength.

(Plan 7.)

For understanding more correctly the nature of this undertaking, the magnitude of which was felt from the first, some description of the city of Nagpoor will here be proper. The central part is surrounded by an imperfect wall of about three miles, with round towers. Without this inclosure are extensive suburbs, which extend the circumference of the city to about seven miles. Its principal strength, considering the nature of the garrison, consisted in a number of well-built houses, each of which, if defended, required an independent attack; and there are perhaps no troops in the world better calculated for their defence than a body of Arabs in India. Of these, three thousand were estimated to be present on this occasion. Within the walls, and near the centre, was the palace, which formed a species of citadel, and from its situation, as well as the nature of the works, promised to the possessors of it the command of the city. But the difficulty of approaching it formed an insuperable bar to its acquisition by any means like a *coup-de-main;* for the avenue leading to it from the gates, consisted of narrow streets, composed of houses from which a most destructive loss must have been sustained, before an attempt could have been made to escalade it. It was therefore proposed to advance cautiously, and to clear away gradually, by means of artillery, such obstacles as might oppose themselves to a conflict, at the last, on more equal terms. The *bund,* or dyke, of the tank called Jumma Talao, which lies between the city and the Seetabuldee hills, offered several favourable circumstances for the proposed attack by the gate called Jumma Durwazza. It makes two angles inclosing the water of this reservoir, by which two sides form approaches, and the other a parallel, to the west face of the city within three hundred and fifty yards; while its elevation gives it a considerable command over the scattered houses of that quarter, and an advantage over the ground opposite the remaining sides, for the purposes of attack.

Operations against the City.

On the west face, it was therefore resolved to commence the operations. Accordingly, on the 19th of December, the whole of the requisite materials having been prepared, the first advance was made from the Seetabuldee, to a point on the dyke within eight hundred yards of the Jumma
(1.) Durwazza, and a howitzer battery was constructed, with an intrenchment for a sufficient number of men to protect it. On the 20th, a further advance was made, of four hundred and fifty yards, which established the attack within three hundred yards of the gate, or Jumma Durwazza, and occupied the part of the dyke parallel to the wall. This operation was naturally attended with more delay and difficulty than that of the first day, as the sappers were much exposed to the fire from the houses, and the work in consequence was frequently interrupted. The advantages attending it were however considerable, as good cover was at once enjoyed for the ammunition, stores, and troops on duty; and for the batteries was obtained a ready-formed breastwork, requiring no further labour than was necessary to cut embrasures. On the 21st, all operations were suspended, the enemy having expressed a desire to evacuate the city. The negotiation having terminated fruitlessly, on the 22d a howitzer battery was con-
(2, 2, 2) structed, to dislodge them from different buildings, and the entire eastern extremity of the *bund* was intrenched. At the same time the enemy were driven from the houses between the batteries and the city-wall, and detach-
(4, 4, 4) ments under Colonel Scot and Major Pitman occupied positions for the prevention of their return. During the night, five of the enemy's captured
(3.) guns were placed in battery to bear on the gateway and adjoining defences. On the 23d, the whole structure of the arch was brought down by their fire, and presented a breach apparently practicable. A lodgment here promised considerable facility towards battering in breach the palace, which was only two hundred and fifty yards distant; and the necessary preparations were made for that purpose.

Unsuccessful assault of the Jumma Durwazza (5)

Major Pitman's detachment was directed to occupy, on the following morning, a strong extensive building, in advance of his previous position; and Lieutenant-colonel Scot's detachment was ordered to gain possession of the Toolsee Baugh, near a gate of that name in the centre of the southern face. The object of these attacks was, to drive the enemy from some positions they still occupied without the walls, to the annoyance of the besiegers; to close on the enemy, and to distract them by a double attack. For the breach was allotted one company of the Royal Scots, five companies of Native infantry, with a detail of sappers and miners; and in the trenches, as a reserve, another company of Europeans and four companies of Native infantry. The three movements were to take place at the same moment. The signal for the advance was given at half past eight A. M., when the storming party darted forward from the trenches, and immediately gained the top of the breach. A few men followed the engineer, Lieutenant Davis, to the bottom of the rubbish on the other side; but the enemy kept up so warm a fire under cover, that the storming party sought for shelter behind adjacent walls, and were called off by the Brigadier-general, under whose immediate inspection the assault had been made. Lieutenant-colonel Scot's attack on the Toolsee Baugh, which was made with two companies of Europeans, two Native flank companies, and a Native battalion, succeeded completely; but as the position was reported to be untenable, and the storm of the Jumma Durwazza had failed, the detachment was ordered to return to its original position. Major Pitman's detachment, which had likewise executed its orders, was directed to adopt the same course; and the troops assumed the positions they had occupied before the assault. The loss of the besiegers, from the 19th to the 24th, amounted to three hundred and seven*, including ten European commissioned officers; but that of the enemy, on account of the advantages of their situation, probably did not exceed fifty.

Camp of the Enemy's Horse beaten up by Major Munt's detachment (Map VIII.)

While the operations of the siege were in progress, Brigadier-general Doveton's attention had been likewise directed to the security of some Bringarry supplies of grain, which had been for some time assembling, and were heard of on the 21st, in the direction of Ramteak, where the principal force of the enemy's horse was collected. A respectable body of these

* Vide Appendix. F.

advanced on that day so near the British camp as to be visible from the top of Seetabuldee; and the Brigadier-general considered that a favourable opportunity offered itself for making an impression on them, and at the same time for securing the convoy. A detachment, consisting of the 6th regiment of Native cavalry, the Wallajahbad light infantry, and four horse-artillery guns, was placed under the orders of Major Munt, who marched it off in the beginning of the night by Corumna and Warreegaum, at which latter place many of the enemy had found protection after the action of the 16th. The detachment arrived at two o'clock A. M. of the 22d, and passing under the walls of the fort, was immediately in front of an encampment of horse, which was accessible alone through the ravines that surrounded it. The horse-artillery opened a fire on it, in front, within thirty yards, while the cavalry made a *detour*, by the left, to intercept the fugitives, and the light infantry a similar movement by the right, to clear an inclosure thickly planted, where several of the enemy had sought refuge. The surprise was so complete that they could offer no opposition; and their flight, towards Ramteak, was made at the expense of a heavy loss. Major Munt re-assembled his detachment, and proceeding in search of the convoy, without halting, arrived within eight miles of Ramteak at eight A. M. The enemy had, however, received the alarm, with the fugitives from Warreegaum, on which they instantly decamped. As their precipitation precluded any repetition of the attack, the Major took nine thousand Bringarries under his charge, and on the following morning escorted them into camp at Nagpoor.

Capitulation of the Arabs.

Though the attack of the 24th had failed in its immediate object, the determination it evinced had made a serious impression on the garrison. On the following day, they renewed their offers to evacuate the city; and in order to be heard with more confidence than they were entitled to from their former overtures, they sent out their principal chief, or Peerzadah, to conduct the negotiation. The arrangement of the capitulation occupied till the 29th, when the following terms were granted: A gratuity of fifty thousand rupees; security for their personal property; a safe conduct under a British officer to Mulkapoor, and their discharge there on the promise of not entering Asseerghur. The three thousand Arabs marched out by the Booteah gate on the 30th at noon, when the city was immediately occupied by the detachment under Lieutenant-colonel Scot, reinforced by the 22d Bengal Native infantry, and some additional flank companies. Judicious arrangements were also made for the prevention of any disturbance between the inhabitants and the new garrison.

Reflections on the Attack of the City and its Failure.

The siege and capitulation of Nagpoor deserve some special reflections, though there remain to be related hereafter other striking instances of the obstinacy of Arabs, and of the petulancy with which they have been attacked. Their first demand was for the payment of their arrears and the security of their private property. This being acceded to and their arrears discharged, they immediately advanced a demand for a gratuity of fifty thousand rupees when called on to evacuate the city.* Such an occurrence as the hostility of a place which might be almost called an open town, some parts of its wall being only three feet high, had never been contemplated. The division under Brigadier-general Doveton was therefore so far unprepared for it, that his small battering-train and engineer's park were still in the vicinity of Akolah, and no less than fifteen days were necessary to bring on these equipments. There was accordingly a strong inducement to attempt the reduction of the place with as many of the captured guns as might be fit for use in the hands of the British artillerymen; and as the fortitude of Arabs had, at this period of the war, been less known, they might be expected to submit when they saw a determination evinced to use the means of force. The enemy might also have made more resistance than they appear to have done, in the suburb leading to the Jumma Durwazza. Their relinquishment of that position without a contest, might indeed be considered as an indication of their intention to withhold their serious opposition and subsequent capitulation till the besiegers should approach the palace. Still these considerations will not justify the attack of a breach, distant three hundred yards from the nearest part of the trenches, with the approach to it through a street raked by a fire of musquetry, without any place in its immediate vicinity to be occupied in security if found impracticable, without the knowledge of cover on the other side, and with the necessity of constructing an artificial lodgment, should such be attempted, under an insupportable fire of musquetry from places of absolute security. For this cover must have been procured within the walls, as the breach formed a space too inconsiderable for that purpose, and was even taken in

* It is stated on good authority, that when desired to give a receipt for their arrears, they sent two leaden balls; which, with other circumstances, has induced the belief, that they were secretly instigated by the Rajah to oppose the execution of his mock endeavours to get rid of them.

reverse by some of the enemy who subsequently dared to come out. If it be said that too much reliance was placed on the observation, that "fortune favours the brave," the enemy may be expected to dispute that title, or at least to claim a full participation of it. They subsequently expressed their astonishment, in no very flattering terms, that the assault so boldly undertaken should have been so soon relinquished; while they eulogized the conspicuous conduct of Lieut. Bell, of the Royals, who was killed in the breach. The abandonment of the attack, whether it be or be not called premature, proceeded from a cause which will always affect the best troops. They saw no advantage to be obtained; and however lavish was the engineer of his own safety, there was no prospect of gaining cover. The responsibility attaching to the Brigadier general on this occasion, will not implicate his judgment. He long resisted the representations of his engineer *; but his disposition, which rendered him far from self-opinionated, induced him to accede to the confident importunities of the professional officer. Whatever might have been his regret at this failure, he disdained to throw off himself any of the responsibility attaching to it, and eulogized in his report both his adviser and his troops.

Reflections on the Capitulation.

The Arabs had now favourable grounds for renewing their offer of surrender on the following day; and though the acquiescence in their continued demand of the gratuity must have been more galling than ever, there were strong reasons for acceding to it. In fact, the caprice and faithlessness with which they had made their first demand, had left no security against a repetition, should it even be granted. But now the enemy must have known, that more means would be brought forward to ensure their reduction; and that therefore, in proportion as the present circumstances were favourable to them, the protraction of their surrender would merit more vindictive treatment: so that the same state of affairs afforded an argument for acquiescence in their demands, and for confidence in their faith. It was a most important object to get them out of a position, which otherwise must give occupation to half the field forces of the Deckan, while in other quarters there were most pressing demands. The period during which the forces might be thus engaged would not, probably, be less than four or five

* This officer, full of petulance and courage, was afterwards killed at the siege of Malleygaum, while discharging his duty with that characteristic zeal and self-devotion which knew no controul.

weeks, including the time required for the arrival of the battering-train. It might even be longer, without imagining a second Saragossa; for though the Arabs have no patriotic sentiment, they possess a degree of fortitude derived from other causes of equal efficacy. The scattered field army would have had time and encouragement to re-assemble; and under this view so many chances appeared productive of a protracted struggle, that the Brigadier-general might find sufficient cause for disregarding the sentiments of his division, had they been obtruded on him, and for coinciding with the Resident in favour of the measure which was ultimately adopted. The feelings of the troops, situated as they were, were naturally adverse to a compromise. Many instances are to be found of a similar disposition under similar circumstances; but as the responsibility rests solely on the commander, he must be considered as the only proper judge; nor do troops always justify their seeming impatience, when brought back to an attack where they have been once unsuccessful.

March of the Arabs to Khandesh

Lieutenant Sheriff, of the Commissariat, was deputed by the Brigadier-general, to accompany the Arabs as far as Mulkapoor, in order to exact the performance of their engagements, and to give them the promised security. They commenced their march from Nagpoor, on the 1st of January; and on the 21st, the majority of them arrived at Mulkapoor by the route of Akolah. During the march, two bodies separated, and went off independently towards Hydrabad. Their conduct was, at first, very unruly; and their manners and appearance so barbarous and uncouth, as might well be calculated to embarrass an individual, attended by an inconsiderable escort. They were however reduced to much order and obedience, considering their habits; and on parting from Lieutenant Sheriff, they evinced their esteem for his character, and gratitude for his treatment of them, by requesting his acceptance of such articles as were in their power to offer. They were latterly accompanied by Lieutenant Hamilton's *russalah* of horse, to prevent the execution of any design they might have formed, of gaining Asseerghur from Mulkapoor. On their leaving that place, some misunderstanding regarding the road to be pursued to Khandesh was the cause of a few of their men being wounded; but the mistake was cleared up, and they pursued their route to the westward. They were now in a part of the country where they had a prospect of immediately procuring new service against the British cause. It was full of strong holds, and the course of operations had not yet made it a theatre of hostilities; Colonel Deacon's detachment, which had been originally sent to Khandesh to replace the Fourth Division, having, as already mentioned (p. 81), been subsequently ordered to take the place of the Second Division.

March of Col. Deacon's Detachment from Hurdah to Jafferabad. (Map VII.)

It will be recollected that the detachment in question marched from Hurdah, on the 20th of November, (p. 81.) by the route of Kundwah. As far as that place, the nature of the country and the disposition of its inhabitants had been already ascertained. The detachment was here joined by Sulabut Khan's contingent, which had been previously detached. On the 26th of November, Colonel Deacon was at Beekungaum, and on the 28th, at Kurgoun, both of them respectably sized towns; but even their names were till then unknown to the British. This line being quite free from the enemy's troops, every facility which the confined resources of the country permitted, was afforded to the progress of the detachment. On the 3d of December it effected the descent of the Seindwah Ghat, without having suffered any molestation from the Beels*, who infest the hilly tracts, and generally annoy the rear of a line of march. This part of the country, however, afforded no supplies. The detachment was therefore obliged to divide in search of them; Sulabut Khan's contingent proceeding down the Taptee to Seerpoor, and the British brigade to Talneir. There it crossed that river, and halted from the 5th to the 7th, to favour the rejunction of the Nuwaub. Lieutenant-colonel Deacon marched, on the 8th, to Betawud, and to Maundul on the 10th; while Sulabut Khan, on the 9th, crossed the river to Pattun, and arrived the following day at Soangheir, where the two corps were distant from each other only six miles. The disposition of this part of the country had begun to manifest itself since the detachment crossed the river. At Sindkeir, near Pattun, Sulabut Khan's camp was fired on; but apologies were subsequently made for this aggression. A communication was now open with Captain Davies above the Ghats; and the present position appearing generally advantageous for the fulfilment of his instructions, Colonel Deacon resolved to halt here for further orders. These he received on the 11th, and on the

* The Beels, or Bheels, are savage tribes, supposed Aborigines, who principally inhabit the mountainous tracts between the Deckan and Goozerat, and between the Deckan and Malwah: their arms are bow and arrows.

following morning commenced his march for Jafferabad by Ummulneir, Perkundah, Pohoor, and Adjunta, where he arrived on the 17th, followed at a short distance by the Nuwaub. On ascending the Ghats, he received repeated advices of the movements of the Peishwah, from the vicinity of Poonah, towards the northward, supposed to be for the purpose of favouring the junction of his ex-minister Trimbuckjee, of whom, however, little had been heard in the Khandesh during the march through that province. Accounts also arrived of the passage of a body of about one thousand Pindarries up the Ghats, east of the Dewul pass. There they were too far advanced, and moving too rapidly, to afford any prospect of their being overtaken. This party had departed from Malwah in November; and passing round the left flank of all the British troops, had crossed the Nerbuddah above Hindia, and passed close by Asseerghur, into Berar. Colonel Deacon arrived, on the 21st of December, at Jafferabad; and on the 28th, for greater abundance of forage, changed ground to Akolah, a small place six miles distant in a southerly direction.

CHAPTER IX.

HOSTILITIES WITH HOLKUR.

Dispositions for the March from Oojein. Reflections on the March of Armies in India. March to Gunnye. Fruitless Negotiations with Holkur's Vakeels. Reconnaissance on both Banks of the Seeprah. State of Affairs at Holkur's Head-quarters. Murder of the Baee. March to Hernia. Second Reconnaissance on both Banks of the Seeprah. Preparations on the Eve of the 21st of December. Final Communication with Holkur. Commencement of the Action with Holkur's Horse. Passage of the River. The Enemy driven from their Position. Partial Stand and subsequent Flight, pursued by the Cavalry and Light Infantry. Situation of the Baggage during the Action, and Loss on both Sides. Reflections on the Battle of Mehidpoor. Errors on both sides. British Light Infantry are select Infantry. Bravery of the Troops, the principal Cause of British Victories.

Dispositions for the March from Oojein.

THE situation in which the army found itself at Oojein, surrounded by flying parties of horse from Holkur's camp at Mehidpoor, rendered necessary the adoption of special measures to secure the skirts of the camp, and for the protection of foraging-parties. The outline pickets were augmented; and to the rear picket were allotted details from all the light corps, independent of others from corps of the line. The escort of the foraging-parties was likewise sufficiently strengthened to give them protection, had they on all occasions availed themselves of it; and a couple of guns were added for this service, in order to deter the enemy's horse from a near approach.

Whatever might be the professions of Holkur's Government, the actual state of things could only be considered, at best, as a sort of war in disguise. Therefore, when the army halted on the 13th of December, the previous arrangements were ordered, preparatory to the expected crisis of a more open hostility; and Sir John Malcolm, as second in rank, was appointed to command the line. The following order of march was also directed to be observed, when the army should move on the next day; and will serve to shew the disposition usually adopted in India, under similar circumstances. The advanced-guard was composed of the details coming on duty under the new field-officer of the day, and was followed by the cavalry and horse-artillery. Next succeeded the infantry of the line, headed by the rifle-corps, and followed by the park, which was covered by a battalion, when not moving between the infantry brigades. The pickets coming off duty, with some guns attached, formed the rear-guard, under the orders of the field-officer of the previous day. All the baggage of the army was directed to move on the reverse flank; and beyond it was the corps of Mysore Silladar horse.

Reflections on the march of Armies in India.

There are so few great roads in India, and the country is, in general, so little enclosed, that convenience has introduced into general adoption the practice of marching on a single line; preserving the proper flank clear, and having all the baggage extended over the country on the reverse flank. There cannot perhaps be a better disposition, if the intention be to pass the enemy supposed to be on the proper flank, and to gain a certain position in front. But if the army be marching to find the enemy in his own country, or in a country in his interests, it is impossible to foretell in what direction he may present himself. The truth of this was evinced during the war of 1799, when occasionally either flank was indifferently threatened; and on the 2d of April, the day the British army moved from the Cavery opposite to Socillay, it was found necessary to remove the baggage from the left to the right during the march, which prevented a greater progress than three miles in that day. The enemy to be most apprehended, on the line of march, are bodies of horse, whose whole attention is given to cause distress by attacks on the baggage. They appear unexpectedly on either flank, or on both flanks at once; and instances have occurred where they have passed through the line. There are cases, however, when two or more parallel roads have been found indispensably requisite; and, in consequence, the expedient of opening the necessary ways across the country, has been resorted to, if its nature permitted that operation. To this arrangement recourse has been had, especially when a battering-equipment accompanied the army in the enemy's country. It was found of great importance on the march from Hooleadroog to Seringapatam, in February 1792. There were opened, on that occasion, three parallel roads: that to the proper flank for the troops and light artillery, the centre road for the heavy guns and all heavy ordnance carriages, and the road to the reverse flank for all lighter store-carts and private baggage-carts. Beyond this line was the great mass of baggage, covered by the part of the cavalry not on other duties, and the infantry of the reserve, for whom no local preparation was considered as necessary. In March 1799, a separate road was not prepared for the battering-train, going to the last siege of Seringapatam; but the troops marched in two columns, of which the grand army composed one, and the Nizam's contingent the other, having the baggage between. In both cases the annoyance to be feared was from the enemy's numerous horse, acting on the baggage flank if left uncovered. Had any attack in front been apprehended, it is evident, as it is acknowledged, that as many and as short parallel columns as possible, with all baggage in their rear, would form the most favourable disposition under such circumstances. The fact is, that a British army has never been attacked on its march. When the enemy resolved on giving battle, they assumed a position which they considered favourable to oppose further progress. There, so far from anticipating the formation of the British line in order of battle, they always awaited an attack, rather than quit, by a forward movement, the advantages of their position. Though this disposition, on a single line, has been described as applicable to the case of India, it is not meant to be understood as peculiar to that country. Similar circumstances will render its adoption equally convenient in other countries, for divisions * much larger than a British army so situated. Movements in many columns are particularly adapted to a campaign of manœuvre—a character of operation rarely met with in India at any period, and certainly not since the death of Hyder Allee.

March to Gunnye. (Map IV.) (Plan 10.)

The army marched on the 14th by the high road towards Mehidpoor, and re-crossed the Seeprah river into camp at Gunnye, distant about four miles from a town in its front, named Paun-Bahar. It was here encamped in the following order, with the river in its rear and on its left, while on the right were deep and impassable ravines: the rear pickets having possession of the fords of the river, and the front pickets the roads leading in the direction of the enemy.

---

* The French army in 1812 consisted of ten *corps d'armée*, each from twenty to thirty thousand men, besides large divisions of cavalry, and they entered Russia in as many columns; yet the greatest part of this immense army gradually concentrated at Smolensk, and from thence marched on a single line (with little exception) to Moscwa.

Right	Four Horse-artillery Guns.
	1st Brigade of Cavalry.
	2d Brigade of Cavalry.
	Head-quarters, Horse-artillery, and Six Guns.
	1st Brigade of Infantry.
	The Park.
	2d Brigade of Infantry.
	Four Horse-artillery Guns.
Left	The Rifles.

The loss of cattle, particularly camels, by the enemy's horse, continued to augment, notwithstanding the precautions used for their security. Every circumstance, indeed, tended so much to promise an early engagement with an insolent enemy, that Sir Thomas Hislop ordered the line to be under arms on the 15th, in order that he might ascertain, from personal inspection, their state of preparation for that contingency.

Fruitless Negotiations with Holkur's Vakeels.

Pursuant to the invitation given to Holkur's Government, that agents should be sent on their part to adjust any differences which might be supposed to have led to the unsatisfactory posture in which the mutual relations between the two States existed; the Vakeels, Behraun Bapoo, Meer Zuffer Allee, and Jeswunt Rao, arrived in the camp. They were received on the 15th by Sir John Malcolm, to whom was entrusted, pursuant to his appointment from the Governor-general, under Sir Thomas Hislop's orders, the conduct of the negotiations which immediately followed. The articles of complaint urged on the part of the British Government were,—Neglect of the duties of the alliance, in not replying to the letter of the Governor-general and the Resident at Delhi: Negotiations with the Peishwah when he had in the most treacherous manner commenced a war with the British Government, against whose interests such negotiations appeared to have a hostile intention: The collection also of a large army, avowedly designed to proceed towards Poonah, at a time when Holkur's Government was not at war with any State. These allegations were asserted on the principle, that the British Government had a right to treat under the character of an offended Power requiring reparation for designed, if not overt, acts of hostility; that from the nature of the present situation of affairs, immediate actions, and not mere professions, were necessary to establish confidence in any engagement into which the Government of Holkur might enter; and that the treaty, if concluded, must be speedily executed, as any delay would be injurious to the progress of the general plan of operations in Malwah. In the course of the negotiations, which continued during five days, ten articles were proposed to the Vakeels, which it will be unnecessary to enumerate here, as no treaty immediately followed. They will have their place more properly hereafter. The Vakeels kept up a constant communication with their camp, distant about twenty miles; and discussed the several points of the negotiation with an apparent anxiety, for which there was probably no other grounds than the desire which all Mahratta Governments have to gain time. They accounted for the delays which attended this conference, by the difficulty of uniting the councils of the Regent, in which Ram Deen and Roshun Beg were decidedly hostile, while Ghuffoor Khan, a relation of Ameer Khan, was said to be on the side of peace. They accounted for the assembling of the army by saying, that after the Baee had last rejoined it, corps after corps had assembled round her; and that she had invited them to do so, as the only means of preventing them from plundering her country; to which Meer Zuffer Allee added the hint, that an army was useful "to aid friends and resist enemies." The period at which the negotiation should be considered as broken off, had been successively fixed and postponed, in order to avoid any precipitation of extremities. It was at length to be apprehended, that any further tolerance of the delays artfully brought forward would be construed into doubts, on the side of the British commander, of his own strength. This could not fail to embolden the party of Holkur, and to encourage the re-assembly, in Malwah, of all those elements of hostility and disorder which had been already dispersed or deterred. A Native Power can never account for the forbearance of another, except by the supposition of weakness. This idea might be encouraged on the present occasion, by the losses of cattle daily experienced in the British camp. These were carried off by the enemy's horse; for their position was surrounded by flying parties, and all communication with Oojein, only seven miles in the rear, was entirely cut off, except through the means of a respectable escort.

Reconnaissance on both Banks of the Seepiah.

On the 19th, therefore, the Vakeels were dismissed, and preparations made for marching on the following morning to find the enemy. Such various accounts were received of their movements, that it was doubtful on which side of the river they would ultimately stand. As the nature of the country was unfavourable to movement, two reconnaissances were now sent out to explore the approaches on both sides of the Seeprah towards Mehidpoor. A comparison of the reports decided in favour of the high road down the right bank, as shorter and easier for guns, though more confined by hills, which, in the present instance, was rather advantageous, as it contributed to cover the baggage against the enemy's horse.

State of Affairs at Holkur's Head-quarters.

It will be proper here to notice the proceedings in the enemy's camp during the period of the negotiations, and of the events which immediately preceded them. It has been already mentioned, that their corps of infantry and guns were under the command of several chiefs, of whom those of most influence were Ram Deen, Roshun Beg, Roshun Khan, and Ghuffoor Khan, who formed the war faction. With these chiefs may also be noticed the *Barra Bhye* (twelve brothers), an association supposed to consist of twelve thousand horse; which evidently appear to have been overrated, by a reference to the strength of Holkur's army. These were influenced by Ram Deen, whose name was subsequently always coupled with theirs. Gunput Rao exercised the functions of minister, and had many political enemies; but the Baee's attachment to him supported his power. Tantiah Jogh was considered as paymaster of the forces, a situation of considerable importance under a Native Government; but being suspected by the war faction to be in correspondence with the British, they had sufficient weight to confine him to his tents. Ghuffoor Khan continually represented his relative Ameer Khan, as on his march to join the army; and Holkur was not undeceived on this head till the 12th of December, when a letter arrived from the Ameer, declaring his engagements with the British Government, and his resolution to abide by them. Still the Maharajah's Government, proudly affecting independence of the conduct pursued by other Native Powers, persevered in their resolution to oppose the British army. Holkur's horse had always been esteemed the best in India; and during the last Mahratta war, though this chief had been reduced to sue for peace, he had gained some advantages in the field, and had not suffered those severe losses experienced by Scindiah and the Bhooslah. His army therefore considered their character quite unimpaired, and declared their *esprit de corps* with proportionate confidence. This has already been seen, during the negotiation, in the language of Meer Zuffer, who likewise, in writing from his camp to Sir John Malcolm, called to his recollection that he had to deal with the army of Holkur. But their efforts were likely to be paralyzed by the distress of the troops for want of pay.

Even after the junction of Roshun Beg's party on the 28th of November, they had again separated, in order to extort by this means some cash, and halted in the first days of December at Burroad, during the march of the rest of the army from Deeg to Mehidpoor. At this place he subsequently rejoined; and was present during the absence of the Vakeels, whose conferences were treated by the army with great indifference.

Murder of the Baee.

The Baee offered to the infantry at Mehidpoor, six annas* in the rupee of the sums due to them, and to the horse an entire discharge of their arrears, on arriving at Oojein and Indoor, having received bills from the Peishwah, payable at the former place. Yet, however the troops might, for the present, have been willing to be satisfied by that arrangement, the chiefs were averse to her measures, as they saw their own degradation in her endeavours to acquire the protection of the British Government. The method they adopted to defeat her schemes and those of her ministers, was most effectual. They seized their persons on the 19th of December, and during the night held a consultation how their prisoners should be disposed of. The result was, that they conveyed the Baee publicly to the bank of the river on the following morning, and there struck off her head. It was, at the same time, determined that Tantiah Jogh should succeed Gunput Rao as Minister; but Roshun Beg, who wished to see Ram Deen in that situation, brought the other candidate a prisoner to the infantry lines, and plundered his property. Such violent measures necessarily produced great disgust in some parts of the army, and some chiefs sent off their baggage as from an insecure situation; but that *esprit de corps*, of which notice has already been taken, kept their forces together for the approaching crisis.

Second Reconnaissance on both Banks of the Seeprah. (Plan 11.)

In this situation were the affairs of Holkur, when the British camp moved, on the 20th, a short distance to Hernia, and encamped in a valley with some scattered hills in the rear and the Seeprah in the front. On the right and left were deep ravines running into the bed of the river. From the left went out the road to Oojein, from the right that to Mehidpoor; a cross road entered the camp from the rear, and passed the river in front of the centre by the only ford within several miles. These avenues were consequently occupied by the pickets; and such other dispositions were made, as promised to secure the baggage against the insults of the enemy's horse.

* About two-fifths.

The *campement* * was always attended by a *russalah* of Mysore horse on the line of march, and their usual orders were to take up a position for observation, at a distance less than a mile from the new ground, in the direction of the enemy, and to be there till the pickets were posted. The party on duty this day, mistaking their orders, did not return in time; and being attacked, by a superior number, were driven in with some loss. This was the first aggression unconnected with a view to plunder, and was followed in the afternoon by a sort of random excursion, which swept along the skirts of the camp, and had little other effect than to create some alarm among the followers, and to keep the in-line pickets on the alert. A second reconnaissance was ordered, from this ground, to ascertain if the enemy's position could be approached by the left bank of the river, on which side they were understood to be posted. The party for this purpose, composed of cavalry and light infantry, crossed the river in front of the camp, and advanced along by-roads about eight miles. Finding themselves still as distant from Mehidpoor as when in the camp, owing to the winding course of the river, and ruggedness of the country, the reconnaissance was abandoned in that direction. Another circumstance of apparent importance to its object, was the separate intelligence from three villages, that the enemy had absolutely changed their position to the right bank. The party accordingly recrossed the river at the nearest ford, and having gained the high road from Mehidpoor, returned by it to the camp, convinced that it was still the best approach for the army. The information received at the villages probably arose from movements among parts of the force, in consequence of internal differences, and of their precautionary measures against a sudden attack. They had patroles moving all night on both sides of the river, supported by large bodies of horse, who lay on the right bank. A detachment from Scindiah's corps, under Anna Bukhshee, which joined on the 17th, also occupied for a few days that position.

Preparations on the Eve of the 21st of December.

As the next day's march was to bring the British army to Mehidpoor, in order eventually to carry as many men as possible into the action, all pickets, camp, staff and regimental guards and orderlies, were directed to join their colours. For the rear guard, forty of the least effective rank and

---

* This word has no corresponding expression in English, on which account it is used here, and signifies the detachment with all the officers of the Quartermaster-general's department and camp-colourmen of corps, &c. sent forward to mark out the ground for the camp.

file from each Native corps, with two guns, five hundred Mysore horse, and all such sick and convalescents as were able to bear arms, were directed to be paraded at assembly-beating, in front of the park, under a captain and a subaltern from each infantry brigade, and six non-commissioned officers from each battalion. These details were likewise destined for the protection of the sick and baggage, in case of a battle, when they would necessarily take post. If the position of the army on the 20th was in some respects favourable, it had one disadvantage; the difficulty of quitting it. In order to facilitate the accomplishment of this operation before day-light on the following morning, openings were made, from the left of each brigade, to the great road. This work, superintended by the officers appointed to conduct them to their places in the line of march, occupied the pioneers till it was dark; and much of the night was spent by the troops in those preparations which had been ordered for the following day.

Final communication with Holkur.

On the morning of the 21st of December, about half an hour before day-break, the army was in motion. Sir John Malcolm was directed to place himself at the head of the advance guard, which consisted of a large detachment from the line. At the same time the *campement* was ordered to attach itself to the brigadier-general, instead of proceeding in advance, as had been usual. In this manner the march was conducted about eight miles without seeing any of the enemy. But a courier arrived from Holkur with a note, dated the same morning, which was couched in general terms, of nugatory import,—such as that Ameer Khan had been invited to come and settle the differences; and observing among other things, that the precipitancy of the British army in advancing, savoured but little of a friendly disposition; that it had prevented him from sending back Meer Zuffer; and that though he had hitherto restricted his own troops to their position, yet their ardour was too impatient of restraint to be much longer controuled. To this communication, the most intelligible part of which was the implied defiance at its conclusion, Sir Thomas Hislop directed a note to be returned in exchange, which Sir John Malcolm, long experienced in Native correspondence, had ready with him, under the date of the preceding day, adapted to the foreseen state of affairs. It contained, simply, a short recapitulation of the endeavours used to settle matters amicably, which had been frustrated by the injudicious councils of the Maharajah, and an invitation to avail himself of the renewed offer of British protection, by abandoning an army which he confessed himself unable to controul. With this the courier returned at speed, the head of the line never having slackened its pace during this interchange of communications.

Commencement of the action with Holkur's horse. (Plan 12.)

About nine, the advance ascended an eminence over which the road passed. From hence there opened a commanding view of the valley in which was situated the town of Mehidpoor, on the right bank of the Seeprah; the course of which was here marked by an avenue of trees. This plantation masked the main position of the enemy; but all the plain in front was occupied with their horse, either in large bodies or in detached parties of skirmishers. These came forward, in the most confident manner, close to the head of the advance; for they soon discovered that there was no intention of fighting them in detail. A halt was here made, to allow the line to come up, as from hence it would be necessary to form the plan for future movements. (*A*) From the summit of a small hill in this vicinity, Sir Thomas Hislop was enabled to obtain a general view of the enemy's dispositions. They appeared behind the river in two lines, of which the infantry and heavy batteries formed the first, and the cavalry in masses the second. The next consideration was, how to pass the Seeprah; because, though the information respecting the two fords in their front was still unsatisfactory, it was evident that to cross by any ford, either above or below, would be the manœuvre of at least an entire day, harassed by their horse, and met by a counter-manœuvre or flight on the part of the enemy; the army of a Native Power never having accepted battle from a British army, under [illegible] of position. It was therefore resolved that the cavalry, with some horse-artillery and light infantry, should be advanced, to clear the intermediate plain, and to cover a closer reconnaissance of the features of the enemy's position, and the means of approaching it. For the first of these purposes Sir John Malcolm was directed to move with half the cavalry towards the right, (*D.*) where the majority of the horse were assembled in the plain, and in occupation of some small villages. These hamlets were soon (*B. B.*) cleared by parties of light infantry, and the skirmishers retired on their main bodies. These would have been charged, had the ground admitted (*F.*) it; but it was found that they were secured by an impassable ravine in their front, and the guns were accordingly opened, which obliged them to disperse and retire. A part descended along the right bank of the river, (*a, a.*) round the town of Mehidpoor, and the rest rejoined their army. While these manœuvres took place to the right and front, the other brigade of (*E.*)

cavalry inclined to the left, to gain the bank of the Seeprah, at the village of Dooleit; where the commanding ground favoured the ascertainment of those objects with which the officer conducting the reconnaissance was charged. It accordingly pushed forward to reach that point before the enemy should be driven by Sir John Malcolm across the river; and in its advance some detached parties of horse crossed the head of the column to retire to the left, and were those which subsequently attacked the baggage. From hence the enemy's dispositions were distinctly viewed; and from the bed of the river, the ascents of its steep banks at the nearest ford were partially seen in reverse; while the retreat of the horse across it, gave a favourable conclusion as to the road and the depth of the water. It was also ascertained that the more distant ford to the right offered no prospect of being useful. Though conveniently situated for the retreat of the enemy's horse, it could be seen that none of them retired by it. A further circumstance of much importance, in favour of the left ford, was a long spit of sand under the opposite bank, which, as the stream flowed close to the near bank, offered a convenient situation for the partial formation of the troops.

Passage of the river.

In the mean while, the line of infantry was advancing under Sir Thomas Hislop's personal command, and had arrived within about six or seven hundred yards of the river, when he was rejoined by Sir John Malcolm, and received the report of the reconnaissance. He immediately decided that the army should pass by the single ford; and the light brigade was
(H) ordered across to seize the opposite bank, while a small battery was established on the near side to cover its movement. This service was performed without any opposition, except that of a powerful cannonade, of which many shots crossed the river. The enemy's front was generally at the distance of 800 yards from the left bank, to which it was nearly parallel. A little beyond their left flank, the river took a sudden turn towards their rear, and continued in that direction for a mile and a half, where was a deep ford, but without any road, down the bank, for guns. On their right was a deep ravine which run into the bed of the river; and
(I.) near their centre was a ruined village, which might be termed the key of their position, as it had some elevation, and was directly in rear of the main ford. The enemy were aware of its importance, filled it with infantry, and flanked it by their principal batteries. The British cavalry and horse-artillery
(K.) crossed after the light brigade; the former ascending the bank to the left, where they were partially skreened by some rising ground between them

and the enemy, and the latter forming battery in front of the ford. At the same time a battery was formed on the right bank considerably below the ford, to keep down in some measure or to divert the cannonade, which played with concentrated effect where the troops were passing. It is necessary here to mention, that the banks of this river, like those of most others in Malwah, are at least twenty-five feet high. The means of getting out of the bed is generally by the mouth of some ravine, of which there happened here to be two of several branches. Of these the light brigade were ordered to take possession, in order to clear the bed of the river for the remaining brigades of infantry. These were crossing at about twelve o'clock, and were directed, by a countermarch, to bring their right in front. As soon as this manœuvre was performed by the first brigade, Sir Thomas Hislop gave his orders for the attack of the enemy along their whole front, with what troops had crossed, leaving the second brigade of infantry, to follow as a reserve. (M.) (G. G.)

To Sir John Malcolm was given the immediate command of the two brigades of infantry destined to the attack of the enemy's left, and the ruined village; and while the 1st brigade ascended the bank, and took sufficient ground to the right for its formation into line, the light brigade arose from the ravines, and formed battalion columns of companies on its left. The whole of this operation was performed with great steadiness, under a fire of both round shot and grape from several batteries. By this time the horse-artillery were nearly silenced or dismounted; for their light pieces were unequal, however well served, to stand against the heavy calibers in their front. The range of the cavalry had likewise been found by the enemy's guns. For some time they suffered from a party of the enemy, who came down the ravine which flanked both positions, and maintained a galling fire till driven off by a company of infantry brought up for that purpose. A smooth glacis of about seven hundred yards now separated both armies, when Sir John Malcolm's division commenced the attack, by a rapid but orderly advance on the ruined village and the enemy's left, which was latterly brought forward to enfilade this expected operation. The desperate service was performed with suitable determination; and if the troops of this division wanted the support of a friendly battery, they were animated by the cheering example of their leaders,* among whom must be

The Enemy driven from their position.

* See in a Memorandum to Appendix G. the division of the army into brigades at this time.

counted Lieutenant-colonel M'Gregor Murray, whose services were given for this occasion to Sir John Malcolm, by whom he was placed with the detachment of the Royal Scots on the right. Many were knocked down by a destructive fire of grape; but the remainder carried the village and batteries at the point of the bayonet. (N, N, N, N.) The enemy's infantry were likewise driven from their position; but none of their artillerymen abandoned their guns, and such as were not killed attempted to recommence a fire after the infantry had fled. On the left, the British cavalry, who had been joined by the Mysore horse, were ordered to follow the movements of the infantry, and to make a simultaneous charge against the enemy's right. The decision and rapidity of their movement carried them, with little loss, to the rear of the opposed batteries. Some troops and guns, near the enemy's centre, still held their ground, having as yet been unattacked; but on (N.) the 2d brigade's ascending from the bed of the river, they advanced in that direction. The infantry in their front, finding both their flanks turned, retired before them, while the Golandauze served their guns to the last. Such of the enemy as were to the left of the ruined village, fled along the bank of the river; but their centre pressed towards the right, with which it retired along the high road to Alloat. In this direction the British and Mysore cavalry hung on the enemy, who, intent only on flight, offered no opposition; and the 2d brigade followed still as a reserve. Sir John Malcolm's division (P) advanced likewise about a thousand yards beyond its point of attack, and then halted to re-form.

Partial Stand and subsequent Flight, pursued by the Cavalry and Light Infantry

As Sir Thomas Hislop ascended the high ground in rear of the enemy's position, he observed, in the hollow towards the river, their camp, which had not been previously visible, still standing. Immediately he sent orders to Sir John Malcolm to move down upon it; at the same time the cavalry got sight of it, where they were in pursuit. Considering its attack more important than the service in which they were engaged, they abandoned the pursuit of the enemy, to the Mysore horse, and turned to their right on the standing camp, distant at least a mile and a half. They arrived before Sir John Malcolm's division, but found it deserted; when a fire (d.) opened on them unexpectedly from a battery further down the river, where some of the enemy still made a stand. The cavalry again advanced against this position; but, finding its front covered by ravines, they drew off under (O.) cover of a village to await the arrival of the infantry advancing under Sir John Malcolm. Sir Thomas Hislop likewise hastened to this point, imagining, from the briskness of the firing, that the enemy's left had only retired on a second position. He accordingly ordered on a detachment of light infantry and some field-pieces to turn their right flank, while the remainder of the 1st and light brigades advanced on their front. These dispositions obliged the enemy to fly across the river by which their left flank had been covered. It appears that this premeditated stand had been made only with a view to cover that part of their retreat, as the ford was extremely difficult; and that to facilitate its success, these guns had been previously placed in battery. Sir Thomas Hislop ordered a fresh pursuit of the enemy by the cavalry and two light infantry corps, under that active officer Sir John Malcolm; but the passage of the river proved so tedious that none of the enemy were overtaken on the right bank, though they were followed as long as day-light remained. (Q.)

Situation of the baggage during the action, and loss on both sides.

(Plan 13.)

The line now returned to the field of battle, and encamped nearly on the enemy's position, but fronting in an opposite direction. The sick and baggage likewise crossed the river from the ground which they had occupied during the action, near the village of Dooleit, and where they were as secure as a small guard well posted could render them. Several shot, which went over the cavalry, fell among them; and they were partially attacked by some of the enemy's horse, who remained on that side of the river. These were beaten off by the five hundred Mysoreans, and little impression beyond confusion was produced by their attempts. The cavalry and light infantry returned about eight o'clock; the pickets were posted as usual, and the troops lay on their arms during the remainder of the night, after having been deluged during two hours by as severe a fall of rain as can be imagined in the heaviest monsoon. The loss of the enemy was estimated at three thousand men; and one of their chiefs, Roshun Beg, who commanded the batteries about the ruined village, was severely wounded. Young Holkur, who was in the action on horseback, fled with the principal bodies of horse to Alloat, after the capture of the guns, which amounted to sixty-three of all calibers, with many tumbrils of ammunition. The loss* of the British army was seven hundred and seventy-eight men killed and wounded, including thirty-eight European and twenty-seven Native officers; and most of the wounds were desperate, being chiefly made by gun-shot or grape.

* Vide Appendix. G.

Reflections on the Battle of Mehidpoor.

The battle of Mehidpoor demands many reflections, as well from the importance of its consequences, as from its being the only general action of primary order in India since 1804; during which period the organization of the British army had undergone several alterations, and received some improvements. The most striking feature of the battle was the bold measure of passing a difficult river by a single ford, in front of an enemy powerfully posted. This has with some been the theme of admiration, and with others of animadversion; for, in the present enlightened age, no common subject of morals is considered more legitimate for general criticism than the dispositions of a commander in the field, however remote they may be from the circumstances of common life and general study. The particular information which can be conveyed in a public dispatch, on such an occasion, must be very confined, partial, and liable to misinterpretation; whereas the old practice of giving concisely the general results*, offers every thing of which

* The Duke of Marlborough thus reports the Battle of Blenheim, in his letter to Mr. Secretary Harley, dated August 14th, 1704. "In order thereto, we went out on Tuesday early in the morning, with forty squadrons, to view the ground, but found the enemy had already possessed themselves of it; whereupon we resolved to attack them, and accordingly we marched between three and four yesterday morning from the camp at Munster, leaving all our tents standing. About six we came in view of the enemy, who, we found, did not expect so early a visit. The cannon began to play about half an hour after eight. They formed themselves in two bodies: the Elector, with Monsieur Marrin, and their troops, on our right, and Monsieur de Tallard, with all his own, on our left, which last fell to my share. They had two little rivulets besides a morass before them, which we were obliged to pass over in their view, and Prince Eugene was obliged to take a great compass to come to the enemy; so that it was one o'clock before the battle began. It lasted, with great vigour, till sun-set, when the enemy were obliged to retire, and by the blessing of God, we obtained a complete victory."—The rest of this short letter describes the loss of the enemy. The Battle of Malplaquet, being of less importance than that of Blenheim, is reported by his Grace in a still shorter letter, to Mr. Secretary Boyle, dated September 11, 1709. "This motion of the enemy kept our army for two nights under their arms; and in the evening, as soon as the twenty-one battalions and four squadrons we were expecting from Tournay, were come within reach, it was resolved to attack them; and the necessary dispositions being made, we accordingly began at eight this morning. The fight was maintained with great obstinacy till near twelve o'clock, before we could force their retrenchments, and drive them out of the wood into the plain, where their horse were all drawn up, and ours advancing upon them. The whole army engaged and fought with great fury, till past three in the afternoon, when the enemy's horse began to give way, and to retire towards Maubeuge and Valenciennes, and part of them towards Condé. We pursued them to the defilee of Bavay with great slaughter, all our troops behaving themselves with the greatest courage."

a distinct judgment can be formed at a distance, without attempting an unfair scrutiny. The reasons which induced the measure adopted at Mehidpoor, have already been noticed, and little remains to be added. The ford below the enemy's position was impracticable for guns, and would have required an entire day to render it passable; a work which could not be performed in front of their overwhelming batteries. In order to march to that point, it would likewise have been necessary first to have possession of Mehidpoor, close under the walls of which place the road passes. This might have occupied the whole day, and thus the period would have been extended, during which the baggage and cattle were exposed to the depredations of the enemy's horse, made more bold by such dilatory conduct. The ford of Moondela, four miles above Mehidpoor, was difficult of access on both banks. None but by-paths led to it through a rugged country; and a *detour* of not less than ten miles would have been necessary, by this means, to approach their position. But supposing this manœuvre performed in the presence of numerous horse, what prospect could there be that the enemy would not, likewise, pass the river—an operation as easy and short to them, as it would have been difficult and tedious to the British army? Having done this, the river was still interposed, their position as strong, and their retreat more certain than from the left bank. It is even probable that they contemplated this alternative, in consequence of the reconnaissances made on both banks; and this supposition seems to be corroborated by the important circumstance of their not destroying the descents into the principal ford in their front. With regard to the second ford in their front, of which mention has been made, subsequent experience verified the conclusion formed respecting it. Only one man at once could descend the bank, the water was breast high, the bottom consisted of large slippery stones, and after an entire day's labour of all the pioneers, it was found impracticable to get a single captured gun across it. On this account they were all conveyed by the more distant, but main ford. After the army had crossed, any flank movement would have been absurd. They were within range of large grape from heavy guns; no situation could have been worse, and the shortest way out of it was by a direct attack. This succeeded, as it has always succeeded with British troops on a plain. It is conformable to their genius; and there is more science shewn by consulting, under such circumstances, this national disposition, than in the display of an acquaintance with the stratagems of war. This feeling extends to the Native troops in the British service; for though it may not proceed from their physical constitution, they receive the *esprit de corps* from their European officers, as they enter the service in youth, with flexible minds. The qualities required, on the present occasion, were such as should enable the troops to endure with patience a destructive fire in the first instance, and afterwards to affront palpable danger with alacrity. This expectation was justified; and it may be asserted, that the same result would have ensued, had there not been a single pound of powder exploded by the army on the 21st of December.*

Errors on both sides.

When a Native army receives battle, its position is generally marked by an obstacle along its front, difficult to be surmounted, and inclosing a glacis, or a plain, to give complete effect to its batteries. Its flanks are seldom to be turned without a considerable *detour*, such as would give time for a corresponding movement; and the rear is always open for a retreat, or secured by a fortified town.† This description contains the general character of a judicious disposition; but Indian armies shew themselves deficient, by neglecting to take the full advantage of it. They seldom oppose the passage of the obstacle in their front except by a cannonade, nor attack their adversary before he has recovered his order. On the present occasion the enemy should have filled the ravines with infantry, and brought forward his right wing as he did his left; by which he might have crossed the fire of his batteries in the ford, and all along the bank. Nor would this have subjected him to an enfilade from the opposite side of the river; the ruins of a village offering good cover to that flank. This disposition would likewise have deprived the British cavalry of the ground on which they

---

* The same may be said of the battles of the Golden Rock and Sugarloaf Rock, in 1753 and 1754; and of the victory of Assye, which followed, as on the present occasion, an attack unsupported by batteries; but what will be said of the battle of Corunna, defensive on the British side with only four guns against several heavy batteries? This observation is given merely as illustrative, and has no tendency to detract from the general usefulness of artillery; which, with the small detachments of British troops, occasionally and necessarily exposed to the attack of greater numbers, becomes even more important in India than in Europe. As well might the circumstance of there not having been a mounted dragoon in action at the battles of Alexandria and Maida, be urged as derogatory to the usefulness of cavalry.

† Some exception to this general remark may, no doubt, be found in the battles of Laswarree and Assye, where, by a flank movement of the British troops, the enemy was forced to change his position; but which perhaps he would not have attempted, had not the infantry been commanded by European officers.

formed; and it was this oversight on the part of the enemy which justified and determined Sir Thomas Hislop in attacking as he did. Having criticised the faults of the enemy, let not those of the British side be overlooked. The 1st brigade should not have been countermarched in the river; by which the whole army was longer exposed to the cannonade. Had they ascended the bank, left in front, like the brigades before them, the head of their column would at once have stood on its ground. After this a deployment to the right would have been both more safe and expeditious than any other movement, within grape range, to take ground for a formation into line. The cavalry were not under the command of a single head; and it accordingly depended on the good understanding between the two Brigadiers, whether the two brigades would act in concert. As it happened, no conduct could surpass theirs in charging the enemy; but their exertions on his rear were not marked by the arrangement which might have been expected from a single leader.* Under a single authority, likewise, a maintenance of the pursuit would probably have been preferred to the attack of a standing camp, as distant from them as it was near the infantry, who were in full possession of the field of battle, with an enemy flying in disorder at all points visible to the whole army. The enemy's cavalry suffered nothing in the action, for they kept aloof; and when the batteries were stormed, they immediately fled, which exposed their infantry to bear all the loss, when they were subsequently pressed by the Mysore horse, who continued the pursuit. They escaped by abandoning their elephants, camels, and *huckeries*, which were laden with valuables.

---

* It may be well to refer here to the method adopted by Major (now Brigadier-general) Doveton, commanding the body of cavalry composed of the Madras body-guard and the 1st regiment of Native cavalry, employed to *cut-up* the column of infantry issuing from Panjalum Courchee, on the storm of that place by General Agnew, in 1801, and flying much in the same disorder as the enemy's infantry from the field of Mehidpoor. The tail of the retreating column was successively cut off, and independently destroyed by successive squadrons; by which means every sword was brought into active employ. No attempt was made to oppose the head of the column, which might then have been induced to act with unanimity; but the operation in systematic detail was prosecuted in the rear for a distance of about five miles, during which the parts successively severed could never escape or be succoured, and each squadron, as it had completed one service, was carried forward to another.

British Light Infantry are select Infantry.

It has been seen that the light infantry and rifles acted, on this occasion, like troops of the line; and it is also true that they have never acted otherwise since their formation.* They are, in fact, select infantry, and nothing else. Formed as they have been by draughts from other corps, the old men have brought with them all the habits of the regular battalions, and the recruits have of course followed the example of their seniors. It is not a particular exercise, dress, and arms, which make light infantry or riflemen. There must be a disposition for desultory action, and confidence in individual resource, entirely different from that sympathy which carries men together in a body. It may be granted that such a disposition is to be acquired; but not by men who have already formed habits in corps of the line. Thus, had the light brigade, on the 21st of December, been really light troops, they would not have stormed the enemy's batteries. If, therefore, the British light infantry are neither used as light troops, nor fit to be so used, it were better for them still to keep their musquets and bayonets, as the arms best suited to the duties they perform. They have always marched well, because they are young and active men; but by no means better than flank companies of the line.† The French make excellent light troops, for that service appears conformable to their genius; but the same cannot be said either of the English, or of the class of Natives into whom English feelings, before an enemy, are infused by their officers. They love at once to encounter the very worst to which they can be exposed, and arguing from their own feelings, consider as ineffectual the cautious and indirect ma-

* In proportion as a corps of infantry, however denominated, expends a greater portion of its ammunition, it may be considered ignorant and untrained in light-infantry service.

† It is even asserted by officers who have seen both on service, that when infantry of the line have had their knapsacks carried for them like the light infantry, they have out-marched them. This affords an useful hint against relieving men habitually from that moderate encumbrance; for when called on for an exertion, they no longer receive that additional stimulus and elasticity which a man, or any other animal, feels on being suddenly lightened. In elucidation of this remark, a reference may be made to Major H. Smith's march from the night of the 12th of April 1817, with flank companies of his own corps (1/14th Madras Native infantry), and of the 1st battalion of the 2d, and the 1st battalion of the 3d Bombay Native infantry, to surprise a hostile body. At the expiration of four days and some hours, he had marched one hundred and fifty miles, and successfully attacked the enemy, of whom seventy were killed and several prisoners taken. These companies had carriage for their knapsacks, and the march was performed in the hottest time of the year.

nœuvres of light troops. The same disposition was found in the infantry corps organized for Native Powers by a few British adventurers. They made and received desperate assaults which quite astonished their employers; and during twenty years active service, when the number of French and British officers in Scindiah's army were equal, only four of the former to fifteen of the latter were killed.*

Bravery of the Troops the principal Cause of British Victories.

From what has been premised, it will be concluded, that more victories have been gained in the field by British armies in India through the bravery of the troops, than by manœuvres of the commander. In fact, the armies are too small for extensive manœuvre beyond cannon range. That they are continually permitted to deploy within it, also shews that the enemy to be coped with are deficient in a most important part of military conduct, a deficiency which obviates the necessity of abiding by those rules and precautions which are respected in Europe. An Indian army is completely under the eye of the commander, as much as a single division is in Europe. There is, consequently, no room for those calculations which are so important in the case of a large army. It may be argued, perhaps, that the addition of an ally's contingent augments the number of fighting men who are to be arranged; but it must at the same time be allowed that they cannot be manœuvred. The utmost to be gained from them is the occupation of a position, which may hold in check the same number and description of the enemy. Almost all Lord Lake's victories will be found an illus-

* It is a pleasing fact to find the British character maintained by British subjects in all parts of the world, and under the most cheerless circumstances; and the hard service and brilliant exploits performed by these men and their corps, would do honour to any army. It would be a mistake to suppose that *De Boyne's* corps were officered entirely by Foreigners, because his name is French; and whenever they have suffered severely, the names of the officers killed and wounded are found invariably to be British. In the action between Holkur's and Scindiah's troops, in September 1802, we find on the latter side Colonel Vickers, Major Harding, and Major Armstrong; and on the former, Dawes, Catts, and Douglas, all of whom were killed, with six hundred of their men, out of fourteen hundred killed and wounded. Only one officer survived, and Major Harding was killed on the other side. In the previous year also, Holkur had attacked, under the walls of Oojein, a corps of Scindiah's consisting of four battalions, commanded by Colonel Hessing's son. Notwithstanding an immense disparity of numbers, these battalions never broke. Three-fifths were killed, one-fifth wounded, and out of eleven officers, seven were sabred at their guns. Their names were Captains Graham, Urquhart, and M'Pherson, Lieutenants Montague, Lany, Doolun, and Haden, all British subjects.

tration of this position; for he gained them all by a direct attack, which he himself led. Yet, if he rejected, or were ignorant of the stratagems of war, he possessed, in an eminent degree, that powerful influence of character which calls forth the exertions of troops, through their affections and admiration. They not only performed for him every thing possible, but repeatedly offered themselves to evident destruction, in his presence, as in the forlorn assaults of Bhurtpoor.

Whence can arise this extraordinary power of one man over others, or how is its cause to be analyzed? Elevated birth and titles cannot confer it, nor can riches purchase it: study cannot acquire it, and the most industrious exertions fail to accomplish it. No, it is a natural quality of the individual, an endowment from heaven, and as little to be obtained through human means, as the mind of a Locke, or the person of a Hercules.

CHAPTER X.

PEACE WITH HOLKUR.

Advance of the Goozerat Division. Its recall by the Bombay Government. Subsequent Permission to advance, and March to Rutlum. Arrangements at Mehidpoor, and Reflections on the Retreat of a Native Army. Pursuit of the Enemy by a Light Detachment. Advance and Junction of the Head-quarters of the Deckan Army, and Goozerat Division. Separation of the Goozerat Division, and Re-junction of Sir John Malcolm's Detachment at Mundissoor. Negotiation ending in a Treaty with Holkur. The Reduction of his Power a striking Example. Supply of the Army in Malwah. Reference to Colonel Monson's disastrous Expedition. Considerations respecting the general Conduct of Operations in India. Comparison of the War with Holkur in 1804 and 1817. View of the Progress of the Holkur State from its Establishment.

A Reference has been made (p. 58) to the circumstances which prevented the early re-assembly of the Goozerat division at Baroda. Its advance was further delayed by the occurrences in the Deckan. These induced Colonel Morris, with the concurrence of the Resident, to postpone its march till subsequent advices should be received from Sir Thomas Hislop. But Major-general Sir William Grant Keir, on his arrival to assume the command, immediately decided on carrying that division forward to a position on the confines of Malwah. There, at least, it might be within easy communication, and be enabled to co-operate promptly, if called for. This measure appeared the more necessary from a consideration of the nature of the country surrounding Goozerat, the entrance to which might be easily closed against the receipt of intelligence, and is full of obstacles to the rapid progress of troops. The high road towards Oojein, which in the former Mahratta war had been pursued by Colonel Murray's and General Jones's forces, appeared to Sir William Grant Keir, as it had to Sir Thomas Hislop (p. 89), the most expedient on the present occasion. The Major-general, accordingly, commenced his march by that route on the 4th of December.

Advance of the Goozerat Division

(Map II.)

He crossed the Kurrah river on the 8th, after three marches; and on the following day entered the Burreeah jungle; the whole of which is at all times infested by a predatory race called Bheels, whose name has been introduced already in describing the march of Colonel Deacon's detachment through the Seindwah Ghat. This jungle rendered the road extremely confined, and the progress difficult, during two marches; in the first of which the baggage of the division was partially plundered, while several men and followers were killed and wounded by the inhabitants. On the 10th an open country succeeded, and continued for the two following marches, (Map IV.) which brought the division to the vicinity of the Dawud Ghat, separating the territory of Scindiah from Goozerat. This pass was descended on the 13th, and the force encamped at Dawud. It was here overtaken by a dispatch from the Government of Bombay, recalling Sir William Grant Keir to the occupation of a position near Jerroad on the Veesamuttra, within sixteen miles of the cantonment of Baroda.

Its recall by the Bombay Government.

This measure was prompted by the threatening appearances among the Deckannee States, and was the immediate consequence of intelligence having arrived at Bombay, of the rupture at Nagpoor. It was apprehended, that if the Goozerat country were left destitute of a British force, the contagion of Mahratta feeling might extend even to the Guickwar Government; and there were circumstances brought to light which rendered justly suspected the dispositions of, at least, the subjects of that State. At Soangheir in particular, a station which communicated immediately with the Poonah territory, the Guickwar troops decidedly spoke of their expectation of orders to join the Peishwah, and to support the Mahratta against the British cause. They were actively employed in encreasing their numbers, and offered high pay for military service. In fact, the same crisis of affairs, in some respects, appeared to the Government of Bombay to be approaching in Goozerat, as had occurred at Poonah and Nagpoor, viz. that the assembly of troops for co-operation would be augmented into the means of hostility. The return of Guickwar troops, according to the Resident's estimate of the 20th of November, amounted to nine thousand horse and foot, independent of the two thousand horse which were intended to accompany the British force. Of that number one thousand seven hundred and forty-eight were stated to be at Soangheir; whereas the intelligence received by the officer commanding at Bearra, represented them on the 26th to be equal to five thousand of all descriptions. In the direction of

Pahlanpoor and Katteiwar, the remaining principal points of defence, there was no reason to expect a state of things more favourable. The contingent of two thousand horse had not marched with the British force; and the alacrity which the Guickwar Government exhibited, in undertaking active and extensive levies, was as suspicious as it was superfluous.

Under these circumstances the orders for the recall of the field force were dispatched from Bombay on the 8th of December. Two days afterwards, however, there followed a modification of those instructions; which left Sir William Grant Keir still at liberty to advance, in case the Resident should consider the interests at Baroda secure, with a reinforcement from the division in the field. This variation in the orders was produced by the receipt of letters from Sir Thomas Hislop, written after his knowledge of the rupture at Nagpoor, and by the apprehension of the injury which the plans of the Governor-general might sustain, should the Goozerat force be suddenly withdrawn. Sir William Grant Keir, on receiving the first order, countermarched two stages to Jerree. There he received, on the 17th, the second order, with a letter from the Resident, which induced him to exercise the discretion given him, and to return to Dawud. He arrived there, for the second time, on the 19th of December, having detached to Baroda a reinforcement, consisting of eight hundred Native infantry and a detail of artillery, which reduced his force to four thousand and sixty-nine British troops. From this place the communication with the Head-quarters of the Deckan army became direct, though, at first, not expeditious; and orders were received to advance immediately by Rutlam, to favour the negotiations with Holkur, which were in progress. Pursuant to these instructions, the force advanced on the 20th; in three marches reached Petlawad, and in two more, arrived, on the 24th, at its destination. The small battering-train, and a considerable portion of the commissariat stores, had been left in the rear at Godra, as not likely to be required in advance, while they obstructed materially the progress of the force. The grain, however, being subsequently called for from the Head-quarters, under the apprehension of a future deficiency of that article, was ordered on by the first favourable opportunity.

Subsequent permission to advance, and march to Rutlam.

Having now conducted Sir William Grant Keir's force to a position where its immediate co-operation was calculable, it is proper to return to the occurrences which followed the battle of Mehidpoor. The first object was the organization of a light corps to follow up the success of that day, and to

Arrangements at Mehidpoor, and reflections on the retreat of a Native Army.

prevent the enemy from re-assembling; while arrangements were made for the care of the wounded, and the establishment of a post, which should be a rendezvous for all detachments coming from the rear, and a place of security for the deposit of the captured ordnance and field-hospital. On the day following the action, a corps of Native infantry, with guns, was posted on an eminence commanding the town, into which guards were sent to prevent plunder, as well as to establish the British authority. The most capacious dwelling-houses were selected and cleared out for the accommodation of the wounded, and orders were given to repair the defences of the place. The captured brass guns were brought into the fort, and those which were of iron were burst on the field of battle. So much had the force been [illegible] by the exertions of the 21st, that some days elapsed before a detachment could be prepared to pursue the enemy. This delay was of little importance, considering the nature of the retreat of an Indian army. So great, in general, on these occasions, is the dispersion, that some days are commonly required to ascertain, for the guidance of the pursuers, in what direction the principal body has fled. In vain should we look for those dispositions, which are expected from the regular army of an European power, to cover its retreat, and to repress the confidence of a victorious adversary in its rear. There will be found no stratagems to mask its route, cover its baggage, gain an advance, lay an ambuscade, or mislead its pursuer; no efforts to check his progress, by the occupation of a defile or a wood, the destruction of a pass or a ford, the blowing up or burning a bridge*. On the contrary, all impediments to flight are successively abandoned, and it becomes literally a *sauve qui peut*. This misconduct will be attributed partly to the want of discipline in an Indian army, and of arrangement in its leaders, which leaves every individual to rely more on himself than on his commander. It will also depend, in instances† like the present, on the nature of the victory, which was gained

* It must be confessed there are seldom any to be blown up or burned.

† In the same manner an attacking army, if after prolonged efforts it be attacked in return, has little means of making an orderly retreat. During repeated assaults, it loses sight of its defensive dispositions, becomes unhinged and incapable of acting in another direction with method. Examples to this effect will suggest themselves in the flight of the French armies, after the battles of Leipsic and Waterloo; for there will always be room for great distinction between the retreat of a beaten army, and of one which has not fought.

by a simultaneous charge of every point of the enemy's line. If they give way before this, there is an end of all immediate opportunity of making dispositions; and the subsequent re-assembly (if it take place) will be at some predetermined rendezvous, or point of general importance. Such was Ramteak after the action of the 16th of December at Nagpoor, and Seeta-Mhao on the present occasion.

Pursuit of the enemy, by a light detachment (Map IV.)

On the 26th of December, a light detachment was formed, and placed under the orders of Sir John Malcolm, for the pursuit of Holkur's army, on the following morning. This force consisted of the 2d cavalry brigade, the 1st battalion of the 3d regiment, and the 1st battalion of the 16th regiment of Native infantry, both light corps, with four horse-artillery guns, and two thousand Mysore horse. To this corps, a reinforcement was ordered, from the Goozerat division, of two squadrons of his Majesty's 17th dragoons, and a Native flank battalion. These were directed to join at Koondla, on the 27th, if practicable; but a delay in the receipt of the order prevented them from arriving there in time; and they followed Sir John Malcolm to Seeta-Mhao, whither he had advanced with great rapidity. From hence it was the Brigadier-General's intention to make a night-march, on the 29th, to Mundissoor; but learning that the enemy had, in the mean while, continued their flight, in a north-westerly direction, towards Mulharghur, he directed his march by Narghur, and arrived there on the 30th. Here it was ascertained that the enemy had countermarched with the intention of proceeding to Purtabghur, leaving only a body of horse at Mulharghur, and proposing to be joined at Mundissoor by the followers and bazars, which had fallen in the rear. A corresponding movement was therefore made on the latter place, to which the Mysore horse, and a squadron of Native cavalry, under Captain James Grant, were sent in advance on the morning of the 31st. By a rapid march they succeeded in surprising and capturing the whole of the cattle, bazars, &c. under the walls of Mundissoor, which place belonged to Scindiah. Sir John Malcolm likewise arrived on the same day, and was here overtaken by orders to halt for further instructions.

Advance and junction of the Head-quarters of the Deckan Army and Goozerat Division

The arrangements which Sir Thomas Hislop found necessary at Mehidpoor, were not completed till the 27th. On the 28th, the army marched in the direction of Taul, proposing to meet the Goozerat division on the Chumbul, in the vicinity of that place, to which Sir William Grant Keir had been requested to direct his movements. He was at the same time required to order on his heavy train to Dawud, for such further operations as might eventually occur in Malwah, should the enemy not submit, on being beaten out of the field. The weather, at this period, was extremely inclement, as has been already noticed, when describing the latter operations against the Pindarries. The army accordingly did not arrive at Taul till the 30th, having advanced by the route of Mundawal. On the same day it was met by the Goozerat Division, which marched on the 28th from Rutlam by Jowra, and took possession near that place of four guns with some ammunition, which had been abandoned by Holkur's troops. The Chumbul separated the head-quarters of Sir William Grant Keir and Sir Thomas Hislop; and in the course of the day it was resolved, that Sir John Malcolm's pursuit of the enemy should be suspended, as only calculated to bring on partial affairs, and to prevent a more decisive action, for which the strength and composition of his force was held to be insufficient. Sir John Malcolm's division had been found too weak to cope with Holkur's army, when he first approached it, during his pursuit of Cheettoo Pindarree; but the posture it maintained then was very different from what could be expected after its defeat; and Sir John was, no doubt, equal to the reduction of its dispirited remains, at the end of December. Both columns marched again on the 31st, in the direction of Mundissoor, and encamped within two miles of each other, on the banks of the Soamlee river, four miles in rear of that place: Sir Thomas Hislop's head-quarters having arrived on the 1st of January, and Sir William Grant Keir's on the 2d.

Separation of the Goozerat Division, and rejunction of Sir John Malcolm's Detachment at Mundissoor.

In the mean while Holkur, finding the activity of Sir John Malcolm's pursuit, which had already reduced him to great distress, followed up by the remainder of the army, had made overtures of submission. The preliminaries of a treaty having been accordingly furnished to him for adoption by Sir John, they were brought back, a little altered, on new-year's-day, by Meer Zuffer Allee, with Holkur's signature. There now remained no enemy in this quarter but the Pindarries. Against them, consequently, it was resolved to direct whatever troops could be applied to this purpose, without withdrawing from Holkur's vicinity such a controul as should enforce the conclusion of a treaty already so happily commenced. Sir William Grant Keir was accordingly directed to march with his division, on the evening of the 3d, towards Jawud, near which place Cheettoo was known to be encamped; and on the following day the army changed ground to Mundissoor, where Sir John Malcolm's detachment rejoined.

(Plan 14.)

Negotiation, ending in a Treaty with Holkur.

By this time the orders of the Governor-general were received, respecting the terms to be given to Holkur under a new state of things; and Tantiah Jogh having arrived in camp by invitation, on the 3d, no time was lost in proceeding to a conclusion. The terms proposed were, the confirmation of the engagements with Ameer Khan; the cession to the British Government of the claims of Holkur upon the Rajahpoot States; the cession to Zalimsing, Rajah of Kotah, of four districts formerly rented by him; the confirmation, under the guarantee of the British Government, to Ghuffoor Khan and his heirs, of his *jaghire*, amounting to near four lacs of rupees per annum, on the condition of his maintaining a quota of horse; the cession of the tribute of Nursinghur; and the cession to the British Government of all Holkur's possessions within and to the south of the Sautpoora range of hills, including Khandesh, Umbur, Elloora, and all his other possessions in that quarter. (Map VII.) During three days, these terms were discussed with much earnestness and ingenuity; and, respecting some of them, a considerable stand was made by Holkur's ministers, particularly those which regarded Meer Khan and his relation Ghuffoor Khan, both of whom they reviled with great acrimony, as disloyal to their sovereign. Ghuffoor Khan had been the first to induce Holkur's mind to submission, by refusing to fly with him beyond Purtabghur; and under his influence Meer Zuffer Allee acted, in personally opening a channel for negotiation. These two Mahometans were not less bitter than the Mahrattahs, whom they denounced to Sir John Malcolm as "the worst of infidels." Whatever shew of discussion, however, Holkur's party might use, they were sensible that they must submit to the terms prescribed; and their objections were generally accompanied with an appeal to the generosity of the Governor-general, and by no means to the alternative of a further contest. For this indeed their master was entirely unprepared, as the remains of his infantry were no longer acting under his orders. They were, on the contrary, with Roshun Beg at Rampoora, where (Map IV) this officer had sixteen guns, and usurped the authority of that town. On the 6th, the treaty was concluded; and, on the following day, copies were interchanged by Sir Thomas Hislop and Tantiah Jogh in a public manner, under the ceremony of a royal salute from the park, with the attendance at Head-quarters of all the field and staff-officers of the army. It consisted, in all, of seventeen articles; and provided, in addition to the terms already enumerated, that the Holkur State should receive the protection of the

British Government, by means of a military force, to be conveniently stationed for that purpose; that a British Resident should be received by Holkur; that he should submit his differences to British arbitration, and hold no communication with other Powers, nor receive any European or American into his service, without the concurrence of the British Government; and that he should maintain a quota of three thousand horse at their requisition, but no further force than his revenues could afford.

The Reduction of his Power a striking example

Thus was reduced to a state of innoxiousness and dependance a Government which had long been a prey to internal feuds, and a receptacle for all the elements of disorder and danger*. With all its weakness this Government had taken pride in its independence, which rested on that most vicious of all foundations, the power of inflicting more harm on peaceable neighbours, than its own situation made it liable to receive. As expressive of this state of things, the late Holkur signified to Lord Lake in 1805, that his country and property were on the saddle of his horse. He also wrote to General Wellesley, that, in the event of hostilities, countries of many hundred *coss* should be overrun, plundered, and desolated. So much misrule obtained throughout his dominion, that his revenue was insignificant compared with his territorial possessions, and perhaps not greater than the countries left to him were capable of producing, under proper management. His system was plunder and exaction; and the expense of the force he maintained for this purpose, was much greater than the contributions which he levied through their means. Unable thus to pay them, they were reduced to plunder for their own subsistence, and consequently became indifferent to his orders. When they found their own existence depended on a combined exertion, they assembled round him; but if their interests were separated, no fealty could be expected under such disorganization. Accordingly it has been seen, that Ameer Khan, his principal Sirdar, abandoned him in the hour of need, to secure for himself and his heirs the guarantee of the British Government. The situation to which Holkur was thus reduced, could not fail of producing a forcible effect on the minds of all the Native Powers of India. The rapidity of his downfal was such, that the

* The result of a complete victory over Holkur's army, considering its constitution, was foretold by the present Duke of Wellington, in 1804, when offering a memorandum for a campaign against that Chief.

account of the commencement of hostilities could only be considered as the near precursor of their termination; and this under circumstances calculated to impress them with despair of the success of any future struggle against the British Government. In his front were drawn up the forces of the three Presidencies, at a distance of more than one thousand miles from two of them. In his rear were the extremities of India, composed of [illegible] deserts where he could find no resources, and which were inhabited on one side by a people at war with all strangers, and on the other by the natural enemy of the Mahratta name. A more forcible exposition of the British power could not be desired than the present state of things exhibited. Nine divisions were in the field between the Punjub and the Kistnah. Each of these were composed of a proportion of every arm, and equal to meet independently any body of the enemy which could be brought collectively into the field. To them no corner of India appeared impervious; and the only imaginable obstruction to their progress, was the probable scarcity of provisions in a barren country. Even supplies they carried with them, by means of a system, to which the irregular government of a Native Power could never give effect. Thus the bazar of a British camp has sometimes been the only seat of plenty in a tract of many hundred miles, depopulated by a dreadful famine*.

From the destructive ravages of Pindarries, it might be concluded that Malwah, within and on the borders of which they were established, would have been found uncultivated, and its towns deserted. This, however, was by no means the case: and though the grain was in many instances hidden or refused, the superabundance of forage near all the villages proclaimed the extent of its production. Rice was scarcely to be seen, but wheat grew in considerable quantities, and was soon adopted by the Native troops as their common food. In fact, after the Army of the Deckan had crossed the Nerbuddah, such was the abundance that prevailed, both for men and cattle, through the activity of a well-arranged commissariat, that Sir Thomas Hislop's mind was relieved from any anxiety on this important object. Supplies which were at first called forward from distant quarters, became even a real incumbrance. Under the apprehension of possible scarcity, at the opening of the campaign, the Government of Bombay had been requested

Supply of the Army in Malwah.

* Such was the case in the Deckan at the close of the Mahratta war of 1804.

to form a commissariat depôt at Soorut. A similar application had been addressed to the Resident at Hydrabad, for the collection of grain, through the Nizam's officers, at the points of Nandeir, Ellichapoor, and Mulkapoor. The latter supplies were not collected before the troops returned, and the former were never brought forward; so that perhaps no troops in India ever before carried on their operations with so little dependance on their depôts. This was a happy result of able arrangements, and freed the troops acting from the southward, from the fetters of a rigid attention to a formal base and line of operations, so unsuitable to the nature of the service to be performed, particularly at a season when all the rivers were fordable.

Reference to Colonel Monson's disastrous Expedition.

Some satisfaction will be derived from the reflection, that the termination of hostilities with Holkur took place in a quarter where the British army formerly suffered its greatest disgrace, under less favourable circumstances, of which want of provisions was not the least. Whatever faults were to be attributed to Colonel Monson for the disasters which attended his ill-fated detachment in 1804, the superior Authority cannot be absolved from the responsibility of the deplorable consequences which followed this expedition. Colonel Monson was detached into the heart of Holkur's country, immediately previous to the filling of the rivers, with five Native battalions, and not a single European corps or a mounted soldier, except such irregulars as had lately been received into pay, and were therefore ill suited to be trusted in a situation so dangerous to their fidelity. He was to have co-operated with Colonel Murray from Goozerat; yet there appears to have been no combined plan established for them. Neither officer was consequently aware of the intentions of the other, and each retired to avoid the consequences of an unsupported contest. Under the circumstances of Colonel Monson's situation, if he was ordered to advance across such streams as the Bunnass and the Chumbul, it was his duty, in the absence of express orders to the contrary, to establish on their banks such posts as should give security to the means of recrossing them, to depôts of grain, and to small escorts following his rear. The strength of his force after these deductions should have determined the distance of his advance; for an offensive operation, or manœuvre, must ever be preceded by defensive dispositions. When he commenced his retreat, the badness of the roads soon obliged him to abandon his guns, and with them the means of keeping the enemy at a distance; while the desertion of his horse deprived him of the means of ascertaining their intentions and more distant movements. Always, however, when the troops were called on to act, they acquitted themselves with valour and effect; for the Bengal Sepoys fight well, and despise irregular horse as much as any infantry in the world. But after the passage of the Bunnass, so many difficulties accumulated around them, that they lost all confidence in themselves, and in a leader who was unable to encourage them in their own language; and their further retreat was a complete rout.*

It was this disaster which taught the Native Powers, and particularly Holkur's army, to consider a British force as no longer invincible, or British measures as infallible; and when this was followed by the defence of Bhurtpoor, the impression was confirmed. Such, however, was the idea entertained of the perseverance of the British Government, that it had the credit of always contemplating with restlessness, the means of repairing the injury its reputation had sustained. Thus, whenever the object of any of its military preparations was not immediately obvious, it was the fashion to refer it to Bhurtpoor—a habit, which, probably, ceased only with the recent reduction of Hattrass. This published to India, most opportunely, that a strong profile was an insufficient security against the means and science at the disposal of the Governor-general.

Considerations respecting the general conduct of operations in India.

It will follow, from what has been related, that however successful a direct attack of an Indian army in the field may invariably prove, able general arrangements † are the indispensable basis of the successful termina-

---

* The force with which Colonel Carnac penetrated from the Jumnah to Seronge in 1781, was precisely of the same strength with Colonel Monson's, and in many respects found itself similarly situated there; for it was harassed on all sides, deprived of supplies, and abandoned by the Native allies whose friendship was calculated on. In this distress it recurred to the unfailing expedient of offensive manœuvre, and at night-fall marched to attack Madhajee Scindiah's camp, thirteen miles distant. This succeeded agreeably to the most sanguine expectation, for the enemy were dispersed, leaving many guns, ammunition, and elephants on the ground; after which, the premeditated retreat from Scindiah's territories became unnecessary.

† These are, in fact, nothing more than "a good beginning:" an expression which, however trite and proverbial now, was equally considered an old saying in the time of Polybius. "For when the ancients said that a work begun was half completed, their intention was to warn us that, in every undertaking, our greatest pains should be employed to make a good beginning. And though this manner of expression may be thought by many to be raised beyond truth, yet, in my judgment, it rather falls below it. For we may boldly say, not only that a work begun is half completed, but also that the beginning is connected closely even with the end. For how can we

tion of a campaign. These arrangements must, no doubt, be decided by principles which have received the confirmation of experience since the art of war was reduced to a science. Yet their successful application, under circumstances so different from those which gave them birth, can only be the result of great natural sagacity or experience. A British division which keeps the field, is frequently so small as to be incapable of making a considerable detachment. Yet without detaching or falling back, it cannot bring up its convoys, which occasionally must move some hundred miles through a hostile country, between the source of supply and the front of the operations. This is one of many considerations, which are fairly calculated to startle a commander unversed in the conduct of a campaign in India; for whatever alternative be adopted, seems to involve the loss of whatever advantage may have been gained. The success which attended the advance of General Wellesley's convoys in 1803, will appear more surprising than accountable. Their escorts were always weak; the distance of their march was considerable; and they were frequently attacked and threatened by enemies, whose disparity of numbers seemed to admit of no hopes of safety. Yet either by general good arrangement, by particular stratagem, by the undauntedness of the troops, or perhaps by the fortunes* of the General, they arrived in safety. They were, however, generally commanded by able and experienced † officers; and supposing it was always possible to

---

properly begin, unless we have viewed our undertaking to its utmost bounds; and known from whence the work is to proceed, to what limits we design to extend it, and what also is the end proposed?"—Hampton's Polybius, ii. p. 200. 8vo. edit.

* Fortune is a most desirable ally, however uncertain she may be considered; and though in the selection of a commander, her attachment to him may not openly be acknowledged as a motive, the circumstance will have its weight, where Court influence does not interpose against public opinion. The ancients were not so squeamish of confessing her influence; and Cicero, a philosopher as well as an orator, in giving instructions for the composition of a funeral oration, desires that, in the case of a General, he shall be extolled for his good fortunes, as well as for his bravery and skill.

† Captain Baynes, with a few companies of Native infantry and four hundred Mysore horse, repulsed the attack of five thousand of the Rajah of Berar's horse, on the 31st of October, 1803; and brought in safety his convoy of fourteen thousand bullocks to Aurungabad, whither General Wellesley's camp had fallen back from Berar to favour this junction. In the same year, treasure amounting to three lacs and a half of rupees was dispatched from the British territory towards Hydrabad, for the use of the army in the field, under an escort of a single company of Native in-

make the selection, it may be concluded, that in their abilities the commander had placed much of his reliance for success.

While giving due credit to the troops and the plans which reduced Holkur's power in so short a period, compared with a less effectual campaign against him in 1804, the great change which had taken place in his army, as well as in that of other Native Powers, must not be overlooked. Comparison of the Wars with Holkur, in 1804 and 1817.

Jeswunt Rao Holkur certainly had superior military qualities; and under his personal command the army of his State arrived at the summit of its celebrity. His victory over Scindiah and the Peishwah in 1802, had given him great reputation; and he cunningly deferred his hostilities till the British army had been much exhausted by a campaign, in which the forty battalions of Perron had, after several severe actions, been destroyed. The regular battalions in Holkur's service had been commanded by Europeans as well as those of Scindiah; but these being all British subjects, who refused to fight against a British Government, they were put to death by the orders of Holkur, who relied on his own skill, independent of the aid of foreigners. This was only in character with the previous events of his life; for his birth was illegitimate, and his rise effected by his natural cun-

---

fantry, commanded by Lieutenant Wight. Near Paungul, this rich convoy, laden on bullocks, was attacked by a body of fourteen hundred men, on the 11th of December, and defended during two hours with a loss of twenty-two men out of one hundred; but the enemy was repulsed and the treasure saved, though it was subsequently obliged to take post till reinforced by an additional escort from Hydrabad.

The example on the side of Bengal is less striking, because all convoys were drawn from the Jumnah, a comparatively short line; and this difference renders it the more necessary to be mentioned, lest no greater dangers, than a small detachment can repel, should be inferred to exist, from the foregoing instances. One convoy of one hundred camels was lost on the 4th of October, 1804, within a short distance of the Commander-in-Chief's camp, near Muttra; and a convoy from that place, of twelve thousand bullocks, escorted by a regiment of Native cavalry and a battalion of Native infantry, was, within a few miles of the camp at Bhurtpoor, attacked by Meer Khan, with eight thousand horse and foot, and saved only by a seasonable reinforcement of a regiment of dragoons and another of Native cavalry. In like manner a convoy of military stores, treasure, and grain, on eight hundred carts, and fifty thousand bullocks, escorted from Agra, for the siege of Bhurtpoor, by a regiment of dragoons, two regiments of Native cavalry, and three battalions of Native infantry, was attacked by all the horse of the Rajah of that place, and of Holkur's and his other auxiliaries; and was only rescued from destruction by the movement of all the remaining cavalry, and two battalions, under General Lake's personal command.

ning, activity, and ambition. With such qualities, he wrested the government from the legitimate and elder brother, Cashee Rao, whose timidity and weakness were unable to support a contest, and who in fact had resigned his claim in favour of Scindiah. The regular battalions were gained over, notwithstanding the inflexibility of their commander, Dudranee, who fled to Perron when he could no longer controul the sentiments of his corps. This officer it was who originally raised them for the service of Tokajee Holkur, Jeswunt Rao's father, in 1791, when they consisted of four battalions only, but were gradually encreased to the twenty-four which took the field in the last Mahratta war. The sudden rise of his power was therefore as remarkable as his precipitate downfall; and having now brought under view his power during the Mahratta wars of 1804 and 1817, it may be acceptable to the reader to have a cursory retrospect of the progress of the Holkur State, traced from a remoter period.

View of the progress of the Holkur State from its establishment.

Jeswunt Rao's father, Tokajee Holkur, was the first of the name who had any transaction with the British, during a long government of thirty-one years, from 1766 to 1797; and he was the nephew of the first of the Holkurs, Mulhar Rao, who received lands in Malwah for his services, as the leader of a northern Mahratta army. This establishment of the family took place about the year 1736; and in the life of the first chief, there was no collision with the British interests. It was during Tokajee's government that important transactions between the Bombay Residency and the Mahrattas had their commencement. Holkur, like all the other Mahratta chiefs, was interested in the contest of the Peishwah Ragobah, whom the British Government supported, for certain cessions about Soorut and Bombay; with which he purchased their assistance in 1775. These cessions were in the following year relinquished, with the exception of Salsette, by the Treaty of Poorunder concluded with the ministers of Poonah, Ragobah's enemies. In 1779, the unfortunate expedition from Bombay for Ragobah's re-establishment, was the commencement of a war in which Holkur was again engaged against the British. He offered no opposition to the march of General Goddard from Calpee to Soorut that year; but was conjoined with Scindiah in operations against him in Goozerat in 1780. In 1781 General Goddard was employed to command an expedition against Poonah, which it was expected would be deprived of Holkur's assistance, by a *demonstration* made against his own territories in Malwah, from the side of

Bengal. This expectation was, however, unfounded, for Holkur despised the menace, and assumed a position at the head of the Boar Ghat, to oppose the passage of the British army from Bombay. In this he was worsted by a spirited attack of General Goddard, which carried all his batteries; and after the general peace, negotiated in 1782-3, he never appears acting against the British, till the last Mahratta war, when he had risen to that importance from which the present war has obliged him to descend.

BOOK II.

CHAPTER I.

PURSUIT OF THE PEISHWAH TO THE REDUCTION OF SATARA.

Flight of Bajee Rao to the Southward; pursued by the Fourth Division. Flight and Pursuit to the Northward. Return of the Peishwah towards Poonah, and consequent Alarm there. Gallant Defence of Koreigaum. Successful Retreat to Serroor. Reflections on this Exploit. European Troops in India, how to be considered. Return of the Fourth Division to Serroor. March of the Deckan Reserve from Chinnoor to Punderpoor. Countermarch to secure a Convoy. Pursuit of the Peishwah to the Southward. Reflections on the Service of Cavalry. On Horse-artillery. The Peishwah turned to the Northward. The Pursuit resumed by the Fourth Division. Junction of both Divisions, and Reduction of Satara.

THE operations of the Fourth Division and of the Reserve of the Army of the Deckan, were unconnected with those of the divisions in Malwah. It has therefore been found convenient to defer a description of them, till they might be brought under one view. These operations, after the Peishwah's flight from Poonah, consisted of a pursuit so unremitting as to offer few incidents on which the narrative may rest. Yet the unvarying circumstances which may possibly impair the interest of this chapter, are those which entitle the troops employed to the praise of fortitude and perseverance. In the relation of this part of the work no prolixity could render it more deserving of attention. Yet while this reason may be sufficient to account for the summary manner which is here proposed, it must be confessed that the materials are, on some occasions, too scanty for a more diffuse method. This observation particularly applies to the Fourth Division, whose marches, as well as those of the Reserve, were incessant; and so harassing, as to leave little leisure for recording, or even for reporting minutely, the result of their exertions. The country, likewise, was so much occupied by scattered parties of the enemy, as to render extremely difficult the transmission of the smallest paper of intelligence; and where it did pass, considerable delay, and risk to the bearer, attended its progress.

Flight of Bajee Rao to the southward, pursued by the Fourth Division.

(Map VI.)

Brigadier-general Smith's arrangements at Poonah having been completed on the 21st of November, he commenced his march on the following day, in search of the enemy, who were understood to be at Mahaollee, near Satara, where the Nepunkur joined him with one thousand Arabs and two thousand horse. On the 24th the Brigadier-general was at Rajwarrah, where he halted to rest his troops, after the fatigues undergone, through the whole of the previous day, in getting his heavy guns up the little Boar Ghat. On the 25th the division made a march of twenty-four miles, during which it came in sight of two thousand of the enemy in front, whom the Brigadier-general pursued with the cavalry, horse-artillery, and light battalion, but without coming up with them. A larger body hung on his rear during the latter part of the day, but without depriving him of many bullocks. On the 27th the division halted at the foot of the Salpee Ghat, which it ascended the following day, under a shew of opposition from a body, who threw some rockets, and increased towards the end of the march to the number of three or four thousand; while in the rear there was an equal number. On that and the following night, the Peishwah was at Poossasaollee, which he left before day-light of the 29th, by the road to Merritch, with five thousand horse, composed of the Nepunkur's* and Putwurdhun's*; confiding to Gokla*, with the main body, the service of obstructing the march of his pursuers. This chief, with the Vinchoorkur* and the elder Gorparah*, placed themselves at the Neivee pass, expecting that the division would march that way; but it made a *detour* by the right, and disappointed this arrangement, arriving in four marches from the Salpee Ghat at Poossasaollee, where it halted on the 2d of December.

Flight and pursuit to the northward.

In the mean while, the Peishwah, flying south from Brigadier-general Smith, found himself necessitated to double towards the northward by Punderpoor. For, at this time, the Reserve under Brigadier-general Pritzler,

* See the Description of the Peishwah's Forces, p. 16.

was advancing from the Kistnah, as will be hereafter described; and further to the east was the Nizam's frontier. The division followed the Peishwah to Punderpoor, and halted there on the 8th and 9th, having been greatly incommoded and harassed during the march, by large bodies of horse, which surrounded it, and contracted its means of procuring provisions. On the 9th at night, an attempt was made to beat up the *bivouac* of the principal body of the enemy under Gokla, distant about ten miles. For this purpose a detachment of six hundred men, with two gallopers, was placed under the orders of Lieutenant-colonel Wilson, of the Bombay European regiment. But a smaller body, belonging to the Vinchoor chief, being found in the road, the necessity of attacking them prevented the surprise of the main body.*

Flight and pursuit to the Northward.

Learning at Punderpoor that the Peishwah had gone to Peirgaum, the division followed in that direction, crossing the Neerah at Soorut, and the Beemah at Kundoogaum. As from hence he continued his flight towards Nassuck on the Godavery, the pursuit was maintained without a halt, to Serroor, where the division arrived on the 17th, and was joined by the 2d battalion of the 15th Madras Native infantry, which had encamped there since the 6th. This arduous march of three hundred miles in twenty-six days was performed with the incumbrance of heavy guns; for on leaving Poonah, it was a matter of great uncertainty what measures would be adopted by the Peishwah, who had the option either of keeping the field, or of standing a siege in one of his numerous strong forts. As that measure appeared no longer probable, Brigadier-general Smith dropped his train at Serroor, and made other arrangements for a more expeditious pursuit. These occupied him till the 21st, when he received a convoy of provisions from Bombay. Thus prepared, the next day he left Serroor, under the command of Colonel Fitzsimon, with orders to detach the 2d battalion of the 15th Madras Native infantry to Peirgaum on the Beemah, to join the Reserve shortly expected in that quarter; and marched lightly equipped, passing Ahmednuggur on the 24th, and crossing the Pheira on the 26th, at Colar. He was induced to follow this route, from understanding that the Peishwah had proceeded to the left by Kullum and Jooneer, where there were several passes, which, it was reported, the enemy had broken up. It was also

* See Appendix H. 1. for Casualties to this date.

in the Brigadier-general's view to interpose between the Peishwah and the Ghats of Khandesh. On the arrival of the division on the Pheira, the enemy, finding it already north of him, abandoned his intention of visiting Nassuck, and fled precipitately to the southward.

Return of the Peishwah towards Poonah, and consequent alarm there.

The division continued its march up the river to Sungumneir. It being ascertained there, that the Peishwah, having been joined by Trimbukjee's infantry, had suddenly taken the road towards Poonah, the division followed him, as expeditiously as possible, through a rough and confined country. The passage of the Wassoora Ghat, on the 29th, was attended with considerable difficulty; the rear guard not rejoining till noon the following day, from the necessity of dragging all the guns, through the Ghat, by hand. To obviate further delay, the division was formed into two parts: one * continued the direct pursuit under the Brigadier-general's personal command; and the other † descended the Ghats under Colonel Boles, to prevent the Peishwah's return towards Khandesh by an eastern route. The head-quarters of the division marched by Wuttoor and Kullum, and on the 2d of January, reached Chakun; the Peishwah having arrived there, on the 30th of December, with the supposed intention of repossessing himself of the capital, which was within eighteen miles of that place. The division was, at the same time, distant one hundred and twenty-eight miles. As the Peishwah was also accompanied by the whole of his army, and had a powerful influence among the inhabitants, much solicitude was naturally excited in the mind of the commanding officer, for the safety of the important charge confided to him.

Colonel Burr had, at this time, under his command three Native battalions, including one of the auxiliary corps, with some light artillery. Also Major Cunningham had arrived at Poonah, on the 28th of December, with seventeen hundred irregular horse, for the purpose of mustering and paying them there. The Colonel, doubtful of Brigadier-general Smith's movements, was only certain of his being at a considerable distance; which appeared so remote, as to favour the supposed designs of

---

* Consisting of the horse-artillery, the second regiment of Madras cavalry, his Majesty's 65th regiment of foot, the light battalion, and the 1st battalion of the 2d regiment of Bombay Native infantry.

† Composed of the foot-artillery, the Bombay European regiment, and two Native battalions.

the Peishwah. In this state of affairs, he considered himself authorized to augment his means by calling to his aid another battalion of Native infantry from Serroor. Accordingly, at his requisition, Captain Staunton marched with the 2d battalion of the 1st Bombay Native infantry, two guns under Lieutenant Chisholm, of the Madras artillery, and Lieutenant Swanston's detachment of two hundred and fifty reformed horse.

Gallant defence of Koreigaum. (Plan 15.)

This detachment left Serroor, on the 31st of December, at eight P. M.; and at ten the following forenoon, had reached the high ground overlooking Koreigaum, at twenty-seven miles distance from Serroor. Captain Staunton (*A*) was now presented with a most cheerless prospect. In the valley below, lay the whole of the Peishwah's army, consisting of twenty thousand horse and nearly eight thousand foot, encamped on the right bank of the Beemah, (*E E E E.*) above the village of Koreigaum; under the walls of which, the high road to Poonah crossed the river by a ford. Luckily for this detachment, the road to the village, which was on the left bank, was unoccupied by the enemy. Captain Staunton pushed for the walls of Koreigaum, and succeeded in gaining that position, before it fell entirely into the hands of the enemy. They were little aware of the approach of the detachment; but soon concluding what measure it would adopt, they likewise detached some infantry to secure the village. Both parties accordingly succeeded in occupying a part; and the village was immediately afterwards surrounded by bodies of horse and foot, with two heavy guns. The Peishwah ascended an eminence at some distance to await the contest, and to encourage the (*D.*) troops by his presence; while his principal chiefs gathering round him, flattered his hopes with the early destruction of this small but resolute band.

The village of Koreigaum is very irregular, and composed of terraced buildings, some of them substantial and surrounded with a wall. It also contains a small *choultry*, of which the British gained possession; but the most commanding situation was left to the enemy. Good positions were however obtained for the two guns, to command the avenues by which the enemy might approach in force; but even this advantage was greatly reduced, by their being exposed to a sniping fire from neighbouring walls. The village became extremely crowded; both horse and foot, as well as baggage, cattle, and followers, being obliged to take shelter in it; and a multitude of the enemy pressing on them with daring impetuosity. Situated as the two parties were, the British had every reason to expect, that even a desperate resistance must soon be overcome; and Captain Staunton failing in his endeavours to drive the enemy from their strong positions, was reduced to the measure of defending his own.

In this state was the detachment, at twelve o'clock at noon, cut off from the water, under a burning sun, after a long night march and no subsequent repose. On entering the village, it consisted of five hundred Native infantry, and twenty-six European artillery, besides the horse, who had no room to act, and were unsuitably armed for defence, when dismounted. These troops were commanded by eight European officers, including two assistant-surgeons, who were more usefully employed in encouraging the fighting men, than in attending the wounded. The infantry of the enemy, who advanced to the attack of the village, are represented as three bodies of one thousand men each. They were all, probably, Arabs, for that corps with the Peishwah was estimated at three thousand. No regular description can be expected of such a conflict. It consisted, on one side, of impetuous attacks, repulsed by desperate sallies from the other; for, when closely pressed, the detachment, in order to gain room, was obliged to charge with the bayonet. This measure, therefore, was frequently repeated, and with success; but as a charge must always be led by an European officer, the majority of these became disabled by death, or wounds, in successive attacks. So much execution was done by the guns, that the enemy found no important impression could be made till they were taken. These, therefore, became the object of all the direct attacks; as well as of the galling fire kept up, with aim, from behind some walls. In one of these assaults a gun was taken, Lieutenant Chisholm was killed, and his severed head sent off as a trophy to the Peishwah; but the gun was immediately afterwards retaken by a successful charge, and the enemy driven out with much loss by the way they came in.

In the course of the day, Lieutenants Swanston and Connellan, and Assistant-surgeon Wingate, who were severely wounded, were placed for safety in the *choultry*; but this small building fell into the enemy's possession in one of their successful attacks. Conceiving that this advantage ensured to them the victory, they gave way to the desire of plunder, and put Mr. Wingate to death, in a spirit of cruelty. The same fate awaited the two remaining officers, when Captain Staunton, Lieutenant Jones, and Mr. Wylie, the only officers left unhurt, vigorously charged the enemy in turn, recovered the *choultry*, with all the lost ground, and rescued the lives of their companions. Yet, with all the success which had hitherto attended the defence of Koreigaum, the loss was so great, and the exertion attended with so much exhaustion from want of water and refreshment, that some of the men, both European and Native, considered resistance hopeless, and expressed a desire to apply for terms. Their commanding officer, however, such is the result of education, formed a better judgment of the state of their affairs: while he encouraged them to persevere, he represented the forlorn prospect of a surrender to barbarous and cruel enemies, exasperated by the contemplation of their own losses. This exhortation had the desired effect, and the enemy began to doubt the success of further attacks. They however maintained their original position in the village till nine P. M., when they finally evacuated it to seek repose and refreshment; apprehensive, probably, of being exposed to attacks in their turn, if they remained longer. Under cover of the night the detachment got a supply of water, and made preparations for renewing the contest next morning, being now in possession of the whole of the village. But the enemy were satisfied with the attempts which had been already made; and day-light on the 2d discovered them preparing to move off on the Poonah road. This had now become necessary, as on that day Brigadier-general Smith arrived at Chakun. (Map VI)

From subsequent accounts it appears, that the Peishwah's army were to have marched, on the previous day, from Koreigaum, though their movement was deferred unusually late; and that, had the detachment arrived there an hour later, this severe contest would never have occurred. Captain Staunton was entirely ignorant of the position of the Fourth Division. It was therefore incumbent on him to provide for his retreat to the point from whence he marched. His want of ammunition and provisions precluded his remaining where he was, and the continuance of his progress to Poonah was impracticable, seeing the enemy already occupied that road. It seems, at the same time, that they expected this measure to be attempted; as they lay all that day and night at Loonee. They, also, endeavoured to induce the detachment to move to the same place, by sending in spies, as from Major Cunningham, with an invitation to meet him there, and to march into Poonah. Captain Staunton appeared to acquiesce, and made his arrangements for the conveyance of his sick; for some, who were able to ride, on bullocks; and for the remainder, in blankets slung to a pole, to be carried by their comrades. But, as night fell, instead of fol- Successful Retreat to Serroor lowing the expected route, he took that of Serroor, and at nine o'clock the next morning the detachment entered that place, with their guns and wounded, with drums beating and colours flying. Lieutenant Patterson here died of his wounds, but the two remaining wounded officers recovered. Of twenty-six artillerymen, twelve were killed and eight wounded; of Native infantry, there were fifty killed and one hundred and five wounded; and of the reformed horse, ninety-six killed, wounded, and missing: while the loss of the enemy was estimated at six or seven hundred men. This will be easily accounted for, by adverting to the situation in which their attacks were necessarily made, in avenues raked by the two guns. On one of these occasions they are represented as having suffered a dreadful loss. An artilleryman serving his gun, half filled it with grape, and let them approach within a dozen yards of the muzzle before he applied the match; nor did it miss fire to disappoint his coolness, but discharged the unusual contents where no effect could be lost. It seems that this detachment marched with what would generally be held a superabundant supply of ammunition, both gun and musquet; the deficiency of which has been, on so many occasions, the cause of unavoidable surrender. The 2d battalion of the 15th Madras Native infantry, which had marched on the 23d of December for Peirgaum, returned by forced marches on the evening of the 2d to Serroor, having been called in from its insulated position, by repeated expresses, on the approach of the Peishwah.

Reflections on this Exploit.

It would be difficult to form any opinion but one, respecting the inflexible defence of Koreigaum. Thus the public, as well as every constituted authority, though differing in the expression of their sentiments on many occasions, concurred in bestowing their unqualified and enthusiastic commendation of the behaviour both of officers and men. In the general alacrity to acknowledge their services, the hackneyed expressions of applause appeared insufficient and unsatisfactory. In order to strain the imagination to the utmost, this brave detachment is represented as having defeated the attacks of the Peishwah's entire army. Such [illegible], probably, arises from a common quality of the human mind, which renders it incapable of forming a distinct idea, when under the influence of admiration; for there can be no greater mistake than to imagine the attack of Koreigaum by all the Peishwah's forces. His choicest infantry, amounting to near four times the numbers of the British force, assailed them, on all sides, with an impetuosity and perseverance, to be surpassed only by that with which the assaults were repelled. It does not even appear that this division of the enemy was ever relieved or reinforced. There were probably no more, brave enough to take their places. Reinforcement was also unnecessary, where already more were present than could act simultaneously. The twenty thousand cavalry were distributed over the plain, on both sides of the river; but none of this arm could be brought into action. The utmost effect which could have been produced by this developement of the whole army, was to appal, through the eye, a handful of men, with whose numbers there was no parity. But this handful was composed of soldiers who required to be addressed through other senses, and despised a display which could only impose on the ignorant and untried. The unembellished report* of the commanding officer, clear as it is modest, will always command, from the intelligent, higher admiration than any figurative exhibition. The facts were such, that their unadorned exposure presents the most forcible appeal for well-earned applause.† If a similar defence occurred in European warfare, and proposed for its object the detention of the enemy from some other point of great importance, it would be justly appreciated on that account; but in the absence of that, or some other object of equal moment, it is a question if such determination would be held excusable. The apparent hopelessness of the situation would afford sufficient arguments for the necessity of a surrender; and the detachment might, or might not, according to circumstances, be permitted to march out with the honours of war. But this reasoning applies to civilized warfare, where prisoners of war are treated with respect; whereas, with a Native enemy, no dependance can be placed on their promises of security. Whenever they have been trusted, immediate slaughter, or cruel treatment, has been the invariable consequence. The faith of a British officer is so well established, that Native garrisons will surrender to a British force; but, per-

---

* Vide Appendix. I.

† There appears a sort of fatality attached to the name of Koreigaum; for in a village of that appellation did Captain O'Donnell and Lieutenant Morgan, of the Madras Establishment, with a company of Native infantry, and details from corps in camp drafted into new corps, take post in 1803, on their march from Ahmednuggur. They were attacked by twelve hundred horse, and three times their own number of foot, at intervals, during two days, and as many nights, till relieved by a detachment sent to their assistance, after having in three sallies killed a number of their enemies equal to their own strength.

haps, there is no example of a body of troops, in the field, laying down their arms. When defeated, they expect no quarter; and the irregularity of their flight is such, as to afford no opportunity of offering them terms. Their chief is generally, on such an occasion, the first to fly; and there remains no one to be answerable for the rest, or to whom the victors can offer terms.

European Troops in India, how to be considered.

The characteristic, common to the defences of Koreigaum and Seetabuldee* is, that the positions were maintained without any European force, except the detail of artillery and the European officers. The corps which were engaged on these occasions have shewn themselves to be brave troops; and there are, no doubt, many more as good, on the establishments to which they belong. Yet it would be a dangerous precedent, to draw, from these events, arguments against the necessity, at all times, of a strong force of Europeans in India, even though an insulated instance might be shewn of a Native behaving better than an European corps. On this subject, some reasoning has been already adduced; and the opinion ought to be ever maintained, that the possession of India will be risked, whenever the number of Europeans shall be diminished. They are in the Indian army what, in ground, is the key of the position, in which the power is concentrated. They answer to the centre of gravity in physicks, which being supported, the body is held in equipoise. Did they even produce no other effect than the emulation excited by their presence, it would be deplorable impolicy to withdraw from the Native troops so strong a stimulus. European troops have ever maintained a high character in India for bravery and discipline, which are seldom separated; and they are always maintained under the immediate eye of their officers, who have few objects in this country to distract their attention. It is only required that their services should be properly applied: they were never meant for pursuing Pindarries. The irregularity of such services would injure their discipline; besides that, the train required for their provisions would render quite nugatory such an attempt. The European foot in India will act in the capacity of grenadiers†,

* The same remark applies to Colonel Montresor's defence of the position of Seedaseer with three battalions of Bombay Native infantry, on the 6th of March, 1799, against the Soolaun's army, during six hours, until relieved by General Stuart.

† Marshal Villars calls them, "*l'arme de l'infanterie.*"

which formerly in Europe composed a distinct corps*. The dragoons, in like manner, should be considered as the heavy horse; and, in a general war, they will never want an opportunity of being so used. Why more of them were not brought, in advance, from the Madras establishment, can only have arisen from the anticipation, that the operations of the war would be of too desultory a nature for their employment.

Return of the Fourth Division to Serroor.

On the 2d of January, B[illegible] Smith learned at Chakun the situation of Capt. Staunton's detachment, on the previous day, at Koreigaum, whither he hastened on the following morning to his relief. Finding that he had returned to Serroor, the head-quarters of the division halted on the 4th, having marched sixty-one miles during the last three days, after a constant movement of ten days since it left Serroor. On the 6th, it returned to that place, and halted there on the 7th, when it was rejoined by the detachment

---

* The late Tippoo Sooltaun shewed no bad idea of the use, though not of the management, of Europeans, when he declared, that had he a corps of them in his service, he would carry them all in *doolies*, and, on the proper occasion, slip them, like the hunting tiger, at their prey. The playfulness of the European character, compared with that of the Asiatic, throws an air of frolic over the most desperate undertakings. One of these was the storm of the rocky height near Careeghaut, on the 15th of May, 1791, occupied by the Sooltaun's forces, and crowned by a powerful battery. The preparations for this service were contemplated by the present Nuwaub of Ellichapoor, Sulabut Khan, then a young man, with a degree of wonder which seemed, in a manner, to suspend his faculties. When the attack succeeded, and he recovered from his astonishment, his first question to the late Sir Barry Close, near whom he happened then to be, was: " For friendship sake tell me, candidly and confidentially, were those countrymen of yours made drunk previous to the assault? for whether I consider the desperate nature of the service, or the gaiety with which it was undertaken, I am alike at a loss to attribute their conduct to men in their sober senses."

The following extract from Orme's account of the battle of the " Golden Rock" affords another example of this characteristic: " In such circumstances, the officers unanimously agreed in opinion with their general, that it was safer to make a gallant push, than to retreat before such numbers of enemies: and the soldiers seeming much delighted at this opportunity of having what they called a fair knock at the Frenchmen on the plains, Major Lawrence took advantage of the good disposition of the whole, and, giving due commendations to their spirit, ordered the grenadiers to attack the rock with fixed bayonets, whilst he himself, with the rest of the troops, wheeled round the foot of it, to engage the French battalion. The soldiers received the orders with three huzzas; and the grenadiers, setting out at a great rate, though at the same time keeping their ranks, paid no attention to the scattered fire they received from the rock, nor made a halt until they got to the top of it; whilst the enemy, terrified at their intrepidity, descended as they were mounting, without daring to stand the shock of their onset."—Book IV. A.D. 1753.

under Colonel Boles. As the further pursuit of the Peishwah brought the Fourth Division into co-operation with the Reserve, it will here be proper to recur to Brigadier-general Pritzler's movements from the Dooab*.

March of the Deckan Reserve from Chinnoor to Punderpoor. (Map VI.)

The Reserve Division, on the 20th of November, recommenced its march from Chinnoor; the cavalry-brigade having, two days before, proceeded in the direction of the Calachaboottra Ghat, pursuant to the original plan, which has been noticed (pp. 58, 59.) It had however scarcely moved, when intelligence was received of the rupture at Poonah. It was immediately directed to march upon Nowlie, on the Kistnah, with a design to cross that river. But that Ghat was, on examination, found less favourable than the Dunnoor or Tuguduhal Ghat, on the high road between Bellary and Poonah. Thither, accordingly, the Reserve proceeded, by the route of Moodgul, and arrived, on the 25th, on the right bank of the Kistnah. The passage of the river occupied till the 5th of December; the light artillery, under Lieutenant-colonel Dalrymple, having, three days previously, joined from Bellary. The delay of this operation, though the elephants and camels were enabled to ford immediately above the ferry, arose from the scarcity and small size of the boats, of which twelve only could be procured. This division was now prepared to advance in the direction of Poonah, for which purpose the Resident there had addressed a requisition to Brigadier-general Pritzler. After crossing the Kistnah, the Brigadier-general had reason to expect that he should be early annoyed by the enemy's horse, as affairs had reached that crisis when, under a Native Government, every armed man, who has a horse, leaves his home to profit by the confusion of the times. Five marches brought the force, on the 11th, to Beejapoor, by Chimblighee and Ballottee. During the last day's movement, some thousands of the enemy appeared on the left; but on finding preparations made to attack them, they retired with precipitation, pursued by the British cavalry. Brigadier-general Pritzler continued his march without interruption till his arrival, on the 17th, at Punderpoor, by the route of Jallihal and Hooljettee, having been in motion without a halt twelve days.

Countermarch to secure a Convoy.

At this time a convoy of grain and supplies, under the charge of Lieutenant Kensey, and two companies of the 2d battalion of the 12th regiment, which followed the route of the Reserve from the Ceded Districts, had arrived

---

* Literally, " Two Waters," being, in this instance, the country situate between the rivers Toombudra and Kistnah.

within a march of Beejapoor, when the Lieutenant found its safety threatened by parties of the enemy hanging on his progress. He accordingly took up a position, for his better security. The intelligence of this measure reached Brigadier-general Pritzler at Punderpoor. A detachment was, in consequence, sent to the relief of Lieutenant Kensey, on the 21st of December, under the command of Captain Baker, of the rifle corps. It consisted of four companies of that battalion, and one squadron of the 7th regiment of Native cavalry. On the 24th, the division fell back to favour the junction of the convoy, and arrived on the 27th at Hooljettee, where it halted on the 28th. The division was enabled, by the approach of the convoy, to return on the 29th towards Punderpoor, and reached that place on the 1st of January, when it was overtaken by the escort with all the commissariat supplies.

Pursuit of the Peishwah to the Southward.

After a day's halt at Punderpoor, preparatory to an active march in search of the enemy, Brigadier-general Pritzler recommenced his movement on the 3d of January. On the following day, he arrived at Auklooss, having learned that the Peishwah was on his return southward; for that chief had, only the day before, left Koreigaum. In order to intercept him, the march was still continued up the Neerah, and the division arrived, on the 6th, in the vicinity of Fultun. There finding that the Peishwah was passing the head of the column to the southward, the direction of the Salpee Ghat was taken, in order to follow him. He arrived, on the 7th, at Mahaollee, in the vicinity of Satara, having again divided his force to favour his flight. The rear detachment, as on a former occasion, in front of Brigadier-general Smith, made a shew of opposition, at the head of the pass, on the 8th, when the Reserve ascended. The cavalry were sent to attack the enemy's horse, who were in considerable bodies. Coming up with one of these, it cut to pieces about fifty of them; but an impression was made on the baggage, many grain-bullocks being driven off, with some stragglers. The Peishwah did not await, at Satara, the ascent of the Salpee Ghat by his pursuers; but, on the night of the 7th, fled again down the left bank of the Kistnah, and reached, on the 11th, the vicinity of Merritch. Brigadier-general Pritzler followed him, by forced marches, by Poossasaollee, Tan-gaum, Malgaum near Merritch, and Erroor on the Kistnah, which he crossed on the 15th; the Peishwah having passed, at the same place, two days before. From hence this chief sent off his infantry, unable to keep up with so rapid a flight, to Neepaunee; and fled himself across the Gutpurba, near Gokauk, as if to Badaumee; leaving a large corps under Gokla and the Vinchoorkur to dispute the progress of his pursuers. This corps, accordingly, on the 17th, after the Reserve had taken up its ground, appeared in broken parties, and approached to reconnoitre the camp. At first the cavalry pickets were ordered out, while the enemy endeavoured to drive off some camp cattle. They were afterwards supported by the rest of the cavalry; and the line was ordered under arms, when the numbers of horse increased. They at first shewed two large divisions, about two miles from the camp. One of these, Major Doveton, with one squadron of his Majesty's 22d dragoons, and two squadrons of Native cavalry, charged and routed. After this, re-forming his corps, he proceeded to the left to attack the second, which manœuvre carried him to a considerable distance. On turning to rejoin the line, he found a third body of the enemy, formed from parts of the other two, interposed between him and the camp. To free himself from this body, he charged a third time, and returned with the loss of only three men; while that of the enemy was computed at from fifty to a hundred. Estimating this exploit by the loss which attended its success, it appears very inconsiderable; but it was expected to deter the enemy from again making a *demonstration,* which put the troops, after a long march, to considerable inconvenience. There is, indeed, no doubt that the freedom with which the cavalry of the Reserve were always detached, contributed to keep its line of march much more free from annoyance than that of the other division engaged on the same service. This visit was, however, a sort of farewell, as on the following day the enemy's horse went off to interpose themselves between the Peishwah and nearer enemies.

Reflections on the Service of Cavalry.

To an eye unaccustomed to contemplate large numbers of Native horse in solid though irregular bodies, they must appear a formidable object * for the attack of a few squadrons; but a consideration of their composition removes the impression; while to an officer like Major Doveton, who had served long in India, habit had rendered such reasoning superfluous. An allusion has already been made to that want of sympathy between the parts of an irregular body, which prevents them from depending on the assistance

* On this point Orme has a similar remark—" Whosoever has seen a body of ten thousand horse advancing on the full gallop altogether, will acknowledge, with the Mareschals Villars and Saxe, that their appearance is tremendous, be their discipline or courage what it will."—Vol. I. page 293.

of each other. Its size prevents the attack of a small but compact corps from being otherwise than partially received; and as an equal front of an irregular body can never stand such a shock, the part menaced must give way. The body is thus broken, and each part acts on the principle of avoiding an exposure to the sole and concentrated brunt of the action. While the part immediately attacked flies, did the remainder fall on the rear of its pursuers, the chace must be immediately abandoned. This, however, would imply a degree of combination, the absence of which is supposed; and the facility with which disciplined squadrons divide, reassemble, charge, and halt, by a single trumpet-sound, keeps each part of the enemy in that constant alarm of being separately attacked, which reduces all its efforts to the object of self-preservation. It was, therefore, no want of individual courage which produced the misbehaviour of the enemy, either on this occasion or on that of Captain Fitzgerald's charge at Nagpoor; but the apprehension, however paradoxical it may appear, of being obliged to contend against odds. Our cavalry are too few in number to authorize the experiment of loose skirmishing. If that were tried, it would soon be found that those horse, now so despicable in a body, would be most formidable in detail. The best arm against the enemy's skirmishers are the horse-artillery, which will always oblige them to withdraw. If to these be attached a party of either horse or light infantry, or both, as an active reserve, the cavalry may attack and pursue with little risk.

On Horse-artillery.

These reflections give occasion to mention the subject of horse-artillery, and its application in Indian warfare. In fact their greatest impression is made by *demonstration**; but as long as that impression is great, it matters little how it is effected. In the absence of numerous cavalry, they perform, in a reserve, a most important part to that arm, as above-mentioned. They will be thrown forward, with proper support, to great advantage, for the acquisition or temporary maintenance of a point during other formations. Their use also will be truly understood in a general action, by having a battery of them in reserve, to be produced where not expected, on the critical

* An important use of horse-artillery in Europe is the means it affords of reducing a discomfited enemy to the necessity of laying down their arms; for the rapidity of its movement deprives them of the hopes of escape by flight; but it has been already shewn, that no *demonstration* can make a body of fugitive troops in India surrender themselves prisoners of war after an immediate defeat.

occasion of any special effort. All these services have a character of vivacity, and not of perseverance, for which horse-artillery are little calculated; being more exposed to injury than the unassuming foot-artillery, whose solid worth is proved by their ability to make a deep and lasting impression. The horse-artillery partake of the shewy nature of the cavalry. Their whole system of manœuvre and instruction, appointment and dress, is calculated by rapidity and noise to compensate for the want of precision and weight.

The Peishwah turned to the Northward.

The Reserve continued the pursuit of the Peishwah, and on the 19th of January crossed the Gutpurba to Caogully; where, finding he had recrossed, and was returning towards the Kistnah, the division likewise marched to that river, and arrived at Gullagullee on the 23d, having recrossed the Gutpurba at Moodagolah. Though this unremitting march had turned the Peishwah back to the northward, and therefore averted the danger that seemed to threaten the British territory by his approach to its frontier, the pursuit was by no means relaxed till arriving at Seedapoor, on the 27th, by a march up the Kistnah, it was ascertained that the enemy, who had passed Kuttanee seven days before, were now followed by the Fourth Division, under Brigadier-general Smith. The Reserve halted on the 28th and 29th, having marched three hundred and forty-six miles in twenty-five successive days.

The Pursuit resumed by the Fourth Division.

On the 8th of January, Brigadier-general Smith had recommenced his march from Serroor, having with his head-quarters, as formerly, a lightly equipped division, and leaving with Colonel Boles the less active part of the force, in charge of the battering-train, to act as a reserve, and cover Poonah by movements in that neighbourhood. The march was conducted without molestation from an enemy, or any extraordinary occurrence, till the 21st, when the division arrived, by the route of Peirgaum, Fultun, Raja Nuddee, and Sheitpool, at Keeleigaum. There it was ascertained that the Peishwah, in his flight from the Reserve, had crossed to Kuttanee, on the left bank of the Kistnah. From hence he fled to Erroor, and there made a shew of pitching his tents, giving out, with a view of drawing the Fourth Division in that direction, that he was proceeding to Neepaunee. He struck his tents again after a few hours; and when he calculated on having misled his pursuers, he suddenly turned to the northward, and went with great celerity by Islampoor and Kuraur to Satara. Brigadier-general Smith, in the mean while, made a forced march of twenty-eight miles on the 22d, to Augur, there receiving faithful intelligence of the ultimate route of the Peishwah up the right bank of the Kistnah. On the following day he directed his march on Merritch, very much harassed by the enemy's horse pressing on his rear-guard. On the 24th they were on both flanks, in numbers estimated at ten thousand. They likewise closed on the rear, till the division found itself obliged to take up ground, by the difficulty with which the baggage advanced in a rugged country, incessantly threatened by the enemy. The line then moved out to repel these attacks, which were more daring than on any former occasion, as the enemy stood the fire of five six-pounders and a howitzer for a considerable time. They, however, effected their object in preventing further progress during that day; for the rapid strides made by the division alarmed them for the safety of the Peishwah, who depended now, as formerly, on Gokla's exertions to impede the advance of his pursuers. The Brigadier-general had previously received instructions from Mr. Elphinstone, to re-organize two corps, with the assistance of the Reserve; one of which should contain all the means of pursuit, and the other all the necessary equipment for a siege. Colonel Boles was accordingly directed to bring forward the battering-train for that purpose. The pursuit of the Peishwah carried the Brigadier-general to meet it by the route of Poossasaollee, and the Salpee Ghat, to Lonud. There he arrived on the 30th, having gained considerably on the fugitive, notwithstanding the constant skirmishing kept up with the enemy's horse, who galled the line of march with rockets, and a fire from distant matchlocks. The Peishwah fled by Fultun; and his horse, who were latterly diminished perceptibly, endeavoured to follow him by the shortest road, after passing Satara. From this they were cut off, and obliged to make a *detour* to get down the Ghats, which threw them, on the 29th, into the valley in which the division was encamped. In this situation the cavalry, horse-artillery, and some flank companies of Europeans and Natives, were sent against them. A part escaped, at speed, in great consternation, to the front; others fled back by the road on which they had advanced. The remainder, with some baggage, sought shelter among the hills, where they fell into the hands of the infantry sent in that direction.*

* See Appendix. H. 2. for casualties to this date.

Junction of both Divisions, and Reduction of Satara.

Having met Colonel Boles's detachment at Lonud, the division halted from the 31st to the 3d of February. On that day it commenced its counter-march to Rymutpoor, where it arrived on the 6th, and halted on the 7th. The Reserve, under B[illegible] Pritzler, was marching since the 30th of January on the same point by Ynapoor, Tausgaum, and Poossasaollee; and on the 7th of February it joined the Fourth Division. On the 8th and 9th, both divisions were at Koreigaum*; and on the following day encamped within three miles of the fort of Satara, which surrendered that evening after receiving a few shells. The place contained twenty-five pieces of ordnance, of different calibers; and the garrison, consisting of four hundred Sebundies†, were permitted to march out with their arms; for, having shewn themselves so little inclined to use them, it was considered unimportant how they went off. The Rajah of Satara's flag was hoisted on the 11th, under a royal salute; and it was also proclaimed to the neighbouring inhabitants, that the fortress was to be considered as the head of a sovereignty, sufficient for the comfort and dignity of the descendants of the ancient Rajahs.

It is generally known that these had been for some generations confined by the Peishwahs, who still acknowledged a nominal superiority; but so little were they brought into notice, that their existence has been merely inferred‡ from the Peishwah's going to Satara to receive the investiture of office. This, however, appears to be the first occasion of any interference on the part of the British Government respecting them; or, indeed, of any transaction with this line§ of Sevajee, if we except that chief's two attacks of the British establishment at Soorut in 1668 and 1670.

---

* This place will not be confounded with Koreigaum, the scene of Captain Staunton's achievement. (p. 179.)

† Troops employed in the collection of the Revenue.

‡ See Note at the end of Rennell's "Sketch of the Mahratta History."

§ The Rajahs of Nagpoor are likewise descendants of Sevajee, as are those of Colapoor. See Wilks's South of India, chap. xxvi.

CHAPTER II.

EXPULSION OF THE PINDARRIES FROM THE LEFT OF THE CHUMBUL.

Separation of Ameer Khan's Army. Detachment of a Light Force from the Centre and Third Divisions of the Grand Army, under Major-general Brown, and Recall of Colonel Philpot's Detachment. Major-general Brown's Attack of the insubordinate Remains of Holkur's Army at Rampoora. Advance of the Head-quarters of the Second Division to Sanganeir. Advance of the Goozerat Division to Burra-Sadree. Captain Grant's Detachment at Jawud. Re-assembly of the Second Division at Shapoorra. Lieutenant-colonel Russell's Detachment from the Deckan Army at Purtabghur, and Reinforcement of Captain Grant's Detachment on the Advance of the Guickwar Contingent. Operations of the Goozerat Division in Meywar. Return of Captain Grant's Detachment to Mundissoor. Parties of Kurreem and Wassil Mahomud's Durrahs flying to the Eastward, are attacked and dispersed with much Loss by a Detachment from the Fifth Deckan Division. Preparations for the Countermarch of the Head-quarters of the Army of the Deckan. Return to Mehidpoor, and Detachment under Major Lushington and Captain Grant to the Goozerat Frontier. The Army at Oojein. Movements of Captain Grant's Detachment. The Army at Indoor. Movements of Major Lushington's Detachment. Sir John Malcolm at Neemuj. Major-general Brown's successful Attack of Jeswunt Rao Bhao. Return to the Chumbul. Sir John Malcolm at Jawud. Operations of the Second Division of the Grand Army in Meywar. Submission of Beema Baee's Force to Sir William Grant Keir. Reflections on the Pursuit of the Pindarries.

THE Marquis of Hastings' head-quarters were still in the neighbourhood of the Sind, throughout December, though a movement of a few miles was made for change of ground from Sonaree to Oochar in the middle of that month; this position being as convenient for regulating and directing the operations in Malwah, as it had been found for controuling Scindiah. A communication by *dawke* * was maintained with all the divisions and de- (Plan 17.)

* By post.

tachments, and the means of reinforcement or re-organization were at all times in readiness, to be applied where required.

Separation of Ameer Khan's Army.

The most satisfactory communication followed Sir David Ochterlony's communication with Ameer Khan, whose acquiescence in the terms of an arrangement proposed to him at an early stage of the war (p. 97.) has been already noticed. The fulfilment of them, however, had been for some time suspended by the events in the Deckan towards the end of 1817, which encouraged his several chiefs to hope for a more gratifying occurrence than the separation of the army to which they belonged. They were, however, so little prepared to oppose the enforcement of the proposed measure, that the service of the Reserve was reduced to a few movements and *demonstrations*, which will be dismissed with that conciseness demanded by their want of connection with the military events of the war. Sir David Ochterlony moved from Rewarree, on the 27th of November; and on the 29th was at Shajehanpoor. From thence his march was continued, by Niranpoor and Jehroul, to Jypoor; near which the Reserve encamped on the 10th of December. It was from this position that arrangements were devised for reducing to submission the Ameer's insubordinate army. Two of its principal divisions* were encamped, apart, under Rajah Buhaudoor and Mehtab Khan; and Sir David Ochterlony, under pretence of seeking forage, moved his force between them. Whether this measure had an influence in controuling them may be doubtful. In this position, however, he remained till they had delivered up all the guns required of them; and a separation of the majority of their forces succeeded as a matter of course. At Ludhanah were received the Governor-general's final instructions of the 8th of January, for the organization of several *russalahs* of irregular horse, eight battalions of the Ameer's infantry, and a corps of Golandauze. This measure gave immediate employment to the most formidable portion of that Chief's army, and the arrangement was completed with a degree of dispatch which probably disappointed those who had calculated on a considerable opposition, in that quarter, to the British interests.

* The remaining division of Ameer Khan's army, with forty guns, under Jumsheed Khan, subsequently submitted to a detachment from the Reserve, commanded by Lieutenant-colonel Knox, on the 9th of April at Samber.

Detachment of a Light Force from the Centre and Third Divisions of the Grand Army under Major-general Brown, and Recall of Lieut.-colonel Philpot's Detachment (Map III.)

Connected with the recall of Major-general Marshall and the Third Division, to the point from whence it had followed the track of the Pindarries, was the formation of a force equipped for rapid movement, under Major-general Brown, to continue the pursuit. This consisted of troops to be drawn from the Centre and Left Divisions. The 3d regiment of Bengal cavalry and the dromedary corps marched from Sonaree on the 18th of December; and arrived, on the 26th, by the route of Cheemuck, Narwur, and Sipperee, within ten miles of Shahabad. Major-general Brown was here joined by the corps and detachments from the Third Division *. This arrangement having nearly stripped the Centre Division of its cavalry, Major Cumming's party was ordered, on the 19th, to join Colonel Philpot, who was directed, under date of the 22d, to bring in the united detachment to the Head-quarters' camp. Major-general Brown continued his march towards the Chumbul by the Lodanah Ghat, Beechee-Tal, and Narghur; and, on the 1st of January, was at Chippa-Burroad. Here he received the accounts of the defeat of Holkur's army, and the flight of the Pindarries to join its remains. He therefore prosecuted his march without a halt, till he arrived in the vicinity of Soneil, where he was in communication with Colonel Adams, at Gungraur, on his left, and, on his right, with Captain Tod, at Rowtah.

Major-general Brown's attack of the insubordinate remains of Holkur's Army at Rampoora. (Map IV.)

Major-general Brown halted at Soneil, during the 6th and 7th, and determined to continue his march, in a westerly direction, on the 8th and 9th, which brought his force to Peeplea. There intelligence was received, of the insubordinate part of Holkur's army under Roshun Beg, Roshun Khan, and Pein Sing, being still at Rampoora. This place being about twenty miles distant, the Major-general left his camp at one in the morning of the 10th, and came before the place, unexpected by the enemy, a little after day-break, with the 3d cavalry, the dromedary corps, and two companies of infantry mounted behind the dromedary riders. Parties immediately surrounded the place, to prevent the escape of the enemy; but the principal part of them had gone off a few days before, with ten

* These were, the 4th Native cavalry, four *russalahs* of Cunningham's horse, the 1st battalion of the 18th regiment of Native infantry, and the galloper brigade; making, in all, a force of two regiments of Native cavalry, four *russalahs* of irregular horse, the dromedary corps, one troop of gallopers with two twelve pounders of horse-artillery, one battalion of Native infantry, and a company of pioneers.

guns, to Ahmud. On the Major-general's entering the town, the garrison fled to a [illegible] hill; up which they were pursued, and about one hundred and fifty were here *cut up*. Several fled on foot where cavalry could not pass, leaving their baggage and about one hundred horses in possession of the victors, and about two hundred killed and wounded. The strength of the enemy, on this occasion, was estimated at two hundred horse and four hundred foot. Consequently, as they attempted no opposition, there was scarcely any casualty on the other side. Pein Sing remained a prisoner.

After this affair, information was obtained of the enemy's guns being deposited at Ahmud*, the chief of which place declared his willingness to give them up. A party was, accordingly, sent to receive them; but, finding the carriages in bad order, they burnt them and spiked the guns, or rendered them otherwise unserviceable. Roshun Beg fled towards Meywar with a few followers; and Major-general Brown halted at Rampoora till the 14th, having been rejoined, on the 11th, by his baggage and his remaining corps.

Advance of the Head-quarters of the Second Division to Sanganeir.

Towards the end of December, as will be recollected, the head-quarters of the Second Division of the Grand Army were at the Gynta Ghat (p. 104), on the Chumbul, after the discomfiture of the Pindarries, in their attempts to cross that river below Kotah. Finding now that the enemy of every description were driven into the confined country towards Meywar, Major-general Donkin determined on closing the northern outlets of that tract; as Major-general Brown and Colonel Adams could guard the eastern avenues, while to the south were divisions from the Deckan and Goozerat. Major-general Donkin accordingly recrossed the Chumbul, on the 29th of December, at the Peepulda ford, having called in his detachments from the Gummuch Ghat and Pattun. He was encamped, on the 31st, at Boondee, with the whole of the division, except the 2d battalion of the 12th regiment, which still continued to occupy the pass at Lakeiree. On the 1st of

---

* The name of this place being little known, it may be worthy of notice, that it is the residence of the remains of a once powerful family, who held as a *fief*, from the Rana of Oodeipoor, the greater part of Rampoora. His ancestors were celebrated in Aurungzeib's wars in the Deckan; and this Chief, besides the Rajah of Boondee, is the only other Rao-Rajah of the empire. He has now a scanty livelihood at Ahmud, the sole place left of all his once ample possessions.—Captain Tod's report.

January, the division's head-quarters, the cavalry brigade, the horse-artillery, and six flank companies of infantry, two of which were Europeans, ascended the Boondee pass, and took the road of Shapoorra; followed by the commissariat supplies, escorted by the 1st battalion of the 25th regiment. On the following day, the foot-artillery, his Majesty's 14th foot, and the 1st battalion of the 27th regiment, ascended the same pass, but took the route of Dubblanna under the orders of Colonel Vanrenen. Major-general Donkin continued his march past Shapoorra to Sanganeir, where he arrived on the eighth of January. Being still without any direct communication with the British troops acting from the southward, he considered it expedient to suspend any further advance, lest he should pass the point of co-operation.

Advance of the Goozerat Division to Burra Sadree.

To render more intelligible this part of the operations, it will be proper to recur to the movements of the Goozerat Division. This advanced from Mundissoor on the 3d (p. 164), in search of Cheettoo's *durrah*, which was understood to be in the direction of Jawud. At the same time, a detachment of three troops of Native cavalry, fifteen hundred Mysore horse, and a weak battalion of light infantry under Captain James Grant, was put in motion to find Kurreem Khan's *durrah* in the vicinity of Jerroot. To Sir William Grant Keir's force were added one thousand Mysore horse, its own irregulars, the Guickwar contingent, being still in the rear; and it arrived at Buntwarree on the 5th, without gaining any satisfactory information of the enemy. On the following morning, at two A. M., Sir William Grant Keir proceeded in the direction of Burra-Sadree, leaving the guns and heavy baggage, to follow his march, under an escort of five hundred Native infantry. The darkness of the night, the ruggedness of the country, and the narrowness of the roads, which were little better than pathways, prevented him from reaching the object proposed, which was distant upwards of forty miles from his point of departure. He accordingly, after a march of more than twenty miles, encamped at Munjerree. There he received such contradictory accounts of the movements of Cheettoo and his followers, that the force halted on the 7th. In the course of that day intelligence was received, which induced the Major-general again to attempt the surprise of the enemy, by a forced march. At ten P. M., the 17th dragoons, six companies of the 47th, and the Mysore horse, marched under his personal command towards Dherah; where he arrived at nine on the following morning. The enemy had already fled precipitately, leaving five guns and some baggage, which were secured. It was understood that more of their property was in the town, which, as well as Satola, was, with good reason, suspected to have given them assistance and protection.

Captain Grant's Detachment at Jawud.

In the mean while, the detachment under Captain Grant, which marched on the night of the 3d from Mundissoor, in search of Kurreem, arrived at Palsodah on the 4th, when it appeared that he was in the vicinity of Jawud. The march was recommenced at 9 P. M., and concluded at day-break the following morning. When Captain Grant arrived at Jawud, he found that Kurreem had moved off, on the previous morning, in consequence, as was concluded, of information given him of the approach of his enemies, by a *hurkarrah* (spy) of Jeswunt Rao Bhao, who commanded Scindiah's troops in that quarter. Intelligence was here received that Kurreem had joined Cheettoo; but where they were, could not be discovered, so much were the inhabitants in their favour, and so many dangers must the British *hurkarrahs* incur, in order to trace their motions. This detachment was therefore under the necessity of halting till the 9th; but its presence near Jeswunt Rao Bhao seemed to have the good effect of preventing his active interference in favour of the Pindarries.

Re-assembly of the Second Division at Shapoorra.

In this situation were the troops from the southward, when Major-general Donkin arrived at Sanganeir. Sir Thomas Hislop, considering that the interception of the Pindarries might be assisted by the positions of the Second Division of the Grand Army, endeavoured to keep the Major-general acquainted with all the movements in pursuit of that enemy. He therefore directed the several officers commanding on detached service, to open a communication with him. It appears, however, that he received no intelligence of these operations till the 11th. On the 12th he moved to Poor, in the direction of Oodeipoor, with his regular cavalry, horse-artillery, and flank companies; leaving the Native battalion at Sanganeir, to keep open communications, and to prevent the escape of fugitives by that point. The battalion left at the Lakeiree pass, was, at the same time, ordered to the vicinity of Boondee, to facilitate the advance of supplies. The foot-artillery and infantry under Colonel Vanrenen, were also ordered to bring on the commissariat depôt from Dubblanna to Sanganeir. From thence, orders had been sent to the irregular horse under Colonel Gardner, which were fifteen miles in advance, to march on the 11th upon Dhaneta, near Chittoor, where a large body of Pindarries were said to be assembled; but on their arrival at Nath-Durarra, on the 13th, it was ascertained that the joint *durrahs* had proceeded in a southerly direction. On the same day, Major-general Donkin's head-quarters were at Dhoseer, near Gungapoor, where they halted on the two following days. During this time it was fully ascertained, that the Pindarries had fled in two parties; one in the direction of the Goozerat frontier, and the other in that of Malwah. Major-general Donkin, accordingly, returned to Sanganeir, on the 17th, recalling Lieutenant-colonel Gardner's horse. On the 21st he was at Mooah; and on the following day he arrived at Shapoorra. The 2d battalion of the 12th, which had been stationed at Dubblanna, was divided; five companies being ordered to Hindoon to receive the charge of treasure, while the remainder, with the field-pieces attached, returned to the Head-quarters on the 30th, when the division still lay at Shapoorra.

Lieutenant-colonel Russell's Detachment from the Deckan Army at Purtabghur, and Reinforcement of Capt. Grant's Detachment, on the Advance of the Guickwar Contingent

Sir Thomas Hislop had anticipated the probable flight of the Pindarries to the southward. To intercept them, in that event, he ordered a detachment, consisting of two squadrons of cavalry, four horse-artillery guns, the 1st battalion of the 16th light infantry, and a battalion of the Russell brigade, under Lieutenant-colonel Russell, to proceed, on the morning of the 7th, to Purtabghur. This detachment remained there on the 8th, and returned on the following morning, under orders from the Head-quarters; there being no longer a prospect of advantage from its absence. At the same time, arrangements were made for reinforcing Captain Grant's detachment, and for enabling it to continue longer on its present service. An additional troop of cavalry, and a month's supply of grain for his horses, were sent to join him on the 9th. Sir William Grant Keir was also requested to return to him the one thousand Mysore horse, as soon as they should be relieved by the arrival of the Guickwar contingent. This corps had followed the march of the Goozerat Division, escorting a large supply of commissariat stores, and met with no interruption on the march. Their progress had been slow, in consequence of the long train of miserable carts, and bullocks, of which it was composed; and both escort and convoy were obliged to halt, from the 6th to the 9th, at Mundissoor. From hence the majority advanced under Mr. Williams, with expedition, to join Sir William Grant Keir, while the convoy followed under a detachment of four hundred horse.

Operations of the Goozerat Division in Meywar.

Sir William was now at Deodah, where he was obliged to halt on the 10th, in consequence of the severe exertions of part of his force, which had joined, the previous day, after a march of thirty miles. The followers had likewise been attacked by the Bheels, and several were wounded. Yet the most perplexing circumstance was the apparent hopelessness of overtaking the Pindarries, who occasionally broke into several parties, in order to escape. From the last accounts of Cheettoo, he was in the neighbourhood of Suloombur, extremely distressed by the privations he had sustained, and meditating an incursion into Goozerat, to avoid his immediate difficulties. Under all views of the case, the Major-general resolved on following in that direction. He arrived at Bheinder on the 12th, where it was ascertained that the enemy had gone to the jungles skirting the Goozerat frontier. He was here obliged to halt for the supplies following his march, and to await the reports of scouts sent out for intelligence. A letter was subsequently received from the Rana of Oodeipoor, who was heartily averse to the incursions both of Pindarries and Mahrattas. It satisfactorily stated, that Cheettoo had left that part of the country for the direction of Banswarra, and that he was attended by three thousand horsemen, and two thousand followers of other descriptions, some elephants, and camels. They were, however, in the greatest distress for provisions, and so apprehensive of a surprise that they seldom unsaddled their horses. On a report that they had thrown some of their property into the village of Khurauber, a distance of twenty-two miles, the flank companies were sent thither; but were disappointed of part of their object, though it was ascertained that the Pindarries had suffered considerably from the Bheels, in their passage through the jungles, which they had been obliged to enter. The detachment rejoined its Head-quarters at Deodah, whither the division marched on the 16th. Here another party was formed to make a forced march to Seetakoond, a place upwards of twenty miles distant, where both Pindarries and their families were said to be concealed. This expedition was equally unsuccessful, though it remained undoubted that the information acted on was correct; but the nature of the country was so rugged, and covered with jungle, that there was scarcely a village in that quarter; and of the few to be found, the inhabitants had fled. From hence the Mysore horse were sent off to Mundissoor, the Guickwar contingent having joined; and Sir William Grant Keir marched on the 17th towards Purtabghur. This was the nearest route by which he could move to the southward, owing to the intricacy of the country into which his operations had carried him. He did not, however, quit this theatre of the war without one more exertion to clear it of Pindarries. Having heard of a body of them left at Mundapie, a village of Jeswunt Rao Bhao's, the Major-general placed himself, on the 19th, at the head of a light detachment of four squadrons of his Majesty's 17th dragoons, and eight hundred infantry, and marched twenty miles from Parlee before he came in sight of the place. As soon as the troops appeared, the Pindarries rushed from the town, and were pursued by the cavalry, who killed about a hundred. Some horses and camels were surrendered by the chief of the place, as belonging to the fugitives; but Sir William refrained from chastising him as an ally of the enemy, on account of a certificate, he possessed, from Captain Caulfield, the British agent at Jawud. The remainder of the division marched in the mean while to Warree, on the Purtabghur road, where it was joined on the 21st by the head-quarters; and on the 23d the entire force was at Neemuj.

Return of Capt. Grant's Detachment to Mundissoor.

Captain Grant received intimation of the reinforcement and supplies ordered to join him, when he was preparing to return from Jawud to Mundissoor, after fulfilling his first instructions. On the 11th he marched to Chittoor, on having received information that the Pindarries were there. Instead of these, he met a party of Colonel Gardner's horse, which had arrived from Major-general Donkin's division, on the same intelligence. Accounts similar to those which have been already mentioned were received here, that Cheettoo's *durrah* had fled to the southward; but it was understood that a considerable body under Namdar Khan, a nephew of Kurreem Khan, had passed to the eastward by Nandawarrah, and some of the Mysore horse were taken by them near Palsodah. The reinforcement of regular cavalry and the supply of grain joined at Chittoor; and Captain Grant, considering himself here too much in Major-general Donkin's line, marched on the 13th to Neemakeirah, as a more central position for intelligence. On the 15th he proceeded to Jawud for the same purpose, knowing likewise that Jeswunt Rao continued to protect the Pindarry interests, and that in the absence of a British detachment he would probably extend his protection to the fugitives from Rampoora and other quarters. But the detachment's longer continuance on this service having become unnecessary, he received orders, on the 15th, to return to Mundissoor, which place he reached on the 18th.

Parties of Kurreem and Wassil Mahomud's durrahs flying to the Eastward, are attacked and dispersed with much loss, by a detachment from the Fifth Deckan Division.

Were it possible to trace the several routes of the Pindarries during the time of their flight, such particulars would, perhaps, give but little additional interest to this account of the operations against them. When pressed, they fled collectively, if possible; otherwise they broke into parts, again to unite. In some instances, from inability to proceed, or under the apprehension of suddenly falling in with British troops from an opposite quarter, parties of them lurked in small numbers about remote villages, or lay in the thickest jungles, exposed to the most severe hardships, till their enemies had passed by. Cheettoo's *durrah*, generally speaking, kept distinct from the rest; while Kurreem's and Wassil Mahomud's were combined, as at the opening of the campaign. The latter, on Captain Grant's approach, fled from Keillee near Jawud, and took a westerly direction, till the British troops had evacuated the tract between them and the Chumbul, when they doubled suddenly back by Neemuj. Some of these, the Mysore horsemen saw near Palsodah. They were then making their escape to the Chumbul, which they crossed north of Gungraur, and encamped at Goorareah. In this situation they were heard of by Colonel Adams, who detached the 5th Bengal cavalry, at eleven P. M. of the 12th of January, under the command of Major Clarke, with instructions to march on the village of Ambee, about which they were said to be plundering. The intelligence, on this occasion, was very faithful, and the means of its conveyance appear to have been well arranged; for the Major was met by a report of the position of the enemy, during the night, and continued his march till within a few miles of them. Here he halted for the approach of day; and at five o'clock moved down upon them in two divisions, when they were just preparing for their march. The surprise was complete: the left division first cut in among them, and a body flying from it encountered the right division, from which it suffered severely. The pursuit was maintained for twenty miles, which, with the immediate return to camp, and the previous march from it, made a distance of more than fifty miles in thirteen hours. The whole number of the Pindarries were estimated at fifteen hundred; and of these one thousand were concluded*, from a comparison of the reports of their pursuers,

* This is one of the few instances in which the loss is not exaggerated by Native report. The means resorted to by Major Clarke appear the most worthy of credit; yet Captain Tod's *akhbars*, which agree nearly as to the whole number, make no more than two hundred killed. Namdar Khan was supposed to be among these; but his name subsequently occurs in frequent

to have been slain. Major-general Brown, who was at Rampoora when this party approached the Chumbul, likewise marched to intercept them, on the first intelligence of their movements. On the 14th, he was at Sanjeet, where he received intelligence of the success of the other attack, and halted on the 15th, to derive some supplies from Sir Thomas Hislop's camp, then in his vicinity.

Preparations for the Counter-march of the Head-quarters of the Army of the Deckan.

Affairs had now arrived at that stage, when the presence of the Head-quarters of the Deckan Army, so far advanced as Mundissoor, was no longer considered necessary. The Governor-general therefore directed that they should return to the southward, leaving sufficient troops with Sir John Malcolm, for the settlement of Holkur's distracted Government, and for making such other arrangements as should provide for the public service in that quarter. The Marquis of Hastings was the more induced to decide on this measure, by the state of affairs in the Deckan, where the Peishwah yet kept the field, and Asseerghur still maintained a posture of hostility. After the treaty of Mundissoor, an officer* was deputed to reside with Holkur; and with him was detached an escort of three companies of the 1st battalion of the 14th Madras Native infantry. When the Maharajah subsequently moved to Rampoora, those companies being relieved by others from Colonel Adams's division, rejoined their head-quarters. During this period, Holkur's minister had been engaged, with the assistance of the British Government, in reducing his master's extra troops; several of whom went off voluntarily, on finding matters approaching to an adjustment. Ram Deen, accompanied by the *Barra Bhye*, went to the southward. Roshun Beg, after his discomfiture at Rampoora, took the same direction to join the Beema Baee, Holkur's sister, who maintained an armed force in the vicinity of Myheyswur. With Sir John Malcolm were left four horse-artillery guns, the 3d regiment of Native cavalry, the 1st battalion of the 14th MadrasNative infantry, the Russell brigade, and two thousand Mysore horse. He was also placed in immediate communication with the officers commanding all the other forces in that quarter, for general co-operation in the public service. These were, Colonel Adams, who was still at Gungraur, awaiting the arrival of his supplies; Major-

---

akkbars, and he is now in the enjoyment of a pension from the British Government, in consequence of his submission.

* Major Agnew, who was subsequently relieved by Mr. Wellesley, appointed by the Governor-general to be Resident with Holkur.

general Brown, who was near Narghur, prepared for active service; Sir William Grant Keir, who was at Neemuj, and directed to give his immediate attention to the defence of Goozerat; and Major-general Donkin, who was in the vicinity of Sanganeir. Orders were at the same time dispatched to Colonel Deacon, directing him to march immediately with his detachment, including the Ellichapoor contingent, from Jafferabad (p. 137) towards Ahmednuggur; and eventually to Poonah, accompanied by Captain Davies's horse.

Return to Mehidpoor: and Detachments under Major Lushington and Captain Grant to the Goozerat Frontier.

These arrangements being made, the Head-quarters and First Division of the Army of the Deckan marched, on the 16th of January, from Eedagherry near Mundissoor, to Peeploattee. From hence it was deemed advisable, while the march continued to Oojein, that light detachments should be sent towards the confines of Goozerat, to clear that part of the country of any enemies who might be lurking there, in expectation of the British troops passing them to the southward. The head-quarters of the 4th cavalry, with one squadron of the 8th, making in all two squadrons and a half, and four companies of rifles with two horse-artillery guns, were placed under the orders of Major Lushington, and directed to sweep round by Rutlam, the entrance of the Dawud Ghat, and to return to camp by Nolye. Orders were likewise sent to Sir John Malcolm, to direct Capt. Grant, with three troops of the 3d cavalry and two thousand Mysore horse, the 1st battalion of the 3d Native infantry, and two [illegible] to march from Mundissoor by Banswarra; and from thence, leaving Rutlam on the right, to rejoin the Head-quarters at or near Oojein. The remaining pass into Goozerat by Dungarpoor, the movements of Sir William Grant Keir's division were expected to cover. The detachment of one thousand Mysore horse, which had been with it, were ordered to proceed straight to Mehidpoor, on which Sir Thomas Hislop's march was directed; while the troop of the 4th cavalry, which had been detached with Captain Grant to Chittoor, was ordered to follow the Head-quarters by the most direct route. The march was continued, on the 17th and 18th, to the Chumbul, which was crossed at the Jao Ghat. Here the force was joined by details from Hindia and Mehidpoor, which escorted a small convoy of supplies from the rear. Orders were from hence dispatched to Major Lushington, to endeavour to gain [illegible] of the Goozerat battering-train, which was understood to be at, or near Dawud, and to bring it on to the camp, as at this time the siege of Asseerghur was in contemplation. Corresponding instructions were addressed to Brigadier-general Doveton. He was directed to march with his battering-train from Nagpoor on Mulkapoor, detaching, after he should pass the Wurdah, as a light reinforcement to the Fourth Division, two squadrons of the 6th cavalry, the 1st battalion of the 12th light infantry, and a detachment of the reformed horse. These were ordered to proceed by the most direct practicable route towards Poonah, in compliance with the desire of the Marquis of Hastings, that every possible aid should be given to the operations immediately against the Peishwah. In order to augment the number of battering-guns, Captain Sydenham, the Political Agent in Berar, was called on to procure from the Nizam's Authorities, as many pieces of ordnance as might be serviceable at Aurungabad, and to send them down the Ghats towards Mulkapoor. The force continued its route, without a halt, to Mehidpoor, and arrived there on the 20th, crossing the Seeprah above the town by a Ghat, to repair which the pioneers had been sent in advance, the previous evening.

The Army at Oojein.

It was one of Sir Thomas Hislop's first objects to visit the hospital, where he had the satisfaction of finding such of the wounded cases as had not been desperate, in a course of recovery, under the careful and judicious treatment of Surgeon Stevenson, who had been specially selected for this charge. Had any stronger proof of the attention which had been given to this duty been required, his Excellency received it in the unanimous petition of the patients, that he would bestow on their surgeon his protection, in return for the kindness they had received from him. Unassuming merit could not have a more gratifying and appropriate reward; intrinsically more estimable than any formal commendation, flowing from Authority.

The Head-quarters and First Division halted till the 23d, engaged in those final arrangements for the public service in Malwah which were incomplete on leaving Mundissoor. With the corps in that direction a communication was hitherto maintained, while the course of operations was gradually assuming a new shape, under the immediate instructions of the Governor-general. On the 24th the march was continued; and on the following day the camp was established in the vicinity of Oojein, where it remained till the 28th. The army changed ground to San-Moakee, a distance of five miles, to withdraw the troops from the temptations of a populous city; and halted two days, to enable the Goozerat battering-train to shorten its distance, and the detachment under Captain Grant to rejoin.

Movements of Captain Grant's Detachment.

That officer, pursuant to orders addressed to Sir John Malcolm, had marched from the vicinity of Mundissoor on the 20th, by the great road towards Banswarra, in the first instance; but on arriving at Soankeir, the intelligence received represented Cheettoo's *durrah* to have passed southward, along the hills bordering on Goozerat, and at the last accounts to be at Petlawad. Captain Grant therefore adopted the route of Rutlam, as the most direct for either intercepting his enemy or for pursuing him into Goozerat. On the 23d he was at that town; where he ascertained to his satisfaction, that Cheettoo, after levying a contribution at Petlawad, had taken the road by Indoor, as more likely to bring him among friends. Captain Grant continued his march to Nolye, where he arrived on the 25th. He there learned, that the Pindarries had left Indoor for the Jam Ghat, leading to the Valley of the Nerbuddah; but that Beema Baee, Holkur's sister, was raising contributions throughout the neighbouring country, by means of a force which probably contained many of the troops lately serving the Maharajah. Captain Grant's instructions not extending to this case, he rejoined the Head-quarters on the 29th, by the route of Attoad, and his detachment was broken up.

The Army at Indoor.

On the 30th, Sir Thomas Hislop received from the Governor-general a letter, dated the 23d, leaving the siege of Asseerghur optional, and calling his Excellency's attention to many important objects in the Deckan. Sir Thomas, therefore, deemed it advisable to exercise the discretion confided to him, by postponing to a future period the attack of that fortress, and carrying his troops with all expedition to Khandesh. The advance of the Goozerat and Aurungabad battering-trains was consequently countermanded. The detachment of the 3d cavalry and six hundred Silladar horse returned on the 31st to rejoin Sir John Malcolm's force, leaving with the Head-quarters two thousand Mysoreans, including those which had been detached formerly from Hindia to Nagpoor. Half of these returned, under charge of Captain Munn, with three thousand Bringarries from the Nagpoor country; and were halted at Hindia, waiting with other details for further instructions, which were forwarded from the camp on the 31st of January. A considerable quantity of private baggage and head-quarters' equipage had been left there, on the First Division crossing the Nerbuddah; and as it was proposed to re-cross that river lower down than on the former occasion, it became necessary to provide for the re-junction of every thing left there. The officer commanding at Hindia was therefore directed to place those equipments under the charge of a detachment, consisting of the company of the Madras European regiment, a company of the 2d battalion of the 14th regiment, three hundred Mysore horse, all recovered men of corps in camp, and the depôt corps. This battalion, whose name has not been hitherto introduced, consisted of men recruited for general service in the Madras Army, but who were maintained embodied, previous to their distribution to corps. The whole detachment, commanded by Captain Wilson, was directed to march by Kundwah and Kurgoun; bringing up the convoy to the latter place as soon after the 10th of February as possible, that the army might not be delayed in waiting for it. This arrangement having been ordered, as well as the distribution of some commissariat supplies collected and prepared at Hindia, the army marched in three days from the vicinity of Oojein to Indoor, encamping there, from the 2d to the 5th, to admit of the re-junction of Major Lushington's detachment, which was ordered in. (Map VII.)

Movements of Major Lushington's Detachment. (Map IV.)

This detachment, on leaving the camp at Peeploattee, marched to Rutlam; where, on the 19th, the Major could procure little intelligence, regarding Cheettoo, from Scindiah's officers at that place; who were neither civil nor inclined to inform against the Pindarries. He was here overtaken by the orders to look out for the Goozerat battering-train, and marched, on the following day, towards Petlawad, where he arrived on the 21st. Learning here that a body of Pindarries were passing towards Nolye, from the westward, he left all his baggage and incumbrances on the ground, under protection of a small party, and marched on the same night towards Taundla, as the point by which all the roads in this quarter pass. This expedition however failed of its immediate object, and Major Lushington returned to Petlawad, to meet the train, which arrived at that place on the 27th; the carriages very much shaken from the badness of the roads. These being re-fitted, the detachment and convoy proceeded on the 30th, and were on the 31st at Budnawur, where further want of repairs made a halt necessary, on the following day. At this place, however, Major Lushington received his orders to re-join immediately; and leaving the convoy, he arrived in the camp at Indoor on the 5th of February. The intelligence subsequently received at Rutlam by Sir William Grant Keir, represented that the news of Major Sealy's advance with a convoy of treasure and stores by Dawud, had early reached the ears of Ram Deen with the *Barra Bhye*, and Cheettoo, who meditated an attack on it; but that the seasonable arrival of Major Lushington's detachment in that quarter, prevented the execution of the project. That it should have succeeded is very improbable; but that it would have given considerable annoyance cannot be doubted.

Sir John Malcolm at Neemuj.

After the march of the Head-quarters of the Army from Mundissoor, Sir John Malcolm passed over to the camp of Major-general Brown at Aorah, to confer respecting the future dispositions of the forces; and returned on the 19th to dispatch Captain Grant's detachment. On the following day he changed ground to Oondla, where he was joined by the one thousand Mysore horse from the Goozerat force, and marched on the 24th to Keimpoor. On the 28th, in the forenoon, Sir John Malcolm arrived with his force at Sunjeet, and heard a cannonade maintained in the direction of Jawud, distant about thirty-five miles. This he naturally attributed to the presence of Major-general Brown's division in that quarter; and though confident in the strength of that corps, yet under the supposition of its being possibly engaged in the attack of an enemy strongly posted with guns, he immediately continued his progress. After a second march of sixteen miles, he was met by a dispatch from the Major-general. This was so satisfactory, that Sir John halted, with the intention of retracing his steps to Sunjeet, should his further advance be deemed unnecessary. Such being the case, he subsequently moved on the 31st to Peepleea, and on the 5th of February to Neemuj.

Major-general Brown's successful attack of Jeswunt Rao Bhao.

Major-general Brown had marched from his camp at Aorah on the 19th of January, after his interview with Sir John Malcolm. Proceeding by the route of Reechry, Narreinghur, Palsodah, and Neemuj, he arrived, on the 25th, at Jawud. He here found that the conduct of Jeswunt Rao Bhao was as unsatisfactory as he had been taught to expect; and that so far from realizing any of his promises of acting against the Pindarries, he actually connived at their secretion in his camp. Accounts were at this time received of a body of Pindarries at Murpah, under a chief named Tukoo; and a detachment under Captain Ridge, consisting of a regiment of cavalry, three companies of infantry, and the dromedaries, was sent to attack them. The enemy had notice of their approach, in time to fly; and the detachment finding in the town some unarmed followers, *tattoos*, and camels only, returned towards Jawud. It was fully ascertained that the officers in the Bhao's camp, who were the immediate protectors of the Pindarries, were Bhao Sing and Imaum Bukhsh. Thes

persons were accordingly required to be given up. Some days passed in fruitless communications, without the Major-general's vigilance being relaxed; till, on the 29th, he received a report that Bhao Sing, with his party, were saddling, preparatory to their flight. The Bhao had been, previously, given to understand, that the movement of any part of his camp before the adjustment of the affair in question, unless with the acquiescence of the Major-general, would be the signal of attack. In pursuance of this declaration, he sent down a squadron of cavalry to reinforce the pickets, (Plan 18) (B.)
and to deter the party proposing to fly. As this squadron passed, three (3.)
guns and a fire of matchlocks opened on them, and at once declared a preparation for hostilities. The enemy had, in fact, received from Koomulneir a reinforcement of six hundred horse, while Captain Ridge's detachment was out, and now proposed bringing the infantry of Bhao Sing's detached camp under the walls of the town, which was however prevented by the alertness of the British troops. The remainder of the enemy had now drawn up behind a *nullah*, with the infantry on their right towards the town, (2.)
and their horse on the left towards the plain, while the Major-general prepared to move down on them. He sent two guns to reinforce the pickets, and ordered two squadrons of the 4th cavalry and some Rohillah horse round the town, to gain the rear of Bhao Sing's camp. Before the line could be formed for attack, the fire of two twelve-pounders with Shrapnell shells, supported by smaller artillery, drove the enemy from their position; the infantry flying into the town, and the horse galloping off. The latter were immediately pursued by the cavalry, under Captain Ridge; but as these had returned only two hours before, after a forced march of twenty-five miles, he relinquished an unavailing pursuit, for the enemy were mounted on fresh horses. He therefore directed his attention against the detached position, in which there remained six guns, supported by two (4.)
weak battalions of infantry. The cavalry crossed the *nullah*, and drew up (E.)
in front of them, detaching a party to enter from another quarter. This combination so completely succeeded, that, in a few minutes, the remnant of the enemy was destroyed, and their guns, camp equipage, and baggage taken. In the mean while, Major-general Brown moved towards the gate of the town, where he called on Jeswunt Rao to surrender unconditionally, or to expect the storming of the place. Finding that his messenger was fired on, at the same time that evasive answers were given, he ordered one twelve-pounder to be *run up* to the gate, while the remaining ordnance swept the (C.)

defences about it. The Bhao fled by the opposite gate towards Koomulneir, ineffectually pursued by part of the 3d cavalry, while the storming-party entered by the Rampoora gate, and defeated all attempts at opposition. The loss of the enemy, on this occasion, was estimated at one thousand men, while that of the British was only thirty-six *.

Return to the Chumbul. (Map IV)

The presence of so large a force at Jawud being no longer required, the Major-general left there the 3d regiment of cavalry, with two galloper guns, and a company of Native infantry, with some irregular horse; and marched, on the 3d of February, towards Rampoora, by Monassah and Kukreisur. On the 8th the light division marched from Rampoora to the left bank of the Chumbul. There it halted for further instructions, and Major-general Brown subsequently left it on this ground to rejoin the Head-quarters. It is impossible to contemplate the short operations of this detachment of the Grand Army, without a [illegible] that it performed considerable service to the general cause. Its march from the Sind, with the exception of one halt, was diligent; and its conduct, against the enemy, very gallant. The decision of Major-general Brown, both at Rampoora and Jawud, was as marked, as his motions were prompt; forming a combination of circumstances that rarely fail of success, when unopposed by physical obstacles of an insuperable nature. The character, in short, of this limited service, was rapidity: the detachment came unexpectedly into the theatre of operations, acted a brilliant part, and vanished again as quickly. Its motions and effects were like those of a rocket among a body of enemies; and prepared the Bhao's, and Bapoo Scindiah's troops, subsequently to surrender, the moment they were summoned.

Sir John Malcolm at Jawud.

In order to strengthen the impression made on Jeswunt Rao, Sir John Malcolm marched from Neemuj on the 10th, with the majority of his troops, lightly equipped, to Neemakeirah. Finding there that, in consequence of his communication to Major-general Donkin, of the position of the Bhao's affairs, that officer was better placed for the proposed service than himself, he countermarched to Jawud. There he arrived on the 17th, for the settlement of the various political arrangements which succeeded the operations of the troops.

---

* Vide Appendix. K.

Operations of the Second Division of the Grand Army in Meywar.

Sir John's letters to Major-general Donkin overtook that officer on the 5th of February, at Mattakeira, whither he had moved from Shapoorra. On the following day he changed his course towards Koomulneir; and on the 11th, Ryepoor, a fort usurped by Bapoo Scindiah, in Meywar, surrendered to a detachment sent for its reduction. It was immediately delivered over to the Rana of Oodeipoor. The surrender of the forts of Dyalghur and Rajnuggur, in like manner, followed a summons from the head-quarters of the division, on its arrival at Kaneraollee on the 13th. These places had, likewise, been usurped from Meywar; the former by Jeswunt Rao, and the latter by Bapoo Scindiah. The division halted on this ground, in consequence of information received from Sir John Malcolm, that letters were immediately expected from the Bhao for the surrender of Koomulneir. These having been received, a detachment, under Lieutenant-colonel Casement, C. B. was sent off to take possession of the place, which was occupied accordingly.

Submission of Beema Baee's Force, to Sir William Grant Keir.

Sir William Grant Keir received the instructions addressed to him, relative to the especial protection of the Goozerat provinces, at Neemuj. From thence he marched, on the 24th of January; and the next day arrived at Peeloo. Thence he marched to Rutlam, by Dundoora and Soankeir, halting on the 31st and 1st of February. Pursuant to the intentions with which he proceeded to Rutlam, a separation was there made of his force, placing under Lieutenant-colonel Corsellis a detachment consisting of the 3d brigade, the greatest part of the artillery, and four hundred Guickwar horse, to look to the avenues by Banswarra, and the country to the westward. Another detachment, composed of a squadron of his Majesty's 17th dragoons, two hundred and fifty light infantry of the flank battalion, and one thousand Guickwar horse, proceeded under the Honourable Lieutenant-colonel Stanhope, by Rajoad, to the neighbourhood of Dhar. This place it was expected to gain when the head-quarters of the force should arrive at Rajoad. The objects of this movement were, to cover the more southern entrances into Goozerat, by Chota-Oodeipoor and Allee-Mohun; and to check the proceedings of Beema Baee, and the fragments of Holkur's late army under Roshun Beg. This arrangement was completed by the arrival of Sir William Grant Keir's head-quarters at Budnawur, on the 3d of February, and of Lieutenant-colonel Stanhope's detachment on the same day at Dessye, twenty miles to the southward of Rajoad. The

Major-general found Beema Baee encamped in his [illegible] with a considerable force. Unfurnished at this time with instructions how to treat her, he confined his communication to the desire that she would restrict her troops from excursions in the direction of his camp. To this she replied, that she herself had been invaded by others, and deprived of considerable property; that she was therefore necessitated to take the field in her own defence; and that her behaviour was not to be compared to the conduct of such as had plundered her and the surrounding country. After this declaration of her own propriety of conduct, she marched off in a westerly direction, to enjoy more freedom of action than was admitted by her vicinity to the British camp. Sir William Grant Keir received his instructions regarding her force, on the 7th, from Sir Thomas Hislop, then encamped at Indoor. These were formed on the wishes of the Holkur Government, that the troops should be dispersed, and that she should be sent to Rampoora, the residence of her brother. In pursuance of these orders, the Major-general marched on the 7th to Burmundle, and from thence by Juknada and Purwut, through a close and difficult country, to Jabooah, where he arrived on the 10th, in the vicinity of her camp. In this position her troops remained perfectly quiescent; for the celerity with which they had been followed, left them no opportunity of being otherwise; and she received the terms proposed with submission. She waited on Sir William Grant Keir with two hundred followers, for whose and her own subsistence, as her finances were much deranged, she received an allowance of two hundred rupees a day. Her troops, about two thousand five hundred men, moved off to Taundla, and dispersed, as if returning to their homes; while she accompanied Sir William Grant Keir to Rajghur, on the 14th, and afterwards Colonel Elrington, to Budnawur, whither he was sent with a detachment for the protection of the hospital and depôts temporarily established there. From thence she was escorted by a party from Colonel Corsellis's brigade, directed to convoy her to Rampoora.*

---

* It may be satisfactory to the reader, that some further particulars should be given of what would appear in Europe so extraordinary a case, as a woman, about twenty years old, commanding an armed force in the field; for Beema Baee did not confine her functions to merely residing in the camp, and thereby giving its proceedings the colour of her authority. She is represented as riding, "*à la fourchette*," at the head of her troops, with a sword by her side and a lance in her hand, on a well-dressed charger. She is the daughter of the late Jeswunt Rao Holkur, but

Reflections on the Pursuit of the Pindarries.

It might now be safely averred, that the Pindarries were expelled from the left bank of the Chumbul, and were in fact unable to exist, any where, in a collected number. It has been seen that the result of one part of the operations was, to drive them in that direction. As they were now driven back again, the former measures might appear nugatory, were not the difference of their situations, at those periods, considered. They were, at length, reduced to such distress, from the loss of property, and the harassing life to which they had been exposed, that they had not wherewith to procure subsistence. If they assembled in sufficient numbers to take it by force, they were immediately heard of, and pursued by the British troops; while, if they attempted it in small parties, they were exposed to be defeated, and deprived of their horses, by the inhabitants of the country. It mattered little whither they were pursued, or from whence they were expelled; it was the principal object to give them no repose anywhere; and this appears to have been effectually accomplished by the most appropriate measures that could have been adopted. Had they been a regular enemy, whose wants and composition would force them to the adoption of a systematic plan of defence or flight, a [illegible] plan, consisting of much

---

not by the mother of the present Mulhar Rao, Toolsee Baee, who was murdered at Mehidpoor. She was married to Khshen Rao, governor of the country south of Dhar; but was at this time a widow, enjoying a *jaghire* about Petlawad, and was said to tipple a little, in addition to her other masculine accomplishments. Her military deportment is a matter of no great singularity in India; and the Begum Sumroo, whose battalions were destroyed at the Battle of Assye, is said to have recommended herself to Scindiah, by mounting a breach with her troops, after the death of her husband, and was therefore continued in the command of them, and in possession of rich *jaghires*. What will be said to the existence of a corps of female infantry at Hydrabad, regularly trained in the manual and platoon exercises, and in the performance of elementary movements? The following is an official account of them in 1815:—"The late Nizam had two battalions of female Sepoys of one thousand each, which mounted guard in the interior of the palace, and accompanied the ladies of his family whenever they moved. They were with the Nizam during the war with the Mahrattas in 1795, and were present at the Battle of Kurdlah, where, at least, they did not behave worse than the rest of the army. One of these battalions was commanded by Mama Burrun, and the other by Mama Chumbebee, two of the principal female attendants of the Nizam's family. The present Nizam still keeps up a reduced establishment of those women; and Moneer-ool-Moolk has also a party of them. They are dressed as our Sepoys formerly used to be, and carry musquets; and they do the French exercise with tolerable correctness. They are called *Zuffer Pultuns*, the victorious battalions, and the women composing them are called *Gardunees*, a corruption from our word guard. Their pay is five rupees a month."

fewer troops than were employed against them, would have sufficed for their reduction. The case being otherwise, it early became evident, that the simplest, as well as most effectual mode of procedure, was the application of as many light detachments as possible to the incessant attack and pursuit of them. To inclose such an enemy, a system of *cordons* would always have proved ineffectual. The attention necessary to guard every point, would have precluded the means of harassing them, and have proved at the same time nugatory; for, with fresh horses, they would have always found openings through which to escape. In the course of the operations against them, one party frequently drove them towards another; and though it seldom happened that either came up with their main body, they were obliged to relinquish their means of subsistence, and to dive, in scattered parties, into the thickest and least pervious wilds for personal safety. Even here famine was by no means their only foe. They found, to their sorrow, that their enemies, however habituated to enjoy a considerable share of luxuries in the field, could lay down their equipments, and explore their most remote retreats. The division of Sir William Grant Keir was nearly two months in this condition, and scarcely ever at rest, till the jungles on the confines of Malwah were clear of Pindarries. These might well consider natural impediments as affording an insecure protection. They found even a general-officer in command of a respectable force, foregoing every convenience and legitimate excuse for maintaining his head-quarters in situations of comparative comfort, to penetrate, with a detachment of dragoons and light infantry, into the deepest recesses of wood and mountain. The climate of India is said to enervate; and there is little doubt that the physical powers of Europeans are impaired by it. Let, however, any officer, who has seen the real service of India, and of other parts of the globe, declare, if he ever witnessed, out of the former country, more of unaffected self-devotion to the public interests, and less of that despicable self-reservation conveyed by one acceptation of the expression "Old Soldier," than in a British camp in India.

CHAPTER III.

DISLOCATION OF THE GRAND ARMY.

Retirement of the Head-quarters of the Marquis of Hastings, and Centre Division of the Grand Army, from the Sind. Return of the Second Division to Quarters. March of the Fifth Deckan Division to the Bheitwah in pursuit of Kurreem's and Wassil Mahomud's Pindarries. Cheettoo's Durrah dispersed near the Nerbuddah. Operations of Lieutenant-colonel Mac Morine from Hoossingabad. Return of Brigadier-general Hardyman's Force to Quarters. Return of Brigadier-general Toone's Force to Quarters. Operations of Major Macpherson from Hoossingabad. Expulsion of Gunput Rao's Party from the Nagpoor Territory. March of the Second Division of the Deckan Army from Nagpoor, for the Reduction of the Ceded Districts West of the Wurdah. March of Colonel Pollock's Detachment, and Progress of the Second Division to Ootran. Establishment of Holkar's Authority about Indoor, entrusted to the Goozerat Force. Head-quarters of the Deckan Army recross the Nerbuddah. Progress of the First Division to the Taptee. Unexpected Hostility of the Garrison of Talneir. Reconnaissance and Description of Talneir. Attack of the Place. Assault by the Gates. Reflections on this Service. Considerations on "Coups de Main" in general. Comparison of the usual Means employed. Reflections on the Engineer Establishment in India.

AS the objects for which the Grand Army had been assembled, approached the period of their accomplishment, the Head-quarters of the Marquis of Hastings began to draw off from their advanced position towards the Jumnah. The instructions to Sir Thomas Hislop, for the return of the First Division of the Deckan Army to the southward, had been dated from Oochar; and there the Governor-general, on the 25th of January, still remained.

Retirement of the Head-quarters of the Marquis of Hastings, and Centre Division of the Grand Army, from the Sind. (Map III.)

On the 1st of February his Lordship and the Centre Division were encamped at Launch; and on the following day at Kunjaollee, remaining there in expectation of the period when it would be proper to dissolve the existing formation of the army. On the 12th, as the first step to its separation, a brigade under Lieut.-colonel Dewar was composed of the 2d battalion of the

1st, the 1st battalion of the 26th, and the 2d battalion of the 13th regiments of Bengal Native infantry. This, with the 7th regiment of Native cavalry, and battering-train, which had been left at Samptur *, was ordered to proceed to join Major-general Marshall, when the remainder of the division should march. This corps was placed under Brigadier-general Watson, and was destined, with other corps from Beirseeah, for the reduction of the Ceded Countries on the Nerbuddah. The order followed, on the 14th, for the final dislocation of the Centre and Right Divisions. The horse-artillery and rocket-troop, his Majesty's 8th dragoons, the 14th foot, and the 1st battalion of the 25th Native infantry, were directed to march to Meerut; his Majesty's 24th dragoons, the 87th foot, and the 1st battalion of the 8th Native infantry, to Cawnpoor; the 4th Native cavalry, and the 2d battalion of the 12th Native infantry, to Muttra; the 1st battalion of the 7th to Etawah, the 1st battalion of the 24th to Agra, and the 1st battalion of the 29th to Keitah. By this arrangement, the 2d battalion of the 25th regiment of Native infantry remained, with the body-guard, as the Governor-general's escort, when the Head-quarters should leave the army. The subsequent march was conducted by the route of Nuddee-Kagoug, where the encampment was, on the 15th and 16th; and, on the following days, by Bheer, Sheikhpoor, Sunkerpoor, and Ooreeah, on the left bank of the Jumnah. On the 25th the Governor-general arrived at Cawnpoor, by Akburpoor and Chinchirdee, and halted during the remaining days of February. On the 1st of March his Lordship again moved towards Lucknow, by Heerapoor and Nyaserye; and on the 6th reached that capital, where a halt of four days succeeded.

(Map II.)

(Map II.)

Return of the Second Division to Quarters.

While the corps of the Centre Division were thus in progress to their several stations, Major-general Donkin received orders for breaking up the Second Division, on the 25th of February; and marched, on the following day, in prosecution of his route to such a point as should be convenient for its separation, after the receipt of treasure which he expected to meet on the way. On the 26th he was rejoined at Lama, by the detachment under Lieutenant-colonel Casement, which had been sent to receive the fortress

* The heavy ordnance and engineer park were thrown into Samptur after the army left Seeonda on the Sind; an arrangement which was not then specified, that the relation of other matters, with which it was unconnected, might not be interrupted, and as, in fact, its vicinity might still admit of its being considered present.

of Koomulneir. This was found to be a place of very difficult access, from any quarter, there being no road for wheel-carriages within two miles. On the following day the march was continued by Maundul, Shapoorra, and Kirkee, to Todah, where the division arrived on the 7th of March. On this ground it was joined by the wing of the 2d battalion of the 12th regiment, sent (p. 199) to bring up the treasure—that indispensable spring in the machinery of every army, but more especially in that of India. In no country in the world is the provision made for the payment of troops on field service, so abundant and efficient. Seldom does a month pass beyond the regular period of issuing the monthly pay; and the effects are seen in the discipline which this regularity renders not only practicable but easy. At the same time, to say that the army, without this regularity, could not be maintained in the field, would be idle. In former times, they were occasionally* a year without a settlement of their pay; but they were subsisted by issues from the public stores; and, it is apprehended, less strictness of discipline was then enforced than at present, with regard to the appropriation of grain in the villages. Be this as it may, so uninterrupted has been the operation of the present system, owing to superior riches, and a better knowledge of this branch of the arrangements of Government, that a departure from it would, at first, be considered as an intolerable hardship. At Todah the division was separated into two parts, of which one, consisting of his Majesty's 8th dragoons, the 14th regiment of foot, and the 1st battalion of the 25th Native infantry, marched, under the orders of Colonel Westenra, for Meerut, by Chaksoo, Doonsa, and Almar, and, on the 24th of March, was at Feerozpoor. From hence it was directed to continue its route by Bullumghur, and to cross the Jumnah at the Tilput Ghat. It arrived at Meerut on the 5th of April. The remaining troops were, with some exceptions, placed under the orders of Colonel Vanrenen, for movement to their respective stations. The artillery, excepting four six-pounders, marched to Agra, and arrived there on the 27th. A detachment, consisting of a wing of the 2d battalion of the 12th regiment, with four guns, manned by Golandauze, a company of pioneers, and Gardner's horse, remained under Major Harriott at Tonk Rampoora, which place surrendered to Colonel Vanrenen. The troop of Native horse-artillery marched by Rampoor Bampoor to join

* Such was the case in Colonel Fullarton's detachment in the southern part of the Peninsula in 1783. See Wilks, vol. ii. p. 494. 4to. edition.

the 3d regiment of cavalry left at Jawud by Major-general Brown. There remained with Colonel Vanrenen, the 1st regiment of cavalry, and half the 2d battalion of the 12th Native infantry, with which he pursued the high road to Muttra, where he arrived on the 12th of April. These movements were followed, at some distance, by the march of the detachment left by Major-general Brown at Rampoor Bampoor; the 4th cavalry marching on the 4th of April for Muttra, in the expectation of reaching that place by the end of the month.

March of the Fifth Deckan Division to the Bheitwah in pursuit of Kurreem's and Wassil Mahomud's Pindarries.

(Map IV.)

Colonel Adams was joined in camp at Gungraur on the 16th of January, by the expected detachment, under Major Logie, escorting provisions from the rear, of which his division stood much in need. The detachment consisted of six hundred Native infantry and six guns, and placed this portion of the Fifth Division of the Army of the Deckan, on an efficient footing for the performance of any further service. It was now refreshed after the severe march it had performed, in very inclement weather, to the neighbourhood of the Chumbul; having necessarily halted at Gungraur since the 6th, with exception of the detachment which, under Major Clarke, had so successfully exerted themselves, on the 13th, against the Pindarries (pp. 201, 202). While that body was attacked, another corps of Kurreem's and Wassil Mahomud's *durrahs* passed to the southward of Gungraur; satisfied that Colonel Adams's means were not sufficient to make two detachments after them. Independent of these bodies, a third, belonging to the same chiefs, passed along the frontiers of Goozerat, and crossed to the eastward, along the Ghats of Southern Malwah, when they were sufficiently ahead of their pursuers. To the second of these, the remains of the first joined themselves, and now formed a sufficient object for the attention of the Colonel, who, being no longer required near the Chumbul, was at liberty to return towards the Nerbuddah. In pursuance of Sir Thomas Hislop's instructions to follow the Pindarries in their south-easterly direction, Colonel Adams marched his division on the 18th to Burroad, and on the following day to Augur. He here left some infantry and artillery details under Major Popham, to follow by moderate stages, and continued his march, with a single halt at the Bheitwah on the 27th, to Durrajpoor, eight miles south-east of Bhilsah, by Saurungpoor, Shoojalpoor, and Islamnuggur; making an average of nearly eighteen miles a-day, for nine days of consecutive marching, from the Chumbul to the Bheitwah. This decisive pursuit of his object shewed the Pindarries that there was no inclination to relax in operations against them; and such as had gained the confines of

(Map III)

the Bhopal territory, gladly availed themselves of the road of submission, opened to them by the liberal policy of the Governor-general. For this purpose Colonel Adams, on arriving at Durrajpoor on the 28th, halted his division; and with the Nabob of Bhopal and Captain Josiah Stewart *, the Political Agent there, formed one party to a negotiation with the Pindarries, who might now be inclined to abandon, for a peaceful and industrious life, the habits of disorder which had proved fatal to so many of them.

Cheettoo's durrah dispersed near the Nerbuddah.

This procedure, accordingly, put an end to the operations against those two *durrahs*; but Cheettoo was still a legitimate object of attack. He had now, likewise, by a circuitous route, thrown himself on the upper part of the Nerbuddah. Driven from Banswarra and the country about Rutlam and Taundla, he carried his *durrah* in a collected state into the district of Oonchode, and was reported to have three thousand horse and five elephants. One party, which entered the Baglee district, were said to have lost there two of their elephants, with other property, taken from them by the petty Chief of that district. With fifteen hundred men, Cheettoo descended the Ghats to Kunnoad, on the 24th of January. On the following day, intelligence of his position was brought to Major Heath, commanding at Hindia, distant twenty-two miles. A detachment of eight hundred and fifty men was immediately formed, consisting of details of the Madras European regiment, of the 1st battalion of the 7th regiment, of the depôt corps, and of Silladar horse, with which the Major marched, and came on the enemy at eight P. M. They immediately dispersed, leaving a few killed; and in their encampment, two elephants, one hundred and ten camels, and one hundred and thirty horses. Their flight was ineffectually pursued in the darkness of the night, and the detachment on the following day returned to Hindia. After this blow, Cheettoo fled up the Ghats to join his adherents left in that quarter; and his dispersed party again collected about him. He was heard of in the neighbourhood of Dowlutpoor Keiree and Anwas, on the 13th of February, by Colonel Adams, who ordered a

* This officer had been Persian Interpreter at the Head-quarters till after the Battle of Mehidpoor, when he was selected to fill the vacant situation of Political Agent at Bhopal. His natural disposition well fitted him for the work of conciliation: possessing one of those happy but rare tempers which immediately addresses the heart. He was subsequently appointed to the charge of political affairs with Scindiah, as a suitable successor to Captain Close, from previous experience in that court, joined to a thorough knowledge of Oriental languages and Indian politics.

detachment under Captain Roberts, consisting of five companies of infantry and five *russalahs* of irregular horse, to look out for him. This movement obliged him to return again to the westward, where more misfortunes awaited him.

Operations of Lieutenant-colonel Mac Morine from Hoossingabad. (Map VIII.)

The course of this narrative having returned to the affairs of the Upper Nerbuddah, a suitable occasion offers for describing the occurrences, at the beginning of the year, between Hoossingabad and Jubbulpoor. It will be recollected (p. 120), that Brigadier-general Hardyman's force, on finding his immediate advance to Nagpoor no longer necessary, had returned to the river; and that Colonel Mac Morine's detachment had arrived at the depôt with the convoy from the eastward. A considerable portion of this was dispatched in the latter part of December, under an escort composed, in part, of details*, to join the Fifth Division by the route of Bhopal. Another part was forwarded by the way of Beitool to Nagpoor. At the same time, a supply of grain carried by Bringarries, which had latterly been collected at Hoossingabad for the Advanced Division of the Deckan Army, was put in motion for Hindia under an escort of two companies of Native infantry and some irregular horse. These arrangements being made, Colonel Mac Morine marched towards Gurhwarra, in the latter days of December, to attack all bodies of the Rajah's troops assembled with hostile views. On arriving at that place, he ascertained that the force under Saddoo Baba, at Sreenugger, was about to receive a large reinforcement from Heerapoor, under a chief named Madhoo Rao; and the Colonel being deficient in cavalry, he applied to Brigadier-general Hardyman for assistance in that arm. In consequence of this application, one squadron of the Bengal 8th joined him, after a short halt at Beirkeirree; and he immediately directed his march on Sreenugger. Approaching that place on the morning of the 5th of January, he found the enemy drawn up in force † to oppose his progress; their left, where were two guns, *appuyed* on the *ghurrie*,

* It almost always happens, that the small convoys sent forward in the course of a campaign, are escorted by details. The posts from whence they advance contain field-hospitals as well as depôts; and all officers and small parties from the rear proceeding to join, collect at such points. These, with recovered men, are sometimes of sufficient strength to form the entire escort required; otherwise they contribute materially to it.

† They were represented, from report, by Colonel Mac Morine to Brigadier-general Hardyman, to be three thousand horse and four thousand foot, with ten guns. The number of ordnance was found to be only half, and perhaps the same proportion of men will approach the truth.

and on the right, their horse. There were likewise three guns in the *ghurrie*, which, with the others, opened as soon as they could do so effectually. The British force, consisting of one squadron of cavalry, three hundred Rohillah horse, the 1st battalion of the 10th regiment, a division of the 2d battalion of the 23d regiment, and four six-pounders, advanced in two columns; their guns in the centre, with the cavalry on the left. The latter were directed to make a *detour* round the enemy's right flank, which induced their horse to retire; and they were pursued with some loss. Their infantry, finding themselves thus abandoned, and the two columns approaching them in front, broke also, leaving in their position their guns and baggage. Their loss was estimated at three hundred. That of the detachment was twelve killed and wounded. The enemy dispersed over the country, and left the Colonel for some time without an object of sufficient importance to be attacked. He retained, however, the squadron of cavalry lent by Brigadier-general Hardyman, whose division was now without that arm, in consequence of the previous detachment to Nagpoor of the head-quarters and remaining squadrons of the 8th Bengal cavalry under Major O'Brien. This officer completed his march on the 3d of January, without having suffered any interruption on the way; and as at this time the affairs of the capital, where there was now a large force, had been settled, he was directed to return with his regiment on the 14th.

Return of Brigadier-general Hardyman's Force to Quarters.

Brigadier-general Hardyman was detained till the 10th of January at Jubbulpoor, in the expectation of commissariat supplies and treasure; still proposing to prosecute his march to Nagpoor. From thence he was without official communication, though Native reports induced him to conclude, that a cessation of hostilities had there taken place. He now received the Marquis of Hastings's instructions to fall back on Belharree, should he not have an immediate prospect of striking a blow at the enemy on the left bank of the river. He was induced, however, to exercise the discretion allowed him, and to continue at Jubbulpoor, though there was no tangible enemy, as he learned that new Authorities, deputed by the Rajah of Nagpoor and the Resident, were on their road to the Nerbuddah, to take charge of the districts on its banks, in consequence of the flight of the former Native officers. As the tract of country in question was to be, immediately, ceded to the British Government, Mr. Jenkins expressed apprehensions that measures of extortion would precede the transfer, were they not checked; and the Brigadier general accordingly remained at Jubbulpoor, to witness and promote the new establishment of affairs. On the 22d, a detachment of Native infantry, under Captain Black, summoned the fort of Belharree to receive terms for its evacuation. These were immediately accepted, and the place was occupied by a party of British troops. On the 27th the two squadrons of the 8th cavalry rejoined from Nagpoor, under Major O'Brien; and matters remained in the state which has been described, during the early part of February. Reports being then received that a body of horse and foot had assembled at Heerapoor, near the mouth of the Heron river, Brigadier-general Hardyman, having been likewise rejoined by the squadron lent to Lieutenant-colonel Mac Morine, marched on the 13th to Kisroad, near the Jhansee Ghat, on his route to attack them. The enemy, however, fled towards Saughur, and the detachment returned on the following day to Jubbulpoor. From hence, it was the Brigadier-general's intention to send a detachment to Mundalah, in the hopes of finding that place likewise disposed to surrender; but this measure was prevented by the receipt of instructions from Lord Hastings, dated the 13th, directing the separation of this force; for it will be recollected, that at this time the dislocation of the other divisions was likewise ordered. His Majesty's 17th foot, under Lieutenant-colonel Nicol, accordingly marched on the 20th for Ghazeepoor; and on the following day, accounts were received from Mundalah, that certain difficulties attending the payment of the garrison, rendered some delay likely to occur in the surrender of that place.

Return of Brigadier-general Toone's Force to Quarters. (Map I.)

Contemporary with the orders to Brigadier-general Hardyman, were those addressed to Brigadier-general Toone for the return of his force from the field. In pursuance of these orders, he directed his several detachments, on the 25th of February, to join his head-quarters at Oontarree. Yet, as some of these were at a distance of sixty miles, he was unable to proceed towards Dinapoor before the 6th of March; leaving one wing of the 2d battalion of the 4th Native infantry at the disposal of Major Roughsedge, commanding in that quarter of the frontier.

Operations of Major Macpherson from Hoossingabad. (Map VIII.)

While the enemy had been dispersed, and the country reduced to some degree of quiet about the Upper Nerbuddah, a small party shewed a hostile disposition below Hoossingabad. A chief, named Kundoo Pundit, occupied the fort of Seeonee, with a small force, which Major Macpherson, commanding at Hoossingabad, resolved to dislodge. He marched from that place with as many men as he could withdraw from garrison duty, and a small train, to attack the enemy; and, on the 21st of January, came before Seeonee. On summoning Kundoo Pundit, that chief desired a few hours to prepare for his departure. These were granted; but at their expiration, the Major finding evasions practised towards him, brought his guns into a position within three hundred yards of the south-east bastion, while he sent his Rohillah cavalry in parties to the opposite side to intercept the retreat. The battering commenced at four P. M.; and after two hundred rounds had been fired, the breach was still impracticable. It was now nearly dusk, when the enemy, in number about two hundred and fifty, evacuated by small parties; one of which, amounting to fifty, was attacked by the Rohillahs, and left fifteen dead on the ground. Several, likewise, took refuge in the town, where the Major allowed them to remain unmolested, on account of the peaceable behaviour of the inhabitants; who he was afraid might suffer, were any troops brought among them to search for those who had been in arms. Kundoo Pundit fled to the village of Bainradhur, distant fifteen miles, and was joined with one hundred and fifty horsemen, by Purrum Sookh, who had been formerly expelled the district. They were followed, however, by the Rohillahs, led by Captain Newton, who came to their position about two o'clock in the morning of the 23d, and was received with a fire from matchlocks, which wounded two troopers. The enemy were ultimately defeated, with the supposed loss of fifty men, and Purrum Sookh taken prisoner. In the fort of Seeonee were found four guns, besides ginjals, rockets, and some stores. One elephant, with a few camels, were likewise abandoned to the captors.

Expulsion of Gunput Rao's Party from the Nagpoor Territory.

On the march of the Arabs from Nagpoor, there appeared to be no enemy in the vicinity of the capital. At Ghirhur, about thirty-six miles distant, in a south-easterly direction, a chief, named Gunput Rao, collected a considerable body of predatory troops, both horse and foot. To disperse these, Brigadier-general Doveton ordered a detachment of four squadrons of Native cavalry with six horse-artillery guns, three companies of his Majesty's Royal Scots, the 2d battalion of the 24th Madras Native infantry, and five companies of the Berar brigade, to march on the morning of the 6th of January, under Lieutenant-colonel Macleod. On the approach of the detachment, the enemy broke up in small parties; the chief, with about three hundred men, taking a westerly course; and the Colonel returned, on the 13th, to the camp at Nagpoor.

March of the Second Division of the Deckan Army from Nagpoor, for the Reduction of the Ceded Districts West of the Wurdah.

(Map V.)

The presence at the capital of the Second Division of the Deckan Army contributed to establish the new order of things till the 22d, when the Resident considered its continuance there no longer indispensable. Brigadier-general Doveton therefore marched on that morning towards Ellichapoor, leaving a reinforcement with the Nagpoor brigade of two horse-artillery guns, the detachment of reformed horse, and one battalion of Berar infantry. This battalion was relieved a few days afterwards by the 2d battalion of the 24th regiment, under Lieutenant-colonel Mac Dowall. The division prosecuted its march by Amneir and Hewerkeir to Kaotah, three miles from Ellichapoor, where it was joined, on the 2d of February, by the battering-train, and was thus in a situation to effect those measures which had been pressed on the Brigadier-general's adoption by the Resident at Nagpoor. These were the assumption of the Ceded Districts in Berar, which had been held by the Rajah since the treaty of Argaum, and the establishment of the Nabob of Ellichapoor's authority in such of them as should be found convenient, pending the decision of the Governor-general. Such were the districts of Akoat, Argaum, and Wurnur: while the fourth, being Bhaut-Koolee, and near Oomrouttee, was to be given over to the Nizam's agent, Govind Bukhsh. With this view, Major Pitman was detached from Amneir with one battalion of Berar infantry, while the other was brought on to Ellichapoor, to assist the Nabob's troops in the occupation of the remaining Cessions. Besides the districts below the Ghats, there were certain places above, such as Meilghat and others, on the Taptee, which were occupied by the Peishwah's troops, and required to be assumed and likewise placed in charge of the Nabob; but the disposal of the forts of Gawulghur and Narnullah were reserved for a special arrangement.

March of Colonel Pollock's Detachment, and Progress of the Second Division to Ootran.

From Ellichapoor, a detachment was made, on the 3d of February, under Lieutenant-colonel Pollock, of two squadrons of the 6th Native cavalry, and the 1st battalion of the 12th Native infantry, with orders to proceed towards Poonah by the most direct route, for the purpose of reinforcing the Fourth Division in the pursuit of the Peishwah. On the 4th, Brigadier-general Doveton moved to Khanzuman-nuggur. From thence he detached a party, under Captain Jones, with one company of the 2d battalion of the 13th regiment, and the Berar battalion, to receive, on the Rajah's order, the fort of Gawulghur. The place was immediately surrendered; and the Berar battalion, with the exception of three companies, returned to the camp. Narnullah surrendered, in like manner, to one company of the 1st battalion of the 11th regiment, and three companies of Berar infantry, on the 7th, when the division was at Argaum. Possession was also taken of all the low country, as had been proposed, by the assistance of detachments from the division, while it continued its march. Lest, however, these arrangements should be disturbed by the armed parties lately dispossessed, and who had retired among the hills, Major Pitman was directed to keep the troops under his personal command, as well as the reformed horse under Lieutenant Hamilton, in motion, through the districts of Oomrouttee and Akolah, to support the newly established authorities. These orders were issued, on the 11th, from Bohungaum; and the Brigadier-general continued his march to Mulkapoor, where he halted on the 15th. He was here joined by details of the First, Second, and Third Divisions, escorting a convoy, consisting of commissariat supplies for the First Division, and some stores, intended for the purposes of siege. At the same time he received Sir Thomas Hislop's orders to advance to Ootran on the Gheernah, in consequence of the temporary relinquishment of the views on Asseerghur, and the expediency of intercepting or dispersing the *Barra Bhye* under Ram Deen, who had crossed the Nerbuddah, near Myheyswur, with the supposed design of joining the Peishwah. The Second Division continued its march on the 16th, and arrived by the route of Sunnoad and Lohara, on the 20th, at Ootran, where it halted for further instructions.

Establishment of Holkur's Authority about Indoor, entrusted to the Goozerat Force (Map IV.)

Though Ram Deen had proceeded towards the quarter to which Brigadier-general Doveton's attention was directed, he left many partizans in the vicinity of Indoor, of which place he had been governor previous to the war. To defeat their secret efforts, and to establish permanently in those districts the new Government of Holkur, so much time would be required, as to preclude the performance of that service by the presence of the Head-quarters of the Deckan Army, which was urgently required to the southward. Sir Thomas Hislop accordingly addressed his instructions for this purpose to Sir William Grant Keir. That officer was directed to give his particular attention to the points of Ragooghur, Beitmah, and Kalunode, where the adherents of the Ex-governor lay in parties not exceeding five hundred, watching an opportunity of re-establishing their principal authority. His brother, Mukin Lal, who conducted the affairs of his party, remained in Oojein, where he was secure from molestation; and Major-general Sir William Grant Keir was recommended to advance his head-quarters towards

Indoor, in furtherance of the objects of his instructions. As a last attempt against the Pindarries in Malwah, a detachment was placed under Captain Grant's orders, on the 3d of February, and consisted of the Mysore horse, a troop of the 8th cavalry, and a few light infantry. This detachment was directed to attempt the surprise of Cheettoo's *durrah* in the Baglee jungles, and afterwards to follow the route of the army.

Head-quarters of the Deckan Army recross the Nerbuddah (Map VII.)

These arrangements being made, Sir Thomas Hislop recommenced his march towards the Nerbuddah, on the 6th; and on the following day descended the Sumroad Ghat, at the foot of which the division was obliged to halt on the 8th, to enable the rear-guard, and a large portion of the baggage, to join. This pass was barely practicable for carriages, and so narrow, that much delay occurred in descending it. The Bheels made some attempts to harass the rear; but, finding at every point a party prepared to repel them, their endeavours were very feeble. From the river Chorud, at the foot of the Sumroad Ghat, were addressed to Brigadier-general Doveton those orders which had induced him to march to Ootran. The accounts, at the same time, of the situation of the Peishwah, rendered the movements of Lieutenant-colonel Pollock's detachment not immediately applicable to operations against him; while Lieutenant-colonel Deacon's detachment was well advanced for this purpose. The former was therefore directed to be recalled by a route calculated to intercept the progress of Ram Deen and the *Barra Bhye*, as a service of more immediate importance to the public interests. In two more marches, the Head-quarters and First Division arrived at the river; and the cavalry and light troops immediately crossed by the Raveir Ghat to the right bank. Here Captain Grant's detachment rejoined, having ascertained the dispersion of Cheettoo's *durrah* ever since the blow they received at Kunnoad; the hostility of the surrounding country having also obliged them to subsist in small parties in the heart of the jungle, about the Ghats near Baglee. The lower part of the Nerbuddah was found to be very rocky; and though the water at this ford had become low enough for the passage of bullocks, it was necessary to relieve them of their burdens, such especially as carried ammunition and grain. On this account, and owing to the difficulty with which the carriages were conveyed over slipping rocks, in the bed of the river, the division was detained on its banks, from the 10th to the 13th of February, on which day the march was continued to Mohallah. On the 14th, the instructions of the Marquis of Hastings were received, desiring that the forces under the command of Sir John

Malcolm and Colonel Adams should be left under his Lordship's immediate orders. The Third and Fifth Divisions were consequently struck off the strength of the Army of the Deckan; the Head-quarters of which had now withdrawn from any connexion with the theatre of their operations. All controul over the Goozerat force likewise ceased, pursuant to the condition under which the command of it had been assumed by Sir Thomas Hislop, when its immediate co-operation was required.

Progress of the First Division to the Taptee (Plan 10.)

The Head-quarters of the army arrived on the 18th at Kurgoon, where it was joined by the convoy from Hindia, escorted by Captain Wilson's detachment already mentioned. A company of the 2d battalion of the 14th Native infantry was detached from the camp with treasure to Hindia; and Lieutenant Mackintosh, commanding it, was directed to proceed afterwards by the route of Meil, from Charwah to Ellichapoor, to ascertain a line of movement hitherto unexplored by any British troops. On this ground, the intelligence of Ram Deen's movements was more satisfactory than any which previously it had been practicable to obtain. He was represented, after having passed the Nerbuddah, near Myheyswur, to have crossed the province of Nemar to the Doolkoat Ghat, in the Sautpoora mountains; and to be accompanied by about one thousand five hundred men, with two guns, many laden carriages, and treasure to the amount of four or five lacs of rupees. A detachment, consisting of the Mysore horse and three companies of light infantry, was placed under the command of Captain James Grant, with orders to pursue him through the hills, and from thence to Choprah in Khandesh, whither he was reported to have proceeded. This was not the most direct route for overtaking this body, in the direction it was expected to follow; but as the Head-quarters proposed descending the Scindwah Ghat, as Brigadier-general Doveton was at Ootran, and as Lieutenant-colonel Pollock's detachment was ordered to return by the Cassurbarree Ghat, it was supposed the enemy might be forced back, and would return by the route he went, should it be left open to him. The country on both sides of the Sautpoora mountains being extremely rugged and confined, Sir Thomas Hislop deemed it advisable to separate the division into two parts for greater facility of movement. He marched, on the 20th, with the light-artillery brigade, cavalry, light infantry brigade, and Europeans of the first brigade; leaving under Colonel Macdowall, the Native corps of the first brigade, three hundred Mysore horse and pioneers, to bring on the park and all the heavy baggage. These divisions rejoined

(Plan 20) on the 22d at Seindwah, which being ceded by the treaty of Mundissoor, was, on the following day, delivered over by Holkur's garrison, and occupied by the 2d battalion of the 14th Native infantry, under Major Ives. On the 24th, the light artillery, cavalry brigade, and rifles, were ordered to march to Punnaghur, beyond the Seindwah Ghat, leaving a party to protect the pioneers employed in improving the pass; and the Head-quarters encamped immediately at the top, on the same day. On the 25th, the march was continued down the Ghat to Punnaghur, and the cavalry rejoined. This descent was found so easy, after the previous labour of the pioneers, that the division was enabled to march on the following morning to Kurroand, and on the 27th to Talneir.

Unexpected hostility of the Garrison of Talneir.

In passing through such parts of the country as were considered free from an enemy, the baggage of individuals was allowed to take the risk of going in front of the line of march, as long as it did not obstruct the progress of the troops; and, therefore, wherever the country opened, all the good cattle which got early in motion were well advanced before the line came to its ground. Even in more difficult situations, the activity of private servants produced the same effect; and on approaching Talneir, the head of the column of baggage arrived at the opening of the small plain surrounding that place, while the troops were still two miles in the rear. The proposed ground for this day's encampment was on the left bank of the Taptee, opposite the fort of Talneir; under the walls of which, the road leads down to the only ford by which the river was here passable. A sick officer in a palanquin was passing alone towards the new ground, to gain some shelter before the heat of the day should set in; but was obliged to turn back by a fire of matchlocks directed at him from the walls of the place. At the same time, a gun opened with round shot on the head of the baggage entering the plain, and obliged it, likewise, to fall back. The unexpected occurrence of this hostile *demonstration* on the part of Talneir, was announced to Sir Thomas Hislop nearly at the same time by a spy, who, having been out for intelligence in that quarter, ascertained the intentions of the garrison. It never was apprehended that this insulated place would be so rash as to oppose the advance of a respectable force, particularly as Seindwah, a fort of much greater supposed importance, had immediately surrendered on the production of Holkur's order. Sir Thomas Hislop, in the first instance, sent a summons to the Killedar, with an intimation of the consequences which would attend his attempt at resistance.

His Excellency, at the same time, directed the proper officers to make a close reconnaissance of the place, while the head of the line should halt out of reach of fire.

One side of Talneir fort rises out of the Taptee, and the three other sides are surrounded by a hollow way, varying in width from one hundred to one hundred and fifty yards. The walls rise to the height of about sixty feet above this hollow, and the interior of the fort* has the same elevation. The only entrance is on the eastern side, and secured by five successive gates, communicating by intricate traverses, whose inclosures gradually rise to the height of the main wall. A winding ramp, interspersed in some places with steps, ascends through the gates to the *terre-pleine* of the rampart. Great Native ingenuity had been exercised to render this part as strong as possible, apparently under the idea that the profile of the rest rendered it secure, notwithstanding the absence of a ditch. The ground immediately surrounding the hollow way, is cut by deep ravines, which run into it. The intermediate parts are crowned with clusters of houses, which form the town of Talneir, distant from the fort about three hundred and fifty yards. The country surrounding the town is flat, but separated from it by other ravines which branch off in various directions. The reconnoitring party descended into the ravines, and from them ascended into the town opposite the north-west angle, driving out a small party of the enemy, who opposed their advance by a sniping fire from behind the walls of

Reconnaissance and description of Talneir (Plan 21.)

---

* Many fortresses, called *ghurries* in the Deckan, bear a general resemblance to Talneir. Perhaps a more accurate idea may be formed, by imagining a mound of earth of about one hundred and fifty yards diameter, and about sixty or seventy feet high. That the sides of this are scarped off by labour, and the prominent parts shaped into flanking towers. Let the whole be *revêted* and surmounted by a parapet, and the *ghurrie* will only want an entrance. A gateway pierced in the *revêtment* of a re-entering angle, something lower than the interior of the fort, will form the inner communication; and on each side will be projected a tower to flank it, and to plunge a fire into the next. This will be formed in a lower wall, the extremities of which will terminate in the *revêtment* of the place, inclosing a small space; and it will be likewise flanked by projecting towers independent of the defences being loop-holed. These works, it is evident, may be frequently repeated; and the form of the traverses, as well as the relative positions of the gates, continually varied; but the general practice avoids placing two successive gates exactly opposite, and the outer aperture is invariably on lower ground than that next within, to favour the ascent. On some occasions so much earth may be scarped off as to form a high glacis, which makes the space left between it and the wall, virtually a ditch; but in very few cases is a ditch actually excavated around a *ghurrie*.

inclosures. It was ascertained that the enemy had no guns on the western face, which was in fact the strongest; the water was here conveniently situate, and the ground on the bank of the river comparatively clear. Sir Thomas therefore resolved on encamping the division in that direction, and in attacking the place by the north-east angle, for no answer was returned by the Killedar to the summons which had been addressed to him.

Attack of the Place.

While the troops, except the details on duty, were going to their lines, to cover the preparations for the attack, two five-and-a-half-inch howitzers, with ten six-pounders, which were the only caliber in camp, were moved down the bed of the ravines; for thus the roads pass. They were then carried (b, c, d.) to positions in the town, where the houses gave tolerable cover to batteries, which opened within two hundred and fifty and three hundred yards of the north-east angle. In the course of a few hours, during which several casualties had occurred by the well-aimed fire of matchlocks from the walls, the enemy were nearly silenced; but no progress had been made in reducing the garrison, which, it had been concluded, would surrender, on viewing a serious *demonstration* against them. Further examination of the place discovered that the outer gate was in a ruinous state, and promised cover in the traverses; while a commanding position immediately opposite to it, overlooked the nearest defences, and from thence some of the inner gates could be seen.* These circumstances having determined Sir Thomas (e.) Hislop to attack by the gates, two guns were opened, with considerable effect, on the traverses, while two others were brought by a *detour* to a position, from whence they might be *run up* with facility to the gate, for the purpose of blowing it open. At the same time a storming-party, consisting of the flank companies of his Majesty's Royal Scots, and of the Madras European regiment, under Major Gordon of the former corps, was (h.) brought down to the same place, and lay in shelter there till called for. Indifferent as the enemy had been to the fire directed against their defences in general, and the north-east tower, which was ineffectually battered with field-pieces, the preparations against the gates did not fail to alarm them, and they sent out to demand terms of capitulation. In reply they were informed, that unconditional surrender alone would be accepted; and they

* Such, in the present instance, was the injudiciousness of having the outer walls lower than those within.

were invited to avail themselves of this offer before the assault of the gates should commence.

The evening was now advanced, and the enemy probably trusted to the approaching darkness, for an opportunity of abandoning a place which they considered untenable. It was necessary to prevent this occurrence; and the guns and storming-party were ordered to advance to the gate. This was done, without loss; the excellent practice of the artillery keeping down at this time all fire from the fort. It was found that a passage for single files existed between the wall and the gate-frame, in consequence of its ruinous state; and no opposition being offered from within, the storming-party, followed by the pioneers, entered it without difficulty, though tediously. During this time the rifle corps, under Major Snow, made an unsuccessful circuit of the fort, to observe if there were any other point by which the place was assailable; while a detachment of cavalry was stationed on the opposite bank of the river, to cut off any attempt at flight. After the passage of the storming-party, endeavours were used to blow open the outer gate, that the guns might be advanced to the remainder. Before, however, that was effected, the storming-party had passed through the second gate without opposition. At the third it was met by the Killedar, with a number of Bumjans and artificers, whom he had forced in on the previous evening. Assault by the Gates.

Lieutenant-colonel Conway, the Adjutant-general of the army, with Lieutenant-colonel Macgregor Murray, and several others, had entered with the storming-party; and it was still doubtful whether resistance would ultimately be made, for at this time there was none. They accordingly passed through the fourth gate, which, as well as the second, appeared so much out of repair, as to be incapable of being shut; but at the fifth, or last gate, they were stopped, though the wicket was opened. A hurried conversation about terms of surrender now took place. It was probably little intelligible under the circumstances of noise and apprehension which attended it. Colonel Murray, under this state of uncertainty, concluding that there was an urgent necessity for establishing a footing such as would secure eventual success to the attack, should the enemy hold out, entered by the wicket, with Major Gordon, and about three grenadiers; but refrained from drawing his sword, to shew that he had no intention of breaking off the parley. He expected to be followed by as many men as should be able to maintain themselves in a confined situation; but four or five persons only had got in, when the enemy, apprehending the consequences, attacked most furiously, and in a moment laid them all dead, except Colonel Murray, who fell towards the wicket covered with wounds. They attempted then to close the wicket; but their efforts were rendered ineffectual by a grenadier, who thrust his musquet (with a happy presence of mind) into the aperture, and secured that hope, while Lieutenant-colonel Mackintosh* and Captain Mac Craith forced it open. It was held in this state during the time that the Captain was, with one hand, dragging Colonel Murray through it, and warding off blows with his sword in the other. A fire was now poured in through the wicket, which cleared the gateway sufficiently for the head of the storming-party, under Captain Macgregor of the Royals, to enter; and the place was carried without further difficulty, but at the expense of that officer's life. As soon as the supporting detachment could open the gate, many troops poured in, the garrison were shortly put to the sword, and the Killedar was hanged on the same evening to a tree on the flag-staff tower.

Reflections on this Service

There were about two hundred and fifty men killed in Talneir, and the loss in British troops amounted to twenty-five†, including seven officers. The enemy shewed an unaccountable degree of negligence, in not fortifying, within, such gates as were closed; and why they fired on the army, it is impossible to say, unless it were to extort favourable terms. When these were refused, there was no alternative, but unconditional surrender, or an attempt to evacuate the place at night, should it hold out so long. They probably knew the nature of the guns which could be brought against their walls, and never expected so daring an attempt as an attack by the gates. But the greatest of all follies was the opening a wicket to parley, when they had no further retrenchment in their rear to retire on with security. It is possible their indecision arose from a division in their councils; and the departure of the Killedar from among them supports this conclusion; the determination of which, were it of much importance, is now impracticable. As to the conduct of the British force, they were reduced to a case of ne-

* This officer, belonging to the commissariat, accompanied the storming-party, like a few other staff officers, without orders; and while no apology will be attempted here for such an irregularity, it is necessary to admit, that to their presence may be materially attributed the fall of the place, after the regimental officers who led, had been killed or otherwise disabled.

† Vide Appendix. L.

cessity; being unexpectedly saluted, at the end of a march, by a fire in front, which they could not avoid without a countermarch. Whether this would have been disgraceful, it would, at all events, have been extremely impolitic, as well as distressing; for no water was procurable, except at the last day's ground, or from the Taptee, the access to which was opposed. Under these circumstances, the necessity for [illegible] this place was unquestionable, and there were only two coercive methods; that of immediately using the unsuitable means present, or of waiting till those better adapted should be brought from Ootran. The latter measure would have caused a detention of eight days from the important object of the early reduction of the Peishwah's field army, besides the opposition expected from every remaining *ghurric* on the route through Khandesh.

The instances, in India, of places being successfully assaulted, are by no means rare*, and will account for the frequency of the attempt. Other motives arise out of the great value of time in the scheme of British operations, and the important moral effect produced in their enemies, by bold enterprize. The event, however, is little calculable†; and it must be allowed, that successful resistance is as favourable to the enemy's cause, as a contrary result has been supposed to be, to the opposite side. This state of the case very much reduces the question to a comparison of chances, which, in war, is, on special occasions only, a legitimate ground of action; for the whole object of military science is certainty of result. In the Mahratta war of 1803, a striking instance occurs, in the assault of Alleeghur, on the 4th of September, by the Bengal army. This place was taken, by the gates, with severe loss; but to have reduced it, regularly, might have been attended with as much, and would have affected the entire campaign, of which it was nearly the opening. The attack of the walled *pettah* of Ahmednuggur by escalade, which nearly opened the same campaign on the side of the Deckan, was exposed to little chance of failure, though attended with

Considerations on Coups de Main in general.

* A remarkable instance occurs in the attack of Carangooly, in 1780, by a detachment from Sir Eyre Coote's army; in Colonel Wellesley's attack of Rannee Bednoor, in 1800; and several other cases, unnecessary to be enumerated.

† Sir Eyre Coote failed in the attack of the fortified Pagoda of Chillumbrum, in 1781, with considerable loss; and a similar result attended the attack of the fortified summit of Moogral Hill, in the Chittoor Pollums, by Colonel Moneypenny's detachment, in the beginning of 1805. The fortress of Panjalum Courchy, in the Tinnevillee district, furnishes more than one instance of successful resistance.

2 H

heavy loss. The walls were low*, and their narrowness at the top, which was probably unknown, was the greatest difficulty they opposed. Under such circumstances, an escalade, at several points, is almost sure of success; but with *ghurries*, whose walls are sixty or seventy feet high, the attempt is out of the question; and even in the instance of places of moderate elevation, scaling-ladders have been found too short, in a number of instances, which are very descriptive of the precipitancy of British assaults.

Comparisons of the means employed.

A ladder, beyond a certain length, becomes unwieldy, and the rearing it difficult; because its mass, from a well-known law in physics, does not increase in the same proportion as its power, which must be adequate to the weight to be borne, and relative to the extent of bearing. The latter element is materially affected by the distance † of planting scaling-ladders, to which much importance attaches. Though the proper use of scaling-ladders is for a surprise, they have been frequently used in India for daring assault. Their consequent importance has been the cause of frequent and ingenious attempts to render them at once portable, and applicable to different heights. French inventions for this purpose were found at Seringapatam, and in British arsenals others have been made of pieces to be put together; but none of these succeeded like the inflexible bamboo-ladder, with all the occasional inconvenience of disproportionate length. These are strong enough, when rolled with spun-yarn for a length of thirty-five feet, bearing as many men as can ascend at once. They are also comparatively light, from being hollow; while every piece of machinery must not only be made of solid timber, but, moreover, double at the joinings; thus multiplying the weight and dividing the power ‡. To the attack of high *ghurries*,

---

* The recent "Memoir of the late War in India" says, "The *pettah* wall was very lofty." Its average height is under twelve feet.

† "The distance from the foot of the ladders to the walls should be equal to half of their height. For this is the most just proportion with respect to the men that are to mount upon them. If the distance be greater, the ladders will too easily be broken under the weight. If less, they will then be so erect, that the soldiers, as they ascend, must be continually in danger of falling headlong down."—Hampton's Polybius, iii. p. 80. 8vo. edition.

The above rule would require the ladder to be one-eighth longer than the height of the wall, merely to reach its top.

‡ The discovery of the law in physics, here referred to, and which is attributed to Galileo, is related by Montucla, with several ingenious reflections:—"Galiléo tire de sa théorie quelques conséquences que nous ne devons pas omettre: la première est que des corps semblables n'ont pas

therefore, scaling-ladders are inapplicable. Breaching-batteries also, to make a sufficient slope in a *revêtted* mound of earth, into which every shot penetrates, as into a butt for practice, however successful they may ultimately prove, require more patience* than is generally compatible with a

---

des forces proportionnées à leurs masses pour résister à leur rupture; car les masses croissent comme les cubes des côtés semblables; les résistances, *cæteris paribus*, ne le font qu'en raison des quarrés de ces côtés; d'ou il suit qu'il-y-a un terme de grandeur au-delà duquel un corps se romproit au moindre choc ajouté à son propre poids, ou par ce poids même, tandis qu'une autre moindre et semblable résistera au sien, et même à un effort étranger. De-là vient, dit Galiléo, qu'une machine qui fait son effet en petit, manque lorsqu'elle est executée en grand, et croule sous sa propre masse. La nature, ajoute-t-il, ne sauroit faire des arbres ou des animaux démesurément grands, sans être exposés à un pareil accident, et c'est pour cela que les plus grands animaux vivent dans un fluide qui leur ôte une partie de leur poids. Nous pourrions encore remarquer que c'est-là la raison pour laquelle de petits insectes peuvent, sans danger de fracture, faire des chutes si démesurées, en égard à leur taille, tandis que de grands animaux, comme l'homme, se blessent souvent en tombant de leur hauteur. Une autre vérité curieuse qui suit de cette théorie, c'est qu'un cylindre creux, et ayant la même base et superficie, résiste davantage que s'il étoit solide. C'est, ce semble, pour cette raison, et pour concilier en même temps la légèreté et la solidité, que la nature a fait creux les os des animaux, les plumes des oiseaux, et les *tiges* de plusieurs plantes," &c.—Histoire des Mathématiques, tom. ii p. 190. 4to. edition.

* The importance of time is the common enemy of regular sieges. Those of the British army in Spain was a mixture of regular approach and insult; for the case was generally reducible to the alternative, of either undertaking the reduction of a place in a restricted number of days, or of refraining from the attempt altogether. These generally succeeded with British troops; and perhaps they alone, or Russians, are suitable to it. Nor is it in these days only that this character has been acquired, in support of which are the following curious extracts from the Harleian Miscellany, (vol. x. pp. 418, 420.) The city of Ypres was besieged by Marshal Turenne, commanding the French army, to which was attached a corps of English, under Major-general Sir Thomas Morgan, sent by Cromwell to assist against the Spaniards; and the Marshal, under great apprehensions that Don John of Austria would "break through one of his quarters to relieve the city," intimated the same to Sir Thomas. "Then Major-general Morgan told him, his condition was somewhat desperate, and said, that a desperate disease must have a desperate cure. His Excellency asked what he meant? Major-general Morgan did offer him to attempt the counterscarp upon an assault, and so put all things out of doubt with expedition. The Major-general had no sooner said this, but Marshal Turenne joined his hands, and looked up through the boards towards the heavens, and said, Did ever my master, the King of France, or the King of Spain, attempt a counterscarp upon an assault, where there are three half-moons covered with cannon, and the ramparts of the town playing point-blank into the counterscarp? Further he said, What will the King, my master, think of me, if I expose his army to these hazards? And he rose up and fell into a passion, stamping with his feet, and shaking his locks, grinning with his teeth. He said, Major-general Morgan had made him mad; but, by degrees, he cooled, and asked the Major-general whether he would stay to dinner with him; but the Major-general begged his pardon, for

comparison of other exigencies of the service to the importance of a small garrison. There remain two other methods which promise early success. These are, bombardment and mining: the first on account of the confined area of all elevated *ghurries*, containing no proof-buildings; and the other, from the facility of entering their *revêtment;* to which, at the same time, there are scarce any means of offering effectual opposition, there being seldom any ditch. It appears, however, that in India, these are branches of the military profession the least understood and practised.

Reflections on the Engineer Establishment in India

In an army which has generally found a wider field for the display of bravery and discipline, than occasion for scientific resources, the Engineering branch of the service is not likely to meet all the encouragement which it deserves, or which, in fact, is necessary. It may, indeed, be fairly asserted, that this establishment is far below its proportion in India, and seldom able to furnish for field service, officers possessing the rare combination of talents and experience, while permanent employment in Civil

---

he had appointed some of the officers to eat beef at his tent that day." The assault, however, was agreed to, and " Marshall Turenne asked Major-general Morgan, How many English he would venture? The Major-general said, he would venture six hundred common men, besides officers, and fifty pioneers. Marshall Turenne said, that six hundred of Monsieur la Ferte's army, and fifty pioneers, and six hundred of his own army, and fifty pioneers, would be better than two thousand men. Major-general Morgan replied, they were abundance to carry it, with God's assistance." After this, the Marshal proposed he should advance by an approach occupied by the French; but " Major-general Morgan begged his pardon, and said, he desired to fall on with the English entire, without intermingling them," and insisted, for that purpose, on exposing himself to the danger of advancing between two approaches. This ended with the Major-general and his men leaping " pell mell into the counterscarp, amongst the enemy. Abundance of the enemy were drowned in the moat, and many taken prisoners, with two German Princes, and the counterscarp cleared. The French were in their approaches all this time. The English fell on upon the half-moons, and immediately the red coats were on the top of them, throwing the enemy into the moat, and turning the guns upon the town. Thus the two half-moons were speedily taken." " Then the French fell on upon the other half-moon, but were beaten off. The Major-general considered that that half-moon would gall him in the day-time, and therefore did speak to the officers and soldiers, that it was best to give them a little help; the red coats cried, ' Shall we fall ôn in order, or happy-go-lucky?' The Major-general said, ' In the name of God, happy-go-lucky;' and immediately the red coats fell on and were at the top of it, knocking the enemy down and casting them into the moat. When this work was done, the Major-general lodged the English on the counterscarp; they were no sooner lodged, but Marshal Turenne scrambled over the ditches to find the Major-general; and when he met with him, he was much troubled the French did no better; for indeed they did just nothing."—Relation of Sir Thomas Morgan's progress in France. London, 1699.

works is considered as paramount to the Military demands of the service. With all the Madras troops in the field, during this war, there was no officer of engineers above the rank of Lieutenant; yet even this is tolerable, compared with the state of the engineer department with the Grand Army, before Bhurtpoor, in the former war under Lord Lake. His Lordship, in his public dispatches, attributed his failures at that place to this deficiency*; and for doing this, might have abundant reason, without any reproach attaching to that respectable corps. The fault lies in the system throughout, in which sufficient importance is not given to the engineer branch of the military service. Individuals belonging to it possess abundance of talent; encouragement and extension are alone required to convert the British attacks of fortified places, now characterised only by a spirit of self-devotion, into elevated instances of generous principle, combined with one of the highest efforts of human ingenuity and cultivated intellect.

---

* A late History of India, in describing this deplorable siege, thus mentions this circumstance: "As general causes, he (Lord Lake) chiefly alleges the extent of the place, the number of its defenders, the strength of its works, and lastly, the incapacity of his Engineers; as if a commander were fit for his office, who is not himself an Engineer." (Mill's History of British India, III. p. 688, 4to edit.) This remark probably arises from ignorance of the distinction between the theoretic and executive parts of engineering. A Commander in Chief should, no doubt, judge of the propriety of a plan of attack, as far as general reconnaissance, and examination of the projects submitted to him, will supply the means: but by whom is all the particular information to be collected on which these projects are to be formed? and being collected, by whom shall it be put together, with all the comparisons and calculations of means that are necessary to the perfection of a plan of attack? By whom are to be distributed, superintended, and directed, the various details which should be unremittingly and simultaneously prosecuted? Many officers, and many ranks, are required for the performance of these duties, the lowest of which, for its due execution, requires a knowledge of the higher; and well might the deficiency of the Engineer establishment be given as the cause for the failures at Bhurtpoor, though it is none for Lord Lake's undertaking that siege with insufficient means. With equal, if not more justice, might the General be expected to command, personally, every separate piece of artillery at the siege: but in either case, supposing it practicable, who is to perform the extensive and superior functions of Commander in Chief, which appear to be left out of the account?

CHAPTER IV.

ESTABLISHMENT OF THE RAJAH OF SATARA, AND EXPULSION OF THE PEISHWAH FROM THE POONAH TERRITORY.

Re-organization of the Fourth Division and Reserve. Siege of Singhur. Capitulation. Reduction of Poorunder. Occupation of the remaining Forts between Satara and Poonah. Colonel Deacon's Marches North of the Godavery, and Departure of Sulabut Khan. March in Pursuit of Gunput Rao to Ahmednuggur, and Return of Sulabut Khan. Reduction of Places between Ahmednuggur and Poonah. Operations of Lieutenant-colonel Prother's Detachment in the Southern Kokun. Operations above the Ghats. March of the Fourth Division from Satara, in Pursuit of the Peishwah. Cavalry Combat at Ashtee. Parallel between the Defeat of Gokla and Dhoondeah Waugh. Reflections on this Affair, and its Result. Considerations respecting the British and Mahratta Governments. Re-establishment of the Rajah of Satara. Movements of Lieutenant-colonel Pollock's Detachment. March of the Head-quarters of the Deckan Army through the Valley of Khandesh. March of the First and Second Divisions to the Godavery. Movements of the Enemy, and of the Fourth Division. Re-organization of the Hydrabad and Poonah Divisions. Termination of Sir Thomas Hislop's Command of the Army of the Deckan.

THE description of the operations against the Peishwah was discontinued at the reduction of Satara, when he was again flying in a northerly direction.

Re-organization of the Fourth Division and Reserve.

The Fourth Division and Reserve having joined, were favourably circumstanced to re-organize their composition, and to benefit by the experience acquired from their preceding exertions. The result was, the formation of two corps; one consisting of all the parts best adapted to a siege, and the other, of those calculated for a renewed and vigorous pursuit of the fugitive. For this purpose the cavalry of the Reserve was transferred to the Fourth Division, and a brigade of Bombay Native infantry, with the battering train, was transferred to the Reserve in return. With the Fourth Division was now left a compact and efficient light force, consisting of the horse-artillery, two squadrons of his Majesty's 22d dragoons, the 2d and 7th regiments of Madras cavalry, twelve hundred Poonah auxiliary horse, and two thousand five hundred infantry. The force remaining to compose the Reserve, consisted of—

		European Rank and File.	Total Rank and File.
Artillery	Madras Establishment of Europeans .	116	194
	Bombay . . ditto . . . . . ditto	78	
The Madras Brigade	Division of the Rifle Corps	—	1775
	European Flank Battalion	823	
	2d Battalion of the 12th Native Infantry	—	
Bombay Brigade . .	Bombay European P[illegible] . . .	419	1766
	2d Battalion of th[illegible] R[illegible] of . Bombay Native Infantry	—	
	2d Battalion of the 15th Regiment of . Madras* Native Infantry	—	
	Total Force . .		3735

with a train of one ten and four eight-inch mortars, two heavy five-and-a-half-inch howitzers, four eighteen and four twelve-pounders, four light five-and-a-half-inch howitzers, and ten six-pounder field-pieces. To this force was attached three hundred and sixty-one Madras and Bombay pioneers, and five hundred Poonah auxiliary horse. The commanding engineer was Captain Nutt, of the Bombay establishment; and the artillery was commanded by Lieutenant-colonel Dalrymple, of the Madras Presidency, who was well experienced in the description of service about to be undertaken.

The Fourth Division having moved off, on the 13th of February, in pursuit of the enemy, the Reserve marched on the following morning from Satara, by the Salpee Ghat and the Neerah Bridge, Eerrec, Seeraola, and Seewarrah, to Singhur, before which place it arrived on the 20th. This movement was luckily accomplished without any molestation from an enemy, though the line of march, with the train, stores, and provisions, equalled in length an extent of four miles; and the latter part of the road, lying among hills, was difficult, from its intersection by numerous ravines. The fortress of Singhur stands on the summit of a mountain, which terminates, to the west, one of the ranges of hills running from the east between

Siege of Singhur.

(Map VI.)

(Plan 22.)

* The 2d Battalion of the 7th Bombay Native infantry was ordered from Poonah, to relieve the 2d Battalion of the 15th Madras Native infantry.

Poonah and the Neerah river. Its altitude is very great; and the access to it, along pathways on high and precipitous ridges, which ascend from the southward and eastward. Its greatest extent, from west to east, is about a thousand yards, and from north to south, about eight hundred; but the irregularity of its shape, which conforms to the direction of the scarped sides of the rock on which the walls stand, deprives it of a diagonal which would be proportional to those dimensions in a regular figure. Its area is therefore comparatively confined, and, moreover, occupied by rugged eminences which rise within the walls. It contains no bomb-proofs; but shelter may be obtained for a small body of men, under ledges of the rocks. The Head-quarters of the Reserve were established on the banks of a *nullah,* about two miles and a half from the fort, in a south-easterly direction; and as one of the avenues from its eastern extremity, or Poonah gate, communicated with the northern valley, six companies of the 2d battalion of the 7th Bombay Native infantry, and a body of auxiliary
(A.) horse, invested it on that side. On the crest of the ridge, opposite that extremity, at the distance of eight hundred yards, a post and battery were established, of one eight-inch mortar, one five-and-a-half-inch howitzer, and two six-pounders, which opened on the 21st. On the following day, four companies of the 2d battalion of the 15th Madras Native infantry marched for Poonah, and were replaced by the remaining four companies of the 2d
(B.) battalion of the 7th Bombay Native infantry. The mortar-battery, which opened on the same evening, consisting of one ten and three eight-inch mortars, and three five-and-a-half-inch howitzers, was placed under cover of a hill, south-east of the fort. On the 24th, Captain Davies, with one thousand eight hundred Nizam's reformed horse, joined Major Shouldham's post, in the northern valley; from which, two six-pounders were ordered to Poonah. Opposite the south-west angle, at the distance of one thousand
(E.) yards, a battery was established, of two twelve-pounders, and two six-pounders, which opened on the 25th of February. To the right of this, distant from the gateway seven hundred and one thousand yards, were the
(C. D) two [illegible] of two eighteen-pounders each; and they opened, on the 28th, against that point.

Capitulation. There were expended, by the 1st of March, fourteen hundred and seventeen shells and two thousand two hundred and eighty-one eighteen-pounder shot, when the garrison, amounting to twelve hundred men, hung out a white flag. They were permitted to march out on the following day, with private property and personal arms, when a British detachment took possession of the place. This was a result as favourable as could have been expected, and a happy commencement of the siege-part of the war. The loss was nothing; though the working party every night were generally one hundred Europeans, and two hundred Sepoys, besides the pioneers. The garrison contained seven hundred Gossyes, and four hundred Arabs. These engaged to proceed to Ellichapoor, accompanied by an agent from the British Government; and to bind themselves, by the delivery of hostages, not to enter any Native service.

Reduction of Poorunder.

The next place which claimed the immediate attention of the Reserve, was Poonadur, or Poorunder. This, likewise, was a hill-fort connected with a neighbouring range. The division commenced its march on the 6th; and made detachments, *en route*, to complete the investment, previous to its arrival in position before the place. From Hinchundee, Major Elridge, with four companies of the Bombay European regiment, and four companies of rifles, marched through the Poorunder Ghat to the northward of the fortress. From Bungoallee, also, a detachment, under Major Thatcher, consisting of three companies of the Bombay European regiment, and five companies of Madras and Bombay Native infantry, marched, on the 8th, for the southward of the fort. The head-quarters, and remainder of the division, continued the march during the 9th, 10th, and 11th; and arrived by the way of Jejoorree, in a position north of the forts of Poorunder and Wuzeer Ghur, distant three miles. Within four miles of the camp, at the village of Sassoor, there was a strong stone building, in which a party of two hundred men, Arabs, Scindees, and Hindoostanees, had shut themselves up, with some small guns, and made a shew of opposition. The walls were so substantial, that six-pounders were found incapable of affecting them. Eighteen-pounders were then brought up; but, though these also appeared to make as little impression on the walls, they had sufficient effect on the minds of the garrison, to induce their surrender at discretion. The operations against the forts were short, and may be related in a few words. On the 14th of March, a mortar battery opened on them; and on the 15th, Wuzeer Ghur admitted a British garrison. As this place commanded Poorunder, the Killedar* was necessitated to accept the terms

* When Sevajee was besieged in this place by Dilcir Khan, a Mogul officer, he was in like

given to the garrison of Wuzeer Ghur; and the British colours were hoisted on the 16th. The example of these places had a salutary effect on the remaining forts in that quarter. Major Thatcher's detachment marched on the 20th from its position west of Poorunder, towards Pandaughur, by the Kamateeka Ghat; and on the 23d, arrived before the place, which was evacuated on the night of the 24th. Within another march were the forts of Kummulghur and Kalinjah, distant from each other about six miles. Major Thatcher's detachment encamped between these places on the 25th. As the result of this movement, the former was evacuated on the same night, and the latter on the night following.

Occupation of remaining Forts between Satara and Poonah.

The division recommenced its march on the 21st, and returning by the Neerah Bridge and Salpee Ghat, encamped on the 24th, within two miles of Chundun and Wundun, two hill-forts, which were evacuated that night. On the 26th, a position was assumed before Wyratghur, by a march in two divisions; the line passing through a defile impracticable for guns, and the heavy train and cavalry making a circuit of the hill on which the fort is situated. Preparations were made for its immediate attack; but they were rendered unnecessary, by its surrender on the same evening. The division halted on the 27th and 28th, to admit of the rejunction of Major Thatcher's detachment, which had been successfully employed in obliging the garrison of Kundulghur to evacuate that place, distant about sixteen miles from Wyratghur. Thus in the limited period of six weeks, between the time of leaving the vicinity of Satara till the division returned, ten forts were reduced, and garrisons established.*

Colonel Deacon's marches North of the Godavery, and Departure of Sulabut Khan.

No convenient occasion having occurred to introduce an account of Colonel Deacon's operations, since the detachment he commanded remained near Jafferabad at the end of December, (p. 137) they may now be brought forward without affecting the unity of the narrative. The Peishwah, it will be recollected, had at that period gone to the northward,

---

manner obliged to surrender, in consequence of Wuzeer Ghur being first taken: it was on that memorable occasion that Sevajee was sent a prisoner to Delhi.

* In Singhur and Poorunder, two companies of the 2d battalion of the 15th Madras Native infantry, each. In Pandaughur, Kummulghur, and Wyratghur, two companies of the 2d battalion of the 9th Bombay Native infantry, divided among them. In the forts of Chundun, Wundun, and Nanghurrie, a company and a half of the same corps, equally distributed.

as far as the Pheira, followed at a considerable distance by Brigadier-general Smith, who was desirous of intercepting his communication with Khandesh. In order to contribute to this object, Mr. Elphinstone pressed Lieutenant-colonel Deacon to move directly to the westward, while the Fourth Division was advancing from the southward. The Lieutenant-colonel accordingly marched on the 30th of December, with his own detachment, and that of Sulabut Khan, and arrived at Roza on the 2d of January. On the following day the detachment was at Lassoor, and halted there on learning that the Peishwah had fled again southward, for then he attacked the Bombay battalion at Koreigaum (p. 179). At the same time, Captain Davies's detachment was at Byzapoor, one march further west. It consisted of sixteen hundred reformed horse, four hundred infantry, and two guns. Colonel Deacon halted till the 12th, when, in consequence of orders from Sir Thomas Hislop, he moved to Ranjengaum, for the purpose of resuming a position near the head of the Ghats, and arrived on the 19th at Pangree, where the roads from Adjunta and Jypoor-Koatly join in the direction of Jalnah. He here received, on the same day, a requisition from Brigadier-general Doveton for the return of the Nuwaub Sulabut Khan to Ellichapoor, to assist in the assumption of the districts ceded by the Nagpoor Rajah, and to cover that part of Berar against the apprehended incursion of the chief, Gunput Rao, who had fled in that direction (p. 223) from Ghirhur. The Nuwaub accordingly, on the 22d, marched with his force towards Ellichapoor; but Gunput Rao was heard of on the same day moving by Sirpoor to join the Peishwah, with a considerable body of horse. On the following day, Colonel Deacon received Sir Thomas Hislop's orders to carry his force to the southward, by Ahmednuggur, in consequence of Lord Hastings' desire that as great a reinforcement as possible, should be sent to the divisions acting against the Peishwah. As these instructions included Sulabut Khan, an express was dispatched to overtake the Nuwaub, and to request that he would send back five hundred of his best horse, to accompany the detachment. This modification of the orders Colonel Deacon received, arose from the urgency of Brigadier-general Doveton's requisition, and a consideration of Sulabut Khan's ill health, and the inefficiency of some of the infantry on a fatiguing service. He was, further, unwilling to have the company of the Nuwaub, who was attended by too many elephants, and circumstances of eastern pomp, to suit the operations

(Map VII

of a light detachment. But the old Chief scorned the proposition of going into quarters during the continuance of the war, and insisted on returning with all his force.

March in Pursuit of Gunput Rao to Ahmednuggur, and Return of Sulabut Khan. (Map VII.)

Lieutenant-colonel Deacon did not wait for his junction; for having received intelligence, on the evening of the 23d, of Gunput Rao being lately at Nair, twenty-four miles east of Jalnah, he marched his detachment immediately in search of the enemy, and the next morning reached Pepree, fifteen miles south of that place. Learning here that they had crossed the Godavery, proceeding towards Bheer, he continued his march in the afternoon, arrived on the 25th at Punchoor, and on the following day at Moongy-Pyetun. On the 28th the Lieutenant-colonel was overtaken by a dispatch from Captain Sydenham, Political Agent at Aurungabad, representing the depredations committed by the garrison of Newassa, said to consist of about seven hundred men, of whom two hundred were Arabs. It was also understood, that one thousand five hundred of the Peishwah's horse were on route to join them from the vicinity of Ahmednuggur. As their existence in this position prevented the assumption of this part of the Poonah territory, Colonel Deacon was pressed to attack them. With this view, he marched on the 29th up the Godavery to Toka, and was there joined by Captain Davies's detachment, which had been ordered on from Byzapoor. On the 30th he marched against Newassa, the garrison of which place fled, as he came in sight, to a neighbouring jungle; but they were overtaken by a party of the reformed horse, who *cut up* about one hundred, with the loss of eighteen killed and wounded. This service completed, the detachment continued its march to Ahmednuggur; where, on the 6th, Sulabut Khan rejoined, and orders, dated the 3d, were received from Brigadier-general Smith, to detach Captain Davies to join the Fourth Division with all the reformed horse, escorting such grain as was ready to be dispatched from Ahmednuggur. The horse accordingly marched to Poonah; but, instead of immediately joining Brigadier-general Smith, they contributed to the investment of Singhur, as has been already related.

Reduction of Places between Ahmednuggur and Poonah. (Map VI.)

At Ahmednuggur Colonel Deacon was in immediate communication with Mr. Elphinstone, who recommended to his primary attention the occupation of the country lying between the Pheira and Bheemah rivers, and the expulsion of any parties of the enemy who might shew themselves. The first measure in execution of this service, was the attack of Kurrah, on the 12th of February, after a long march that day from Ahmednuggur.

The detachment was followed by two howitzers; but, they not arriving early, Colonel Deacon tried the experiment of taking off a part of the loose defences of the *ghurrie* with his galloper six-pounders. The garrison, being three hundred men, were apprehensive of more coercive means coming up for their reduction; and in order to gain better terms before their arrival, proposed to capitulate immediately. They were permitted to retire, with their arms and private property; and the place, double-walled, was found capable, if resolutely defended, of an opposition superior to the means of subjugation which could have been immediately produced. Lieutenant-colonel Deacon was on the 20th and 21st at Serroor; and came before the fort of Chakun on the 25th, having received from Poonah a detachment of the Bombay European regiment and some howitzers and guns, the heaviest of which were twelve-pounders, iron and brass. This fort was deservedly considered strong, particularly at the gates; and was surrounded by a good ditch. The wall and defences were of substantial masonry, and the garrison made a shew of a determined resistance; one of their guns, however, was disabled on the first day, and on the same evening preparations were made for the establishment of a breaching battery within two hundred and fifty yards of the western face, where was the point to be attacked. The brass twelve-pounders were first brought down to battery, early on the 26th, in order to take off some collateral defences, and the enemy still maintained the fire which they had commenced on the previous day, though its execution was very trifling. At the same time a position was given to the 2d battalion of the 17th Madras Native infantry, and a company of Europeans, on the south, while the Nizam's battalion, which had accompanied Captain Davies, occupied a post on the north side. At ten o'clock, however, the garrison considered they had made sufficient resistance, and desired terms; but, as they were required to lay down their arms, the capitulation was delayed till the afternoon, when they marched out and grounded, as desired. Four or five Europeans were killed and wounded. After this service the detachment proceeded to Poonah, to refit for further operations in the direction of Jooneer; and detached the heavy guns against the neighbouring hill-forts on the road to Bombay.

(Plan 23.) (C) (2, 2, 2.) (3, 3, 3.)

Operations of Lieutenant-colonel Prother's Detachment in the Southern Kokun. (Map VI.)

The fortress of Lhoghur is situate thirty-six miles west from Poonah, near the road to Bombay, on the left of which it lies distant two miles and a half. It was at this time besieged by a small force under Lieutenant-colonel Prother, fitted out with laudable exertion by the Government of Bombay. At the opening of the war, this corps consisted of parts of the 1st battalion of the 5th, and 1st battalion of the 9th regiments of Native infantry, equal to five hundred and sixty rank and file, details of his Majesty's regiments thirty-three, seventeen men of his Majesty's 17th dragoons, and eleven Native cavalry, belonging to the Governor's and Commander in Chief's guards; for even these were applied to the exigencies in the field. There remained for the duties of Bombay, only three hundred and fifty of the marine battalion. This small detachment was destined, in the first instance, to cover the British possessions in the Upper Kokun, and to keep open the communication towards Poonah. This service was effected, at first, by a detachment made up of details of regular and irregular horse, and mounted infantry. These were commanded by Captain M'Neil, who ascended the Ghats in December, and advanced nearly to Poonah; from whence other detachments were sent by Lieutenant-colonel Burr, to contribute to the same object. A post of infantry was established at the bottom of the Ghat; and a redoubt, constructed near Kondallah at the top of the Ghat, was occupied by a party from Lieutenant-colonel Prother's detachment, which received the addition of two companies of the 2d battalion of the 4th regiment. In the early part of January, the enemy being only in small force below the Ghats, the Lieutenant-colonel received instructions to proceed against such places in the Southern Kokun as he was capable of reducing. The first of these was Kottella, which was approached through a difficult country on two sides. It made a shew of resistance; but was evacuated, on the 20th of January, without occasioning any loss. This place was occupied by a Native officer's party, and the detachment marched, in the beginning of February, by Calliapoor and Nanoosee, to Pallee; from the garrisons of which place and Boorup, parties were detached to obstruct its progress through thick jungles. Without halting at Pallee, the Lieutenant-colonel, with three hundred men, marched towards Owchilghur, distant twenty miles from that place, through a difficult country; but, being met by the Killedar, who surrendered it, the party returned to Pallee, after establishing a small garrison in it and Soneghur, which likewise surrendered. Pallee still making opposition, a mortar-battery was established against it; and after two hours' bombardment, the place surrendered on the 8th of February. The fall of Boorup followed on the 15th, in the same manner, by the fire of a battery, established on the

13th. These successes having given affairs so favourable a posture below, the detachment was found applicable to offensive operations above, the Ghats. A division of his Majesty's 89th regiment of foot, three hundred and seventy strong, arrived at Bombay, on the 13th of February, from Quiloan, in consequence of an application to the Madras Government, which was promptly complied with. This reinforcement, added to an ordnance train, put Lieutenant-colonel Prother in a condition to ascend the Ghats.

Operations above the Ghats

On the 4th of March, the detachment arrived before Lhoghur, all the ordnance and stores having been brought up the Boar Ghat with considerable labour. In order to hasten the reduction of Lhoghur, detachments of the 2d battalion of the 6th and the 2d battalion of the 1st regiments of Native infantry, with a detail of the Poonah artillery and two companies of the auxiliary brigade, were sent from Poonah to join Lieutenant-colonel Prother, whose train consisted of seven mortars and four heavy guns. In the immediate vicinity of this fort was that of Eessapoor; and in the course of the attack, this was occupied without resistance. Its occupation was immediately followed by that of Lhoghur, on the 5th; the garrison of which evacuated, after viewing the situation proposed for the battery against their gateway, and finding their out-posts driven in by the detachments which invested that place on all sides. This result was the more satisfactory, as the guns had not yet been brought up—a labour which, from the natural impediments of the environs, would have been attended with much delay and difficulty. This service was followed by the voluntary surrender of the forts of Takoonah and Toonga, which were subsequently restored to the owners, who came in to Mr. Elphinstone. Two other forts, Ragh and Muchee, were occupied in their stead; for they likewise made no resistance. Koaree, a hill-fort twenty miles south of the Boar Pass, and situated at the summit of the Ghats, was the next object of attack. Its difficulty of access, from the valley of Karlee, promised considerable obstruction to the progress of the detachment; and one attempt to communicate with the road, leading to it from Poonah, proved ineffectual. Another avenue being discovered, the Lieutenant-colonel came before the place, on the 11th, with an advance party, which drove in the enemy's out-posts, leaving the remainder of the detachment to follow, under Major Hall, of his Majesty's 89th foot, and which arrived on the following day, with the exception of the heavy train. Even this had been greatly lightened, by leaving at Lhoghur the two eighteen-pounders, and one of the thirteen-inch mortars, with every other article not absolutely necessary for the service in contemplation. On the 13th, a fire from the smaller mortars opened against the place, and produced immediately an evident conflagration: while another battery was in a state of forwardness, opposite the north-eastern gateway, which was the principal access to the fort. On the following morning, at day-break, this likewise opened with good effect, from one thirteen, one ten, and two eight-inch mortars; and in the afternoon the enemy's magazine was seen to blow up, which, at eight P. M., induced the garrison to demand a suspension of hostilities, which was followed, an hour afterwards, by their surrender. They were about six hundred men, supposed to include some of those who had fled from Eessapoor and Lhoghur. The loss of the detachment, on this occasion, was twelve* men, including one officer of engineers slightly wounded; and that of the enemy amounted to about thirty-five. The fall of Koaree was followed, on the 17th, by the occupation of the dependant hill-fort of Gunga, which was evacuated on the previous day. To the terror inspired by shells, is to be attributed the early fall of this place, which had fair pretensions to be considered a fortress of strength, and it was even said to be mined about the gateway. A place of importance it certainly was held to be, from its extent, and command of a principal Ghat leading into the Kokun; and on its fall the troops from Poonah returned immediately to that station. Thus were closed the operations of this detachment above the Ghats; and as the subsequent service in the Kokun was unconnected with those demanding immediate attendance, their resumption will be postponed to a future occasion.

March of the Fourth Division from Satara in Pursuit of the Peishwah.

While the Fourth Division was detained in the vicinity of Satara, the Peishwah was in the country about Pundapoor and Sholapoor; where he was reported to have levied a heavy contribution; and Brigadier-general Smith followed by moderate marches, in order to gain on him with fresh troops. The march was prosecuted by Salpa and Rednee to Yellapoor, where the light force arrived on the 19th of February, and received intelligence of the Peishwah having taken a westerly route from Sholapoor. The Brigadier-general accordingly made a corresponding movement the same night; but learning on his way that the enemy had suddenly turned on Kurkum, he likewise changed his direction, passed the Beemah at Karaollee,

* Vide Appendix. M.

near Goorsalla, and heard that the Peishwah was the previous evening at Ashtee. The march was continued, without intermission, by Mundapoor; and at eight o'clock on the forenoon of the 20th, the Brigadier-general had the satisfaction of hearing the enemy's *nagarras** beating below a hill which covered him from their view. They were not, however, entirely unapprised of his approach; and though unable altogether to avoid a conflict, they were not without time to make some preparation for it. They had proposed to march that morning, and had accordingly struck their tents and laden their baggage. The Peishwah, however, did not consider himself safe in a palankeen. He therefore mounted a horse, and fled precipitately with a sufficient guard, leaving Gokla with from eight to ten thousand horse, to cover his retreat, and, if possible, that of the baggage. When this measure was recommended to Bajee Rao, Gokla, thinking probably the entire Fourth Division, with its baggage, was advancing, assured him he would amuse the Brigadier-general, who would, as usual, open his guns; but when the British cavalry alone were discovered moving over the hill, he found other dispositions must be adopted. His force was divided into several bodies, which made a *demonstration* of mutually supporting each other; and between them and the British cavalry was a *nullah* of difficult passage, which it was necessary for the attacking body to cross. (Plan 21.)

In this situation of affairs, Brigadier-general Smith's corps was advancing in regimental columns of threes at forming-distance, the two squadrons of his Majesty's 22d dragoons in the centre, the 7th Madras Native cavalry on the right, and the 2d on the left. On the outer flanks, and a little retired, were the Bombay horse-artillery and galloper guns, the former on the right under Captain Pierce, and the latter under Captain Frith on the left. Thus disposed they approached the enemy, and were about forming, when Gokla, with a body of two thousand five hundred horse, containing several ensigns, advanced from opposite the left, cleared the *nullah*, and charged obliquely across the front to the place where the 7th cavalry were unprepared to receive them, delivering a volley from matchlocks as they passed. About three troops were imperfectly formed; and these, with the rest of the regiment, advanced through broken ground and ravines, (Cavalry Combat at Ashtee.) (A A A) (2, 2, 2) (B B)

* A species of drum.

as the enemy circled round their right flank, to which they couched their
(3, 3, 3.) lances and gained the rear. This manœuvre threatened immediately the
right flank and rear of the 22d dragoons, then engaged to the front; but
Major Dawes, with the presence of mind of an old soldier, threw back the
right troop, and bringing forward the left, charged in turn. Here Gokla
was foremost to receive the attack; and met in conflict a young officer of
the dragoons, Lieutenant Warrand, who had the honour of receiving from
him a contusion on the shoulder; but Gokla had many more antagonists,
and fell, with several mortal wounds*, at the head of his corps. Brigadier-general Smith was on the right as the enemy made their charge; and before
he could quit that position, received a sabre cut on the back of his head.
During the confused mixture of dragoons, Native cavalry, and enemy's
horse, which prevailed for some minutes, the 2d cavalry had formed on the
left, and threw out a squadron which checked some parties of the enemy
still in the rear of the other regiments; but the fall of the Chief deprived
(4, 4, 4) them of further hopes, and they fled towards the left, in which direction
their main body, who never came into action, left the field pursued by the
(a, a, a.) 2d cavalry. A squadron of this corps received a cluster of the opposite
party, which proved to be the Rajah of Satara, his brothers and mother,
all of whom voluntarily sought the British protection. The remaining regiments, as soon as they recovered a little order, likewise commenced the
pursuit. They found a body in the hollow beyond the village of Ashtee,
which had never been engaged, and still made a shew of covering the retreat
of the baggage. But these fled on a nearer approach; and twelve elephants,
fifty-seven camels, and many palankeens, fell into the hands of the pursuers. The enemy were followed about five miles, but no further impression appears to have been made on them, beyond greater dispersion. The
horse-artillery on the right had been ordered, in the first instance, not to
fire, as it would prevent the immediate charge of the cavalry; and the difficulties of the ground opposed its subsequent passage of the *nullah* in time
to be brought into action; but the gallopers on the left found greater facility of crossing, and opened with some effect. The enemy lost about two

---

* He received three pistol-shots and two sabre-cuts; and as he fell he is represented as covering his head gracefully with his shawl.

hundred killed, including some Chiefs besides Gokla, while the British loss amounted to no more than fourteen Europeans and five Native cavalry killed and wounded. The cavalry returned to the field of action, and encamped near Ashtee, where they were rejoined by their infantry and baggage from the rear.

Parallel between the Defeat of Gokla and Doondeah Waugh.

Thus closed this brilliant affair, which, while attended with little loss, had the important result of liberating the Satara family, and terminating completely the enterprise of the Peishwah's horse. There are but few similar actions to be met with in Indian warfare; and that which most resembles it, has never appeared on the page of military history. In 1800, Colonel Wellesley was engaged in operations against a chief, named Dhoondeah, who assembled the remains of Tippoo Sooltaun's dispersed army, and endeavoured to establish a principality for himself amidst the general disorder. After several places, in his interest, had been reduced, he found himself, on the 10th of September, 1800, enclosed between unfordable rivers, and in presence of the British cavalry, with the Colonel at their head. The cavalry, consisting of his Majesty's 19th and 25th (now 22d) regiments of dragoons, and the 1st and 2d regiments of Madras Native cavalry, formed, at the same time with the enemy, who were already getting in motion to attack, as a last resource, when the British gallopers opened from both flanks, and produced in them a perceptible hesitation. The critical moment was seized with three huzzas*; and the whole line

* To huzza on approaching an enemy will not be considered a very military practice: though, on some occasions, its effects are undeniably salutary. It is so truly English, however, that were it even more objectionable, it would, perhaps, be neither desirable nor easy to be abolished. In order to shew its antiquity, it is here convenient to recur to Sir Thomas Morgan's Progress in France in 1657 and 1658; though more ancient histories will probably record a similar custom. Previous to the battle of Dunkirk, when the French and Spanish armies were drawn out, and the action about to begin, "Major-general Morgan, seeing the enemy plain in battalia, said before the head of the army, 'See, yonder are the gentlemen you have to trade withal.' Upon which the whole brigade of English gave a shout of rejoicing, that made a roaring echo betwixt the sea and canal. Thereupon the Marshal Turenne came up, with above an hundred noblemen, to know what was the matter and reason of that great shout. Major-general Morgan told him, it was an usual custom of the red-coats, when they saw the enemy, to rejoice."—(*Harleian Miscellany*, vol x. p. 414.) But exclamations on going into action will be found among other nations. Thus the Turks have the cry of "Allah," and the Native troops in the British service in

of cavalry charged, and came at speed on the enemy, who, unable to face this formidable assault, were retiring in the greatest confusion. Their Chief was killed, as in the present instance, and his party dispersed with considerable loss; and the service was so complete, as to enable the troops to return immediately into quarters. One cause which prevents one body of cavalry from receiving the charge of another with firmness, arises from the nature of a horse, which, notwithstanding his education, is justly classed with animals who herd. He is, consequently, disposed to go with the crowd. It follows, therefore, that the body of horse which stands at the commencement of the rapid approach of another body, as the distance decreases, evinces an inclination to turn and gallop off in the same direction with those in motion. Of this propensity, familiar illustrations may be observed every day. If, on the contrary, both bodies be put in motion to meet each other, the horse performs his duty, in conformity with the impulse of his nature, and the responsibility of declining the shock must be borne by the rider. If, however, some of the leading horses are actuated by their fears (which belong likewise to their nature), as is generally the case in approaching a fire of musquetry, and they halt or turn, few, if any, of the other horses will go on; but it is also supposed, that there is, at the same time, a check of the hand unconsciously applied. The contagion of example will be likewise observed, at the passage of unfordable rivers, when a body of horse will swim intrepidly, if well led; but if the leaders turn, so will all the rest. Colonel Wellesley's arrangements, on the occasion cited, were as near perfection as such situations admit; and if those of Brigadier-general Smith, on this occasion, were less perfect, it is very questionable whether that circumstance affords any cause for regret.

Reflections on this Affair, and its Results.

The great object of bringing the enemy's horse to action was obtained; and with Gokla's fall the most important procurable result was accomplished. It mattered little, whether a few hundreds of the enemy more or less were put *hors de combat;* and the advantages gained could not be

India, that of "Deen," signifying "The Faith;" which, though it refers to the Mahomedan belief, is not the less used by the Hindoo casts in the same ranks. The French likewise cry "Vive le Roi;" but any sentiment will be too weak in utterance to produce the mechanical effect on the nerves, of a simultaneous shout, which dissipates apprehension, excites alacrity and sympathy, and declares unanimity.

expected, under any arrangement, to be acquired at a smaller loss. Had Brigadier-general Smith formed his line sooner, (and that he did not, appears to be, in general, considered as the cause of the confusion which ensued to the right,) it is a fair question, whether Gokla would not have fled, instead of hazarding an action? and as Native horse so rarely charge a British force, encouragement might easily be imagined for delaying that evolution till the worst ground was cleared. If Brigadier-general Smith was ignorant of the art of manœuvring cavalry, and he is said not to have pretended to it, there will be no cause for surprise, that more method was not observed in bringing them into action, supposing him to have interfered beyond ordering the direction of the attack, the disposition of the guns, and the amount and position of the reserve; since the remaining orders for execution must be given by a cavalry officer. Without pursuing this disquisition further, it will be granted that he had, on his side, all the arguments derivable from success, and that he was opposed by the most able manœuvre which could be expected from his antagonist, Gokla, justly denominated by his master, the Sword of the Empire.

While the light force of the Fourth Division advanced by moderate, but regular marches, from Ashtee, by Hingengaum and Barramuttee, towards Poonah, Bajee Rao fled, in the first instance, by Pureinda to Moongy-Pyetun on the Godavery, and from thence towards Nassuck, in the greatest confusion. His people were now tired of this unprofitable course of life, and began, immediately after his defeat, to return to their homes.* The intention of setting up the Rajah of Satara had already been published; and as he had now fallen into the hands of the British Authorities, there appeared no obstacle to a measure so much at variance with the fealty previously acknowledged to the Peishwah. A proclamation, suited to the times, had been issued on the fall of Satara, and at the period when the Rajah was rescued, nine days afterwards, it was in general circulation. This document contained an exposition of the conduct of the Peishwah since his accession to the Government, and of the circumstances that brought on the war. Arguments were thence drawn for the necessity of his deposition; and

* The impression produced by that event is described in an animated manner, in the translation of two intercepted letters, published in a Bombay newspaper, March 7, 1818, for the authenticity of which the Editor pledges himself. Vide Appendix. N.

the means of carrying the same into effect were exhibited with too much truth and force, to leave room for doubt of their success. The new order of things was explained, and the inhabitants of the Poonah territory were called on to conform to it. *

Considerations regarding the British and Mahratta Governments.

The object of all political Manifestoes is to make out a case; and this contains the British side of the question. The other side is never publicly exhibited; for the Native Powers have yet to learn the practice of this diplomatic weapon. It may be easily imagined, without supposing any fundamental misrepresentation on the part of the author of the British manifesto, that it might be met by a very plausible counter-statement, had the Native Powers an experienced and well-informed advocate. At present the epithets of "treacherous" and "faithless" are so commonly applied to the conduct of Mahrattas, that, whatever foundation there is for the general imputation, by no discrimination are any of their acts exempted from that character. Yet how easy would it be, to draw a parallel between their conduct, as on many occasions it has been thus represented, and that of European Powers, which is not only considered with toleration, but even applauded. When a Power, by its weakness or vices, finds itself on a footing inferior to its neighbours with whom it may have political intercourse, and unsupported by a greater Power, the usual consequence will be its partial subjection; and if it has once been independent, it will necessarily be on the watch for opportunities to throw off this dominion. As necessarily will the other Power adopt the requisite measures for defeating these attempts, and disabling the adverse State from repeating them. Such a state of things must necessarily generate grounds for the imputation of treachery, as the powerful party cannot, with safety, relinquish its predominancy, nor the weaker, its secret machinations; for force is always balanced by fraud. Many weak States, in contact with a powerful one, will naturally league together, and excite each other to resist the common enemy; but always at a disadvantage, from less union among themselves than if they formed parts of a single Power. This has been forcibly illustrated in both the Mahratta [illegible] the British Government; nor was it less so in Europe during the power of Buonaparte, till the irresistible occasion of unani-

* As a rapid view is taken, in this proclamation, of events highly interesting, a place is given to it in the Appendix. O.

mity arose out of his reverses in Russia. His *exposés* on all occasions were extremely specious, and if civilized enemies furnished him with such grounds of plausibility, it may be admitted that the Native Powers of India, who scarcely ever recognize the check of public opinion, were liable to discard every consideration of good faith which could interfere with their political conduct. In fact, whatever may be said for the Mahrattas, they do not, themselves, even affect to regard any arguments but those which accord with their own narrow conception of political expediency. These are frequently less imposing than that used by the Peishwah's Vakeel on the 5th of November, when he announced his master's intentions by telling the Resident, " that his Highness had heard of the approach of General Smith, and the near arrival of the battalion from Serroor; that this was the third time that we (the British) had assembled troops at Poonah, and that the last time we had surrounded the city. His Highness was therefore determined to bring things to an early settlement."*

Re-establishment of the Rajah of Satara

(Map VI.)

Brigadier general Smith's head-quarters were, on the 4th of March, at Beilsoor. As his movement to this place approached the position of the Reserve, Mr. Elphinstone now came over, with an auxiliary battalion and Captain Davies's horse, to receive the Rajah of Satara, who still accompanied the Brigadier-general. The Fourth Division, on the 6th, continued its march towards Serroor, where it arrived on the 8th, and halted on the 9th; while the Rajah, with Mr. Elphinstone, proceeded to join the Reserve, which they found, on the 11th, near Jeioor, on route to besiege Poorunder. They remained with this force till its subsequent arrival in the vicinity of Satara, when the Rajah was established in the seat of his Government, and Captain Grant, of the Bombay Establishment, placed with him, to assist his councils and direct his conduct. The Rajah, a man in the prime of life, was accompanied by two brothers and his mother; the latter of whom appeared to have more ambition than her son, who seemed to be of a dull disposition, and to possess scarcely any education. He shewed little knowledge of the world, and was perhaps almost unacquainted with the Mahratta history; but his mother made large claims, and expressed her expectations that the family should be re-established on the footing it enjoyed in its greatest fortune. The impolicy and impracticabi-

(Plan 26.)

* Mr. Elphinstone's Report to the Governor-general, 6th of November, 1817.

lity of complying with such desires, require no explanation; and an idea of the extent and situation of the territory allotted for their maintenance, will be best formed by a reference to the maps. Under the protection of the British Government, they were relieved from a thraldom which had continued at least as long* as their power; and a sovereignty was revived, which was, at least, as legitimate as the majority of Indian dynasties.

(Map VI.)

Movements of Lieutenant-colonel Pollock's Detachment. (Map VII.)

The flight of Bajee Rao, north of the Godavery, was contemporary with the arrival of the Head-quarters and First Division of the Army of the Deckan on the Taptee, where the events at Talneir detained Sir Thomas Hislop till the 2d of March. Apprehending that similar service might occur on the route through Khandesh, his Excellency directed Brigadier-general Doveton immediately to detach his battering-train towards Aumulnair; and it was, subsequently, ordered to halt at Pahrola. Brigadier-general Doveton was, likewise, recommended to make a westerly movement, as the demands of the service appeared likely to occur in that direction. In fact, he received intimation from Captain Gibbon, at Ahmednuggur, that Bajee Rao was, on the 27th, at Copergaum, with the supposed intention of flying to Hindoostan. On this intelligence, the Brigadier-general immediately recalled Lieutenant-colonel Pollock's detachment, which, it will be recollected, had marched towards Poonah, after leaving the Head-quarters of the Second Division (p. 223). On the 4th of February, this detachment ascended the Lackenwarree Ghat; and, on the 13th, was at Jafferabad. The Lieutenant-colonel was obliged, from hence, to abandon the most direct route to Ahmednuggur, in order to have one of his gun-carriages repaired at Jalnah, where, on the 15th, he received instructions from Head-quarters to direct his attention to the movements of Ram Deen and the *Barra Bhye.* With that view, he marched to the head of the Cassurbarree Ghat, where he learned that this part of the enemy were at Chandoor. He therefore continued his route to join Brigadier-general Doveton, at Ootran; his instructions not permitting him to remain longer detached. As some of the enemy's horse, a few days afterwards, passed the small *ghurrie* of Heurah, which was garrisoned by a Native officer and fifty Bombay Native infantry, a party from this small detachment sallied on the enemy, who were plundering in

* Sevajee wrested a small government from his father, in 1645, and his coronation took place in 1674. The power of the Peishwahs is generally dated from about 1730.

its vicinity, and drove them off, killing four and wounding seven, whose horses they likewise took.

March of the Head-quarters of the Deckan Army through the Valley of Khandesh.

The Head-quarters and First Division of the Deckan Army crossed the Taptee on the 3d of March, and advanced by Kurrumkeirree to the vicinity of Pahrola, where it arrived on the 6th. Finding Bajee Rao was still north of the Godavery on the 1st, Sir Thomas resolved to press him on this side, and, if possible, to defeat his supposed intention of flying beyond the Nerbuddah. With this view, all the sick, and other impediments to a rapid movement, were ordered to march, under the protection of the 2d battalion of the 13th regiment, by the most direct route to Jalnah; and, on passing through the camp of the Second Division, to take up all the sick of that force. The First Division was to march up the Bhoree river, in the direction of Malleygaum; and the Second to ascend the Gheernah, towards Bhal. To that division was, at the same time, returned the small battering-train; for the impression produced by the vigorous proceeding at Talneir, caused the immediate evacuation of all those places, from which opposition on the march had been anticipated. Thus the preliminary arrangements for the occupation of Khandesh could be effected *en route*, notwithstanding a rapid progress through that province. The First Division accordingly marched from Pahrola on the 7th, and was joined by the detachment under Captain James Grant, which had been sent down the direct pass to Choprah (p. 227), in search of Ram Deen and the *Barra Bhye*. This Chief having continued his progress by Aumulnair and Chandoor, to join the Peishwah, Captain Grant remained near the Taptee till he was called forward on the advance of the Head-quarters.

March of the First and Second Divisions to the Godavery

The division was, on the 8th, at Boar-Roond; and during the march of the following day, a report was received of Bajee Rao moving easterly towards Byzapoor. He had approached Malleygaum to favour the junction of Ram Deen, and to collect the garrisons of such forts about the Khandesh Ghats, as were not intended to stand a siege. Having effected these purposes, he retired towards the Godavery, from the approach of enemies more numerous than even those from whom he had escaped. He proceeded to the southward, and was followed by the *Barra Bhye*. The camp had even been marked out for the First Division, on the morning of the 9th, at Sy[illegible]gaum, on the banks of the Gheernah, when Sir Thomas Hislop sent forward orders from the rear for selecting ground several miles in advance directly towards the Ghat. At the same time, instructions were dispatched to the left, to inform Brigadier-general Doveton of this movement. He was required to detach immediately, the 6th regiment of cavalry to join the First Division, by the route of the Cassurbarree Ghat, and to follow with his own head-quarters and remaining corps. No water was found, in this direction, nearer than the village of Jamderree; and as this place was twenty-seven miles from Boar-Roond, the line did not arrive at its ground till late in the afternoon. On the 10th, the First Division marched eighteen miles to the foot of the Cassurbarree Ghat, where the 6th cavalry joined; and on the following day ascended to Parlah. On the 12th, the camp was established at Byzapoor, at which place it still remained on the 13th. From thence, a detachment of Native infantry, consisting of two companies of the 1st battalion of the 3d regiment, was sent to occupy Chandoor and Galnah, which places, agreeing to receive [illegible]. were occupied accordingly. On the same day, the Second Division was at Parlah, having advanced by Perkundah, Bhal, Syegaum, and Kassarree, at the rate of fifteen miles a day. Brigadier-general Doveton moved on the 14th to Belloanee; and here meeting orders to march on Copergaum, he arrived there on the next day instead of following the Head-quarters.

Movements of the Enemy and the Fourth Division.

(Map VI.)

This arrangement arose out of intelligence that Bajee Rao had been for some days at that place; for it was, in former times, one of his favourite retirements, and he was never likely again to behold it. While it formed the point of direction for the movement of the Second Division, the First marched on Fooltamba, another Ghat on the Godavery, lower down. There Sir Thomas Hislop received information, on the 15th, that the enemy had passed on, in great confusion, towards Jausgaum. They were marching in two divisions; one consisting principally of horse, and the other of infantry and guns. Both corps were passing Heurah during the day and night of the 12th; but they appeared to keep clear of Peer Mahomed, the Subidar commanding there, who had interrupted their excursion on a former occasion. They were next heard of near Rakisboan on the Godavery, where Bajee Rao himself encamped on the 14th, and was joined by Ram Deen; but a considerable portion of his horse overspread the country north of the river, for the purpose of plunder. One body of them suddenly appeared at Jalnah, to the great alarm of the open cantonment at that place, where the sick details from both divisions had arrived, on the 16th, by the route of Adjunta. As the rapidity of the enemy's movements had entirely thrown out the divisions from the northward, Sir Thomas Hislop directed

Brigadier-general Doveton to move down the river, to Fooltamba, that a new separation of the force might be adapted to the actual state of affairs: Bajee Rao being now expelled from the Poonah territory. To account for this result, it should be recollected that Brigadier-general Smith was, on the 9th, at Serroor; and there received intelligence that the enemy was flying down the river. For he was now pressed, at once, from both north and south; and though he might still have passed in the latter direction by Jooneer, he had no encouragement to try that route again; as there was now a moveable force, near Poonah, under Lieutenant-colonel Deacon. Several places* also, on that line, had entered, with few exceptions, into terms of composition with Mr. Elphinstone. But independent of the positions of his immediate enemies, he found objections to his longer adopting the routes he had so often passed over; for the country, in their neighbour-hood, was exhausted by both parties, and his former contributions had left him nothing to glean, either in men or money.

Brigadier-general Smith marched, on the 10th of March, from Serroor; and passing Ahmednuggur on the 12th, descended the Neembadeorah Ghat on the following day. He continued his march by Nandoor and Teetroney to Rakisboan, where he encamped on the 18th and 19th, to gain further intelligence of the enemy, who, after having made *demonstrations* on Bheer to distract attention, suddenly fled on the 15th, by Gumsangy and Goouj, to Keir. As Bajee Rao had now apparently abandoned Poonah, the Brigadier-general directed Lieutenant-colonel Deacon to conduct his detachment to Ahmednuggur, which movement commenced on the 20th, and was effected in four marches. *(Map V.)*

The situation of the Head-quarters of the Army, at Fooltamba, appeared to Sir Thomas Hislop favourable for executing the orders of Lord Hastings, which had been received on the 13th of February. These directed that, whenever the proper occasion should offer, the conduct of affairs in the Deckan should return to the Authorities in whom they had been vested previously to his Excellency's arrival. Also, that the divisions of Brigadier-generals Doveton and Smith should be reinforced by every corps and piece of ordnance, not necessary for his own escort in returning to the territories of Fort Saint George. As a first measure, for this purpose, the 4th and **Re-organization of the Hydrabad and Poonah Divisions.**

* Hurreschund, Chawkund, Jeodhur, Hurrussur, Koongoorghur, Narrodee, Narreinghur, and Owsurree.

8th regiments of cavalry were ordered to march on the night of the 16th, to overtake Brigadier-general Smith by the route of Ahmednuggur. At the same time, the squadrons of those corps which had been detached under Colonel Deacon's command, since the formation of his corps in November, were directed there to join them. On the arrival of the Second Division at Fooltamba, on the 17th, it encamped on the left bank of the river opposite the First Division on the right bank; and was joined next day by a detachment of horse-artillery, the 6th cavalry, foot-artillery, park and stores, flank companies of the Royal Scots, detachment of the Madras European regiment, the Palamcottah and Trichinopoly corps of light-infantry, the Mysore horse, and first battalion of pioneers. At the same time was formed the subsidiary force for Nagpoor. Of this, some of the corps were already there, and the remainder were to be supplied from the force placed under Brigadier-general Doveton. Its amount was fixed at one regiment of cavalry, half a troop of horse-artillery, two companies of foot-artillery, one company of pioneers, and five battalions of Native infantry; and the future movements of the Hydrabad Division were expected to be favourable to the progress and junction of the remaining corps and details. The direction of Bajee Rao's flight to the eastward, rendered the movement of the above force by Jalnah advisable. Accordingly it marched under Brigadier-general Doveton's personal command towards that quarter, on the night of the 18th, leaving the remainder of the division, under Lieutenant-colonel M'Dowell, to follow with as much expedition as possible. Owing, however, to the unsatisfactory accounts of the position and designs of the enemy, as well as to subsequent variations in the orders under which Brigadier-general Doveton marched, he halted at Aurungabad from the 20th to the 23d of March, and did not arrive at Jalnah till the 25th; from hence the details for Nagpoor were put in motion under the command of Major Goreham. They consisted of a half troop of horse-artillery, a detail of foot-artillery, with two five-and-a-half-inch howitzers and four six-pounders, the 1st battalion of the 11th regiment of Native infantry, and the depôt corps. The Brigadier-general was met at Jalnah by Brigadier-general Smith, whose division encamped at Karlah, fourteen miles south-east of Jalnah, and who arrived for the purpose of concerting a combined operation of both forces, suited to the present state of the common service on which they were engaged. After halting on the 19th at
(Map V.) Rakisboan, he had marched, in the first instance, in an easterly direction,

by Kirkee and Ashta, to Peeplegaum, where he encamped on the 23d and 24th. While Bajee Rao having passed through Pandra Nandagaum, at the junction of the Doodna and Poornah, proceeded in the direction of Bassim, his army being divided into several bodies. The B[illegible] now suspended his pursuit, and countermarched by Purtoor, where he arrived on the 27th.

Termination of Sir Thomas Hislop's Command of the Army of the Deckan.

The First Division having been reduced, by the transfers to the Second and Fourth Divisions, which have been described, to a mere escort for the Head-quarters, consisting of the rocket troop, squadron of dragoons, and rifles, Sir Thomas Hislop left the Godavery on the 20th, and repaired by Lassoor, Elloora (or Errolla), and Dowlatabad, to Aurungabad, where he arrived on the 26th. From hence his Excellency issued, on the 31st of March, his final orders as Commander in Chief of "The Army of the Deckan;" and directed the discontinuance of that designation. The corps, commanded by Brigadier-generals Doveton and Smith, were ordered to revert to their former footing, previous to his Excellency's assumption of the chief command; and Brigadier-generals Munro and Pritzler were directed to maintain their existing relations to each other, and to Brigadier-general Smith. Though Sir Thomas Hislop still reserved to himself the right of resuming his powers in the Deckan, during his further [illegible], should the emergency of the public affairs require that measure, he was probably convinced that the occurrence of that necessity was very improbable. During the period while his Excellency exercised the extensive controul delegated to him by the Supreme Government, such uniform success had attended his measures, as to "extinguish the necessity" of those powers, by the "completion of the object;" for there was now the prospect of "a cessation of all Military operations in the Deckan, excepting those against the Peishwah, which must necessarily be conducted in concert with the arrangements to be prosecuted by Mr. Elphinstone, for the introduction of the authority of the British Government into the Poonah territories."* The operations, under Sir Thomas Hislop's personal command, commenced with the expulsion of the Pindarries, and terminated with the expulsion of the Peishwah, which produced a revolution in the Mahratta Empire the most important since its establishment. His Excel-

* Lord Hastings's letter of the 2d of February, 1818.

lency was not unmindful of the able assistance he had derived from the officers commanding divisions of his army, in the execution of the duties pointed out to him by the Governor-general, and evinced his high opinion of their services in the most public manner. He had the gratification of finding that applause confirmed by the Supreme Civil and Military Authority in India, while it pronounced the merits of the Lieutenant-general himself so well established by the events of the war, that the "offer" of "praise might seem superfluous." *

* General Order by the Governor-general and Commander in Chief in India, dated February 21st and 22d, 1818.

CHAPTER V.

ESTABLISHMENT OF HOLKUR'S AUTHORITY IN WESTERN MALWAH, AND EXPULSION OF THE PEISHWAH FROM THE DECKAN.

Sir John Malcolm's Movement from Jawud to Oojein. Detachments from the Goozera Force at Indoor, in Search of Pindarries. Junction of Colonel Huskisson's Detachment, and Return to Baroda. Dispatch of the captured Ordnance and Field Hospital from Mehidpoor. Lawless Tribes in Western Malwah. Reduction of the Soandees. Expulsion of Cheettoo from the right Bank of the Nerbuddah. Return of the Russel Brigade to the Deckan. Hostile Design of the Nagpoor Rajah defeated by the Seizure of his Person. March of Colonel Adams's Force to Hingenghat, and of Colonel Scot to Chanda. Combined Arrangements of the Hydrabad and Poonah Divisions for the Attack of Bajee Rao's Army. Brigadier-general Doveton's March from Jalnah to Panderkaorah. Brigadier-general Smith's Progress down the Godavery. Dispersion of Bajee Rao's Army by Colonel Adams's Attack at Seonee. Result of this Action. Pursuit of Bajee Rao's Army by Brigadier-general Doveton's Force. Pursuit taken up by Brigadier-general Smith. Return of the Hydrabad Division to Jalnah. Return of the Poonah Division to Serroor. Reflections on the Peishwah's Conduct. His Military Stratagems. Reflections on the Marches of Armies. Comparison of those in Europe with those in India. Bad Roads, and consequent heavy Gun Carriages, the Impediments to the Movements of Indian Armies.

THE Narrative of operations in the Deckan having arrived at a period when it may be conveniently suspended, the present Chapter will commence with the description of those events which occurred north of the Nerbuddah, immediately after the departure of the Head-quarters of the Grand Army, and of the Army of the Deckan, from Malwah. The Governor-general, on his excursion through the province of Oude, was still within easy communication wth Sir John Malcolm, to whom, as his Lordship's Political Agent, the immediate conduct of affairs in the late theatre of operations was entrusted ; and with this charge, the command of all the Madras troops north of the Taptee.

Sir John Malcolm's Movement from Jawud to Oojein.

The presence of the Brigadier-general on the confines of Meywar, continued to be indispensable for some weeks after the departure of Sir Thomas Hislop; and the efficacy of his measures was evinced by the surrender of Jeswunt Rao Bhao on the 14th of February, and of Kurreem Khan, the Pindarry chief, on the following day. The success of previous military operations had been so complete, that no farther service in that quarter remained to be performed. Yet, for harmonizing the various elements of discord, the pacification of turbulent and disappointed individuals, and the silent direction, into peaceful ways, of habits long marked by violence and injustice, there was abundant occasion for the influence of character--that power felt in every state of society, but especially in that particular stage of civilization which exists in most parts of India. Happily the proper remedy was at hand, and was sought with confidence. It becomes therefore necessary to pass thus cursorily over a state of things, which contributes nothing, immediately, to military history, till the march of Sir John Malcolm's division towards Mehidpoor. This movement commenced on the 23d of February, while with a light detachment Sir John proceeded from Jawud to the Court of Holkur, to settle his final [illegible] for the quarter he was leaving. He overtook the division at Mehidpoor on the 1st, and accompanied it to Oojein, where he arrived on the 8th of March, and met Sir William Grant Keir, who had advanced his force to that point on the 4th, for the purpose of this interview.

(Map IV.)

Detachments from the Goozerat Force at Indoor, in Search of Pindarries

This notice of Sir John Malcolm's movement to the southward being premised, the Narrative may be pursued, without interruption, respecting the operations of the Goozerat force, after the departure of Sir Thomas Hislop, when, it will be recollected, that Sir William Grant Keir was required to direct his attention to the country about Indoor. Arriving there on the 22d of February, he found the influence of Ram Deen's agents, in that quarter, fully equal to what had been reported, and that they were, moreover, actively supported by Scindiah's officers at and near Oojein. Troops which had been dispersed to a distance, were gradually drawn nearer, though with a caution that still rendered the defeat of their machinations difficult, as well as dilatory. Wherever any assembling body was heard of, a detachment was sent to disperse it. Lieutenant-colonel Elrington marched with one party towards Budnawur, on this service; and another party, under Lieutenant-colonel Stanhope, was sent to the vicinity of Ragoogur, to beat up the Pindarries, who had returned after their discomfiture at Kunnoad. At Baglee, about thirty miles east of Indoor, on the 28th, the last-mentioned officer met a detachment under Captain Roberts, from Colonel Adams's division, which had followed Cheettoo since the 13th (p. 220), and was engaged in endeavouring to prevail on the local Authorities to deliver up the Pindarry Chief, concealed in impervious jungles. Not anticipating any success from negotiation, the Lieutenant-colonel moved the same day to Erwas, where Kooshall Sing, the Thakoor (head man) of the town and district, was supposed to have perfect information of the enemy's haunts. In consequence of intelligence obtained by these movements, parties were detached to the several avenues by which the enemy could escape; Lieutenant-colonel Stanhope returning himself to Baglee, whither a further reinforcement, with provisions, was dispatched to him by Sir William Grant Keir. No immediate effect having attended this arrangement, the Lieutenant-colonel changed his ground, and was, on the 8th of March, at Seymlee; while Captain Roberts's detachment returned towards Bhopal by Shujawulpoor and Ashta. Lieutenant-colonel Stanhope received a report, during the night, that a body of Pindarries, under Cheettoo, were assembled at Jee, distant thirty miles, and situate south-west from Indoor. The enemy, hearing of his approach, fled to Hursulla, whither they were pursued without intermission; and notwithstanding the length of the previous march, the Colonel, with some dragoons, succeeded in coming up with them, and two hundred are represented to have been *cut up*, without any loss on the part of the pursuers.

Junction of Colonel Huskisson's Detachment, and Return to Baroda

During this period, Sir William Grant Keir was joined at Oojein by his Majesty's 67th foot, and a detachment of Bengal infantry and irregular horse, which marched in the middle of February, under Colonel Huskisson's command, from the Reserve in Rajahpootana. The route of this corps was by Tonk, Boondee, and Kotah; the Mokunda pass, Soneil, and Augur. It was conducted, without interruption, through countries either friendly or awed into passiveness. The 67th regiment, having been transferred to the Bombay establishment, had been ordered to join Sir William Grant Keir, for the purpose of proceeding to its destination under his command. The Major-general having also received the Governor-general's instructions, to return into Goozerat with his division, except such part as the Political Agent should deem necessary in addition to the Madras troops in Malwah, he marched, on the 12th, towards Debalpoor, to collect his detachments, and make his final arrangements. He was here rejoined by Lieutenant-colonel Stanhope; and having ascertained the resources of the route by Chottei-Oodeipoor, he commenced his march on the 16th by that point for Baroda, leaving at Nolye the Native brigade, the Guickwar contingent, and the battering-train, at Brigadier-general Malcolm's orders. The division encamped, on the 20th, at Tanda, and, on the 22d, at Kookshee. On the second march from thence, the road became difficult and confined by jungle, and continued so, with occasional variation, till the arrival of the division, on the 29th, at Oodeipoor. From hence the country became gradually more open and cultivated during its further approach to the sea coast; and the division completed its march on the 7th of April, having passed by the route of Banderpoor, Dubbooree, and Ruttunpoor. From Baroda the Bengal troops were directed to return to Malwah; the 17th dragoons and half the flank battalion were sent to Kaira, and his Majesty's 67th foot to Bombay; to which place Sir William likewise removed his head-quarters.

(Map II.)

Dispatch of the captured Ordnance and Field Hospital from Mehidpoor.

(Map IV.)

The force remaining under Sir John Malcolm's command, on the departure of the Goozerat Division, consisted of a detachment of Madras horse-artillery, one regiment of Madras Native cavalry, a half company of Bombay European foot-artillery, and seven battalions of Native infantry; of which three belonged to the Madras establishment, two were the Russell brigade, and two belonged to the establishment of Bombay. Independent of these was the detachment left by Major-general Brown (p. 210), at Rampoora. It was, therefore, found practicable to dispense with the Russell brigade, whose return to their head-quarters, near Hydrabad, was now deemed advisable. Their conduct had been very creditable throughout the campaign; and the march of the 1st battalion was considered a favourable opportunity for the dispatch of the Mehidpoor captured guns towards the Carnatic. This battalion was ordered to march on the 18th, by the Oonchode pass, to Hindia; and from thence, by Charwah and Boorhaunpoor, in prosecution of its further progress, which will be hereafter noticed. The remaining battalion, and flank companies of the First, continued for some time longer, under Captain Hare, in Malwah. The next movement was the march of the sick, wounded, and convalescent, from the Mehidpoor hospital. This commenced, on the 25th, under the conduct of Captain Green, and the escort of a company of the 2d battalion of the 6th regiment, with one hundred Mysore horse. The party was directed to follow the same route as the captured guns, which, owing to the imperfect state of the carriages, it would probably overtake. These arrangements being completed, Sir John Malcolm found himself disengaged for other considerations, and the whole of his force applicable to the accomplishment of his views. He had, for the exercise of his talents, a wide field; to understand which, it will be necessary to advert to the state of Western Malwah, from a period anterior even to the power of the Pindarries.

Lawless Tribes in Western Malwah. (Map IV.)

When the Mahrattas carried their arms into that part of the country, the inhabitants who did not submit, fled to the hills, and became there a people of robbers, who transmitted to their posterity lawless habits, as an hereditary possession. The chief of these were the Soandees, who gave the name of Soandwarrah to a tract of country, lying between the Chumbul and Cala Sind rivers. There, owing to numerous fastnesses, and the difficulties of the country, they had succeeded in maintaining a state of disturbance during more than half a century. The Bheels, who occupy the hills forming the confines of Goozerat, the Deckan, and Malwah, and are by some considered to be the Aborigines of the country*, seldom venture into the plains; while the Soandees are so habituated to those incursions, as to maintain a force of two thousand horse. Between the southern hills of Malwah and the Nerbuddah, Cheettoo, and his Pindarries, still lay concealed in jungles impenetrable to a regular force, enduring the severest privations, in the hope that attention towards them would relax, and that then all the hidden partizans, who had mixed with the general population for safety, would again declare themselves, and join his *durrah*. Several Powers might be supposed desirous of the reduction of the Soandees to a state of innoxiousness, but most of all, the Rajah of Kotah, who owned several valuable districts in the infested tract. Holkur and Scindia were likewise proprietors, but the latter in a degree comparatively small.

Reduction of the Soandees.

The Bombay brigade, with six hundred irregular horse, were allotted to the attack from the side of the Chumbul, should the Soandees, on this *demonstration*, exhibit any hesitation to submit; and the 2d battalion of the 6th regiment of the Madras Native infantry, with some [illegible], was directed to attend to the central parts by a movement from Mehidpoor. In co-operation with this corps, was a contingent under a Chief,

* The *Grassies* is another general name by which the plundering tribes of Malwah are denominated.

named Mirab Khan, supplied by the Rajah of Kotah. This was the only efficient aid brought forth; for though Holkur's Government was materially interested in these operations, it was not in circumstances to come forward, actively. Against such enemies, the detail of military operations cannot afford much interest or instruction; and they were marked by no event of importance, excepting the storm of Nuralla by the Kotah troops. The walls of this petty fortress were very contemptible; but the assailants had guns as contemptible, to bring against it. The utmost effect they could produce, was a breach scarcely practicable. Under the apprehension of the garrison escaping during the night, while the arrangements for the attack were incomplete, Mirab Khan ordered the assault, in the afternoon, under serious disadvantages. The breach was defended, with perseverance, during two hours; and the gallantry of the assailants put to its extreme test; but it stood the trial, and prevailed, with a loss of two hundred men, including several officers. The garrison were killed to a man; and in this country no further example was necessary. To have destroyed all the lawless men in arms by hostile measures, would have been a work of nearly general extirpation, which was no part either of Sir John's plan, or of his instructions. The object of both was, as far as practicable, to reclaim; and where those turbulent inhabitants proved themselves to be incorrigible, to pursue them with vigour, and to excite a general hostility against them. These measures succeeded in a shorter period than could have been expected, and were hastened by a judicious consideration of those circumstances of anarchy, under which so deplorable a state of things had arisen, and had been fostered. With the Chief of Lalghur, a principal leader, an amicable arrangement was effected, through the intervention of Holkur and Zalim Sing. Many horsemen delivered up their steeds on the terms held forth; and in the space of six weeks, thirteen petty fortresses had surrendered, of which five were razed to the ground.

Expulsion of Cheettoo from the right Bank of the Nerbuddah

This desirable success was attributable, in some degree, to the circumstance of the Soandees having a local attachment, which was not the case with the Pindarries. These, however, as has been seen, were tired of their hardships. Kandir Bukhsh, the principal leader of the Holkur Shahee, embraced the example furnished to him by Kurreem Khan; and was with him sent off to Goruckpoor to reside on a pension, far removed from their former scenes of rapine and disorder. Even Cheettoo, after his last discomfiture by Lieutenant-colonel Stanhope's detachment, preferred the line of submission, in imitation of others. He repaired to Bhopal, to surrender himself on terms; but finding these unequal to his expectations, or changing his mind as to the happiness of a peaceful life, he suddenly decamped, to rejoin his associates in scenes of greater interest and adventure. Sir John Malcolm, by the forwardness of his arrangements in other quarters, was enabled to direct his immediate attention to crush, by the same measures he adopted towards the Soandees, the remains of the Pindarries, between the Malwah Ghats and the Nerbuddah. On the 1st of April, he directed his march towards Baglee, with three battalions of Native infantry, a regiment of cavalry, and two thousand irregular horse. Colonel R. Scott, with a respectable detachment, was posted at Indoor, from whence he was directed to push forward parties into the jungle, in co-operation with those detached from the Brigadier-general's head-quarters. The detail of those operations affords no important incident; and the reader is probably satisfied with past descriptions of marches and countermarches against those freebooters, which will have ceased to convey either amusement or instruction. It will be sufficient to state, that their result was the submission of another chief, named Rajum, and the flight of Cheettoo across the river, with an inconsiderable number of followers, containing no person of importance. Connected with the accomplishment of this object, was a partial arrangement with the Bheels of Southern Malwah, which suspended their hostility against the convoys and followers of the British detachments, and withdrew their support from the Pindarries, some of whom they even delivered up. This might be sufficient to account for the flight of Cheettoo south of the Nerbuddah, where he had been supposed to have fewer partizans, and less means of concealment, than previously existed on the northern bank. But he had another inducement, which was the approach of Bajee Rao, in the latter part of April, towards Asseerghur; and, near his army, Cheettoo expected to find, at least, a temporary relief from his pressing troubles.

Return of the Russell Brigade to the Deckan

This event will render necessary a return to the operations of those divisions, whose active exertions had produced it. Yet, previously to suspending an account of the affairs in Malwah, it must be noticed, that, on the 20th, the head-quarters of the Russell brigade marched for Hindia, accompanied by six hundred irregular horse, forming part of Holkur's contingent. The escort, with the captured guns, and the sick details, were ordered to halt at that place till the arrival of the reinforcement. The combined detachments were subsequently instructed, for their further security, to continue their march towards Boorhaunpoor, with no greater separation than might be prescribed by the scarcity of water at that dry season of the year.

Hostile Design of the Nagpoor Rajah defeated by the Seizure of his Person

The Peishwah's flight towards Bassim has been related; the particulars of his further movements, while the Hydrabad and Poonah divisions remained near Jaulnah, being little known. The direction of his march, however, towards the Nagpoor frontier, tended to corroborate suspicions, which had been for some time past entertained, respecting the sincerity of the Rajah's conduct towards the British Authorities. The operations connected with the reduction of the territories ceded by Appah Sahib, on the Nerbuddah, will be related hereafter; but it is necessary here to mention, that there was, on the part of the Rajah's Authorities, such a general spirit of opposition to the accomplishment of this part of the treaty, as could only be imagined to proceed from secret instructions. Extraordinary preparations were likewise in progress at Chanda; and many circumstances concurred to induce the supposition, that these measures of hostility were likely to extend to the heart of the Nagpoor possessions. Whatever doubts might have been entertained, notwithstanding a mass of suspicious appearances, they were brought to a period, by the Resident's receiving from Mr. Elphinstone an intercepted letter, addressed by the Rajah to the Peishwah, inviting him to repair to Chanda, and promising to meet him there with all the troops he could muster. This discovery demanded instant measures for the counteraction of such a plan; and the decisive resolution was adopted, of seizing Appah Sahib's person. The usual British force in the city of Nagpoor was, one battalion of Madras Native infantry; and on the morning of the 15th of March, two additional companies of Bengal Native infantry, commanded by Captain Browne, of the 22d regiment, were sent to the Rajah's palace. These were accompanied by a Gentleman from the Residency, charged with the duty of persuading the Rajah to surrender without opposition. This mission having failed, Captain Browne proceeded, agreeably to his instructions, to enter the palace, and, penetrating into the inner apartments, seized his person. He was immediately conveyed to the Residency-lines, where he remained a close prisoner for a few days; and was afterwards sent off with his ministers, Ram Chunder Bang and Narrain Pundit, on the road to Allahabad, escorted by one squadron of cavalry, and four companies of Bengal Native infantry.

March of Colonel Adams's force to Hin- [illegible] to Chanda. (Map VIII.)

This state of affairs induced the Resident to call for the advance of Colonel Adams's force from Hoossingabad, where it had arrived in the beginning of March, after its field service beyond the Nerbuddah was completed. The Colonel, accordingly, commenced his movement towards the capital, on the 23d, with the 5th cavalry and two* battalions of Native infantry, followed by the 1st battalion of the 23d regiment, escorting the ordnance train. As his approach strengthened the posture of the British interests there, advantage was taken of this effect, to detach towards Chanda, on the 29th, a small force under Lieutenant-colonel Scot, consisting of the 6th Bengal Native cavalry and one squadron of the 8th, a *russalah* of auxiliary horse, the 1st battalion of the 1st regiment Madras Native infantry, and the six flank companies of the remaining corps, with three horse-artillery guns. The object of this measure was to disappoint Bajee Rao's supposed design of entering Chanda, where active preparations were on foot for both offensive and defensive operations. The spirit of the garrison was evinced on the 2d of April, by opening their guns as the British detachment approached to take up its ground; and a skirmish ensued, on the following day, in the plain. The garrison were represented to be in readiness to take the field, on Bajee Rao's approach; and to have from twenty to thirty field guns, with their cattle and every equipment complete. Lieutenant-colonel Scot made his dispositions to prevent the eventual entry of the enemy: yet, owing to the extent of the place, it is probable his force would have been found insufficient; and the principal use of this position was, the distraction it was calculated to produce in Bajee Rao's designs. In the mean while Colonel Adams having arrived at Nagpoor, on the 5th of April, halted on the following day, and on the 7th continued his march to Hingunghat, where he arrived on the 9th. He immediately directed Lieutenant-colonel Scot's detachment to join him, and requested Brigadier-general Doveton to order the march of the Nagpoor details, under Major Goreham, towards Hingunghat, to be disposed of from thence as the public service should require.

(Map V.)

Combined di- [illegible] and Fourth divisions for the attack of Bajee Rao's army.

In the mean while Brigadier-generals Doveton and Smith had concerted their plans for further operations against Bajee Rao, who, during several days at the end of March and the beginning of April, lay with his camp at

* The flank battalion and 1st battalion of the 19th regiment.

Ydelabad and Wun on the Wurdah. His army was represented to be again considerable in numerical strength, as his scattered parties had re-joined; and he was accompanied by Gunput Rao, with his followers, from the Nagpoor territory. His horse were allowed to amount to, at least, twenty thousand; of which one half were of a description superior to the rest; but of infantry and guns he had few, except what supplied certain guards; the majority, unable to accompany his rapid movements, having been sent off, in the middle of March, to Sholapoor, from the Godavery. The cattle of Brigadier-general Smith's division were almost exhausted, on their arrival near Jaulnah, where a halt became necessary, for their re-establishment. But there were other arrangements to be made of equal importance. The sick, which had latterly accumulated with the increasing heat of the weather, were to be placed in the hospital; a fresh supply of cash was necessary; and a re-organization of the provision department, for a line of distant operations, perpendicular to the line of supply, demanded peculiar attention. There were two suppositions in regard to Bajee Rao's probable movements; one, that finding no support at Nagpoor, he would re-cross the Godavery; and the other, that he would fly into Malwah, across the Nerbuddah. With this view the Brigadier-generals agreed that the Hydrabad Division should approach the Upper Wurdah, through the Berar Valley, to prevent the first probable measure; and that the Poonah Division should hold a course nearly parallel, to the right, to counteract the second. In order to bring forward as many cavalry as possible, the 2d and 7th Madras regiments were transferred from the Poonah to the Hydrabad Division; and the 4th and 8th regiments were ordered to join Brigadier-general Smith, from Ahmednuggur.

Brigadier-general Doveton's march from Jaulnah to Panderkaorah. (Map V.)

With this reinforcement Brigadier-general Doveton marched, on the 31st of March, from Jaulnah; his light force now consisting of the horse artillery, the 2d, 6th, and 7th regiments of Madras Native cavalry, with a galloper battery of six guns, three companies of his Majesty's Royal Scots, the flank companies of the Madras European regiment, and the 3d, 12th, and 16th light infantry corps. He encamped, on the 1st of April, at Palliskeir, and at Maiker on the 6th. On the 8th, from the camp, on the Adoal *nullah*, instructions were sent to Major Goreham's detachment of corps and details to prosecute its march direct on Nagpoor, for hitherto its movements had been regulated by the advance of Brigadier-general Doveton's head-quarters. These orders, on the following day, were countermanded, in consequence of a dispatch from the Resident at Nagpoor; and the Major was directed to proceed towards Colonel Adams's force, by the route of Nachingaum and Tukul Ghat. The march of the Hydrabad Division was continued without a halt, by Seiloo and Karinjah, and without further incident than the occasional reports of the movements of Bajee Rao's army, which nevertheless avoided quitting the jungles and difficult country on the right bank of the Wurdah. There are few tracts of the Deckan which have been less explored than that in question, which contains the termination of the Berar range of hills. This, after holding a direction from west to east, turns suddenly to the southward on arriving at the Wurdah, and interposes itself between that river and the Pein Gunga, till at length they join at its termination. The several ramifications of this range covered with jungle, render this corner extremely difficult of access; on which account it was probably selected by Bajee Rao, as a temporary place of security; for he was now situated little better than a chief of Pindarries. Brigadier-general Doveton, finding that he persevered in maintaining this position, altered the direction of his route at Karinjah, on the 12th, and in two marches arrived at Doodgaum. From hence the march was continued by Pohoor to Panderkaorah, where, on the 17th and 18th, every preparation was completed for sudden and expeditious movement. Extra ammunition was served out, and the Natives were directed to hold prepared two ready-dressed meals. During the latter part of the march an intimate communication had been maintained with Colonel Adams; and repeated dispatches had been sent to Brigadier-general Smith, with the view of keeping him informed of the position of the enemy, and the progress of the combination against them.

The Poonah Division marched, on the 2d of April, from Karlah, towards the Godavery, in order to favour the junction of Major Lushington's cavalry brigade from Nuggur. It arrived at Nandeir on the 15th, by Purtoor, Peepulgaum, and Pinglee, having halted occasionally for the same purpose. Major Lushington's brigade, on the 1st of April, left Ahmednuggur; and, with considerable difficulty, descended the Satmulla Ghat into the Valley of the Godavery. The brigade crossed that river at Moongy-Pyetun, and, on the 9th, endeavoured to overtake Brigadier-general Smith at Seiloo; but finding him still in advance, it was unable to come up with him till the following day, when it joined at Perbonie, and accompanied

Brigadier-general Smith's Progress down the Godavery.

him to Nandeir. On the 16th and 17th the march of the division was continued to Modul, where it halted for further events and intelligence.

Dispersion of Bajee Rao's Army by Col. Adams's Attack at Seonee.

Lieutenant-colonel Scot marched his detachment from Chanda on the 12th, and arrived at Hingunghat on the 14th, in pursuance of the orders he had received. At the same time Colonel Adams was in possession of undoubted information regarding the position of the enemy; his arrangements for acquiring intelligence having at length taken complete effect, after being for some days distracted by reports of Bajee Rao's intended movement towards Hindoostan. During the latter period, this Chief had been in constant motion between the Koonee river and the Wurdah, in consequence of the accounts which he continued to receive of the approach of his enemies. According to their tenor, he directed his marches and counter-marches, encamping sometimes in a collected, and at others in a divided state. On the 13th he appears first to have received decided information of Colonel Adams's position; on which he left Anjee-Andoora on the Wurdah, and proceeded by easy marches to Seonce. There, on the 16th, he was informed of Brigadier-general Doveton's approach to Panderkaorah. On the previous day, Colonel Adams marched from Hingunghat to Allunda, and awaited there the arrival of his spies, who brought him information of the enemy being at Seonee. The march was recommenced at nine P. M., and continued during the night, till it reached Peepul-Kote before day-light on the following morning; when the Colonel halted a short time to refresh the troops, and to bring to the front the cavalry and horse-artillery, which had been in the rear during the night. The march had been scarcely continued five miles in the direction of Seonee, when the advance of both parties met within one hundred and fifty yards of each other; for the enemy were now flying from Brigadier-general Doveton. These were pursued back to their main body preparing for the march; and a division of them formed with the apparent design of resistance. Colonel Adams brought forward the 5th cavalry, with the three horse-artillery guns, which opened with grape and shrapnell, at the distance of a few hundred yards, and caused the enemy to break in some confusion; while the remaining regiment of cavalry was directed to make a *detour* by the left, and to attack the enemy in flank. The movements of the officer to whom this essential measure was intrusted, are represented as having failed in seconding the Colonel's generous ardour at the head of the 5th regiment; which, with the horse-artillery, recommenced the attack, as often as the enemy re-assembled, and obliged them to retire from one position to another several times. At length they finally gave way, as well as the rest of Bajee Rao's army; which, with the numerous followers, had fled on the first onset in every direction, leaving five brass six-pounders, their elephants, camels, and treasure, in possession of the victors.

Results of this Action.

Great praise has been given to the horse-artillery for their service on this occasion; and from a comparison of several accounts of this affair, whatever loss was sustained by the enemy is chiefly attributable to their fire. The nature of the country was certainly unfavourable for the charge of cavalry; yet the guns, by admirable exertion, were advanced, and the cavalry may be said to have only covered them. Some skirmishing took place on the flanks; but the horses were too much fatigued to continue the pursuit after having cleared the Valley of Seonee; for they had already marched from Alunda thirty-one miles of road distance. It is probable that the loss of the enemy, on this occasion, was not very considerable; and this is unworthy of much regret, for the object was attained, of dispersing Bajee Rao's army and giving opportunity of returning to their homes, to those who were tired of following his fortunes. His personal guards accompanied his flight at the beginning of the action; but the great body of his horse, as at Ashtee, opposed themselves to the progress of his pursuers, and gave him time for escape. Subsequent accounts represented him as having fled, on the first day, about thirty miles, to Meinly, in a westerly direction, followed by such troops as still resolved to accompany him. Among this number was Gunput Rao, but not his force; for they returned in small parties to the Nagpoor country, greatly disgusted with the hardships they had lately suffered. Ram Deen, with the wreck of his party, fled by the direct road towards Boorhaunpoor; while Bajee Rao, still keeping a westerly course, passed Mahoor on the third day, and Oomerkeir on the fourth (the 20th of April.)

Pursuit of Bajee Rao by Brigadier-general Doveton's Force.

(Map V.)

Brigadier-general Doveton marched, on the 19th, to Boree, with a view of gaining the road by which Bajee Rao was flying. He there divided his force into two parts; one of which, consisting of the horse-artillery, cavalry brigade, galloper battery, and the 3d and 12th light infantry corps, lightly equipped for rapid movement, he reserved under his personal command. The remainder of the division, under the orders of Lieutenant-colonel Fraser, was directed to bring on all the heavy baggage, while the light force should maintain the pursuit. This force was subdivided by the detachment under Captain Grant, consisting of the Mysore horse, reinforced by a brigade of gallopers, two squadrons of cavalry, and two companies of light infantry, which were directed to keep a more southerly route by Dooulee, Garce, Moorchund, and Betgaum; and to form a parallel column on the left of the Brigadier-general's march. On the 20th, after a march of twenty-nine miles, his head-quarters were at Tar-Saollee; on the 21st, at Dyegaum, a march of twenty-six miles; on the 22d, at Daunkey, where Captain Grant's detachment rejoined, distant from the last ground twenty-five miles. On the 23d, a march of twenty-eight miles brought the light force to Saptee, on the Pein Gunga, within eight miles of Oomerkeir. The pursuit was here suspended, from actual inability to continue it, the horses being completely exhausted, and the men nearly reduced to the same state. It was likewise necessary to await the arrival of supplies with the rear division; for the hopes of overtaking the enemy, having been grounded on the efficacy of a strenuous exertion at the first, almost every sort of supply, except what the troops carried, had been out-marched. But if the Brigadier-general's force was reduced to a state of temporary inaction, that of Bajee Rao was scarcely in a better condition. He was two days earlier in motion than his pursuers, and had longer previous rest; yet he only left Oomerkeir at three o'clock of the morning when Brigadier-general Doveton arrived there; and his route was easily tracked by the numbers of exhausted and dying, or dead, cattle, found in the several villages he passed. His force became daily reduced, not only by the loss of those who were unable to accompany him; but also from the desertions of others who were either disgusted with the service, or unable to procure, in company with so large a body in rapid movement, subsistence for themselves and horses.

Pursuit taken up by Brigadier-general Smith

Brigadier-general Smith remained, some days after the affair at Seonee, without intimation of the route pursued by the enemy. In the mean while he had marched to Beilky, where he halted from the 19th to the 22d. Learning, at length, that the principal force was moving in a westerly direction, followed by Brigadier-general Doveton, he retraced his steps, at the average rate of eighteen miles a day, till his arrival at Rattee on the 26th. After this, he crossed to the south bank of the Godavery, to interpose himself between Bajee Rao and the corps of infantry and guns he had left to the southward of that river, on abandoning his ancient territory. The Brigadier-general continued his march to Keir, where he arrived on the 28th, and learned, in the afternoon, that a large body of the enemy had passed that forenoon, within eighteen miles of his camp, towards the Dharoor Ghat. A light detachment was immediately formed for pursuit; and a body of auxiliary horse, under Lieutenant-colonel Cunningham, reinforced by four hundred infantry and two guns, was detached by a route to the left, to come in the rear of Dharoor. The Brigadier-general marched at ten o'clock at night, and arrived at seven o'clock in the morning of the 29th, at Soanput, within about twelve miles of which, at Hinghenee, the enemy had *bivouacked* the preceding night. After baiting the horses, the pursuit was continued, and reports were received on the march, that the fugitives had passed on to Dharoor; but the cattle were unable to proceed further, having accomplished sixty miles since the previous morning, including the march into Keir. The force *bivouacked* at Hinghenee, for the night, but was again early in motion to ascend the Ghat, which, being difficult for the passage of guns, caused a considerable *detour* on their account. At eight A. M. of the 30th, the Brigadier-general met Lieutenant-colonel Cunningham's detachment, which, after a march of seventy miles, had arrived at Dharoor on the evening of the 29th, about an hour after the enemy had decamped. The Colonel succeeded, however, in taking about sixty or seventy prisoners; from whom it was ascertained, that this body had dispersed in many directions to gain their respective homes, and that Bajee Rao, finding himself so closely pressed, had fled with his immediate guards and attendants to the northward. The division accordingly halted to enable its rear to rejoin, and occupied the same ground till the 4th of May.

Return of the Hydrabad Division to Jaulnah.

Brigadier-general Doveton having, in like manner, halted at Saptee, for his rear-guard, was rejoined by it on the 25th of April, and marched again on the 27th, in the direction of Jaulnah, having ascertained the direction of Bajee Rao's flight towards Boorhaunpoor. The Brigadier-general was in want both of money and provisions; and he so regulated his movements, that he might be met by treasure from Jaulnah, and joined by such supplies of grain as had been collected for the use of his division. The remainder of his march was performed by moderate stages, without a halt, by Nandapoor, Ahoonda, Asseigaum, Saoonghee, and Chicooly, to Jaulnah, where he arrived on the 11th of May.

Return of the Poonah Division to Serroor.

The reasons which dictated to Brigadier-general Doveton the expediency of a return to Jaulnah, were equally forcible for Brigadier-general Smith's return to Serroor. While he prepared to execute this measure, he sent out Lieutenant-colonel Cunningham, with the Poonah auxiliary horse, some infantry, and four galloper guns, between the Neerah and Kurrah rivers, on the left of his proposed route, and Captain Davis, with his reformed horse, through the Beer district by the right. He commenced his march on the morning of the 5th; and on the 9th, at Cheecheepoor, received the satisfactory intelligence of Captain Davis's detachment having, after a march of thirty miles, come up with a body of two thousand horsemen near Yellum. While preparing to charge them, a white flag was advanced, and the leader, Appah Dessye Nepaunkur, with Chimmajee Appah, Bajee Rao's youngest brother, surrendered themselves, with all their force. From Ahmednuggur, where Brigadier-General Smith's head-quarters were on the 12th and 13th, the division marched twelve miles, on the 14th, to Serola; and a serious accident occurred on arriving at the ground of encampment. Some fire fell on a powder-barrel, which immediately exploded. This event was quickly followed by others of a similar nature, till the explosions became general and extended to the tumbrils. The affrighted cattle fled in all directions, carrying their combustible loads throughout the camp, and putting to flight whomsoever they approached. The horses of the cavalry, and horse-artillery, broke from their pickets to avoid the fire, and produced a scene of confusion which was scarcely overcome during two hours. At the conclusion of this uncontroulable disaster, the casualties in men were found to amount to no more than seven; but the cattle which carried the powder-barrels were inevitably blown up, and the tumbrils were broken to pieces, and scattered, as at the close of a desperate action. After this unlucky occurrence, the march was continued to Serroor, where the force arrived on the 16th of May.

Reflections on the Peishwah's Conduct.

Having now described the expulsion of Bajee Rao from the Deckan, some reflections appear necessary on a series of events, of which no exact parallel is to be found in history. His military operations were neither so ably conducted, nor so long protracted, as the struggle of Mithridates against the Roman armies. They yet, however, bear more general resemblance to that part of history, than to any other which immediately suggests itself, on account of the common feature of a Prince long pursued through his own and the adjoining territories, and at length obliged to fly, with a reduced force, into foreign wilds, among an uncivilized people: for such were the Scythians, and such are the Bheels. But though his character and conduct will shrink from a comparison with the King of Pontus, yet Bajee Rao must be allowed to have shewn considerable art in the style of warfare he adopted. Deficient in personal courage, he was unable to set an example in offensive war; even considering as such, a system of active operation against the supplies and detachments of an enemy unremittingly engaged in pursuit. For this purpose, the daring character of a leader should be seconded by the venturous spirit of many subordinate chiefs; but the soul of a Sevajee was no longer to be found among the Mahrattas of the nineteenth century. They must, therefore, be considered as incapable of conduct, which, to casual observers, will appear the most easy, most advisable, and most natural choice. In the former Mahratta war, some attempts were made to adopt such a line of proceeding; but in the war of 1817-18, it does not appear to have been even meditated: a difference which must be attributed to the superior power of the Mahrattas, in 1803-4. As long as Gokla lived, the activity of his horse was manifest, on the flanks and rear of the British force; but its object was rather to delay the marches of the enemy, than to cut off any part of them, or of their supplies; and after his death, there is no sign of even so contemptible a *demonstration*. The Peishwah must have confided in an immediate and general hostility of all the Mahratta States against the British Power; and he committed himself, to give the signal for its unanimous declaration. But, even among more civilized and better-regulated Governments, it has appeared, that perfect union* against a common and powerful enemy is not always to be expected; and Rajee Rao found himself unequal to cope with the forces, which the indecision of his allies left applicable to operations against him, alone. Under this state of things, he was reduced to the condition of a fugitive, and all his efforts were adapted to the prolongation of his continuance in a country, where he had the greatest number of partizans, and the most abundant means of subsistence.

In order to screen himself from immediate attack, he detached the best portion of his cavalry to occupy the attention of his pursuers; and this manœuvre was attended with as much success as it merited. Nor was it confined to general arrangement alone, but was adopted with much effect, on the particular occasions of the two attacks of his army, by Brigadier-general Smith and Colonel Adams, when he was enabled to make his escape, by the devotion of a part of his troops. Though the command of his forces, His Military Stratagems.

* Witness the nugatory attempts of Austria, Russia, and Prussia in 1805 and 1806.

in front of an enemy, devolved thus on his chiefs, the conduct of his flight was entirely managed by himself; and he cannot be denied the praise of having exhibited much ingenuity and stratagem in his several dispositions, of which their protracted success was a sufficient evidence. His style of movement cannot be better described, than in the words of the Officer principally instrumental in the reduction of his power:—"Bajee Rao takes great pains, personally, to consult the village *puteils**, on the nature of different routes, not one of which he follows, for the purpose of deceiving us in the pursuit. His movements since he left Copergaum, and the deception he made, of throwing bodies of troops in different directions upon the same ultimate point of march, have been quite masterly. Not a soul in his camp knows his direction of march till he is in motion himself, when the whole follow. His personal baggage is generally in front, and his treasure-elephants are flanked by his horse. He then follows. A few select infantry, in ordinary marches, are about his person; and then, generally, Nepaunkur's and his own horse. The rest follow in any order they happen to march under. Gokla generally covered his rear; and, if attacked, always went off in a different road from that Bajee Rao was on †." The length of his marches was sometimes considerable; but, though not extraordinary, was generally sufficient to secure him against the attacks of his enemies, as long as, by such an exertion, he could throw them on one and the same line. Examples of this occur in his passing the head of Brigadier-general Pritzler's column, on the 6th of January, when flying from B[illegible] Smith; and in his passing the head of Brigadier general Smith's column, on the 21st of the same month, when flying from Brigadier-general Pritzler. When, however, he found, in the beginning of March, that two additional divisions were entering the theatre of operations against him, his extended movements no longer promised the same advantage, and he sought, in a distant asylum, a respite from such pressing dangers. He never allowed his movements to be hampered by his guns and infantry, of whom he was attended by much fewer than of cavalry. He threw them off, and took them up again, as he found most convenient; for he never formed the intention of

---

* Head men of villages.

† Brigadier-general Smith to Brigadier-general Doveton, March 26, 1818.

hazarding their safety by the defence of a position. Indeed, the Mahrattas have never shewn much acquaintance with the art of moving rapidly a well-organized force of every arm. The Rajah of Nagpoor's army, in 1803, was out-marched by General Wellesley, notwithstanding all the impediments to movement with a British force; and it is improbable that the Peishwah could have made more expedition than the Bhooslah, had he ever contemplated a battle.

The practice of this branch of the art of war, received more illustration from the Mussulman chiefs of Mysore, than from any other Power in India. Hyder's march of one hundred miles in two days and a half, to frustrate Sir Eyre Coote's intentions against Chillumbrum in 1781, and the march of Tippoo's entire army, sixty-three miles in two days, before General Meadows, in November 1790, may be selected as striking instances, out of a general system of efficient organization. Of the rapid movements of horse, there will be no difficulty in finding examples in all ages. General Smith marched after Ameer Khan, in the beginning of 1805, seven hundred miles in forty-three days; and this exertion was rendered more extraordinary by its being undertaken with the same corps, with which, but a short time before, Lord Lake had pursued Holkar five hundred miles to Furruckabad. What still further adds to the merits of this service, is the consideration of its performance by regular cavalry, which in general require their supplies to accompany them; while irregular horse, who can better trust to the resources of the country through which they pass, enjoy greater facilities of movement. The truth of this observation is evinced by many instances during the Moghul conquest of the Deckan, the early Mahratta operations, Abdalla's invasions of Hindoostan, and the Pindarry* excursions of the present day. The marches of the ancients throw little light on this subject, because they were unaccompanied by trains of artil- Reflections on the Marches of Armies

* For extraordinary circumstance, there is perhaps no account of the movements of horse comparable with that recorded of a body of thirty thousand from Gengis Khan's army, that made a circuit of the Caspian Sea in the thirteenth century. "They had trampled on the nations that opposed their passage, penetrated through the gates of Derbend, traversed the Volga and the Desert, and accomplished the circuit of the Caspian Sea by an expedition which had never been attempted, and has never been repeated."—Gibbon's Decline and Fall, &c. vol. xi. p. 412, 8vo edit.

lery, and must therefore be regarded as infantry alone. Among those minutely ascertained, is the march of Septimius Severus, at the end of the second century, from the Danube to Rome; a distance of eight hundred* miles, accomplished at the rate of twenty miles a day without intermission. The progress of Julian †, from the Rhine to Mount Hæmus, for the attack of the Emperor Constantius in the fourth century, is another memorable example.

Comparison of those in Europe with those in India.

After the introduction of extensive trains of artillery, the establishment of a balance of power in Europe was gradually advancing, and the operations of armies became in general proportionably confined. The instances therefore of distant marches with artillery, are but few; and even some of those were effected with so many interruptions, as to furnish no elucidation of the present question. Such was the march into Italy of Charles VIII. of France, at the end of the fifteenth century; the progress of Gustavus Adolphus to the Upper Danube, during the Thirty-Years' war; and that of Charles XII. to Smolensk, at the commencement of the eighteenth century. At the latter period, however, occurs the Duke of Marlborough's famous march from the Lower Rhine to the Upper Danube, previous to the battle of Blenheim, in 1704; when it was his object to anticipate the movements of the French for the reinforcement of Monsieur Tallard. It was accordingly executed with all possible expedition; yet the distance of two hundred and fifty miles through a friendly country, from Bedburg, near Cologne, where the army was assembled, to Gross Seinssen, near Donawert, where it came into immediate co-operation with the Austrians, was not performed under twenty-eight days; giving an average of nine miles a day only, including occasional halts for the indispensable refreshment of the troops. To descend to later times, the French army completed the passage of the Niemen on the 24th of June, 1812; and the centre divisions, with the Emperor, arrived at Witepsk on the 31st of July—a distance of about four hundred and twenty-five miles; while the Prince of Ekmuhl's corps arrived at Mohilow, on the Borysthenes, on the 23d of July, a distance of near four hundred miles. These elements give an average of eleven, and thirteen miles a day; and the latter movement, which is among the most rapid, performed by a *corps d'armée*, was

* Gibbon's Decline and Fall, &c. vol. i. p. 186, note, 8vo edit.

† Gibbon's Decline and Fall, &c. vol. iv. p. 26, 8vo edit.

executed by a strenuous exertion to intercept the junction of Prince Bagratien's corps with the Russian head-quarters. This rate must therefore be taken as the maximum of what an army can perform; and, no doubt, required all the organization of the French service, under the late Emperor, for its accomplishment. Yet this does not exceed the progress made by small armies in India, notwithstanding the enervating quality of the climate, and the abundant equipments of the troops. Brigadier-general Smith's division, it has been seen, marched, with its small battering-train, three hundred miles in twenty-six days, at the rate of eleven miles and a half a day; and Brigadier-general Pritzler's force, with light field-pieces, three hundred and forty-six miles in twenty-five days, being, on an average, fourteen miles a day.

Bad Roads and consequent heavy Gun-Carriages, the Impediments to the Movements of Indian Armies

Heavy trains of artillery will, in all countries, impede the progress of an army; but especially in India, where the cattle are so weak. A consideration of the number of bullocks* which are required for the movement of a [illegible] will be quite conclusive on this head, without entering into a demonstration of the loss of power in the length of yoke chain, and at every turn and irregularity of the roads. These are so rough in many parts of the Deckan, that gun-carriages of extraordinary strength are required, and occasion a slowness of movement at present unknown in Europe from the same cause. The very distance they have to move, independent of the roughness of the roads, will account for the necessity of their substantial form. The horse-artillery, with Brigadier-general Smith, marched two thousand two hundred and fifty miles in seven months—a movement of which there is probably no example in the world; and which therefore stands in evidence of the impracticability of employing gun-carriages in India constructed like those of Europe within the last half-century. As the æra at which field-artillery became lightened in the west, was the Seven-Years' war, this circumstance will account, in some degree, for the more rapid marches performed during the campaigns which followed the French revolution, than in those of the Succession-war: but in India the case remains unaltered; not because the guns are heavy, but because light carriages are insufficient for their conveyance.

* Sixty Carnatic bullocks in yoke to an iron twenty-four-pounder, fifty to an iron eighteen, and forty bullocks to an iron twelve-pounder.

CHAPTER VI.

REDUCTION OF THE SOUTHERN MAHRATTA COUNTRY.

Brigadier-general Munro's Situation at Dharwar in December 1817. Commencement of Operations by the Reduction of Places South of the Mulpurba. Incursion of a Body of Pindarries into the British Territory. March of Brigadier-general Munro's Force beyond the Mulpurba. Capture of Badaumee. Occupation of the Country between the Mulpurba and Gutpurba. Operations before Belgaum to the Construction of breaching Batteries. Reduction of the Place on Capitulation. Reflections on this Success and consequent Arrangements. March of Brigadier-general Pritzler's Force from Satara for the Investment of Wassota. Fall of that Place and Liberation of the Prisoners. Return to Satara and Separation of the Madras and Bombay Troops. Junction with Brigadier-general Munro's Force. Collected Amount of the Reserve. March to Sholapoor, and Description of the Enemy's Strength and Position. Escalade of the Pettah. Defeat of Gunput Rao's Attack. Flight and Dispersion of Bajee Rao's Infantry. Reflections on the Arms of Cavalry. Surrender of Sholapoor. Considerations on the Number of Mahratta Forts. Importance of Fortresses in general. Application of these Reflections to the Case of India.

THE great difference which exists between the military service in India, before and since the commencement of the first Seringapatam war, arises out of circumstances connected with the increased power and resources of the British Government. Almost all the operations which preceded the peace of 1784 with Tippoo Sooltaun, were crippled or controuled by the want of supplies, the deficiency of force, and the absence of a maturely organized staff. Success was, therefore, chiefly to be expected from the personal exertions and talents of the commanding-officer; and when Sir Eyre Coote exercised the powers with which he was vested during his last campaigns in the Carnatic, he afforded a lively exemplification of the state of things, a description of which is now to be attempted. Most of the officers of those days have left the stage, and the recollection of the former circumstances scarcely exists.

But an insulated instance in the late war, will prove that the best spirit of the old times still remains, and that to produce the same results, only required the recurrence of the same emergencies.

Brigadier-general Munro's Situation at Dharwar in December 1817

Since closing the Third Chapter of this work, no mention has been made of Colonel Thomas Munro, who, on being relieved by Brigadier-general Pritzler in the command of the Reserve, (p. 60,) returned to Dharwar, to regulate the countries which had been ceded by the Peishwah in the Treaty of June 1817. With the receipt of his Brigadier-general's commission, in the beginning of December, he was again appointed to the command of the Reserve; but the course of events had hitherto deprived him of the opportunity of joining it, and he found himself, with a nominal command over Brigadier-general Pritzler, apparently immovable, with no more than a couple of field-pieces, and a single battalion, at his head-quarters. The reader will, probably, expect that he would immediately have prescribed to the Reserve, or a portion of it, a line of movement, which would have enabled him personally to assume the important command destined for him by the highest Authority in India; and such would probably have been the ordinary course of proceeding under such circumstances. But Thomas Munro is not a man of ordinary stamp, and his conduct on this occasion was strictly conformable to the approved service of thirty-eight years. The whole scope of his instructions to Brigadier-general Pritzler, referred immediately to the primary objects of the public interests; and in sedulously providing for these, he lost sight of the outward marks of personal importance, which dazzle and captivate even minds of a superior order. With regard to individuals, personal qualities alone are the deserving subjects of history; for it matters little to posterity, what were the decorations, rank, or titles of the possessors of power, unsupported by the sterling riches of native energy and sagacity, which can neither be conferred nor taken away. If the latter Roman emperors, and the latter Ptolemies, catch a cursory or casual attention, they are regarded as objects of disgust, instead of admiration. The costly attire, and ceremonious distance of elevated station, are incapable of concealing the baseness of the mind, or the despicable nature of arrogant imbecility, whose best protection from the contempt of mankind is the oblivion in which it is allowed to repose. The impediments and obstacles in the way of fame, are necessarily numerous, and difficult to be surmounted. The progress to public notice and esteem is checked and interrupted by the emulation of rivals, the want of riches or elevated birth, the institutions of society, the characteristic diffidence of worth, joined to the accidents of education and entrance into the world: yet there is a buoyancy about talent, difficult to be depressed on ordinary occasions, and certain of discovery in public exigencies—that triumphant period for vigorous souls; and Munro was called from the peaceful occupation of a Civil commission, to pursuits which he had long relinquished. He found himself at Dharwar, opposed, in the first instance, by the influence of a chief mamed Cassee Rao Gokla, who was newly appointed by the Peishwah Sir-Soobah and Foujdar* of the Southern Mahratta country, and commanding, therefore, all its force and resources. The country was studded with forts, all of which, though not of a superior order, were secure against hasty insult, and therefore required to be breached in order to be reduced; while, independent of his want† of troops, Munro had not even the assistance of a staff-officer, in organizing such means as his activity and ingenuity should create. But he had a most able second in Lieutenant-colonel Newall, who, after having been appointed by the government of Madras to the special command of the fortress of Dharwar, which he had himself reduced, was permitted to relinquish it for more active and important service in the field.

Commencement of Operations by the Reduction of Places South of the Mulpurba.

(Map VI.)

While Brigadier-general Munro procured from Bellary a small battering-train, and the detachment of the 2d battalion of the 12th Native infantry, which had been left at Soondoor since the beginning of November, he was engaged in raising Peons (a description of irregular infantry), as a sort of auxiliary force, which might relieve his few regulars from unimportant duties, and garrison some of the places he might succeed in reducing. A party of these Peons, placed in Naulgoond, were threatened and harassed by a body of horse of Cassee Rao Gokla's; and Lieutenant-colonel Newall, with five companies of the 2d battalion 4th regiment, two guns, and a five-and-a-half-inch howitzer, was charged with the duty of removing this pressure. This was effected by his march from Dharwar, on the 22d

* Civil and Military Governor.

† The confidence with which the result of Munro's measures was anticipated, notwithstanding every disadvantage of circumstances, suggests the Great Frederick's reply to Marshal Schwerin, who complained of having received only twenty thousand men, instead of thirty thousand, which had been promised him. "In my calculations of force, I always estimate Marshal Schwerin at ten thousand men."

of December, and arrival at Naulgoond on the 24th. Connected, at the same time, with this movement, was the protection of the battering-train advancing from Humpsagur; to which place a detachment was made for the reinforcement of its escort; and Lieutenant-colonel Newall returned to Dharwar. As the train approached, he was again sent out, on the 31st, to meet it, with three companies of the 2d battalion of the 4th, and two pieces of ordnance; and, on the 3d of January, he received charge of the train, and the detachments by which it was accompanied, at Colaspoor. These consisted of three troops of the 5th Native cavalry, the three companies of the 2d battalion of the 4th regiment, sent forward on the 23d, and two companies of the 2d battalion of the 12th Native infantry. The battering-train contained, two iron eighteen-pounders, two iron and two brass twelves, with two mortars, accompanied by the head-quarters, and four companies of the 2d battalion of pioneers. Brigadier-general Munro having now collected sufficient force for offensive operations, opened the campaign by the siege of Gudduck, to which place he marched on the 5th; and it surrendered on the 6th, after a battery against it was completed. Cassee Rao's horse appeared, but made no stand; and, on the 7th, the force came before Dummull. After about four hours' firing from two batteries, on the morning of the 8th, the garrison, amounting to four hundred and fifty men, capitulated, and engaged not to serve against the British during the war. This favourable commencement was followed by the reduction of Hooblee, where Brigadier-general Munro arrived on the 13th, having been joined, on the march from Dummull, by a seasonable reinforcement of two hundred Mysore regular infantry. The Killedar, on being summoned, promised to surrender on the following morning; and fulfilled his engagement, by marching out with three hundred men, the remains of a more numerous garrison, of whom a large portion had deserted, from want of pay, which the Killedar was unable to levy on the surrounding country, from its being in possession of the British detachments. The fall of Hooblee was followed, on the next day (the 15th), by the submission of Misiree Kotah, which received the same terms of security for private property; and both places were occupied by parties of the newly-levied Peons. After these operations, the Brigadier-general returned to Dharwar, to re-organize his measures for a fresh departure; and halted there till the 4th of February. In the interim, successive reinforcements were sent to meet treasure and commissariat supplies, expected from the Ceded Districts, by the route of Humpsagur; and, latterly, Lieutenant-colonel Newall, with the remainder of the force, except the train and pioneers, was detached to bring it forward, in consequence of the movements of several parties of horse about the country, in numbers difficult to be ascertained.

Incursion of a Body of Pindarries into the British Territory.

It will be recollected that a body of Pindarries, having passed the left flank of the British troops beyond the Nerbuddah, had ascended the Berar Ghats, in the middle of December, in their course to the southward. Their progress had excited little notice during the marches and countermarches of the Peishwah and his pursuers, near the country through which they passed; and their advance to the frontier of the British territory was unobstructed and unknown. They left Jalnah, eighteen miles to the right, passed between Punderpoor and Beder, crossed the Kistnah at Gookee, and the Toombudra, on the 6th of January, at Balloonsee. They plundered Harponelly, and some lesser towns between that place and Chittledroog, while pursued by a troop of the 5th cavalry; and divided themselves into lesser parties, to embrace a longer tract of country, and more easily to evade their enemies. In this, however, their success was by no means complete; for near Nundiaul, which place they plundered, they were attacked by a detachment of horse and foot from Dodeiree, and about fifty of them were killed. Parties of them subsequently appeared at Herroor and Hoasdroog, and further west, towards the boundaries of Mysore. On the 17th, they were attacked by a small detachment, under Captain Hurdis, and suffered considerably, both in the loss of men, horses, and booty. After this, they were retiring in all directions; till, on the 25th of January, the British territory was clear of this pest. Their hasty departure was produced by the unremitting activity of the various detachments, which the foresight of the Madras Government had maintained in readiness for active movement at every point. Nor were their arrangements calculated only to defeat Pindarries, but the supposed intentions of the Peishwah likewise, when, with his army, he crossed the Gutpurba in the early part of this month, and excited well grounded apprehensions of an immediate attack. If he ever entertained this design, which was not ascertained, the relinquishment of it may be fairly attributed to his knowledge of the energetic measures of the Madras Government; which, considering the extensive drain of troops from that Presidency, was truly laudable and important. A party of the Pindarries, who recrossed the Toombudra on the 18th of January, marched north, leaving the Soonda jungles about six miles on their left. On the 20th, accounts were received, by Brigadier-general Munro, of their progress and recent positions; and at eight o'clock that night, he detached Captain Gorton, with three troops of the 5th light cavalry, to intercept them passing between Dharwar and Hooliaul. The party arrived at their *bivouac* at three A. M. of the following morning, and commenced an instantaneous attack. This terminated in a pursuit of an hour, through a close jungle, which greatly impeded its effect; for the loss of the Pindarries amounted only to about twenty men and forty horses. Their departure from the British territory was of great importance to Brigadier-general Munro, as it enabled the Madras Government to dispense with the 2d battalion of the 9th Native infantry, and the detachment of his Majesty's 22d dragoons, which were destined for the reinforcement of his small force.

March of Munro's Force beyond the Mulpurba

Lieutenant-colonel Newall's force, escorting the treasure and supplies, having returned to Dharwar on the 31st of January, Brigadier-general Munro recommenced his operations, on the 5th of February, by a march toward Badaumee on the Mulpurba, which place he proposed to reduce. His force, independent of small garrisons, now consisted of three troops of cavalry, twelve companies of Native infantry, of which four were Mysorean, four companies of pioneers, four heavy guns, four field-pieces, and a howitzer. With these he proceeded by Naulgoond and Holloor, where he encamped on the 8th. The pioneers employed this day, in opening the road in advance, were driven in by a party of horse. To reconnoitre their strength and designs, a picket of thirty Native cavalry were immediately ordered out, accompanied by Captain Middleton, the officer on duty for the day. This picket was unfortunately induced to follow the small parties of the enemy who presented themselves; and thus became exposed to the attack of an overwhelming number. These lay in ambuscade, and repeated an expedient which has been so often practised against British cavalry in India, that it would be wonderful it should have succeeded at so late a period, did not the events of every day shew how little benefit is derived from the experience of past times. The picket, however, retreated in good order (though pressed so closely as to be obliged to form three several times), and gained the camp with the loss of nine men and eight horses, killed and wounded; compensating as far as possible, for imprudence, by intrepidity. A troop of the 5th cavalry was immediately ordered out to repel the enemy; which measure being the natural consequence of the previous occurrence, they were prepared to retire before it, and Captain

Munro, who commanded, after pursuing till night-fall, made no more impression on them than the destruction of a few of the worst mounted. On the 9th of February the force arrived at Belloor, the garrison of which, consisting of four hundred horse, and three hundred foot, made their escape over the [illegible] hills towards Badaumee; and the Brigadier-general halted on the 10th and 11th, to complete his preparations for its siege. Thither he marched on the following day; and the advanced party was opposed by a small detachment of the enemy's foot posted in a pagoda, and supported by a body of four hundred horse. They were covered, in front, by a deep *nullah*, passable at one point only; and while a gun was brought up and opened, to cover the passage, the light-company of the 2d battalion of the 4th Native infantry was prepared to attack the entrenchment with the bayonet. This succeeded with little loss; and the enemy retreated under a heavy fire, leaving four dead on the ground.

Capture of Badaumee.

Badaumee consists of fortified hills, with a walled town at the foot of them, containing an inner fort; and it was deemed necessary, in the first instance, to attack the lower defences. The previous means at the Brigadier-general's disposal, were increased by the arrival, on the 15th, of two weak squadrons of his Majesty's 22d dragoons, and a company of the 2d battalion of the 9th regiment, followed, two days afterwards, by the head-quarters, and seven companies of the same corps. The batteries, which were erected against the place, played in breach till the evening of the 17th, when the way in was concluded to be practicable. On the morning of the 18th, a storming party* advanced from the rear of the batteries, as the day dawned. In eight minutes they surmounted the breach; for the garrison appeared to be unprepared, and such men as were in the neighbouring works were immediately killed. Those in the streets were attacked with the same spirit and expedition, and driven to the upper forts, to which they were so quickly pursued, the scaling-ladders all the while advancing with the storming party, that the enemy, apprehending such daring conduct

* Consisting of twenty-five men of the 22d dragoons, dismounted, with flank companies of the 2d battalion of the 4th, and 2d battalion of the 9th regiments of Native infantry. The advance was composed of the dragoons, and a havildar's party from each of the Native detachments; the whole headed by a party of pioneers carrying ladders. Four companies of the 2d battalion of the 4th, and three companies of the 2d battalion of the 9th regiments, were held in reserve to support the assault.

would be followed by an immediate escalade, called out for terms of capitulation. They were allowed to march out with their arms, and, by ten o'clock A. M. the Brigadier-general was in possession of all the forts, in which were found fourteen guns of various calibers, and seventeen ginjaul pieces. Two companies of the 2d battalion of the 12th regiment were allotted for the garrison of this place, which was deservedly esteemed one of the strongest hill-forts in India, and almost impregnable with a determined garrison. The loss was four Europeans, and five Natives, killed and wounded.

Occupation of the Country between the Mulpurba and Gutpurba.

Baggrekotah, on the Gutpurba, was the next object of Brigadier-general Munro; and he marched his force in that direction on the 21st of February, when he was joined at Hingengaum by the remaining two companies of the 2d battalion of the 9th regiment. On the following day he came before the place, which surrendered without offering any resistance. It was found to contain eight guns and ten ginjaul pieces. One company of the 2d battalion of the 9th regiment being placed in garrison, the Brigadier-general halted till the 25th, engaged in various arrangements for the permanent possession of the country he had subdued. The repair of some gun-carriages, which broke down on the 26th, obliged him to remain at the next stage of Soolikeiry till the 1st of March; after which he continued his route up the right bank of the Gutpurba to Gokauk, where his force encamped on the 7th and 8th. A weak company of the 2d battalion of the 9th regiment was detached under Lieutenant Stott to Hangul, to check the excursions of the garrison of that place, amounting to near eight hundred men; and it arrived in position on the 8th. This weak party drove in an out-post, and was attacked in turn by the garrison, who sallied in the afternoon; but they made so little impression, causing the loss of only two men, that they soon retired, and next morning surrendered the place; convinced, probably, that they would otherwise be visited by the entire force, and receive worse terms. Munro crossed the river at Gokauk, and marching two days up the left bank, recrossed to Goarree-Ghurree, and encamped at Padshapoor on the 11th. This place, which is the head of a district, immediately submitted; and all the dependent country was placed under the management of new Authorities established by the Brigadier-general. The same measures were adopted in the country through which he had passed; for the rapid fall of the first forts which had been attacked, prepared places less strong, to receive, with alacrity, the establishment of the British Authority.

Operations before Belgaum, to the Construction of Breaching-Batteries.

There remained still, however, in the country between the Mulpurba and Gutpurba, a place of considerable strength, which was likely to give employment to the force for some time; and as Brigadier-general Munro deemed it inexpedient to leave any fort in his rear, in opposition to his arrangements, he marched towards Belgaum, situated in the direction of the (Plan 26.) Western Ghats. He arrived before the place on the 20th, and took possession of the *pettah* without delay, in order to gain cover as near the fort as practicable, before commencing further operations. It was found to be in perfect repair, possessing a broad and deep wet ditch, surrounded by an esplanade of six hundred yards; and was garrisoned by sixteen hundred men. The pi- (A) oneers were set to work to prepare a battery of three twelve-pounders, at a Mosque opposite to the north face; and to favour their progress, a five-and-a-half-inch mortar and a six-pounder opened from the *pettah*. On the 21st, the battery opened within eight hundred yards of the fort, and was answered by five guns, which were nearly silenced in the course of the following day. On (B.) the night of the 22d, an enfilading-battery of two guns was completed in the *pettah*, and raked completely the north face and gateway. A gun opened (3.) on it from a cavalier within the works, and the fire of the twelve-pounder battery was returned from the curtain, left of the gate. These efforts were, (F) however, partially defeated on the 24th, when the approach was commenced, and carried one hundred and forty yards. On the following day, the enemy had only ginjauls firing, and the approach advanced one hundred and twenty yards. On the 26th, the garrison again shewed artillery; and (3) opened from the flag-staff battery, which had been nearly destroyed by the previous fire of the twelve-pounders. They likewise produced a new gun on the right of the gate; but could not impede the progress of the approach, which was carried forward one hundred yards through very hard ground. On the 27th, the mortar was moved from the enfilading to the twelve-pounder battery, and threw shells all the night, while an advance of one hundred yards more was made. This was prolonged one hundred and twenty yards next day, the enemy's fire was reduced to two guns; and on the 30th, one hundred and twenty yards more were added, without any extraordinary occurrence. On the 31st, the magazine in the Mosque, belonging to the twelve-pounder battery, blew up; and the garrison instantly sallied to take advantage of the confusion, which they supposed that it had occasioned. On their arrival within one hundred yards of that point, the battery-guard, under Lieutenant Walker, of the 2d battalion of the 4th regiment, and the artillery detail under Lieutenant Lewis, advanced to meet them, and drove them again into the fort, under a heavy fire of guns and small-arms, from the walls. Colonel Newall, who witnessed this act of gallantry, eulogized, with the two officers already mentioned, the conspicuous conduct of Lieutenant Macky, of his Majesty's 53d regiment, who, unable to join the detachment of his corps with Brigadier-general Pritzler, took his tour of general duty in Brigadier-general Munro's force.

The repair of the twelve-pounder battery, after this accident, occupied the 1st of April, during which day an eight-inch mortar was opened, the five-and-a-half inch mortar removed back to the enfilading battery, and the approach carried on fifty yards. This was now so well advanced, that a breaching-battery was commenced and finished on the 2d, for two eighteen- (C.) pounders, within five hundred and fifty yards of the wall. It opened, on the left of the gateway, with great effect, on the following morning. But the garrison had still two guns able to fire on the side of the attack; and as they annoyed considerably the breaching-battery, two twelve-pounders (D.) were brought into battery one hundred yards to the left, to silence them. This effect succeeded on the 4th, when a large part of the outer wall, left of the gate, and some of the inner wall, were brought down. On the next day the destruction was still more augmented, all the batteries having continued firing, and shells being thrown during the whole of the night. The same activity was continued during the 6th; and before day-light, a twelve-pounder was got into battery, within one hundred and fifty yards of the gate. This opened on the 7th, but unfortunately burst after firing fifteen rounds. The breach of the curtain was extended, notwithstanding the garrison still maintained a smart fire. On the 8th, the original twelve-pounder (E.) battery was abandoned, and two of the iron guns from it were brought into the battery near the gate. They opened next day, with excellent effect, on the curtain to the right, where the enemy's ginjauls and matchlockmen had previously had good cover, and made a practicable breach in the outer wall. On viewing this result, the Killedar sent out to propose terms; which not being agreed to, the batteries continued, on the morning of the 10th, to fire as usual, till the Killedar surrendered at discretion. A detachment of British troops took possession of the outer gateway on the same day; and, on the next, the pioneers were employed in opening both entrances, as they were built up within, and strongly barricaded. On the 12th of April the garrison marched out, and acknowledged to have had twenty

Reduction of the Place on Capitulation

killed and fifty wounded during the siege, while, of the British troops, there as a loss of twenty-three.*

Reflections on this Success and consequent Arrangements.

Thus was happily concluded this important service, in effecting which, the want of ordinary means was compensated by extraordinary labour and zeal in all ranks. The exertions of the artillery, and detail of his Majesty's 22d dragoons, serving in the batteries, was unremitting, for there were no means of affording them any relief; and the labours of the pioneers were equally meritorious in constructing, in addition to several batteries, an approach through extremely hard ground, which, however narrow, was seven hundred and fifty yards in length. Brigadier-general Munro, as already noticed, took the field without any staff; he was even without a professional engineer, a circumstance, considering the nature of the service in which he was engaged, especially to be regretted, had he not possessed, in the assistance of his second in command, a resource which supplied, as far as possible, this, as well as other, deficiencies. Accordingly the Brigadier-general did not fail to express, in the most unqualified manner, how much he was indebted to Lieutenant-colonel Newall, "for the judgment, zeal, and energy, with which he personally directed every operation." The return of ordnance on the works amounted to thirty-six pieces, mostly of large calibers, and of ginjauls and small brass guns, sixty more. The place was, moreover, supplied with stores in a superior manner; and, notwithstanding the progress that had been made, it was justly a matter of congratulation, that the garrison surrendered without further opposition. The three eighteen-pounders were latterly so much run at the vent, that three fingers might be introduced into them, and they had consequently lost considerably in effect. The walls were, every where, solid and massive, and being upwards of a mile and a half in extent, afforded the garrison abundant room to avoid the effect of shells. The consequences of this service obliged the force to halt at Belgaum, till the 17th, to re-organize the means of future operations, and to establish permanently the benefits to be derived from it. A company of the 2d battalion of the 4th regiment, with a party of pioneers, were sent on the 14th to Humpsagur, to escort guns and treasure, from thence to Dharwar; a company of the 2d battalion of the 9th regiment was placed in possession of the fort of Belgaum; and the

---

* Vide Appendix. P.

Brigadier-general recommenced his return, on the 18th, to the Gutpurba, which he crossed on the 21st, and arrived on the following day at Nugger Manaollee. Here he was joined by the remainder of the Reserve, under Brigadier-general Pritzler; whose movements since the latter end of March, it will be proper to mention, before the operations of the combined force are further described.

March of Brigadier-general Pritzler's Force from Satara for the Investment of Wassota.

This part of the Reserve marched, on the 29th, from the vicinity of Satara, having halted there on the two previous days (p. 255), and encamped, on the 30th, at Tambia, on the high road to Wassota, the reduction of which was its immediate object*. This fort is situate on the summit of a lofty mountain in the Western Ghats, about three thousand feet high, on the Kokun side; and on the eastern side, about two thousand feet from the base of the hill; but like most other hill-forts it is commanded. Its greatest strength consists in its elevation, and in the difficulties of approach; for, in almost every direction, it is surrounded by inaccessible mountains, with the exception of a few passes, so narrow and rugged as to be easily defended, and extremely difficult to be surmounted, though presenting no other opposition than that of nature. A detachment † was sent forward on the 31st, under Colonel Hewitt's command, to invest the place. The remainder of the division continued at Tambia, about twenty miles south-east of Wassota, yet the nearest point at which the encampment and the park could be formed. In the afternoon Colonel Hewitt's detachment reached Indoolie, a small village within two miles and a half of Wassota; and drove in an out-post of the garrison. Two companies of the seventh were left in

---

* The force assembled for this service was composed of two corps of Europeans, viz. the flank battalion and Bombay European regiment, half a battalion of rifles, four battalions of Native infantry of the line, that is, the 2d battalion of the 12th Madras, the 2d battalion of the 7th, and 2d battalion of the 9th Bombay, and an auxiliary battalion from Poonah. To this force was attached seven hundred Poonah auxiliary horse and four companies of pioneers; and the ordnance amounted to twenty-nine pieces, of which four were iron eighteen-pounders, and two were iron twelves; there were one ten-inch, and four eight-inch mortars, two heavy five-and-a-half-inch howitzers, two brass twelve-pounders, and the remainder were field-guns and light howitzers. Lieutenant-colonel Dalrymple, of the Madras Establishment, commanded the artillery, of which there were two hundred and seventy Europeans, and three hundred and seventy Natives, of both Presidencies. Captain Nutt, of the Bombay Establishment, was chief engineer.

† Consisting of six companies of the European flank battalion, two companies of rifles, flank companies of the 2d battalion of the 12th, and the 7th Bombay Native infantry.

possession of the post, and the remainder of the force returned to Tambia, five miles from Wassota, there being no nearer place fit for encampment. (Plan 26) The investment was accordingly postponed till the 1st of April, when three (A. A. A) outposts were established; one at Old Wassota, distant seven hundred yards, and commanding the place; the second at the same distance, and commanding the road up to the gateway; and the third to the right of it, distant no more than four hundred yards from the walls.

Fall of that Place, and Liberation of the Prisoners.

A summons was sent forward to the Killedar; but it was refused admittance, while all the pioneers and *dooly*-bearers were engaged in making a road towards the place, and continued to be so employed the following day. On the 3d, the head-quarters of the division were moved forward to Tambia; and the mortars and howitzers were conveyed across the mountains to the same place, by means of elephants. The next day a strong working-party was employed on the pathway to Old Wassota, up the mountain, to complete the work commenced on the 1st; and some light guns and ammunition were got up. The Rajah of Satara, whose family were confined here, arrived in the camp, and a detachment of rifles and auxiliary horse were sent into the jungles, to search for eighteen elephants that had been carried off, by their keepers, from Pandaughur, immediately before that place was (B.) reduced. On the 5th, the battery from Old Wassota opened with good effect, and one of the largest buildings in the place was fired by the bombardment. The garrison returned few shots from their large guns, but kept up an unremitting fire from their ginjauls and small arms, and were all day busily employed in improving their defences. The bombardment continued on the 6th, when, it being found that the previous arrangements had been insufficient to intimidate the Killedar, the pioneers were directed to complete the road from the camp, for the advance of the battering-guns. This was, however, unnecessary; for on the following morning the garrison surrendered unconditionally, and a company of Bombay Native infantry took possession of the fort. The loss of the enemy amounted to seventeen killed and wounded, and that of the British force to four only. Among the prisoners liberated, were the two officers, Cornets Morison and Hunter, whose captivity has been already noticod (p. 71), and who were restored to their profession and society, after an almost hopeless confinement. They were the first to meet the party advancing to receive possession of the place, among whom were some intimate friends; but such was their altered appearance, in consequence of their past hardships, that they were scarcely to be recognized.

This circumstance only heightened the interest of so singular a meeting, which was inexpressible for several moments. The impression was so pathetic, as to extend to the common soldiers, who witnessed the scene, and testified how much they participated in the event by an acclamation, as sincere as it was clamorous.

Return to Satara, and Separation of the Madras and Bombay Troops

Great importance was attached to the fall of Wassota, it being considered, by the inhabitants of the Poonah territory, as one of the strongest fortresses of the Peishwah, and therefore one of his treasure depôts. On account of its supposed strength and remote situation, he likewise made it the place of confinement of the Rajah's family, who were liberated on the present occasion, and accompanied him to the seat of his Government. A recollection of the last siege of this place may afford some notion of its strength; for it then held out nearly eleven months, in the hands of a rebel, against the Peishwah's army of ten thousand men, commanded by Gokla, his best general; and ultimately surrendered, when no great progress was made in the siege, beyond the establishment of batteries. The 7th was occupied in the removal of the mortars and guns, from the batteries, back to the park, and in preparations for recrossing the mountains. This was effected during the two following days; and on the 10th, the force returned to Satara, having reduced the fortress of Parlee by the detachment of a party of infantry under a Native officer, to whom it surrendered. The detachment of rifles and auxiliary horse, which had been sent off a few days before, rejoined with the elephants they had gone in search of, after a most fatiguing and long march among the hills. At Satara, the Bombay troops, excepting the 7th Native infantry, were encamped separately from those of Madras; and the Rajah was formally placed, by the Commissioner, on the *musnud*, with the usual ceremonies, at which the Brigadier-general and the principal officers of the force attended. On the 11th of April there was a halt, during which visits of ceremony were exchanged with the Rajah; and on the 12th, the force recommenced its return towards the southward, by the Valley of the Upper Kistnah, for the reduction of more forts during its progress to join Brigadier-general Munro.

Junction with Brigadier-general Munro's Force

On the second march from Satara, the encampment was at Mussoor, which fort, as well as the hill fortress of Wassuntghur, surrendered in the course of the day. On arriving at Korar, on the 14th, the garrisons of Kola and Seedasheeghur abandoned those places. At Copergaum, on the following day, the submissions were received of Machendurghur, Battee Seraollee,

Islampoor, Wanghy, and Walwa; and garrisons were established in all these, as well as in the other places. From hence the march was conducted, without intermission, by Islampoor, Atta, and Secredwar, to Nugger-Manaollee, where, on the 22d, the junction was formed with Brigadier-general Munro's head-quarters. The rapid fall of so many places verified a well-known observation, that, as long as there is no army to keep the field, the forts will quickly submit; for now they seemed to want only a pretence for surrendering. A party of Peons was even formed equal to this service; and Brigadier-general Munro did not fail to embrace the opportunity of establishing them [illegible] the country within the influence of the prevailing impression. Among others was the hill-fort of Kalla Nundidroog, about twenty-five miles west of Belgaum, containing a garrison of three hundred and fifty men, who surrendered, on the 22d, to a party of irregulars, detached early in the month to invest it.

Collected Amount of the Reserve.

The Native infantry, with Brigadier-general Munro's force, had been very much reduced, in consequence of the numerous detachments he had been obliged to make for the occupation of forts, and for escorts; and it has been seen that, of Europeans, he was always deficient, having been obliged to avail himself of the voluntary and meritorious conduct of the detachment of dragoons, who acted both as artillery and grenadiers. He was therefore unable to push the war, with any prospect of success, against an enemy, which might take the field, or occupy a fortified position, with many guns and regular corps of foot. The junction of Brigadier-general Pritzler's division of the Reserve, supplied him with these means; and the return of Bajee Rao's infantry and park to the Beemah, offered him a respectable and worthy object for their employment. The troops which joined from Satara were, the two companies of artillery, under Lieutenant-colonel Dalrymple; the European flank battalion, composed of the flower of four regiments, who, notwithstanding the difficulties of maintaining long, in a state of regularity, a corps composed of various details, had been as remarkable throughout the service, under Major Giles's command, for their discipline and order, as for their gallantry; the four companies of rifles, the 2d battalion of the 22d Native infantry, the 2d battalion of the 7th Bombay Native infantry, and a detachment of pioneers. Two iron eighteen-pounders and two mortars were likewise brought from the Bombay battering-train—a desirable acquisition, considering the unserviceable state to which the heavy guns had been reduced at Belgaum.

The force halted on the 23d, 24th, and 25th, to give time for the arrival of the scaling-ladders from Belgaum, and to organize its several parts for an immediate march to the Beemah; where, on the 25th, Bajee Rao's infantry and guns were encamped south-south-west of Sholapoor. The march was recommenced, on the 26th of April, by Ryebaugh and Ynapoor, near which place the Kistnah river was crossed. From hence the route was pursued, without intermission or halt, by Partanelly, Zettee, and Gardee, to Seedapoor, on the Beemah, which was passed on the 7th of May; while the enemy fell back on Sholapoor, to make their final stand. On the next day, the force crossed the Seena, at Pattree; and, on the 9th, took up ground within two miles of the enemy's position, which Brigadier-general Munro immediately and closely reconnoitred with a squadron of dragoons, half the flank battalion and rifles, with the flank companies of the remaining corps, under a continual fire from the place. A summons, with an offer of terms, had been previously sent forward by a Native officer*, who was cruelly murdered by Arabs under the walls. The Fort of Sholapoor is an oblong of considerable area, with a wall and *fausse-braye* of substantial masonry, flanked by capacious round towers. A broad and deep wet ditch surrounds the place, and the north and east sides are covered by an extensive *pettah*, surrounded by a good wall, and divided in the same manner into two parts, of which one is immediately contiguous to the fort. To the southward, communicating with the ditch, is a tank, surrounded on three sides by a mound, which, in its extent, formed a respectable breastwork to the enemy's position under the walls. Their force, thus strongly posted, amounted to eight hundred and fifty horse, five thousand five hundred and fifty foot, including twelve hundred Arabs, and fourteen guns, independent of the garrison, estimated at one thousand. Major de Pinto, a country-born descendant of Europeans, commanded the regular infantry; and the Native chief, named Gunput Rao Phansee, was the hereditary commandant of the Peishwah's artillery.

March to Sholapoor, and Description of the Enemy's Strength and Position

(Plan 29.)

(1, 1, 1)

* This officer, named Cheyn Sing, was Subidar of the 2d battalion of the 4th regiment, and had been, on many occasions throughout the campaign, selected for the performance of a similar duty, on account of his singular intelligence and address. The reader will be gratified by learning, that his next heir has been liberally pensioned by the Government, in gratitude for the Subidar's devotion to their service.

Escalade of the Pettah.

At three o'clock in the morning of the 10th of May, the British troops destined for the attack began to get under arms. The 2d battalion of the 12th Madras, and the 2d battalion of the 7th Bombay Native infantry, with the exception of their flank companies, remained in charge of the camp under Lieutenant-colonel Fraser. The remaining troops were formed in the following order. For the escalade of the *pettah* walls, under the general orders of Colonel Hewitt, two columns, commanded by Lieutenant-colonel Newall and Major Giles, each composed of two European flank companies, two companies of rifles, one incomplete battalion of Native infantry, and one company of pioneers. For the support of the escalade, a reserve, under the personal command of Brigadier-general Pritzler, consisted of a squadron and a half of dragoons with gallopers, two European flank companies, four Native flank companies, four six-pounders, and two howitzers. The escalading columns took up positions at the distance of one thousand yards from the point of attack, till the day broke; when they moved briskly for-
(a, a.) ward, preceded by the pioneers, carrying scaling-ladders, while the reserve,
(b, b) from a position opposite the same face, opened a smart fire on the front and flanking defences. The ladders were planted with promptitude; and the heads of both columns topped the walls at the same moment. As soon as a sufficient number of men were formed by each, possession was taken of the towers to the right and left, parties were sent to open the gates, and the whole entered in a short time. The right column, under Lieutenant-colonel Newall, followed the course of the wall by the right; and having gained that which divides the *pettah*, occupied three large houses in the quarter contiguous to the fort. Major Giles, with the left column, (which was accompanied by Colonel Hewitt,) separated into two parts; of which one kept along the wall on the left, and the other advanced up the central street to the opposite extremity, after forcing the gate which divided the *pettah*. The outer gate was also forced open, and the column, both parts of which here rejoined, passed through, and dislodged, by the detachment of a company of European grenadiers, a party of the enemy posted in a neighbouring suburb.

Defeat of Gunput Rao's Attack.

While these events occurred within the *pettah*, without, Gunput Rao
(2, 2, 2) left his position near the fort, and making a *detour* by the eastern side,
(3, 3) placed himself, with seven guns and a respectable body of horse and foot, opposite to the reserve, on which he immediately opened a fire. Brigadier-general Munro, finding himself neither strong enough in men to storm this

position, nor his guns sufficiently numerous to silence the fire, withdrew the reserve under the wall of the *pettah*, and sent to Colonel Hewitt for a reinforcement. Before this arrived, one of the enemy's tumbrils blew up, and the opportunity was considered favourable for attacking them with the bayonet. Brigadier-general Pritzler headed the dragoons, and Lieutenant-colonel Dalrymple, the infantry, joined by the artillery-men from the guns, while Brigadier-general Munro directed the charge in person, cheered vociferously by the Europeans, whose delight at the veteran's presence among them, on such an occasion, was an excuse for the noisy freedom with which he was hailed. The enemy, in the mean while, had lost their commander, who was severely wounded, and their second in command killed by a cannon-shot. They began to draw off their guns, but not in time to prevent three of them from falling into the hands of the reserve, while their foot were driven into a garden and inclosures, from whence they maintained a fire of musquetry. At this time Lieutenant-colonel Newall joined with a reinforcement of Europeans and rifles from the *pettah;* and immediately attacked and dislodged them. The enemy retreating to their original position, near the fort, passed the south *pettah* gate, of which, at this time, Colonel Hewitt was in possession. He being seasonably joined by a field-piece, ran it out, and opened it quickly, to their great annoyance. A gate leading into the inner *pettah* was taken possession of by a company of the 69th regiment, and three companies of Native infantry; but the range of their position being found by an enemy's gun, and their small arms from behind cover, it was abandoned, and the troops confined to the occupation of the main street, and the avenues leading into it. The enemy maintained possession of such parts of the *pettah* as their matchlocks from the fort could reach; and the remainder continued to be occupied by the British troops. The reserve returned to camp, which had in the mean while changed ground from the west to the north side of the place, and was here joined by Doolie Khan, an officer in the Nizam's service, with eight hundred irregulars, of whom three hundred were horse.

Flight and Dispersion Bajee Rao's Infantry

Some faint attempts were made by the garrison, during the day, to extend their possession of the *pettah;* but these proving unsuccessful, their friends without evinced a design of quitting their position, the security of which became doubtful after the events of the forenoon. As soon as intimation of this movement was received in the camp, the detachment of dragoons, and as many auxiliary horse, with the two galloper-guns, were ordered out under Brigadier-general Pritzler; and Doolie Khan's horse was directed to follow as quickly as possible. The enemy were not overtaken nearer than seven miles from the camp; for they had left their guns behind them, in order that their flight might not be impeded. The gallopers opened on their rear with grape, while a half-squadron took ground on each flank of the retreating column, which maintained an unsteady fire of matchlocks. When the half-squadron came in contact with the enemy, the guns limbered up, and followed as a reserve with the remaining half-squadron and Doolie Khan's horse, till these, likewise, and the auxiliary horse, joined in the general destruction of this ill-advised body. It was completely dispersed before night put an end to the pursuit on the banks of the Seena river; and near a thousand were left dead on the field. Subsequent accounts represent those who remained, and who might be considered annihilated as a military body, seeking their homes in small parties, not exceeding ten or fifteen men, many of whom were wounded. The cavalry got back to their lines at ten o'clock that night, and thus closed this eventful day, the various operations of which, in rapid succession, might rival the artful bustle of the last act of a play.

Reflections on the Arms of Cavalry.

Brigadier-general Pritzler, in reporting his successful pursuit of the enemy, states that, after the charge, the men " made use of their pistols;" and, in fact, all the regular cavalry in India, both European and Native, adopt the same practice. The best writers on cavalry service in Europe, consider the sword as its proper and primary arm, for execution among a broken enemy, as well as for the charge; and so much has the pistol been regarded as an emergent reserve only, that, with light-horse, it has been proposed there should be only one allowed to each individual. The experience of many campaigns goes, however, to prove that most execution is to be done in India by the pistol; and the neglect of the sword must arise from a cause not prevailing in Europe. Almost every soldier in the service of a Native Power, has his head secured by many folds of cotton cloth, which not only pass round, but likewise over it, and under the chin; and a protection for the back of the neck is provided of similar materials. The jacket is composed of cotton, thickly quilted between cloths, and so substantial as almost to retain the shape of the body, like stiff armour. To penetrate this covering with the edge of the sword, is to be done only by the practice of cutting, which forms no part of the instruction of regular cavalry in the British service; whereas it is considered a most essential point by an irregular horseman. In this, the most difficult part is not only to apply the edge directly, but to carry it through, which may confidently be declared to be impracticable *, or the result of chance, with the supple wrist prescribed in the British sword-exercise. The Native practice not only prescribes a stiff wrist, but a stiff, though not a straight, elbow, for a cut that shall disable; but this supposes an adversary on the same level, and is not the case of cavalry against infantry. As the sword is thus held, the motion of it proceeds from the shoulder: the distance from thence to the hilt becomes the radius of a revolving circle, of which the blade forms part of the periphery; and on this principle, the application of its edge ensures to it all the power of a wheel in mechanics, by which the hardest substance is penetrated. This is no untried theory, but the explanation of an efficacious practice, introduced by its own utility among a people incapable of referring it to any scientific principle. All the manual of drawing and returning the sword, inevitably deprives it of sharpness, and leaves it incapable of putting an adversary *hors de combat;* which circumstance will probably suggest the expedient of preferring the use of the point. Unfortunately, however, the present dragoon sword is incapable of entering a cotton-quilted jacket by that means, in consequence, likewise, of its elasticity, and the broadness of its point. It is trusted that this explanation will account for the prevailing use of the pistol, which has given rise to this digression, and may likewise point out the means of restoring to the sword its rightful importance. The strength of a British arm is sufficient, perhaps, to drive even a blunt and broad point, with all the disadvantage of indirectness arising from a curved blade; but if, by daily cleaning, this becomes easily flexible, it will bend beneath the impelling force, instead of overcoming the opposed resistance. That national weapon, fitted for the world's awe, is blunt enough, but straight forward; and as unbending as the stubborn souls, and nervous arms, whose proper instrument it is.

---

* The truth of this position may be proved by the adoption of a common expedient in India. Let a wall narrowing to the top be raised three feet high of clay, carefully cleared of any gravelly substance, and of as much thickness, and no more than will enable it to stand to dry. When the crust only of it has become crisp, which will be the case after a few hours' exposure to the sun, let a soldier, expert in the sword exercise, try to cut deep in it; and he will find that, till he has acquired the habit of a stiff wrist, his sword will invariably turn.

Surrender of Sholapoor

No time was lost, after the attack of the *pettah* of Sholapoor, before operations were commenced against the fort, of which the southern face was selected as the most favourable for an approach; there being, on that side, considerable cover, and the ditch being there partially dry. On the 11th, a battery of one mortar, one howitzer, and two six-pounders, was established behind the *bund* of the tank, to keep the enemy within their walls, and to afford cover to the working-parties and advanced-posts. This was further enlarged, on the same evening, for three additional mortars, which opened on the following morning with some effect. On the 13th, an approach was made towards the fort, and the commencement of a breaching-battery was laid, under cover of the fire from the mortars and six-pounders; the *practice* from which, on this day, was so admirable, as to silence the enemy at many points. An enfilading-battery was also marked out for two twelve-pounders and two six-pounders, and was half-finished towards evening, while the garrison were busily employed in throwing up retrenchments. This, as well as the breaching-battery, was completed during the night; and both opened, on the morning of the 14th, with unremitting vigour. By noon, the breach of the outer wall was reported practicable; and at the same time the enemy, viewing the rapid progress which had been made, sent out to demand terms. They were promised security for themselves and private property, with which they marched out on the following morning. The principal officers received passports to proceed to Poonah, and the troops dispersed to their several homes. The number of guns in the fort, from a one to a forty-two pounder, amounted to thirty-seven, including eleven field-guns; besides which, there were thirty-nine wall-pieces, rom a one-pounder to three-pounders. The reduction of this respectable and important fort deprived Bajee Rao's troops of their last rallying-point in the Southern Mahratta country; while the losses they had suffered, during the operations at this place, completely disheartened all the abettors of their cause. The loss of the British troops, as of the enemy, occurred almost entirely on the 10th, and amounted to one hundred and two men*, including four officers, which, however to be regretted, was far from being incommensurate with the service performed.

* Vide Appendix Q.

Considerations on the Number of Mahratta Forts.

No territory of similar extent in India, or perhaps in any part of the world, possesses so many fortresses as that which belonged to the Peishwah before the war. Of this multiplied number of strong holds, the cause must be sought in the nature of the country, combined with events in the history of its inhabitants. The first of these causes appears insufficient; for the country, including the Western Ghats, both north and south of the tract in question, differs immaterially from it, in general feature and construction, without being marked by the same efforts of human art; and with regard to the last cause, its peculiarity consists principally in its being the cradle of the Mahratta Power. The author possesses no historical memoirs which record the origin of such numerous fortified places, many of which are indubitably Mahratta-built. Arguing, however, from the history of other nations who have existed on distant conquests, and maintained for this purpose large armies of horse, the Mahrattas will appear a singular exception to the general conduct, under similar circumstances. That they required strong holds, in the commencement of their power, when they subsisted principally on the plunder of the plains, in which they were too weak to maintain themselves, permanently, against the Mussulman forces in the Deckan, is natural and comprehensible. Subsequently, however, they have never been attacked in their fortresses by a Foreign Power, till they came in contact with the British Establishments in India. In their early history, they acquired some places by force, and many by artifice. When their power became established, and subsequently disunited, many new places of strength were constructed; but their wars of sieges almost entirely occurred in their internal dissensions.

Importance of Fortresses in general.

The importance of fortified places in a State, is a question which has been freely discussed, since the art of their attack and defence has been brought to its present state of perfection. Immediately after the French Revolution, it was fashionable to decide against their utility, in consequence of the little opposition they made to the inundation of French armies and French warfare. But these means of conquests must be considered as only accidental; for they proceeded out of a state of things which rarely occurs, which no Government can produce at pleasure, and which paralyzed the conduct of the defending, as much as it invigorated the efforts of the offending party. The rapid occupation, therefore, either of Italy or Spain, cannot be taken as conclusive on this subject; and when the affairs of Europe began to seek their natural state, armies, against which, under other circumstances, the fortresses on their line of march would have been satisfied with a few discharges of artillery, were now detained from other operations by tedious, and occasionally unsuccessful sieges. Those of Cadiz, Dantzig, Sarragossa, and Hamburgh, may be sufficent instances for the present purpose; and the advantage derived from the reduction of those which fell, may at best be questionable, when compared with the price of the purchase. There are few countries so circumstanced, that their army can maintain the field against a powerful invasion, without forts to contain and secure its supplies. The reduction of these becomes, therefore, in general, the first step of the offensive operations; as their support, by every practicable means of reinforcement or diversion, is the object of the defensive measures. It is observed in return, and with truth, that every frontier, or other place reduced, becomes the means of further conquest, in the hands of the invader, and the point of a new base for the prolongation of his line of operations. But it must not be forgotten, that the gaining time, in defensive war, is the most important acquisition, from a variety of causes, both political and military; which may, and probably will, more than compensate for the loss of a fort gained by the enemy with breached ramparts, broken counterscarp, filled ditch, ruined interior, and expended stores, with the necessary and disproportionate injury of a large army, compared to the numbers of a garrison. There is no doubt, however, that on a question liable to be affected by an endless variety of circumstances, the ingenuity and extensive knowledge of modern days will be able to bring forward so many arguments on both sides, as may well suspend the judgment of, at least, the careless reflector. The general opinion of States, however, from the earliest to the latest times, as declared in their conduct, has been favourable to the importance of fortresses, notwithstanding the heavy expense of their maintenance, or original construction, which has never been effected in the course of a single century. If, therefore, the importance of fortified places be granted, the priority of possession seems to secure their advantage; for, in fact, the argument derived from their liability to be taken, applies, in a certain degree, to every defensive operation of war, or even of the individual.

Application of these Reflections to the Case of India.

This reasoning is, perhaps, more applicable to Europe than to India, where the boundaries of governments have been so changeable, as to have precluded the fortification of a frontier, had that measure formed any part of their principle of defence. But it does not appear to have been ever thought of; nor would it have been suitable to their conduct in other respects. A system by which a foreign enemy shall be detained on a frontier, by long foresight and provisions for the security of the internal resources, and protection of the inhabitants, of a kingdom, is, indeed, little compatible with a conduct which desolates the country, and plunders the subject, through inattention, misrule, or a temporary policy, which seldom looks beyond the present exigency. Under such circumstances, in India, as in every part of the world, the strongest holds will be in the recesses of a kingdom, instead of its exposed parts. They will be considered as places of security for the treasures, families, and lives of the chief and other officers of the government, in cases of emergency, more than as military positions to ensure the possession of the country. The revolutions of time have thrown, indifferently, on the skirts, and in the interior of the existing political divisions of India, extensive fortresses. These, when built, were the very heart and last stake of a principality; but they have been allowed to run to decay on losing their original destination. The number of forts in India, which are in perfect repair, is very few, compared with the numerous ruins scattered throughout its kingdoms—a state which has arisen, as well from the expense attending their maintenance, as from their inutility, and defective plan and construction. Many of these were considered, in their day, as completely impregnable, except when stratagem* occasionally succeeded; but European science, enterprise, and perseverance, have removed the illusion; and the Natives of India have seen places of the least imposing appearance make the greatest resistance. The possession of fortified mountain-summits, towering in the air, inspired a garrison, in former times, with a contempt of all coercive endeavours to reduce a place with a single and narrow avenue, guarded by unscalable precipices, and, to all appearance, remote from the reach of batteries. They might even be tempted to address their besiegers, in the language used to Alexander by

---

* Prior to the introduction of the systematic attack of fortified places in Europe, the history of its wars abounds in examples of successful stratagem; and the Natives of India were equally fertile in expedients for the reduction of places which resisted their coercive attempts. Among numerous instances, the capture of Rhotas by an officer of the Emperor Acbers, is worthy of admiration: Sevajee supplies others; for he always preferred cunning to force, and was successful in more instances than in the acquisition of Poonadur.

the garrison of Sogdia, who tauntingly enquired "whether he had furnished himself with winged soldiers for the storming of that rock? for otherwise they had no cause to be afraid, it being out of the power of all other mortals to ascend it by force." The capture of Gwalior*, in 1780, was not dissimilar to that of the Sogdian rock; and the Mysore war of 1791-2 demonstrated to India, that hill-forts are as contemptible, considered as places of [illegible] as they are useless for the purposes of a depôt. It has been seen, in the course of this Narrative, with what rapidity numerous hill-forts were reduced; and more instances remain to be related. The place which made the longest resistance was Belgaum, and evinced the importance, even in Indian warfare, of a fortress in the plain. The time was, when a similar post was of equal importance to the British possessions; and during the prevalence of a system of œconomy, which leaves every fort, with few exceptions, to dilapidate, under a reasonable confidence in the efficacy of a well-organized army, it may not be unsalutary, if, with all the change of circumstances, an occasional reflection be given to the incalculable services of a few garrisons, during the arduous campaigns of General Coote.

---

* See Rennell's Memoir of a Map of Hindoostan, p. 234, 4to edition. The note in which is related the escalade of this place by Major Bruce, under Colonel Popham's command, is too long for insertion here, but worthy of reference as an instance of a well-concerted surprise gallantly executed.

CHAPTER VII.

SUBJUGATION OF THE KOKUN, AND THE NORTHERN PARTS OF THE POONAH TERRITORY.

Operations of Lieutenant-colonels Kennedy and Imlach from Severndroog and Malwan. March of Colonel Prother's Detachment to Ryghur. Capitulation of the Fortress. Its former Importance. Dislocation of the Kokun Field Force. Return of the Reserve to Dharwar and Hooblee. Detachments in the Jooneer and Ahmednuggur Districts. Sir Thomas Hislop's Return to the Madras Presidency. March of Lieutenant-colonel Mac Dowell's Detachment to the Khandesh Ghats. Siege and Capture of Rajdeir. Countermarch to the Godavery. Siege and Surrender of Trimbuck. Inadequacy of the Means of further Operations. Defence of Soangheir. Description of Malleygaum. Investment and Construction of the Batteries. Unsuccessful Assault of the 29th of May. Abandonment of the Attack of the West Face. Successful Operations after the Arrival of the Bombay Train. Comparison of the Force of both Parties and Loss of the Besiegers. Qualities of an Engineer. Lieutenant-colonel Mac Dowell's Detachment assumes its Monsoon Position.

THERE were four independent detachments engaged at the same time in the reduction of Bajee Rao's forts. The relation of the fall of those which submitted to Brigadier-generals Munro and Pritzler has been concluded in the last Chapter; and there remains now to be described the subjugation of such as were in the Kokun, on the Upper Godavery, and in Khandesh.

The operations of Lieutenant-colonel Prother's detachment have been brought up to the 17th of March (p. 248), when a British garrison was placed in the fort of Koarree, on the summit of the Western Ghats. From hence, its future objects lay in the low country, where already some confined but successful operations had been conducted by Lieutenant-colonels Imlach and Kennedy, the officers commanding at Malwan and Severndroog. This place had been taken by a small detachment from Lieutenant-colonel Prother's force, before it ascended the Ghats; and was established as the head-quarters of a newly-raised battalion, into which were judiciously

Operations of Lieutenant-colonels Kennedy and Imlach from Severndroog and Malwan.

(Map VI.)

received the unfortunate deserters, whom the persecuting conduct of the Peishwah's officers to their families had induced to quit their colours. When Lieutenant-colonel Kennedy found himself in sufficient force, with the aid of a party of Europeans and of men from the Cruizers off Vittoria, he attacked the fort of Muddunghur, and took it by surprise, with a trifling loss, on the 15th of February. The fort of Ramghur was taken by escalade on the 4th of March; and its fall being followed by the immediate evacuation of Paulghur, the whole country between the Bancoot and Anjenwail rivers fell into British possession. These events were followed, on the 11th of March, by the surrender of Raussulghur; but the neighbouring hill-forts of Thomanghur and Myputghur were too imposing and too resolute to be attacked, with any prospect of success, by such limited means as were at the Lieutenant-colonel's disposal, after establishing so many small garisons as he was obliged to detach. Colonel Imlach was as little prepared for offensive measures; and owing to his insufficiency of force, and the total want of heavy guns, he had been obliged to tolerate the existence of an enemy's post in the neighbouring fort of Seedghur till the month of March, when adverse winds obliged a detachment of his Majesty's 89th regiment, bound for Bancoot, to put into Malwan. The Lieutenant-colonel directed their immediate disembarkation, and renewed the designs he had formerly been obliged to abandon. He was in a condition to move to Seedghur on the 15th; and on the next day opened a battery, which, by noon, produced so much effect on the wall, that the garrison evacuated by the opposite side. On the 28th, he proceeded to Bhugwuntghur; where, on the same day, having driven in the enemy's outposts, that place was likewise abandoned. Its fall was followed by that of Deoghur, which was evacuated; and of Ramghur. Compta, and Acheera, which capitulated on the first appearance of the detachment, by this means placed in full occupation of the province of Salsee. No further service of importance offered in this quarter beyond the dislodgement of a body of the enemy, who, from a position on the opposite bank of the Deoghur river, fired on the passing shipping; and the detachment of the 89th was re-embarked for Bancoot, to join Lieutenant-colonel Prother, now engaged before Ryghur.

March of Lieutenant-colonel Prother's Detachment to Ryghur.

This fort was represented as one of the strongest in India, and contained for the defence of its extensive works one thousand men, of whom many were Arabs. From the importance attached to it, the wife of Bajee Rao was placed there for her better security, with considerable property.

But it became necessary to reduce some smaller places, before Ryghur could be immediately invested; for the siege of which more troops would probably be required than were now under Lieutenant-colonel Prother's command. When the ordnance and commissariat departments were in a proper state for further operations, they were dispatched by the Boar Ghat as the most practicable for carriages, and the troops descended by that of Jamboosarrah, as the most direct. On the 12th of April, both divisions rejoined at Paullee, where they halted till the 14th, on account of the extreme fatigues incurred by the ordnance department, in surmounting the many obstacles opposed to its progress. As the force continued its march to Tella, it was, occasionally, opposed by small posts of the enemy. One of these, on the evening of the 16th, was taken by a reconnoitring party; and on the 17th, a stronger body, behind a stockade near Indapoor, was successfully attacked by a detachment under Captain Rose, of his Majesty's 89th regiment. His party consisted of the light company of that corps, and the flank companies of the 1st battalion of the 5th Native infantry. After properly disposing them for this service, he carried the post at all points; while a party of Guickwar horse succeeded in *cutting up* some fugitives, and taking some prisoners, among whom was a Chief of distinction. From this place to Tella the road being extremely difficult for guns, the Lieutenant-colonel, with a small detachment, proceeded, on the 18th, without them, and found the place evacuated. Goorsalla, in its vicinity, after a few discharges, followed the example; and both forts were found well supplied with provisions and ammunition. Maunghur, a hill-fort near the foot of the Ghats, was likewise taken possession of by a detachment sent for that purpose. The force moved from Indapoor to Mahar, on the 23d; and during the night, Major Hall, of his Majesty's 89th regiment, with a detachment of two hundred Europeans, and as many Sepoys, was sent to examine the immediate environs of Ryghur, which was now within a moderate distance. At day-break, on the 24th, he drove in the enemy's first post, and found, near the *pettah*, a body of about three hundred drawn up to oppose him. These he charged and routed, killing about twenty, with the loss of three men of the 89th, wounded. Having placed a party in possession of the *pettah*, he fell back, with the detachment, three miles, for want of water. A party of Guickwar horse at the same time brought in some camels, horses, and two elephants, from an excursion to a few miles distance.

Capitulation of the Fortress.

On the 25th, the camp was established as near Ryghur as the ground admitted, and the place was invested without loss of time by the separation of the force into several detachments; an arrangement which was also indispensable, on account of the scarcity of water at any one point. A small post, on the ridge of the hill, was driven in, and a battery for mortars constructed, with so narrow a front, owing to the confined nature of the situation, that they were necessarily placed on the line of each other's fire. The want of sufficient force was calculated to delay the operations against this place, and thus to defer the period of its submission much beyond that of the forts which had previously surrendered. Under this apprehension, the Government of Bombay, with zealous promptitude, sent off a seasonable reinforcement of six companies of his Majesty's 67th foot, which had recently landed from Goozerat. The arrival of this body, on the 4th of May, was followed by the detachment of his Majesty's 89th regiment from Malwan; and while an additional mortar-battery was established on the opposite side of the mountain, some heavy howitzers were expected from Bombay. In the mean while, however, no exertion was omitted to get up those in the camp into suitable positions; and the bombardment was maintained with an unremitting spirit, which, while it harassed the garrison, materially injured the mortar-beds. During the siege, a body of the enemy from the forts of Kangoorree and Purtabghur collected in the rear of Lieutenant-colonel Prother's force, and at length shewed themselves at Pooladpoor, near Mahar, on the coast, where there was a British post. Lieutenant Crosby, who commanded there, immediately marched against them with his detachment, consisting of seventy-five Native infantry and one hundred and forty Guickwar horse, whose attack put them to flight with the loss of twenty killed and fifteen prisoners. A passport was offered to the garrison of Ryghur for the departure of Bajee Rao's wife, which being refused, she was not permitted to leave the place. On the 7th, a shell having set fire to her habitation, she is said to have had sufficient influence to bring the Killedar to consent to a capitulation, the terms of which were arranged after an occasionally interrupted negotiation of two days.

Its former Importance.

The conditions under which the garrison agreed to evacuate Ryghur, were, the preservation of their arms and private property, permission to the Killedar Sheikh Abood, and his attendants, to reside at Poonah, where also the wounded were to remain till cured, and to Bajee Rao's wife, likewise, to pass, with her immediate followers, by Poonah. She was found seated among the embers of the late conflagration: for she refused to quit the site of her previous edifice, and was scarcely sheltered from the inclemency of the air by a wretched hut, subsequently erected for her abode. In this situation, however, she affected to maintain the outward shew of princely rank; and on taking her departure for Poonah, she was accommodated with the captured elephants and camels, and attended by a guard of honour. The remaining terms of the capitulation were likewise duly fulfilled, and, on the 10th, possession was taken of this famous fortress. Of its former grandeur, traces alone were to be discovered; for every building, one granary excepted, had been reduced to ashes by the bombardment. The palace of Sevajee, with some religious buildings of contemporary date, had been allowed many years since to decay; and the tomb of the founder of the Mahratta Empire was scarcely, and doubtfully discernible. It has been found difficult, by any description, to give an adequate idea of this extraordinary fort, more familiarly known, in Indian history, by the name of Rairree, as it is invariably denominated by Orme, who has much mistaken its geographical position. At the commencement of the Mahratta power, its unusual dimensions contained an entire army; and all the excursions of Sevajee were made from this place, which was the secure repository of his treasures and his plunder. In former* times, to attempt its speedy reduction would have been considered as the unavailing effort of insanity, so prevalent was the idea of its justly reputed strength, and of the insuperable obstacles of its situation. In the fallen fortunes of its master, in the nineteenth century, a period of fourteen days, and a few mortars, protected by a small detachment, proved sufficient for its easy capture.

There still remained in the Kokun, several places of inferior note, such as Linginna, Kangoorree, Chanderghur, and Myputghur. Against these the force would have been marched, had the advanced state of the season admitted of further operations. They were, however, subsequently evacuated, or they submitted to detachments, being useless without the possession of the surrounding country, which soon after fell quietly under the direction of the Civil officers of the British Government, and was only dis-

Dislocation of the Kokun Field Force.

* Ryghur was taken at the close of the 17th century by a Moghul General, after a tedious siege; and this event is supposed to have caused the removal of the seat of Mahratta Government to Satara.

turbed by the incursions of the Ramoossees, a plundering tribe from the hills. While the field force was, on the 21st, at Mhar, where the train was deposited, and at Kondar on the 23d, the necessary arrangements were in progress for the return of the troops and their equipments to Bombay; and Paullee was selected as a favourable position for the cantonment of such corps as should stay out the approaching monsoon. These were, the 1st battalion of the 9th, and two companies of the 2d battalion of the 4th regiment, under the Lieutenant-colonel's command; and the European troops returned to Bombay.

Return of the Reserve to Dharwar and Hooblee

The approaching period of the rains, on the western side of the peninsula, rendered alike necessary the return of the reserve to Dharwar, after the fall of Sholapoor. There remained no further service of importance to be performed in that quarter. Brigadier-general Munro, therefore, leaving there the Bombay battalion, which was serving with the force, commenced his march, on the 17th of May, in two divisions; of which, the 2d battalion of the 4th regiment, with two guns, composing one, proceeded, under Lieutenant-colonel Newall, by Yendee and Beejapoor. The head-quarters and remaining corps marched by Sangaollee to Serdone, where the Brigadier-general left them, on the 25th, to meet the Commissioner at Satara. On the 30th, he returned to Erroor, on the Kistnah, where the division had halted since the 28th, on which day they were likewise rejoined by the 2d battalion of the 4th regiment. It has been seen, that Appah Dessye Neepaunkur deferred his submission (p. 278) till Bajee Rao's force was entirely broken up. As he thus deprived himself of the advantages held forth in the proclamation, it was considered as an indulgence to leave him even a share of his original possessions. For the settlement of the remainder, it was necessary that Brigadier-general Munro should march to his capital, Neepawnee, which he had long been engaged in fortifying. His works were not yet completed; and as the force continued in its vicinity during the 1st and 2d of June, some officers were sent over to examine a place which bore the character of great strength. The surrender of Manaollee to a detachment having completed the Brigadier-general's present business with this Chief, the reserve marched next morning in the direction of Hooblee, where it arrived on the 15th, by the route of Padshapoor, Sangaollee, and Dharwar. Lieutenant-colonel Newall, with the 2d battalion of the 4th regiment, resumed possession of the latter place, into which was thrown the heavy guns and ordnance stores; and the head-quarters and remaining corps cantoned at Hooblee for the approaching rains.

On the separation, at Satara, of the Bombay troops from those of Madras, after the fall of Wassota (p. 297), they proceeded to Poonah, for further service in the districts bordering on the Ghats north of that place. Six companies of the Bombay European regiment, one company of foot-artillery, and one battalion of auxiliary Native infantry, with a respectable train, marched from thence on the 24th of April, under Major Elridge, to the northward; and found, on reaching Jooneer, that it had been evacuated. His subsequent reduction of the forts of Hennee, N[illegible], Hurrychunder, Chowan, and Joodhun, the two last of which only made a shew of opposition, established the British authority early in May, through the whole country south of the range of hills which separate the Beemah and Godavery rivers. The detachment returned to Poonah on the 15th, from whence the 2d battalion of the 15th Madras Native infantry, and a Berar battalion, were sent to Punderpoor, to canton for the rains. This movement formed part of a general distribution of the Poonah force, which took place in the latter end of May, and which, as will be evident from the following enumeration of corps and positions, completely occupied the conquered country:— Detachments in the Jooneer and Ahmednuggur Districts

Serroor	Head-Quarters of the Force. Head-Quarters of the Cavalry Brigade. Horse Artillery. Remains of Foot Artillery. His Majesty's 65th Regiment. Light Battalion. Right Wing of the 1st Battalion of the 7th Bombay Native Infantry.
Satara and neighbouring Garrisons	A Detachment of Auxiliary Horse. One Battalion of Bombay Native Infantry. One Auxiliary Battalion.
Ahmednuggur	Detail of European Artillery. One Battalion of Auxiliary Infantry. N. B. The five Companies of the 1/7th Native Infantry to be stationed here also, when no longer required against Dhunnagee.
North-West Detachment for Nassuck, Jooneer, &c.	One Battalion of Bombay Native Infantry. Two Six-Pounders. A Party of Captain Swanston's Horse.

Poonah, City Cantonments, and Dependent Garrisons	Details of Artillery and Pioneers. One Regiment of Light Cavalry. One European Regiment. Three Battalions of Bombay Native Infantry.
South-East Detachment, Head-quarters, Punderpoor	Captain Sherriff's Auxiliary Horse. Two Six-Pounders. One Battalion of Madras Native Infantry. One Battalion of Auxiliary Ditto. Captain Blake's Battalion of Nizam's Infantry.
South-West Detachment, below Satara........	Captain Spiller's Horse. Two Six-Pounders. One Battalion of Bombay Native Infantry.
To reduce Dhumagee, Purtaub Row	Major Macleod's Horse. The Battalion from Ahmednuggur, with exception of its Outposts. Two light Howitzers, two heavy Twelve to Eighteen-Pounders, and Proportion of Artillery-men.

The only remaining corps of Madras infantry in the Poonah territory, between the Godavery and Kistnah, was the 2d battalion of the 17th regiment of light-infantry, which continued at Ahmednuggur, with Lieutenant-colonel Deacon, after the march of the cavalry brigade from that place, in the beginning of April. This corps was here employed in supporting the arrangements of the Collector of the district. In pursuance of this duty, the Lieutenant-colonel, on the 1st of April, detached three companies of Native infantry, with two hundred of Sulabut Khan's horse, to relieve the garrison of Aumulnair, situate at the distance of forty-five miles, in an easterly direction. On arriving, next morning, within fifteen miles of that place, Lieutenant Bourdieu, who commanded the party, learned that the garrison had been forced to surrender, and that the enemy were engaged in plundering the surrounding villages. He succeeded in attacking some of their horse, of whom a few were killed; and on the 3d, having re-established a British garrison of Peons in Aumulnair, he returned immediately to Ahmednuggur. Sulabut Khan, having been rejoined by his party of horse, now marched on his return to Ellichapoor. At Aurungabad he met Sir Thomas Hislop, who halted there till the 15th of April, to confirm the several arrangements which he had recently organized for the public service.

Sir Thomas Hislop's Return to the Madras Presidency.

Notwithstanding the flight of Bajee Rao from his late dominions, there were several parties of the enemy moving about in uncertain directions, which induced Sir Thomas, considering the weakness of his escort, to order the 2d battalion of the 17th regiment to meet him at Toka. That corps accordingly, on the 16th, joined the head-quarters at that place, and continuing the march by regular stages, arrived, on the 26th, at Poonah, by the usual route of Ahmednuggur and Serroor. Sir Thomas, having resolved to return by sea to a point on the Malabar coast within the Madras Presidency, quitted Poonah on the 2d of May. A few days previously to his departure, he placed the detail of horse-artillery, the squadron of his Majesty's 22d dragoons, and the second battalion of the 17th regiment, at the commissioner's disposal, for the interception of parties of Bajee Rao's horse, which were returning to the southward after their defeat at Panderkaorah. This and other arrangements being completed, he descended the Boar Ghat, escorted by the rifles, and arrived on the 7th at Bombay; from whence having embarked on the 12th, he landed on the 17th, with the Madras staff, at Cannanoor. The rifles, after Sir Thomas Hislop's embarkation, returned to Poonah, where they met the horse-artillery and dragoons on the 22d, and with them proceeded by Satara, Merritch, and Dharwar, *en route* to Bangaloor, without meeting an enemy on the march, or interruption of any description, besides the filling of the Toombudra, at Hurryhur. At the same time, the 2d battalion of the 17th regiment, which was left by the dragoons at Peirgaum, marched to join Lieutenant-colonel Mac Dowell's detachment, which was then employed in the subjugation of Khandesh.

March of Lieutenant-colonel Mac Dowell's Detachment to the Khandesh Ghats. (Map VII.)

The Lieutenant-colonel, as will be recollected, was left in charge of corps and details of the Hydrabad Division, on the march of Brigadier-general Doveton to Jaulnah, in the latter end of March. He pursued, for a few days, the route of Aurungabad from Fooltamba, till a new plan for the reduction of Khandesh and the countries about the Godavery, induced Mr. Elphinstone to direct the movement of the detachment to those quarters, though its strength appeared inadequate to the subjugation, by coercive means, of the late Peishwah's adherents. When Lieutenant-colonel Mac Dowell, on the 30th of March, countermarched from Sirrisgaum, near Aurungabad, his force consisted of one company of foot-artillery, two companies of the Royal Scots, three companies of the Madras European regiment, the 1st battalion of the 2d Native infantry, four companies of the 2d battalion of the 13th regiment, five companies of pioneers, and a few hundred irregular horse. He had, likewise, a small battering-train of two eighteen and two twelve-pounders, with two mortars, four howitzers, and some field-pieces; and the small corps of sappers and miners. He arrived, on the 2d of April, at Byzapoor, on his route towards Unkye, a hill-fort on the summit of the Khandesh Ghats. It contained a small garrison, and commanded one of the principal passes descending into the low country. On this account it was considered of peculiar importance; and Lieutenant-colonel Mac Dowell summoned it, as he approached the *pettah* at the foot of the hill, to form his encampment. Some attempts at evasion from the garrison were met by a display of impatient determination; and the British troops proceeded to occupy the place on one side, as it was evacuated on the other. This proof of the impression which prevailed in the country, was highly satisfactory. Filled as it was with hill-forts, an opposition from all, however trifling, would have required larger means than those by which it could be met. The minds of the inhabitants also would have remained in a state of suspense, the prevention of which was very desirable. A party of forty Native infantry, under a European officer, was left in the place, wherein were found fourteen pieces of ordnance, with a large store of ammunition, and some treasure.

Siege and Capture of Rajdeir.

The detachment halted till the 7th, and, on the three following days, marched to Chandoor, where it encamped on the 10th. In the vicinity of this place, were two hill-forts, Rajdeir and Inderye. These having been uninfluenced by the example of Chandoor, it appeared necessary to reduce them; and the detachment moved, on the 11th, against the first of these, which had the character of impregnable. (Plan 29.) The place is formed by nature; being merely a high precipitous mountain, possessing no works except such as have been constructed for the defence of a narrow traversing footpath *, cut through the rock with great labour, and secured by gates. Above

* The entrance into the fort of Rajdeir differs from that of the famed Dowlatabad, by being open at the top; while the other is completely subterranean. The passage into Dowlatabad contains several iron gates; and the method proposed for their defence, is the ignition of combustible matter heaped behind them whenever they shall be threatened. But independent of the passage into Rajdeir being capable of a similar expedient with iron gates, it is much more defensible from being exposed over head to the precipitation of stones, none of which could be avoided by the assailants.

these, and all along the precipice which commands the passage, stones are piled, which alone would afford the means of sufficient opposition. Loopholes and embrasures are also cut through the solid rock, to rake the traverses successively. The fort of Rajdeir is abundantly watered; and, at this time, was supplied with a year's provisions. It was therefore evident, that the principal means of reducing such a place were those of intimidation, the best instruments of which were shells, which were, luckily, in abundance. The summons sent forward was rejected with contempt; and the refusal to surrender, was followed by an active fire of ginjauls and small arms, from some out-posts, situate among rocks, on the more advanced hills. To get possession of one of these was the first object; and from thence to extend the advanced posts to such others, as were calculated to confine the enemy within their walls. Also to gain possession of such positions as should be fit for the construction of batteries. The first point was obtained the same evening, by a company of Native infantry; and a lodge- (*A*)
ment was completed with the loss of only one man. At the foot of the hill, a battery of four heavy guns, three mortars, and four howitzers, to (*B*.)
cover the further advance of new lodgements, opened on the morning of the 12th. Preparations were also made for storming one of the posts of the enemy immediately under a prominent angle of the superior precipice, and distant from it about two hundred and fifty yards. Below this, and between it and the point already occupied, was another ridge of intermediate height, the extremity of which was occupied by two detachments. One of these was the first post, reinforced to one hundred and twenty men, under Captain Coombes; and the other, a detachment commanded by Major Andrews, consisting of two companies of Europeans, (*C*)
and one company of Natives. At a preconcerted signal of three discharges of cannon, both parties advanced rapidly against the enemy's post, which they evacuated in time to secure their retreat into the fort. They restricted their fire now to occasional discharges from above, and some shots *lobbed* into the camp; but they could not prevent the preparation of a new bat- (*D*)
tery at the advanced point; and a six-pounder was got into it at nine P. M. by taking the carriage to pieces, and carrying up its parts by hand. The garrison were, however, no longer inclined to resist, and sent out to demand terms; such as arrears of pay, for periods uncertain and indefinite. But as nothing more than the preservation of their private property, and liberty to repair wherever they preferred, would be granted to them, they were

sent back, with the indulgence of two hours, to consider these terms of capitulation. They had scarcely gained the interior of the fort, when it was observed to be on fire. There were frequent explosions, and those within endeavoured to gain the outside, in the greatest terror and confusion. Their sortie was effected with much difficulty, owing to the obstructions of the passage; which shortly became so warm, that a party sent to seize it amidst the confusion, was unable to endure the heat. Under cover of the night, the greatest part of the garrison escaped; forty were brought in prisoners, by the irregular horse, next morning, and seven were found alive in the place. It was never ascertained how this conflagration was occasioned. It was probably the effect of the shelling, which for some time previously might have remained dormant. Within were twelve pieces of ordnance of various calibers; and some treasure was discovered among the ashes. This important fort thus fell into the hands of the besiegers, with a loss to them of only five Europeans and two Natives, including Lieutenant Steele, an officer on the staff, wounded. The fort of Inderye was moved by the example within its view; for its garrison likewise evacuated, on beholding the conflagration of Rajdeir.

Countermarch to the Godavery (Map VI.)

This successful progress enabled the Lieutenant-colonel to direct his immediate attention to the vicinity of the Godavery. In the Valley of Khandesh, at the same time, through the means of the Civil officers, and the employment of some irregular troops, every advantage was taken of the terror inspired by the rapidity of the military operations, to reduce to subjection those places where less coercive means were sufficient. Goorup, and some other places, evacuated voluntarily. So numerous, indeed, were the forts which adopted this measure, that it was difficult to find garrisons for them all. After halting at Rajdeir till the 15th, the march was recommenced, by Sheilloo, Bunneira, and K[illegible] gaum. to Nassuck; within one mile of which the encampment was formed, on the 19th of April. On the same day a detachment was made, under Major Andrews, of one hundred Europeans, two hundred and fifty Native infantry, and as many irregular horse, which marched at sunset to overtake a predatory corps of Arabs and Hindoostanees, who were collected near the western hills, about twenty-four miles from the camp. The detachment returned, however, the following day to Nassuck, without attaining the object of its movement; the enemy, on its approach, having returned into the fort of Trimbuck. The importance of the early reduction of this place, induced Lieutenant-colonel Mac Dowell to march thither without further delay. The engineers were, therefore, sent forward, with an escort, from Khumballa, the first stage in that direction, to reconnoitre the environs, with a view to the investment on the following morning.

Siege and Surrender of Trimbuck.

(Plan 35.)

On the 22d, the detachment took up its ground fronting Trimbuck, on the north-eastern side of the hill; and the reconnoissance was extended during the day, notwithstanding a well-directed fire from the fort, which also gained the range of the camp. In the evening a party, composed of fifty Europeans, and as many Native infantry, was sent to occupy a position opposite the gateway on the south side, and to construct cover for two six-pounders which accompanied them. In the course of the night, all the heavy guns and mortars were placed in battery, to bear on the gate in the north-west side, situate in a re-entering curve; and on the morning of the 24th, they opened, under considerable disadvantage, owing to the great height of the hill. (*A*) The town of Trimbuck was immediately in front of the camp, in a small valley, which it entirely filled. Above it, is a hamlet, half way up the ascent, which it was deemed necessary to possess immediately. Accordingly, during the forenoon, Major M'Bean was placed in charge of a detachment, composed of one hundred Europeans, and one hundred and twenty Native infantry, to protect the working-party, proceeding with the necessary materials to make the proposed lodgement. It being ascertained that the hamlet was unoccupied, a small party was sent up, in the first instance, to attract the less observation. (*C*) No sooner, however, had the remainder ascended, and given a commencement to the work, than they were attacked with a fire of wall-pieces, matchlocks, and rockets, accompanied by a discharge of stones and rocky fragments, from the impending cliff. The working-detail were now obliged to desist, and it became necessary to withdraw the party, with exception of fifty European and Native infantry, who covered the construction of the battery when recommenced in the night. One mortar and one six-pounder were brought into it, and, by midnight, other ordnance were in progress up the hill. Previously to this, the detachment, on the south side of the hill, had established their two six-pounders within six hundred yards of the gate on that face. (*B*) This was, however, partially protected from their fire, by a prominent rock projecting in front of it: but the enemy's means had not been at all impaired, and their fire always recommenced as soon as the batteries ceased firing at them. Their constancy, however, was exhausted; and, early on the morning of the 25th, they sent out persons to treat for terms. After a few messages, and attempts at a protracted negotiation, they accepted the same conditions which had been granted to the garrison of Rajdeir, and delivered up one of their gates, at nine A. M. to an officer and twelve men. The south gate was appointed for their departure, but so well had it been secured inside, by heaps of stones, that they had not completed a clear way for themselves before three o'clock P. M. when five hundred and thirty-five men, bearing arms, marched out with the most creditable regularity. Within were found twenty-five pieces of ordnance, from a thirty-three down to a one-pounder, with a sufficiency of ammunition. The loss* with which this important fortress was gained, amounted to thirteen Europeans and nine Natives, including two officers.

Inadequacy of the Means of further Operations.

If, however, the loss was small, the state to which the heavy guns and their carriages were reduced, was an inconvenience of great magnitude. There were no means of replacing them, and all the required service was not yet performed, though the rains were fast [illegible]. The siege of hill-forts is particularly destructive to gun-carriages, for, in order to give the pieces sufficient elevation, it becomes necessary to sink the trails into the ground, or, where this may be impracticable from the rocky site of the battery, as at Trimbuck, to raise the wheels on sand-bags, to reach a wall eight hundred feet above the level of the platforms. The expedients necessary on similar occasions of insufficient means, are numerous, and, perhaps, as little practised in Europe, as the depriving a howitzer of its elevating screw to make it perform the service of a mortar, as was practised at Nagpoor. In this state of things it was, therefore, satisfactory to find, that no more hill-forts offered resistance; for seventeen strong places† of this description surrendered, after the fall of Trimbuck. Another difficulty, however, presented itself in finding the means of occupying so many posts; for there were no regular troops to spare from other service, and irregulars raised for this purpose were unworthy of trust. This expedient, unsatisfactory as it was, could not, however, be avoided, as a temporary measure, while application was made to Brigadier-general Doveton for more Native

* Vide Appendix. R.

† These were Haruss, Wajeerah, Bowleyghur, Cownye, Eyewattah, Achlah, Marundah, Rowlah, Towlah, Caheenah, Caldher, Hatghur, Ramsey, Kuneirah, Bapeirgun, Gurgurrah, Tringlewarree.

infantry; and two companies of the 2d battalion of the 13th regiment were ordered to join the Colonel from Jalnah, with all expedition, pending the supply of greater reinforcement.

The want of this arm had already been experienced in the valley; wherein the town and fort of Soangheer, after admitting a small garrison, had nearly been lost. Lieutenant Rule, of the 3d Native infantry, by a forced march from Galnah, with a part of his detachment and fifty irregulars, received possession of the place from its head authorities, on the 13th of April; and drove out of the town a small party of Arabs, who disputed the occupancy of one quarter. In the fort were eleven guns, and in the *pettah* five more, with many ginjauls and wall-pieces, besides abundance of ammunition for them, which the Lieutenant carefully removed into the fort; the only place he could venture to secure, with a havildar and ten of his men, aided by twenty irregulars. On his return to Galnah, the Arabs, who were still about the Taptee in considerable numbers, heard of the smallness of the garrison. On the 17th, they advanced in numbers, said to be two thousand, with scaling-ladders to take a place, in the possession of which they had been so promptly anticipated. They easily carried the town, killing the irregulars who were in it, and turned the guns on the fort. Owing, however, to the previous removal of the ammunition, these were useless in their hands; while the havildar kept up so brisk a fire from the fort, that they were at length obliged to quit the town, after having plundered such part of it as was least exposed. The havildar's party nearly expended their musket-ammunition, and had every reason to expect a renewal of the attack. To repel this, a reinforcement was sent from Galnah, of fifteen additional regulars, besides fifty irregulars with ammunition. Nor were these measures superfluous; for, on the 21st, the Arabs were again approaching, at the same time that a body of the Poonah auxiliary horse arrived there, from Lieutenant-colonel Mac Dowell's head-quarters. This, with other events shewing how much more powerful the enemy were in the Valley of Khandesh than above the Ghats, induced the Lieutenant-colonel to descend, immediately after the reduction of Trimbuck, to a position which might be convenient for his camp during the rains, and suited to overawe the disaffected.

Defence of Soangheer.

The detachment recommenced its march, on the 29th of April, and returned to Chandoor by the same road it had formerly pursued, with exception of a *detour* to the left, by Dindoorree, between Nassuck and Bunneira.

Description of Malleygaum

During the 10th and 11th of May, the encampment remained at Chandoor; and, on the 15th, was established at Debarree, within one march of Malleygaum, from whence the chief Native Authority, or Zumeendar, Raj Buhaudur, arrived, to give an account of the state of affairs in that quarter. The fort and town were in possession of a body of resolute Arabs, prepared to try the extent to which resistance might succeed against the small British force assembled for the subjugation of the province. For this purpose, they had selected the strongest place in the Valley of Khandesh. The plan of the

(Plan 31.) fort is quadrangular, having on one face, and on half of the two adjoining, the river Moassum, which at this place forms a convenient curve. On the opposite side is the town, which nearly encompasses the remainder of the fort, by approaching the river at its two extremities. The fort consists of two lines of works, the interior of which, a square of about three hundred feet, is built of superior masonry, and surrounded by a *fausse-braye* seven feet high, and a dry ditch twenty-five feet deep by sixteen wide. The outer line is built of mud and stone, having flanking towers; and it approaches within a few yards of the town on one side, and of the river on the other. It is only of moderate elevation; but the inner fort is sixty feet high, with a *terre-pleine* sixteen feet wide, to which there are no means of ascent, except through narrow covered staircases of difficult access. Within were abundance of bomb-proofs; the guns were few and badly mounted; but the matchlocks, in the hands of the Arabs, were sure of hitting their mark. Such was the place before which Lieutenant-colonel Mac Dowell took up his position of siege, on the 16th of May, with means quite insufficient for its reduction; but with which a trial was deemed expedient, seeing how much had already been effected by a commanding tone.

Investment and Construction of the Batteries.

The camp was formed with its left on the junction of the rivers Moassum and Gheernah; and a post was established to prevent the entry of reinforcements, while bodies of irregular horse were ordered to patrole round the town, for the same purpose, during the night. The camp was however moved, on the 17th, to the right bank of the Moassum, which placed that river, then low in water, between it and the fort; and on the same night, from fifty to one hundred men joined the garrison. The materials for the batteries being collected, on the 18th, in sufficient quantity, as soon as it

(*B*) was dark, an enfilading-battery of two eighteen-pounders, one eight-inch mortar, and two eight-inch howitzers, was constructed for the south face;

(*A*) and another, of two twelve-pounders, for the west face. Both of these were

four hundred yards from the works; at which distance was likewise marked out, a place of arms in the centre of a *tope* (grove of trees), which was si- (C)
tuate between the camp and the river. At eight P. M., the garrison sallied on the covering party near the place of arms, and directed the fire of their guns at the two batteries. A reinforcement arriving at the same time from the camp, the sortie was repulsed with spirit; but with the loss of Major Andrews wounded, and the misfortune of the commanding engineer, Lieutenant Davis*, killed. On the 19th, the two batteries opened, and were answered from the fort, by seven guns. A company of infantry took possession of a breastwork in rear of part of the village of Sumungseer, a little higher up the river; and repulsed, that night, a second sortie, which was not unexpected; for, as it became dark, all the posts were strengthened. The body of auxiliary horse, which had been sent to Soangheer, returned this day, and with them two weak companies of the 2d battalion of the 14th regiment, from Seindwah. Next day, the enfilading-batteries continued to fire, but seldom, on account of the scarcity of shot; and, in order to relieve the larger guns, some six-pounders were brought into position. The remainder of the village of Sumungseer, having been deserted (D)
by the inhabitants, was taken possession of by the Arabs, on being repulsed from the breastwork. Also at ten A. M., they again tried to dislodge the company of Native infantry, in which, however, they failed, the post being strengthened by two field-pieces. In the mean while, the approaches were advanced; and, on the 21st, a parallel was completed, along the bank of the Moassum, containing a battery at each extremity; of which, that on the left for three guns, raked the bed of the river, and the other was prepared for breaching the opposed angle of the fort. On the 22d, the guns of (E)
the fort having found the range of the camp, obliged it to fall back four hundred yards. The [illegible]y opened with little effect against the towers, which were round and of good masonry. It was, therefore, subsequently directed against the intermediate curtain. One of the enfilading-batteries was converted into a mortar-battery, and the other was dismantled. An additional post was established on the bank of the river, (G)
near Sumungseer, to confine the garrison. Some field-pieces were attached (F)
to it, with a view to their bearing on the gate of that side of the fort. This

* See previous mention of this officer, p. 134.

extension of the attack was adopted in consequence of the arrival of the two companies of the 2d battalion of the 13th regiment from Jalnah, which had been ordered from thence by Brigadier-general Doveton, as already mentioned; and was a seasonable reinforcement.

Unsuccessful Assault, on the 29th of May.

The duty now fell extremely severe on the troops, who were kept continually on the alert, by the sallies of the garrison. The 23d was distinguished by few incidents beyond the effect of the breaching-battery, which brought down a part of the curtain, and discovered the *fausse-braye* of the inner fort, and the arrival of a body of irregular horse, who were part of Holkur's contingent, which had been detached from Sir John Malcolm's force. This arrival was followed, the next day, by the battalion of the Russell brigade, which had escorted the captured guns to Jalnah, and was ordered on this service, as here was the most important demand for all the troops which could be spared from other quarters. An explosion took place in the fort, owing to the fire of the howitzers, of which some more were placed, on the 25th, in an *epaulment* to the right of the breaching-battery. On the 26th, the breach was carried through the wall of the inner fort; and the arrival of the 2d battalion of the 17th Native infantry in the camp, was a most important addition in the article of means, which, as far as regarded troops, were now superior to the resources in artillery and ammunition. The twelve-pounder shots were all expended, and every heavy gun was run at the vent; so that on the 27th, the improvement of the breach entirely depended on the eighteen-pounders, from which it was dangerous to fire the small quantity of ammunition remaining; and in this state every endeavour was used to effect a slope on the flanks of the breach, to facilitate the ascent of the *terre-pleine*. This object was adhered to, all the next day, and shells were occasionally thrown to prevent the construction of any retrenchments. The parties for the attack of the fort and town were told off in the evening, and *bivouacked* at their respective posts for the assault of the following morning. The column for the attack of the breach, commanded by Major Greenhill, remained in the parallel on the bank of the river. It consisted of one hundred Europeans, and eight hundred Sepoys, principally of the 2d battalion of the 17th regiment. The column destined to storm the *pettah*, consisting of five hundred Sepoys from the three corps in camp, was commanded by Lieutenant-colonel Stewart, and crossed the river, lower down, to a point on the left bank, eight hundred yards from the walls. The third column, commanded by Major M'Bean, which had for its object the escalade of the outer wall, near the river gate, took post near the six-pounder battery up the right bank, and consisted of fifty Europeans and three hundred Sepoys. Each column was headed by a party of pioneers, with tools and scaling-ladders, and led by an engineer officer. Major Greenhill's column was provided with bundles of long grass, to be applied, as might be necessary, in filling up trenches, and, after a warm fire of two hours from the breaching and mortar battery, against the point of attack, it moved forward at broad day-light. As it approached the outer wall, Lieutenant Nattes ascended the breach in front, and, having gained the summit, made a sign not to be followed, as there were insuperable obstacles previously unknown. This gallant young officer, who was the senior engineer since Lieutenant Davis's death, fell, like his predecessor, in the daring discharge of a desperate duty; and the storming party not having noticed his signal, continued to advance under a fire of small arms, by which the commanding-officer was wounded. While the column was under partial cover, the scaling ladders were dropped from the top of the wall, but disappeared, which unfavourable circumstance being reported to Lieutenant-colonel Mac Dowell, at the battery, he directed the attempt to be abandoned, and the troops returned with exemplary order. Lieutenant-colonel Stewart's attack was earlier commenced, and more successful. Before day-light he had obtained possession of a part of the *pettah;* and subsequently succeeded in gaining the whole, assisted by Major M'Bean's column; this party having, on the failure at the breach, co-operated in the attack of the town from the left.

After these events, the relative situation of the parties appeared little different from what it was on the investment of the place; or the difference, if any, was in favour of the enemy. The breach of the outer wall, as has been seen, was only practicable in its direct ascent; but though the descent, on the other side, was impracticable, the height of nine feet would by no means have accounted for the disappearance of the ladders, had not there been a trench excavated within to deprive them of a footing. The enemy had likewise cut off the breach by a retrenchment, flanked by two guns, which would have been sufficient to destroy the head of the column, had it attempted to descend; and the numerous matchlocks, of unerring aim, placed behind this work, to pour a concentrated fire on the summit of the breach, could not miss whoever exposed himself under such disadvantages. A proof of this was seen in the fate of the engineer, who Abandonment of the Attack of the West Face.

alone received seven balls, and will account for the precipitancy with which the ladders were dropped out of hand. No progress was made in filling up the moat, beyond the small quantity of rubbish which fell from the *fausse-braye;* and indeed its respectability, as well as its distance from the outer wall, was now for the first time fully ascertained. Of the inner line, nothing but the upper part had been yet seen; and though the breach was a good one, if it could have been approached, there was no way to get from it on the *terre-pleine* to the right and left; and the descent on the other side was still more difficult than that of the outer wall. Under all these circumstances, it was esteemed fortunate, that no lodgement was attempted between the two lines, as it would have been attended with a severe loss, and ultimately useless; for the guns were unserviceable, the ammunition was expended, the soil so mixed with rock as to preclude mining, and the access through the bed of the river so exposed, as to render all communication from the parallel insecure. Why this side, indisputably the strongest, was selected for the attack, remains unexplained, with the death of the engineer. No reason has been suggested, except the existence of the *tope* of large trees on the bank of the river, which afforded convenient materials for the siege. It was now, therefore, deemed proper to recommence from the side of the *pettah;* and to make such preparatory dispositions as should accelerate the capture of this stubborn place, during the interval which must elapse previous to the arrival of the new train, already on its route from Ahmednuggur. This necessary aid had been applied for, during the construction of the breaching-batteries, on the 21st of May; when, in consequence of the opinion of Lieutenant-colonel Crosdill, the commandant of artillery, it was concluded, that should the garrison persevere in their defence, the means, in artillery, were insufficient for their reduction.

Successful Operations after the arrival of the Bombay Train

(*H, H, H, H*)

On the 29th, as a preliminary measure, all the guns were withdrawn from the batteries, with the exception of the six-pounders in the post of Sumungseer. On that night and the next day, the several avenues connecting the fort with the town, were barricaded; and, on the 1st of June, the camp was removed across the river to the vicinity of the Gheernah, which was close to its rear. This measure was the more necessary, in consequence of the advanced season of the year, when the rains might be expected, and the consequent filling of the Moassum would separate the besiegers from the fort. It was deemed proper, however, to leave a post there for some time. In the first instance this consisted of fifty rank and file of his Majesty's Royal Scots, the 2d battalion of the 13th regiment, the battalion of the Russell brigade, and some auxiliary horse; while Holkur's irregular contingent, with two companies of the 2d battalion of the 14th regiment, encamped on the north side of the *pettah*. The construction of a redoubt was, at the same time, commenced in the rear of the old (I.) breaching-battery. While the place was, by these dispositions, completely blockaded, new *emplacements* were prepared for a fresh attack from the opposite side as soon as the expected train should arrive. The garrison had time, during this cessation of fire, to reflect on their situation, and were alive to its danger. They, accordingly, endeavoured to open a communication; but the answer to their advances leaving them no reason to expect any terms, they declined an unconditional surrender, and recommenced hostilities. On the 4th of June, the redoubt being finished, all the troops (I.) on the right bank of the Moassum, with exception of the Russell battalion and the Poonah auxiliary horse, were withdrawn to the camp; and, on the next day, two howitzers opened on the fort from the *pettah*. On the 6th, the galleries of three mines were commenced, from the nearest points of the town, against the three opposite towers of the outer line of works; but, on account of a stratum of rock, that on the right was alone continued on the following days, and was the only occupation of the besiegers, except completing the new batteries, till the 10th; when Major Watson's detachment, consisting of the 1st battalion of the 4th Bombay Native infantry, a detail of artillery, with four eighteen-pounders, two twelves, and six mortars, which marched from Ahmednuggur on the 1st of June, arrived in the camp. On the same night, the mortars were brought into battery, and (K.) opened, on the following morning, an unremitting discharge, which, at eleven A. M., fired two of the enemy's magazines. The explosion overthrew to its foundation, a large portion of the eastern curtain of the inner line, exposing to view the interior of the place. Two of the eighteen-pounders were immediately brought into position, to the right of the mortar-bat- (L.) tery, to take off the defences near the breach. The remaining two were carried down the bank of the river still further to the right, to breach the (M.) outer line. So much good effect attended the fire of these, that, on the evening of the 12th, a deputation came from the garrison, and continued a negotiation till the following day, respecting the stipulations of surrender. At length it was agreed, that a Native officer and twenty men should be admitted into the inner fort. The British flag was, accordingly, hoisted on

2 U

one of its towers, at three P. M. of the 13th. On the next morning, the British line was drawn up near the outer gate; and, at nine o'clock, the garrison marched out and formed in front of it. They then grounded their arms, and were conducted to a quarter of the *pettah* allotted for their accommodation.

Comparison of the Force of the Parties, and Loss of the Besiegers.

Thus fell Malleygaum, after open trenches of twenty-five days; during which both besiegers and besieged had as unremitting service, as falls to the share of most operations of a similar nature. The garrison amounted to three hundred and fifty men; and the detachment, at the commencement of the siege, to no more than one thousand men and officers, exclusive of two hundred and seventy pioneers. The successive reinforcements of ninety Native infantry on the 22d of May, of four hundred on the 24th, of five hundred and forty on the 26th, and of six hundred on the 10th of June, still made it amount only to two thousand six hundred and thirty; a number by no means commensurate with the strength of the enemy, considering the usual * proportion allotted to the reduction of a place of such respectable strength. It is probable, likewise, that even more means would have been required to reduce the garrison to an unconditional surrender, had not the explosion of the magazines precipitated their decision. The loss with which this acquisition was purchased was more proportionate to the numbers which ought to have been present, than to those which were actually there. It amounted †, from the 18th to the 29th of May, to two hundred and nine killed and wounded, including officers; among whom were the successive commandants of the detail of sappers and miners. These, as well as the remaining officers of engineers, had exhibited a conspicuous *esprit de corps*, the more laudable as it was unaided by any of those mechanical impressions derived from parade, imposing evolutions, or martial sounds, which are not without their effect on all troops.

---

* The following extract from *Cormontaingne* is applicable to this subject, and suggests the instance of the unsuccessful attack of Burgos during the Peninsular war. "Si petite que soit une place, lorsqu'il faut l'attaquer dans les formes, on n'y sauroit employer moins de 10 à 12 mille hommes et quelques régimens de dragons, n'y eût-il que 3 à 400 hommes dans ce poste; et cette petite armée se trouvera assez fatiguée lorsqu'il faudra suffire à une attaque dans les régles. Il est vrai que ces sortes de places sont ordinairement des forts ou châteaux d'une assiette favorisée par la nature et par l'art; ce qui occasionne la petitesse de la garnison."—L'Attaque des Places, p. 1.

† Vide Appendix. S.

Qualities of an Engineer.

It is indispensable in the engineers' department, more than in any other branch of the military profession, that every individual, and the officers in particular, should possess that cool and considerate courage, which estimates justly the dangerous chances of every undertaking, without being appalled by the results of the calculation. Not only, also, must the bravery derived from the animal spirits be complete, but there must be that fortitude of sentiment, which is the rare lot of an individual, which, justly founded, [illegible] him from the rest of his species, and grounded in error, is a baneful and presumptuous obstinacy, rendering the possessor unfit for a situation wherein his opinion will often determine a commanding officer to risk the lives of half his troops. The various sources of courage have been so frequently and ably investigated, that no advantage will arise from a repetition of observations already common-place. If, however, their application in military affairs has been less hackneyed, the present digression may be entitled to indulgence. Every day's experience shews that most men, however vulgar, are capable, under due instruction and proper treatment, of being made good soldiers, so far as acting well in a body is deserving of that character. Yet, how few * can be selected from any walk in life, capable of independent action; otherwise, Knights-errant would have been held in less estimation than once they were, and even a good non-commissioned officer would now be a less difficult acquisition than it is. The more, therefore, an individual is left to his own resources, so in proportion is the possession of courage necessary. In this state is pre-eminently the Engineer, from the time when, as the exclusive mark of deliberate hostility, he establishes the directions of the first parallel, to the completion of a lodgement in the body of the place. The solitary fate of the Miner, who meets his antagonist and his death in the grave of his own digging, has nothing parallel above ground, where the eyes of spectators and sympathy of numbers, inspire boldness and encourage exertion. The more the mind has leisure to contemplate danger, the more it is likely to be appalled. This circumstance will easily account for the ordinary result of a council of war, and for the greater difficulty in maintaining a defence, in comparison with that of making an active assault.

---

* This truth must have struck Mareschal Villars forcibly, when he observed in one of his letters, " Vouz trouverez de très bonnes gens de leur personne ; si on leur ordonne de se jeter dans le plus grand peril, il n'y balanceront pas ; s'ils sont seuls, ils n'attaqueront pas une chaumiere "

While the engineer incurs the dangers of both, he is expected, by the exercise of an undisturbed judgment, to derive from every event, accidental or prepared, the most favourable consequence. Like the pilot in a sea-engagement, he must keep his mind abstracted from the business of attack and defence, from personal fears, and the ambition of dazzling actions. This is the province of the troops of the line, and particularly of the cavalry, who, even acting on the defensive, must adopt offensive movements. If these observations are founded in truth, the mental qualities sufficient for service on horseback are more common than those which are required for the various contingencies of service on foot; [illegible]: that in all times and circumstances, with a few exceptions, the former has been deemed a more noble occupation than the latter. But this is not the only instance of honour being conceded to situation, without comparison of worth.

Lieutenant-col. Mac Dowell's Detachment assumes its Monsoon Position.

There was now no further occasion for the service of the Bombay troops, which had barely time to return to monsoon quarters; for which they countermarched on the 16th: but the train and ordnance stores remained with Colonel Mac Dowell for operations after the rains. The Poonah auxiliary horse were sent, on the 19th, to Pahrola, and the Holkur contingent to Soangheer. The battalion of the Russell brigade took the route of Aurungabad; and the head-quarters of the detachment marched on the same day to Wakhary, in the direction of the Panjun river, on the banks of which it established its monsoon position.

CHAPTER VIII.

REDUCTION OF THE PLACES IN THE INTEREST OF APPAH SAIB BHOOSLAH.

Re-organization of Major-general Marshall's Division. Subjugation of the Saughur District. Treacherous Conduct towards Major O'Brien, of the Killedar of Mundalah. Investment of the Fort of Mundalah by General Marshall's Division. Establishment of the Batteries. Storm of the Town, and Surrender of the Fort of Mundalah. Trial of the Killedar for Rebellion and Treachery. March of the Saughur Force towards Chouraghur, which is consequently evacuated. Escape of Appah Saib, Ex-Rajah of Nagpoor. Lieutenant Johnson's successful Attack of the Pindarries at Goruckpoor. Arrival of the Force at Saughur, and Major Lamb's unsuccessful Attack of Satunwarree. Evacuation of Satunwarree, and Return of Major Lamb's Detachment. Creditable Behaviour of Scindiah's Contingent. Uselessness of Native Auxiliary Horse, in general. Considerations respecting the Maintenance of Irregular Horse in the British Service. March of Colonel Adams's Force against Chanda. Establishment of the Batteries against the Town. Capture by Storm. Comparison of the Attack of Indian and European Forts. Causes which produced the imperfect Defence of Places during the Campaign. Return of the Nerbuddah Division to Hoossingabad.

HAD an exclusive attention to the order of time been preferred, to a respect for the connexion of events, the operations of the Bengal troops, remaining in the field, after the departure of the Marquis of Hastings from the confines of Malwah, would have been earlier resumed.

Re-organization of Major-gen Marshall's Division.

(Map III)

The formation of Brigadier-general Watson's detachment, has been described (p. 216), with the dislocation of the rest of the Grand Army, except the corps at Beirseah, under Major-general Marshall, to join whom it marched, in the middle of February, from Kanjaollee on the Sind. The route of the detachment passed by Sumptur to Burwasaghur, where it arrived on the 19th; from thence, on the 23d, by Teerree, Estoon, and the Maltown Ghat, to a town of the same name, on the 2d of March; and, on the 5th, to Kimlassah, where it joined Major-general Marshall's head-quarters.

(Map VIII.) The Major-general had been, since the early part of January, at Beirseah, where, with the 6th brigade of infantry, a detachment of Baddeley's horse, and a park of two twelve-pounders, two six-pounders, and two five-and-a-half-inch howitzers, he had been ordered to controul the neighbouring country, and prevent the re-establishment of the enemy's posts which had already been dislodged. He was there joined by Scindiah's contingent under Captain Blacker, on the 11th of February; and in the latter days of the same month, he commenced his march for the settlement of the Saughur district, and assumption of the countries which, from the events of the campaign, had become the property of the British Government. These were, principally, the Cessions by the Rajah of Nagpoor, in the Valley of the Nerbuddah, the reduction of which promised employment for a military force. There was also the prospect of having eventually to reduce some of Scindiah's insubordinate places, such as Raatghur and others, that were the asylums of predatory bands, in whose neighbourhood the maintenance of good order was impracticable. On the 3d of March, the Major-general was at Koorwye, on his route to Kimlassah, where his entire means for the service on which he was about to engage, amounted to one regiment of Native cavalry*, five battalions of Native infantry†, three thousand four hundred irregular horse‡, and a train of from five to six hundred carriages§.

Subjugation of the Saughur District.

As the country of Saughur possesses many forts, the magnitude of the battering-train was a material circumstance in the composition of the force. It was also expected to have important weight in prevailing on the ruler Bennaik Rao, to accept the proposed terms of surrendering his strong places, and receiving for himself, and his principal, (a female) a pension, which should descend, in due proportion, to their heirs. The approach of the force

* The 7th.

† The 2d battalion of the 1st regiment, 2d battalion of the 13th, 1st battalion of the 14th, 1st battalion of the 26th, and 2d battalion of the 28th regiment.

‡ Three thousand were Scindiah's contingent, and four hundred Baddeley's horse.

§ These contained the stores attached to two twenty-four-pounders, four eighteen-pounders, four twelve-pounders, four six-pounders, two eight-inch, and four five-and-a-half-inch howitzers; and three ten-inch, three eight-inch, and eight five-and-a-half-inch mortars.

to Saughur, had the desired effect of awing into submission, where resistance would have been madness; and the necessary orders for the surrender of the several places being prepared, they were delivered to the officers charged with the duty of receiving possession. Each of these, commanding a battalion, was reinforced by two field-pieces, and a *russalah* of the 3d Rohillah horse. Major Rose marched, on the 13th, to the eastward, in which direction was situate Reply, Pattereah, Damoho or Dunmow, and Sonado, while Major Lamb, on the same day, took a western route towards Jysingnuggur, Koorge, Turrah, and Jelindar. In the direction of Huttah were, likewise, the forts of Nersingnuggur and Jellasankur, besides those of Kimlassah, Airin, Jelhoreeah, Deogah, Chindrapoor, Growlah, &c. in other quarters. After this arrangement, and providing for the defence of Saughur, the Major-general continued his march on the 15th, with the remainder of the force, in the direction of Dhamaunee, which, as well as Benaiku-Pattum, had been ceded by the Rajah of Nagpoor; and having crossed the Korear *nullah* on the 18th, he came, on the 19th, in the vicinity of the place. The fort of Dhamaunee is triangular, and (Plan 32.) situated on a small eminence, to the form of which, on the eastern extremity, the direction of the wall corresponds. On the other side is the town, encompassed by a loose stone wall, mostly in ruins, following the limits of the acclivity where it is less abrupt; but the ramparts of the fort are, in some places, fifty feet high, and generally fifteen feet thick, with capacious round towers. The fort is again divided by internal lines of works, which render the eastern quarter, in which is comprised the Killedar's residence and magazines, and where the precipice is two hundred feet high, the strongest and most difficult of access. Beyond the town is a tank, of which the garrison cut the *bund* (dyke) on the 18th, to let the water into the dell, but which attempt was attended with no material advantage, and above the tank was established the encampment. The interval till the 23d, was employed in collecting materials for the siege; and on the same day, in consequence of a close reconnoissance, the place was completely invested by the establishment in the town, on the west side, of the (*a*, *a*) 2d battalion of the 28th regiment, and on the remaining two sides of Scin- (*b*, *b*, *b*.) diah's contingent. The south face was selected for the attack; as on that side a ridge offered a commanding situation, within four hundred yards, for the principal batteries, and cover for the mortars and covering party. A battery was, accordingly, constructed in the assigned place, on the night

(B.) of the 23d, and, next morning, two twenty-four pounders, and four eighteen pounders, opened on the south-west bastion, to enfilade the western face. To these were added, against the eastern defences, the fire of a brass twelve-pounder, and two five-and-a-half-inch howizers, from a (C.) position more to the right, and the occasional discharge of mortars from the rear. Six hours incessant firing induced the Killedar to surrender unconditionally. This service completed the subjugation of the Saughur district, for the present occupation of which were left, under the command of Major Lamb, the 1st battalion of the 26th regiment, five companies of the 2d battalion of the 1st regiment, and three companies of the 1st battalion of the 14th regiment, with eight hundred irregular horse, partly Baddeley's, and partly Scindiah's contingent. With the head-quarters of this detachment at Saughur, were nine companies of Native infantry, and five hundred horse, which belonged to the British levy in Scindiah's name; two companies, and the remaining three hundred horse, were left at Dhamaunee; and the rest of the infantry were distributed among the several smaller places of the district.

Treacherous Conduct of the Killedar of Mundalah towards Major O'Brien

The division continued its march, on the 27th, towards the Nerbuddah, where its presence was emergently required; and arrived, on the 30th, by the route of Oodun and Saeepoora, in the vicinity of Gurrakota. It will be recollected, that on the departure of Brigadier-general Hardyman from Jubbulpoor, some communication had been holden with the Authorities of Mundalah, which had for its object the acquisition of that fortress at the expense of the arrears due to the garrison. The affairs of the Cessions on the Nerbuddah subsequently fell into the hands of a Commission, of which the President was Major O'Brien, who proceeded in the latter end of February to execute the conditions required by the supposed capitulation. So confident was he in the faith of the Killedar, that he was satisfied with an escort, composed of a troop of the 8th cavalry and sixty Native infantry, which he took up at Pinree on his march; and with them proceeded to Nandia, within three miles of Mundalah. Several messages and reciprocal assurances of sincerity were subsequently interchanged; and all was confidence on the part of the Major, till the 1st of March; when, riding out with a small party of troopers, he was undeceived by the hostile approach of a body of horse and foot, with two guns. After loading, the party made their escape, pursued by the enemy, who endeavoured to cut them off; and immediately prepared for action. An attack soon followed, which was successfully repelled with creditable constancy for a considerable time. To the assailants it was attended with so much detriment, as to facilitate the subsequent retreat, which was conducted with much order and perfect safety. Lieutenant Kempland was wounded with a spear; but any other loss was inconsiderable. This treacherous proceeding might have been imagined, at the time, to originate solely in the contumacy of the Killedar. Even in this case, it would not have been considered less necessary to adopt early measures of coercion for his chastisement; but the intelligence conveyed to the Governor-general respecting the secret practices of the Rajah of Nagpoor, and the resistance of the fortress of Chouraghur, afforded sufficient grounds for suspecting that a systematic scheme existed of obstruction, if not of extensive hostility, against the British Power.

Investment of the Fort of Mundalah by Gen. Marshall's Division

Major-general Marshall's division was considerably diminished in Native infantry, by the detachments which had been made. There was still, however, sufficient, with an abundant supply of stores, for the remaining service; and with these he continued his march without unnecessary delay. On the 6th of April, he was at Goobree; at Kuttinghy, on the 7th; and, on the 9th, at Jubbulpoor, where he was joined by a squadron of the 8th cavalry, and the 2d battalion of the 8th regiment of Native infantry. On the 13th, Brigadier-general Watson was detached, from the camp on the Moolye *nullah*, with all the cavalry and light companies of corps in camp, to invest the fort of Mundalah on both sides of the river; which he effected in the completest manner on the following day, after a harassing march of eighteen hours over bad roads. A party of the enemy's horse, which were encamped under the walls, made a shew of attacking a post in charge of a party of Scindiah's contingent, but were driven in with loss; and a fire was kept up from the walls, which was attended with little effect. The remainder of the division with the train, following by the same road, which lay parallel to the river at no great distance, was at Sohrah on the 15th; on the 16th, at the Cheereah Ghat; and, on the 18th, the head-quarters arrived before Mundalah, though the numerous store-carts were not able to rejoin for some days afterwards. The town and fort of Mundalah, whose garrison was estimated at two thousand men, are separated by an artificial ditch; but, taken collectively, they form an equilateral triangle. Two sides of this are washed by the Nerbuddah, which makes a sudden change of course at the apex formed by the fort, opposite to which it receives the accession of a small stream, called the Bunjeer river. The fort is thus situate on an island

(Plan 33.)

in the Nerbuddah, whose waters enter the ditch, which is only to be passed by a narrow causeway at the eastern extremity. The north side of the town, or base of the triangle, is a straight line of works, which connects the bank of the river before and after its abrupt turn. In front of this wall is a contemptible ditch; and more dependance appears to have been placed in the natural security derived from the river, than in the artificial disposition of the works. The principal entrance of the town is in the centre of this wall, which contains, at frequent intervals, the usual flanking defences of round towers; but this is entirely exposed to be taken in reverse from the opposite bank, both above and below the fort, as no works cover the town along the river. Several small villages lie in the neighbourhood of Mundalah, and they contributed to the facility of its investment. Across the Ner-
(A) buddah, and opposite the west face of the fort, is the village of Marajpoor, in rear of which was one company of infantry. More distant, and on the left
(B.) bank of the Bunjeer, were the head-quarters of the Mahratta contingent. Opposite the southern angle of the fort was the hamlet of Ponwah; and, to
(C) its right, that of Surkwah, in the rear of which were a squadron of cavalry and two companies of infantry. On the right bank of the Nerbuddah, about twelve hundred yards above the town, is situate the village of Khyree,
(D) which was occupied by a squadron of the 7th cavalry and a company of infantry. The village of Benaika, about two thousand yards distant, in a
(E.) north-east direction, was occupied by Major Cumming, with a squadron of cavalry and a company of infantry. Between this and the last-mentioned
(F) village, were a company of infantry and one hundred Rohillah horse, on the skirts of a jungle. Six hundred of Scindiah's contingent occupied another
(G) jungle in front of the gate, from which it was distant fifteen hundred yards, throwing forward, at midway, an advanced post, which immediately watched the motions of the enemy. On the right of this body, and on the
(H) right bank of the river, were two companies of infantry, commanding the nearest Ghat; and, on the opposite side, were the head-quarters of Bri-
(I.) gadier-general Watson, with a squadron of cavalry, which completed the circle of investment. Such was the disposition of the troops detached in advance, and which subsisted after the arrival of Major-general Marshall, who, with the remaining troops, encamped on the left bank.

Establishment of the Batteries.

The necessity of providing an extraordinary supply of materials, for the numerous and extensive batteries proposed to be simultaneously established, added to the tardy arrival of the store-carts, prevented the commencement of any works before the 25th of April; on which day, every preparation was complete for a rapid prosecution of the siege. As soon as it became dark, all the pioneers and miners, assisted by every Sepoy of the battalion companies of corps not on other duty, were carried down to the different positions, already selected for the batteries; and thirty-two pieces of ordnance were on their platforms soon after day-light, notwithstanding the fire of the garrison as soon as the positions of the working-parties were discovered. The western extremity of the town wall, where it terminates at the bank of the river, having been selected as the most favourable point to be breached; battery No. 1, of two eighteen-pounders, one twelve-pounder, and two six-pounders, was established immediately opposite to it, at the distance of five hundred yards. Battery No. 2, for the double purpose of breaching and enfilade, was placed on the prolongation of the western extremity of the wall, likewise on the opposite side of the river, here about three hundred and fifty yards wide; and contained two twenty-four-pounders, two eighteen pounders, two eight-inch, and two five-and-a-half-inch howitzers. No. 3, the mortar-battery, was established in a hollow, close to the village of Marajpoor, on the right of No. 2, and consisted of three ten-inch, three eight-inch, and eight five-and-a-half-inch mortars. As this was partially exposed to the fire of the fort, a twelve-pounder was placed about one hundred yards to its right, to check any annoyance from the enemy, and was denominated No. 4. No. 5, was two six-pounders near the village of Ponwah, which bore directly on the causeway connecting the town and fort; and No 6, was the same number of field-pieces, advanced, under cover of strong ground, to within four hundred and fifty yards of the eastern extremity of the northern wall.

Storm of the Town, and Surrender of the Fort of Mundalah.

By two P.M. of the 26th, so much impression had been made on the point of the wall, against which the breaching-batteries were directed, that the Major-general concluded, that two more hours firing would render it practicable. He, therefore, without loss of time, crossed the troops intended for the attack, to the right bank of the river. They halted in rear of the previous posts; and the column for the assault, commanded by Colonel Dewar, consisted of four companies of the 2d battalion of the 1st regiment, eight companies of the 2d battalion of the 13th regiment, and three of the 1st battalion of the 14th regiment of Native infantry; while the reserve for its support, under Colonel Price, was composed of five companies of the 2d battalion of the 8th regiment, and eight companies of the

2d battalion of the 28th regiment. Both were placed at Brigadier-general Watson's orders, and waited, in anxious suspense, the preconcerted signal from Captain Tickell, the commanding engineer, that the road in was clear. This officer, and Lieutenant Pickersgill, of the quartermaster-general's department, had both examined it under cover of the enfilading-battery, which cleared the *terre-pleine* of the enemy; and they were enabled, from actual experiment, to declare its practicability. The same fire facilitated the ascent of the storming-party, a portion of whom secured the ramparts, and the rest descended into the town, where the enemy were unable to resist the impetuosity of the attack. This devoted part of the garrison, after an ineffectual attempt to maintain their ground, endeavoured to gain the fort; but, to their dismay, they found the gate shut against them, and that while driven forward to the ditch, by their assailants, they were at the same time exposed to the unremitting fire of battery No. 5. Their destruction was unavoidable, and among their number was said to be Annund Sing, an old officer of the Rajah of Berar, and one of the most hostile to the British cause. The only remaining portion of the enemy within the town, were two hundred and fifty who occupied the part of the rampart least exposed to the enfilading-battery. These, on the advance of the assailants along that work, evacuated the place by a sally-port at the eastern extremity. But their fate was not less unfortunate than that of their brethren, for they were soon discovered by Major Cumming's post, and that at Khyree, the cavalry from both of which moved down, and dislodging them successively from several covers, at length drove them into the river, where they perished, with the exception of fifty, taken prisoners. It was now dark, and the storming-party remained in possession of the town for the night, during which one of the outposts near the river, opposite the fort, observed a small boat crossing to the left bank. Among the four persons who were immediately seized on its touching the shore, was the Killedar Sahib Roy Hazerree, who said he came to offer an unconditional surrender of the fortress. Whether this, or a desire of escaping, was his intention, may be as doubtful as immaterial; but there was sufficient reason to suppose the events of the day had made an important impression on the minds of the garrison. In fact, they never fired another shot; and early next morning, eleven hundred Sepoys voluntarily evacuated, unarmed, with Nuthoo Ram, the second in command, at their head. Their loss, during the operations against the town, was estimated at five hundred, while, on the British side, it amounted to only seventeen*, killed and wounded. In the fort and town were found twenty-six guns of various calibers, from a sixty-eight to a two-and-a-half pounder, and shot in abundance, sufficient to have admitted of some days further firing.

Trial of the Killedar for Rebellion and Treachery.

In the execution of this service there was nothing to be [illegible]; for there was no essential measure omitted, and none appeared superfluous, and, as General Marshall justly observed in his reports, "not a single mischance occurred to disappoint expectation." To few operations, however successful, can the same remarks be applied; and among the principal circumstances which contributed to this complete accomplishment, must be reckoned the extent of the ordnance train, which surpassed whatever had hitherto been brought forward during the campaign. The remaining causes must be sought in the judicious dispositions, the good behaviour of the troops, and in whatever influence good fortune may be allowed to claim, in a course of events where her interposition by no means appeared obtrusive. On the 28th, the Killedar was brought to a court-martial, for rebellion against the British and Nagpoor States, in having refused to surrender his fort; and was acquitted, it appearing that he had acted under the orders of the Rajah, who, moreover, had placed another chief at Mundalah, to controul his conduct. This was Annund Sing, who was killed in the defence of the town. On the charge of treachery towards Major O'Brien, an acquittal was likewise pronounced, on that officer's declaration of his conviction that the prisoner was unconcerned in it. The charges against Nuthoo Ram, the second in command, were for instigating the Killedar to the acts for which he was tried; but, as the principalwas acquitted, his accessary likewise was deemed innocent, and both were handed over to the Civil Commissioner. General Marshall† now obeyed an order he received, to return to the important command of the troops at Kawnpoor, and left Mundalah on the 30th of April, when the command of the Saughur force devolved on Brigadier-general Watson, who had little prospect of further service previous to the approaching rains.

---

* Vide Appendix. T.

† This officer likewise commanded at the bombardment of Hattrass, in the month of March 1817; and judging from these two instances, he appears to have a just knowledge of the proper application of ordnance for the reduction of Indian forts.

March of the Saughur Force towards Chouraghur, which is consequently evacuated.

(Map VIII.)

The object which claimed the first attention of the Brigadier-general, was the reduction of the fort of Chouraghur, situate among the hills which form the southern boundary of the Valley of the Nerbuddah. The only British troops in its vicinity were those of Colonel Macmorine's detachment, which were too few, and too deficient of the requisite means, for any effectual impression on a place of strength; while Colonel Adams was importantly engaged on the Wurdah, as will be hereafter related. Lieutenant-colonel Macmorine had been sufficiently employed in opposing the practices of the Ghoands, in the neighbouring hills. Their hostility was principally directed by Chine Shaw, a relation of the powerful Chief of Hurrye; but they avoided giving the Colonel an opportunity of defeating them. The success which attended one attack, was calculated to produce and confirm their caution; for Lieutenant Wardlow commanding the post of Chichellee, marched in the evening of the 4th of April, and after making thirty miles before day-break next morning, suddenly came on a party of the enemy at Bussoreeah, where he destroyed a considerable number.

The same difficulties as had been experienced in conducting the ordnance-train to Mundalah, delayed its return from that place to Jubbulpoor; the intermediate country being composed of hills and wilds, through which the river forces its passage with many abrupt windings, particularly towards the source. This induced Brigadier-general Watson to divide his force for the march through that country, as had previously been practised by General Marshall. Placing the engineers and ordnance parks under the charge of Lieutenant-colonel Dewar's brigade, he marched with the remainder of the force on the 1st of May; encamped, on the 4th, at the Battye *nullah;* and arrived at Jubbulpoor, on the 7th. Here he halted, till the 9th, for the rear division, which was brought forward with the greatest labour and persevering exertions at the drag-ropes; in which the troops participated with praiseworthy cheerfulness. The force again moved forward by Nutwarra; and, having crossed the river, arrived, on the 12th, at Chindwarra, where, on the same day, it was again overtaken by part of the park. The Brigadier-general, in the mean while, had opened a direct communication with Colonel Macmorine, whom he ordered to join near Chouraghur; and he separated from the rest of the force, to accompany his head-quarters on a rapid advance, the whole of the cavalry, the 1st battalion of the 14th regiment, the engineers, pioneers, and two twelve-pounders. With these, added to the Lieutenant-colonel's detachment, he proposed to come before the place on the 14th, and to possess himself of the town while the train, expected to rejoin on the 16th, should be *en route*. But these, and some arrangements for the supply of water, which was in great scarcity at this season among the hills, were no longer necessary. For, at Garurwarra, on the 13th, Brigadier-general Watson learned, that his approach had induced the garrison of Chouraghur to evacuate on the previous day; and Colonel Macmorine announced his having taken immediate possession with two companies of the 10th. In the town were found twelve guns; and in the hill-fort, three miles distant, were twenty-eight.

Escape of Appah Saib, Ex-Rajah of Nagpoor.

The Saughur force returned without delay to the Nerbuddah, which it crossed the next day at the Keirpaunee Ghat. In this situation, information was received of the escape of the Ex-Rajah Appah Saib, from the detachment which, it may be recollected, (p. 270) was escorting him from Nagpoor. He had suborned the guard which mounted over him, on the 12th, at Rachoor, about thirty miles south of Jubbulpoor; and when it came to be relieved at three A. M. on the following morning, he paraded with it, unnoticed, in the dress of a Sepoy. The non-commissioned officer of the new guard looked into the tent where Appah Saib was supposed to be asleep; and a long pillow, covered with bed-clothes, was shewn by one of the attendants, with a request that his master, who was a little indisposed, might not be disturbed. The eight Sepoys, who had assisted his escape, fled with him; and found a party of horse and foot in a neighbouring ravine ready to receive him. The coincidence in the time of this event with that of the evacuation of Chouraghur. gives them the appearance of a combination, which has not been ascertained. As soon as this intelligence arrived at Jubbulpoor, a troop of the 8th cavalry was sent in quest of the fugitive; and the cavalry, with the escort, were likewise in active search, without being aware of his real route. Brigadier-general Watson countermarched, on the 15th, to Garurwarra, leaving a portion of Scindiah's contingent, at Keirpaunee, under Lieutenant Johnson, to look out for some Pindarries, of whose movements about Deorree, there was a rumour; but seeing no prospect of intercepting the Ex-Rajah, he returned, on the 18th, to Keirpaunee, and next day was at Baumanee, on route to Saughur.

No sooner was this event passed, than reports pressed in from several quarters, of the approach of the Ex-Peishwah to the Nerbuddah, on his route to Gwalior, to claim Scindiah's protection. For the discomfiture of such a design, Saughur was a favourable point. The Brigadier-general therefore continued his march, on the 20th, by Deorree; by Jeitpoor Koprah on the 21st; and, on the 22d, by Reillee; though he previously detached to Hoossingabad the 7th regiment of Native cavalry, under Major Cumming, and five companies of the 2d battalion of the 1st regiment, with orders to arrive there on the 24th, in readiness to meet the requisitions which might be expected from Sir John Malcolm.

Lieutenant Johnson's successful Attack of the Pindarries at Goruckpoor.

The commencement of this movement approached the haunts of the Pindarries, who were plundering in the confines of the Deorree and Bhopal districts; and the occasion appearing favourable for dispersing or destroying them, four hundred picked horsemen of Scindiah's contingent were detached, on the 21st, under Lieutenant Johnson, with orders to make a forced march, in the view of surprising them. At sun-rise the following morning, after a march of forty-four miles, he reached their *bivouac* at Goruckpoor, which he instantly attacked; and while he dispersed one party, he found himself exposed to the fire of another, from a rocky eminence immediately commanding the scene of conflict. The fugitives were pursued by a portion of the party, while, with one hundred dismounted men, he attacked those among the rocks, sword in hand; and as these stood the assault, they were cut down to a man. After this exploit, in which the enemy had thirty men killed, and an unknown number wounded, with the loss of forty horses taken, the party countermarched, the same day, eighteen miles, having lost ten men and six horses killed and wounded, and completed a march of sixty-two miles in twenty-four hours.

Arrival of the Force at Saughur, and Major Lamb's unsuccessful Attack of Satunwarree

While at Reillee, Brigadier-general Watson received information, from the Political Agent at Bhopal, of the hostility evinced by some garrisons in the Beirseeah district, for whose reduction there was an emergent necessity, and who amounted to near a thousand men, under the general name of Baugrees. They had gradually assembled, since the march of General Marshall's head-quarters towards Saughur; and those in Satunwarree, eighteen miles west of Beirseeah, were particularly bold in killing three men of Captain Roberts's detachment from Colonel Adams's division (p. 265), which had invested the place without the expectation of such serious opposition. The force arrived at Saughur on the 24th; and while the battering-train was still in the rear, the troops were held in readiness for eventual movement against the Ex-Peishwah; but his approach in that direction appearing no longer probable, detachments were prepared to proceed against the hostile garrisons. Major Lamb was charged with this service; for which he marched on the last day of May, with a detachment composed of details of artillery, miners, and pioneers, the 1st battalion of the 26th regiment of Native infantry, and one thousand five hundred of Scindiah's contingent, with two eighteen-pounders, four twelves, four mortars, and two field-pieces. The Major arrived before Satunwarree, on the 8th of June, after a march of eighteen miles; and was joined by the small force from Colonel Adams's division. This consisted of two companies of the 1st battalion of the 19th regiment; three companies of the 1st and 2d battalions of the 23d regiment; five *russalahs* of the 1st, and a division of the 2d Rohillah horse, which arrived on its march from Rampoora to Saughur. The presence of these irregulars had enabled him to dispense with the assistance of the division of Scindiah's contingent; and Lieutenant Johnson, commanding it, was sent, during the march, to summon and invest the remaining places, Gurrah and Hirautghur Kuveeza, Kooloo-Kheiree and Munjulghur, agreeably to the further instructions he was taught to expect from Captain Henley, the Political Agent at Bhopal. Major Lamb found the garrison of Satunwarree in possession of some posts outside the place, which commanded the only supply of water there; and he commenced operations by dislodging these, during the absence of the train, which did not come up till late in the evening. The enemy suffered some loss on this occasion; while on the other side there were six Sepoys wounded, and proof was received what excellent marksmen were among the Baugrees, who, subsisting much on the deer they shoot in the neighbouring jungles, had acquired a fatal certainty of aim. During the night of the 9th, the batteries being prepared, they opened at day-break on the following morning; and maintained an incessant fire till five o'clock in the afternoon, when Captain Tickell, the senior engineer, reported the breach to be practicable. The commanding officer concurred in this opinion, after a personal examination, which induced him to resolve on an immediate assault. The storming-party was composed of the grenadier company of the 1st battalion of the 26th regiment, augmented to two hundred men, and a detachment of the 1st battalion of the 23d regiment, equal to one hundred and fifty men. These were to be supported by a reserve of two hundred men from the remaining corps, to be stationed in readiness at the breaching-battery, while the rest of the detachment were under arms. The head of the storming-party, preceded by pioneers with ladders, were allowed to approach within thirty yards of the wall, under cover of a quick discharge of grape on the breach; but suddenly a destructive fire was poured on the head of the column, which instantly knocked down thirty-two men of the first and second sections, composed of the 1st battalion of the 26th regiment. The rear of the column were the first to retire, and sought shelter among the adjacent houses, where they were joined by the rest; and no entreaty of Captain Watson, and their other officers, could induce them to quit this cover. Lieutenant Manson, of the Pioneers, was killed near the breach, whither four or five Sepoys only accompanied their European leaders; and the hour of night-fall not being far distant, Major Lamb allowed the party to remain, till the darkness admitted of their retiring without further loss. This had indeed been severe, amounting to eighty-six killed and wounded, including two officers *; and the enemy probably suffered also, for they exposed themselves to a heavy fire, in the most dauntless manner, on the breach.

Evacuation of Satunwarree, and Return of Major Lamb's Detachment.

The usual practice of an Indian garrison, after such an event, is to evacuate during the night; and there might be a multitude of examples brought forward in support of this observation, without gaining a nearer acquaintance with the train of reflection or argument which produces a measure so inconsistent. If their original intention be to avoid the attack, which must ultimately enforce their submission, why not abandon the place, as they do not ask for terms, before they have suffered from the first assault? Were their object so respectable, as that of diverting the force sent against them from other service in a general cause, there would be no room for enquiry; but in this instance, as well as in many others, the effort appeared to be entirely insulated and desperate. It may be imagined that a point of honour induced them to try their strength, in the first instance; and that having repelled the assault with unexpected slaughter, their daring, which must have been strained to its utmost pitch, has suddenly suffered as violent a depression, and they have fled in terror at their own exploits. Major Lamb did not fail to argue justly respecting their probable intentions; and disposed his troops, during the night, for their interception. The garrison made the expected sortie; and about one-half, if not more, are said to have escaped being killed or made prisoners. The entire num-

* Vide Appendix. U.

ber of Baugrees, besides fifty inhabitants of the fort, was estimated at two hundred and fifty [illegible] ... of whom the commandant, Undah Jemadar, was wounded, and his brother, with twenty others, were killed before the evacuation. Major Lamb's detachment returned to Beirseeah, while that under Captain Roberts proceeded to Hoossingabad; and as the monsoon shortly afterwards commenced with violence, this period will be chosen as the conclusion of the campaign in this quarter, though occasional movements of a partial nature took place during its continuance, which promoted the settlement of the country, notwithstanding the reverse which has been related; and which may be considered a desirable event for the narrator, already apprehensive of having wearied his reader wirh too monotonous a series of successes.

Creditable Behaviour of Scindiah's Contingent

The division of Scindiah's contingent, under Lieutenant Johnson, was more fortunate. Gurrah, the first fort to which he came, was attacked with offers, remonstrances, advice, and menace; to which its Killedar reluctantly submitted. A similar result attended the proceedings against the remaining places, which was especially promoted by the Political Agent's presence with the detachment, and the regular conduct of the contingent, which gave a confidence never previously justified by the behaviour of irregulars paid by a Malwah State. The gallantry and willingness they evinced on all occasions, since their formation, exhibited a striking difference between the same people left to themselves, and under the regulation and direction of British officers. Such is the consequence of their punctual payment, remuneration for the loss of their horses in action, their supply with good pistols and ammunition; and, above all, their confidence in the result of whatever is undertaken by a leader, who they are convinced has the skill and information to ensure success, or the necessary support at hand, in case of failure, to secure them from destruction. They have naturally all the feelings of light cavalry, regular or irregular, respecting their insecurity at night at any distance from infantry; and, very properly, this arm has generally been attached to them in a small proportion; but their service in attacking is quite independent of either foot or guns, as was proved before the campaign in a most brilliant affair under Captain Davies*,

---

* "The gallant affair which lately took place in Khandesh, is a practical proof of the value of the services which may be expected from it (the Nizam's reformed horse). A party of six hun-

and in the recent instance at Goruckpoor (p. 344), where they were taught to dismount and assail infantry sword in hand.

Uselessness of Native Auxiliary Horse in general

The conduct of irregular horse, in the service of Native Powers, was contemptible in every instance, since the commencement of the campaign; but as an auxiliary force, without any of those regulations which have been enumerated, they are in fact hurtful, in consuming the forage and provisions for which they make no return. It was vainly expected in Lord Cornwallis's first campaign, that they would perform the duties of light troops, and ten thousand were procured from the Nizam; but " they soon shewed themselves unequal to the protection of their own foragers on ordinary occasions; and after the lapse of a few days from leaving Bangalore *, they never stirred beyond the English pickets, consuming forage and grain, and augmenting distress of every kind." In the second Seringapatam war they were more useful, because placed under the superintendence of an able and active officer, the late Colonel Walker. The next occasion of their being employed, was during the Mahratta campaign of 1803, when doubts regarding their conduct were of sufficient importance to affect the† plan of the campaign. At that time, the Mysore horse were an exception to the general description of Native auxiliaries; for they were composed of the men who had served both Hyder and Tippoo, and learned, in an excellent school, the duties of light troops. But, as these men died off, the corps lost proportionally in character; and the principal impression they are now calcu-

---

dred, under the personal command of Captain Davies, after a rapid march of fifty miles, charged a body of Trimbuckjee's adherents nearly four times their strength, strongly posted and prepared to receive them. The enemy was almost immediately broken and repulsed, and left four hundred killed and badly wounded on the field, besides those whose wounds were not so severe as to prevent them from escaping. Both Captain Davies and Captain Pedlar, the only one of his European officers who had then joined him, received severe wounds, from which they are now only just recovering. I have no doubt, that on any occasion on which this corps may be employed, it will exhibit a decided superiority over any description of irregular troops against whom it may be brought."—Resident at Hydrabad to Sir Thomas Hislop, June 14, 1817.

* Wilks's South of India, ii. p. 137.

† " The Nizam's horse are very useless, which annoys me a good deal, and creates a doubt of the propriety of sending Colonel Stevenson on the proposed expedition to Berar, at least till we shall have beaten the enemy in the field. If they were all to follow Colonel Stevenson into Berar, we should effectually relieve the Nizam's territory; but we might meet with a misfortune, of which there could not be a chance, if the cavalry were worth any thing."—Letter from General Wellesley to General Stuart, September 15, 1803.

lated to make, will arise from the uniformity of their dress, which gives a unity of appearance of some importance. In Tippoo's service, they used to ride up as enemies to the British line of march, in the most dauntless manner; but during this campaign, it was impossible to make them, as friends, quit the line of march without placing a British officer at their head. With that encouragement they were bold enough, and followed their leader, Major James Grant, into the range of the cannonade, at Mehidpoor. Of the remaining contingents of horse, during this war, little can be said. Brigadier-general Hardyman, on his march to Jubbulpoor, was abandoned by the Rewah contingent, with the exception of a few men; and Major-general Donkin reported, that he could not trust the Bhurtpoor contingent to perform even the trifling service of escorting a few bullocks in his rear.

Considerations respecting the Maintenance of Irregular Horse in the British Service

It may be considered no part of the business of this work to advert to the policy which may have weighed with Government, in enforcing the supply of the auxiliary contingents of horse. An obvious design was to give employment to a class of the population of India, who must otherwise follow predatory habits; to abolish which, was the principal view of the campaign. The great deficiency of British force rendered an augmentation necessary; and this was the only convenient means of deriving it from the resources of the neighbouring States, who should have been as much interested as the British Government, in destroying the Pindarries. There was no method of rendering their services effectually available to the proposed end, or of guarding even moderately against their hostility under adverse circumstances, except the placing them under British officers and guaranteeing their pay. Their fidelity can never be depended on with the same confidence which may be placed in some corps of auxiliary infantry, who have been recruited at a distance, are disciplined to act like British battalions in the line, and to look to the British Government as, in reality, their lawful sovereign. The irregular service of the horse is too much allied with the nature of the Country Government and inveterate prejudice, to admit of its being permanently corrected, without difficulty. The Nagpoor contingent never came forward during the war; that of Poonah was only partially produced, even by the measure of recruiting beyond the Peishwah's influence; and of a part of the Nizam's reformed horse, in the course of the campaign, suspicions were entertained; while, on the whole body, the officer best authorized to judge, placed no dependence in case of an open defection on the part of the Nizam. Since the termination of the war, Government have gradually carried on the work of reduction; the ultimate extent of which, whatever be intended, has, prudently, not been yet promulgated. But, probably, it will never be proposed entirely to abolish this arm; for under proper regulation, of which abundant experience has already been obtained, there can be no doubt of their usefulness for certain services, at a less expense than that of a regular trooper. The necessity of light troops of this description is acknowledged in every army of Europe, while the British army is almost the only one which is unable or unwilling to maintain it. That paternal feeling for the inhabitants of the seat of war, will always be opposed to the employing troops whose subsistence shall be left to chance, or, in other words, to the produce of plunder. The same principle extended to India, considerably cramps the employment of irregular horse in the British service; for they are allowed to take nothing without payment, and therefore fall back on the bazars of the regular army for their support, unless they find open markets wherever they go*. One of the principal dangers to be guarded against is, the introduction of too much regularity and discipline; which, while it is insufficient to make them troops of the line, will spoil them as light troops. The more regularity is enforced, the more will the Government impose on itself the necessity of providing for multiplied wants, the absence of which should be the pride of light troops. In Hyder's and Tippoo's service, the Silladar horse were not permitted to plunder their own country, while war was waged in it; yet they were by no means tied to the main army. They harassed the British line of baggage continually; and towards evening, drew off to a distance of ten or twelve miles, to avoid surprise at night, though they slept holding their bridle-reins. Perhaps, however, this perfection may be impracticable in the British service; and the permanent, though imperceptible effect of a rigid system of regulation may be superior to the occasional advantages, however great, to be derived from an attention to more temporary and obvious expediency.

March of Col. Adams's Force against Chanda (Map V.)

This Chapter being dedicated to the affairs of the Nagpoor country, in which the operations north of the Nerbuddah have been brought to a termination with the commencement of the rains; the present will be a fit

* The Author trusts it will not be concluded from these observations, that he is an advocate for the Cossack system; his object being to elucidate the state of the case.

occasion for describing those in the southern quarter, directed by Colonel Adams. This officer, after his dispersion of Bajee Rao's army at Seonee, encamped at Andoorree on the Wurdah, from the 20th to the 26th of April, and arrived, on the 28th, by Alleepoor, at Hinghenghat, where the 1st battalion of the 23d regiment, with the ordnance train, had already arrived from Hoossingabad (p. 271.) He was joined, on the 3d of May, by Major Goreham's detachment, composed of the corps and details of the Madras Establishment, destined for the Nagpoor subsidiary force; which had been detained a few days at Boorgaum, awaiting the arrival, from Oomrouttee, of an eighteen-pounder, whose services were likely to be required at the expected siege of Chanda. The Colonel was at Deogaum on the 6th, and arrived before this place on the 9th of May, with an efficient force, composed of the troops of both the Bengal and Madras Presidencies, amounting to one thousand Native cavalry *, a troop of horse-artillery †, of which half was European and half Native, a complete company of European foot artillery ‡, three thousand Native infantry §, two companies of pioneers ||, and two thousand irregular horse, with three eighteen-pounders, four brass twelves, six howitzers, and twelve six-pounders. This extensive town, equal in size to Nagpoor, is situate between two small rivers, the Eerree and Jurputtee, which join at the distance of half-a-mile from its southern extremity. At the northern extremity is a deep and extensive tank, and beyond it some hills commanding the place, at the distance of nine hundred yards; and between them and the fort are thick groves of trees. On the east face are suburbs, interspersed with trees, and separated from the town by the Jurputtee river; and opposite the south-east angle, distant seven hundred and fifty yards, are other hills, beyond which the encampment was ultimately established. Within the place, at equidistance from the north and south faces, but nearer

(Plan 34)

* The 5th and 6th regiments, and a squadron of the 8th.

† The Europeans, Madras, and the Natives, Bengal.

‡ Bengal and Madras Establishment.

§ The 1st battalion of the 19th regiment, six companies, 1st battalion of the 23d, six companies, flank battalion, Bengal Establishment, five companies; and the 1st battalion of the 1st, and 1st battalion of the 11th regiments, and four flank companies, Madras Establishment.

|| One company Bengal, and one Madras Establishment.

the eastern than the western wall, is situated a citadel, called the Balla Killa; and the rest of the interior consists of straggling streets, detached houses, gardens, and plantations. The walls of Chanda are six miles round; and as their direction is frequently broken, and they are surmounted by a high parapet, their effectual enfilade becomes impossible. They are built of cut free-stone, well cemented, are from fifteen to twenty feet high, and flanked by round towers, capacious enough for the largest guns. Of these there were eighty on the works; and the garrison, of whom a few were Arabs, amounted to two thousand men.

Establishment of the Batteries against the Town

While selecting a suitable point for the attack, the first battery was erected, on the 13th, at night, on the southern hill, and admitted one eighteen-pounder, two howitzers, and one six-pounder, to amuse the enemy (A) while the necessary collection of materials for the siege was in progress. Both shells and red-hot shot were thrown into the town, to intimidate the garrison, who returned the fire with as little effect, for no conflagration succeeded these attempts. Connected with these dispositions was the establishment of a post in the suburb, called Baboolpett, consisting of the battalion of Bengal light infantry, and one squadron of cavalry, under Captain Doveton, whose vigilance so near the city was an important advantage. (F.) Some days were spent in reconnoitring; and, at length, the south-east angle being determined on for the breach, on the night of the 17th a battery of four twelve-pounders was constructed within four hundred yards of (B.) that point, to destroy the collateral and flanking defences, and to enfilade the south face. To this was added a howitzer battery, at the distance of six hundred yards on the capital of that angle. (D) Independent of these, was an [illegible]y of three six-pounders, on the prolongation of the eastern face, and distant four hundred yards; (C) but though three of the enemy's guns were dismounted, little impression appeared to be made on the garrison, for the effect of the four twelve-pounders was very unimportant. During the night of the 18th, the breaching-battery of three eighteen-pounders was completed within two hundred and fifty yards of the angle attacked; and it opened at day-break next morning; the working-party having suffered a few casualties during the night, from small arms. At four P. M. of the same day, the way in was practicable, and the storming-party in readiness to enter. But the assault was delayed till the following morning; while during the night an incessant fire was maintained, to prevent the garrison from forming a retrenchment which they ineffectually attempted. Lieutenant-colonel Scot was appointed to command the storming-party, consisting of two columns, of which the right was composed of Bengal troops, the left of those of Madras; and each was supported by a battalion, and a half company of pioneers, of their respective establishments. Lieutenant-colonel Popham, commanding the right column, had under his orders four companies of Bengal grenadiers, followed by pioneers with ladders, and the 1st battalion of the 19th regiment of Native infantry. Captain Brook commanded the left column, consisting of four flank companies, followed by pioneers with ladders, and the 1st battalion of the 1st regiment of Native infantry. The 1st battalion of the 23d Bengal, and the 1st battalion of the 11th regiment of Madras Native infantry, followed; while with the advanced sections was a detail of artillery-men, provided with spunge-staves and nails, for either turning the enemy's guns, or for spiking them. A reserve consisted of the Bengal light-infantry battalion, four troops of the 5th cavalry dismounted, and two horse-artillery guns; the whole commanded by Major Clarke: and for the protection of the camp, were left the infantry pickets, a squadron of the 5th cavalry, and three hundred of the Nizam's horse; while the remaining cavalry, viz. the 6th, and Nizam's irregulars, were distributed around the place, to *cut up* the fugitives.

The storming-party, in sections, marched from camp at the appointed time, in two columns, the heads of which were equally advanced; and in this order they crossed the Jurputtee to the foot of the breach, up which they were conducted, at break of day, by Lieutenant-colonel Scot, whose gallant offer of commanding on this dangerous service had been accepted with alacrity. So far the advance had been effected with immaterial loss; for a tremendous fire, from all the guns which could be brought to bear on the breach and defences, had been previously poured in for half an hour. The garrison were, however, entirely prepared, and maintained a warm discharge of small arms on the head of the columns; which separated, notwithstanding, to the right and left as preconcerted, under their respective commanders. Lieutenant-colonel Scot took the personal command of the supporting battalions, which marched up the central street of the town; while the reserve took possession of the breach. The right column, in proceeding along the rampart, met with considerable opposition from bodies of the garrison, who, being driven back, appeared to cross over towards the western rampart, where they encountered the left column. This had

Capture by Storm.

attempted, at first, to keep along the *terre-pleine;* but finding its progress impeded by long *fraises,* it descended into the place, and keeping close along the foot of the rampart, was not only able to drive the enemy from the works, but from houses on the right, which were occupied to their annoyance. In this manner it had proceeded two miles, before it encountered any opposition materially to obstruct its progress; but, at length, a heavy body, probably that which had retired before the right attack, shewed a determination to dispute their further advance. Captain Charlesworth, and Lieutenant Watson, of the Madras Establishment, were here wounded severely: but the column still pressing on, the enemy were driven back; for, all this time, their further stand would have endangered their being taken
(*II.*) in reverse, as the right and supporting columns were closing in to the same point. No further attempts of any importance were made to rally; and the garrison shortly dispersed to seek safety in flight, by letting themselves over the walls, for every gate and sallyport, two excepted, had been built up. The Killedar Gunga Sing, with about two hundred of them, were killed, and one hundred taken prisoners, within the hour which elapsed from entering the fort till it was completely occupied; but the number who fell outside were much inferior, partly on account of the thick jungle, on the northern face, and of the great extent of the walls, which obliged the cavalry to scatter, in small and distant parties, for the investment. Among the fugitives was a Ghoand Rajah, in whose palace was found considerable property; among the rest, nine lacs of rupees, dug up a few days after the storm. There were found, also, an extensive variety of European manufactures, such as glass, and some pictures; for this ancient capital being considered as the citadel of the kingdom, had become the grand repository of whatever was considered rare or valuable. The British loss *, by which this acquisition was made, amounted to an inconsiderable number, compared with its importance, as depriving the enemy, before the monsoon, of their principal fortress, connected in opinion with the existence of the Nagpoor dominion.

---

* Vide Appendix X.; in which are not included the names of Assistant-surgeon Anderson killed, and Lieutenant Fell, attached to the Pioneers, wounded.

Comparison of the Attack of Indian and European Forts.

The period which elapsed from arriving before Chanda, to breaking ground, appears longer than was obviously necessary, or than would be considered excusable in European warfare; but there is a wide difference between approaching a fortified city of six miles circumference, thickly wooded on some sides, and coming before a place of moderate size, and perhaps regular shape, of which an accurate plan is in the possession of the besiegers, and which may enable an engineer to calculate the day of storming the counterscarp, nearly as well as to decide on the point of attack. Almost every fortress in Europe has been frequently attacked, and frequently taken; and the journals of former sieges will probably shew how they are to be again approached with certainty of success. This is not the case in India: no instruction can arise from a knowledge how a place was formerly besieged, beyond the information where batteries have been established *, which, with regard to hill-forts, is of some importance. Yet these examples will not shew every position to which a gun can be carried by European exertion, skill, and perseverance †; and the establishment of batteries in points formerly considered inaccessible, has, on many occasions, been effected, to the astonishment of the garrison. The greater the regularity of any fortified place, the more certainty is afforded respecting the length of its practicable defence, and, at the same time, an equal certainty as to the time in which it may, with proper means, be reduced. The whole operations on both sides are conducted by measured and calculable steps, which even mines can scarcely obstruct. But in the siege of an irregular walled city, which may contain an army, and offers unlimited means of successive retrenchment, so much depends on accident, and the comparative bravery of the two parties, which are elements of most uncertain value, that the remaining data of calculation become both weakened

* When Gokla besieged Wassotah, he established his batteries in the same places, subsequently selected by the engineers of Brigadier-general Pritzler's force.

† Officers who served in General Wellesley's army in 1803, will probably recollect an anecdote of the late Colonel William Wallace, who was charged with the execution of certain operations on one side of the hill-fort of Gawilghur. It was necessary that a heavy gun should be transported to a difficult position; and it so long baffled all endeavours for its conveyance over precipitous heights, that the artillery-officer, in despair, reported the accomplishment to be impossible. "Impossible, sir!" repeated impatiently the veteran Colonel, who had all his life maintained the most elevated sentiments regarding implicit obedience—"Impossible, sir! Have I not the order for it in my pocket?" and doubtless the result evinced the efficacy of the order.

and diminished. How often have British storming-parties been foiled by the enthusiasm of a petty garrison, and been successful against garrisons of the most formidable appearance! *

Causes which produced the imperfect Defence of Places during the Campaign.

It has been already observed, that the forts of India are like those of Europe before the introduction of regular fortification. Both are marked by the absence of outworks, for their additional lines were constructed within, instead of without, the body of the place, and furnished a succession of retrenchments, the last of which were possibly more strong than the first. If between these lines the garrison were exposed to the effects of shells in a confined situation, that inconvenience was not less the share of the besiegers, after they came to possess the outer lines. But on the other hand, if there be a ditch between the two walls, as at Seringapatam, most of the shells will find their way into it, and burst innoxiously. So little discipline obtains in Native armies, that their courage is very uncertain: bearing, on some occasions, the most exalted and devoted character, as at Satunwarree, where they crowded on the breach which was ploughed by grape; and, at other times, marked by the most pusillanimous traits, under the most advantageous circumstances, as has been frequently seen in the course of this campaign. But the enemy not only wanted discipline, but all those provisions for their support in cases of extremity, and for their supply with military stores, and other *et ceteras*, which speak confidence to a garrison, and proceed from the same provident combination and fore-sight, which acknowledge the necessity of discipline as one of the most material elements of an efficient army. The variety of the calibers of the guns in all their forts, and the consequent confusion of their shot, and quantity of powder for their charge, added to the frailness of their carriages, which soon rendered them unserviceable, deprived their exertions of all weight. The positions of their guns were another source of weakness. In some instances exposed on high cavaliers, for the sake of an uselessly extensive range, or otherwise confined in a tower, where the effects of a shot from the besiegers were scarcely avoidable, but seldom capable

* At the last siege of Seringapatam, that fort was stormed when there were but three day's provisions for the fighting-men remaining; and the assault may be pronounced to have become emergently necessary. Yet, had not by chance a way been left for crossing the inner ditch, whose existence was previously unknown, the event of that day must be deemed beyond all calculation.

of being directed to flank correctly its collateral salient angle, whether from injudiciously constructed embrazures, or insufficiency of space. These considerations are more applicable to the Mahratta wars, than to those of Mysore, the despots of the kingdom recognizing the superior skill of Europeans, and devising those alterations and additions to their forts, which gave them respectability and strength.

Return of the Nerbuddah Division to Hoossingabad

On the 24th of May, Colonel Adams marched his division from Chanda, leaving for the garrison of that place the 1st battalion of the 11th regiment of Madras Native infantry, and arrived by the route of Hingenghat, at Nagpoor, on the 1st of June. Here he left the 6th Bengal cavalry and squadron of the 8th, the 1st battalion of the 23d regiment of Bengal Native infantry and battering-train, with the Madras troops, under Lieutenant-colonel Scot; and, after two days' halt, continued his march, with the expectation of arriving at Hoossingabad before the commencement of the heavy rains. The 5th Bengal cavalry preceded his movement, being under orders to Bundah, on the northern frontier of Bundelcund; and the head-quarters and remainder of the division completed their march, on the 15th of June, by the route of Mooltye and Shawpoor. During his return towards the river, Lieutenant-colonel Macmorine, who had been left in the vicinity of Chouraghur on the evacuation of that place in the middle of May, was constrained, at the end of that month, to return to his cantonment, at Garurwarra, hopeless of effecting any service at so late a season of the year. The movement of a detachment under Major Richards, on Buttaghur, which obliged Appah Saib to retire from thence further into the hills, closed the operations from that quarter. One Ghoand Chief, called the Dillum Rajah, had come in, shortly after the Cession of the Valley. His example, however, was not followed; for several other Chiefs, who at first were less decided, were awed into the adoption of the Ex-Rajah's cause, by the influence of the Chief of Hurrye and the Killedar of Chouraghur, who threatened to lay waste the country if they declined to join their party. Under this discouraging prospect, a reward of two lacs of rupees, and a *jaghire* of ten thousand rupees per annum, was offered, under the sanction of Government, for the apprehension of Appah Saib; but the sequel will shew that the Barbarians, among whom he resided, were too much bound by their sense of fidelity, to be gained by a temptation, which, in more civilized States, might have proved irresistible.

CHAPTER IX.

SUBMISSION OF THE PEISHWAH, AND DISSOLUTION OF THE MAHRATTA CONFEDERACY.

March of the Hydrabad Division from Jaulnah to Boorhaunpoor. Bajee Rao's Application to Sir John Malcolm for friendly Intercession. Considerations which dictated the Conduct observed by Sir John Malcolm. Disposition of Sir John Malcolm's Division during the Negotiations. Interview between Bajee Rao and Sir John Malcolm. Ultimatum dispatched to the Ex-Peishwah. His reluctant Surrender on Conditions. Reflections respecting the Necessity of the Terms granted. Return of the Hydrabad Division to Quarters. March of Sir John Malcolm with the Ex-Peishwah towards the Nerbuddah. Mutiny of the Arabs. Suppression of the Mutiny. Reflections on this Service. Arrival at Mhow, and Confirmation of the Convention. Comparison of the British with Native Governments. Difficulty attending a fair Judgment respecting Indian Affairs. Mutability of Indian Empires.

THE reader is congratulated on having arrived at the last Chapter on the subject of the Campaign. If the previous details have afforded any interest, it is hoped that some curiosity may still exist, to trace the termination of the Ex-Peishwah's struggle for sovereign power; a struggle which, however ill fated, has yet been seen to continue after reiterated declarations of adverse fortune.

March of the Hydrabad Division from Jaulnah to Boorhaunpoor.

His flight seemed restricted within a magic circle, from which he appeared destined never to be emancipated. He fled twice to the northward, and twice to the southward. To the westward was the ocean; and to the eastward, where the land was wide, and contained well-wishers to his cause, he had met with one of his severest defeats. Again, he sought the north; and after a flight of several hundred miles, he found himself, on the borders of Khandesh, not far distant from the extreme point of a previous visit, but more closely beset by enemies than on the former occasion. To describe the means by which this was effected, it becomes necessary to return to the operations of Brigadier-general Doveton's Division, which (Map V.) were discontinued with its arrival at Jaulnah on the 11th of May. However harassed it had been by the late marches, the period of repose was not yet arrived; for the accounts of the enemy's progress and re-assembly, called emergently for further exertion. The order of march was accordingly republished, at the season in which troops generally establish their monsoon quarters; and after only two days' halt, the Hydrabad Division got in motion again, on the 14th of May. At Kodally, on the 16th, the detachment under Lieutenant-colonel Heath, which escorted the sick details and captured guns from Mehidpoor, passed through the camp on their way to Jaulnah. This officer, who had commanded the post of Hindia, was directed by Sir John Malcolm to deliver it to the next officer, and to place himself in charge of the several parties which arrived from Malwah (p. 270), at the end of April. He prosecuted his march, by Charwah and Peepload, without the occurrence of any extraordinary event; but at Boorhaunpoor, on the 6th of May, he learned the arrival of Bajee Rao at Changdeo. This Chief's route from Oonerkeir had been conducted by Ahoonda and Bonee, where his brother separated from him (p. 278), and from thence by Chartana, and between Meiker and Jafferabad, till he descended the Dewul Ghat. He encamped at Belloon on the 4th of May; and next day, at Changdeo, he heard of Lieutenant-colonel Heath's approach. The apprehension of an attack induced him to ascend the Ghats of Sautpoora immediately, and there he had leisure to repose after his harassing flight from the Deckan. From Kodally, the Hydrabad Division arrived in two marches at Adjunta, and halted there one day. On the next, it continued its route by Samroad and Hurtallah, where, on the 23d, a detachment was prepared to march against a party of the enemy, supposed to be near Beawul, beyond the Taptee; but it was subsequently countermanded, on intelligence of their having dispersed, at the approach of the division. On the 25th, the Brigadier-general crossed the Taptee; and encamped on its right bank, at a short distance above the city of Boorhaunpoor, preparatory to his projected attack of Bajee Rao. This chief was then encamped in the vicinity of Dhoolkoat and Bonee, with an estimated force of five thousand (Map VII Compartment) horse and four thousand foot, of whom half were Arabs; and immediately arrangements were made for marching against him that same night, with a selection of such troops as were still fit for so strenuous an exertion. The detachment was formed, and the hour of movement fixed for the rising of the moon, when the march was countermanded, in consequence of the receipt of intimation, that Bajee Rao was engaged in a negotiation respecting the terms of his surrender to Sir John Malcolm.

Bajee Rao's Application to Sir John Malcolm for friendly Intercession

To account for this circumstance, the situation of Sir John Malcolm's force, when the approach of Bajee Rao was first reported, must be recollected (p. 269). From his position at the head of the Malwah Ghats, Sir John, on that occasion, detached, without delay, the 1st battalion of the 14th regiment of Madras Native infantry, to occupy the post of Mundleisur and the adjoining fords of the Nerbuddah; and marched his force, in the first instance, to Mhow, about twelve miles south-west of Indoor, where he proposed to establish his monsoon cantonment. It was here he learned the certainty of Bajee Rao's arrival at Dhoolkoat, which was the first satisfactory information of the precise point towards which his flight was directed. While Brigadier-general Watson was requested to contribute to the chain of posts from the upper part of the Nerbuddah, every exertion was used to complete it along the lower part of its course. The 3d Madras cavalry was detached to Hindia, in order that, reinforced from them with some infantry, it might assume a favourable position for closing in on the enemy. To enable a battalion at Hindia to make a suitable detachment, two companies were sent, to reinforce it, by Sir John Malcolm, who likewise detached six companies to occupy the Oonchode pass, one company to that of Peepalda, thirty miles to the west of it, in the same range of hills, three companies to the Ghats, in the Dhar district, and a ford at Chikaldah on the Nerbuddah, about fifty-five miles west of Myheyswur. These dispositions, which were completed before the middle of May, enabled Sir John Malcolm to assume an appropriate tone towards the agents of the fugitive Chief, who sought the British camp at Mhow, with earnest entreaties that he would interpose his good offices for the re-establishment of their distracted affairs. They were received on the night of the 16th of May; and were permitted to use all their eloquence, to extenuate the criminal conduct of their master; who, they said, had been always averse to the war, as they attempted to prove by a reference to the known cowardice of his character. They concluded with a request, that Sir John would visit their fallen Prince, and offer the consolation of an old friend. But he deemed that this measure would have the bad effect, of inducing the belief, that a reconciliation with Bajee Rao was still a desirable object for the British Government, independent of its being calculated to withdraw him from the immediate direction of those military dispositions, which might eventually require the most vigilant conduct. To counteract the first supposition, the Vakeels were distinctly informed, that Bajee Rao must abandon all expectation of ever again enjoying Princely dignity or Sovereign rule; and they were furnished with a copy of the proclamation, declaring him deprived of government, and the country conquered, from which position there was no longer a possibility of retracting.

Considerations which dictated the Conduct observed by Sir John Malcolm.

These were points on which Sir John had no doubt of the Governor-general's intentions; but there were others of a more questionable nature, respecting which he was unfurnished with any instructions. He was not, however, a person who naturally dreaded responsibility: and in his present situation, to await the arrival of orders, was to abandon all the power, which the forbearance of the monsoon left in his hands. The ill-disposed parties in Malwah had been crushed; and Scindiah had remained without a reasonable hope of successful hostility, on the Marquis of Hastings withdrawing the troops from his frontiers: but the inconsistency of Native Governments promised no satisfactory security against the recommencement of the war, should the Ex-Peishwah gain the plains of Malwah. His escape across the Nerbuddah during the monsoon, was either probable, or its prevention depended solely on a strict guard of the river during that inclement season, along a course of many hundred miles; while, in his present situation, it was deemed totally impracticable to reduce him before the monsoon; and his existence, even in a position however invested, was calculated to maintain a state of suspense throughout the Deckan and Malwah, extremely disadvantageous to the British interest. By the arrangements in progress, he would be ultimately hemmed in as long as the dry weather continued; but he was confident against the first effects of an attack, having secured a hasty retreat into Asseerghur, which could not be besieged during the rains. To understand this singular situation, a topographical description must be given of the position of Dhoolkoat, which is surrounded by hills of difficult access. Bajee Rao's rear was on Asseerghur, with which it had a direct communication of only nine miles; and the approach to it on that side, from which Brigadier-general Doveton's force was distinct only one march, necessarily passed under the guns, and even musquetry of the lower defences, or through a ghat which, though between the enemy and the fort, was of long and difficult ascent. His flanks were secured by impervious hills and jungle; and the few passes which led to the front, as well as that from Calachabootra in the rear, were guarded by desperate bands of Arabs, capable of maintaining a protracted, if not a successful, defence. In either event, Bajee Rao was determined to fly into Asseerghur, the Killedar of which was ardent to obtain and deserve the honour of being the champion of the Peishwah and the Mahratta cause. From these and other considerations, which might be further extended with considerable force, (were the defence of a transaction, the conduct of which has been occasionally questioned, to precede the military exposition of the means by which it was brought to a termination,) Sir John Malcolm concluded that the earliest possible reduction of Bajee Rao's power, was paramount to any narrow calculation of the expense at which it might be purchased. He even judged that this reduction might be prevented by the unfortunate protraction of a contest, the expense of which was as real, though its duration was less certain. In pursuance of this resolution, he dispatched an officer with the Vakeel, to the Mahratta camp, and charged them, among other conditions, to declare, that Bajee Rao would not be permitted to reside in the Deckan, and that it was expected he would surrender, were they in his power, Trimbuckjee Deinglia, and the murderers of the two Vaughans.*

Disposition of Sir John Malcolm's Division during the Negotiations.

It was Sir John's promise and intention, to meet the Ex-Peishwah at the Nerbuddah, in a private manner, to arrange the inferior conditions of his surrender, should he consent to the preliminary articles, and come unattended; but the Vakeels had departed a few days only, when the intelligence was received of the escape of the Ex-Rajah of Nagpoor. This event appeared of so much importance, that Sir John immediately sent after-orders for the Vakeels to proceed alone, and his assistant to await their return with the acquiescence of their master in the terms offered to him. It was now necessary, not only that his escape should be prevented, but that Appah Saib (the Ex-Rajah of Nagpoor) should be prevented from joining him; and the early formation of the cordon of troops became proportionably pressing. The 1st battalion of the 14th regiment of Native infantry was accordingly directed to cross the river from Mundleisur, and to approach, by moderate movements, the Mahratta camp; while Lieutenant-colonel

* The reader is referred back to pp. 5, 71, for further information on these two heads.

Russell's detachment was instructed to advance towards the same point from Hindia. Sir John repaired himself towards Mundleisur, where he arrived on the 22d, when the distribution of his force was then in three lines, as follows:

Along the Nerbuddah:—Head-quarters at Mundleisur, with one company of infantry at the Chicalda ford on the right, one at the Raveir ford on the left, and four companies at Hindia.

In advance:—The 1st battalion of the 14th regiment, and flank companies of the Russell brigade at Gogaum, with a small post of irregular horse at Beekungaum; and the 3d cavalry, with eight companies of Native infantry, and two guns, at Charwah.

Above the Ghats, in the rear:—The Bombay brigade of infantry at Mhow, with advance posts at the Jam and Sumroal passes; having on the right two companies at Boree, with one company below the Ghats at Baug; and on the left two companies at Peepulda, five companies at Oonchode, and the Rohillah* cavalry, and Bhopal contingent, at Ashta.

Interview between Bajee Rao and Sir John Malcolm.

Sir John Malcolm was at this time aware of the approach of Brigadier-general Doveton towards Boorhaunpoor, as was, likewise, Bajee Rao; who, apprehensive of an attack from that side, was anxious that intimation should be sent to the Brigadier-general, of the existence of the negotiation. Being informed that this must depend on his moving towards Sir John, to shew his sincerity, he got in motion accordingly. Having by this means induced a Native officer, charged with a letter for Brigadier-general Doveton, to dispatch the same, he instantly halted, having only advanced three miles; and this communication it was, which prevented Brigadier-general Doveton from attempting a night attack, on the 25th, from Boorhaunpoor. This transaction, with the delays of the Vakeels, convinced Sir John, that to bring matters to a speedy conclusion, the Ex-Peishwah must be pressed closely; and while he directed Lieutenant-colonel Russell to advance towards Boorgaum, he carried his own head-quarters, on the 27th, to Beekungaum. Here he was met by the Vakeels, who declared their master's disposition to conform to the terms generally proposed, and requested that the assistant might be sent back with them. Sir John Malcolm acquiesced

* These were the five *russalahs* forming Captain Roberts's detachment returning from Baglee, p. 265.

in this request, and moved, on the 29th, to Metawal, within fifteen miles of the Mahratta camp. Two more days were lost in fruitless negotiations, before Bajee Rao consented to advance to meet the British commander. Even this concession was marked by evident tokens of apprehension; and he stipulated that he should come only five miles, and but half a mile distant from his hills; while Sir John Malcolm, leaving his force at Metawal ten miles in the rear, should advance with a small escort. Unreasonable as was this proposal, it was not rejected; and the interview took place agreeably to appointment, on the afternoon of the 1st of June, near the Keiree Ghat, where he had established a battery to cover his retreat, in case of need. Previously to this measure, which probably appeared rash to Bajee Rao, he sent his treasures into Asseerghur; and, however he might have expressed acquiescence in the terms which had been communicated to him, in order to induce Sir John Malcolm to come forward, his subsequent conduct shewed his mind was not yet prepared to abandon the flattering illusion of Princely * ceremony. He affected a *durbár* on coming to the ground; and seated himself under a canopy, on a thick stuffed bedding, maintaining the form of addressing himself through a third person, for Sir John's information, as if he were still in the plenitude of power at Poonah. This melancholy farce was maintained about a quarter of an hour; after which he retired with Sir John into a tent, to discuss, with ease and privacy, the important topics of his future fate. This private conference lasted two hours, during which the conversation principally referred, on Bajee Rao's side, to the subject of his bitter misfortunes, and his hopes that Sir John Malcolm, as his only friend, would intercede in his favour. He pressed his solicitations with a degree of eloquence, which could have been little expected from his previous habits of supercilious form in conversation. This, however, was natural to him, and is the portion of every inhabitant of India, in a much greater measure than falls to the share of the natives of Europe, of similar rank in life. He warmly invoked the sentiments of disinterested friendship, as his sole resource in hours of difficulty, when not only the tribe of flatterers had absconded, but even adherents of old attachment were forsaking a distressed master. He designated Sir John

* A recent instance, in another hemisphere, affords an additional proof, were such necessary, of the reluctance with which the forms of grandeur are relinquished.

as the repository of this inestimable and solitary treasure; for, of his three earliest and best friends, he alone remained, Colonel Close * being dead, and General Wellesley in a distant land. But his mind was not yet humbled by all his misfortunes, to the measure of relinquishing, without a struggle, the hopes of maintaining the name of Peishwah, and residing at Poonah; and Sir John's remonstrances on the fruitlessness of his perseverance, appeared to have made insufficient impression, when they separated to return to their respective camps.

Ultimatum dispatched to the Ex-Peishwah.

Bajee Rao had, however, declared that Trimbuckjee Deinglia's cause was separate from his own; and that he had no control over that Chief. Sir John, thus left entirely at liberty to attack him, pending the negotiation, advanced Lieutenant-colonel Russell's detachment on one side of Asseerghur, near which Trimbuckjee was encamped, while he dispatched intimation of the state of affairs to Brigadier-general Doveton, on the opposite side, which placed him likewise at liberty to act against the Deinglia and his followers. To Bajee Rao, Sir John Malcolm dispatched, in a formal shape, a copy of the terms on which his submission, within twenty-four hours, would be accepted. These were founded on the communications previously made to him; but they also engaged to secure him a pension of not less than eight lacs of rupees (about a hundred thousand pounds) per annum for himself, and a liberal consideration of the situation of principal Jaghirs, his old adherents, and Brahmins of remarkable character. As Major Cumming's detachment had now arrived at Kotra, from Brigadier-general Watson's division (p. 343), Sir John was prepared to push the negotiation to immediate extremities; for the detachment previously at Gogum was brought forward to Metawal, and Lieutenant-colonel Russell was advancing from Appla-Debla to Boorgaum, which closed the investment of Dhoolkoat as much as was practicable; Brigadier-general Doveton being at this time as near the Mahratta camp, as the nature of the country, and the position of Asseerghur, permitted him to lie. These movements had the desired effect on the minds of the Ex-Peishwah and his principal

* The late Major-general Sir Barry Close, Bart., during whose nine years' residence at Poonah in a political capacity, the Peishwah had been rescued from the hands of Holkur, and his affairs placed in that train of prosperity which furnished him with the power of exciting hostility against the British Government, when he ceased to appreciate the benefits of their connexion.

officers. A constant series of messages ensued, which were uniformly met by the most decided adherence to the terms offered. This inflexibility was, however, combined with friendly remonstrances to the Vinchoor and Poorundhur chiefs, against permitting their master to pursue a course of infatuation, which it was their own interest, as well as his, that he should avoid; and their answers are no less worthy of record, from the generous attachment which they evinced. While they declared that they would endeavour, by kind persuasion, to soften him into a submission which was unavoidable; they deprecated the idea of assuming a tone of harsh control towards a fallen prince. The Vakeel of the Vinchoorkur said, that his master's family, in serving that of the Peishwah during five generations, had, on all occasions, spoken boldly; but that now, when he was oppressed by the visitation of fate, not only silence, but even submission to unmerited reproaches, was an incumbent duty. The last act of the night of the 2d of June, was the dismissal of an agent of Bajee Rao's, who had been permitted to reside at Sir John's head-quarters for a few days, that his master's fears and suspicions might be allayed, by the constant intelligence of the military dispositions, which he was allowed to collect and transmit, with the greatest *minutiæ*, through messengers constantly employed.

His reluctant Surrender on Conditions.

Agreeably to his promise, Sir John marched, on the morning of the 3d, to the vicinity of the Keirree Ghat, where he had invited Bajee Rao to surrender himself, and where they had met two days before. Instead, however, of the Chief, his Vakeel appeared, and alleged that his master was willing to come as required; but that he was in a state of the greatest trepidation at the recent military movements, and solicitous to have another twenty-four hours, as this was an unlucky day. "A most unlucky day it shall prove for your master, if he fail to come in," was the reply of Sir John, who further demanded, with a shew of indignation, whether he apprehended treachery. This *Anundrao* (the Vakeel) denied; but said that there might be orders, received from the Governor-general, to place Bajee Rao under sentries, which would disgrace him for ever. "Tell him," said Sir John, "that I have no such orders; and that the settlement I have ventured to make on anticipation, was too liberal to allow of my thinking it possible that any mortal, in Bajee Rao's situation, should attempt to fly from it; and if he did, he would forfeit all future claims, and the British Government would be relieved from a large disbursement, which it voluntarily incurred through a respect for its own dignity." The report of this conversation decided the hesitating Chief. At eleven o'clock of the same forenoon, he came from among his hills, and encamped, in the plain, near the British lines, with four thousand horse, and three thousand infantry, containing twelve hundred Arabs. These, a few days afterwards, were increased to nearly two thousand, by the junction of some parties that had been detached to guard distant passes. Trimbuckjee Deinglia, with others, applied for terms; but receiving no assurance, except of life, he made his escape, on finding measures in progress for his attack. Ram Deen, the Chief of the *Barra Bhye*, who had still remained with the Ex-Peishwah, and was a rebel to the Holkur Government, surrendered on a promise of pardon; and rejoined the Mahratta camp, now augmented to a considerable force. This inconvenience was greater than had been expected or stipulated; but Sir John, in the expectation that these troops, in the natural course of events, would shortly fall off, preferred their temporary presence, to the embittering their Chief's last moments of intercourse with them, by a harsh interference for their removal.

Reflections respecting the Necessity of the Terms granted.

However the amount of pension conferred on Bajee Rao, may be with some a subject of regret, as imposing on the British finances an unnecessary burden; there will be found abundant cause for admiring the temper and ability discovered towards that Chief; and which, at length, obliged him to accept what Sir John Malcolm thought a cheap price for the conclusion of a contest, which, if continued, would be fraught with dangers certainly incalculable. The recommencement of the Mahratta war, after Lord Lake's army retired to monsoon quarters in 1804, may be a case not entirely parallel; but it is sufficiently similar to shew the extent of evil, which the premature, though unavoidable, suspension of active operations, is capable of producing. If any part of Sir John Malcolm's reasoning, for the necessity of prevailing on Bajee Rao to compound his claims of sovereignty for one hundred thousand pounds per annum, and a liberal provision for adherents, Brahmins and principal Jaghiredars, be considered unsatisfactory, it will probably be that which regarded the strength of Bajee Rao's position, and the certainty of his retreat into Asseerghur. This may have been the case latterly, when he was so much alarmed as to send his treasures into that fortress. But Brigadier-general Doveton did not apprehend an unfortunate issue, when he formed his detachment to attack the Mahratta camp on the night of the 25th, with a promptitude that does credit to his arrangements. That, with great self-command, he suspended that attack, on receiving a note from the subaltern officer sent forward with the Vakeels, may be a subject of regret, though it will probably be approved, in consideration of his ignorance of the contingencies, on which the dispatch of that communication was made to depend. There would have been no faith broken by his contempt of it; for Sir John Malcolm was no further engaged than his specific offers implied; and the acquiescence in them would have removed Bajee Rao out of the reach of attack. This transaction, if other considerations were wanting, was sufficient to convince Sir John of the necessity of his own presence near the scene of action; as well to secure the British interests entrusted to his charge, in the capacity of Governor-general's Agent, as to avoid the indecency of leaving the conduct of his senior general-officer, dependent on the discretion of a European subordinate, delegated to a Native subordinate. The pass direct from Boorhaunpoor to Dhoolkoat was practicable; and it was suggested to Brigadier-general Doveton, towards the conclusion of the negotiation, that he should endeavour to interpose between Asseerghur and the camp of Trimbuckjee, who had equal facilities of entering that fortress with Bajee Rao. This shews that the connexion of the Mahratta camp with Asseer, along a distance of nine miles, was not considered entirely secure against interruption. But the local information which then existed, was extremely defective; and it would be unfair to argue from what may have been subsequently obtained, if even this were conclusive. Such, however, in general, is the injustice of those who criticise public acts, while of the information which really existed, the self-elected judges are partially or entirely ignorant. A short intercourse with the world is sufficient to discover the occasional elevation of imbecility to places of trust and difficulty. This evil, there can be little doubt, would be more extensive, were there no assumed judicature to deter the governing power from the selection of incompetent instruments; or to drive these, with irresistible clamour, from a situation of which they are unworthy. Far from an instance of this description, is the case of Sir John Malcolm. His long course of important and valuable services has secured, through the severe ordeal of successive trials, a name which, while it claims the character of public utility, is equally celebrated for those virtues of private life, which are not always considered the indispensable* qualifications of a servant of Government.

* Hear the opinion of Marshal Villars, who was as little of the courtier as any man who

After this tribute to his merits—leaving him with the Ex-Peishwah's apprehensions to calm, a body of turbulent Arabs to controul, and a multitude of other troops to disband; all which, if the exercise of talents be their best reward, promised ample gratification—the Narrative will, for the present, attend the return of the Hydrabad Division towards Jalnah, where it was instructed to take up monsoon quarters.

Return of the Hydrabad Division to Quarters.

While negotiations were prosecuted north of the Sautpoorra hills; to the southward of them, Brigadier-general Doveton had remained in a continual state of preparation for immediate action, till the 6th of June, the day on which intimation arrived of Bajee Rao's surrender. During this interval, the proposition was received for attacking Trimbuckjee, and the necessary arrangements were made with proper dispatch. On the morning of the 3d, a detachment, composed of the 7th regiment of cavalry, with four galloper guns, a company of Europeans, the 1st battalion of the 16th regiment of Native infantry, and one thousand Silladar horse, was placed under the command of Major Doveton, who was directed to attempt the passage by Asseerpetta, as that least likely to interfere with Bajee Rao's position, which lay comparatively westward. A few hours afterwards, the camp moved to Calachabootra, on the high road to Dhoolkoat; but Major Doveton's detachment was unable to pass through Asseer; for as soon as it arrived there, all the guns of the fort which could be brought to bear on it, were fired incessantly, and prohibited all approach. The Major accordingly retired upon Nusserabad-Boree; and next day passed the new camp to Patur, two miles in advance; where, on the 5th, the 1st battalion of the 7th regiment of Native infantry, from Sir John Malcolm's head-quarters, relieved the 1st battalion of the 16th regiment of Native infantry, two galloper guns were returned, and the remaining flank-company of the Madras European regiment joined. On the following day, rumours which had previously prevailed, of Trimbuckjee's escape, were confirmed; and the Patur detachment, now commanded by Lieutenant-colonel Heath, was

carried a baton. "Qu'importe au Roi que l'on soit méchant? Vous trouverez les qualités du plus grand Général du monde, dans un homme cruel, avare, perfide, impie. Qu'est ce que tout cela fait? J'aimerois mieux pour le Roi un bon Général, qui auroit toutes ces pernicieuses qualités, qu'un fat, que l'on trouveroit dévot, liberal, honnête, chaste, pieux. Il faut des hommes dans les guerres importantes; & je vous assure que ce qui s'appelle des hommes sont très rares."—Lettre à M. le Comte de Marsan.

ordered to march to Beawul, whither the enemy were supposed to have fled: for in that direction there were many armed bodies who had not yet been subdued by the course of operations in Khandesh, which had hitherto been confined to the southern parts of that province, where Lieutenant-colonel Mac Dowell was now engaged in the siege of Malleygaum. To that point, Lieutenant-colonel Heath was directed to carry his detachment, after his pursuit of Trimbuckjee, whether successful or fruitless. Under these instructions, he marched, on the 9th, between the Taptee and Sautpoorra mountains, reinforced by the flank-companies of the Russell brigade, and three hundred Poonah auxiliaries. B[illegible] Doveton, at the same time, took the direct road towards Jalnah, with the remainder of the force, and was joined at his first ground by a convoy of treasure from that place, escorted by two companies of the 1st battalion of the 3d regiment Native infantry. The division, pursuing the same route by which it had come from Jalnah, arrived, on the 11th, at Hurtallah, and halted there the three following days, in consequence of intimation received from Colonel Adams, that the Ex-Rajah of Nagpoor, having fled from the Mahadeo hills, was supposed to have taken a south-westerly direction. No corroboration of this report succeeding, the march was continued, by nearly the same stages formerly adopted; and the division arrived, on the 26th of June, at Jalnah, having ascended the Adjunta Ghat on the 21st. At the same time, Lieutenant-colonel Heath, having failed of discovering Trimbuckjee, or his adherents, concluded his march at Kurgoun, near the Taptee, and six miles from Neesserabad. There he took a position for the monsoon, agreeably to the subsequent orders he received; for at this period his reinforcement was no longer required by Lieutenant-colonel Mac Dowell, who had left Malleygaum; but the flank-companies of the Russell brigade, and the thousand Mysore horse, were sent forward by his camp, as the high road to their respective head-quarters.

March of Sir John Malcolm with the Ex-Peishwah towards the Nerbuddah.

After Sir John Malcolm had called in the several detachments from his head-quarters, his collected force amounted to one regiment of Native cavalry, a battalion of Native infantry, seven field-pieces, and six hundred irregular horse; for the 1st battalion of the 7th regiment of Native infantry, and the detachment of the Russell brigade, as already mentioned, were sent across the hills to join the Hydrabad Division, to which they had been transferred. All arrangements being complete, the march was commenced on the 4th of June, by Beekungaum and Seeonee, towards the Raveir

Ghat, on the Nerbuddah. This movement was conducted, for several days, by moderate stages, without any extraordinary occurrence; Bajee Rao's camp, which marched late in the day, being invariably separate from that of the British troops. Yet scarcely any diminution was made in the numbers of his followers, notwithstanding Sir John's occasional remonstrances on the embarrassments they were likely to produce. The Ex-Peishwah seemed averse to any measure calculated to dispel the illusions of sovereignty, which he could yet scarcely believe to have vanished with the late treaty. The shadow still afforded a soothing deception, which required, for its banishment, some external event, independent of his unwilling mind; or perhaps he even considered this as the least painful manner of being divested of his troops, the impropriety of whose admission into Malwah he would probably confess. Experience must have shewn him that Arabs, at all events, were a body with whom it was difficult to make a settlement, and that, in all likelihood, the intervention of Sir John's means and influence would be requisite to compromise the impending disagreement. This interference would also save him from the necessity of anticipating an active exertion, so different from the usual policy of a Mahratta Government, in which, through habit, he still imagined himself to preside. These troops, amounting to about two thousand men, had been hired for Bajee Rao's service, some months previously, by Trimbuckjee; and they demanded their arrears of pay from that date: instead of which it was offered to them from the day they had joined. The comparative justice of the claim and offer, were it of importance for examination here, might not be easily determined, as it would depend on express stipulations, or on the prevailing custom in similar cases, which would generally be found in favour of the offer. But a turbulent body, like the Arabs, are not always to be satisfied by the payment of just demands; and instances are not uncommon of their rising in their exactions, in proportion to the degree of acquiescence.

Matters arrived at an extremity, on the 9th of June, at Seeonee, when the Arabs, instead of marching, as had been ordered, clamorously surrounded Bajee Rao's tent, threatening personal injury, if their demands were not satisfied on that ground, which was within ten miles of the Nerbuddah. They accompanied this violent conduct with declarations, that any movement on the part of the British troops, for his liberation, would cause his instant destruction, and that of all the helpless people about him. The

Mutiny of the Arabs.

contagion of their example spreading to the Rohillahs, in a short time the whole of the infantry were in a state of mutiny. Sir John Malcolm, though not apprehensive of the extreme crisis which was approaching, was not without the expectation of some disturbance on this morning. While, therefore, he dispatched his baggage to the next ground, with the irregular horse, and part of the infantry, he retained the regular cavalry, with six companies of the battalion, and two galloper-guns. In this predicament were affairs when Bajee Rao applied for assistance, at the same time that he intreated no coercive movement might take place, to bring on the fate with which he had been threatened; and Sir John, finding that he had not sufficient force to awe the mutineers, sent off a dispatch for the return of the troops which had marched. The day passed in messages to Sir John, from Bajee Rao, declaring his apprehensions; and from Sir John to the Arabs, menacing them with extirpation if they proceeded to violence. Towards the evening, however, he had such communications with the refractory principals, who were themselves comparatively reasonable, as to enable him to send consolation to the encircled Chief, whom he assured of a favourable settlement on the following morning.

Suppression of the Mutiny.

The Mahratta camp was established along the bank of a *nullah*, or ravine, much divided by small water-courses, and interspersed with scattered jungle, highly favourable to the efforts of irregular troops; but to the west, the ground gradually rose into a commanding position. This Sir John assumed, at day-break, on the 10th; and was joined by the troops who had countermarched, which completed his corps to four hundred regular Native cavalry, seven hundred regular Native infantry, with seven guns and six hundred irregular horse. These he extended, in a single rank, to increase their apparent numbers, as his object was intimidation, under the apprehension of the results of mutineers' despair. This expedient was not without the desired effect, and the principal Jemidar, Syed Fyze, advanced to demand a parley, while some of his own lawless bands opened a fire, which wounded two Sepoys. The troops were under such admirable discipline, that no attempt was made to resist this aggression, though the guns were loaded and the matches lighted; but all communication was refused, till this irregular firing should be discontinued; and as the Chief dispatched an attendant for this purpose, he was permitted to approach. Bajee Rao had already paid the greater part of their demands; and the remaining subject of difference consisted of trifling matters, which both parties were satisfied to refer to the arbitration of Sir John, who willingly assented to become the umpire. Syed Fyze galloped off, on this assurance, to withdraw his people from their position round Bajee Rao's tent; but these refused to be removed, till all their leaders had received a promise of security against attack, after they should relinquish the pledge they already held. As Sir John instantly gave his hand to every Jemidar, their men were drawn off without more delay; and the Mahratta Chief, attended by some horse, came in front of the British line, delighted at his emancipation from such barbarous thraldom. To make the contrast of the treatment to be derived from his own troops and from the British Authorities, more striking, Sir John received him with a general salute; and he acknowledged the error he had committed in neglecting previous admonition, with expressions of gratitude for the benefits recently conferred. His first mark of obedience was moving off instantly to the opposite bank of the Nerbuddah; while the British Commander was engaged in granting passports to the remaining troops, and in witnessing the departure of the Arabs and Rohillahs towards, what they called, their respective homes.

Reflections on this Service.

When the mutineers came to cool, after the heated state of irritation to which they had been raised, they expressed themselves equally indebted with Bajee Rao, for the lenity and temper with which they had been treated. Nor were these sentiments entertained without sufficient grounds; for, undoubtedly, Sir John Malcolm had the means of annihilating a considerable portion of them, and of dispersing the remainder. But they knew well the character he bore among the Natives of India; and that nothing less than the most indispensable necessity, could force him into the measure of sacrificing so many lives, and among them, most probably, the numerous innocent and defenceless victims, who, from restraint, were unable to avoid the scene of conflict. Proud and sincere tribute to character! demonstrated at the hazard of life, and superior, as an evidence of individual merit, to the most gaudy trappings of victory! If there were general reasons to apprehend, that the occasional practice of lenity would weaken the hand that bestows it, or render it less useful for the public service, the present instance would oppose itself to that conclusion; for the happy termination of this formidable insurrection may be fairly referred to the influence of character and talents of a higher stamp than fall to the share of the narrow-minded Martinet. That discipline is indispensable among soldiers, cannot be questioned; but the ability sufficient to maintain, in ordinary cases, the efficacy of rules, through the previously established forms of courts martial and military punishments, sinks into nothing before that power which controuls a tumultuous multitude, or directs a military body under circumstances which have suspended the ordinary respect for orders. It will not be inferred from these observations, that severity is never required; on the contrary, its frequent necessity, as the sole remedy, is freely [illegible] But the talents which are required to apply it in the supposed cases, are not those of the vulgar disciplinarian, who considers the whole art of war to consist in the inflexible observance of subordination. There are few men of the military profession who have seen service, and observed characters, whose experience has not shewn them officers in whom they could not have expected the virtue of forbearance, when a pretext so plausible had been furnished for the gratification of coercion, that natural disposition of the human mind; to subdue which, are required all the powers of education, and the influence of civilized society. But though the page of history exhibit instances, where political expediency was consulted, with less convenient concealment than might have attended the intentional sacrifice of the Ex-Peishwah, through the instrumentality of an Arab mutiny; far be the thought, that any public servant of a British Government* could be found so base and depraved as to prostitute his conscience for the evasion of the promised pension, however embarrassing it might prove. Such conduct would discover his false and contemptible opinion of the Government he served; and, if known, expose him to the execration of his own countrymen, more than of any other nation.

Arrival at Mhow, and Confirmation of the Convention.

Sir John Malcolm and Bajee Rao pursued their march, from the Raveir Ghat, on the Nerbuddah, towards Mhow, with more confidence in each other than they had previously felt; and after three marches, arrived there by the Simroal pass in the hills of Southern Malwah. Bajee Rao was here permitted to halt for a month, previously to his departure for Hindoostan, as well to compose his mind, and settle the many cares incidental to an

* However the reader may think a gratuitous defence of the British character unnecessary, his reflections on the events of the late wars in Europe will supply him with instances in another country of a respect for present expediency, at the expense of the vulgar principles of morality. Such conduct is commonly called Machiavelian, by those who never read the works of the Florentine Secretary, but adopt an assumed interpretation as ill-founded as the vulgar opinion respecting the philosophy of Epicurus.

irrevocable banishment from the scenes of youth, of former enjoyments, and of sovereign rule; as to await the orders of the Governor-general, who was at Goruckpoor when he received the intimation of the treaty which had been concluded, subject to his confirmation. Nor was this sanction withheld, whatever might have been the reasoning of Lord Hastings on the claims of the Ex-Peishwah, or on the position of his affairs when terms so liberal were offered him, in the conviction of their being ratified. Those who know the character of the Governor-general as well as Sir John did, and there are many who have had a better opportunity of gaining that knowledge, will not hesitate to form an opinion of the conduct, which, under such circumstances, his Lordship would adopt. It must be with difficulty, and under inexorable circumstances, that the virtues of the individual can be entirely sunk in the public character; and a life marked by chivalric sentiments of honour, gave a security for the credit of the British name, proof against every sordid calculation of immediate profit.

Comparison of the British with Native Governments

Thus was terminated the grand Mahratta confederacy, by the abdication and exile of its principal member; which left the remaining parties without an excuse for combination against the British Government, founded on their internal and ill-understood connexion. However inconsistent might appear the actions of the Mahratta Powers, in warring against each other, and in attacking the Peishwah, whose office they professed to revere, there can be no doubt of the influence which his conduct had over all the other members; for its effect was too visible; and some of their intermediate communications are mixed with the language of reproach, for imputed indifference to the fate of the first officer of the Mahratta nation. The remaining Chiefs are insulated in politics, as they are in territory; and the exercise of common vigilance, added to the experience which has been gained of the sources of disorder, promises to secure the peace of India by the termination of those feelings of lawless insolence which have marked the character of her military class for many ages. The abolition of this useless description of subject, if they deserve such a name, will be the proper object of British policy, as the most effectual method of extending the blessings of industry and peace. Such has been, on all occasions, the language of the British Government, in accounting for its acts in India; and it has not escaped the notice of its opponents, that such is the language of all conquerors. Without denying this allegation, it seems that the most pertinent subject of investigation is, whether it steadily pursue the most suitable and legitimate method of accomplishing that good which is undeniable. The immorality of conquering more than can be governed, is unquestionable; and seems conclusive against many other Powers, who have established themselves temporarily in India, as well as in other parts of the globe, without inquiring into the other important principles of national equity, which may have been violated. The more gradually and steadily dominion is enlarged, the more likely is the Power which exercises it, to enjoy the means of confirming its authority, and discovering its faults; and this case must be allowed to bear a stronger resemblance to the British Government of India, than to either Mahomedan or Mahratta. The conquests of these Powers were suddenly made, and suddenly lost. They were at times beaten back, and subsequently recovered their ground according to the events of a battle, by which, perhaps, an army was annihilated. In the intervals, there was no rule deserving the name of government; and, in many cases, the subject found no personal security but in the profession of arms. Not only were dynasties changed among the same people, but the succession was a continual source of contest, which prevailed both among Mahomedans and Mahrattas, notwithstanding their inveterate wars with each other, and left scarce a discernible barrier against the despotism of a ruler, excepting public opinion, which gained no access to his ear till the extremity of his reign, or a consideration of individual interest, seldom well understood. Whatever despotism has been occasionally exercised in India, political folly, which is likewise a source of misery to the subject, will be less frequently imputed to the British Government; and perhaps this will be found oftener on the side of forbearance, than on that of assumption, or miscalculated strength. The return of British armies from countries they have occupied, is a circumstance which scarcely any Native can comprehend; and he declares his inability to explain it, by referring to the unaccountable customs of an extraordinary people. The body of laws and regulations which have gradually arisen out of events, give a solidity to its power, and permanency to its government, by establishing a uniform principle of policy, which circumscribes, within narrow bounds, the caprices, the passions and errors of individuals, and encourages the subject to place his dependance on a fixed rule of action, which he can understand, and which may not be transgressed.

Difficulty attending a fair Judgment respecting Indian Affairs.

When subjects connected with India were less understood than they are at present, a Governor-general was brought to trial for misdemeanors, which may be pronounced to be now impracticable. Yet even of those he was acquitted, notwithstanding all the talents employed in his prosecution. After an accumulated knowledge of Indian affairs had been obtained, both respecting those and succeeding times, the venerable Hastings was selected to be the privy-councillor of his Sovereign; and his memory was subsequently honoured by monuments, to be erected on the very stage of his alleged criminality, and at the seat of the directing power, which he was supposed to have disgraced. The ordeal undergone by a distant Government, whose most secret correspondence and instructions are printed in England, has nothing like it in a home administration, where even verbal explanation, of political transactions with a foreign power, is sparingly given. If to this be added the common gratification of attacking Authority, there will be little cause to wonder that the usual course of writers in Europe, who have not witnessed the vicinity of irregular and corrupt governments, has been that of reviling the efforts occasionally made, to avert the evils flowing from such a neighbourhood. The difficulty, also, which the reading world would experience, in procuring access to records which might furnish grounds for an independent opinion, is sufficient to throw them on the mercy of authors who court the popular side, and give such extracts of documents as suit their designs. The line which should accurately define the allowable encroachment on abstract principles of morality, for the accomplishment of an unquestionable good, appears, from the conduct of nations, to be still undetermined. In the affairs of this world there is no unmixed excellence; and it must be the lot of governments, as of individuals, to obtain as much good as they can. The price at which it shall be acquired, must determine the advantage of the purchase; and there is but little probability of the cost being under-rated by a British public, ever alive to what affects the honour and character of the nation. This delicacy of feeling respecting distant acts, however it may create a theme for declamation at home, cannot deprive the British Government of India, of a celebrity for liberality and humanity among the reflecting Natives; at the same time that they observe, that whatever Power comes in contact with it, gradually declines. This may be undeniable; but were not the numerous governments of India as ephemeral before? and why should unsound principles, or the absence of all principle, have a different effect now from what they had formerly?

Mutability of Indian Empires.

The circle, or retrogression, by which States arrive at their dissolution, is a hackneyed subject, admitting of scarcely any novel remark in these times, when princely conventions are tried as an experiment, for the everlasting maintenance of the established order of things. With regard to India, however, its fate has always been that of revolution; nor has it ever possessed the name of a kingdom. China has always upheld the integrity of her state, notwithstanding the changes of dynasty, and invasions of Tartars. Persia, with all its variations of limits and of title, is a kingdom as ancient as any of which there is a record; but the "kingdom of India" never existed as a name, though the inhabitants have been described from the earliest periods of history. The uncertain accounts of its first states have rewarded the researches of the industrious, whom any story, however doubtful, relieves from the painful solicitude of total ignorance. The march of the Mahomedan conquests cast a gleam which partially lighted its own events, and assisted in the discovery or verification of more distant occurrences. There are, subsequently, the alternate empires of Moghuls and Putans, the kingdom of Bengal, and the principalities of the Deckan; with numerous others, which rose and fell, combined and separated, with continual and rapid variation of frontier, and change of capital. Shall the conclusion to be drawn from these examples be the downfall of the British Empire in India, like a Mahratta State? To answer this question without hesitation, would discover a confidence of judgment which the author disclaims; but it may be asserted that such a catastrophe, if it ever happen, will proceed from causes widely different from those which have produced the destruction of previous empires. Circumstances which were once considered monstrous in idea, are now familiar in existence; and the freedom of the press can be cited as an undeniable instance, of which the explanation may be found in the altered state of the British power, and of that of Native States. It is certainly calculated to abolish that barbaric ambition still so dear to these, by diverting their attention to other objects, through the free dissemination of knowledge; and the abundant introduction of European inventions has a real, though not a striking effect. If opposite results may be anticipated from opposite causes, on one account will the British conquerors of India deserve, from the original (Hindoo) population, a different sentiment from that with which the Mahomedan conquerors were contemplated. The support and confirmation of their priesthood and church endowments, forms an obvious contrast with the intolerant destruction of their temples, and occasional suppression of the exercise of their religion. But the ties of gratitude are easily broken; and while every freedom, their degree of civilization renders them capable of enjoying, is conferred by the prevailing policy; may a powerful body of European troops be ever maintained, to guard against the incalculable operation of caprice, inconstancy, and superstition!

Some apology for so long a digression from military affairs, may appear necessary, and will, it is hoped, be found in the example of liberality which introduced these reflections, and which should be set off against the instances of aggrandizement, which may generally be traced to the patriotic motive of preventing the recurrence of extensive and hostile combinations, from the dangers of which a previous escape had been with difficulty effected.

CHAPTER X.

EXPULSION OF APPAH SAIB FROM THE NAGPOOR TERRITORY.

Reasons for continuing this Memoir after the Dissolution of the Mahratta Confederacy. Distribution of the British Forces. Elevation of the young Rajah of Nagpoor. Destruction of Captain Sparkes's Detachment. March of British Detachments into the unsettled Districts. March of Brigadier-general Doveton's Light Force from Jalnah to Ellichapoor. Detention of this Reinforcement by inclement Weather. Destruction of the Enemy's Garrison of Mooltye. Captain Gordon's successful Attack of Compta. Major Wilson's successful Attack of Ambaghur. Major Wilson's successful Attack of Puriee. Evacuation of Amlah before Captain Jones's Detachment. Major Bowen's successful Attack of Boordye. Lieutenant Cruickshanks's successful Excursion into the Hills. Arrival of Cheettoo Pindarry at Patchmurree. Unsuccessful Efforts of the Ghoands North of the Hills. Last Efforts of Appah Saib at the Close of 1818. *Combined Dispositions for his Attack and Interception. Siege of Jilpy-Aumneir by Lieutenant-colonel Pollock's Detachment. Renewal of Operations in Khandesh. Reduction of Ummulneir, and Separation of the Field Force. Combined Movement into the Mahadeo Hills. Appah Saib's Escape from Patchmurree. Brigadier-general Doveton's March to Boorhaunpoor. Reflections on the Events described in this Chapter.*

Reasons for continuing this Memoir after the Dissolution of the Mahratta Confederacy.

WHEN a work arrives at a period which seems to include the termination of all, or most, of the transactions forming the subject of its previous descriptions, the reader, if not the writer, generally feels a disposition to dispense with any further prosecution of his inquiries. He will rather be satisfied with the information already attained. Such is frequently the case with the history of a campaign. This must, at all events, conclude with the suspension of active hostilities, or the return of the troops to quarters; and such, in fact, is part of the definition of the term; the recommencement of operations being frequently considered as the suitable beginning of a fresh Memoir. It cannot, therefore, be denied, that the continuation of a description of the war of 1817, 18, and 19, is exposed, in a certain degree, to the before-mentioned common objection. The author, however, hopes to shew sufficient cause for the further prosecution of his subject, and an indispensable obligation on his readers who have gone so far, to continue, for some time longer, a salutary exercise of patience. Treaties, it is true, have been concluded with the principal Powers; the Mahratta Confederacy has been dissolved; and, with the exception of some jungles and strong places, the whole of Malwah and the Deckan have been occupied by the British troops. But the affairs of the Nagpoor dominions were left in an unsatisfactory state; many parts being still in the possession of the adherents of Appah Saib, who was himself supported by the Ghoands, occupying the range of mountains that bound to the southward the Valley of the Upper Nerbuddah. Treaties remained to be concluded with some of the minor States of Central India; some places were still to be wrested from the hands of the Arabs; and Bajee Rao was yet to quit the theatre of the war, before its termination could be decidedly pronounced, or any reasonable hopes entertained of the permanent peace of India. These exigencies, it will be seen, disturbed the repose of the troops in their monsoon quarters. With some divisions, indeed, it may be said, that their campaign was not concluded, since they were obliged to resume their operations in all the severity of the season.

Distribution of the British Forces.

Previous, however, to the account of these operations, it will be proper to take a view of the actual distribution, at the commencement of the monsoon, of the troops destined to be subsequently employed. Their strength was, indeed, very much reduced, in comparison with the force brought forward on the same theatre eight months before, though the number of corps were nearly equal on both occasions. The details of the previous chapters will have rendered the following statement intelligible. To them it is only necessary to add, that a detachment, consisting of three companies of the 2d battalion of the 20th Native infantry, a corps of six hundred Sebundies, and four hundred irregular horse, were sent in the middle of May, to Ruttunpoor, under Captain Edmunds, appointed the Collector of that district. These were not mentioned before, as they were then considered more connected with Civil arrangements than they have subsequently proved, and were, indeed, unconnected with military operations.

(Map II.)

Saughur and Dependencies, under the Command of Brigadier-general Watson........	Detail of Horse-Artillery. Four Squadrons of Native Cavalry. Two Companies of Foot-Artillery. Five Battalions of Native Infantry. One Russalah of Irregular Horse.
Mhow and Dependencies, under the Command of Brigadier-general Sir J. Malcolm, K.C.B. and K.L.S.	Two Brigades of Horse-Artillery (Four Guns). Three Squadrons of Native Cavalry. One Company of Foot-Artillery. Four Battalions of Native Infantry (two Madras and two Bombay). One Company and a Half of Pioneers. Three Thousand Two Hundred Irregular Horse.
Hoossingabad and Dependencies, under the Command of Lieutenant-col. Adams, C.B.	Three Brigades of Native Horse-Artillery (Six Guns). Four Squadrons of Native Cavalry. One Company of Foot-Artillery. Five Battalions of Native Infantry. One Thousand Five Hundred Irregular Horse.
Khandesh, under the Command of Lieutenant-colonel A. Mac Dowell	One Company and a Half of Foot-Artillery. Five Companies of European Foot. One Company of Sappers and Miners. Three Battalions of Native Infantry. Five Companies of Pioneers. Five Hundred Irregular Horse.
Nagpoor, under the Command of Lieutenant-colonel H. S. Scot ...	One Troop of Horse-Artillery (Eight Guns). Four Squadrons of Native Cavalry. One Company of Foot-Artillery. Six Battalions of Native Infantry. One Company of Pioneers.
Jalnah, under the Command of Brigadier-general Doveton.......	One Troop of Horse-Artillery (Eight Guns). Eleven Squadrons of Native Cavalry. Five Companies of European Foot. Three Battalions of Native Infantry. Two Companies of Pioneers.

Elevation of the young Rajah of Nagpoor.

The first subject which claims attention, relates to the affairs of Nagpoor. On the 25th of June, Bajee Rao, a youth of ten years of age, and grandson of the late Rajah Ragojee Bhooslah, was placed on the *musnud**,

* The Mahratta term of *gaddee* (or throne) might be more properly used on the present occasion, were it equally familiar to the European ear with the Persian word *musnud.*

in the room of Appah Saib. The young Prince received, likewise, on this occasion, the name of Rajah Ragojee Bhooslah. The ceremony of his accession was attended with all the forms of Native state, noise, and demonstrations of joy, suited to the event. But the measure of elevating a new ruler under the regency of his mother, was not sufficient to ensure the possession of the country, or to intimidate the adherents of the former Chief. Throughout the months of June and July, their numbers and boldness increased in an evident degree; the inclemency of the weather being such, that no active measures to prevent this evil were attempted, or very practicable. Appah Saib generally resided in the neighbourhood of Daolagherree, a sacred place, and at Patchmurree, situate in the heart of the Mahadeo hills. There he was surrounded by a body of Arabs and Ghoands, said to amount to many thousand men. Parties of these took occasion from the inertness of the British troops, at this season, to possess themselves of some important places, and among others of Meilghat, Meirsee, Atnere, Satnere, and Amlah. At the same time active levies of Arabs, and others, were conducted by Appah Saib's partisans at Boorhaunpoor, and wherever there were any men of the military class thrown out of employ; while the recent discharge of Bajee Rao's force supplied an abundant field for recruiting. (Map VIII.)

Destruction of Capt. Sparkes's Detachment.

The first occurrence of importance was in the Beitool district, which a body of Arabs and others entered from Meilghat, and proceeded to levy contributions throughout the country. The post of Beitool was at this time garrisoned by a detachment from the Nerbuddah Division, commanded by Captain Sparkes. With about one hundred and seven men of the 10th Bengal Native infantry, he marched on the 19th of July to check these incursions. On the second day he crossed the Taptee from Bherran, and was immediately threatened by a party of horse, whom he beat off. These, however, were soon afterwards succeeded by larger bodies, both of horse and foot, containing a considerable proportion of Arabs, who immediately commenced the assault. This was maintained about an hour; after which the enemy, perceiving no impression made on this small detachment, threatened to close on them. Captain Sparkes, apprehensive of the result of such an effort in his position, sought a more commanding situation on a neighbouring eminence; in gaining which he was wounded in the leg. A continual fire was necessary to keep the enemy at a distance; while the maintenance of it was the sure precursor of the detachment's destruction, when their supply of ammunition should be expended. On this the Arabs probably calculated; for as the musquetry slackened, they closed in with eagerness. Further particulars of this melancholy affair are little known. Captain Sparkes and his detachment were cut off to a Naigue and eight Sepoys. Even the followers, with the exception of a few fugitives, were destroyed. There were other small posts in the neighbourhood, which, after this event, were in danger of being cut off by the enemy. They were now in considerable strength above the Ghats; and notwithstanding the unremitting continuance of the rains, it was found necessary that immediate reinforcements should be sent thither, and also into other quarters, to recover the lost ascendancy.

March of British Detachments into the unsettled Districts.

Intelligenee of this disaster no sooner reached Colonel Adams at Hoossingabad, than he detached Major Mac Pherson with four companies of the same battalion to which Captain Sparkes's detachment belonged, and a squadron of the 7th Bengal cavalry, to ascend the Ghats. After passing them, the Major left at Shawpoor a post of thirty Sepoys with some followers, who immediately afterwards were cut off. A reinforcement of three flank companies and two guns were subsequently sent to join him, under Captain Newton. This officer, however, on approaching the Shawpoor Pass, received such intelligence of the appearance of the enemy, said to be in possession of it, that he thought it expedient to await the arrival of additional force, for which he accordingly applied to Colonel Adams. Major Cumming was immediately detached with another squadron of the 7th, and four more companies of infantry with two guns. On their junction, the combined detachment ascended, and proceeded without molestation towards Beitool. Major Mac Pherson, who was on the 24th at that place, arrived with one battalion, one squadron, and two guns, at Meisdee on the 27th, to recover from the enemy that part of the Ceded Countries for which he was appointed a Commissioner. From Nagpoor, Captain Hamilton, likewise charged with the regulation of Ceded Territory above the Ghats and in the direction of Deoghur, proceeded on the 20th of July towards that quarter, with an irregular battalion, three hundred reformed horse, and two hundred regular Sepoys, with four guns. At the same time another party, under Captain Gordon, was sent to take possession of the post and district of Lanjee towards the East; while Sulabut Khan was pressed to co-operate to the westward from Ellichapoor, with what troops he could spare. A detachment, consisting of two hundred auxiliary horse, and one hundred irregular infantry, likewise marched from Nagpoor to Pandoorna. A few days afterwards, on the menacing movements of the enemy, this was augmented by a squadron of cavalry and two flank companies of infantry. A similar necessity occurred for detaching, on the 27th of July, a further reinforcement from Nagpoor, under Captain Pedlar, to join the party with Captain Hamilton at Sindwarra. This reinforcement consisted of a squadron of the 8th cavalry, with one hundred regular infantry, and five hundred of the Nagpoor auxiliary horse. These, joined to Captain Hamilton's force, made the whole detachment amount to three hundred regular infantry, an irregular battalion with four guns, a squadron of cavalry, and eight hundred horse. The remaining party at this time employed in the field, south of the Ghats, was detached from Chanda towards Chamoassee. It consisted of about two hundred men from the 1st battalion of the 11th regiment, and as many of the Nizam's irregular horse belonging to a *russalah* which had arrived, at the commencement of the monsoon, from the previous pursuit of the Peishwah. In the northern quarter, Major O'Brien, commanding at Jubbulpoor, was requested to advance as many troops as he could prudently withdraw from that station, to Chuparra. These amounted on the 6th of August, when he arrived there, to one squadron of the 8th cavalry, four companies of the 2d battalion of the 8th, and 1st battalion of the 10th Bengal Native infantry, and ninety Rohillah horse; while Captain Roberts's Rohillah cavalry were distributed between Chouraghur, Barra, and Tuttypoor, supported by the troops at Garurwarra and Sohagpoor.

March of Brigadier-general Doveton's Light Force from Jalnah to Ellichapoor.

(Map VII.)

By such extensive demands on the troops at the capital, their strength had been reduced to so low an ebb, that any further deduction was considered imprudent. For, at this time, there was sufficient reason to be convinced, that in Nagpoor as strong a party existed in favour of Appah Saib, as of the new Government; and that their active practices to gain an ascendancy, could only be counteracted by a commanding force. The Resident, therefore, considered himself justified in addressing a requisition to Brigadier-general Doveton for the advance of a portion of the Hydrabad Division, on Ellichapoor, to restore a predominancy to the British interests. This they had certainly now lost, through a considerable portion of the Nagpoor and Ceded territories. The Brigadier-general, accordingly, marched on the 7th of August from Jalnah, with a troop of horse-artillery, the 3d regiment of Native cavalry and gallopers, four foot-artillery guns, five companies of the Royal Scots, and the 1st battalion of the 3d, 1st battalion of the 12th, and 1st battalion of the 16th light infantry corps; and took the high road to Ellichapoor by the Lackenwarree Ghat. He had detached, two days previously, in his front, the 6th cavalry, with orders to march direct on Nagpoor by Meiker. Lieutenant-colonel Heath's detachment, which, in the month of June, was left north of Nusserabad, being likewise in motion at the same time, was directed to march by Mulkapoor to join Brigadier-general Doveton on his route to Ellichapoor. A minute relation of the hardships and privations suffered by these troops would convey no instruction, and therefore will not be attempted. As their march was considered indispensable, their sufferings were unavoidable. The guns, equipage, and baggage, were continually falling in the rear; and every comfort, at the time most necessary, was entirely wanting. Under the same circumstances in Europe, cover of some description would be found in towns and villages; but in India, if the tents are detained in the rear, the troops necessarily remain exposed. Nor is there any remedy, as the villages are small, the houses incapable of containing more than their proper inhabitants, and large public edifices are no where existing to supply the deficiency. But even were the case otherwise, the customs of the inhabitants are such, that any attempt to enter their dwellings would cause all the villages, on the line of march, to be abandoned, and excite the hostility of the whole country. Cases must, no doubt, occasionally arise, beyond the reach of human foresight; but the events of this war have sufficiently shewn, were the caution necessary, how indispensable, previous to the assumption of monsoon quarters, is the provision for the contingencies of the inclement season. This subject cannot be too forcibly impressed on the minds of those with whom rests the dispositions for the defence of the country. If not destined to share the hardships of the troops, caused either by their mistakes or neglect, they will find the less room for self-esteem, when enjoying comparative comfort. The distress and difficulties of the force under Brigadier-general Doveton at length arose to such a height as to force him to halt at Akolah, from the 15th of August; for, in fact, the roads were completely impassable. After a few days the movement was recommenced; but on coming to the Poornah, the roads were again found impracticable for wheel-carriages of any description. He now pushed on with the troops alone, leaving all the park and artillery on the right bank of the river; and arrived at Ellichapoor on the 3d of September.

Detention of this Reinforcement by inclement Weather

In the mean while the destination of the 6th cavalry was changed to Pandoorna, and on the 19th the 1st battalion of the 16th regiment was sent from Akolah to join it. Both corps were the next day at Mortizapoor, and continued their march together without further interruption. A detachment of Berar troops closed in likewise on the Nagpoor territory, by Captain Doveton's march, on the 15th of August, from Risoor to Oomrouttee. He commanded eight companies of infantry, with two field-pieces, and six *russalahs* of irregular horse. Lieutenant-colonel Heath overtook the ordnance park on the river, and continuing his march with it, by slow degrees, arrived after several days halt, on the 13th, at Ellichapoor. He had sent forward the 7th cavalry and flank companies of the Madras European regiment, which joined Brigadier-general Doveton's head-quarters on the 11th. On the 14th, four companies of the Madras European regiment, and the 2d battalion of the 17th regiment *, from Lieutenant-colonel Mac Dowell's camp on the Panjun *nullah*, arrived together at Ellichapoor. Here they were weather-bound again, though nearer the scene of action than when above the Berar Ghats. The Nuwaub's contingent, which made a few marches at the requisition of Mr. Jenkins, was for the same reason obliged to halt, after having had its ammunition and equipage entirely destroyed.

Destruction of the Enemy's Garrison of Mooltye (Map VIII.)

The first object of the detachments which ascended the Ghats from Hoossingabad and the Wurdah, was the expulsion of the enemy from Mooltye, which they had seized from a party of Sebundies, on the 8th of August, in the face of a respectable detachment at Beitool. The combined parties of Majors Cumming and Mac Pherson, arrived before the place several days previously to Major Munt, who commanded the 6th Madras cavalry, and was directed to advance there, instead of halting at Pandoorna. As Major Cumming approached Mooltye, he sent on a reconnoitring party of a troop of cavalry, who, on the 18th, were encountered near that place, by a body of horse and foot, which came out to oppose them. The horse,

* This division of the Madras European regiment had arrived at Jalnah before the monsoon, for the relief of one wing of the Royal; but these were likewise detained on account of the demand for troops in advance.

in numbers about three hundred, were soon dispersed, with thirty killed; and a few discharges from the field-pieces induced the infantry to withdraw into the fort. The rest of the detachment arrived on the 20th; but the Major did not hold himself strong enough either to attack or to invest this position, as his troops were much exhausted and reduced by sickness. He, therefore, awaited the arrival, from Nagpoor, of the further reinforcement, under Captain Baker, of one squadron, half a battalion, and two guns, which marched early in this month for Pandoorna. The garrison were not, however, disposed to expect that occurrence; and, on the morning of the 23d, evacuated both fort and town, to join their party where it was more secure. The place was occupied, after the day broke, by a British detail; and a detachment was formed to pursue the fugitives in a north-easterly direction. Captain Newton, the commander, had a squadron of cavalry, and a company of light-infantry, for this service, on which he moved on the night of the 23d. Early on the following morning, after a march of twenty miles, he discovered the enemy, amounting to about one hundred and fifty horse, and two hundred foot, on the opposite side of the Bell *nullah*, near Hurna. This, though deep, the squadron immediately crossed, undiscovered; and as soon as it gained the opposite bank, Lieutenant Lane, commanding, formed it for a charge, which instantly followed. The result was complete. One hundred and seventy-one were killed on the spot, and many of those who escaped must have carried off severe wounds. While this example was made of one party of the enemy, another was overtaken, about twelve miles north of Mooltye, by a squadron under Lieutenant Ker, who likewise destroyed about fifty of them.

Capt. Gordon's successful Attack of Compta.

The enemy were at this time in possession of the fort of Compta, from whence they overran all the neighbouring country. Captain Gordon, who was on the march to occupy that place and Lanjee, found a body of four hundred men, Mussulmans, Gossyes, and Mahrattas, drawn up, to oppose him, behind a deep *nullah*, near the village of Nowurgaum. He accordingly left his treasure, and provisions, under the protection of twenty-five regulars, all his matchlocks and his gun. With the remainder, consisting of twenty-five of the 6th Bengal cavalry, two hundred and twenty-five regular infantry (of which two hundred were of the newly-raised Nagpoor brigade), and six hundred irregular horse, he advanced against the enemy, who had good cover in the ravines, connected with the bed of the *nullah*. They fired at each other for about a quarter of an hour; after which, the horse, in two parties, plunged into the stream, and gained the enemy's rear. The infantry, in the mean time, forded in front, carrying their cartridge-boxes and musquets on their heads, to save them from the water. About one hundred of the enemy were killed, and some prisoners were taken. From them it was ascertained, that they were strangers, who had been engaged, in the service of Appah Saib, by his agents in the city of Nagpoor. This success was obtained with the loss of no more than four Sepoys. Captain Gordon's progress towards Compta continued to be so much impeded by the weather, that he was unable to arrive there before the middle of September. He was then reinforced by two companies of the 1st battalion of the 1st Native infantry, under Lieutenant Thulier, sent from Nagpoor to overtake him. As, in the mean while, the enemy had extended a chain of posts from Ambaghur to Chandpoor, Rampylee, and Sahungurree, a second detachment* was sent out, under Major Wilson, on the 17th. His instructions were to attack and dislodge all the enemy's parties along his route, to the most distant point of their line. But Captain Gordon proceeded to the attack of Compta, before the arrival of the Major; and his dispositions for this purpose were carried into execution at day-break of the 18th. The town of Compta is surrounded by a wall and partial ditch, and contains a small *ghurrie*, like most other Mahratta towns. To attack the town, in the first instance, the force was divided into three parties, of which the left, under Lieutenant Thulier, was composed of one hundred and sixty Madras Native infantry, and two hundred of the Nagpoor brigade, The centre party consisted of a company of the same brigade, and a gun; and the right, of matchlock men, under a Native Chief, named Appah Annund Rao. The left column was provided with fascines, carried by every second man; and as they approached the ditch of the town, which was very contemptible, these were precipitated into it, and the troops passed over without difficulty. After entering the *pettah*, they separated into two parties. One of these took the right, and the other the left, and drove the enemy before them with much gallantry and some loss; while the fugitives, who took to the plain, were intercepted by the irregular horse, from whom they suffered considerable injury. The enemy had two bat-

* This consisted of five companies of the 2d battalion of the 1st regiment, a strong company of the depôt corps, and a complete squadron of the 6th Bengal cavalry.

teries in the town; one of which was opposed to the centre party, and the other to that on the right. Both these were stormed, as soon as the left column got into the town. The *ghurrie*, alone, now remained to be reduced; and a gun was brought up to the gate to blow it open; but this failing, an elephant took its place, and forced open the outer barrier. There was still, however, another gate; but while the assailants were devising the means of forcing that, likewise, the garrison surrendered, on the promise of personal safety. This was a very important success, as the Killedar had much influence over several of the remaining garrisons of this quarter, whose submission he immediately promised. The number, stated to have been in the town, is probably overrated at two thousand men, of whom the loss was estimated at four hundred. The number of British troops killed and wounded amounted to sixty-one.*

Major Wilson's successful Attack of Ambaghur.

On the 24th of September, six days after this event, the detachment commanded by Major Wilson arrived in the neighbourhood of Ambaghur; and he proceeded to reconnoitre the place, which was garrisoned by five hundred men. This fort, situate on a hill, is surrounded, to a considerable distance, by a thick jungle; but, in its immediate vicinity, on the south and east sides, there is a cultivated valley, half a mile broad. The hill on which the fort stands, is covered with wood, which conceals the dependant village at the bottom, and several posts with guns, which the enemy had established to command the inferior plain. The camp was pitched out of range of cannon shot, and the detachment was divided into two parties, of which one was destined to cover a close reconnoissance. This consisted of a troop of cavalry and half of the 2d battalion of the 1st Madras Native infantry, of which the light company was advanced in small parties *à la débandade*, while the remaining three formed a reserve to it. The enemy retired before these dispositions at the foot of the hill, after giving an ineffectual fire and abandoning a few small guns, and extended themselves on an eminence, connected by a barrier with Ambaghur. The reconnoissance ascended the principal hill; and establishing itself near the gate of the fort, was interposed between the place and the enemy on the other eminence, who had evidently adopted that position for the security of their retreat. This *demonstration* of abandoning Ambaghur, where a few men

---

* Vide Appendix. Y.

still remained, induced Major Wilson to order up the pioneers with scaling-ladders and axes, while he brought forward the remainder of the detachment. Before these could arrive, the garrison had already made their sortie through the opposite sallyport; and the wicket of the near gate having been cut open, the reconnoitring party were in possession. This place was thus obtained, without bloodshed, by twelve o'clock, and the detachment was available for the further duty it was ordered to perform.

Major Wilson's successful Attack of Pourree.

Nothing extraordinary, however, occurred before the 7th of October; when Major Wilson came before Pourree, and made his arrangements to examine the enemy's position, while he was expecting a reinforcement from the rear. But here, as in the former instance, the reconnoissance terminated in a successful assault. This place consisted of a partially walled town, having the gate on the north-west side; and in the opposite quarter a *ghurrie*, in a dilapidated state. On the south side ran the Wyne Gunga; where was a ferry of difficult access, except through the town. A ridge of earth covered the north side; and behind it the enemy were drawn up with a few small guns, as the detachment made its dispositions. The infantry were in two parties, of which that on the right was the 2d battalion of the 1st regiment of Madras Native infantry, and the 6th cavalry were opposite the gate; while the Moghul horse were destined to pass round the town, on the enemy being dislodged. When the detachment advanced, their opponents fled into the town, and were pursued through the streets, at the same time that the cavalry were let in through the gate by the infantry, who had passed over the inferior impediments. They made no further resistance elsewhere, but fled towards the ferry; and the *ghurrie* was scaled, as the Moghul horse were endeavouring to overtake the fugitives, having forced a barrier-gate. In this, however, they failed, from the intricacy and difficulty of the avenues; but, a small party of them arriving at the edge of the ferry, a few of the enemy were there destroyed; and two boats, which were overloaded by the eager crowd, sunk with about forty of them, who were all drowned. Their entire loss was estimated at about one hundred and fifty. That of the detachment amounted to twelve killed and wounded. The operations, in this direction, were nearly terminated by these successes; notwithstanding which, Major Wilson received from Nagpoor, where already a wing of the Madras European regiment and the 1st battalion of the 3d Madras Native infantry had arrived on the 2d of October, a reinforcement of two companies of that corps, which marched on the 4th from the capital. With these he proceeded immediately against Barhampoorree and Sahungurree, which severally submitted on his approach. Purtabghur had been, in like manner, reduced, on the approach of Captain Gordon's detachment, on the 21st of October. As this fort was found in good repair, and well supplied with water, which rendered it of importance for occupation, it was, from want of regular troops, entrusted to some irregulars of Beekrah, a Takoor chief, who had shewn himself staunch to the new Government, notwithstanding the threats of Chyne Shaw, a partizan of Appah Saib, of much influence in the country.

Evacuation of Amlah before Captain Jones's Detachment

These successes, to the eastward, had all the effect that could be expected; and the expulsion of the enemy from places on the plain, reduced them to considerable distress. All the cattle and provisions, which they had originally carried off from the villages of the more open country, were now expended; and for some time they had been obliged to gain subsistence by making excursions to the vicinity of the British posts. To check these, the troops were on the alert, and since the arrival of Major Munt's detachment on the 9th of September at Mooltye, there were sufficient troops for this purpose, as Major Cumming's detachment was by this time enabled to return to Beitool. Previously, however, to his countermarch, a detachment under Captain Jones, of the Bengal Establishment, consisting of a squadron of cavalry and two companies of infantry, was sent to dispossess a body of five hundred of the enemy, of the post of Amlah, about twelve miles north-west of Mooltye, before which it arrived at eight o'clock in the morning. This *ghurrie*, contemptible as a place of strength, owing to the dilapidated state of its walls, was, however, situated between two deep *nullahs*. These suddenly beginning to fill, as soon as the detachment crossed, Captain Jones was apprehensive of being cut off from his baggage before he had completed the projected service. He therefore preferred to re-cross the *nullah*, and encamp out of reach of the fire of the garrison, rather than to attempt an assault by a *coup de main*, and accordingly remained inactive throughout the remainder of the day. During the night, however, the enemy lost confidence, knowing the weakness of their position. They also, probably, imagined that additional force was coming against them; for they evacuated before day-break, when the place was peaceably occupied by the British troops.

Major Bowen's successful Attack of Boordye.

A similar party of the enemy had taken possession of Boordye, within sixteen miles of Mooltye. From thence Major Bowen was detached in the middle of September, in quest of them, with a squadron of cavalry, and one hundred light-infantry. He found the enemy drawn up in front of the village prepared to receive him. Having placed a half squadron on each flank, in this order he advanced, directing the cavalry to pass round the village, when, with the light-infantry, he should charge in front. This manœuvre had the desired effect. The charge of the infantry drove the enemy through the street, and the cavalry were ready to take them up on the opposite side, where about three hundred were *cut up*, and a lasting effect produced by so signal an example.

Lieutenant Cruickshanks's successful Excursion into the Hills.

This event was followed by Lieutenant Cruickshanks's excursion, who, with a detachment consisting of one hundred and eighty infantry, fifty of the 7th Bengal cavalry, and eighty Rohillah horse, marched, on the 20th of September, from Dorol, to surprise some distant posts of the enemy among the hills. After an almost unremitting march of thirty hours, he arrived near Juna-Ghurree. There he found the chief, Dajee, with three hundred and fifty* men in front of the village. This post was situate in a deep valley, to which the only access for troops is through the opening by which the detachment entered. There, two difficult *nullahs* run parallel to their front, within range of their fire, which consisted of ginjauls and matchlocks. The same manœuvre which had been practised by Major Bowen, was here adopted. The regular cavalry were sent to the right, the Rohillahs to the left, and the infantry crossed the *nullahs* in front. The enemy were driven through the village, and endeavoured to gain the hill in the rear; but the horse intercepted and destroyed about two hundred and fifty. Lieutenant Cruickshanks burned their cantonments, and marched on another body, distant three miles, which, in advancing, he had passed on his right. This body was commanded by a chief named Gubba, who occupied a village on the side of a mountain. While the enemy opened their fire, the infantry of the detachment divided into two parts; one of which ascended the hill from the left, while the other advanced in front. The cavalry, at the same time, were held in reserve, to act according to circumstances. But the enemy had been, on this occasion, too prudent to trust themselves in the plain; and on being nearly

* There were originally five hundred; but the Ghoands, amounting to one hundred and fifty, fled on the first appearance of the detachment.

approached, fled up the mountain, and abandoned their store of provisions, their plunder, and two ginjauls. Both these services being accomplished, with scarce any other loss than that of Lieutenant Lane, of the Bengal cavalry, wounded, the detachment returned to its position, having marched forty miles in thirty-eight hours, and performed the services which have been described.

Arrival of Cheettoo Pindarry at Patchmurree.

Under these circumstances, and as the season for penetrating the hills was yet distant, both parties had abundant leisure to make their dispositions for what was expected as the final operation. But the Ex-Rajah, and his adherents, were probably much discouraged by their late reverses; and the difficulties they continued to experience in procuring subsistence, rendered their situation distressing. Yet Appah Saib still had his emissaries employed in increasing the number of his troops, to prevent the junction of whom was the natural concern of the British posts: as by their means he might be more in a condition to undertake excursions, or even to force his way out of the circle within which he was invested. Of the small parties which contrived to evade the posts, necessarily at a considerable distance from each other, there was probably little information; but in the middle of October, a more important body was reported to be crossing the *cordon*, and excited an attention proportionate to its consequence. The intelligence was, however, too late; and a party of about seventy followers of Cheettoo Pindarry, succeeded in joining the Ex-Rajah from the westward, through the jungles about Asseer *, and thence by a north-eastern road to Patchmurree. Where this marauder had secreted himself since his expulsion from Malwah by Sir John Malcolm (p. 269), is of little importance; though it may be inferred that he had lain about the Sautpoorra hills and jungles, under cover of Bajee Rao's army and the fort of Asseerghur, till he found a convenient opportunity of sallying forth. At the same time a *demonstration* was made on the British posts on the south side of the Mahadeo hills, which, from the coincidence of time, might be imagined to be intended as a diversion in favour of Cheettoo's junction. The enemy had effected an understanding with some persons in Deoghur, already an English post, which was even in the rear of some other positions, and of Sindwarra, whither Captain Pedlar's detachment had marched

* This place should not be confounded with that of the same name near Boorhaunpoor.

in August. For the execution of their design of gaining Deoghur, they assembled at Lonadye, a village ten miles distant, in a westerly direction. A detachment advanced against them under Captain Cuffley, while Captain Pedlar and Lieutenant Cameron proceeded to Deoghur, where a European officer was established in charge of that post, to prevent the recurrence of future treachery. This movement dispersed them. Captain Cuffley burned their cantonments on the 15th of October; the other officers took several prisoners; and it was concluded that none of the remainder returned to Patchmurree.

Unsuccessful Efforts of the Ghoands North of the Hills.

The enemy, seeing no further prospect of success to the southward of the hills, turned their efforts to the northern side, on which Colonel Adams had encamped his head-quarters, with two hundred cavalry, two hundred infantry, and four horse-artillery guns, with a few Rohillahs, at Sindkeir, in the middle of November. On the 23d of that month, Chyne Shaw, the Ghoand chief, suddenly appeared before Chouraghur, with two thousand followers, who surrounded the place, in the hopes of intimidating the garrison, which consisted of no more than a Native officer and thirty men. These, however, maintained a good countenance, and during twenty-four hours, deterred the enemy from an assault, by a constant fire of such guns as were on the walls. Their situation, in the mean while, was made known to Lieutenant-colonel Mac Morine, who immediately detached a relief of two hundred infantry and fifty Rohillahs, under Lieutenant Brandon. This officer, by a diligent march, arrived there in time on the 24th, and found the enemy drawn up to receive him. He formed his men against these formidable odds, and commenced his attack by five volleys, which had the effect he expected, of producing a certain degree of irresolution; of the indications of which he took advantage, by instantly charging with the bayonet. The success of this measure was proved in the destruction of one hundred and fifty of the enemy, with little comparative loss. They never returned again to the attack of the fort; in which a reinforcement having been placed by Lieutenant Brandon, he returned with the rest of his detachment to his head-quarters. Their next appearance was in the neighbourhood of Futteepoor, in the beginning of December, which immediately claimed the attention of Captain Roberts, commanding a detachment at Sohagpoor. He, accordingly, marched against them with a party of Rohillah horse. Finding these insufficient for his purpose, he was obliged to suspend his attack, till the arrival of some infantry and guns on the 8th, when a few discharges from the artillery, which the enemy stood till they found themselves within reach of grape, effected their dispersion.

Last Efforts of Appah Saib at the close of 1818

As a last resource, the Ex-Rajah was engaged in practices among the British troops, to suborn their allegiance; but in this he had little more success than Bajee Rao on a previous occasion. Two or three men of the 6th Bengal cavalry went over to him, and sent invitations to others in that regiment to join them; but the bearers of their letters were detected; and though these were subsequently delivered, with a view to ascertain the sentiments of the parties to whom they were addressed, they produced no impression; and the only answer the messengers received was: not to return, as such communication was calculated to endanger the lives of those whose names were introduced. Notwithstanding the satisfactoriness of this experiment, the Resident deemed it advisable to require the removal of this corps from Nagpoor, where Appah Saib had so large a party. It, accordingly, changed position to the Beitool district, with the 6th Madras cavalry, which arrived at the capital on the 4th of January. The other movements which affected the power of the new Government towards the end of 1818, was the arrival, from Chanda, of half of the 1st battalion of the 11th Madras Native infantry, at Nagpoor, on the 8th of November; and this was followed by other changes of less importance. On the 27th of December a detail of artillery and two six-pounders marched to relieve a similar party of the Bengal Establishment, in the Chaoteesghur district; and next day the remainder of the 2d battalion of the 1st Native infantry proceeded to join its battalion head-quarters at Pourree. On the 31st of December Major Wilson returned to Nagpoor with the infantry portion of his detachment, excepting some parties left on the Wyne Gunga, at Ambaghur, Pourree, and Barhampoorree, by the 2d battalion of the 1st regiment; and at Wyratghur by the 1st battalion of the 11th Native infantry. The squadron of cavalry had previously returned, as had, likewise, Captain Gordon's detachment, after taking possession of Lohargurree and Dungurghurree, and leaving small garrisons in Compta and Lanjee. This would be the proper place for taking a summary view of the operations of Captain Moxton's detachment in Chaoteesghur, and of Captain Saunders's detachment in the Chanda district, were they immediately connected with the defeat of Appah Saib's active adherents. But in fact they were more directed to the establishment of the new order of things, than to the expulsion of the ostensible enemy; and, in some instances, even to the subjugation of parties, that had been equally hostile to the Ex-Rajah during his government.

Combined Dispositions for his Attack and Interception.

With the beginning of the year 1819, were proposed to be undertaken the combined movements into the hills, which should close this long protracted struggle. Three detachments were destined to enter from the northern points of [illegible] Garurwarra, and Chuparra, two from the southern points of Mooltye and Deoghur, while Brigadier-general Doveton, leaving a detachment in Berar, should ascend, with the rest of his force, the Dhoolghat to Jilpy-Aumneir on the Taptee, to intercept the enemy, should they attempt to gain Asseerghur. (Map VII.) In pursuance of this arrangement, Brigadier-general Doveton marched, on the 21st of December, from the vicinity of Ellichapoor, leaving under Lieutenant-Colebrooke, for the protection of Berar, the galloper battery, three troops of the 2d Native cavalry, and the Nuwaub Sulabut Khan's cavalry and infantry. Instead, however, of ascending the Injardie hills, with his whole force, he halted at Warkeira, on arriving there on the 30th of December; and on the 2d of January detached Lieutenant-colonel Pollock, with three troops of the 2d Native cavalry, the Wallajahbad light infantry, one company of the 2d battalion of the 17th regiment, three companies of pioneers, and one hundred horse and one hundred and fifty foot of the Ellichapoor contingent, to take possession of Jilpy-Aumneir, and make the proposed dispositions. This detachment ascended the Dhoolghat, and arrived, through a wild uncultivated country, on the 6th of January at noon, before the fort. This was held by a body of armed men, who had seized it during the prevailing anarchy throughout the Cessions to the British Government and its allies.

Siege of Jilpy-Aumneir by Lieutenant-col. Pollock's Detachment. (Plan 35) (1, 2, 3)

Jilpy-Aumneir, situate at the confluence of the Taptee and Gurgah rivers, is washed on two sides by their waters; on a third, is a deep and difficult ravine; and on the fourth side, where is the entrance, is a double line of works; and in front of them, a stockade. This face, which is shorter than the other three, is that alone towards which the access is easy; and it was selected to be attacked, as the garrison refused to submit, and the walls were too high for an escalade. A few scattered houses, called the *pettah*, are near the bank of the Taptee, from one hundred to one hundred and fifty yards from the north face of the fort; and about two hundred yards from the south-east angle, on the bank of the Gurgah, is a building called the *Dargah* (a Mahomedan mausoleum). Of these two positions, the

possession was taken, without difficulty, on the day of arrival; while the camp was established about six hundred yards in the rear, stretching from one river to the other. Next day, a disposition was made for completing
(A.) the investment of the place. For this purpose, a picket of cavalry and infantry was thrown across the Gurgah, opposite the fort, at a village called the Shar; and the Ellichapoor contingent was, in like manner,
(B, B, B.) placed across the Taptee, on the 8th; for both these rivers were fordable near their confluence. The object of these arrangements, as well as of a six-pounder battery constructed, on the night of the 9th, in front of the *pettah*, was to induce the garrison to surrender, before the arrival of the additional guns and troops expected from Jalnah; and the positions of the several posts were such, as to impede the communication of the garrison with the
(I.) rivers. On the 10th, a gun opened on the defences about the gateway;
(1.) which being but thin, were easily damaged. Grape was also fired in the same direction, occasionally, to increase the annoyance. On the 11th, at
(C.) night, an additional battery of six-pounders was constructed; and on the following morning, it likewise opened against the defences adjoining the gateway, of which considerable masses came down. At eight o'clock, the garrison desired to have permission to retire with their arms and private property, and a parley ensued; but no more than their lives being promised them, which they refused to accept without other favourable terms, hostilities recommenced. In the evening, the most strict injunctions of alertness were given to all the posts, in the apprehension that the garrison would attempt a sortie that night; and that at the Shar was reinforced, as most likely to encounter the enemy. In the west face of the fort was a small sallyport, leading down to the Taptee by a flight of steps, which was entirely concealed from view by a thick jungle that extended also along the bank of the river. Immediately after night-fall, the garrison, in small numbers, commenced descending through this way; and by eight o'clock, were all clear of the place. From thence they silently held their way, unobserved, down the bed of the stream, and were too late discovered ascending the opposite bank. A pursuit was attempted, but it proved unavailing beyond the capture of a few prisoners; for as soon as they left the river, by the ravines which joined it, they dived into thick jungles, which effectually secured their further flight. The garrison were certainly entitled to no better terms than had been promised them; for they had delayed their offer of surrender till the arrival of the detachment under

Lieutenant-colonel Crosdill, who, as senior officer, assumed the command, and made every disposition for opening, on the following morning, the guns and howitzers which he had brought with him.

Renewal of Operations in Khandesh. (Map VII.)

It will be recollected that this officer, with the battering-train of the Hydrabad Division, was attached to the force under Colonel Mac Dowell, employed at Malleygaum immediately before the monsoon. The foot-artillery and guns had remained with him throughout that inclement season, in the expectation of further sieges, on the return of the fair weather. The detachment, on the 1st of October, moved back to Malleygaum; and there awaited the result of some negotiations with the garrison of Ummulneir, the principal refractory post in Khandesh, and the junction of reinforcements, which might render the eventual siege less tedious and destructive than had been that of Malleygaum. Ummulneir had belonged to the Peishwah, but was in immediate possession of a chief named Raj Buhandoor, who, for twenty years, had held it with a garrison of Arabs. The nature of this sort of tenure will be better understood, by observing that on Raj Buhandoor having fallen into disgrace with his Prince, he was ordered to Poonah, where it was proposed to deprive him of his *jaghire*. On leaving his fort, in obedience to orders, he gave strict injunctions to the garrison to surrender it to no one, not even to the Peishwah. This order, however rebellious, was strictly obeyed; for after the Chief had succeeded in re-establishing himself in his master's good graces, they refused to admit even him, on his return. Though he was subsequently acknowledged, they would not now permit him to surrender the place to the British Authorities, to whom he was desirous of submitting. After the failure of many attempts to purchase their submission, they were justly declared rebels, and it was resolved to suppress them. For this service there were now more Europeans than before the monsoon; for as soon as the weather had cleared sufficiently for movement, the head-quarters of his Majesty's 67th foot was put in motion, from Bombay, to reinforce the detachment in Khandesh, in the western parts of which province there was likewise employed, since June, a small detachment of that establishment, composed of four companies of the above corps, and the 2d battalion of the 5th regiment, which arrived from Soonet, under Major Jardine. The 67th arrived at Malleygaum on the 11th of November, where Colonel Huskisson, as senior officer, took the command of the force, which consisted of that corps, six companies of the Madras European regiment, and the head-quarters of the 2d battalion of the 1st regiment. To these were subsequently added part of Major Jardine's detachment, and the flank companies of the 2d battalion of the 13th Madras Native infantry, ordered from that battalion, (at this time stationed in the vicinity of Boorhaunpoor,) to overawe some Bheels who shewed a disposition towards aggression. With these additions, the force under Colonel Huskisson amounted to one thousand European foot, eight hundred Native infantry, and two hundred and fifty irregular horse, with the Bombay battering-train, and what remained serviceable of that belonging to the Hydrabad Division, the pioneers, and detail of sappers and miners. On the 25th of November, the head-quarters of the force marched from Malleygaum; and, on the 28th, came before Buhaudoorpoor. This place, though it contained but a few Arabs, was of some importance, from its strength, and from its containing the residence of a Chief of consequence, and a manufactory of gunpowder. It was, however, passed over till after the siege of Ummulneir, the object of primary consideration; before which the force encamped, on the following day, at the distance of three thousand yards, with the Boarree river intervening.

Reduction of Ummulneir, and Separation of the Field Force.

(Plan 36.)

The *ghurrie* of Ummulneir is a square of only two hundred feet; on three sides is surrounded by the town, the fourth being washed by the river Boarree, on whose left bank it is situate. The wall on this side, as well as the towers at the angles, are *revetted* with stone; but the remaining curtains are of mud, and the works generally are fifty feet high. The interior is filled up to nearly the foot of the parapet, and commands the surrounding town, which is extensive, and inclosed by a wall eight feet high, of which the river face is likewise *revetted* with stone. The gates of the *ghurrie* are three in number, and greatly out of repair, as well as a traverse, projected to cover them. On the opposite bank of the river, here two hundred and fifty yards broad, is a small eminence higher than the *ghurrie*, and therefore commanding it; so that this place might well be considered contemptible in point of strength. The garrison was summoned to unconditional surrender, nor would any attention be given to their solicitation for more specific terms. They found themselves obliged to consent, on the following day (the 30th), to what neither their force nor position could enable them to refuse; for they were only one hundred and fifty men, and all hope of escape was precluded by the posts and patroles with which they were surrounded. They deposited their arms outside of the *ghurrie*, and advanced into the bed of the river, where they were made prisoners; while the grenadiers of the 67th regiment moved across, and took possession of the place. Next day Buhaudoorpoor, which, in most respects, is the counterpart of Ummulneir, surrendered, in the same manner, to the irregular horse under Lieutenant Swanston, which were sent to demand its submission; and as there was now no further occasion for the force in its collected state, it was broken up. The head-quarters returned to Malleygaum, for the occupation of Khandesh, in which were left, of Madras corps, the 1st battalion of the 2d, the 2d battalion of the 13th, and the 2d battalion of the 14th regiments of Native infantry, with the sappers and miners, and some pioneers. The battering-train, escorted by all the Madras artillery, the detachment of the Madras European regiment, and some Native troops, marched, on the 7th of December, under Lieutenant-colonel Mac Dowell, towards Jalnah. This detachment arrived there on the 25th, and, after lodging the heavy train in store, Lieutenant-colonel Crosdill marched again on the 28th, with the whole of the artillery-men brought from Khandesh, two brass twelve-pounders, and two five-and-a-half-inch howitzers, the six companies of the Madras European regiment, and detail of pioneers, with five lacs of rupees, for the head-quarters of the Hydrabad Division, at this time on march from Ellichapoor to Warkeira. On his arrival at this place, on the 8th of January, he received further orders to continue his march, on the following day, to Jilpy-Aumneir, where he arrived, as already related, on the 12th. The fall of this place having enabled him to return immediately with his guns, he left the detachment of the Madras European regiment with Lieutenant-colonel Pollock, and rejoined, on the 21st, Brigadier-general Doveton. (Map VII.)

Having now disposed of the detachment destined for the interception of Appah Saib, should he attempt the Jilpy-Aumneir road, for the description of which disposition, a digression from the immediate operations against that Chief was found necessary, the narrative returns to the movements in the Nagpoor country, which were discontinued with the conclusion of the year 1818. On the 9th of January, the head-quarters of the Subsidiary Force, with the 6th Madras cavalry, four horse-artillery guns, the 1st battalion of the 3d, and the 1st battalion of the 11th Madras Native infantry, six hundred reformed horse, and half a company of pioneers, marched from the capital for Mooltye; and with the exception of the first of these corps, arrived there on the 15th. Major Munt, with the 6th Madras cavalry, and some irregular horse, was left in defence of the lower country; and for the

Combined Movement into the Mahadeo Hills.

(Map VIII.)

better protection of the capital, the 1st battalion of the 16th regiment was sent thither, on the 17th of January, from Mooltye, and replaced in the camp by the flank companies of the Madras European regiment. A double line of posts, chiefly of irregular horse, extended, for the interception of stragglers, from the Wyne Gunga below the Ghats, to the Machna above. For at this time it was strongly suspected that Appah Saib might endeavour, by evading his adversaries in disguise, to gain the southern part of the Nagpoor territory. On the other side of the hills, Colonel Adams took up a position at Babye; and had, with his head-quarters, about fifteen hundred men. Lieutenant-colonel Mac Morine was at Garurwarra with one thousand men, and Major O'Brien, at Lucknadaon, with the same number. Each of these corps had two six-pounders, and two five-and-a-half-inch howitzers, carried on elephants; and they commenced their march on the 2d and 3d of February. Colonels Adams and Mac Morine proceeded directly towards Patchmurree, and Major O'Brien marched on Hurrye. From this place, the Major, keeping a south-west course, which approached the other corps, encountered a body of Ghoands under Chyne-Shaw, who was himself taken, and his party dispersed. Beyond this, no other opposition was made; and while parties from Colonel Scot's force penetrated every recess of the hills from the south, in co-operation with those from the north, Colonel Adams arrived at Patchmurree, in the middle of February, when Appah Saib and his open adherents were no longer there.

Appah Saib's Escape from Patchmurree

That Chief, perceiving, at the end of the previous month, the forward state of the preparations against him, and that the season no longer opposed a barrier to their execution, adopted the measure he had, for a considerable time, contemplated. On the 1st of February he left his position, after plundering his friends the Choands of all their valuables. He passed Boarda on the 3d, accompanied by Cheettoo Pindarry; and was followed through the same place next day, by five hundred Arabs and Hindoostanees. Captain Jones, of the 7th Bengal cavalry, commanded there with a troop of that regiment, and two companies of infantry; and received timely information of the intended flight of the Ex-Rajah; but this intelligence was conjoined with such other circumstances as induced him to march immediately towards Shawpoor; by which route the fugitive was reported to be proceeding. The other road being thus left open, Appah Saib and his Pindarry allies passed the line of posts to Saolleeghur. As soon as Captain Jones discovered the deceitful part that had been acted towards him, by the *Amildar* (Native Civil officer) of Boarda, he countermarched, and intercepted the body of Arabs and Hindoostanees who formed the enemy's rear. They at first drew up to oppose him, and with the cavalry part of his detachment, he *cut up* one hundred of them, while the rest attempted a retreat. At the Dauber Ghat, they again drew up, and were attacked, with the infantry of the detachment, by which they lost one hundred men more, with some prisoners. The remainder dispersed in the jungles, and Captain Jones continued his march in pursuit of the Ex-Rajah. Lieutenant-colonel Pollock likewise received early advice of this flight; which being on a more northerly line than Jilpy-Aumneir, he immediately decided on marching to Peeplaod, where he arrived on the morning of the 4th, and occupied the point from whence the two avenues to Asseerghur branch off by Bamghur and [illegible]. A strong picket of cavalry and infantry was, likewise, posted on a road which passed the village of Eurah, two miles in his rear, and offered another road for flight to the Westward. In this state of preparation the utmost vigilance was maintained, to intercept the enemy. In the mean while, Appah Saib was pursuing his way from Saolleeghur, accompanied by his Pindarry friends, as the best guides through this wild and scarcely pervious tract; and late in the evening of the same day (4th of February) approached the picket, which turned out with great alertness. In this unexpected rencounter, he dashed his horse into a deep ravine; and made his escape with considerable difficulty, while his party dispersed and fled in every direction, pursued by the picket till the darkness rendered further exertion unavailing. A few prisoners were taken, among whom were some of the deserters from the Bengal 10th Native infantry, who had assisted in Appah Saib's escape. These, a few days afterwards, suffered the punishment due to so flagrant an instance of infidelity. A part of the cavalry were sent the next morning, in the direction of [illegible]. to ascertain if the fugitive Chief, and Cheettoo, had taken that route. Finding that place deserted by its Killedar, who was a relation of the Governor of Asseerghur, Jeswunt Rao Laar, the party countermarched to Sewul, whither Colonel Pollock also, on the night between the 5th and 6th, conducted his detachment. As this place was well situated to intercept the progress of any more of the enemy to Asseerghur, where it was concluded Appah Saib had certainly taken refuge, the Lieutenant-colonel halted for the further orders of the commandant of the division.

Brigadier-general Doveton's March to Boorhaunpoor.

Brigadier-general Doveton's head-quarters were still at Warkeira, when he received the intelligence of these movements. He had been joined, on the 27th of January, by a wing of his Majesty's 30th regiment from Madras, as a relief for the division of the Royal Scots, at this time in camp. These were accordingly put in motion, the next day, by the route of Jalnah, where they were to be joined by the 2d battalion of the 14th regiment of Native infantry, from Malleygaum. This corps, which had been left in Seindwah by Sir Thomas Hislop, suffered so severely from fever, that it was withdrawn to Malleygaum, to rescue its remains from destruction. There its sickness continuing unabated, it was ordered to return within the British territory; and at this time had but a few men fit for duty. Few, however, as they were, Brigadier-general Doveton considered them a necessary addition to his force, under the new course of events. He likewise countermanded the march of the Royals, whom he directed to escort the battering-train from Jalnah to Boorhaunpoor. There he arrived, with his own force, on the 14th of February, to await the ascertainment of the actual conduct of Jeswunt Rao Laar, with regard to the cause of Appah Saib. In this suspense the narrative will leave him, to conclude this Chapter with a summary reflection on the many events with which it has been crowded.

Reflections on the Events described in this Chapter

It will be difficult now to say, whether expectations of assistance from other Powers were entertained by Appah Saib, when from the heart of his jungles he sent out his parties to take possession of the surrounding country. This probably would not have been left at his mercy, by any military man, accustomed to reflect on the occupation of a conquered territory. The dispositions made by Brigadier-general Smith, in the Poonah territory, immediately previous to the monsoon (p. 315), form a striking contrast to the absence of a similar measure in the Nagpoor country; which was equally dependent on the British means for its defence, and ultimately required the co-operation of troops, which might have been more than sufficient, with other dispositions. If a contempt of the enemy caused this neglect, the result will agree with what is generally inculcated, as the usual consequence of such an opinion of an adversary. At the same time, it must be allowed, that Appah Saib's subsequent conduct very much justified the contempt both of his means and his judgment. Every project he pursued appeared the result of miscalculation; and its easy defeat exhibited his entire ignorance of the means possessed by the British Government.

There is, in fact, some difficulty in comprehending distinctly the conduct of his parties. They offered themselves freely, on several occasions, to the attack of the British detachments sent against them, when the numbers were nearly equal, without appearing to have made any provision for their retreat. Though they were necessarily beaten by disciplined troops, they continued to try the chance of combat in a manner unaccountable, considering the diminution they were reported to have invariably sustained, and the little loss they caused to their assailants. These unsuccessful efforts would soon convince Appah Saib of the inefficacy of a further struggle. He probably contemplated those encounters only as the means of amusing his enemies, till a fit occasion offered for his escape. For this purpose, he wisely availed himself of the services of the Pindarries, who were well acquainted with the needful stratagems, and the nature of the country to be passed. Under their guidance, he was enabled to traverse one of the wildest tracts in India. But he deferred adopting this measure till long after the opening of the season had exposed him to the liability of being attacked; and he might have deemed the delay of the British movements extraordinary, when he left Patchmurree, on the 1st of February, fifteen days before Colonel Adams's arrival. The period of combined movement, on that place, was originally fixed for the 1st of January, instead of the 2d of February, when it actually commenced. The postponement has been attributed to the preparations necessary for carrying, on elephants, the ordnance attached to the three columns advancing from the northward. This would certainly be worthy of much regret, were there reason to suppose that an earlier movement would have surprised Appah Saib; but there is no ground for that opinion. His intelligence was necessarily correct; and ever since the end of October, when joined by Cheettoo, he may be considered as prepared to fly on the day of combined movement. Whatever inconvenience, therefore, belonged to the delay of advancing against him, was principally the loss of time, with the evils attending the suspense in which the minds of the inhabitants were held, during a state of things so inconclusive. Any observations which can now be made, on the inefficacy of guns, on that occasion, are liable to be considered as derived from the subsequent knowledge of facts then uncertain; for there are many cases in which great sagacity is required to judge of the propriety of dispensing with their aid. They are at times positively prejudicial; but few officers, long accustomed to use them, will voluntarily deprive themselves of the security against a reverse which they confer, to promote the certainty of a success which they impede. The fate of Appah Saib and Cheettoo remains to be related hereafter; but its wretchedness will be easily conceivable. The influence of the British Government in India being parallel to that of the Romans during their prosperity throughout the known world of their day, no enemy to its interests has better means of concealment, or of escape, from its power, than were permitted by the vindictive perseverance with which those despots unerringly pursued their victim.

CHAPTER XI.

TERMINATION OF THE WAR.

State of Scindiah's Dominions. Siege of Gurrakota by the Saughur Force. Defeat of Dhokal Sing's Party by Scindiah's Contingent. Bajee Rao's March through Malwah. March of the Mhow Field-Force to Asseerghur. Assembly of Troops and Ordnance for the Siege. Description of the Fortress of Asseerghur. Assault of the Pettah. Opening of the Batteries. Final Positions of both Camps, and Plan for the Siege of the Upper Fort. Reduction of the Lower Fort. Operations confined to the East and West Attacks. Successful Prosecution of the Siege. Distressed Condition of the Garrison. Negotiations for a Capitulation. Surrender of Asseerghur. Loss of the Enemy, and Recapitulation of the British Forces. British Loss, and Reflections on the Reduction of Asseerghur. Separation of the Force. Considerations on the Result of the War, as it affected the Peishwah. As it affected Scindiah. Holkur. Bhooslah. Rajapoots. Nizam. The Pindarries. Trimbuckjee. Recapitulation of British Acquisitions in the Deckan and Kokun. In Hindoostan. Military Dispositions. Considerations on their Importance. Conclusion.

THE events which occurred north of the Nerbuddah, during the monsoon, had an influence on the immediate termination of the war, so indirect, as to justify a summary description of them, till the march of those forces, which co-operated in the reduction of Asseerghur, the principal subject of this chapter. These events were chiefly, if not entirely connected with the settlement of Scindiah's distracted country; for he was then, and has since continued to be, incapable of restraining the turbulent chiefs and officers, into whose hands many of his troops and districts had fallen. For this purpose, the contingent, commanded by British officers, was kept in a state of motion during the greater part of the rainy season; and its approach, in August, to some mutinous battalions, near Seronge, had the effect of awing them into temporary order. While each Chief, of any enterprise, was endeavouring to establish a *jaghire* for himself, Arjoon Sing, who had once

State of Scindiah's Dominions.

(Map VIII.) been master of Gurrakota and Maltown, deemed the occasion of the mutiny favourable to the recovery of his former possessions, and succeeded in occupying, by stratagem, the first of those places. As Scindiah considered himself incapable of retaking it, the assistance of a Saughur force, under Brigadier-general Watson, was granted to him; and that corps came before Gurrakota, on the 18th of October, having left its cantonment on the 15th.

Siege of Gurrakota by the Saughur Force.

(Plan 37.)

Possession of the town was gained without opposition, on the day the camp was established before the fort, which is situated at the confluence of the Sonar and Guddaree rivers. These streams wash the outer wall on two sides, and towards the land is a wet ditch communicating between them. The longest dimension of this place is about nine hundred yards, and its greatest breadth three hundred. Its general figure is that of a semicircle, of which the diameter is parallel to the bank of the Sonar; and the remainder is composed of broken lines, which touch the Guddaree river, and take the general figure to which it has been assimilated. A *fausse-braye*, or outer wall, twenty feet high, runs along the bank of the river and the scarp of the ditch. This is thirty feet deep and substantially *revetted*: but, excepting in the wet season, the Sonar is easily fordable, near its junction with the ditch, to which point, moreover, a pathway leads down the bed, under cover of the left bank, on which is likewise situate the place. The interior wall, twenty-nine feet high, retains a *terre-pleine*, composed of a mass of stone and mud, varying in thicknesses from six to twenty feet; and its direction is so irregular, excepting on the Sonar side, that in few other places can its parallelism with the outer wall be traced. About sixteen hundred yards from the ditch, a wall extends between the two rivers, and is continued for the space of a few hundred yards along the Sonar. The space thus enclosed between this wall, the fort, and the rivers, is nearly waste; and a gate opens into it from the place, to which it might be denominated the esplanade, if it were rendered more level. Such as it is, Brigadier-general Watson gained easy possession of
(*A*.) it, having, on the night of the 18th, constructed a battery of two twelve-pounders on the left bank of the Guddaree, here fordable, to enfilade the wall which has been described. The camp was in rear of this battery; and the point selected for the attack was the south-east angle, where the
(*C*) ditch joins the Sonar river. On the night of the 23d, a battery for fourteen mortars and four howitzers was completed, on the left bank, and below the junction of the rivers, and was about one thousand yards from the

northern angle of the fort. On that day, likewise, two six-pounders were placed in battery, on the opposite bank of the river, to enfilade the outer (B) wall along the Guddaree; and on the 24th, a similar battery, to enfilade (D) the same wall, between the gate and the Sonar. The breaching-battery for two twenty-four pounders, four eighteen, and two twelve-pounders, was established at the distance of nine hundred yards from the point selected, (E) and was on the right bank of the Sonar. It was ready to open on the morning of the 26th; and on that of the 29th, two twenty-four-pounders opened from another battery, previously prepared, higher up the river, to (F) improve the breach, already sixty feet wide at top. During this period, the fire of the besieged had been quite contemptible, and was attended with only two casualties; but the explosion of a shell in the mortar-battery, at the mouth of the piece, on the morning of the 24th, caused the loss of several artillery-men and Natives, by firing about one hundred shells. On the evening of the 29th, the breach was reported practicable; and the storming-party was accordingly ordered for the assault, proposed to take place on the following morning. For this purpose, it was marched from the camp to a position in the vicinity of the breach, where it *bivouacked* for the night; but the garrison were not prepared to stand a storm, and sent out to demand the terms of being permitted to preserve their arms and private property, and to return to their homes. They were certainly in no condition to insist on these stipulations; but as their opposition had by no means been directed against the British Government, Brigadier-general Watson acquiesced in their demands, in preference to exposing the lives of his troops to the risk of an assault; and hostages were sent to his camp, as a security for the performance of the agreement. At seven o'clock, on the morning of the 30th of October, the garrison, which originally amounted to five hundred men, marched out for their respective homes. They were supposed to have lost near one hundred killed and wounded during the siege.

Defeat of Dhokal Sing's Party by Scindiah's Contingent.

(Map VIII.)

Gurrakota was immediately occupied for Dowlut Rao Scindiah, and the Saughur force, while returning to its former station by the way of Benaika-Pattun and Kurkaree, was engaged in settling such territory as had been disturbed by the opposition of Arjoon Sing; who, with his brothers, now shewed every disposition to conciliate the British Government, and to be satisfied with the provision due to them from Scindiah. To the contingent of this Prince, was by these means left the settlement of the remaining insubordinates of Central Malwah; as Brigadier-general Watson's head-quarters, after arriving at Saughur on the 16th, continued there during the remainder of the year. The majority of this corps, under Captain Blacker, had been posted at some distance from Gurrakota, during the siege of that place, to cut off the garrison, should they attempt a sortie with the intention of flight; but now that the business was concluded here, the contingent (Map IV.) was free to depart for other calls of the service. The most pressing of these was the arrangement of the succession of the Tributary District of Budjuntghur, in consequence of the death of Jye Sing, the late possessor. There were two competitors, of whom Dhokal Sing was the most powerful, having a force of three thousand men, chiefly Rajapoots. In order to remove his pretensions, a pension, and provision for his family, were offered to him by Scindiah's Government. As these were not satisfactory, the contingent was ordered against him, to disperse his force, and besiege his person, provided its movement were not sufficient to reduce him to accept the proposed terms. Captain Blacker marched, with that design, from Seronge to the Parbuttee, where he arrived on the 20th of November, having detached a portion of the force by Ragooghur. Dhokal Sing was, all this time, retiring before the contingent; but was stated as not being far distant when it crossed the Parbuttee, a few miles south of Ragooghur. Captain Blacker now prepared to overtake him by a forced march, and was in motion at five P. M. of the 21st; but at midnight, understanding his adversary was only a few coss in advance, he halted, in order to come upon him after day-break. Dhokal Sing was, however, again in movement, anticipating an attack, and kept his course to the westward, through a thick jungle, in which he was followed till ten o'clock of the 22d, when he was discovered, drawn up in a confined plain of difficult access, with the choice of his small body of horse and foot. At this time the majority of the contingent were far in the rear, owing to the fatigues of the march, which had been latterly much accelerated, and to the difficulty of penetrating a thick jungle in a rough country, where two horses could seldom move abreast. Those, however, which were in front, were the best, and about three hundred and fifty in number; and they were formed for action with all possible expedition. But they were not in motion sooner than the enemy, who charged with a determination that carried a few of them through their opponents, never to return. They were led by Dhokal Sing in person, who, in the conflict, received three severe wounds, which obliged him to quit the field with precipitation. This was the signal for the flight of his party, who dispersed in the jungle, and left on the ground thirty of their best men. The loss of the contingent amounted to fifty; which gives reason to conclude, that had not the adverse Chief been luckily wounded, the result of his daring conduct might have been doubtful, if not successful; for he had certainly the advantage of numbers. Unable to ride in this condition, he was carried on a litter into the heart of the hills and jungles north of Ragooghur, where he dismissed such as rejoined him, in order to elude pursuit with the more facility. The contingent having made some movements about Gogul Chuppra, to cut off his retreat beyond the Chumbul, returned towards Seronge, leaving him, in his reduced state, to the exertions of his rival.

Bajee Rao's March through Malwah

Advancing from the east to the west of Malwah, the narrative of events which succeeded the submission of Bajee Rao to Sir John Malcolm, is here resumed. Their indirect reference, indeed, to the progress of the war equally entitles them to consideration; not only as partially conjoined with the name of Bajee Rao, but, like the operations of the Saughur force, as productive of a state of comparative order, which permitted the march of the troops to a distant object. All the posts which had been established along the Nerbuddah, and the range of Ghats north of it (p. 363), with exception of the 1st battalion of the 14th regiment of Native infantry, at Mundleisur, being called in at the commencement of the monsoon; on the 22d of July, the Ex-Peishwah commenced his march for Hindoostan. He was accompanied by Sir John Malcolm's head-quarters, with one troop of the 3d Madras cavalry, the 1st regiment of Skinner's irregular horse, flank companies of the 2d battalion of the 6th regiment of Madras Native infantry, and the 1st battalion of the 8th regiment of Bombay Native infantry. The inclemency of this season might have furnished an argument for delaying the movement till the weather should clear up; but the necessity of removing Bajee Rao from a quarter where the character of Peishwah was considered with a sort of reverential awe, was paramount to every other consideration. In the neighbourhood of Indoor and Oojein, the difficulty of preventing intrigues and improper communications was early experienced, and imposed the necessity of quitting, as soon as possible, a Mahratta territory, where such was the dangerous state of ignorance in which the inhabitants were held respecting foreign transactions, that the bulk of them were yet unacquainted with the Peishwah's sad reverses. The remaining troops of this force continued at Mhow, under the command of Lieutenant-colonel Corsellis, while Sir John and Bajee Rao prosecuted their march by Nolye and Kachroad to Mundissoor, where they arrived on the 7th of August. A halt was here made till the 24th, for the completion of various arrangements. The 1st battalion of the 19th regiment of Bengal Native infantry, having then joined the detachment, Bajee Rao proceeded towards his destination, with an escort composed of that corps and Skinner's horse, commanded by Major Innes of the Bengal Establishment, while Sir John Malcolm, with the remaining corps, returned by the same road they had advanced, to the cantonment at Mhow, to await the termination of the monsoon.

March of the Mhow Field Force to Asseerghur

A general view has already been taken of the success which attended Sir John's measures, for the suppression of the lawless habits existing in the western parts of Malwah. These, however, still prevailed, to a deplorable degree, on the frontiers of Goozerat, where his exertions had not extended. That nothing might be left incomplete, he commenced, on the 1st of December, with the horse-artillery, the 3d cavalry, and the 1st battalion of the 8th regiment of Bombay Native infantry, a tour through the turbulent parts, to the westward. His progress to Rutlam was by Dhar Amgherra, Bhassawur, Jabbooah, and Petlawud; and he returned to Mhow on the 15th of January, by Budnawur and Beitmah. The fruit of this excursion was an arrangement with several of the Chiefs of the country through which he passed; and the expulsion, through negotiation, of four thousand Arabs, Meckrannees, and other mercenaries, who had actually governed and distressed those districts for several years. This source of evil removed, by the dismissal of these bands to their respective homes, the force remained in readiness for further operations, till the 12th of February; when it marched towards Asseerghur, on the intelligence of Appah Saib's flight in that direction. (Map VII.) Accordingly, on the 21st, it was at Mahurpoor; from whence Sir John repaired to B[illegible] Doveton's camp, at Calachabootra, for the purpose of a conference respecting the future operations of both forces. The immediate consequence of this visit was, the march of the Mhow force to Boorgaum, on the 24th, and from thence, by the Kuttee Ghat, to Sundlepoor, within five thousand yards of the fort of Asseer. Here Sir John's head-quarters continued till rejoined by the Bombay brigade and [illegible] which had been left in the rear; and his ground was then changed, for immediate siege, to a position north-west of the fort. While these movements took place, Lieutenant-colonel Smith, with the 1st battalion of the 14th regiment of Madras Native infantry, and Skinner's irregular horse, was engaged in closing the passes north of Asseerghur, with a view to intercept the escape of the fugitives, supposed to be concealed among the jungles near that place, if not within the walls. In the performance of this service, he made a march of thirty-five miles, on the 15th, and was nearly successful in taking Cheettoo prisoner, while his party dispersed; and Appah Saib likewise narrowly escaped, as was then supposed, into Asseerghur. He and his party were pursued to the gates of the fort, by a detachment of Skinner's irregular horse; but the fire which opened from the place prevented the enemy from being attacked in its vicinity. Many were however *cut up*, during the first surprise, notwithstanding the difficulty of the country which was passed in approaching and pursuing them.

Assembly of Troops and Ordnance for the Siege.

Jeswunt Rao Laar, the Killedar, at the same time, relied on a temporizing policy; in pursuance of which, on the 18th of February, he had sent to Brigadier-general Doveton to demand a passport, that he might wait on Sir John Malcolm at Boorgaum; but he never made use of this permission, and, on the contrary, was active in his arrangement for resistance; denying, all the while, that Appah Saib was within his fort. The delays, however, which he conceived that his duplicity produced in the operations against him, were equally useful to his enemies; who, while they sincerely pursued the way of accommodation, were gradually approached by the means of coercion, in the event of its failure. The Jaulnah battering-train, consisting of seven eighteen-pounders and two twelves, one ten-inch, three eight-inch, and one five-and-a-half-inch mortars, and two eight-inch and three five-and-a-half-inch howitzers, accompanied by two hundred men of the Royal Scots, and one hundred and sixty men of the 2d battalion of the 14th regiment of Native infantry, arrived in Brigadier-general Doveton's camp, on the 1st of March. The Khandesh force moved from Malleygaum, on the 25th of February, towards Ummulneir; and from thence detached the engineers' department, detail of sappers and miners, and eight companies of his Majesty's 67th foot, with a company of pioneers, all of whom joined on the 9th of March. Similar aid was drawn from the Nagpoor Subsidiary Force, whose head-quarters being no longer required above the Ghats, descended by the Baroolee pass, on the 26th of February, with the half troop of horse-artillery, and the 1st battalion of the 3d regiment of Madras light infantry, and arrived at the capital on the 4th of the following month, having left the 1st battalion of the

11th regiment of Madras Native infantry at Mooltye. The flank companies of the Madras European regiment had been sent off, on the 19th of February, to join Brigadier-general Doveton, from the camp; and they were joined on the march by the battering-train from Nagpoor, escorted by a company of the 1st battalion of the 1st regiment of Madras Native infantry. This reinforcement of ordnance, consisting of four eighteen-pounders, two eight-inch mortars, and two heavy eight-inch howitzers, with a company of foot-artillery and Lascars, arrived in the camp on the 11th of March; and was followed on the 17th by the Hoossingabad train, and a detachment under Lieutenant-colonel Grimstrut, of the Bengal Establishment, which had advanced by the Jilpy-Aumneir route. These consisted of a squadron of the 7th Bengal cavalry, a half company of foot-artillery and gun-Lascars, fifteen companies of Bengal Native infantry, and a company of pioneers, with two eighteen-pounders, two twelves, and two five-and-a-half-inch howitzers. As, with these reinforcements, there were abundance of means assembled for the reduction of Asseerghur, the Killedar of which had sufficiently evinced his resolution to avoid any other decision excepting that of arms, the immediate preparations were made, on the night of the 17th, for the attack of the *pettah* next day. This measure might have been undertaken at any period, since the arrival on the banks of the Taptee, and other preparatory steps might likewise have been adopted; but, as an envoy had been on his way from Scindiah, with an order for the surrender of the place, every appearance of precipitation had been avoided. The arrival of this person, and the Laar's extravagant stipulations, soon shewed the fruitlessness of further delay; for he desired that the British forces should be first removed, and that a respectable hostage should be given for his safety. Brigadier-general Doveton's camp was in reality six miles from the place, where it continued several days longer; and from thence were made the arrangements for the attack of the *pettah*. In order to render these understood, some description of the place and its environs becomes necessary; and will be related as succinctly, as the complex nature of this subject will permit.

Description of the Fortress of Asseerghur. (Plan 38.)

The upper fort, in its greatest length from west to east, is about eleven hundred yards; and in its extreme breadth, from north to south, about six hundred; but, owing to the irregularity of its shape, the area will not be found more than three hundred thousand square yards. It crowns the top of a detached hill, seven hundred and fifty feet in height, and round the foot of the wall inclosing the area, is a bluff precipice, from eighty to one hundred and twenty feet in perpendicular depth, so well scarped as to leave no avenues of ascent, except at two places. To fortify these, has therefore been the principal care in constructing the upper fort; for the wall which skirts the precipice is no more than a low curtain, except where the guns are placed in battery. This is one of the few hill-forts possessing an abundant supply of water, which is not commanded within cannon range; but it fully participates in the common disadvantage attending similar places of strength, by affording cover in every direction to the approaches of an enemy, through the numerous ravines, by which its inferior ramifications are separated. In one of these, which terminates within the upper fort, is the northern avenue, where the hill is highest; and to bar the access to the place at that point, an outer rampart, containing four casemates with embrasures, eighteen feet high, as many thick, and one hundred and ninety feet long, crosses it from one part of the interior wall to another, where a re-entering angle is formed by the works. A sallyport of extraordinary construction descends through the rock at the south-eastern extremity; and is easily blocked, on necessity, by dropping down materials at certain stages which are open to the top. The principal avenue to the fort is on the south-west side, where there is consequently a double line of works above; the lower of which, twenty-five feet in height, runs along the foot of the bluff precipice, and the entrance passes through five gateways, by a steep ascent of stone steps. The masonry here is uncommonly fine, as the natural impediments are, on this side, least difficult; and on this account, a third line of works, called the lower fort, embraces an inferior branch of the hill immediately above the *pettah*. The wall is about thirty feet in height, with towers; and at its northern and southern extremities, it ascends to connect itself with the upper works. The *pettah*, which is by no means large, has a partial wall on the southern side, where there is a gate; but in other quarters it is open, and surrounded by ravines and deep hollows, extending far in every direction.

To take possession of the town was the object of the preparations of the 17th; and the troops destined for this service were ordered to assemble at midnight, and to move out, an hour afterwards. The column of attack, commanded by Lieutenant-colonel Fraser of the Royal Scots, consisted of five companies of that regiment, the flank companies of his Majesty's 30th and 67th foot, and of the Madras European regiment, five

Assault of the Pettah.
(Map VII. Compartment)

companies of the 1st battalion of the 12th Madras Native infantry, and the detail of sappers and miners. The reserve, under Major Dalrymple of his Majesty's 30th, was composed of the remaining companies of that corps, one company of the 67th, one of the Madras European regiment, and nine companies of Native infantry, from the 1st battalion of the 7th regiment, the first battalion of the 12th regiment, and the 2d battalion of the 17th regiment, with detachments from the 2d and 7th Madras Native cavalry, and four horse-artillery guns. One hundred pioneers moved in the rear of the column of attack; and the remainder followed the reserve with the Doolies and Puckallies. The object of gaining the town was, to have a convenient position from whence, under secure cover, batteries might be erected to take off the defences, and breach the wall, of the lower fort. On this account, the necessary engineers, materials, and workmen, were attached to the attacking column. While on the southern side this disposition was made, Sir John Malcolm was directed to distract the enemy's attention on the northern side, by the operations of his force; from which he prepared, for this service, the 3d cavalry, the 2d battalion of the 6th regiment, and the 1st battalion of the 14th regiment of Madras Native infantry, the 1st battalion of the 8th regiment of Bombay Native infantry, six howitzers, and two horse-artillery guns. At the appointed hour of the morning of the 18th of March, the troops moved out of Brigadier-general Doveton's camp at Numbolah, which he had occupied since the junction of his first reinforcement; and the column of attack advanced up the bed of the Bateekeirah *nullah*, which runs parallel to the works on the southern side, till, arriving within a convenient distance of the *pettah*, it rushed in by the gate and on both flanks, overpowering every resistance on the part of the enemy. The Reserve at the same time occupied, in two parties, points of the Bateekeirah and Chaokul *nullahs*, which are parallel to each other for some distance before their junction, and sufficiently near the *pettah* to afford eventual support. On the other side of the hill, Sir John Malcolm's force was divided into parties, which occupied all the avenues in that quarter, from the Chaolkan to the Boorgaum road; and from two of these, shells and rockets were thrown into the lower fort during the attack of the *pettah*, in which the 1st battalion of the 8th regiment of Bombay Native infantry, supported by the 1st battalion of the 14th regiment of Madras Native infantry, was especially employed. The troops, on entering the town, found cover so immediately in streets running parallel to the works of the lower fort, that they suffered little loss*, notwithstanding an unremitting fire from the enemy; and Major M'Leod, the Deputy Quartermaster-general, with Lieutenant Bland of the Royal Scots, were the only officers wounded. This day's operations terminated by the recall of the troops to their respective camps, with exception of the column of attack and the 1st battalion of the 8th regiment of Bombay Native infantry, which occupied the *pettah*, a post at the Laal Baugh, and another at the Moote Baugh, where was likewise the howitzer-battery.

Opening of the Batteries.

During the course of the day, a battery for six light howitzers was completed in the *pettah*, and directed against the lower fort; and in the course of the night, an attempt was made to construct another battery for eight heavy guns, on an eminence to the left (north) of the town, and six hundred yards from the lower fort: but owing to the hardness of the ground and insufficiency of materials, the work, when half completed, was destroyed before day-light, and the materials hid in the neighbouring ravines. The streets, enfiladed by the fort, were however barricaded, and a post was established among some houses in advance of the *pettah*, which was occupied during the night; but it was deemed expedient always to withdraw the troops to the most advanced point of the town, at the approach of day-light; the flanking fire of the enemy rendering all communication with that post dangerous, except in the dark. The enemy also considered it too near them; and on the evening of the 19th, made a sally on it under cover of a fire of small arms from their walls. They succeeded in burning some of the houses; but were soon repulsed by the troops from the *pettah*. The heavy gun-battery was recommenced and completed during the night, and another, for eight mortars and howitzers, half finished immediately on the left of the *pettah*. On the 20th, the heavy gun-battery opened, at day-break; and by evening had nearly effected a practicable breach in the lower fort, as well as injured the defences of part of the upper works. The enemy, at the same time, made a bold sally into the *pettah*, and gained the main street, where they were finally repulsed; but, during this service, a deplorable loss was sustained in the death of Lieutenant-colonel Fraser, who was killed while rallying his men in the confusion attending so sudden an attack. The breach of the lower fort having be-

(I) (B) (D) (C) (B) (E.)

* Vide Appendix, Z.

come practicable, a fire was renewed every half hour during the night, to keep it open, and a working-party were engaged in completing the mortar-battery. Before day-break, on the 21st, the enemy evacuated the lower fort, but this circumstance was not then known; and at seven A. M., by an accident, the cause of which was never ascertained, the magazine in rear
(B) of the breaching-battery exploded. Unfortunately, at this moment, the relief of the covering party took place, which exposed a detachment of one hundred men of the 2d battalion of the 15th regiment of Madras Native infantry, to the effects of the explosion of one hundred and thirty barrels of gunpowder. A Native officer and thirty-four non-commissioned rank and file were killed, and another Native officer and sixty-five non-commissioned rank and file wounded. The disaster did not however extend to the battery, which recommenced firing on the enemy, who were perceived descending the hill, on witnessing what had happened. The enemy again occupying the lower fort, the fire from the heavy battery was chiefly directed towards the perfecting of the breach, and silencing the fire from the top of the hill, particularly of two large guns; one in the centre tower of
(1.) the northern face, and the other at the flag-staff bastion.

Final Positions of both Corps, and Plan for the Siege of the Upper Fort

The mortar-battery being complete, in the afternoon of the 21st, a few shells were thrown to ascertain the range, and the 2d battalion of the 13th regiment of Native infantry joined the camp from Russoolpoor. On this occasion, it was deemed necessary to change the positions of the two forces engaged in the siege; and pursuant to the arrangements for this purpose, Sir John Malcolm's division was reinforced on the 22d, and detachments from it took the duties in the *pettah;* while Brigadier-general Doveton's head-quarters were removed to a position three miles and a half north-east of Asseerghur. In the batteries, the eighteen-pounders were silent this day; and the fire was chiefly confined to the mortars, which continued to play with perseverance on the top of the hill, occasionally varying their
(1) range. One gun, in the centre bastion of the north face of the upper fort, having given considerable annoyance to the breaching-battery, an embrasure was opened to silence it, about two hundred yards to its left, during the night; and another, at the same distance on the right, to keep down a fire from small arms, behind the defences of the lower fort, at a particular spot which commanded the *pettah.* Very little interesting occurred during the 23d. Shells were still fired unremittingly, and the breach was kept open; while a howitzer remained loaded with grape in the main avenue

from the lower fort into the *pettah,* for the reception of the enemy, should they attempt a sally. The same observation applies to the service of the 24th; but on the night between that and the following day, a battery was erected three hundred and fifty yards to the left of the breaching-battery, for two eight-inch howitzers and two five-and-a-half-inch mortars. (F.) The reconnoissance of the upper fort had now been completed; and the result was, the plan of conducting the real attack against it on the east side, while a *demonstration* was made on the north side, against a point where the rock failed. Brigadier-general Doveton's personal command embraced both operations. With this view, the 25th and 26th were principally occupied in collecting the requisite materials and in making gabions. Some necessary alterations took place in the position of the park; and the firing continued the same, as for the last few days.

Reduction of the Lower Fort

The next morning, three troops of the 3d Madras cavalry, and the 2d battalion of the 6th regiment of Madras Native infantry, moved to a position at the Bateekeirah *nullah,* for the protection of the working-parties employed to the southward, which was the quarter where Sir John now commanded. A battery was also constructed on that side, to breach in a (G.) second place the lower fort; but the guns were not brought in that night. Two six-pounders were likewise carried on elephants, to a position called *Moghulka Topee* (Moguls Camp), which was subsequently reinforced by two howitzers. On the northern side, at the same time, the engineers' depôt was advanced into a garden called the Rambaugh; and in front of it a battery was thrown up for two twelve-pounders, to silence a large gun (I.) on the north-east bastion of the upper fort. A communication was likewise commenced in the direction of the proposed battery, and finished next day; while, on the southern side, the guns were brought into the new breaching- (G.) battery by creditable exertion, under a fire which did little execution, from its great elevation. On the 29th, the original breaching-battery recom- (B.) menced firing for the perfection of the breach, destined to be stormed on the following day. During the night, two more heavy guns were carried to the left, to assist in that object, as well as to destroy some remaining defences. On the southern side the four-gun breaching-battery played, throughout the day, with happy effect, and by evening, made a practicable breach in the lower wall opposite; a howitzer, to the right of it, commanding the gate of the upper fort. On this night the first ground was broken, for the eastern attack, by the construction of two batteries, one for five,

(*L, M.*) and the other for four eighteen-pounders, both of which were destined to destroy the defences of the flank, on each side of the curtain proposed to be breached. Shells were thrown incessantly into the lower fort, during the night, for the purpose of firing different buildings; and every arrangement was made for the assault on the following day, by Sir John Malcolm, to whom was entrusted the conduct of this important service. The enemy, however, despaired of a successful resistance, and early in the morning abandoned Malleeghur (the lower fort), which was occupied without opposition, at sun-rise, on the 30th, by the British troops, who advanced, under every proper precaution, to guard against a surprise. A fire opened on them from above; but, besides that its great elevation rendered it ineffectual, a reply to it from the British batteries imposed silence in a short time.

Operations confined to the East and West Attacks.

The first measure, after the occupation of Malleeghur, was the disarming of the batteries, which were solely directed against it; and as the subsequent operations against the upper fort brought the troops and working-parties within a short range of small arms, the casualties which succeeded, became more numerous than they had previously been. The two (*B, G*) breaching-batteries were, consequently, dismantled, and during the night the mortars, hitherto in the *pettah*, were brought into the lower fort. On the east side, considerable difficulty was experienced in bringing the heavy guns into the batteries prepared for them on the rocky eminences; and only (*L*) a portion of them ascended; while, on the left of one, a battery for two heavy mortars was prepared. On the 31st, however, the remaining heavy guns were brought up the heights, and opened with good effect; and in (*Q*) front of the Rambaugh, a battery was thrown up for eight mortars and howitzers. At the same time, the Kummurgah (second line of works on the west side) was assailed with shells from the north and south mortar-batteries, and from Malleeghur, and eighteen and twelve-pounders opened with equal perseverance on its defences. In the course of the day the Saughur reinforcement arrived. Brigadier-General Watson, C. B. with his staff, had come in the day before, having marched by Rasseen, Hoossingabad, and Jilpy-Aumneir, in the early part of March, as soon as the siege of Asseerghur was proposed. The troops and ordnance which accompanied him, amounted to two thousand two hundred non-commissioned rank and file, and twenty-two heavy pieces *.

---

* These were, a party of Rohillah horse, two complete companies of European and Native

On the 1st of April the firing was continued, as on the previous days, while two more heavy guns were placed in the *pettah* to annoy the Kummurgah; and during the night, a six-gun battery was constructed at the distance of six hundred yards from the north-west curtain of the upper fort. On the eastern side the eight-mortar battery opened, and a new ten-mortar battery was thrown up in the rear, and to the left of the others. Into this the mortars were brought next day (the 2d), and a magazine was established in their rear. At the same time the guns were brought into the new battery opposite to the north-west curtain, and opened at two P. M. The fire of these, on the 3d of April, destroyed the defences to the right of the intended breach on that side; but its direction against the corner tower being too oblique, two eighteen-pounders were drawn out at night to the right of the battery, and an *epaulement* was thrown up in front for a covering-party, where a new battery was proposed. On this morning the ten-mortar battery opened on the eastern side; and a battery for four additional mortars was thrown up to the right and front of this attack.

(*H*)
(*Q*)
(*P*)
(*H*)
(*P*)
(*R*)

Successful Prosecution of the Siege

So many shot had now been expended, that a common expedient in Indian sieges was resorted to for the repair of the deficiency, and a reward offered for each brought into the camp, according to its dimension, was attended with an abundant return, where camp followers were so numerous. On the 4th, the fire had so effectually destroyed the defences on each flank of the intended breach, on the eastern side, that the breaching-battery for two twenty-four, and two eighteen-pounders, was commenced immediately opposite the curtain selected. At the same time, to keep down some annoyance from the north-east tower, three eighteen-pounders were placed in battery on the right of this attack, to destroy its defences. On the *pettah* side much labour was exerted in bringing up guns to the lower fort; and to convey them from thence to a ridge on its left, a mine was commenced in the wall near its northern angle. This was successfully sprung on the morning of the 5th; and two additional eighteen-pounders were brought up that day, in consequence of which, the new breaching-battery on the advanced ridge was completed. The usual fire was kept up from guns and

(*N*)
(*S*)
(*K*)

---

artillery, the 2d battalion of the 1st regiment and 2d battalion of the 13th regiment of Bengal Native infantry, and four companies of gun-Lascars, pioneers and miners; with two twenty-four and four eighteen-pounders, two eight-inch howitzers, and three ten-inch, three eight-inch, and eight five-and-a-half-inch mortars.

mortars; and in order to keep in check the boldness of some matchlock men, from whom much annoyance was experienced in Mall[illegible]hur, where Lieutenant Hannah, of the 67th, with others, was wounded, a few good marksmen were selected, and posted in suitable situations, with entire success. On this evening, likewise, the breaching-battery newly commenced on the eastern side, was completed; and the left battery, which had hitherto fired at the defences, was advanced to become a [illegible]y.

Distressed Condition of the Garrison

While these operations against the fort were so vigorously carried on, the officer from Scindiah's court had been permitted to enter occasionally, on business supposed to be connected with the ostensible object of his mission; but latterly so little was his character acknowledged, that some of the garrison were desirous of treating him as a partizan of the British Authorities, instead of a messenger from their own Prince. In this respect, his character was as much mistaken, as his supposed powers and instructions were deceitful, which subsequent circumstances explained; but the state of the garrison had now become such, that little importance attached to the part he should act; for the cattle on the hill were starving for want of forage, and the troops, seeing the walls falling before the [illegible] batteries, began to think their own efforts useless. To this was added the extreme annoyance they sustained, from the number of shells that fell about them continually, which, though they did not produce a large amount of casualties, harassed them, and depressed their spirit of constancy. This condition of affairs was understood from a spy, who, after having been detained in irons twenty days, succeeded in making his escape, and likewise reported the great loss they had sustained, in the death of a Jemidar, who had the chief management of their artillery. Jeswunt Rao Laar, therefore, came to the resolution of opening a negotiation; and with this view, desired that an officer named Sooltaun Khan might be permitted to join him from Boorhaunpoor. But, this individual not being present, a respectable servant of the Soobahdar of that city was sent in his room; while, to convince the Killedar that the British Authorities were not to be diverted from their designs by empty *demonstrations*, a double number of shells were thrown from all the mortar batteries. This activity was followed up, on the 6th, by the completion of the new breaching-battery, on the west side, with a magazine in its rear; and on the east side by the arming with two twenty-four pounders, and two eighteen-pounders, the advanced battery prepared during the previous night. At the same time the ten-mortar battery was repaired, and a road opened from the right of the attack towards the breach. Next morning the heavy guns in three batteries opened against the curtain, and made a practicable breach in its retaining wall by evening, while, on the opposite (west) side, the new battery having been likewise armed with eighteen-pounders, fired with happy effect on the wall of the upper fort, from ten A. M. (P.) (K.)

Negotiations for a Capitulation

During the whole of these proceedings, the enemy kept up an unremitting discharge of small arms, which caused some casualties, but these not numerous; and their alarms at the consequences of an assanlt were now so pressing, that the Killedar sent out this evening two Vakeels (agents) to solicit terms of capitulation. Those which he demanded were, liberty for the garrison to preserve their arms, and to depart with their personal property; but any stipulation from him was positively rejected, and Jeswunt Rao Laar was informed in reply, that himself and the principal officers would be sent to their master, to be treated according to his pleasure, but that the troops must surrender their arms under no other assurance than that of personal security for themselves and families. Even this was made to depend on a knowledge of their conduct towards Appah Saib, who was still confidently believed to be in the fort; and the most peremptory menaces of severe execution were denounced against the garrison, if it were discovered that they endeavoured to conceal him. To support this tone, the most active labours were carried on during the night. An approach up the hill was commenced on the west side; and on the morning of the 8th all the breaching batteries of both attacks re-opened with decisive perseverance; but they received orders at eleven A. M. to cease firing, in consequence of the terms offered having been accepted. This unconditional acquiescence in them was signified however by Jeswunt Rao Laar, in order that he might repair to Brigadier-general Doveton's head-quarters, and exert his last endeavours to mitigate their inflexibility; and while he avowed his own readiness to submit to them, he declared his apprehensions that his power over the troops was insufficient to enable him to promise as much on their part. The conference was immediately suspended on this declaration; and Sir John Malcolm, who was present at it, was charged, in the Killedar's presence, with the duty of receiving the surrender of the fort in the manner directed, at six A. M. on the following morning; or in case of its refusal, or of any demur, to recommence hostilities. Orders of preparation for the renewal of the fire on the east side, in this event, were likewise issued; and the embrasures, every where, were put in a complete state of repair. Jeswunt Rao Laar unwillingly re-ascended his hill, and took leave of Sir John Malcolm, in the lower fort, under assurances of the destruction of himself and garrison, should he fail of fulfilling the terms which were the only means of escape left to him.

Surrender of Asseerghur.

These admonitions made the proper impression on his mind; for at four A. M., of the 9th, he sent down a messenger to report that the garrison were preparing to descend. This communication was followed, at five o'clock, by a proposition, that the British flag should be sent up immediately, and that the troops should surrender their arms in the *pettah;* which last suggestion probably arose out of an idea of there being less degradation in this necessity, after having evacuated the fort with arms in their hands. A union flag, protected by one hundred European and an equal number of Native infantry, was accordingly sent up, and erected on the western tower under a royal salute from all the batteries; while the guard took possession of the upper gates. Thus was Asseerghur surrendered; but the garrison did not descend till noon, when a square was formed of Sir John Malcolm's line, to ensure their submission. Brigadier-general Doveton likewise repaired to the appointed position near the *pettah*, and received there Jeswunt Rao and his principal officers, to whom he gave permission to retain their arms. After this, they were directed to bring forward their several parties in succession; and their conduct was marked by the strictest order. Each party that entered the square, grounded its matchlocks, and was permitted to retain articles of private property, shields and daggers, with the promise of a secure escort, and even of subsistence to those who were found in need. But this was all conferred as a boon from the British Government; and each body *salamed* in acknowledgment of the same, as it filed off to make room for the succeeding party. In this manner, twelve hundred Mukranees, Arabs, and Sindees, passed through the square; and the solemnity of the scene was acknowledged by all the spectators to be most impressive. The garrison were followed by numerous women and children, whom they considered perfectly secure under the promise which had been gratuitously made to them; for Appah Saib was certainly not in the fort when it surrendered; and it is still matter of doubt that he was ever admitted within the gates.

Loss of the Enemy, and Recapitulation of the British Forces.

The loss during the siege, on the part of the enemy, amounted to no more than forty-three killed and ninety-five wounded: for they fought under considerable advantages in regard to personal cover, excepting against shells; and it was not therefore owing to the diminution of their fighting men that they surrendered. By the havock made in their walls, they were reduced to this necessity; for on the eastern side the retaining wall had been destroyed, and on the western side it was ready to fall; at the same time that the collateral defences, to a considerable distance, had been completely knocked off. Such was the effect of twenty-two heavy guns, and twenty-six mortars and howitzers, in battery, in the course of eleven days of open trenches; and the ordnance equipment collected towards the end of the siege, exceeded what had, at any former period, been brought together, in the Deckan, with a British army. Had the whole force been assembled before the commencement of the siege, it would have been most suitably enumerated previous to the detail of the operations; but as several parts of it arrived at different times, and a considerable reinforcement towards the conclusion of the siege, it has appeared more convenient here to sum up their amount. Including Scindiah's contingent, which joined the army from Malwah under Captain Blacker, in time to be spectators of the fall of their master's fort, the force amounted to

Horse Artillery, one Troop and a half.
Native Cavalry, eight Squadrons.
Foot Artillery, including one Golandauze Company ... } five Companies.
European Infantry, two Battalions and a half.
Native ditto, eleven Battalions and a half.
Sappers and Miners, and Pioneers.... } thirteen Companies.
Irregular Horse, five thousand.

The ordnance-train consisted of two twenty-four pounders, twenty-two eighteen-pounders, seven twelve-pounders (of which three were brass), sixteen six-pounders, (exclusive of fourteen horse-artillery and cavalry gallopers.)

Four Ten-inch Mortars.
Eight Eight-inch ditto.
Nine Five-and-a-half-inch ditto.
Six Eight-inch Howitzers.
Two Five-and-a-half-inch heavy ditto.
Seven Five-and-a-half-inch light ditto, and
Four Four-and-a-half-inch light ditto.

The artillery was commanded by an officer of great experience, Lieutenant-colonel Crosdill, C. B., and the senior engineer was Lieutenant Coventry, of the Madras Establishment, whose skill and merits were deservedly acknowledged throughout the siege.

British Loss, and Reflections on the Reduction of Asseerghur

The loss on the British side, compared with that of the enemy, was heavy, amounting to eleven European officers, four Native officers, and ninety-five European and two hundred and thirteen Native non-commissioned rank and file killed * and wounded. Nor is this number to be considered disproportionate, either to the importance of the object, or to the operations by which it was accomplished. The eyes of all India were turned on this siege, as the last effort of the Mahratta struggle; and the Killedar was enabled, from the strength of his position, to contemplate the slow progress of the approaches, without having occasion to risk the safety of his garrison by the experiment of sallies. These had been attempted with but little success from the lower fort; and the difficulty which will always attend a sally from a hill-fort, as well as the unprofitableness of the first attempts, discouraged all further repetitions. As the batteries were brought nearer, they became more secure against the ordnance of the place; but not against the small arms, the fire of which from the walls caused the majority of the casualties on the British side. To have made this fire more destructive, some matchlockmen should have been posted behind rocks, and under cover, outside of the walls, with orders continually to shift their position, when occasion offered. But this plan would have been met by a counter-manœuvre, that would probably have defeated it; and the enemy would soon have apprehended the insecurity of their return within the walls, particularly when the besieging-batteries should learn to act in concert with their own marksmen. These considerations, summary as they are, will serve to shew the difficulties of defending hill-forts, especially those unprovided with abundance of bomb-proof buildings. The inequalities of the interior surface, of which, generally, one or two parts command the remainder, joined to the ordinary rockiness of the soil, keep a shell in constant motion till it bursts; and the lower parts, which are most secure against shot, are, consequently, most exposed to the

* Vide Appendix. A. A.

effects of bombardment. Though the number of casualties, therefore, actually produced by the shells, may be very few, the garrison suffers from them a harassing and [illegible]. annoyance, to which the besiegers below them are in no wise exposed, were even well-served mortars generally found in Indian forts. On the present occasion, an important deficiency, on the part of the besieged, was the want of some small guns on serviceable carriages, that might be removed and depressed at pleasure, to bear on the advanced batteries. Instead of these, they had a superabundance * of heavy guns, which were unmanageable in their hands. The Killedar, Jeswunt Rao Laar, with all his deficiency of means, was entirely dissatisfied with the defence he had made; and expressed his fears of Scindiah's displeasure at his surrender. Sir John Malcolm, to whom these were addressed, acquiesced in his fears, though he argued from a different cause; and the Laar rejoined, " Yes, he will reproach me for having fought so ill with so fine a fort! He will say, I ought to have died." On Sir John asking him, if he had not an order from his Prince to deliver up the place to the British Army? he said, " It may be the custom, among Europeans, to obey such mandates; but, with Mahrattas, forts like that," pointing to Asseerghur, " are not given up on orders." It subsequently proved, however, that he had no real directions to surrender; on the contrary, instructions were discovered in the place, from Scindiah, enjoining him to pay no attention whatever to any counter-orders he might receive, but to hold out as long as possible. This duplicity, on the part of that Prince, formed the grounds of Lord Hastings's resolution to retain possession of Asseerghur; and the same was subsequently notified to Scindiah, with the production of his original instructions; for it appears to have been a part of his Lordship's conduct, to return to the right owner the occasional documents of hostile tendency to his government which fell into his possession.

The fall of Asseerghur closes the military service of the Mahratta campaign † of 1818-19, and this work; and there remains little more to be Separation of the Force

---

* Vide Appendix. B. B.

† In using the word campaign here, it will be understood as referring exclusively to the troops employed in the destruction of the remnants of the Mahratta Confederacy; for some other insulated services took place at this period, which, however brilliant, do not directly belong to the object of this work. These were the capture of Nowah and Kopauldroog, in the Nizam's territory, by the

related, beyond the return of the troops to their established cantonments and stations, which may be dismissed in a few words, as nothing ulterior depends on it for explanation. After placing in Asseerghur a garrison of six companies of the Madras European regiment, and the 2d battalion of the 13th regiment of Madras Native infantry, Brigadier-general Doveton was engaged for some days in arranging the separation of a force, composed of troops and ordnance of the three Presidencies, assembled nearly in the most central* point of India. His Majesty's 67th foot marched for Ummulneir, to join Colonel Huskisson's force, in Khandesh, on the 12th; and the Nagpoor train, with the flank companies of the Madras European regiment, and one company of the 1st battalion of the 1st regiment of Madras Native infantry, on the following morning took the opposite direction of Nagpoor, where they arrived on the 7th of May. On the 14th, Sir John Malcolm, after transferring to Brigadier-general Doveton the 3d Madras cavalry, and the 2d battalion of the 6th regiment of Madras Native infantry, commenced his return to Malwah, and arrived at Mhow on the 20th, with a light escort, by the route of Metawal, Beekungaum, and Mundleisur, while Colonel Robert Scot, who rejoined a few days afterwards with one brigade, and the heavy guns and stores, marched by Raveir and the Sumroal Ghat. Lieutenant-colonel Grimstrut likewise, with the brigade and [illegible] train of the Nerbuddah Division, left Asseer on the 14th of April, for Hoossingabad; and Brigadier-general Watson, with the troops and guns from Saughur, followed next morning on the return to their proper stations, where they arrived on the 24th of April and 16th of May respectively. Brigadier-general Doveton moved at the same time south towards Jaulnah, detaching to Secunderabad the wing of his Majesty's

---

detachment and division commanded by Major Pitman and Brigadier-general Pritzler respectively; and the successful expedition from Bombay against Sawunt-Warree, under the orders of that active and enterprising officer, Sir William Grant Keir. As, however, they form part of the military operations of the British Army in India, a place is given to the official reports of them, in the Appendix C.C. D.D. and E.E.; in order that the mention of no service may be omitted until the Temple of Janus was shut. The same explanation applies to the reduction of Madooghur, or Madoorajpoor, by Lieutenant-colonel Thompson's detachment from the Reserve of the Grand Army in July 1818. Vide Appendix. F.F.

* Ellichapoor is nearest the center of gravity of the figure of India.

Royal Scots, which had been detained for the late service. At Autoortee, on the 21st of April, he separated his division into two parts, of which one, consisting of the battering-train, escorted by the 2d battalion of the 6th regiment, and the 2d battalion of the 14th regiment of Native infantry, marched, under Colonel Crosdill, by the route of the Neemghat, Mulkapoor, the Burwund Ghat, and Jafferabad, while, with the remainder, he proceeded by Eedulabad, Samroad, the Adjunta Ghat, and Nalnye, to Jaulnah, where he arrived on the 5th of May.

Considerations on the Result of the War—as it affected the Peishwah

It will be the province of future historians, to describe the remote consequences of the enlarged policy and extensive measures of the Marquis of Hastings, in 1817, 18 and 19, which, as far as military arrangements were concerned, have been the subject of this memoir. Their immediate results fall legitimately under present consideration, which may be indulged without speculating too far on future events. The dissolution of the Mahratta confederacy is the most prominent of these; and the little sensation manifested on the occasion of Bajee Rao's progress through Rajapootanah and the Dooab, to the place of his retirement, exhibited in a striking manner, the predominancy acquired by the British Government. His removal from the scene of hostilities claims, therefore, an important station among the events of the war; and a reference to the protracted struggle of the Ex-Rajah of Nagpoor, with but a contemptible portion of his means and importance, affords a demonstration, which was previously recognized by only a few persons *, of the policy of conferring on the Ex-Peishwah the liberal provision he now enjoys. While it is insufficient to enable him to excite any further serious disturbances, if so disposed, it is abundant for the gratification of all his former domestic habits and pursuits. He accordingly bathes daily in the Ganges, indulges in the highest living of a Brahmin, maintains three expensive sets of [illegible], and is surrounded by low sycophants, without talents or respectability. If these habits be received as a proof of his relinquishment of the objects of former ambition, the change will be happy for himself; for after his submission, and till he

* These few, however, were those best able to judge of so important a subject, and among them are the names of Sir David Ochterlony, Brigadier-generals Munro and Doveton, the Hon. Mr. Elphinstone, Mr. Russell, and Mr. Jenkins.

departed from Mundissoor, he never ceased to grasp at every hope of being restored to Poonah, though his power should be restricted to the government of that city. For this purpose he besieged Sir John Malcolm with applications, through those in his confidence, in order to gain any assurance or expression that should enable him to found on it a future argument for the amelioration of his fate. These being uniformly resisted, as a last resource, he begged to have an opportunity of speaking unreservedly, without being answered. Sir John consented to hear him, without promising acquiescence in this condition; but as he apprehended, after listening*, without interruption, that there was a danger of silence being misinterpreted into a favourable omen, he found himself necessitated to add a distinct declaration of the hopelessness of his return to the Deckan. Benares had been proposed as the place of his residence; but, as he had a rooted aversion to it for that purpose, this point was not insisted on. He preferred Muttra; but as this was refused, in consideration of its being a frontier station, he selected the village of Betoor or Brimatwar, on the Ganges, uear Kawnpoor, where he continues to reside.

As it affected Scindiah

Though Dowlut Rao Scindiah appeared ostensibly in no hostile attitude, it has been seen that he was not less coerced than the other Mahratta Chiefs. He was, in fact, compelled to avoid those measures, which must have ended in reducing his power like that of the others; so that, notwithstanding the humiliation he early suffered, through the treaty he was constrained to conclude, and the subsequent reduction of his favourite fortress, he stood comparatively higher as a Mahratta, than on any former occasion, all his rivals being reduced to a condition from which he had nothing left to fear. The districts wrested from him by the Pindarries were restored, while the loss of Asseerghur, in perpetuity, is the principal injury he has

---

* The manner in which he unfolded his cherished hopes is so characteristic, that it appears deserving of introduction here. " I will," he said to Sir John Malcolm, " relate an event which is drawn from the shasters of my tribe, and which occurred more than five thousand years ago." He then related an allegory from Hindoo Mythology, in which an attendant of the Court of Brahma, after being condemned to the earth for gazing too eagerly on the Goddess Gunga, was from her feeling of remorse at being the cause of his removal from Heaven—(What a natural feeling to the female breast!)—married to that Goddess, and after a short sojournment in the lower regions, restored, through her influence, to his former celestial abode.

sustained; but since the close of the war, he has been humoured in every particular, through the moderate and steady conduct of an officer*, in whose hands the most important interests will be ever safe.

Holkur.

The reduced state of Holkur created no particular interest, after the treaty of Mundissoor; and an obscure attempt at setting up a false Mulhar Rao was soon crushed. Comparative order followed the active operations which expelled the bands of mercenaries, and crippled the power of the lawless freebooters of the west of Malwah; and the establishment of British detachments in that quarter, seems calculated to maintain the present state of things, unless the British controul shall be used by that Government, as the pretence and means for the oppression of the country.

Bhooslah

The Ex-Rajah of Nagpoor, after his narrow escape from the vicinity of Dhoolkoat, was ascertained to have entered Boorhaunpoor, and to have remained there several days, in a Brahmin's house, while Brigadier-general Doveton's force was encamped in that vicinity. From hence he was traced, in the habit of a mendicant, to Hindia, near which he crossed the Nerbuddah, and entered the jungles about Bhopal. An application to the Nuwaub to become his mediator, was unattended with the desired effect; and after his departure from that hiding place, no positive information of his haunts or wanderings appears to have been received, though frequent reports have prevailed of his unexpected appearance in very different directions. The conduct of this Prince appears more infatuated than that of any of the remaining hostile Chiefs; for he had no reasonable hope whatever of even temporary success, when, after his reinstatement in reduced power, he was again discovered in secret hostility against the British Government. His character is represented as weak and cowardly; and his actions throughout this war corroborate the imputation. But he is not, therefore, necessarily devoid of the virtues of constancy and devotion to a cause, which he probably considered paramount to every other consideration, and to which he held himself bound, both by worldly and religious ties. With a few exceptions, none of the Princes of India can be expected, or supposed to bear an attachment of affection to the British Power. They cannot avoid considering its increase as the inevitable cause of their own ruin; and all

---

* Vide Note to p. 219.

that class who pursue public service, and employment of the higher gradations of the state, must always encourage that feeling. This is a case peculiar to the European Government; for though the Mahomedans were equally conquerors, and did not always exercise the virtue of toleration, they governed the country through the means of all Casts indifferently; and Hindoos were not only eligible, but occasionally sought for in the highest offices of state. A similar conduct is incompatible with the permanent system and views of the British Government, which aims at its establishment through means* independent of the occasional wisdom or folly of particular rulers or official servants. Even with those Princes who owe their elevation entirely to the exertions of the British Government, the causes already noticed must have an influence; or if not with them, with their descendants. The Nuwaub Mahommud Allee was the first of these; and the history of the cabals in which his successors were engaged, is fully known. The Rajah of Mysore has had little opportunity of evincing the ingratitude which will be natural to his successors; and all those rulers who have been established, in room of relations who refused to subscribe to the terms on which a limited rule was at their option, can deem themselves in no manner indebted for their elevation, which they may possibly be taught to consider subsequently as having been purchased at the price of odium and disgrace. This sentiment was probably entertained by Appah Saib; and in that case he has expiated his supposed fault, by preferring a life of misery and vicissitudes, to a pension of two lacs of rupees per annum, offered by the British Government, while he was still invested in Patchmurree.

Rajapoots.

Among those who especially benefited by the war are the Rajapoot States; and these have lost nothing, while they have gained considerably. They had long been oppressed by the Mahrattas, and they are now in direct union with the British Government. Some of them, moreover, have acquired additional territory, some a remission of tribute, others have regained lost possessions, and all, an exemption from vexatious tyranny

* The attachment to a system of law and regulation in a British Government is here strengthened by the private objects of the Authorities at home, who find in its support the surest provision for the numerous relations and friends who are destined to be employed, through its operation, in one of the most desirable walks for men of liberal education.

They have generally been the staunch allies of the British Government, when they have had an opportunity of declaring their preference; and it remains to be hoped that they will not change their sentiments,

Of the Nizam's State little is to be said; for its condition, or government, has been altered in no respect by the war. Its power was neutralized by antecedent events, and the active vigilance of the Resident; and the condition of the country continues as wretched as it was before. Exceptions to this are the districts which form the *jaghire* and possessions of the Pitan Nuwaub of Ellichapoor, Sulabut Khan, who has acquired a claim on the consideration of the British, by his invariable attachment to their views. He has accordingly received as his reward, some lands lately belonging to the Nagpoor and Poonah territories; and though still nominally a Jaghiredar of the Nizam, he feels perfectly independent of his power, beyond the outward acknowledgements of subjection. Nizam

Along the banks of the Nerbuddah, the Pindarries have been extirpated, and the occasional movement of British detachments in that quarter, maintains the country clear of them. Those Chiefs who submitted within the period of the proclamation, received the means of living with respectability; and even the inferiors were supplied with the materials for gaining their livelihood by honest industry. Cheettoo, the remaining leader, who continued Pindarry to the last, met a death not unsuitable to the deserts of his previous life. A few days after his narrow escape with Appah Saib from Lieutenant-colonel Smith's detachment, a party discovered in the jungle near Sutwass, whither he fled beyond the Nerbuddah, the head and remains of a body destroyed by wild beasts, which was recognized to be that of the famous Pindarry Chief. His adopted son, who was a prisoner in Sir John Malcolm's camp, acknowledged its identity; and this melancholy fate was further corroborated by the discovery of his horse, and saddle-bag containing several original papers, among which was Appah Saib's correspondence with him. The Pindarries

Trimbuckjee Deinglia, the assassin of Gungadhur Shastree, the Guickwar Vakeel, having acted a part of much importance in the Deckan, and greatly contributed by his counsels to precipitate a rupture between the British Government and the Peishwah, was after Bajee Rao's surrender a vagrant about Khandesh, till the end of June 1818; when he fell into the hands of Lieutenant Swanston, who, with a party of the Poonah reformed horse, Trimbuckjee surprised him in the village of Ahurgaum, after a march of fifty miles in sixteen hours. He was conveyed to Bombay, there shipped off, in March next year, for Calcutta, from whence he was conveyed to Chunarghur, to remain a prisoner for life.

Recapitulation of British Acquisitions in the Deckan and Kokun.

(Map 1.)

Having considered, generally, the consequences of the war, with reference to the Native States of India; its effects respecting the British power will form the suitable conclusion of this Memoir. The augmentation of territory may be understood from what has been already related; but in order to spare the reader the trouble of a reference to many parts of previous Chapters, they will be collected into a single view, with such further explanations as shall appear requisite for the better comprehension of them. With regard to the actual revenue of these acquisitions, the author is without information; nor did it form an object of special enquiry; the military and political importance of their position and extent being alone, immediately, within the scope of the present consideration.

With the conquest of the Poonah territory, the British dominion and possessions have been extended along the western coast * from the northern boundary of the small province of Goa, to the mouths of the Taptee; and inland, to the long established western frontier of the Nizam, from the junction of the Wurdah and Toombudra to the junction of the Wagoor and Taptee. Such places of Khandesh belonging to Holkur, as fell within these bounds, were ceded by him at the treaty of Mundissoor, which likewise transferred all the territory, south of the Sautpoora range of hills and the fort of Seindwah. This, connecting immediately with the British and Guickwar possessions on the western coast, it became of importance to render them as connected in themselves, and distinct from each other, as possible. The means in the British hands for this purpose, arose out of the rights in Goozerat, derived from the subjugation of the Peishwah's power, and the supply of a subsidiary force for the protection and maintenance of the Guickwar state. Accordingly, by a treaty concluded on the 6th of November, 1817, the Guickwar Rajah ceded to the British Government, in perpetuity, all the rights obtained from the perpetual farm of the Peish-

* It is proper to notice here, that these boundaries include some petty States, which are either tributary or protected.

wah's territories, subject to the city of Ahmedabad, as secured by the treaty of Poonah, dated in the previous June; and an exchange was made of certain British districts in the vicinity of Barroda, for the Guickwar remaining share of the city of Ahmedabad and some territory about Soorut, and bordering on the Company's possessions. Turning to the eastward, from Nusserabad, the first new acquisition is the fort of Asseerghur, with a small *arrondissement;* and from thence the connexion with the eastern coast of the Peninsula, and with the previous British possessions under the Bengal Presidency, is formed by the Nagpoor Cessions from Jilpy-Aumneir. This consists of an irregular belt of various breadth, from fifty to one hundred and fifty miles; embracing, in the first instance, both banks of the Taptee, and, subsequently, both banks of the Nerbuddah to its source; from whence the districts of Sergoojah and Jushpoor connect with the British districts of Palamao and Chotah Nagpoor. To the northward, it joins Bundelcund and the Bhopal territory; and to the southward, the reserved dominions of Nagpoor along the Mahadeo range of hills, and the territory ruled by the Nuwaub of Ellichapoor. By the foregoing acquisitions, witb the exception of a tract, thirty-five miles broad, on each side of Asseer, there is an unbroken line of communication through British territory from Bombay to Calcutta, as there is likewise from Madras to Bombay. The former Mahratta war also having been attended with the similar advantage of continuous dominion between Madras and Calcutta, the communication between the three Presidencies may now be considered as complete.

The acquisition of the Peishwah's rights in Malwah, by the treaty of In Hindoostan
June 1817, conferred the means of forming a compact boundary to the British territory on that side, and of establishing a description of confederation with several petty States, of some political importance. The Nuwaub of Bhopal, in return for his faithful exertions against the Pindarries, and for his engagement to supply a respectable corps of troops when required, received five Districts situated on his western frontier, which had been ceded by the Peishwah. The Rajahs of Dutteah, Jhansee, and Simpthur, likewise profited, by being confirmed in the territory they held, for the obligation of supplying a quota of troops when required by the British Government. Nor was this species of alliance confined to the eastern frontiers of Malwah. It also extended along its northern and western boundaries, in pursuance of the policy held in view, during the negotiation

of the treaties with all the Mahratta Powers, of making the relinquishment of claims for tribute on the Rajapoot States, except through the medium of the British Government, an indispensable article of every agreement. The accomplishment of this important object, was accordingly followed by treaties with the several States of Karaollee, Jypoor, Boondee Kishenghur, Jondpoor, Kotah, Oodeipoor, Dungarpoor, Banswarra, and Dhar; which separately entered into engagements of subordinate alliance with the British Government, for the guarantee of their respective dominions against all enemies whatever. The material conditions on their part are found in all of these alliances. They relate to an acknowledgment of the supremacy of the British Government, a renunciation of all communication with foreign States, an acquiescence in British arbitration on all the points of difference with their neighbours, and an engagement to supply, according to their respective means, a certain contingent of troops.

Military Dispositions. (Map II.)

From what has been premised, it will be seen that the several Mahratta States and the Nizam's dominions are, in a considerable measure, encompassed by the British territories; and when these fail, that the deficiency is supplied by the petty States acknowledging British supremacy. Thus the Nagpoor and Hydrabad territories, taken collectively, are entirely surrounded by the British possessions; Scindiah and Holkur by the British territory and petty States, in about equal proportions; and Goozerat in the same manner, and by the sea, which is no less a part of the British dominion. In order to maintain this order of things, several respectable corps, complete with artillery, are distributed through this extensive *arrondissement*, under orders from the Supreme Government through its Political* Agents. Commencing from the great stations in the Dooab, at Ajemeer † is one corps, another at Neemuj, and a third at Mhow, all supplied by the

---

* The Guickwar Contingent, and Poonah Division, and Malleygaum force are under the Bombay Government.

† The original position proposed for this force was Jonk Ramporrah; but when Ajemeer came to be ceded by Scindiah, its superiority as a position was immediately acknowledged. Sir David Ochterlony's division accordingly marched under Lieutenant-colonel Knox, on the 20th of June, towards that place which remained in the possession of Bapoo Scindiah, an officer subject to the Maharaj. The force arrived there on the 1st of July; but owing to the mutinous state of the garrison, who were in long arrears of pay, possession was not obtained till the following evening after the *demonstration* of a battery.

Bengal army. These are succeeded by the Goozerat subsidiary force, the field-force at Malleygaum, and the Poonah division, furnished principally by the Bombay army. The circle is continued by the field-force in the southern Mahratta country, the Hydrabad and Nagpoor subsidiaries, composed of Madras troops; and the detachments from the Bengal establishment, forming the Nerbuddah and Saughur divisions, from whence the *cordon* terminates in Bundelcund. Though, in this general outline, the minor dispositions dependant thereon are not particularized, it will be sufficient to exhibit the powerful command of position in the hands of the British Government; and to shew how small the chance of a future hostile combination, while the spirit shall be pursued of those measures which has dissolved the last.

Considerations on their Importance

Any observation respecting the efficacy of maintaining, in a constant state of equipment and efficiency, the corps which have been enumerated, must be trite and unnecessary. It may, however, be remarked, that thus alone can the troops, composing the Army in India, be formed for service, their habits of home being quite forsaken, and the luxuries and indolence of long established stations in the interior forgotten. Their discipline and manœuvre, which is shaken by their constant separation for internal service, as guards and escorts, must depend on the frontier stations for renewal, and the officers, as well as men, will there alone be necessitated to entertain military sentiments, and to reflect on their profession. But if the service of the Indian troops beyond the frontier is thus necessary, their seasonable relief is not less so, on many accounts. Among the most important of these, is the expediency of preventing the alternative of their becoming either disgusted with a long exile from home, or of their losing the tie which binds them to their family residence within the British territory, and, with that feeling, the chief security for their fidelity. The accomplishment of this desirable object evidently depends on the maintenance of the army in sufficient strength to admit of a certain number of corps being in constant motion, on a line of relief varying from four hundred to one thousand* miles; and however unpopular, on the score of expense, a

* The 1st battalion of the 16th Madras Native infantry, is now on a march of eight hundred and sixty-one miles from Nagpoor to its native station.

discussion of this subject may appear, its importance, it is to be presumed, will not leave it without consideration. To press it here, would probably excite the ready suspicion of a military writer's partiality to his own profession, which would lessen the effect of his reasoning; and the same sentiment might possibly attach to any discussion respecting the diversion of the funds necessary for the augmentation of a commanding military force, into channels of less probable importance. Yet the Natives of India are accustomed to be governed by the sword; they comprehend that species of rule, and it is not saying too much, however apparently paradoxical, to assert, that they prefer it. If the results of those experiments which have been made, shew that a complicated Judicial establishment renders less necessary a large military force, or that there is the smallest evidence of the prosperity or happiness of the subject having thus been increased, it may be hoped that it will be continued. It may also be fairly expected, that what further information shall be acquired will excite a proportionate attention in those whose situation is calculated to permit the exercise of a judgment, more impartial than may be expected either from the class which profit by it, or from that which, by its extensive introduction, has suffered in importance. The system, or rather absence of system, which preceded the present order of things, decidedly required amendment; and, in some respects, improvement has followed: what, however, is good in a certain degree, is necessarily bad in the extreme, to which most innovations have a tendency. A new kingdom has been conquered, and is therefore to be governed; and the opportunity appears favourable for ascertaining, by the adoption of a system consonant with the better feelings and habits of those to be ruled, whether this consideration, or its neglect, shall prove most profitable.

Conclusion

Nothing has been advanced here, which can authorize the imputation of a desire to view the Civil power in a subordinate relation. As a British subject, the author disclaims the sentiment; but, ardently devoted to the prosperity of the British Government of India, and to the happiness of its subjects, he wishes to see its means advantageously applied. No better judge of this important question in politics can be desired, or procured, than the Nobleman, under whose auspices the Indian Empire has attained its present shape and posture. The language of panegyric has been sparingly used hitherto; and the same motives which have opposed its previous admission, prevail, in forbidding the gratification of private feelings, on the present occasion. The Marquis of Hastings recognized the wisdom of the Marquis of Wellesley's policy, and most ably pursued it, when the enemies of the British Government, by their conduct, placed its measures legitimately in his power. They have been skilfully and successfully executed; but will require the vigilant protection of a force undiminished, and of enlightened rulers. In this respect has the India Government enjoyed its full share of favour, and it has ample reason to expect a continuance of this boon from a Country wherein rank is but a secondary recommendation, and the existence of talent and virtue among nobility, however happily exemplified by the Marquis of Hastings, is by no means confined to the instance of his Lordship.

APPENDIX.

APPENDIX.

A. (p. 69.)

Return of Killed, Wounded, and Missing, of the Poonah Brigade, commanded by Lieutenant-colonel C. B. Burr, in the Action with the Enemy near Poonah, on the 5th of November 1817.

Corps.	Killed.				Wounded								Missing, supposed Killed			
	Havildars.	Naigues.	Drummers	Privates	Lieutenants.	Jemidars	Havildars	Naigues	Drummers.	Lascars	Bheasties	Privates				Privates.
His Majesty's 65th Regiment Detachment	-	-	-	-	-	-	-	-	-	-	-	-	-	-	-	-
Artillery Detachment	-	-	-	-	-	-	-	-	-	2	-	-	-	-	-	-
H. C. Bombay European Regiment	-	-	-	1	-	-	-	-	-	-	-	1	-	-	-	-
2d Battalion 1st Native Regiment	-	-	-	1	1	-	1	1	-	-	1	5	-	-	-	-
2d Battalion 6th Native Regiment	-	-	-	4	-	-	-	-	-	-	-	10	-	-	-	-
1st Battalion 7th Native Regiment	1	1	1	9	-	-	1	3	-	-	-	34	-	-	-	-
Major Ford's Battalion	-	-	-	1	-	1	1	-	-	-	-	5	-	-	-	-
Pioneers' Detachment	-	-	-	-	-	-	-	-	-	-	-	-	-	-	-	-
Total	1	1	1	16	1	1	3	4	-	2	1	55	-	-	-	-

Name of the Officer Wounded, severely in the shoulder—Lieutenant Falconar.

(Signed) J. Hallifax,
Major of Brigade

B. (p. 73.)

RETURN of CASUALTIES in the Force under the Command of Brigadier-general LIONEL SMITH, C. B. on the 11th, 15th, and 16th of November 1817.

Camp, near Poonah, 17th of November 1817

CORPS.		Killed	Wounded										Missing	
		Rank and File	Captains	Lieutenant	Subidars	Sergeants, or Havildars.	Rank and File	Lascars	Bheasties.	Drivers	Troopers.	Horses	Rank and File	Horses
11th November.	Auxiliary Horse - - -	-	-	1	-	-	-	-	-	-	8	7	-	2
	1/3d Regiment - - - -	-	-	-	-	-	1	-	-	-	-	-	-	-
15th November.	1/3d Regiment - - - -	-	-	-	-	-	1	-	-	-	-	-	-	-
16th	Bombay Foot Artillery -	-	-	-	-	-	3	2	-	2	-	-	-	-
	His Majesty's 65th Reg. -	-	-	-	-	-	2	-	-	-	-	-	-	-
	Bombay European Reg. -	5	1	-	-	1	12	-	-	-	-	-	-	-
	Light Company 1/3d Reg.	1	-	-	-	1	9	-	-	-	-	-	-	-
	Light Company 1/4th Reg.	2	-	-	1	-	3	-	-	-	-	-	-	-
	2d Battalion 6th Regiment	2	-	-	-	-	11	-	1	-	-	-	-	-
	1st Battalion 7th Regiment	3	-	-	-	-	11	-	-	-	-	-	-	-
	Resident's Escort - - -	2	-	-	-	-	2	-	-	-	-	-	-	-
	Madras Pioneers - - -	-	-	-	-	1	4	-	-	-	-	-	-	-
	Bombay ditto - - - -	-	-	-	-	-	1	-	-	-	-	-	-	-
	Total - -	15	1	1	1	3	60	2	1	2	8	7	-	2

Names of Officers Wounded.

11th November, Lieutenant Spiller, 1/3d, attached to Auxiliary Horse, slightly.
16th November, Captain Preston, B. E. Regiment, severely.

(Signed) H. TOVEY,
D. A. General.

C. (p. 114.)

Return of Killed, Wounded, and Missing, in the Action on the 26th and 27th of November 1817, at Nagpoor.

Corps.		Majors.	Captains.	Lieutenants	Cornets and Ensigns	Adjutants.	Surgeons.	Assistant-Surgeons.	Sergeant-majors.	Quartermaster-sergeants	Subidars.	Jemidars.	Havildars or Sergeants.	Corporals.	Drummers & Trumpeters.	Puckallies.	Rank and File.	Gun Lascars.	Recruit Boys.	Horsekeepers.	Grass Cutters.	Horses.
Detachment three troops, 6th Reg Bengal Cavalry	Killed - -	-	-	-	-	-	-	-	-	1	-	-	-	-	-	-	21	-	-	1	-	20
	Wounded	-	-	2	-	1	-	-	-	-	1	-	3	-	-	-	18	-	-	-	-	11
	Missing -	-	-	-	-	-	-	-	-	-	-	-	-	-	-	-	-	-	-	-	-	11
Detachment Madras Body-guard - - - - -	Killed - -	-	-	-	-	-	-	-	-	-	-	-	-	-	-	-	-	-	-	-	-	-
	Wounded	-	-	-	-	-	-	-	-	-	-	-	-	-	-	-	-	-	-	-	-	-
	Missing -	-	-	-	-	-	-	-	-	-	-	-	-	-	-	-	-	-	-	-	-	-
Detachment Foot Artillery - - -	Killed - -	-	-	-	-	-	-	-	-	-	-	-	1	-	-	-	2	2	-	-	-	-
	Wounded	-	-	1	-	-	-	-	-	-	-	1	1	-	-	-	5	8	-	-	-	-
	Missing -	-	-	-	-	-	-	-	-	-	-	-	-	-	-	-	-	-	-	-	-	-
1st Battalion 20th Regiment Native Infantry - -	Killed - -	-	-	1	-	-	-	-	-	-	-	-	-	-	-	-	15	-	-	-	-	-
	Wounded	1	1	1	-	-	-	-	-	-	1	-	1	-	-	-	14	-	-	-	-	-
	Missing -	-	-	-	-	-	-	-	-	-	-	-	-	-	-	-	-	-	-	-	-	-
1st Battalion 24th Regiment Native Infantry - -	Killed - -	-	1	1	-	1	-	-	-	-	1	-	4	-	1	-	49	-	1	-	-	-
	Wounded	-	1	1	-	-	-	-	1	1	-	2	7	-	-	-	89	-	-	-	-	-
	Missing -	-	-	-	-	-	-	-	-	-	-	-	-	-	-	-	-	-	-	-	-	-
Resident's Escort	Killed - -	-	-	-	-	-	-	-	-	-	1	-	1	-	-	-	8	-	-	-	-	-
	Wounded	-	1	-	-	-	-	-	-	-	-	-	1	-	-	-	31	-	-	-	-	-
	Missing -	-	-	-	-	-	-	-	-	-	-	-	-	-	1	-	3	-	-	-	-	-
Major Jenkins's Battalion - - -	Killed - -	-	-	-	-	-	-	-	-	-	1	-	1	1	-	-	5	-	-	-	-	-
	Wounded	-	2	-	-	1	-	-	-	-	-	-	-	-	-	-	13	-	-	-	-	-
	Missing -	-	-	-	-	-	-	-	-	-	-	-	-	-	-	-	-	-	-	-	-	-
Unattached - - -	Killed - -	-	-	-	-	-	-	1	-	-	-	-	-	-	-	-	-	-	-	-	-	-
	Total - -	1	6	7	-	3	-	1	1	2	5	3	20	1	2	-	303	10	1	1	-	15

Names of the Officers Killed and Wounded.

Killed, Lieutenant Clarke, 1st Battalion 20th Regiment N. I.; Captain Sadler and Lieutenant & Adjutant Grant, 1st Battalion 24th Regiment N. I.; Mr. Assistant-surgeon Niven, unattached.

Wounded—severely, Lieutenant R. W. Smith, and Lieutenant & Adjutant Hearsey, Detachment 6th Regiment Bengal Cavalry—slightly, Lieutenant Maxwell, Detachment of Foot Artillery—slightly, Major Mackenzie, 1st Battalion 20th Regiment N. I.—severely, Captain Pew, Ditto ditto—slightly, Lieutenant Dun, Ditto ditto—severely, Captain Charlesworth, and Lieutenant Thuillier, 1st Battalion 24th Regiment N. I.—severely, Captain Lloyd, Resident's Escort—slightly, Captain Robison, and severely, Captain and Adjutant Bayley, Major Jenkins's Battalion.

(Signed) H. S. Scott, Lieutenant-colonel.

D. (p. 121.)

RETURN of CASUALTIES of the Detachment under the Command of Brigadier-general HARDYMAN, in the Action before JUBBULPOOR, on the 19th of December 1817.

	Commissioned Officers. Europeans. Killed	Commissioned Officers. Europeans. Wounded.	Commissioned Officers. Europeans. Missing.	Commissioned Officers. Natives. Killed.	Commissioned Officers. Natives. Wounded	Commissioned Officers. Natives. Missing.	Sergeants and Havildars. Killed.	Sergeants and Havildars. Wounded.	Sergeants and Havildars. Missing.	Drummers and Trumpeters. Killed.	Drummers and Trumpeters. Wounded.	Drummers and Trumpeters. Missing.	Rank and File. Killed.	Rank and File. Wounded	Rank and File. Missing	Gun Lascars. Killed.	Gun Lascars. Wounded	Gun Lascars. Missing.	Horses. Killed.	Horses. Wounded	Horses. Missing.	Gun Bullocks. Killed.	Gun Bullocks. Wounded.	Gun Bullocks. Missing.
Artillery	-	-	-	-	-	-	-	-	-	-	-	-	-	-	-	-	-	-	-	-	-	-	-	-
8th Native Cavalry	-	1	-	-	1	-	-	-	-	-	-	-	2	4	-	-	-	-	5	10	5	-	-	-
His Majesty's 17th Foot	-	2	-	-	-	-	-	1	-	-	-	-	-	1	-	-	-	-	-	-	-	-	-	-
Total	-	3	-	-	1	-	-	1	-	-	-	-	2	5	-	-	-	-	5	10	5	-	-	-

Officers Wounded.

Lieutenant Pope, 8th Native Cavalry (severely) not dangerously
Maw, 17th Foot, ditto ditto
Nicholson, 17th Foot, slightly

Native Corps.

Subidar Summer Sing (severely) and right arm amputated.

(Signed) H. DESPARD,
Major Brigade.

E. (p. 127.)

Return of Killed, Wounded, and Missing, of the Force under the Command of Brigadier-general John Doveton, in the Action of the 16th of December 1817, with the Troops of his Highness the Rajah of Berar, at Nagpoor.

EUROPEANS.

Division	Corps	Killed: Field-officers	Killed: Captains	Killed: Lieutenants	Killed: Ensigns or Cornets	Killed: Staff: Adjutants	Killed: Staff: Quartermasters	Killed: Staff: Surgeons	Killed: Staff: Assist.-surgeons	Killed: Sergeant-majors	Killed: Quartermaster-sergs.	Killed: Sergeants	Killed: Drummers and Fifers	Killed: Rank and File: Corporals	Killed: Rank and File: Privates	Wounded: Field-officers	Wounded: Captains	Wounded: Lieutenants	Wounded: Ensigns or Cornets	Wounded: Staff: Adjutants	Wounded: Staff: Quartermasters	Wounded: Staff: Surgeons	Wounded: Staff: Assist.-surgeons	Wounded: Sergeant-majors	Wounded: Quartermaster-sergs.	Wounded: Sergeants	Wounded: Drummers and Fifers	Wounded: Rank and File: Corporals	Wounded: Rank and File: Privates
	Horse-Artillery	-	-	-	-	-	-	-	-	-	-	-	-	-	-	-	-	-	-	-	-	-	-	-	-	-	-	-	-
Lieut.-col. Gahan's Division	Bengal Gallopers	-	-	-	-	-	-	-	-	-	-	-	-	-	-	-	-	-	-	-	-	-	-	-	-	-	-	-	-
	Coast ditto	-	-	-	-	-	-	-	-	-	-	-	-	-	-	-	-	-	-	-	-	-	-	-	-	-	-	-	-
	6th Bengal Cavalry	-	-	-	-	-	-	-	-	-	-	-	-	-	-	-	-	-	-	-	-	-	-	-	-	-	-	-	-
	6th Coast ditto	-	-	-	-	-	-	-	-	-	-	-	-	-	-	-	-	-	-	-	-	-	-	-	-	-	-	-	-
	Royals six Companies	-	-	-	-	-	-	-	-	-	-	-	-	-	6	-	-	-	-	-	-	-	-	-	-	2	-	1	21
Lieut.-col. M'Leod's Division	1st Battalion 12th Regiment, or W. L. I.	-	-	-	-	-	-	-	-	-	-	-	-	-	-	-	-	-	-	-	-	-	-	-	-	-	-	-	-
	2d ditto 13th ditto N. I.	-	-	-	-	-	-	-	-	-	-	-	-	-	-	-	-	-	-	-	-	-	-	-	-	-	-	-	-
	1st ditto 22d Bengal N. I.	-	-	-	-	-	-	-	-	-	-	-	-	-	-	-	-	-	-	-	-	-	-	-	-	-	-	-	-
	Flank Companies 1st Batt. 2d Reg. N. I.	-	-	-	-	-	-	-	-	-	-	-	-	-	-	-	-	-	-	-	-	-	-	-	-	-	-	-	-
Lieut.-col. M'Kellar's Division	One Company Royals	-	-	-	-	-	-	-	-	-	-	-	-	-	2	-	-	-	-	-	-	-	-	-	-	-	-	-	5
	2d Battalion 24th Regiment N. I.	-	-	-	-	-	-	-	-	-	-	-	-	-	-	-	-	-	-	-	-	-	-	1	-	-	-	-	-
	Brigade Horse-Artillery	-	-	-	-	-	-	-	-	-	-	-	-	-	-	-	-	-	-	-	-	-	-	-	-	-	-	-	1
Lieut.-colonel Scot's Division	One Company Royals	-	-	-	-	-	-	-	-	-	-	-	-	-	-	-	-	-	-	-	-	-	-	-	-	-	-	-	-
	1st Battalion 11th Regiment N. I.	-	-	-	-	-	-	-	-	-	-	-	-	-	-	-	-	-	-	-	-	-	-	-	-	-	-	-	-
	Detachment Artillery	-	-	-	-	-	-	-	-	-	-	-	-	-	-	-	-	-	-	-	-	-	-	-	-	-	-	-	-
	Sappers and Miners	-	-	-	-	-	-	-	-	-	-	-	-	-	-	-	-	-	-	-	-	-	-	-	-	-	-	-	-
	One Company 2d Batt. 24th Reg. N. I.	-	-	-	-	-	-	-	-	-	-	-	-	-	-	-	-	-	-	-	-	-	-	-	-	-	-	-	-
	Reserve Battery, commanded by Lieutenant-colonel Crosdill	-	-	-	-	-	-	-	-	-	-	-	-	-	-	-	-	-	-	-	-	-	-	-	-	-	-	-	-
	Reformed Horse, under Captain Pedlar	-	-	-	-	-	-	-	-	-	-	-	-	-	-	-	-	-	-	-	-	-	-	-	-	-	-	-	-
	Total	-	-	-	-	-	-	-	-	-	-	-	-	-	8	-	-	-	-	-	-	-	-	1	-	2	-	1	27

NATIVES.

Division	Corps	Killed: Subidars	Killed: Jemidars	Killed: Havildars	Killed: Drummers and Fifers	Killed: Puckallies	Killed: Rank and File: Naigues	Killed: Rank and File: Privates	Wounded: Subidars	Wounded: Jemidars	Wounded: Havildars	Wounded: Drummers and Fifers	Wounded: Puckallies	Wounded: Rank and File: Naigues	Wounded: Rank and File: Privates	Missing: Naigues	Missing: Sepoys	Horses: Killed	Horses: Wounded	Horses: Missing	Remarks
	Horse-Artillery	-	-	-	-	-	-	-	-	-	-	-	-	-	-	-	-	-	1	-	
Lieut.-col. Gahan's Division	Bengal Gallopers	-	-	-	-	-	-	-	-	-	-	-	-	-	-	-	-	-	-	1	
	Coast ditto	-	-	-	-	-	-	-	-	-	-	-	-	-	-	-	-	-	-	1	
	6th Bengal Cavalry	-	-	-	-	-	-	-	-	-	1	-	-	-	4	-	-	11	8	11	One private soldier since dead of his wounds.
	6th Coast ditto	-	-	-	-	-	-	-	1	-	-	-	-	1	2	-	-	14	3	6	
	Royals six Companies	-	-	-	-	-	-	-	-	-	-	-	-	-	-	-	-	-	-	-	
Lieut.-col. M'Leod's Division	1st Battalion 12th Regiment, or W. L. I.	-	-	-	-	-	2	12	-	-	1	-	-	2	17	-	-	-	-	-	
	2d ditto 13th ditto N. I.	-	-	-	-	-	-	1	-	-	-	-	-	1	4	-	-	-	-	-	
	1st ditto 22d Bengal N. I.	-	2	-	-	-	-	6	1	-	-	-	-	2	14	-	-	-	-	-	
	Flank Companies 1st Batt. 2d Reg. N. I.	-	-	-	-	-	-	-	-	-	-	-	-	-	1	-	-	-	-	-	
Lieut.-col. M'Kellar's Division	One Company Royals	-	-	-	-	-	-	-	-	-	-	-	-	-	-	-	-	-	-	-	One Sepoy since dead of his wounds.
	2d Battalion 24th Regiment N. I.	-	-	1	-	-	1	1	-	1	-	-	-	-	12	-	2	-	-	-	
	Brigade Horse-Artillery	-	-	-	-	-	-	-	-	-	-	-	-	-	-	-	-	1	-	4	
Lieut.-colonel Scot's Division	One Company Royals	-	-	-	-	-	-	-	-	-	-	-	-	-	-	-	-	-	-	-	
	1st Battalion 11th Regiment N. I.	-	-	-	-	-	-	-	-	-	1	-	-	-	-	-	-	-	-	-	
	Detachment Artillery	-	-	-	-	-	-	-	-	-	-	-	-	-	-	-	-	-	-	-	
	Sappers and Miners	-	-	-	-	-	-	-	-	-	-	-	-	-	-	-	-	-	-	-	
	One Company 2d Batt. 24th Reg. N. I.	-	-	-	-	-	-	-	-	-	1	-	-	-	2	-	1	-	-	-	
	Reserve Battery, commanded by Lieutenant-colonel Crosdill	-	-	-	-	-	-	-	-	-	-	-	-	-	-	-	-	-	-	-	
	Reformed Horse, under Captain Pedlar	-	-	-	-	-	-	-	-	-	-	-	-	-	7	-	-	8	1	-	
	Total	-	2	1	-	-	3	20	2	1	4	-	-	6	63	-	3	34	13	23	

N. B. The Horse of Lieutenant Horner, Adjutant 1st Battalion 22d Regiment Bengal Native Infantry, not included in the above.

(Signed) J. Morgan, Captain,

Acting Assistant Adjutant-general.

F. (p. 131.)

Return of Killed, Wounded, and Missing, of the Troops under the Command of Brigadier-general John Doveton, from the 19th to the 24th of December, 1817, inclusive.

EUROPEANS. — Killed.

CORPS.	Commissioned: Field-officers.	Captains.	Lieutenants.	Cornets, or Ensigns, Lieuts.-Fireworkers.	Staff: Adjutants.	Quartermasters.	Surgeons.	Assist.-surgeons.	Sergeant-majors.	Quartermaster-sergeants.	Sergeants.	Drummers and Fifers.	Rank and File: Corporals.	Privates.	Total.
General Staff	-	-	-	-	-	-	-	-	-	-	-	-	-	-	-
Brigade Ditto	-	-	-	-	-	-	-	-	-	-	-	-	-	-	-
Engineer	-	-	-	-	-	-	-	-	-	-	-	-	-	-	-
Artillery	-	-	-	-	-	-	-	-	-	-	-	-	-	4	4
Sappers and Miners	-	-	-	-	-	-	-	-	-	-	-	-	-	5	5
His Majesty's Royal Scots	-	-	1	-	-	-	-	-	-	-	-	-	2	8	10
Flank Companies, 1st Battalion 2d Regiment N. I.	-	-	-	-	-	-	-	-	-	-	-	-	-	-	-
1st ditto 11th ditto	-	-	-	-	-	-	-	-	-	-	-	-	-	-	-
1st ditto 12th ditto	-	-	-	-	-	-	-	-	-	-	-	-	-	-	-
Flank Companies 2d ditto 13th ditto	-	-	-	-	-	-	-	-	-	-	-	-	-	-	-
Flank Companies 1st ditto 20th ditto	-	-	-	-	-	-	-	-	-	-	-	-	-	-	-
Flank Companies 1st ditto 24th ditto	-	-	-	-	-	-	-	-	-	-	-	-	-	-	-
1st Battalion 22d Regiment Bengal N. I.	-	-	-	-	-	-	-	-	-	-	-	-	-	-	-
2d ditto 24th ditto N. I.	-	-	-	-	-	-	-	-	-	-	-	-	-	-	-
Detachment 1st Battalion Pioneers	-	-	-	-	-	-	-	-	-	-	-	-	-	-	-
Major Pitman's Brigade, His Highness the Nizam's Service	-	-	-	-	-	-	-	-	-	-	-	-	-	-	-
Total	-	-	1	-	-	-	-	-	-	-	-	-	2	17	19

EUROPEANS. — Wounded.

CORPS.	Commissioned: Field-officers.	Captains.	Lieutenants.	Cornets, Ensigns, or Lieut.-Fireworkers.	Staff: Adjutants.	Quartermasters.	Surgeons.	Assist.-surgeons.	Sergeant-majors.	Quartermaster-sergeants.	Sergeants.	Drummers and Fifers.	Rank and File: Corporals.	Privates.	Total.
General Staff	1	-	1	-	-	-	-	-	-	-	-	-	-	-	-
Brigade Ditto	-	-	1	-	-	-	-	-	-	-	-	-	-	-	-
Engineer	-	-	1	1	-	-	-	-	-	-	-	-	-	-	-
Artillery	1	-	-	1	-	-	-	-	-	-	-	-	2	13	15
Sappers and Miners	-	-	-	-	-	-	-	-	-	-	2	-	-	7	7
His Majesty's Royal Scots	-	-	-	-	-	-	-	-	-	-	2	-	3	46	49
Flank Companies, 1st Battalion 2d Regiment N. I.	-	-	-	-	-	-	-	-	-	-	-	-	-	-	-
1st ditto 11th ditto	-	-	-	-	-	-	-	-	-	-	-	-	-	-	-
1st ditto 12th ditto	-	-	-	-	-	-	-	-	-	-	-	-	-	-	-
Flank Companies 2d ditto 13th ditto	-	-	-	-	-	-	-	-	-	-	-	-	-	-	-
Flank Companies 1st ditto 20th ditto	-	-	-	-	-	-	-	-	-	-	-	-	-	-	-
Flank Companies 1st ditto 24th ditto	-	-	-	-	-	-	-	-	-	-	-	-	-	-	-
1st Battalion 22d Regiment Bengal N. I.	-	-	-	-	-	-	-	-	-	-	-	-	-	-	-
2d ditto 24th ditto N. I.	-	1	-	-	-	-	-	-	-	-	-	-	-	-	-
Detachment 1st Battalion Pioneers	-	-	-	-	-	-	-	-	-	1	-	-	-	-	-
Major Pitman's Brigade, His Highness the Nizam's Service	1	-	-	-	-	-	-	-	-	-	-	-	-	-	-
Total	3	1	3	2	-	-	-	-	-	-	4	-	5	66	71

NATIVES.

CORPS.	Killed: Commissnd: Subidars, or Syrangs.	Jemidars, or 1st Tindals.	Havildars, or 2d Tindals.	Drummers and Fifers.	Puckallies.	Rank and File: Naigues.	Sepoys.	Total	Wounded: Commissnd: Subidars, or Syrangs.	Jemidars, or 1st Tindals.	Havildars or 2d Tindals.	Drummers and Fifers.	Puckallies.	Rank and File: Naigues.	Sepoys.	Total	Missing: Rank and File.	REMARKS.
General Staff	-	-	-	-	-	-	-	-	-	-	-	-	-	-	-	-	-	
Brigade Ditto	-	-	-	-	-	-	-	-	-	-	-	-	-	-	-	-	-	
Engineer	-	-	-	-	-	-	-	-	-	-	-	-	-	-	-	-	-	
Artillery	-	-	-	-	-	-	-	-	-	-	1	-	-	-	13	13	-	
Sappers and Miners	-	-	-	-	-	-	1	1	-	-	-	-	-	-	2	2	-	
His Majesty's Royal Scots	-	-	-	-	-	-	-	-	-	-	-	-	-	-	-	-	-	
Flank Companies, 1st Battalion 2d Regiment N. I.	-	-	-	-	-	-	-	-	-	-	-	-	-	-	-	-	-	
1st ditto 11th ditto	-	-	-	-	-	-	2	2	-	-	-	-	-	-	6	6	3	
1st ditto 12th ditto	-	-	-	-	-	-	-	-	-	-	-	-	-	-	-	-	-	
Flank Companies 2d ditto 13th ditto	-	-	-	-	-	-	-	-	-	-	-	-	-	-	5	5	1	
Flank Companies 1st ditto 20th ditto	-	-	-	-	-	-	-	-	-	-	-	-	-	-	3	3	-	
Flank Companies 1st ditto 24th ditto	-	-	-	-	-	1	1	2	-	-	-	-	1	1	16	17	-	
1st Battalion 22d Regiment Bengal N. I.	-	-	1	-	-	-	6	6	-	-	1	-	-	2	33	35	-	
2d ditto 24th ditto N. I.	-	-	2	-	-	-	11	11	1	2	2	-	-	-	17	17	1	
Detachment 1st Battalion Pioneers	-	-	-	-	-	-	-	-	-	1	-	-	-	-	7	7	1	
Major Pitman's Brigade, His Highness the Nizam's Service	1	-	-	-	-	2	10	12	-	1	4	-	-	2	38	40	-	
Total	1	-	3	-	-	3	31	34	1	4	8	-	1	5	140	145	6	

Officers Killed, ... Lieutenant . . Bell, . . . His Majesty's Royal Scots.
Wounded, ... Major . . . . Macleod, Deputy Quartermaster-general.
slightly, Ditto . . . . . Goreham, Artillery.
severely, Ditto . . . . . Elliot, . . His Highness the Nizam's Service.
slightly, Captain . . . Tolfrey, . 2d Battalion 24th Regiment Native Infantry.

Wounded, severely, . . Lieutenant . . . . . . Cameron, Assistant Quartermaster-general.
ditto, ... Ditto . . . . Davis, . . Engineer.
slightly, . . . Ditto . . . . Taylor, . Major of Brigade to Lieut.-colonel Scot's Brigade.
severely, . . Ditto . . . Fireworker Caulb, . Artillery.
slightly, . . . Ensign . . . . Nattes, . Engineer.

(Signed) F. Morgan, Captain,
Acting Assistant Adjutant-general.

G. (p. 151.)

General Return of the Killed, Wounded, and Missing, in the 1st and 3d Divisions of the Army of the Deckan, under the personal Command of His Excellency Lieutenant-general Sir Thomas Hislop, Bart. Commander-in-Chief of the Army of the Deckan, &c. &c. &c. in the Action of the 21st instant, near the Village of Mehidpoor, on the Soopra River, with the Army of Mulhar Rao Holkur.

Head-quarters of the Army of the Deckan, Camp, Mehidpoor, 23d December, 1817.

Killed.

CORPS.	Lieutenants.	Subidars, or Syrangs.	Jemidars, or 1st Tindals.	Sergeants, Havildars, or 2d Tindals.	Trumpeters, or Drummers.	Rank and File.	Puckallies.	Sepoy Recruits.	Silladars.	Total: Officers: European.	Total: Officers: Native.	Total: Sergeants, or Havildars.	Total: Trumpeters, or Drums.	Total: Puckallies.	Total: Sepoy Recruits.	Total: Silladars.	Total: Rank and File.	Total: Grand Total.	Horses: Officers.	Horses: Regimental.
tillery and Rocket-Troop	-	-	-	-	-	5	-	-	-	-	-	-	-	-	-	-	5	5	3	35
ry Brigade . Squadron H. M. 22d Light Dragoons	-	-	-	-	-	-	-	-	-	-	-	-	-	-	-	-	-	-	-	3
ry Brigade . 3d Regiment Light Cavalry	-	-	-	-	-	4	-	-	-	-	-	-	-	-	-	-	4	4	-	14
ry Brigade . 4th Regiment Light Cavalry	-	-	-	-	-	2	-	-	-	-	-	-	-	-	-	-	2	2	-	7
ry Brigade . 8th ditto ditto	-	-	-	-	-	3	-	-	-	-	-	-	-	-	-	-	3	3	1	5
ent 6th Regiment Light Cavalry	-	-	-	-	-	-	-	-	-	-	-	-	-	-	-	-	-	-	-	1
rtillery	-	-	-	-	-	-	-	-	-	-	-	-	-	-	-	-	-	-	-	-
nfantry Brigade Rifle Corps	-	-	1	1	-	37	-	-	-	-	1	1	-	-	-	-	37	39	-	-
nfantry Brigade 1st Battalion 3d Regiment, or P. L. I.	1	-	-	1	1	25	-	-	-	1	-	1	1	-	-	-	25	38	1	-
nfantry Brigade 1st ditto 16th ditto or T. L. I.	-	-	1	1	-	14	1	-	-	-	1	1	-	1	-	-	14	17	-	-
nfantry Brigade Flank Companies H. M. Royal Scots	1	-	-	1	-	7	-	-	-	1	-	1	-	-	-	-	7	7	-	-
nfantry Brigade Madras European Regiment	1	-	-	2	-	4	-	-	-	1	-	2	-	-	-	-	4	7	-	-
nfantry Brigade 1st Battalion 14th Regiment N. I.	-	-	-	-	-	1	-	-	-	-	-	-	-	-	-	-	1	1	-	-
nfantry Brigade 2d ditto 14th ditto N. I.	-	-	-	-	2	11	-	1	-	-	-	-	-	2	1	-	11	14	-	-
itto ditto 2d Battalion 6th Regiment N. I.	-	-	1	2	-	11	-	-	-	-	1	2	-	-	-	-	11	14	-	-
itto ditto Russell Brigade in regular service of the Nizam	-	1	-	2	-	9	-	-	-	-	1	2	-	-	-	-	9	12	-	-
ichment 22d Regiment Bengal Native Infantry	-	-	-	-	-	-	-	-	-	-	-	-	-	-	-	-	-	-	-	-
Battalion Pioneers	-	-	-	-	-	-	-	-	-	-	-	-	-	-	-	-	-	-	-	-
opal Contingent	-	-	-	-	-	-	-	-	-	-	-	-	-	-	-	-	-	-	-	5
ysore Silladars	-	-	-	-	-	-	-	-	19	-	-	-	-	-	-	19	-	-	-	23
Nizam's Reformed Horse	-	-	-	-	-	-	-	-	-	-	-	-	-	-	-	-	-	-	-	-
Adjutant-general's and Quartermaster-general's Department	-	-	-	-	-	-	-	-	-	-	-	-	-	-	-	-	-	-	2	1
Brigade Majors	-	-	-	-	-	-	-	-	-	-	-	-	-	-	-	-	-	-	1	-
Commander-in-Chief's Personal Staff	-	-	-	-	-	-	-	-	-	-	-	-	-	-	-	-	-	-	-	-
Total	3	1	3	10	3	133	1	1	19	3	4	10	1	3	1	19	133	163	8	94

Wounded.

CORPS.	Camels.	Majors.	Captains.	Lieutenants.	Cornets, or Ensigns.	Surgeon.	Troop Quartermasters.	Staff Sergeants.	Farriers.	Subidars, or Syrangs.	Jemidars, or 1st Tindals.	Sergeants, or Havildars.	Trumpeters, or Drummers.	Silladars.	Rank and File.	Puckallies.	Sepoy Recruits.
tillery and Rocket-Troop	1	-	-	1	1	-	1	1	-	-	-	1	-	-	10	-	-
ry Brigade . Squadron H. M. 22d Light Dragoons	-	-	-	-	-	-	-	-	-	-	-	-	1	-	2	-	-
ry Brigade . 3d Regiment Light Cavalry	-	-	-	-	-	-	-	-	-	-	-	-	-	-	8	-	-
ry Brigade . 4th Regiment Light Cavalry	-	-	-	-	-	-	-	-	-	-	-	1	-	-	5	-	-
ry Brigade . 8th ditto ditto	-	-	-	-	-	-	-	1	-	-	-	-	-	-	4	-	-
ent 6th Regiment Light Cavalry	-	-	-	-	-	-	-	-	-	-	-	-	-	-	2	-	-
rtillery	-	-	-	-	-	-	-	-	-	-	-	-	-	-	-	-	-
nfantry Brigade Rifle Corps	-	-	1	5	2	-	-	2	-	-	3	6	3	-	75	1	-
nfantry Brigade 1st Battalion 3d Regiment, or P. L. I.	-	-	1	2	-	-	-	-	-	-	5	5	-	-	61	-	-
nfantry Brigade 1st ditto 16th ditto or T. L. I.	-	1	1	3	-	1	-	-	-	1	4	3	5	-	56	1	-
nfantry Brigade Flank Companies H. M. Royal Scots	-	-	-	2	-	-	-	-	-	-	-	4	1	-	27	-	-
nfantry Brigade Madras European Regiment	-	-	-	1	-	-	-	-	-	-	-	1	5	-	45	-	-
nfantry Brigade 1st Battalion 14th Regiment N. I.	-	-	1	-	-	-	-	-	-	-	-	1	1	-	9	-	-
nfantry Brigade 2d ditto 14th ditto N. I.	-	-	-	1	-	-	-	-	-	1	3	5	3	-	40	-	-
itto ditto 2d Battalion 6th Regiment N. I.	-	-	-	2	-	-	-	-	-	-	-	2	1	-	31	-	1
itto ditto Russell Brigade in regular service of the Nizam	-	-	-	1	-	-	-	-	-	2	4	1	-	-	54	1	-
ichment 22d Regiment Bengal Native Infantry	-	-	-	-	-	-	-	-	-	-	-	-	-	-	3	-	-
Battalion Pioneers	-	-	-	-	-	-	-	-	-	-	-	-	-	-	2	-	-
opal Contingent	-	-	-	-	-	-	-	-	-	-	-	-	-	5	2	-	-
ysore Silladars	-	-	-	-	-	-	-	-	-	-	-	-	-	47	-	-	-
Nizam's Reformed Horse	-	-	-	-	-	-	-	-	-	-	-	-	-	-	-	-	-
Adjutant-general's and Quartermaster-general's Department	-	-	-	2	-	-	-	-	-	-	-	-	-	-	-	-	-
Brigade Majors	-	-	2	2	-	-	-	-	-	-	-	-	-	-	-	-	-
Commander-in-Chief's Personal Staff	-	-	-	1	-	-	-	-	-	-	-	-	-	-	-	-	-
Total	1	1	6	23	3	1	1	4	-	4	19	30	20	52	436	3	1

Wounded — Total; Horses; Missing.

CORPS.	Total: Officers: European.	Total: Officers: Native.	Total: Sergeants, or Havildars.	Total: Trumpeters, or Drums.	Total: Puckallies.	Total: Sepoy Recruits.	Total: Silladars.	Total: Rank and File.	Total: Grand Total.	Horses: Officers.	Horses: Regimental.	Missing: Rank and File.	Missing: Horses.
tillery and Rocket-Troop	3	-	2	-	-	-	-	10	15	-	-	-	8
ry Brigade . Squadron H. M. 22d Light Dragoons	-	-	-	1	-	-	-	2	3	-	-	-	2
ry Brigade . 3d Regiment Light Cavalry	-	-	-	-	-	-	-	8	8	-	-	-	9
ry Brigade . 4th Regiment Light Cavalry	-	-	1	-	-	-	-	5	6	-	-	-	4
ry Brigade . 8th ditto ditto	-	-	1	-	-	-	-	4	5	-	-	-	12
ent 6th Regiment Light Cavalry	-	-	-	-	-	-	-	2	2	-	-	-	-
rtillery	-	-	-	-	-	-	-	-	-	-	-	-	-
nfantry Brigade Rifle Corps	8	3	8	3	1	-	-	75	98	-	-	-	-
nfantry Brigade 1st Battalion 3d Regiment, or P. L. I.	3	5	5	-	-	-	-	61	74	-	-	-	-
nfantry Brigade 1st ditto 16th ditto or T. L. I.	6	5	3	5	1	-	-	56	76	-	-	-	-
nfantry Brigade Flank Companies H. M. Royal Scots	2	-	4	1	-	-	-	27	34	-	-	-	-
nfantry Brigade Madras European Regiment	1	-	1	5	-	-	-	45	52	-	-	-	-
nfantry Brigade 1st Battalion 14th Regiment N. I.	1	-	1	1	-	-	-	9	12	-	-	-	-
nfantry Brigade 2d ditto 14th ditto N. I.	1	4	5	3	-	-	-	40	53	-	-	-	-
itto ditto 2d Battalion 6th Regiment N. I.	2	-	2	1	-	1	-	31	37	-	-	-	-
itto ditto Russell Brigade in regular service of the Nizam	1	6	1	-	1	-	-	54	63	-	-	-	-
ichment 22d Regiment Bengal Native Infantry	-	-	-	-	-	-	-	3	3	-	-	-	-
Battalion Pioneers	-	-	-	-	-	-	-	2	2	-	-	1	-
opal Contingent	-	-	-	-	-	-	5	2	7	-	-	-	-
ysore Silladars	-	-	-	-	-	-	47	-	47	-	-	-	-
Nizam's Reformed Horse	-	-	-	-	-	-	-	-	-	-	-	-	-
Adjutant-general's and Quartermaster-general's Department	2	-	-	-	-	-	-	-	2	-	-	-	1
Brigade Majors	4	-	-	-	-	-	-	-	4	-	-	-	-
Commander-in-Chief's Personal Staff	1	-	-	-	-	-	-	-	1	-	-	-	-
Total	35	23	34	20	3	1	52	436	604	-	-	1	36

ABSTRACT.

	Officers: European.	Officers: Native.	Sergeants, or Havildars.	Trumpeters, or Drummers.	Puckallies.	Sepoy Recruits.	Silladars.	Rank and File.	Grand Total.
Killed	3	4	10	3	1	1	19	133	174
Wounded	35	23	34	20	3	1	52	436	604
Total	38	27	44	23	4	2	71	569	778

Names of the Officers Killed and Wounded in the Action of the 21st of December 1817, near Mehidpoor, with the Army of Mulhar Rao Holkar.

KILLED.

His Majesty's Royal Scots	Lieutenant Donald Macleod.
Madras European Regiment	Lieutenant Charles Coleman.
1st Battalion 3d Regiment	Lieutenant Glen.

WOUNDED.

Horse Artillery	Lieutenant Gamage	Slightly.
Ditto	Lieutenant F. Worker Noble	Ditto.
Ditto	Troop Quartermaster Griffin	Severely.
His Majesty's Royal Scots	Lieutenant John M'Gregor	Slightly.
Ditto	Lieutenant C. Campbell	Severely.
Madras European Regiment	Lieutenant and Acting Adjt. Hancome	Do. (since dead)
Rifle Corps	Captain Norton	Ditto.
Ditto	Lieutenant and Adjutant Gwynne	Dangerously
Ditto	Lieutenant Shanahan	Ditto.
Ditto	Lieutenant Drake	Ditto.
Ditto	Lieutenant Eastment	Severely.
Ditto	Lieutenant Calder	Ditto.
Ditto	Ensign Gem	Dangerously
Ditto	Ensign Agnew	Slightly.
1st Battalion 3d Regiment, or P. L. I.	Lieutenant Jones	Dangerously
Ditto	Captain Lieutenant Agnew	Slightly.
Ditto	Lieutenant Clemons	Ditto.
2d Battalion 6th Regiment N. I.	Lieutenant and Adjutant M'Maister	Ditto.
Ditto	Lieutenant Mathias	Ditto.
1st Battalion 14th Regiment N. I.	Captain W. Brown	Ditto
2d Battalion 14th Regiment N. I.	Lieutenant M'Intosh	Ditto.
1st Battalion 16th Regiment N. I.	Major Bowen	Dangerously.
Ditto	Captain Cuffley	Slightly.
Ditto	Lieutenant and Adjutant Macglashaid	Ditto.
Ditto	Lieutenant M'Intosh	Ditto.
Ditto	Lieutenant Palmer	Severely.
Ditto	Surgeon Stephenson	Slightly.
Attached to the Russell Brigade	Lieut. Kennedy, H. M. 86th Regiment	Ditto.
Adjutant-General's Department	Lieutenant O'Brien	Ditto.
Quartermaster-General's Department	Lieutenant Gibbings	Severely.
Commander-in-Chief's Personal Staff	Lieutenant Elliot	Slightly.
Brigade-Major	Capt. Evans, Acting Major Bde. Lt. B.	Ditto.
Ditto	Capt. Hunter, 2d Infantry Brigade	Ditto.
Ditto	Lieut. Tocker, Acting M. B. R. B.	Ditto.
Ditto	Lieut. Lyon, 2d Cavalry Brigade	Severely.

(Signed) T. H. S. Conway,

Adjutant-General of the Army of the Deckan.

Memorandum of the Organization of the Divisions of the Army of the Deckan, under the personal Command of His Excellency Lieutenant Sir Thomas Hislop, Bart. Commander-in-Chief, &c. &c. &c. on the 21st December, 1817.

(P. 149.)

Light Horse Artillery Brigade	Ten Guns, Madras Horse Artillery Galloper Guns, 3d Regiment Cavalry Galloper Guns, 8th Regiment Cavalry Rocket Troop	Captain Rudyard, Madras Horse Artillery, commanding.
1st Cavalry Brigade	One Squadron H. M. 22d L. D. under Captain Vernon 3d Regiment Madras Light Cavalry, under Lieut. Clubley	Lieut.-Col. Russell, 3d Regt Cavalry, Brigadier.
2d Cavalry Brigade	4th Regiment Madras Light Cavalry, under Lieutenant Macquay 8th Regiment Madras Light Cavalry, under Captain Martin	Major Lushington, 4th Regiment Cavalry, Brigadier.
Artillery	Madras Artillery, one Company, under Lieut. Bennett Russell Brigade Artillery, in the regular Service of H. H. the Nizam, under Lieut. Sotheby	Major Noble, C. B. Horse Artillery, commanding.
Light Infantry Brigade	Madras Rifle Corps, commanded by Major Snow 1st Battalion 3d M. Regiment, or Palamcottah Light Infantry, under Major Knowles 1st Battalion 16th M. Regiment, or Trichinopoly Light Infantry, under Captain Cuffley	Major Bowen, 16th Light Infantry, Brigadier.
1st Brigade of Infantry of the Line	Flank Companies H. M. Royal Scots, under Captain Hulme Madras European Regiment, under Major Andrews 1st Battalion 14th Madras N. I. under Major Smith 2d Battalion 14th Madras N. I. under Major Ives	Lieut.-Colonel R. Scott, Madras European Regiment, Brigadier.
2d Brigade of Infantry of Line	2d Battalion 6th Regiment Madras Native Infantry, under Major Moodie Russell Brigade in the regular Service of H. H. the Nizam, { 1st Battalion under Capt. Laride, 2d Battalion under Lieut. J. Currie, } Captain Hare Brigade,	Lieut.-Colonel A. M'Dowell, 6th Regt. Madras Native Infantry, Brigadier.
Madras Pioneers	Three Companies under Command of Captain M'Craith.	
Mysore Silladar Horse	Commanded by Captain James Grant, 5th Regiment M. Light Cavalry.	

(Signed) T. H. S. Conway, Adjutant-General.

Adjutant-General's Office, Camp at Mehidpoor,
23d December, 1817.

H. 1. (p. 177.)

Return of Casualties in the Division under the Command of Brigadier-general Smith, C. B., from the 22d of November to the 8th of December, 1817.

Camp, Punderpoor, 8th December, 1817.

Corps.	Killed			Wounded.				Missing
	Troopers	Silladars	Horses.	Farriers	Troopers	Lascars.	Silladars.	Horses.
25th November, Auxiliary Horse	-	-	2	-	-	-	4	-
27th ditto ditto	-	2	-	-	-	-	4	4
29th ditto Horse Artillery	-	-	-	-	-	-	-	1
5th December, Madras Artillery	-	-	-	-	-	1	-	-
Auxiliary Horse	-	-	-	-	-	-	4	-
7th ditto Horse Artillery	-	-	-	-	-	-	-	1
2d Madras Cavalry . . . , .	1	-	-	1	1	-	-	-
Auxiliary Horse	-	-	-	-	-	-	3	-
8th ditto ditto	-	-	-	-	-	-	1	-
Total . . .	1	2	2	1	1	1	16	6

(Signed) H. Tovey,
Deputy Adjutant-general.

H. 2. (p. 191.)

RETURN of CASUALTIES in the Division under the Command of Brigadier-general SMITH, C.B., from the 23d to the 29th of January, 1818.

Camp at Lonud, 31st January, 1818.

CORPS.		Wounded.					Missing.		
				Followers					
23d January,	2d Madras Cavalry	-	-	-	-	-	-	-	1
	Light Battalion	-	-	-	-	-	-	1	-
24th ditto	H. M. 65th	1	-	-	-	-	-	-	-
	1st Battalion 2d Native Infantry	-	1	-	-	-	-	-	-
	Light Battalion	-	2	-	-	-	-	-	-
26th ditto	Horse Artillery	-	-	1	-	-	-	-	-
	2d Madras Cavalry	-	-	1	-	-	1	1	2
	H. M. 65th	-	2	-	-	-	-	-	-
	Light Battalion	-	8	-	-	-	-	-	-
27th ditto	Horse Artillery	-	-	-	-	1	-	-	-
	H. M. 65th	-	2	-	-	-	-	-	-
	1st Battalion 2d Native Infantry	-	1	-	-	-	-	-	-
29th ditto	H. M. 65th	-	1	-	1	-	-	-	-
	Total	1	17	2	1	1	1	2	3

(Signed) H. TOVEY,
Deputy Adjutant-general.

Officer Wounded.
Ensign Newhouse, H. M. 65th, slightly.

N. B. The wounds all slight, and the parties in the ranks, except two Sepoys badly wounded with rockets.

I. (p. 183.)

To Lieutenant-colonel FITZSIMON, commanding, &c. Serroor.

SIR,

I HAVE the honour to report, that in conformity to your instructions, I marched from Serroor at half-past eight P. M. on the 31st of December, in command of the following detachment: the 2d battalion of the 1st regiment, about five hundred, two six-pounders, and about two hundred and fifty auxiliary horse under Lieutenant Swanston. Having proceeded on my way towards Poonah, as far as Koreigaum, by ten A.M. on the 1st of January, my further progress was arrested by the appearance (according to information then obtained) of the Peishwah with a very large army, supposed to be about twenty thousand horse, and eight thousand infantry, with two heavy guns; the whole formed on the opposite side of the river Beemah ready to attack us. I continued my march until I reached the village of Koreigaum, in which I determined to make a stand; and accordingly took post, selecting commanding situations for the two guns. The enemy, perceiving my intention, sent three different bodies of Arabs, consisting of about one thousand each, under cover of their guns, and supported by large bodies of horse, for the same purpose; and I am sorry to say, from their superior information of the nature of the village, succeeded in getting hold of its strongest post; and from which I was unable to dislodge them during the day. We continued incessantly engaged till nine P. M. when we finally repulsed them. At day-break on the morning of the 2d, we took possession of the post the enemy had occupied the day before, but they did not attempt to molest us. On the evening of the 2d, despairing of being able to make my way good to Poonah, and my men having been forty-eight hours without food, and no prospect of procuring any in the deserted village we had taken post in, I determined upon the attempt to retreat; and having collected the whole of the wounded, secured the two guns and one tumbril for moving, I commenced my retreat at seven P. M. being under the necessity of destroying one empty tumbril, and leaving the camp equipage. Under this explanation, I trust I shall be deemed justified in the steps I have taken. Our loss has been heavy indeed, but not more so than might have been expected in a struggle like this; and is as follows:

Killed . . Lieutenant Chisholm, Artillery.
——— Assistant-Surgeon Wingate, 2d Batt. 1st Reg.
Wounded, Lieutenant Patterson . . . . 2d Batt. 1st Reg. dangerously,
——— Lieutenant Connellan } badly, but not dangerously.
——— Lieutenant Swanston }

50 men killed, 2d Battalion 1st Regiment.
12 men killed, Artillery.
62 killed, Auxiliary Horse, not included.

124

105 men wounded, 2d Battalion 1st Regiment.
8 men ditto Artillery.

113 wounded.

Total, 175 men, Auxiliary Horse not included.

In concluding this Report, I beg to assure you that it is utterly impossible for me to do justice to the merits and exertions of the European officers, non-commissioned officers, and privates, that I had the honour and good fortune to command on this trying occasion.

I have &c. &c.

(Signed) F. F. Staunton,
Capt. 1st N. I.

Serroor, 2d January, 1818.

K. (p. 210.)

Return of Casualties in the Detachment commanded by Major-general Thomas Brown, at the Assault of Jawud, and Capture of Jeswunt Rao Bhao's Camp and Guns, on the 29th of January 1818.

CORPS.	Killed.		Wounded.				Missing.
	Rank and File	Horses.	Ensigns.	Havildars	Rank and File	Horses.	Horses.
European Horse Artillery	1	1	-	-	4	-	-
Native Horse Artillery	1	-	-	-	4	1	-
3d Regiment Native Cavalry	1	2	-	-	3	3	2
4th ditto ditto	-	6	-	1	7	1	-
2d Rohillah Cavalry	-	1	-	-	4	4	-
1st Battalion 1st Regiment Native Infantry	2	-	-	-	4	-	-
Pioneers	-	-	-	-	5	-	-
Dromedary Corps	-	-	1	-	-	-	-
Total	5	10	1	1	31	9	2

Officer Wounded.

Ensign J. W. Patton, (commanding Dromedary Corps) severely, not dangerously.

(Signed) Thomas Brown,
Major-general.

(Signed) Edward W. Beatson,
D. A. A. General.

L. (p. 232.)

RETURN of KILLED and WOUNDED in the First Division of the Army of the Deckan, under the personal command of His Excellency Lieutenant-general Sir THOMAS HISLOP, Bart. Commander-in-Chief, &c. &c. &c. in the Operations against the Fort of TALNEIR, on the 27th of February 1818.

Head-quarters of the Army of the Deckan.
Camp near Talneir, 28th Feb 1818.

CORPS.	Killed.				Wounded.			
	Officers.	N. C. Officers.	Rank and File.	Total.	Officers.	N. C. Officers.	Rank and File	Total.
Horse-Artillery and Rocket Troop	-	1	-	1	-	-	2	2
Engineers	-	-	-	-	1	-	-	1
Flank Companies H. M. Royal Scots	2	1	3	6	1	-	3	1
Flank Companies Madras European Regiment	-	-	-	-	-	-	1	1
Rifle Corps	-	-	-	-	-	-	4	1
1st Battalion 2d Regiment N. I.	-	-	-	-	1	-	-	1
1st ditto 16th ditto, or Trichinopoly L. I.	-	-	-	-	-	-	2	2
1st Battalion of Pioneers	-	-	-	-	-	-	1	1
Adjutant-general's Department	-	-	-	-	1	-	-	1
Deputy Adjutant-general H. M. Forces	-	-	-	-	1	-	-	1
Total	2	2	3	7	5	-	13	18

Names of Officers Killed and Wounded.

Killed.

Major Gordon, H. M. Royal Scots.
Captain Mac Gregor, ditto.

Wounded.

Lieutenant-colonel Mac Gregor Murray, Deputy Adjutant-general H. M. Forces, severely.
Lieutenant Mac Gregor, H. M. Royal Scots, severely.
Captain H. O'Brien, Assistant Adjutant-general, severely.
Lieutenant Anderson, Engineers, severely.
Ensign Chauvel, 1st Battalion 2d Regiment N. I. severely.

(Signed) T. H. S. CONWAY,
Adjutant-general of the Army of the Deckan.

M. (p. 248.)

Return of Wounded on the 13th and 14th of March, belonging to the Field Force under Lieutenant-colonel Prother, at the Siege of Koaree.

Corps.	Lieutenants	Sergeants.	Havildars.	Drummers.	Fifers.	Rank and File	DooleyBearers	Bheasties	Total.
Engineers	1	-	-	-	-	-	-	-	1
His Majesty's 47th Regiment	-	-	-	-	-	1	-	-	1
Ditto 65th ditto	-	-	-	-	-	-	-	-	-
Ditto 89th ditto	-	-	-	-	-	5	-	-	5
2d Grenadier Battalion	-	-	-	-	-	1	-	-	1
2d Battalion 4th Regiment	-	-	-	-	-	1	-	-	1
1st ditto 5th ditto	-	-	-	-	-	-	-	-	-
2d ditto 6th ditto	-	-	-	-	-	-	-	-	-
1st ditto 9th dittto	-	-	-	-	-	1	-	-	1
Followers	-	-	-	-	-	-	2	-	2
Total	1	-	-	-	-	9	2	-	12

Killed.

One Drummer, H. M. 89th Regiment.

(Signed) George Moore,
Major of Brigade.

Officer Wounded.

Lieutenant Remon, Engineers, slightly.

N. (p. 253.)

Translation.

Dated from Peempulnair, in the Pergunnah
of Kurkum, 21st February, 1818

Yesterday morning, after the Peishwah had bathed and was eating, the English cavalry arrived, with an intention of seizing him, but he fortunately escaped. The Satara Rajah, with his mother and two brothers, fell into the hands of the enemy. Tents, elephants, colours, nagarrahs, palankeens, and elephants laden with jewels and treasure, and the palankeens of Nur-Narrain, were all lost. We intended to march upon Trimboorna, and had sent off part of our baggage in that direction; but when the alarm took place, the route was altered to Pureinda, near which place we encamped. Grain and grass were given to the horses, and it was intended to move on; however, as I had lost every thing, I quitted the army, and came to this place on my way to Merritch. Our loss has been so great, that not even a cooking-pot remains with us. We had no information;

which was the cause of our misfortune; but some say treachery must have existed. Gokla, with a part of the troops, went out to meet the enemy; and if the others of the army had charged with equal spirit, such a defeat could never have occurred. The English, in gaining possession of Maharaj (Rajah of Satara), have accomplished all their wishes. Where the Peishwah's army is going, is known only to themselves.

The Peishwah, on the first alarm, mounted, and rode two coss at full speed.

The elephants belonging to the Alkote Rajah, carrying the colour and nagariah, were taken, as were the whole of Nepaunkur's.

Some say Gokla is wounded; others, that he is killed.

Dated Peempulnair, in the Pergunnah of Kurkum,
21st February.

By B——e Jasood, I wrote to you at Chinchunee, which you will have received. Yesterday morning, about nine o'clock, the English came from Amkluch to Ashtee, where the army was halting. Our men were eating, when the first report of their being within half a coss reached us. In the confusion which followed, A———m came and gave me more certain information. The army moved off; and when the guns opened upon us, the flight became general: Bajee Rao went from right to left, not knowing how to act; the whole of his family were on horseback. The Satara Rajah, with his mother and two brothers, were also on horseback; but finding escape impossible, dismounted, and, as the enemy were fast approaching, sat down until their arrival; when they were surrounded and carried off. The elephant, carrying the standard of the empire, was taken; the flag only was saved, by being put in charge of a horseman. Five elephants laden with treasure, and ten Hurcarrah camels, were captured. Two of Mahadeo's palankeens, with the idols in them, were taken, together with many others, tents, stores, aftabgeers, &c. In this manner was the wealth of the Sirkar destroyed. The mare of the Sur Luskhur, the nagarrah elephants, treasury department, were all, all lost. The Akulkote Rajah lost two elephants carrying howdahs; it is reported, however, that part of his baggage has arrived in safety. Gokla was wounded, but he has not joined us. Poorundurie, Rastia, and some few Mahrattas, came up at night. Several men of distinction, belonging to Gokla, have fallen; and the troops that arrived from Nagpoor have fully shared in the misfortunes of the day. After this, we halted at Kurwa Roopallee, three coss from Puremda. Soon after sunset, a report of the English approaching created the greatest alarms; and becoming more so about nine o'clock, the baggage was sent off, and at midnight the whole army moved north. My people, R–o, Punt, Yadoo, and Gunajee, began to consider that after this it would be difficult for them to save themselves; and as our villages were near, it would be better to return home. When the last alarm took place, we quitted the army, and went off towards Punderpoor. Where the Peishwah is going, I know not. The whole of our property is gone; jewels, money, to the value of one crore of rupees, have been lost. Let this be forwarded to our master ——— What can I say more?

O. (p. 254.)

Translation of a Proclamation published by the Honourable Company, *Sorsun Suman Usur Myanlyn Ouluf*, or A. D. 1817.

That all persons may become acquainted with this Proclamation, and regulate their conduct accordingly: It is notified, that from the time of the assumption of the Government, by Bajee Rao, sedition and rebellion prevailed in various shapes; that his authority was not, at any time, established in the country subject to his rule; that not very long ago, when Holkur was in a state of rebellion, he abandoned the country, and pusillanimously repaired to Bassein, where he remained dependant upon the assistance he derived from Khunderow Rastay. He then formed an alliance with the British Government; and being joined by the troops of the Honourable Company, was by them re-established in his government. The disorders and disaffection which prevailed, were suppressed, and his authority was restored throughout his dominions in the most beneficial manner. In consequence of the previous disordered state of things, followed by a famine, the country was in a most depressed condition; but its prosperity revived under the Honourable Company's protection. Bajee Rao, however, adopted the system of farming out the districts; and the farmers, on their part, made undue exactions from the inhabitants: still, however, the improvement of the country was materially advanced, so much so, that Bajee Rao was enabled, from the revenues of the country, not merely to defray the expenses of the administration, and to enjoy every degree of personal tranquillity and happiness, but also to amass immense wealth. The Honourable Company's Government did not wish to countenance claims on the Mahratta Chieftains which had long ceased to exist; it was the wish of the Company's Government, that he should regulate his conduct by the principles of equity. In conformity with this feeling, the Guickwar Government dispatched Gongather Shastree to Poonah as its agent, to settle the matters in dispute with that Government, under the guarantee of the Honourable Company. He accordingly repaired to that city; and it was expected the discussion would be brought to a speedy termination, which would have proved infinitely to the advantage of Bajee Rao; but in the mean time the Shastree was assassinated by a public officer of Bajee Rao's, on consecrated ground, at Punderpoor. At the very moment in question, the universal voice of the country, including pilgrims and all those that were on the spot, declared that it could only have been by Bajee Rao's order, that Trimbukjee perpetrated that deed: but still regarding Bajee Rao as an Ally ruling over a large Empire, and entertaining no suspicion that he would be accessary to such a crime, the Honourable Company's Government contented itself with demanding the surrender of Trimbukjee as the murderer; but as he was not immediately delivered up, as he ought to have been, a large army belonging to the Honourable Company was assembled, and Trimbukjee was therefore put into our possession. The expense incurred by the Honourable Company, on this occasion, was very heavy; but in consideration of the existing friendship, it preferred no demand for the same, and was satisfied to accept the person of Trimbukjee, and to replace the alliance on the footing on which it had previously stood. Subsequently to these occurrences, Bajee Rao dispatched letters to foreign Chieftains, urging them to have their army in a state of preparation; while he excited disturbances in his own territories, and had his troops in readiness in aid of the same system; the object of which was to plunge the Company's Government into a state of war, and to expose it to injury. For the purpose of suppressing these disturbances, a British force was equipped and marched to Poonah, and the city was invested, with Bajee Rao in it. At this moment Bajee Rao was in our power, and a force was likewise collected fully adequate, from its strength, to the subjection of the country; but from the time the treaty was signed, Bajee Rao had, on all occasions, acknowledged that he owed his political existence, as well as the happiness and tranquillity he enjoyed, to the Honourable Company's Government, and that he was grateful for the blessings its protection had afforded him. His declarations to this effect were reiterated in various shapes; and in consideration of them, a fresh treaty was concluded in confirmation of that of Bassein, the object of which was to maintain his sovereignty, but to deprive him of the means of exciting disturbances. It was stipulated that the five thousand horse and three thousand infantry, which Bajee Rao was all along bound to furnish as auxiliaries, should be kept up by the Honourable Company; and to meet the expenses of this force, territorial assignments were made; and from that moment the same friendly course of proceeding which had previously existed was renewed; and as the Pindarries had been in the yearly habit of harassing the people in every direction, and especially the territories of Bajee Rao, which had suffered the most severely, the Company's Government determined to adopt the necessary measures for suppressing these freebooters; and Bajee Rao then acknowledged, that the accomplishment of this object would be highly beneficial to him, and promised that his army should also co-operate therein. Under the cloak, however, of an assurance so satisfactory, he remitted to foreign Chieftains that treasure which the Company's protection had afforded him the means of amassing, for objects hostile to its interests, at the same time that he put his own army in a state of equipment; while, for the purpose of removing to a distance the British force, which was in its neighbourhood, he caused it to be joined by a body of two thousand of his cavalry, and they then marched to a remote position. Taking advantage of this opportunity, at a moment when there was neither cause for such a measure, nor any points of difference in discussion, he suddenly equipped his army, put it in motion, and attacked the Honourable Company's troops; he likewise pursued a line of conduct, which has never been adopted in any country. The residence and cantonments of the British representative were plundered and burnt; inhabitants of the Company's dominions, as well as travellers, passing through the country in faith of existing treaties, were seized and imprisoned; whilst others were plundered; two British officers, who were on their way from Bombay, were put to death in the vicinity of Tellagaon, in a manner not even practised in regard to public offenders, and the perpetrators of that crime are yet in his service—it is therefore manifestly established, that their murder could only have been in pursuance of the Peishwah's orders. Trimbukjee Deinglia, the assassin of Gungadhur Shastree, has likewise been recalled to his presence, and has been allowed to continue in the exercise of official functions; and hence he has fixed upon himself the assassination of the Shastree, which public opinion had all along declared could not have been committed without his sanction; he has, moreover, taken steps to call in the Pindarries to lay waste the country. Having thus abandoned the paramount duties of a Sovereign, for the purpose of ruining the Company's Government, that Government is satisfied, Bajee Rao is unfit to reign over this Empire. Upon these grounds, measures are in progress to deprive him effectually of all public authority, and to place the country and forts in possession of the Honourable Company, to be governed by them. With this view, a light force has been dispatched in pursuit of the Peishwah; another has been appointed for the reduction of the forts, and a third has reached the neighbourhood of Ahmednuggur, whilst a large army has also made its appearance in Khandesh. General Munro is employed in reducing the southern provinces, and another force from Bombay is in the Kokun, where it is engaged in settling the country, having already reduced the forts there. In a short period, therefore, there will be nothing remaining connected with Bajee Rao, and measures will be adopted, by the Honourable Company's Government, for the enlargement of his Highness the Rajah of Satara, now in the custody of Bajee Rao; and who, when his liberation shall be effected, will be established in a principality, for the maintenance of his rank and dignity, and the rank and dignity of his court. In prosecution of the measures thus contemplated by the Honourable Company's Government, his Highness's flag has been displayed in the fort of Satara, and satisfactory assurances given to his adherents. In the territories which will belong to the Maharajah, the administration of justice, the controul and government of the country, will be conducted by his Highness. In the territories which will be reserved to the Honourable Company, their authority will be established, without prejudice to any Wutuns, Enams, annual allowances, charges of the temples, alms, or the religious tenets of any sect. Whatever may be equitable, will be duly enforced. The farms granted by Bajee Rao being abolished, the duties will be committed to Kamavisdars, who will confine their collections to the just amount of the revenues. Every individual will be secured from every species of tyranny and oppression. Upon this point, let every person be satisfied. Those who shall be in the service of Bajee Rao shall withdraw from it, and retire to their habitations in two months from this date; in failure of which, their Wutuns shall be seized, and ruin will be their inevitable lot. The Zumeendars (public officers) are, without delay, to send in a detailed list of those in their respective Pergunnahs, who are in the employ of Bajee

Rao, continuing also to report those who may quit his service and return to their homes, as they do so. No assistance is to be afforded to Bajee Rao; and no payments, on account of revenue, are to be made to him. If payment be made to him, no remission will be allowed when the injury sustained by the country, in the present year, shall be investigated. If any revenue be paid to Bajee Rao, credit will not be allowed for the same, but the whole amount thereof collected. The Wutuns and lands of all those public officers who may afford aid or pay money to Bajee Rao, will be forfeited. Dated the 11th of February, 1818, or 5th of Rubecoolkaheir.

P. (p. 294.)

RETURN of KILLED and WOUNDED of the RESERVE DIVISION during the Operations against the Fort of BELGAUM, from the 21st of March to the 10th of April 1818 inclusive.

Camp near Belgaum, 11th of April, 1818.

CORPS.	Killed.							Wounded.					REMARKS.
	Sub-Conductors.	Sergeants	Gunners.	Matrosses, or Privates.	Drummers.	Sepoys, or Gun Lascars.	Total.	Sergeants.	Gunners.	Matrosses or Privates	Sepoys, or Gun Lascars.	Total.	
Detachment H. M. 22d Light Dragoons	-	1	-	1	-	-	2	-	-	3	-	3	
Ditto Foot Artillery	-	-	2	3	1	2	8	-	1	1	2	4	One Matross since dead.
2d Battalion 9th Regiment N. I.	-	-	-	-	-	-	-	-	-	-	5	5	Two Sepoys since dead.
Store Department	1	-	-	-	-	-	1	-	-	-	-	-	
Total . . .	1	1	2	4	1	2	11	-	1	4	7	12	

(Signed) D. NEWALL, Lieutenant-Colonel,
Commanding Detachment.

N. B. The Sergeant returned "Killed" belonged to the Honourable Company's Horse Artillery, and was doing duty with the guns of H. M. 22d Regiment of Light Dragoons.

Q. (p. 304.)

RETURN of KILLED and WOUNDED in the FIELD DIVISION of the Army before SHOLAPOOR, from the 10th to the 15th of May, 1818.

CORPS.	Killed.		Wounded.							
	Sergeants, or Havildars.	Rank and File.	Captains.	Lieutenants.	Sergeants, or Havildars.	Rank and File.	Gun-Lascars.	Officers Horses.	Regimental ditto.	Ditto Missing ditto.
His Majesty's 22d Light Dragoons .	-	-	1	-	-	7	-	3	16	4
Detachment Artillery	-	-	-	-	-	-	1	-	-	-
His Majesty's Flank Battalion . .	-	3	-	-	1	37	-	-	-	-
Rifle Detachment	1	-	-	-	-	8	-	-	-	-
1st Battalion 4th Reg. Madras N. I.	1	3	-	-	-	9	-	-	-	-
1st ditto 7th do. Bombay do.	-	1	-	-	-	1	-	-	-	-
2d ditto 9th do. Madras do.	1	4	-	2	-	15	-	-	-	-
Engineers Department	-	-	-	1	-	-	-	-	-	-
Total . . .	3	11	1	3	1	77	1	3	16	4

(Signed) WAL. JOLLEE,
A. A. General.

(Signed) THOS. MUNRO,
Brigadier-general.

Names of Wounded Officers.

Captain Middleton, H. M. 22d Light Dragoons.

Lieutenants Maxtone and Robertson, 2d Battalion 9th Regiment.

Lieutenant Wahab, acting in the Engineers Department, slightly.

R. (p. 322.)

Return of the Killed and Wounded in a Detachment of the Hydrabad Subsidiary Force, under the Command of Lieutenant-colonel Mac Dowell, at the Attack of Trimbuck, on the 23d and 24th of April, 1818.

Corps.		Europeans.								Natives							
		Majors.	Captains.	Lieutenants.	Ensigns.	Sergeants	Drummers.	Corporals.	Privates.	Subidars.	Jemidars.	Havildars.	Naigues.	Drummers	Puckallies.	Privates.	Grand Total.
Sappers and Miners	Killed	-	-	-	-	-	-	-	-	-	-	-	-	-	-	-	-
	Wounded	-	-	-	1	-	-	1	-	-	-	-	-	-	-	1	3
Detachment Royal Scots	Killed	-	-	-	-	-	-	-	-	-	-	-	-	-	-	-	-
	Wounded	-	-	-	-	1	1	-	8	-	-	-	-	-	-	-	10
1st Battalion 2d N. I.	Killed	-	-	-	-	-	-	-	-	-	-	-	-	-	-	1	1
	Wounded	-	-	-	-	-	-	-	-	-	-	-	-	-	-	2	2
2d Battalion 13th N. I.	Killed	-	-	-	-	-	-	-	-	-	-	-	1	-	-	-	1
	Wounded	1	-	-	-	-	-	-	-	-	-	-	1	-	-	3	5
	Total	1	-	-	1	1	1	1	8	-	-	-	2	-	-	7	22

(Signed) W Maitland,
M. B. 2d Brigade H. S. Force.

Names of Wounded Officers.

Sappers and Miners, Ensign Lake, severely, but not dangerously.
2d Battalion 13th N. I., Major M'Bean, slightly.

N. B. one Sepoy, 1/2d N. I., since dead.

S. (p. 330.)

Return of Killed and Wounded in a Detachment of the Hydrabad Subsidiary Force, under the Command of Lieutenant-Colonel Mac Dowell, at the Siege and Storm of Malleygaum, from the 18th to the 29th of May 1818.

Killed.

CORPS.	Europeans.								Rank and File.				Natives. Nat. Officers.					Rank and File.			
	Lieutenant-colonel.	Majors.	Captains.	Captain-lieutenants.	Lieutenants.	Ensigns and Lieutenants-Fireworkers.	Sergeants.	Drummers.	Corporals.	Gunners.	Matross or Priv.	Total.	Subidars, or Syrangs.	Jemidars, or 1st Tindals.	Havildars, or 2d Tindals.	Drummers.	Puckallies.	Naigues.	Sepoys, or Lascars.	Total.	Grand Total.
Sappers and Miners	-	-	-	-	1	1	-	-	-	-	-	-	-	-	-	-	-	-	-	-	2
Detachment Artillery	-	-	-	-	-	-	-	-	-	-	1	1	-	1	-	-	-	-	-	-	2
Ditto His Majesty's Royal Scots	-	-	-	-	-	-	-	-	-	-	5	5	-	-	-	-	-	-	-	-	5
Madras European Regiment	-	-	-	-	-	-	-	-	-	-	1	1	-	-	-	-	-	-	-	-	-
2d Battalion 17th, or Chicacole Light Infantry	-	-	-	-	1	-	-	-	-	-	-	-	-	-	-	-	-	1	2	3	4
1st ditto 2d N. I.	-	-	-	-	•	-	-	-	-	-	-	-	-	-	-	-	-	1	2	3	3
2d ditto 13th N. I.	-	-	-	-	2	-	-	-	-	-	-	-	-	-	1	-	-	1	8	9	12
2d ditto 14th N. I.	-	-	-	-	-	-	-	-	-	-	-	-	-	-	-	-	-	-	-	-	-
Russell Brigade	-	-	-	-	-	-	-	-	-	-	-	-	-	-	-	-	-	-	2	2	2
Detachment Pioneers	-	-	-	-	-	-	-	-	-	-	-	-	-	-	-	-	-	-	3	3	3
Total	-	-	-	-	4	1	-	-	-	-	7	7	-	1	1	-	-	3	17	20	33

Wounded.

CORPS.	Europeans.								Rank and File.				Natives. Nat. Officers.					Rank and File.			
	Lieutenant-colonel.	Majors.	Captains.	Captain-lieutenants.	Lieutenants.	Ensigns, or Lieutenants-Fireworkers.	Sergeants.	Drummers.	Corporals.	Gunners.	Priv. or Matrosses.	Total.	Subidars, or Syrangs.	Jemidars, or 1st Tindals.	Havildars, or 2d ditto.	Drummers.	Puckallies.	Naigues.	Sepoys, Lascars, &c.	Total.	Grand Total.
Sappers and Miners	-	-	-	-	-	-	2	-	-	-	-	-	-	-	-	-	-	-	1	1	3
Detachment Artillery	-	-	-	-	-	1	1	-	-	-	9	9	-	-	-	-	-	-	2	2	13
Ditto His Majesty's Royal Scots	-	-	-	-	-	1	1	1	1	-	10	11	-	-	-	-	-	-	-	-	14
Madras European Regiment	-	1	-	-	-	-	1	-	2	-	20	22	-	-	-	-	2	-	-	-	26
2d Battalion 17th, or Chicacole Light Infantry	-	1	-	-	-	-	-	-	-	-	-	-	1	1	-	-	-	3	43	46	49
1st ditto 2d N. I.	-	-	-	-	1	-	-	-	-	-	-	-	-	1	1	-	-	-	12	12	15
2d ditto 13th N. I.	-	-	-	-	1	-	-	-	-	-	-	-	-	-	3	-	-	2	19	21	25
2d ditto 14th N. I.	-	-	-	-	-	-	-	-	-	-	-	-	-	-	-	-	-	1	3	4	4
Russell Brigade	-	-	-	-	1	-	-	-	-	-	-	-	1	-	-	-	-	-	9	9	11
Detachment Pioneers	-	-	-	-	-	-	-	-	-	-	-	-	-	-	1	-	1	1	12	13	15
Total	-	2	-	-	3	2	5	1	3	-	39	42	2	2	5	-	3	7	101	108	175

Names of Officers Killed.

Sappers and Miners, Lieutenant Davis.
Ditto Ensign Nattes.
2d Battalion 17th N. I. Lieutenant Kennedy.
2d ditto 13th N. I. Lieutenant Eagan (28th, at Night)
2d ditto 13th N. I. Lieutenant Wilkinson.

Names of Officers Wounded.

Detachment of Artillery, Lieutenant-Fireworker King.
His Majesty's Royals Ensign Thomas.
Madras European Reg. Major Andrews.
2d Battalion 17th N. I. Major Greenhill.
1st Battalion 2d N. I. Lieutenant Dowker.
Russell Brigade Captain Larride.
Ditto Lieutenant Kennedy.

(Signed) W. Maitland, M. Brigade.
2d Brigade H. S. Force.

T. (p. 341.)

RETURN of KILLED and WOUNDED of the LEFT DIVISION of the GRAND ARMY, during the Operations before MUNDALAH.

Camp, 30th of April, 1818.

Artillery Detachment	One Private of Golandauze, and three Ordnance-drivers, Wounded.
Pioneers	One Private Wounded dangerously.
5th Brigade.	
2d Battalion 1st N. I.	Two Sepoys, and one Lascar, Wounded.
2d Ditto 13th N. I. . . .	One Sepoy Killed, one Bheastie Wounded.
6th Brigade.	
2d Battalion 8th N. I	One Havildar, and two Sepoys, Wounded.
1st Ditto 14th N. I.	One Naick, one Sepoy, Killed, two Sepoys Wounded.
2d Ditto 28th N. I.	None.

Total . . . . . Three Killed, and fourteen Wounded

(Signed) W. L. WATSON,
Assistant Adjutant-general.

U. (p. 346.)

RETURN of European and Native Commissioned, Non-commissioned Officers, and Privates, of the Detachment under the Command of Major LAMB, who have been KILLED and WOUNDED before the Fort of SATUNWARREE, between the Morning of the 8th, and Evening of the 10th of June 1818.

CORPS.		Killed.					Wounded.														REMARKS.
		Lieutenants.	Corporals.	Subidars.	Privates.	Total.	Horses.	Captains.	Sergeants.	Gunners.	Matrosses.	Subidars.	Jemidars	Naigues.	Sepoys.	Risaldars.	Sewars.	Miners.	Lascars.	Total.	
Detachment of Artillery	8th June 1818	-	-	-	-	-	-	-	-	-	-	-	-	-	-	-	-	-	-	-	
	10th	-	1	-	-	1	-	-	1	1	5	-	-	-	2	-	-	-	3	12	
Engineer Department, and Miners	8th	-	-	-	-	-	-	-	-	-	-	-	-	-	-	-	-	-	-	-	
	10th	-	-	-	-	-	-	-	1	-	-	-	-	-	-	-	-	2	-	3	
4th Company of Pioneers	8th	-	-	-	-	-	-	-	-	-	-	-	-	-	-	-	-	-	-	-	
	10th	1	-	-	3	4	-	-	-	-	-	-	-	-	4	-	-	-	-	4	
Detachment 1st Batt. 19th Reg.	8th	-	-	-	-	-	-	-	-	-	-	-	-	-	-	-	-	-	-	-	
	10th	-	-	-	-	-	-	-	-	-	-	1	-	1	3	-	-	-	-	5	
Detachment 1st Batt. 23d Reg.	8th	-	-	-	-	-	-	-	-	-	-	-	-	-	-	-	-	-	-	-	
	10th	-	-	-	-	-	-	-	-	-	-	-	-	-	3	-	-	-	-	3	
Light Comp. 2/23d N. I.	8th	-	-	-	-	-	-	-	-	-	-	-	-	-	-	-	-	-	-	-	
	10th	-	-	-	-	-	-	-	-	-	-	-	-	-	1	-	-	-	-	1	
Flank Comp. 1/26th N. I.	8th	-	-	-	-	-	-	-	-	-	-	-	-	2	3	-	-	-	-	5	
	10th	-	-	1	5	6	-	1	-	-	-	-	1	3	35	-	-	-	-	40	
1st Rohillah Cavalry	10th	-	-	-	-	-	1	-	-	-	-	-	-	-	-	1	1	-	-	2	
Total		1	1	1	8	11	1	1	2	1	5	1	1	6	51	1	1	2	3	75	

N. B. The Wounded are, in general, severely so.

Officer Killed.

Lieutenant Manson, commanding Pioneers.

Officer Wounded.

Captain A. T. Watson, 1st Batt. 26th Reg. N. I. (severely, but not dangerously.)

(Signed) W. LAMB, Major, Commanding Detachment.

(Signed) T. LESTER, Lieut. Adj. Detach. Staff.

X. (p. 354.)

RETURN of KILLED and WOUNDED in the Siege and in the Assault of CHANDA.

Camp near Chanda, 22d May, 1818.

CORPS.	Killed.													Wounded												
	Majors.	Captains.	Lieutenants.	Ensigns.	Subidars.	Jemidars	Havildars	Naicks.	Drummers	Privates and Sepoys	Gun-Lascars	Magazine-Men.	Ordnance-Drivers	Majors.	Captains.	Lieutenants.	Ensigns.	Subidars.	Jemidars.	Sergeants, or Havildars.	Naicks.	Drummers	Privates and Sepoys	Gun Lascars.	Magazine-Men.	Ordnance-Drivers
Bengal Foot Artillery . .	-	-	-	-	-	-	-	-	-	3	-	-	-	-	-	-	-	-	-	-	-	-	-	4	2	2
Madras ditto	1	-	-	-	-	-	-	-	-	-	-	-	1	-	-	-	-	-	-	-	-	-	1	-	-	-
Bengal Grenadier Detachmt.	-	-	-	-	-	-	-	-	-	3	-	-	-	-	-	-	-	-	-	2	1	-	11	-	-	-
Light Infantry Battalion .	-	-	-	-	-	-	-	-	-	-	-	-	-	-	-	-	-	-	-	-	-	-	2	-	-	-
1st Batt. 19th Regt. N. I. .	-	-	-	-	-	-	-	-	-	-	-	-	-	-	-	1	-	-	-	-	-	-	5	-	-	-
1st do. 23d do. N. I. .	-	-	-	-	-	-	-	-	-	-	-	-	-	-	-	-	-	-	-	-	-	-	5	-	-	-
Madras Flank Battalion .	-	-	-	-	-	-	-	-	-	1	-	-	-	-	-	-	-	-	-	-	-	-	6	-	-	-
1st Batt. 1st Regt. N. I. .	-	-	-	-	-	-	-	-	-	2	-	-	-	-	1	1	-	-	-	-	-	-	3	-	-	-
1st do. 11th do. N. I. .	-	-	-	-	-	-	-	-	-	1	-	-	-	-	-	-	-	-	-	1	1	-	1	-	-	-
Bengal Pioneers	-	-	-	-	-	-	-	-	-	1	-	-	-	-	-	1	-	-	-	1	-	-	-	-	-	-
Madras ditto	-	-	-	-	-	-	-	-	-	-	-	-	-	-	-	-	-	-	-	-	-	-	-	-	-	-
Nizam's Reformed Horse .	-	-	-	-	-	-	-	-	-	-	-	-	-	-	-	-	-	-	-	-	-	-	3	-	-	-
Total . .	1	-	-	-	-	-	-	-	-	11	-	-	1	-	1	3	-	-	-	4	2	-	37	4	2	2

Major Goreham, commanding the Artillery, died of excessive fatigue and exposure to the heat.

Capt. Charlsworth, commanding 1st Batt. 1st Reg. wounded severely in the shoulder.

Lieutenant and Adjutant Watson ditto ditto.

Lieutenant F. M. Cunny, Bengal Pioneers.

Lieutenant Casement, 1st Batt. 19th Reg. Baggage-master, left hand amputated.

(Signed) JOHN SCOTT,
Dy. Asst. Adjutant-general.

Y. (p. 390.)

RETURN of KILLED and WOUNDED in the Storm of the Town and Ghurrie of COMPTA, on the 18th of September, 1818.

	Peer Khan's Silladars.	Omeon Sahib's Russalah.						Jeejabia Sahib's Russalah					1st Batt. 1st Reg. Madras N. I.				1st. Batt. 20th Mad. Nat. Inf			Nagpoor Brigade				Ambarick Jemidar's Irreg. Inf			Annund Rao's Irregular Infantry			
		Men.				Horses.		Men.			Horses.																			
	Horses.	Russaldars.	Jemidars.	Duffadars.	Sewars.	Horses.		Jemidars	Duffadars.	Sewars.	Horses.		Subidars.	Jemidars.	Havildars.	Sepoys	Havildars	Naigues.	Sepoys	Jemidars.	Havildars.	Naicks.	Sepoys	Jemidars.	Duffadars	Sewars	Russaldars.	Jemidars.	Duffadars.	Sewars.
Killed	-	-	-	-	-	-	-	-	-	-	-	-	-	-	-	2	-	-	-	-	-	-	1	-	-	-	-	-	-	1
Wounded	3	-	-	-	1	2	-	-	1	6	3	-	-	-	2	12	-	-	3	-	2	1	12	-	-	2	-	1	-	11
Total . .	3	-	-	-	1	2	-	-	1	6	3	-	-	-	2	14	-	-	3	-	2	1	13	-	-	2	-	1	-	12

Total of Horses Killed and Wounded . . . . 8.

	Killed.	Wounded.
Subidars	-	-
Jemidars	-	2
Havildars	-	4
Naigues	-	3
Sepoys	4	40
Jemidars of Horse . . .	-	1
Duffadars of ditto	-	7
Sewars of ditto	-	7
Total . .	4	57

(Signed) W. GORDON, Captain,
Commanding Detachment.

Z. (p. 417.)

General Return of Killed and Wounded of the Hydrabad Subsidiary Force in assaulting the Pettah of Asseerghur, on the 18th March, 1819

Camp Nimbolee, 19th March, 1819.

CORPS.	Europeans. Killed. Officers. Lieutenant-colonels.	Majors.	Captains.	Captain-lieutenants.	Lieutenants.	Ensigns.	Assistant-surgeons.	Sergeants.	Drummers.	Rank and File. Corporals.	Privates.	Total.	Puckallies.
General Staff	-	-	-	-	-	-	-	-	-	-	-	-	-
Detachment H. M. Royal Scots	-	-	-	-	-	-	-	-	-	-	1	1	-
Ditto H. M. 30th Regt.	-	-	-	-	-	-	-	-	-	-	-	-	-
H. M. 67th Regiment	-	-	-	-	-	-	-	-	-	-	-	-	-
1st Battalion 7th N. I.	-	-	-	-	-	-	-	-	-	-	-	-	-
Total	-	-	-	-	-	-	-	-	-	-	1	1	-

CORPS.	Europeans. Wounded. Genl Staff. Deputy Quarter-master-general.	Officers. Lieutenant-colonels.	Majors.	Captains.	Captain-lieutenants.	Lieutenants.	Ensigns	Assistant-surgeons.	Sergeants.	Drummers.	Rank and File. Corporals.	Privates.	Total.	Puckallies.
General Staff	1	-	-	-	-	-	-	-	-	-	-	-	-	-
Detachment H. M. Royal Scots	-	-	-	-	-	1	-	-	-	-	-	7	7	1
Ditto H. M. 30th Regt.	-	-	-	-	-	-	-	-	-	-	-	2	2	-
H. M. 67th Regiment	-	-	-	-	-	-	-	-	1	-	-	2	2	-
1st Battalion 7th N. I.	-	-	-	-	-	-	-	-	-	-	-	-	-	-
Total	1	-	-	-	-	1	-	-	1	-	-	11	11	1

CORPS.	Natives. Killed. Officers. Subidars.	Jemidars.	Havildars.	Drummers.	Rank and File. Naigues.	Sepoys.	Total.	Puckallies.	Natives. Wounded. Officers. Subidars.	Jemidars.	Havildars.	Drummers.	Rank and File. Naigues.	Privates.	Total.	Puckallies.
General Staff	-	-	-	-	-	-	-	-	-	-	-	-	-	-	-	-
Detachment H. M. Royal Scots	-	-	-	-	-	-	-	-	-	-	-	-	-	-	-	-
Ditto H. M. 30th Regt.	-	-	-	-	-	-	-	-	-	-	-	-	-	-	-	-
H. M. 67th Regiment	-	-	-	-	-	-	-	-	-	-	-	-	-	-	-	-
1st Battalion 7th N. I.	-	-	-	-	-	-	-	-	-	-	-	-	-	-	-	-
Total	-	-	-	-	-	-	-	-	-	-	-	-	-	-	-	-

CORPS.	Public Followers. Killed. First Tindal.	Second Tindal.	Foot Lascars, or Dooley-bearers.	Public Followers. Wounded. First Tindal.	Second Tindal.	Lascars, or Dooley-bearers.	Horses. Killed.	Wounded.
General Staff	-	-	-	-	-	-	-	-
Detachment H. M. Royal Scots	-	-	-	-	-	-	-	-
Ditto H. M. 30th Regt.	-	-	-	-	-	-	-	-
H. M. 67th Regiment	-	-	-	-	-	-	-	-
1st Battalion 7th N. I.	-	-	-	-	-	1	-	-
Total	-	.	-	-	-	1	-	-

(Signed) J. Doveton,
Brigadier-general.

N. B. General Staff, Major Macleod, Deputy Quartermaster-General, Wounded.
H. M. Royal Scots, Lieutenant James Bland, Wounded.

A. A. (p. 426.)

General Return of Killed and Wounded during the Operations against Asseerghur, in the Forces under the Command of Brigadier-general John Doveton, C. B.

Camp, Asseerghur, 11th of April, 1819.

CORPS.		Killed.											Wounded.																
		Lieutenant-colonels.	Sub-conductors.	Sergeants.	Drummers.	Rank and File.	Subidars.	Jemidars.	Havildars.	Naigues.	Drummers.	Sepoys.	Depy. Quartermaster-general	Major.	Captain.	Lieutenants.	Lieutenant Fire-workers	Sergeants.	Drummers.	Rank and File.	Jemidars.	Havildars.	Drummers.	Rank and File.	First Tindal Gun-Lascars.	Second Tindal Tent-Lascars	Gun-Lascars.	Sirdars.	Dooley Bearers, and Bamboo Coolies.
Hydrabad Subsidiary Force	General Staff	-	-	-	-	-	-	-	-	-	-	-	1	-	-	-	-	-	-	-	-	-	-	-	-	-	-	-	-
	Foot Artillery	-	-	-	1	1	-	-	-	-	-	-	-	1	1	-	-	1	-	8	-	-	-	-	-	-	8	-	1
	H. M. Royal Scots	1	-	-	-	1	-	-	-	-	-	-	-	-	-	1	-	-	-	14	-	-	-	-	-	-	-	-	1
	—— 30th Regiment	-	-	-	-	-	-	-	-	-	-	-	-	-	-	-	-	1	-	6	-	-	-	-	-	-	-	-	-
	Madras European Regiment	-	-	1	-	-	-	-	-	-	-	-	-	-	-	1	-	1	-	7	-	-	-	-	-	-	-	-	-
	1st Battalion 12th, or W. L. I.	-	-	-	-	-	-	-	-	-	-	-	-	-	-	-	-	-	-	-	-	-	-	2	-	-	-	-	-
	2d ditto 17th, or C. L. I.	-	-	-	-	-	-	-	-	-	-	-	-	-	-	-	-	-	-	-	-	-	-	3	-	-	-	-	-
	1st Battalion Pioneers	-	-	-	-	-	-	-	-	-	-	-	-	-	-	-	-	-	-	-	-	-	-	13	-	-	-	-	-
Bengal Division	Foot Artillery	-	-	-	-	-	-	-	-	-	-	-	-	-	-	1	-	-	-	5	-	-	-	-	2	-	6	1	-
	2d Battalion 13th Regiment N. I.	-	-	-	-	-	-	-	-	-	-	-	-	-	-	-	-	-	-	-	-	-	-	2	-	-	-	-	-
	1st ditto 15th Regiment N. I.	-	-	-	-	-	-	-	-	-	-	1	-	-	-	-	-	-	-	-	-	-	-	6	-	-	-	-	-
	2d ditto 15th Regiment N. I.	-	-	-	-	-	-	1	2	2	-	29	-	-	-	-	-	-	-	-	1	3	-	65	-	-	-	-	-
	2d ditto 29th Regiment N. I.	-	-	-	-	-	-	-	-	-	-	1	-	-	-	-	-	-	-	-	-	-	-	-	-	-	-	-	-
	Pioneers	-	-	-	-	-	-	-	-	-	-	-	-	-	-	-	-	-	-	-	-	1	-	15	-	-	-	-	-
Brigadier-general Sir John Malcolm's Division	3d Regiment Light Cavalry	-	-	-	-	-	-	-	-	-	-	-	-	-	-	-	-	-	-	-	-	-	-	1	-	1	-	-	-
	Detachment Horse and Foot Artillery	-	1	-	1	1	-	-	-	-	-	-	-	-	-	-	-	1	-	7	-	-	-	-	-	-	7	-	-
	2d Battalion 6th Regiment N. I.	-	-	-	-	-	-	-	-	-	-	-	-	-	-	-	-	-	-	-	1	-	1	7	-	-	-	-	-
	1st ditto 7th Regiment N. I.	-	-	-	-	-	-	-	-	-	-	-	-	-	1	-	-	-	-	-	-	1	-	11	-	1	-	-	2
	1st ditto 14th Regiment N. I.	-	-	-	-	-	-	-	-	-	-	1	-	-	-	-	-	-	-	-	-	-	-	4	-	-	-	-	-
	Public Followers	-	-	-	-	-	-	-	-	-	-	-	-	-	-	-	-	-	-	-	-	-	-	-	-	-	-	1	-
Bombay Brigade	Foot Artillery	-	-	-	-	1	-	-	-	-	-	-	-	-	-	-	1	1	-	6	-	-	-	-	-	-	4	-	-
	H. M. 67th Regiment	-	-	-	-	1	-	-	-	-	-	-	-	-	-	2	-	2	1	12	-	-	-	-	-	-	-	-	-
	1st Battalion, or Grenadier Regiment	-	-	-	-	-	-	-	-	-	-	-	-	-	-	-	-	-	-	-	1	-	-	2	-	-	-	-	-
	1st ditto 8th Regiment N. I.	-	-	-	-	-	-	-	-	-	-	-	-	-	-	-	-	-	-	-	-	-	-	3	-	-	-	-	-
	Detachment of Pioneers	-	-	-	-	-	-	-	-	-	-	-	-	-	-	-	-	-	-	-	-	-	-	-	-	-	-	-	-
	Public Followers	-	-	-	-	-	-	-	-	-	-	-	-	-	-	-	-	-	-	-	-	-	-	-	-	-	-	-	5
	Total	1	1	1	2	5	-	1	2	2	-	32	1	1	2	5	1	7	1	65	3	5	1	134	2	2	25	2	9

N. B. Major Macleod, Deputy Quartermaster-general, Wounded slightly.
—— A. Weldon, Madras Artillery, ditto.
Captain J. H. Frith, ditto, ditto.
Lieutenant-colonel Fraser, H. M. Royals, Killed.

Lieutenant-colonel James Bland, H. M. Royals, Wounded severely.
—— A. D'Esterre, M. E. Regiment, ditto slightly.
—— Gunsell, Bengal Artillery, ditto ditto.
Captain Burman, 1/7th N. I. ditto ditto.

Lieut. F. W. Lewis, Bombay Artillery, Wounded slightly.
—— T. J. Adair, H. M. 67th. ditto severely.
—— J. Hannah, ditto, ditto ditto.

B. B. (p. 427.)

Return of Ordnance, &c. taken in the Fortress of Asseerghur, 11th April 1819, by the Troops under Sir John Malcolm.

	Guns																					Howitzers										
	384-Pounders	140	110	85	68	44	42	34	32	24	18	14	12	9	8	6	3½	2	1½	1	½	12-Inch	9½	9	8	6	5½	4	3½	3	2	Grand Total.
Brass Ordnance	-	1	-	1	1	-	1	-	-	2	1	-	1	-	2	-	-	-	-	4	1	-	-	-	-	-	-	-	-	-	-	15
Iron Ditto	1	-	1	-	2	1	1	1	1	7	2	1	5	3	5	7	1	3	1	35	11	1	1	1	1	1	4	1	1	3	1	104
Total . . .	1	1	1	1	3	1	2	1	1	9	3	1	6	3	7	7	1	3	1	39	12	1	1	1	1	1	4	1	1	3	1	119

N. B. Round Iron-shot, of different sizes, about 30,000; Ditto Stone Ditto, Ditto, about 6,000; Guupowder loose, in different Magazines, about 2 Cwt.; about 2,000 Wall-pieces, of different sizes; about 4 Cwt. of Grape-shot.

(Signed) J. Crosdill,
Lieut.-colonel Com. Artillery.

Return of Ordnance, &c. taken in the lower Fort of Asseerghur.

	Guns.					Howitzers	Grand Total
	33-Pounders	14	13½	8	1	7-Inch	
Iron Ordnance	2	1	-	1	2	1	7
Brass Ditto	-	-	1	-	-	-	1
Total . . .	2	1	1	1	2	1	8

(Signed) J. Crosdill,
Lieut.-colonel Com. Artillery.

C. C. (p. 428.)

OFFICIAL PAPERS, detailing the Operations of Major PITMAN's Detachment against NOWAH.

To HENRY RUSSELL, Esq. Resident at Hydrabad.

SIR,

I HAVE the honour to report to you, that on the 7th instant, in conformity with your instructions, I assumed the command of the force which had assembled for service against the Naiks, at the village of Tonnah, twenty-four miles north-east of Nandair, and three miles east of Nowsaghee Naiks Fort of Nowah.

On the following day, the detachment took up a position before Nowah, and I was joined by Lieutenant Sutherland with his *ressalah* of reformed horse.

Nowah is a strong mud fort, of the usual construction. A square, with a bastion at each angle, and one on each side of the gateway. The rest of the works consist of a *fausse-braye* extending all round the fort, a covert way, ditch, and glacis. The gateway is protected by an outwork, in which cannon were mounted. The wall of the *fausse-braye* is almost entirely covered by the glacis; and pieces of ordnance, throwing shot of between five and six pounds in weight, were mounted on the different faces.

From the above description it will be evident, that the only mode of reducing the place was by regular approaches. Accordingly, on the 10th instant, a mortar-battery was commenced, about six hundred yards from the north face of the fort, when the enemy advanced and fired upon our working-party. He was immediately driven back into the fort by Captain Hare, with two companies of the Russell brigade. This battery, and one for our eighteen-pounders, one hundred paces in advance of it, were completed during the night. Both began to play at sun-rise the following day, with considerable effect, silencing the enemy's guns, and knocking off the defences.

On the evening of the 11th, positions were established to the right and left of our batteries, and within three hundred yards of the place; and a six-pounder and a mortar-battery were constructed in front of the east face, distant three hundred and fifty yards.

On the night of the 13th, the enemy made a sortie, and attempted to pass our post on the right. He was quickly driven back by Lieutenant Hampton, with three companies of the Berar infantry. He then attempted to pass our post on the left, but retired after receiving a few shots from the party posted there.

During the night of the 14th, an eighteen-pounder battery was advanced to within two hundred and fifty yards of the fort, and lines of communication were formed between our several advanced positions.

On the 16th, a sap was commenced from our post on the right, which has this morning reached to within twenty-five yards of the crest of the glacis. If the soil will permit, it is intended to form a mine to blow in the counterscarp, otherwise the ditch, which is our principal obstacle, must be filled in some other manner. In either case, I hope to be enabled, in a few days, to report to you the successful termination of our operations against the place. Our loss hitherto has been, five Sepoys and three horses killed, and three European officers and fifty-five Native officers, Sepoys and Lascars, wounded.

At ten P. M. of the 19th, about two hundred of Nowsaghee's horse came suddenly and fired on a small guard in the rear of my camp. They were soon repulsed, and Lieutenant Sutherland, with a small party of the reformed horse, pursued them for a few miles; but, owing to the darkness of the night, they got clear off.

Having received information that a party of five hundred of Nowsaghee's matchlock men had taken possession of Omurkair, which is nine or ten coss distant from Nowah, and is represented to be in a dilapidated state, I determined to attempt to carry it by escalade. I accordingly detached Captain Seyer, last night, with eight companies of infantry, his battalion field-pieces, and six hundred reformed horse, and directed him to make the attempt, should there appear to be a fair prospect of success. He will afterwards take up a position to be ready to check the movements of the enemy, who has of late been plundering the country in every direction.

I beg leave to inclose copy of my instructions to Captain Seyer, and have the honour to be,

Sir,

Yours, &c.

(Signed) ROBERT PITMAN,

Major Com. Detach.

Camp before Nowah, January 21, 1819

List of Officers Wounded before Nowah, to the 21st January, 1819.

Lieutenant Kennedy, H. M. 86th regiment, doing duty with the Russell brigade, severely.

Captains Larkins and Johnston, Nizam's Berar infantry, slightly.

To HENRY RUSSELL, Esq. Resident at Hydrabad.

SIR,

I HAVE the satisfaction to report to you that the Fort of Nowah was carried by assault this day, at two P. M. The greater part of the garrison was put to the sword.

With reference to my letter to your address, under date the 21st instant, I have the honour to acquaint you, that, at nine A. M. of the following day, the enemy made a desperate sortie; and sword in hand attacked our working-party at the head of the sap, but was very soon driven back to the fort.

On the morning of the 24th, a man brought me a letter from the Arab Jemidar commanding the fort, requesting permission to send two persons to treat for its surrender. No notice was taken of this letter; but the people in the fort ceased firing, and called out to our men to do the same; and an Arab was sent to me with another letter, of the same purport as the former. To this I returned a written answer, offering to allow the garrison to surrender at discretion. The Jemidar replied by claiming their arrears of pay, and permission to leave the fort with their arms and property of all kinds. I answered that, as he had not agreed to the terms offered, none other would be granted. I have the honour to inclose copies of the notes which passed on this occasion.

On the 25th, our sap had reached the crest of the glacis, where a six-pounder battery was established, and two mortars were brought into it. On that night, the engineer commenced his mine, which was completed on the 29th. The whole of the 30th was employed in battering in breach with the eighteen-pounder, and in demolishing the Rownee or Porkotah wall with the six-pounder. During the night, shells and grape were thrown into the breach; and it was determined to spring the mine, and make the assault, this day at noon.

At eight A. M. two Arabs were again sent to request permission to treat for terms, but they were told that no other could be granted than that of unconditional surrender.

I beg leave to inclose for your information, copies of my orders preparatory to the assault, and after the reduction of the place.

On the mine being sprung, Ensign Oliphant, of the Madras Engineers, rushed forward with the Pioneers, and planted ladders against the scarp of the ditch, which were instantaneously ascended by Captain Hare, and the storming-party, who in a few minutes had surmounted every obstacle, and were in possession of the upper fort. The Arabs continued to defend themselves for a considerable time between the two walls, with the exception of about two hundred, who fled from the gate of the fort. They were immediately attacked by Lieutenant Campbell, who commanded a party of infantry posted for the purpose of intercepting them; and nearly at the same time they were charged by Captains Davies, Smith, and Lieutenant Sutherland, with different parties of the reformed horse, so that not a man of the enemy escaped.

By the best accounts I have been able to obtain, the garrison consisted of more than five hundred men; of these one hundred are prisoners, more than eighty of them are dreadfully wounded, and upwards of four hundred bodies have already been counted.

The conduct of all troops employed has been exemplary, and I trust will obtain for them the high honour of your approbation.

I beg leave to inclose a return of our killed and wounded during the siege, and have the honour to be,

Sir,

Yours, &c.

(Signed) ROBERT PITMAN,

Major Com. a D. N.

Camp Nowah, January 31, 1819.

RETURN of KILLED and WOUNDED of a Detachment of his Highness the NIZAM's Regular Forces, commanded by Major PITMAN, during the Siege of NOWAH, from the 10th to the 31st of January, inclusive.

Camp at Nowah, 31ts January, 1819.

CORPS.	Killed										Wounded																		
	Corporals.	Subidars.	Jemidars.	Havildars.	Horsemen.	Golandauze	Sepoys	Bildars	Total.	Horses.	Captain Commandant	Captains.	Lieutenants	European Privates	2d Rissaldars	Subidars	Jemidars.	Havildars	1st Tindals	Naigues	Horsemen	Golandauze.	Gun-Lascars	Miners	Duffadars	Sepoys	Bildars.	Total.	Horses.
Reformed Horse.																													
Newaub Jullahool Dowlah's Russalah	-	-	-	-	-	-	-	-	-	-	-	-	-	-	1	-	-	-	-	-	5	-	-	-	1	-	-	7	7
Newaub Alleem Ullee Khan's	-	-	-	-	2	-	-	-	2	6	-	-	1	-	-	-	-	-	-	-	23		-	-	2	-	-	26	33
Artillery.																													
Russell Brigade Artillery	1	-	-	-	-	2	-	1	4	-	-	-	-	2	-	1	-	1	1	-	-	5	1	-	-	-	6	17	-
Berar Regular Artillery	-	-	-	-	-	-	-	-	-	-	-	-	-	-	-	-	-	-	-	-	-		-	2	-	-	-	2	-
Infantry.																													
1st Regiment Russell Brigade	-	1	1	-	-	-	10	-	12	-	-	-	1	-	-	1	1	-	-	3	-	-	-	-	-	52	-	58	-
2d ditto ditto	-	-	-	-	-	-	3	-	3	-	1	-	1	-	-	-	2	2	-	4	-	-	-	-	-	48	-	58	-
2d Battalion Berar Regular Infantry	-	-	-	1	-	-	-	-	-	-	-	1	-	-	-	-	-	-	-	-	-	-	-	-	-	-	-	-	-
3d ditto ditto	-	-	-	-	-	-	-	-	-	-	-	1	-	-	-	-	1	1	-	-	-	-	-	-	-	8	-	11	-
	1	1	1	1	2	2	13	1	21	6	1	2	3	2	1	2	4	4	1	7	28	5	1	2	3	108	6	179	40

Names of Officers Wounded.

Captains Currie, Larkin, and Johnston; Lieutenants Sutherland, Kennedy, and Burr.

D. D. (p. 428.)

OFFICIAL PAPERS, detailing the Operations of Major-general Sir WILLIAM GRANT KEIR's Force in the Sawunt-Warree Country.

Extract of a Letter from Major-general Sir WILLIAM GRANT KEIR, to the Honourable MOUNTSTUART ELPHINSTONE, Commissioner at Poonah, dated 3d February, 1819.

" Major Thatcher's brigade having arrived at Choke, on the 26th ultimo, after a very tedious and harassing march, during which the labour of the Pioneers was required in cutting a great part of the road, I lost no time in making dispositions for entering the Sawunt-Warree country. The heavy ordnance and stores required for the siege of Newtee having to proceed by sea, I directed Lieutenant-colonel Imlach to proceed along the coast with his corps, the 2d battalion of the 2d regiment, and some field-pieces, to protect their debarkation; with the rest of the force I determined to proceed by the ford at Kalsee. This disposition was further calculated to embarrass any attempt that might be made to obstruct our advance. Both divisions marched from Choke on the 31st of January, and crossed the Carlee river on the 1st of February. Some advanced picquets of Babna Gopauls appeared opposite the ford by which Colonel Imlach was to cross, and fired on his advance. They were driven back without loss, and a position taken up near the Fort of Newtee, by the Lieutenant-colonel, where every facility presented itself for landing the guns and stores. On my side, no opposition was made. The post of Coodall was evacuated on my advance, and the inhabitants of the country exhibited every friendly disposition. The road however was bad, and the labour of the Pioneers incessantly required to make it practicable for the guns. Owing to this circumstance, I was unable to arrive before Newtee until this morning. Four hundred men, whom I detached under Captain Donnelly by another route, have also taken up a position to the southward of the fort, which is now closely invested on all sides. Every exertion has been made in landing the guns and stores, and the batteries will be thrown up without delay."

(A true Extract.)

(Signed) C. T. METCALFE,
Secretary to the Government.

Camp at Newtee, 4th February, 1819.

To the Honourable MOUNTSTUART ELPHINSTONE, &c. &c. &c.

SIR,

I DO myself the honour of reporting, that an overture was made to me this morning by the Killedar of Newtee, to surrender the place, on permission being granted for the garrison to march out with their arms. I have complied with the condition, and the fort is in our possession. The garrison consisted of three hundred men: of whom one hundred and twenty-five are Pur-Deshees, who have requested passports to return to their country above the Ghats; the rest are inhabitants of this neighbourhood, who have promised to remain at their houses. Although the defences of Newtee are not formidable, they are of a nature to have caused a considerable loss in their reduction. The ordnance and stores are again embarking, to be transported to Rarree.

I have, &c.

(Signed) W. GRANT KEIR,
Major-general.

Extract of a Letter from Major-general Sir WILLIAM GRANT KEIR, to the Honourable MOUNTSTUART ELPHINSTONE, Commissioner at Poonah, dated 10th Feb. 1819.

" Having left a detachment of Sepoys in occupation of the Fort of Newtee, I put the force in motion on the 4th instant, and arrived here yesterday, after experiencing a slight opposition from the enemy, in crossing the salt-marshes to the eastward of the fort. The position I have taken up is nearly that which was occupied by the Portuguese last year. It was my wish to have closely invested the place on all sides; but I find that a much larger force will be required to do this effectually. I am, besides, convinced, from observation, that the active and concentrated employment of all the resources at my disposal, will be called for in the reduction of a place, the defences of which are so formidable. I understand, from some Portuguese officers who visited me this morning from their out-posts, that their trenches were open twenty-nine days, and that they employed in the siege twenty-five pieces of ordnance, of which ten were of the largest caliber.

Sambajee Sawant has declined to receive the summons which I sent in, and preparations for the siege are in progress. The arrival of the ordnance and stores required from Bombay, may be hourly expected.

(A true Extract.)

(Signed) C. T. METCALFE,
Secretary to the Government.

To the Honourable M. ELPHINSTONE, Commissioner, &c. &c.

Camp, Rarree, 14th February, 1819.

SIR,

I HAVE the satisfaction to inform you, that I have this morning taken possession of the Fort of Rarree. Having erected batteries on the night of the 12th instant, an unremitted fire was maintained from day-break on the 13th, and which was so skilfully directed, that, at four o'clock in the afternoon, I considered the general defences to be sufficiently impaired to admit of the outworks being assaulted. This service was executed by two columns under Lieutenant-colonel Clifford, of H. M. 89th Regiment, in a most gallant manner. The troops were drawn up for the attack on the sea-beach, under cover, and so near to the breaches, that the enemy were completely surprised, and in half-an-hour were driven from two strong lines, defended by brick walls, flanked with towers, and under a very galling fire from the fort. This was situated upon a rocky hill, and assailable only along a circuitous causeway, which intersected the ditch, and was occupied by six gateways. To the second of these the enemy was followed by our troops, and a lodgement made in the first. Nothing could exceed the gallantry of all the troops engaged in this successful enterprize.

I received a communication last night, requesting a suspension of hostilities; and I allowed Sambajee Sawant, with a few followers, not exceeding fifty, to march out this morning, having declined to grant them any other terms. The remainder of the garrison made their escape during the night. The whole were said to have amounted to twelve hundred men.

I have, &c.

(Signed) W. GRANT KEIR,
Major-general.

To the Adjutant-general of the Army, Bombay.

SIR,

I HAD the honour, yesterday evening, to forward a brief report of the success of the attack on the enemy's lines before Rarree; and have now the pleasure to acquaint you, that the fort was this morning taken possession of by a detachment from my camp.

The difficulties experienced in the disembarkation of the ordnance and stores, retarded our operations in a considerable degree, but; on the night of the 12th instant, we succeeded in erecting our batteries, and opened on the fort at day-break the next morning, with four battery-guns, and as many eight-inch mortars, which were served with such vigour and precision, as to dismantle the whole of the guns in the outworks in the course of an hour, when our fire was directed against the general defences of the place. About three o'clock a breach was effected in a curtain of the advanced outwork, and a party of three hundred and thirty grenadiers formed for the assault under the command of Lieutenant-colonel Clifford, of H. M. 89th Regiment. The troops moved to the attack about four o'clock, and passed the breach without difficulty, driving the enemy, in considerable numbers, towards the second lines, which were immediately carried, and a lodgement effected within half musket-shot of the upper fort, to which the enemy were pursued, and many bayonetted at the lower gate, which was for a short time in our possession. The spirit and rapidity of the attack, added to the advantageous position which was gained by the advance of our troops, struck the enemy with such terror, that nearly the whole of the garrison evacuated the fort during the night.

This morning Sambajee Sawant proposed to surrender, and was permitted to march out with about fifty adherents, the small remnant of a garrison which is said to have consisted of near twelve hundred men at the commencement of the siege.

I beg leave to inclose a more detailed report of the attack, transmitted by Lieutenant-colonel Clifford, whose conduct on the occasion is deserving of the highest applause.

I have likewise the pleasure to forward a copy of the field-orders, conveying my sentiments on the behaviour of the troops, together with a list of killed and wounded.

I shall march to-morrow towards Warree, in order to accelerate the treaty with that Government, which will, I trust, be speedily brought to a favourable conclusion.

I have the honour to be, &c. &c.

(Signed) W. GRANT KEIR,
Major-general.

Camp, Rarree, 14th Feb. 1819.

RETURN of KILLED and WOUNDED of the Force under the command of Major-general Sir WILLIAM GRANT KEIR, K. M. T. employed on the Assault of the Enemy's Outwork of the Fort of RARREE, on the 13th of February, 1819.

CORPS.	Killed.				Wounded.				
	Sergeants and Havildars.	Rank and File.	Gun-Lascars.	Total Killed.	Lieutenants.	Sergeants and Havildars.	Syrang	Rank and File	Total Wounded.
Artillery and Gun-Lascars	-	1	1	2	-	-	1	1	2
Detachment of his Majesty's 89th Reg.	-	2	-	2	2	1	-	3	6
2d Battalion 2d Regiment N. I.	1	-	-	1	-	-	-	9	9
2d Battalion 6th Regiment N. I.	-	-	-	-	-	-	-	2	2
2d Battalion 9th Regiment N. I.	-	2	-	2	-	1	-	4	5
Pioneers (Madras)	-	1	-	1	-	-	-	1	1
Total	1	6	1	8	2	2	1	20	25

Names of Wounded Officers.

Lieutenant Aylmer Dowdall (severely), H. M. 89th Regiment.

Lieutenant and Acting Adjutant Naylor, H. M. 89th Regiment (severely).

E. E. (p. 428.)

OFFICIAL PAPERS, detailing the Operations of Brigadier-general PRITZLER's Field Force against COPALDROOG.

Head-quarters, Field Division, Camp near Alwundie,
7th May, 1819

To HENRY RUSSELL, Esq. Resident at Hydrabad.

SIR,

I HAVE the honour to acquaint you that the Division under my command, as per margin,* entered the territories of His Highness the Subadar of the Deckan, this morning, and encamped at this place.

I have, &c. &c.
(Signed) T. PRITZLER,
Brigadier-general.

* H. M 22d L. D., three Troops; Detachment 1st N. C., four Troops, Flank Battalion, six Companies; Rifle Corps, eight ditto; 2d Battalion 4th Regiment, five ditto; 2d Battalion 12th Regiment, ten ditto; 2d Battalion Pioneers, three ditto.

Detachment of Artillery ordnance—Iron Guns, eighteen-pounders, four; Howitzers, heavy five-and-a-half-inches, two, Howitzers, light five-and-a-half ditto, two; Brass guns, twelve-pounders, two; Brass ditto, six-pounders, attached to H. M. 22d L. D., two; Brass Mortars, eight-inches, eight, Brass ditto, five-and-a-half ditto, one, Dooab Auxiliary Horse, one hundred.

Head-quarters, Field Division, Camp before Copaldroog,
9th May, 1819

To HENRY RUSSELL, Esq. British Resident.

SIR,

I HAVE the honour to acquaint you, that I encamped before Copaldroog yesterday, and employed the morning in reconnoitring the fort. In the evening I moved down with the intention of carrying the pettah, and establishing a post for a mortar-battery; but I was met by a man who said he was a brother to Veerapa, and that the fort should be given up. I therefore halted, and directed eight companies to proceed, and take possession of it; but on arrival at the gate, they were refused admittance by the garrison, and returned, accompanied by the man who came out to meet us.

Seeing that there was no prospect of getting possession of the fort, as was proposed,

I established a body of troops in the pettah, and occupied the position for the mortar-battery, which was armed, during the night, with nine mortars and two howitzers; a brigade of brass twelves, and a brigade of six-pounders, was also got into the pettah; which, with the mortars, opened their fire between two and three o'clock this morning.

Preparations are now making for the formation of a breaching-battery, which I am inclined to think the wall will not long withstand.

Mahomed Edroos Khan arrived last night, and was joined by his troops this morning, which I propose to send against Behauder Bunda, a hill fort, dependant on Copaldroog, while we are carrying on the siege of the latter place.

I have, &c. &c.

(Signed) THEO. PRITZLER,
Brigadier-general.

Head-quarters, Field Division, Camp before Copaldroog,
11th May, 1819.

To HENRY RUSSELL, Esq. British Resident.

SIR,

ON reference to the subject of my letter of the 9th instant, I have the honour to acquaint you, that, yesterday morning, a breaching-battery of two eighteen-pounders was opened upon the wall of the lower fort; in the evening, a third eighteen-pounder was got into the battery; and I have every reason to hope that the breach will be practicable by sun-set this evening.

I have, &c. &c.

(Signed) THEO. PRITZLER,
Brigadier-general.

Head-quarters, Field Division, Camp before Copaldroog,
12th May, 1819.

To HENRY RUSSELL, Esq. British Resident.

SIR,

AFTER closing my letter of yesterday, I went down to the batteries, with a view to ascertain that the breach was practicable, and that every necessary arrangement had been made for storming the lower fort, which I had directed to take place at day-light this morning, when two men came in to request *cowl*, which was granted to them, on their giving up the two principal gates, and which were occupied by our troops immediately.

Veerapa, who, with about five hundred men, retired into the upper fort, has sent a letter to Mahomed Idroos Khan, and if he does not immediately accept the terms which have in consequence been offered to him, I shall prosecute the siege.

I have, &c. &c.

(Signed) THEO. PRITZLER,
Brigadier-general.

Head-quarters, Field Division, Camp before Copaldroog,
14th May, 1819.

To HENRY RUSSELL, Esq. British Resident, Hydrabad.

SIR,

ON reference to the subject of my letter of the 12th instant, I do myself the honour to acquaint you, that all negotiation ceased with the enemy about ten o'clock yesterday morning, and perceiving that nothing but a very strong and decided measure would prevent a long and protracted siege, I determined to carry as many of the lower works by escalade as could be accomplished; for which purpose, the troops specified in the margin* were placed in the batteries, and at twelve o'clock, they moved out under the fire of all our guns and mortars, commanded by Lieutenant-colonel Fraser, 12th N. I. in two divisions; the first or left attack, under the command of Captain Tew, H. M. 34th regiment—and the second, or right attack, under the command of Captain Cuppaidge, H. M. 53d Regiment. These columns were conducted, the first by Lieutenant Grant, and the second by Ensign Oliphant of the Engineers; and Captain Smithwaite commanded the Pioneers, who carried the ladders.

The left attack moved on without much opposition, till it arrived at the first gate, which was, however, blown open by a galloper gun of H. M. 22d Light Dragoons, under the command of Lieutenant Gregory, to whom much praise is due for having carried it through a heavy fire, and up a road apparently impracticable for any wheel carriages.

The right attack found the wall they were to escalade very high, which rendered the operation slow and tedious. I therefore detached Captain Jones, of H. M. 69th Regiment, with the Reserve, to follow up the left attack, and the whole of the three parties formed a junction at the second gateway; from which they pushed the enemy, who

---

* Left Attack—One Company and a half Flank Battalion, one ditto Rifle Corps, one ditto 4th Regiment N. I., one ditto 12th Regiment N. I.

Right Attack—One Company and a half Flank Battalion, one ditto Rifle Corps, one ditto 4th Regiment N. I. two ditto 12th Regiment N. I.

Reserve, Captain Jones—One Company Flank Battalion, one ditto Rifles, one ditto 4th Regiment N. I.

disputed every inch of ground, through two gates, to the very summit of the hill, where they begged for quarter.

Such a service could not be performed without some loss; and when I reflect upon the strength upon the enemy's works, and the power they had of throwing down stones, I am astonished that it was so trifling, having only six killed and fifty-one wounded, and which can only be accounted for by the spirited manner in which the officers and men did their duty; and I have to lament the loss of a very promising young officer, Ensign Elliot, of the Rifle Corps, who fell, when exerting himself to the utmost, near the second gateway. I have also to lament the loss of the service of Captain Dunn, Assistant Quartermaster-general, and Lieutenant Pringle Taylor, severely wounded, the former employed to explain my orders to the left attack, and the latter, who happened accidentally to be on the spot, was permitted to advance with it; both these officers, as well as Lieutenant Silver, of H. M. 53d Regiment, were wounded, when shewing an example of the most determined bravery to the troops. A squadron of H. M. 22d Dragoons, under the command of Captain Mills, was so placed as to cut off the enemy's retreat in the event of their attempting one, but the attacks were too spirited to give him time to think of it before they were driven up the hill.

Where every officer and soldier employed did their duty to the utmost, it is difficult to point out those who most distinguished themselves, but I feel much indebted to Lieutenant Grant of the Engineers, for the very judicious situation in which he placed the batteries, planned the attacks, and conducted one of them; and he was ably assisted by Ensign Oliphant.

To Major Cleaveland, of the Artillery, much praise is due, for the judgment which he shewed in so well directing the fire from the batteries; and the officers and men of that corps, as well as the Artillery Troop of H. M. 22d Light Dragoons, are entitled to every credit, for the admirable manner in which the guns were served both before and during the attack, and the excellent practice which was made. Nothing could exceed the zeal shewn by Lieutenant-colonel Fraser, Captains Tew, Cuppaidge, and Jones, commanding the different parties; and every thing that could be done by men, was accomplished by the troops under their command.

To Captain Smithwaite, and the Pioneers, I feel much indebted for their unwearied exertions, constantly exposed to a very heavy fire; and much praise is due to Dr. Trotter, and the medical officers generally, whose assistance was, upon every occasion, and in every situation, so promptly afforded.

To the Assistant Adjutant-general, Lieutenant Watson, and Assistant Quartermaster-general, Captain O'Donnoghue, I feel much indebted, for their great exertions, and the able assistance they afforded me, as well as to Captain Dunn, Assistant Quartermaster-general, and to my Aid-de-Camp, Lieutenant Brown, of H. M. 25th Light Dragoons.

I inclose a Return of Killed and Wounded, and Ordnance captured.

I have, &c. &c.

(Signed) THEO. PRITZLER,
Brigadier-general.

RETURN of ORDNANCE captured at COPALDROOG.

GUNS.	Serviceable.	Unserviceable.	REMARKS.
IRON.			
11 Pounder	-	1	
12 ditto	1	3	
9 ditto	1	-	
6 ditto	4	-	
4 ditto	1	-	
3 ditto	2	-	
2 ditto	2	-	
BRASS.			
42 Pounder	1	-	
3 ditto	1	-	
2 ditto	1	-	

(Signed) SAMUEL CLEAVELAND,
Major Commanding Artillery F. D.

RETURN of KILLED and WOUNDED in the Field Division under the command of Brigadier-general PRITZLER, C. B. duriug the Operations against the Fort of COPALDROOG.

H. M. 22d Light Dragoons—Wounded: 1 Lieutenant and 1 Private.

Artillery—Wounded: 1 Sergeant, 1 Corporal, 4 Privates, 4 Privates Natives, and Gun-Lascar since dead.

H. M. Flank Battalion—Killed: 1 Sergeant, 3 Privates. Wounded: 1 Lieutenant, 2 Corporals, and 11 Privates.

Rifle Corps—Killed: 1 Ensign. Wounded: 1 Havildar and 4 Privates.

2d Battalion 4th Regiment N. I.—Wounded: 1 Jemidar, 1 Puckally, and 4 Privates.

2d Battalion 12th Regiment N. I.—Wounded: 1 Subidar and 5 Privates.

2d Battalion Pioneers—Killed: 1 Private. Wounded: 7 Privates, 1 since dead.

Division Staff—Wounded: 1 Captain.

Name of Officer Killed: Ensign Elliot, Rifle Corps.

Names of Officers Wounded: Captain Dunn, Assistant Quartermaster-general; Lieutenant Taylor, H. M. 22d Light Dragoons; Lieutenant Silver, H. M. 53d Regiment, Flank Battalion.

(Signed) J. WATSON,
Assistant Adjutant-general.

Camp at Copaldroog, 14th May, 1819.

F. F. (p. 428.)

OFFICIAL PAPERS, detailing the Operations of Lieutenant-colonel THOMPSON's Detachment against the Fort of Madoorajpoor*.

Extract of a Letter from Lieutenant-colonel THOMPSON, C. B. to Major CARTWRIGHT, Assistant A[illegible]. Dated Madoorajpoor, July 29, 1818.

"I request you will report to Major-general Sir David Ochterlony, Bart. G. C. B. that Ensign Garstin, Field Engineer, having reported the breach in the wall of the town of Madoorajpoor to be practicable early yesterday evening; I ordered a storming-party, consisting of three companies on duty in the batteries, reinforced by another company from the 1st Battalion 27th, and supported by two companies from the 1st Battalion 28th N. I. the whole under the command of Captain Leith, 1st Battalion 28th Regiment, to advance to the assault, at a signal of three guns fired at ten o'clock P. M., in quick succession, from our battery.

I also directed other columns, one under Captain Arden, 1st Battalion 27th, the other under Captain Watson, of the 1st Battalion 28th N. I. each consisting of three companies, to attempt the town by escalade, at two different points, at the same signal being given. I am to add, that all the columns succeeded, no opposition being made, except by firing one or two matchlocks. The enemy either retreated into the fort, or made their escape over the town wall, and got off, favoured by the darkness of the night. After our party got possession, a heavy fire of matchlocks, ginjals, and guns, was opened from all sides of the fort; but the cover afforded by the houses of the town under which our men were posted, prevented its occasioning that loss it otherwise must.

Extract of a Letter from Lieutenant-colonel THOMPSON, to Major CARTWRIGHT, Assistant Adjutant-general, Jyepore. Dated Camp Madoorajpoor, 2d August, 1818.

"I BEG, through you, to offer my congratulations to Major-general Sir David Ochterlony, Bart. G. C. B. on the surrender last night of the fort of Madooghur, to the detachment under my command."

* This fort stood a siege of twelve months against Ameer Khan's army, immediately before the war.

General Return of the **Killed** and **Wounded** of the Detachment under the Command of Lieutenant-colonel **Thompson**, C. B. in the Operations against **Madoorajpoor**, from the 27th of July to the 2d of August, 1818.

Camp before Madoorajpoor, 2d August, 1818.

	KILLED.					WOUNDED.			
	Rank and File.	Gun-Lascars.	Dooley Bearers.	Gun Bullocks.	Total.	Subidars.	Havildars.	Rank and File.	Total.
European Artillery Detachment	-	-	-	-	-	-	-	1	1
Native ditto ditto	-	1	-	1	2	-	-	-	-
1st Battalion 27th Regiment N. I.	-	-	-	-	-	1	-	5	6
1st ditto 28th ditto	1	-	2	-	-	1	-	5	6
Pioneer Detachment	-	-	-	-	-	-	1	4	5
Total	1	1	2	1	2	2	1	15	18

(Signed) W. A. Thompson,
Commanding Detachment.

THE END.

LONDON:
PRINTED BY S. AND R. BENTLEY, DORSET-STREET, FLEET-STREET.

The Codes Of Hammurabi And Moses
W. W. Davies

QTY

The discovery of the Hammurabi Code is one of the greatest achievements of archaeology, and is of paramount interest, not only to the student of the Bible, but also to all those interested in ancient history...

Religion **ISBN:** ***1-59462-338-4*** **Pages:132**
MSRP ***$12.95***

The Theory of Moral Sentiments
Adam Smith

QTY

This work from 1749. contains original theories of conscience amd moral judgment and it is the foundation for systemof morals.

Philosophy **ISBN:** ***1-59462-777-0*** **Pages:536**
MSRP ***$19.95***

Jessica's First Prayer
Hesba Stretton

QTY

In a screened and secluded corner of one of the many railway-bridges which span the streets of London there could be seen a few years ago, from five o'clock every morning until half past eight, a tidily set-out coffee-stall, consisting of a trestle and board, upon which stood two large tin cans, with a small fire of charcoal burning under each so as to keep the coffee boiling during the early hours of the morning when the work-people were thronging into the city on their way to their daily toil...

Childrens **ISBN:** ***1-59462-373-2*** **Pages:84**
MSRP ***$9.95***

My Life and Work
Henry Ford

QTY

Henry Ford revolutionized the world with his implementation of mass production for the Model T automobile. Gain valuable business insight into his life and work with his own auto-biography... "We have only started on our development of our country we have not as yet, with all our talk of wonderful progress, done more than scratch the surface. The progress has been wonderful enough but..."

Biographies/ **ISBN:** ***1-59462-198-5*** **Pages:300**
MSRP ***$21.95***

The Art of Cross-Examination
Francis Wellman

QTY

I presume it is the experience of every author, after his first book is published upon an important subject, to be almost overwhelmed with a wealth of ideas and illustrations which could readily have been included in his book, and which to his own mind, at least, seem to make a second edition inevitable. Such certainly was the case with me; and when the first edition had reached its sixth impression in five months, I rejoiced to learn that it seemed to my publishers that the book had met with a sufficiently favorable reception to justify a second and considerably enlarged edition. ..

Pages:412

Reference **ISBN:** ***1-59462-647-2*** *MSRP* ***$19.95***

On the Duty of Civil Disobedience
Henry David Thoreau

QTY

Thoreau wrote his famous essay, On the Duty of Civil Disobedience, as a protest against an unjust but popular war and the immoral but popular institution of slave-owning. He did more than write—he declined to pay his taxes, and was hauled off to gaol in consequence. Who can say how much this refusal of his hastened the end of the war and of slavery ?

Law **ISBN:** ***1-59462-747-9*** **Pages:48**

MSRP ***$7.45***

Dream Psychology Psychoanalysis for Beginners
Sigmund Freud

QTY

Sigmund Freud, born Sigismund Schlomo Freud (May 6, 1856 - September 23, 1939), was a Jewish-Austrian neurologist and psychiatrist who co-founded the psychoanalytic school of psychology. Freud is best known for his theories of the unconscious mind, especially involving the mechanism of repression; his redefinition of sexual desire as mobile and directed towards a wide variety of objects; and his therapeutic techniques, especially his understanding of transference in the therapeutic relationship and the presumed value of dreams as sources of insight into unconscious desires.

Pages:196

Psychology **ISBN:** ***1-59462-905-6*** *MSRP* ***$15.45***

The Miracle of Right Thought
Orison Swett Marden

QTY

Believe with all of your heart that you will do what you were made to do. When the mind has once formed the habit of holding cheerful, happy, prosperous pictures, it will not be easy to form the opposite habit. It does not matter how improbable or how far away this realization may see, or how dark the prospects may be, if we visualize them as best we can, as vividly as possible, hold tenaciously to them and vigorously struggle to attain them, they will gradually become actualized, realized in the life. But a desire, a longing without endeavor, a yearning abandoned or held indifferently will vanish without realization.

Pages:360

Self Help **ISBN:** ***1-59462-644-8*** *MSRP* ***$25.45***

QTY

The Rosicrucian Cosmo-Conception Mystic Christianity *by* ***Max Heindel*** ISBN: *1-59462-188-8* **$38.95**
The Rosicrucian Cosmo-conception is not dogmatic, neither does it appeal to any other authority than the reason of the student. It is: not controversial, but is: sent forth in the, hope that it may help to clear... *New Age/Religion Pages 646*

Abandonment To Divine Providence *by* ***Jean-Pierre de Caussade*** ISBN: *1-59462-228-0* **$25.95**
"The Rev. Jean Pierre de Caussade was one of the most remarkable spiritual writers of the Society of Jesus in France in the 18th Century. His death took place at Toulouse in 1751. His works have gone through many editions and have been republished... *Inspirational/Religion Pages 400*

Mental Chemistry *by* ***Charles Haanel*** ISBN: *1-59462-192-6* **$23.95**
Mental Chemistry allows the change of material conditions by combining and appropriately utilizing the power of the mind. Much like applied chemistry creates something new and unique out of careful combinations of chemicals the mastery of mental chemistry... *New Age Pages 354*

The Letters of Robert Browning and Elizabeth Barret Barrett 1845-1846 vol II ISBN: *1-59462-193-4* **$35.95**
by ***Robert Browning*** *and* ***Elizabeth Barrett*** *Biographies Pages 596*

Gleanings In Genesis (volume I) *by* ***Arthur W. Pink*** ISBN: *1-59462-130-6* **$27.45**
Appropriately has Genesis been termed "the seed plot of the Bible" for in it we have, in germ form, almost all of the great doctrines which are afterwards fully developed in the books of Scripture which follow... *Religion/Inspirational Pages 420*

The Master Key *by* ***L. W. de Laurence*** ISBN: *1-59462-001-6* **$30.95**
In no branch of human knowledge has there been a more lively increase of the spirit of research during the past few years than in the study of Psychology, Concentration and Mental Discipline. The requests for authentic lessons in Thought Control, Mental Discipline and... *New Age/Business Pages 422*

The Lesser Key Of Solomon Goetia *by* ***L. W. de Laurence*** ISBN: *1-59462-092-X* **$9.95**
This translation of the first book of the "Lernegton" which is now for the first time made accessible to students of Talismanic Magic was done, after careful collation and edition, from numerous Ancient Manuscripts in Hebrew, Latin, and French... *New Age/Occult Pages 92*

Rubaiyat Of Omar Khayyam *by* ***Edward Fitzgerald*** ISBN:*1-59462-332-5* **$13.95**
Edward Fitzgerald, whom the world has already learned, in spite of his own efforts to remain within the shadow of anonymity, to look upon as one of the rarest poets of the century, was born at Bredfield, in Suffolk, on the 31st of March, 1809. He was the third son of John Purcell... *Music Pages 172*

Ancient Law *by* ***Henry Maine*** ISBN: *1-59462-128-4* **$29.95**
The chief object of the following pages is to indicate some of the earliest ideas of mankind, as they are reflected in Ancient Law, and to point out the relation of those ideas to modern thought. *Religiom/History Pages 452*

Far-Away Stories *by* ***William J. Locke*** ISBN: *1-59462-129-2* **$19.45**
"Good wine needs no bush, but a collection of mixed vintages does. And this book is just such a collection. Some of the stories I do not want to remain buried for ever in the museum files of dead magazine-numbers an author's not unpardonable vanity..." *Fiction Pages 272*

Life of David Crockett *by* ***David Crockett*** ISBN: *1-59462-250-7* **$27.45**
"Colonel David Crockett was one of the most remarkable men of the times in which he lived. Born in humble life, but gifted with a strong will, an indomitable courage, and unremitting perseverance... *Biographies/New Age Pages 424*

Lip-Reading *by* ***Edward Nitchie*** ISBN: *1-59462-206-X* **$25.95**
Edward B. Nitchie, founder of the New York School for the Hard of Hearing, now the Nitchie School of Lip-Reading, Inc, wrote "LIP-READING Principles and Practice". The development and perfecting of this meritorious work on lip-reading was an undertaking... *How-to Pages 400*

A Handbook of Suggestive Therapeutics, Applied Hypnotism, Psychic Science ISBN: *1-59462-214-0* **$24.95**
by ***Henry Munro*** *Health/New Age/Health/Self-help Pages 376*

A Doll's House: and Two Other Plays *by* ***Henrik Ibsen*** ISBN: *1-59462-112-8* **$19.95**
Henrik Ibsen created this classic when in revolutionary 1848 Rome. Introducing some striking concepts in playwriting for the realist genre, this play has been studied the world over. *Fiction/Classics/Plays 308*

The Light of Asia *by* ***sir Edwin Arnold*** ISBN: *1-59462-204-3* **$13.95**
In this poetic masterpiece, Edwin Arnold describes the life and teachings of Buddha. The man who was to become known as Buddha to the world was born as Prince Gautama of India but he rejected the worldly riches and abandoned the reigns of power when... *Religion/History/Biographies Pages 170*

The Complete Works of Guy de Maupassant *by* ***Guy de Maupassant*** ISBN: *1-59462-157-8* **$16.95**
"For days and days, nights and nights, I had dreamed of that first kiss which was to consecrate our engagement, and I knew not on what spot I should put my lips..." *Fiction/Classics Pages 240*

The Art of Cross-Examination *by* ***Francis L. Wellman*** ISBN: *1-59462-309-0* **$26.95**
Written by a renowned trial lawyer, Wellman imparts his experience and uses case studies to explain how to use psychology to extract desired information through questioning. *How-to/Science/Reference Pages 408*

Answered or Unanswered? *by* ***Louisa Vaughan*** ISBN: *1-59462-248-5* **$10.95**
Miracles of Faith in China *Religion Pages 112*

The Edinburgh Lectures on Mental Science (1909) *by* ***Thomas*** ISBN: *1-59462-008-3* **$11.95**
This book contains the substance of a course of lectures recently given by the writer in the Queen Street Hall, Edinburgh. Its purpose is to indicate the Natural Principles governing the relation between Mental Action and Material Conditions... *New Age/Psychology Pages 148*

Ayesha *by* ***H. Rider Haggard*** ISBN: *1-59462-301-5* **$24.95**
Verily and indeed it is the unexpected that happens! Probably if there was one person upon the earth from whom the Editor of this, and of a certain previous history, did not expect to hear again... *Classics Pages 380*

Ayala's Angel *by* ***Anthony Trollope*** ISBN: *1-59462-352-X* **$29.95**
The two girls were both pretty, but Lucy who was twenty-one who supposed to be simple and comparatively unattractive, whereas Ayala was credited, as her Bombwhat romantic name might show, with poetic charm and a taste for romance. Ayala when her father died was nineteen... *Fiction Pages 484*

The American Commonwealth *by* ***James Bryce*** ISBN: *1-59462-286-8* **$34.45**
An interpretation of American democratic political theory. It examines political mechanics and society from the perspective of Scotsman James Bryce *Politics Pages 572*

Stories of the Pilgrims *by* ***Margaret P. Pumphrey*** ISBN: *1-59462-116-0* **$17.95**
This book explores pilgrims religious oppression in England as well as their escape to Holland and eventual crossing to America on the Mayflower, and their early days in New England... *History Pages 268*

www.ingramcontent.com/pod-product-compliance
Lightning Source LLC
Chambersburg PA
CBHW060242240426
43673CB00047B/1865
* 9 7 8 1 4 3 8 5 0 1 5 6 7 *